SCOTLAND

Murray Pittock MAE FRSE is Scotland's leading cultural historian. His books include *Culloden*, *Enlightenment in a Smart City*, *The Myth of the Jacobite Clans* and *Robert Burns in Global Culture*.

Further praise for *Scotland*:

'A sweeping overview of Scotland's story . . . Amid his scrupulous recounting of a vast swathe of history, Pittock offers fresh insights.'

Rosemary Goring, *Herald*

'Demonstrates Pittock's concern to emphasise the distinctiveness of Scotland, as well as to highlight the historical significance of the country's external relationships.'

Valerie Wallace, *TLS*

'Rich in detail . . . Lively, free-flowing, and engaging.'

Rab Houston, *BBC History Magazine*

'A monumental achievement . . . This is a tremendous book, a really significant contribution to Scottish history. It will delight, surprise and irritate in equal measure.'

Christopher Whatley, author of *The Scots and the Union*

'A magisterial work which Scots will actively return to again and again, as we redefine our role in Europe and the world in the twenty-first century.'

Billy Kay, author of *The Scottish World*

'In this wide-ranging and engaging book, Pittock expl———— ⸱⸳ survival of Scotland and the projection of ⸳⸳⸳⸳⸳

Ewen Cameron, author of

SCOTLAND

THE GLOBAL HISTORY
1603 TO THE PRESENT

MURRAY PITTOCK

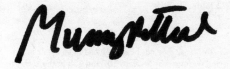

YALE UNIVERSITY PRESS
NEW HAVEN AND LONDON

For information about this and other Yale University Press publications, please contact:
U.S. Office: sales.press@yale.edu   yalebooks.com
Europe Office: sales@yaleup.co.uk   yalebooks.co.uk

Set in Adobe Garamond Pro by IDSUK (DataConnection) Ltd
Printed in Great Britain by Clays Ltd, Elcograf S.p.A

Library of Congress Control Number: 2023935509

ISBN 978-0-300-25417-4 (hbk)
ISBN 978-0-300-27301-4 (pbk)

A catalogue record for this book is available from the British Library.

10 9 8 7 6 5 4 3 2 1

For two global Scots:

Clark McGinn

Global Burnsian and financier

and

Michael Russell

Former Brexit Minister and Cabinet Secretary for the Constitution,
Europe and External Affairs, Scottish Government

CONTENTS

ILLUSTRATIONS

12. *Dido Elizabeth Belle* (1761–1804), attributed to David Martin (1737–97). The Picture Art Collection / Alamy Stock Photo.

13. *Am I Not a Man and a Brother?* Ceramic medallion produced for Josiah Wedgwood, 1787. AF Fotografie / Alamy Stock Photo.

14. Slavery in Surinam, depiction by John Gabriel Stedman (1744–97), of the Scots Brigade in the Dutch Service. CPA Media Pte Ltd / Alamy Stock Photo.

15. Anne-Louis Girodet (1767–1824), *Ossian Receiving the Ghosts of Fallen French Heroes* (1801). ART Collection / Alamy Stock Photo.

16. Arran Distillery Burns-branded whisky. By kind permission of Pauline Mackay.

17. Burns Night Udo Mushaira, Edinburgh 2020. By kind permission of the Scottish Indian Muslim Association.

18. Edwin Landseer, *Deer and Deerhounds in a Mountain Torrent* (1832). Artefact / Alamy Stock Photo.

19. Edwin Landseer, *The Monarch of the Glen* (1850). photosublime / Alamy Stock Photo.

20. *La nouvelle mode ou l'Écossais à Paris*. BTEU / RKMLGE / Alamy Stock Photo.

21. Henry Bell's *Comet*, the first European steamboat passenger service on the Clyde, 1812–20. Chronicle / Alamy Stock Photo.

22. Cowden Japanese Garden, Clackmannanshire, created with the advice of Taki Handa.

23. Members of the Royal Family visit the post office at *An Clachan*, Empire Exhibition 1938. Chronicle / Alamy Stock Photo.

24. The Scottish Avenue, Empire Exhibition 1938. Chronicle / Alamy Stock Photo.

25. The Scottish Parliament, frontage. Designed by Catalan architect Enric Miralles (1955–2000). Colin Palmer Photography / Alamy Stock Photo.

26. Queensberry House, townhouse of the Duke of Queensberry. Author's image.

27. Statue of Donald Dewar (1937–2000), first First Minister of Scotland, by Kenny Mackay, located in Buchanan Street, Glasgow. Author's image.

IN TEXT

ACKNOWLEDGEMENTS

This history is first and foremost a work of scholarship, and reflects not only my own reading and understanding over the years, but also the research of many other people, including Karin Bowie, Tanja Bueltmann, Sir Tom Devine, Angela McCarthy, John Mackenzie, Andrew Mackillop, Steve Murdoch and many others, and the friendship and generosity of Jeremy Black, Joep Leerssen, Ann Rigney, Daniel Szechi, Chris Whatley and many more. Taking a longer view, I have benefited greatly over the years from my longstanding friendships with the late Sir Neil MacCormick and with Bridget McConnell and Michael Russell, as well as from the strong engagements I have had with the External Affairs Directorate in the Scottish Government, including an invitation in 2018 from its then Director, Karen Watt, to brief her department staff on the Scottish brand and how it was regarded abroad at the time in different parts of the world. Within that Directorate, I am grateful to the friendship and support of Brian Dornan as the then Head of Scotland House and his colleagues, to John Webster and his colleagues in Dublin where they hosted the Glasgow–Dublin Creative Cities summit I organized in 2019, to Joni Smith in Washington and Brussels and to Chris Thomson in Glasgow and Washington. I am also grateful to have had the opportunity to be nominated to join the Scottish Government delegation at the United Kingdom–Canada colloquium in 2021, one of many events which has helped me to see ourselves as others see us, as has my engagement with CIVIS, the confederal European university partnership, and with my colleagues and friends in the International Association for the Study of Scottish Literatures. It has also been a privilege to supervise and examine doctoral and advanced students studying Scotland from Canada, China,

France, Taiwan, the United States and elsewhere. Going back to my own student days, I learnt a great deal from the company and friendship of my contemporaries at Glasgow and Oxford, including the diplomats Ian Lindsay and John Rankin, the politicians Liam Fox, Boris Johnson, Charles Kennedy and John Nicolson and the global Scots Clark McGinn and the late Jimmy Walker.

I am also grateful to Heather McCallum, Humanities Commissioning Editor at Yale, for initiating discussion on this project, and to Katie Urquhart and other colleagues at Yale University Press, the National Library of Scotland and elsewhere who have engaged with it from its gestation, as well as to the National Gallery of Scotland, National Library of Scotland, National Records of Scotland, National Trust for Scotland, Glasgow Museums, NatWest Archives, Scottish Indian Muslim Association and Todd Wong of the Gung Haggis Fat Choy movement for granting permissions. My colleagues in the Office of the Vice-Principals and the College of Arts at the University of Glasgow have as ever been most supportive, and the scholarship of Gerry Carruthers and Nigel Leask has been a particular pleasure to engage with in bringing this history together. It is dedicated to Clark McGinn, the founder of the first ever World Debating Competition, former Managing Director of CHC Leasing Ireland, Senior Vice-President of Waypoint Leasing and one of the leading global speakers on Robert Burns, and to Michael Russell, Scottish parliamentarian and government minister: both Leos in the service of Scotland. This book is published on Michael's birthday and within a day or two of Clark's and is a fitting tribute to the different visions of Scotland in the world they have each spent a lifetime advocating and acting to bring about.

INTRODUCTION
GLOBAL SCOTLAND

When the world thinks of Scotland, it often thinks less of a country than of a place: a place with a strong brand, summed up in images of bagpipes, mountains, tartan, whisky. This Scotland, largely developed and exported in the era of the country's great Romantic writers, is the same Scotland that provided the finance, technology and innovation that drove the steam age, leading to the vast expansion in global trade and in-country traffic on water and land which began in Scotland with the first passenger steamboat service in Europe. This latter is the Scotland that – it has been claimed – 'Created Our World & Everything in It'.[1]

These two Scotlands are the same place. This book tells us how that happened, and also explains the national institutions and structures, the education, ambition and displacement, the formal and informal networks that underpinned these two Scotlands, which were once – in the century before the First World War – the same Scotland. The roots of both are found in the same places, and for good reasons. Scotland is a country, but not a state: one of the longest-lived of all global nations yet hardly counted by some to be a nation at all. This book will tell us how the history of Scotland worked, and how that history continued to work when the country disappeared from the map as an independent state and yet built a global brand. Scotland is a normal country, but it has not had the status of a normal country for a long time: yet some of its greatest successes have been built out of that ambiguity of status. Time changes all things, however, and, as we shall see in the latter pages of the book, the changing status of Scotland within the United Kingdom and of the United Kingdom within the world have had major impacts on the achievement and brand of Scotland worldwide which have not yet been resolved.

This is a global history of Scotland. What does that mean? Despite the rise of global history, national histories are the main route by which history is read and understood. And because a national audience (often) and politicians (almost always) want to read about a shared history, national historians are a powerful force in their home states. At the elite Peking University in 2014, over 50 per cent of staff were specialists in Chinese history; at the Australian National University, 67 per cent were specialists in Australian history. In the United States, declining European emigration after 1945 was followed by a decline in European historians across university faculties. Despite a determined turn to the global in the United Kingdom in recent years, British historians continue to dominate, and their changing practices are not always borne out by changing assumptions. The Irish historian Vincent Morley characterized the apparently international outlook of the New British History as propounded by those who 'see no obstacle to that enterprise in the plurality of languages that were spoken throughout the British Empire – which is in itself eloquent testimony to their anglo-centric perspective and preoccupations'. In other words, global history can remain framed by national experience and expectation. That is even more intensively the case in the contemporary political and culture war with respect to global historical practice which takes into account the impact of slavery and empire: the advocates of a 'traditional' history which ignores these factors demand a high degree of introspective insularity, the presentation of 'a thousand years of English history' as an unproblematic entity which cuts out the rest of the world. In the extreme versions of such views, Black lives do not matter in history because they were never 'here'; in the extreme actions of those who oppose these views, the attacks on statuary and campaigns for renaming, apologising and decolonising are all attempts to reclaim public space from the intense insularity of a national history. In aggressively exposing the global consequences of white British or American power, these activists provoke the antipathy of those for whom introspective and self-congratulatory narratives are the very purpose of history, which is otherwise misused. The tensions between global flows of information, money and people and the attempts to control them by national governments, cultures and electorates are thus played out in the historical sphere: as international communication improves, the battle over controlling and reframing information in the terms of a purely national memory intensifies.[2]

In Scotland, Scottish historians are a minority and outside the country they are a rarity: an unusual situation brought about by the political status of Scotland. At the same time, this presents an advantage in that it may make it easier to stand outside a Scottish framework and take on a more global identity, something that Scots themselves have been doing for centuries.[3] This book adopts an approach which frames Scotland not as (implicitly or explicitly) a great global actor, but as a small country with a primarily relational history rooted in 'the world in Scotland, and Scotland in the world'.[4] It acknowledges the importance of the ability of individual Scots to adopt the characteristics of other cultures and the more collective premiss that Scotland has long formed part of the most successful multi-kingdom or 'composite' monarchy in history, a form of political organisation that was once commonplace and is now all but extinct, and which post-Enlightenment historiography has often sidelined or ignored. This history therefore begins in the era of the Thirty Years' War, which led, in the eyes of many in the contemporary West, to a recognizably modern definition of statehood, and which presaged the ending of the Scottish state, while bearing witness in its war, its politics and its conflicts over sovereignty to the survival of the Scottish nation.

All national sovereignties and their histories are contingent and relational rather than absolute, but – as E.H. Dance and his collaborators pointed out in 1967 in relation to the teaching of history in Europe – large states can ignore more of this reality for more of the time than small ones can. Hybridization with local populations and customs has been a longstanding Scottish trait, and thus engages strongly with a key area of enquiry in global history. At the same time, Scottish networking and integration were a double-edged sword, a broadsword. Integrating with native populations was all very well, but Scots also integrated just as well with British imperial expectations and practice, sometimes with a chilling cynicism. General Charles Napier (1782–1853) described the capture of Sind as a 'useful piece of rascality' and defined the actions of the forces he commanded as 'the usual Anglo-Saxon process of planting civilization by robbery, oppression and murder'.[5]

Scottish networks were powerfully exclusive and defensive: they did not often exist to promote the integration of others rather than the domination of Scots. Nor was Scotland's relationship with the historical abuses of slavery and colonialism anything that should inspire moral confidence, however praiseworthy might have been the beliefs and actions of many individual Scots. Scots abroad often maintained or even developed their Scottishness, and the complex and profoundly important dimensions of their informal and formal networks functioned – like Scottish nationhood itself – within a relational framework of limited autonomy but profound effectiveness. How this happened is a key question this book sets out to address. What is distinctively Scottish in the history of these islands in their global context is frequently overlooked, but it is a most appropriate subject for global history, because it was formed in the context of dialogue and relationship with countries across the world. Even as Scotland's embassies began to close in the seventeenth century, paradiplomacy – formal and informal – replaced the country's beleaguered sovereignty. Many minorities, such as Huguenots, Quakers and Ugandan Asians, become disproportionately successful as they integrate into larger and alien ecclesiastical or secular polities. The case of the Scots was like theirs in some ways, but not in others, for a nation with its own institutional and cultural life remained within Great Britain to sustain that history of success in a wider sphere, one sometimes more Scottish abroad than at home. Understanding Scotland as neither quite a 'stateless nation' nor a British region is central to the analysis and history that follows, for much of the country's survival and success from the Treaty of Westphalia (1648) to our own day is the product of neither deprivation nor extinction but of a difficult road between the two, a balancing act that was for a long time sustained – albeit often carelessly – by the wider United Kingdom and its global interests.[6]

This may be the first global history of Scotland titled as such, but the risks attending histories of Scotland which focus on the country's international relations and significance are well-established. Many such histories are lists of individual Scots of rank, achievement or ideas, and are thus celebratory prosopography stitched together – or not – with narrative, an associational cultural memory of celebration, a prolonged 'wha's like us', or in the historian Ted Cowan's acid terms, 'philo-pietistic drivel'. One aspect of this celebration is to attribute the term 'Scot' to those born and brought up elsewhere and in other cultures and contexts, not least those with only a remote genetic link to the home country: by contrast this book will generally only include individuals from Scotland or (on the rare occasions when born abroad) figures with strong and relevant Scottish networks.

Histories which focus on international networks, associations and fields of endeavour for Scots and Scotland are fewer in number, but have grown rapidly in recent years with the work of the historians Tanja Bueltmann, Sir Tom Devine, Marjory Harper, Angela McCarthy, Andrew Mackillop, Graeme Morton, Alex Murdoch and Steve Murdoch and others very much to the fore, though enormous credit still attaches to the pioneering work of John Mackenzie, which predates them all. These have offered a much more complex understanding of issues such as diaspora, emigration and the nature of Scottish associations and networks, and this history is much in their debt. More recently, Andrew Mackillop has sought to conjoin these elements by introducing the notion of human capital – migration as an investment strategy – to Scotland's imperial era global engagements, building on an element in global systems theory, which presents imperial peripheries as trading surplus labour for access to the power structures of the centres of financial and political authority.[7]

There is nonetheless always a risk in country-centred global approaches. In Scotland's case, the acutest problem such histories face is that of celebratory anaphora, the focus on Scots and Scotland as exceptional. The difficulty for the historian here is that Scots and Scotland *are* both demonstrably exceptional – given the country's size – through the data of history, and also invisible to many by reasons of historical and geographical displacement into Great Britain, a relatively modern state whose own historiography has a tendency to construct for itself a continuity which never existed in the past and a unity which is still absent in the present. 'Britain's' conflation of the Roman province of Britannia with the whole island has long been in evidence and indeed remains with us today, both directly and indirectly in phrases such as 'north of Hadrian's Wall' to identify (inaccurately) Scotland. On a larger stage, the historian Sir John Seeley's (1834–95) famous view that

Great Britain acquired its empire 'in a fit of absence of mind' is perhaps better applied in the twenty-first century to the manner in which the UK simultaneously manages to perceive itself as a multinational union and also as 'one nation' which enjoys a unitary historical narrative: a composite state absent-mindedly composing a national history which never existed. 'Mediaeval Britain' is almost a contradiction in terms. The phrase carries vast historiographical risks, including being Anglocentric, ignoring Scottish–Irish–Welsh connectivity, understating the importance of Norway, France and French families and relationships including feudal cross-Channel loyalties, and simply evading the multinational nature of the British Isles. Not to mention projecting concepts dependent on a modern road and rail communications network back into the Middle Ages, when sea transport was far more central to communication and mobility.

The temptation to react against history of this kind is strong, and can lead in Scotland to Scottish exceptionalism, where making the invisible Scot visible can goad the historian beyond recovery into aggrandizement. This creates its own reactions of self-doubt and self-accusation, notably regarding Scotland's participation in colonialism and the slave trade, as well as in more recent times elevating British regional topics (such as housing, heavy industry, economic development) into Scottish national ones to a degree arguably at times unjustified by the 'national' quality of the evidence, and the extent to which any separately 'Scottish' powers of policymaking existed to render diversity possible. British regional inequalities are not necessarily national Scottish ones, nor are all the effects of the British Empire on Scottish life – economic transformation, changing diets, new flora and fauna and so on – distinctively national to Scotland when their effects may have been felt equally in England's regions. Although this book will naturally have to be selective, it will seek to address those elements of the impact of Britain and its Empire in Scotland where these reflect, or had an effect on, distinctively Scottish practice and activity.[8]

One of the core problems of defining Scotland is thus its political status within a larger state. On one level, it is part of a unitary United Kingdom state with certain powers preserved under the 1707 Union and subsequent legislation and now subject to local democratic control; on another level, Scotland is a devolved polity with paradiplomacy and other appurtenances of soft power presenting itself as a quasi-state with longstanding international presence in the global arena through national representation in sporting and other bodies, while domestically retaining a discrete jurisdiction. This ambiguity arises from one fundamental root cause: the country's status as part of an early modern composite monarchy which was both perpetuated and compromised by the terms of the 1707 Union with England which replaced the 1603 regnal Union, and by their subsequent interpretation. The first chapter will address this question in more detail. The UK (and beyond it, the more than a dozen current or former territories of the British Empire in which her Majesty the Queen is head of state) is evaluated in this study as one of the last partial survivors of the multi-kingdom or 'composite' (a term introduced by Helmut Koenigsberger (1918–2014), and popularized by Sir John Elliott (1930– 2022)) monarchy model in Europe; Spain, which is another, does not tend to acknowledge the countries within its state as nations, as the Spanish constitutional court response in striking down elements of the (legitimate) 2006 Catalan referendum made clear. The United Kingdom of the Netherlands (1815–1839), the Commonwealth of Poland–Lithuania (1386/1569–1795), the Kalmar Union (1397–1523), the Twin Kingdoms of Denmark–Norway (1536/37–1814), the Holy Roman Empire and the Habsburg domain of Austria–Hungary have all alike vanished into the past. The United Kingdom has not, and continues to evince certain of the structures of composite monarchy in respect of native traditions, institutions and separate legal systems, which were – as we shall see in Chapter 1 – emplaced by the Union of 1707 into the new state of the 'united kingdoms' of Great Britain.[9]

The book which follows will outline the structures that constituted Scotland's presence on the global stage in terms of this continuing, yet compromised, role as a national entity, and will address the role played by Scottish networks and the careers of individual Scots in a global Scotland in substantive detail with key examples highlighted. In particular, it will take the view that the historic success enjoyed by a Scots elite abroad arose from an intersection between the large-scale domestic provision of high quality education which created a larger educated group than could be satisfied by domestic opportunities, arising in the context of a society with very strong kin and association-based networks. These networks functioned in a manner which accelerated the process of creation and acceptance of innovative practices both domestically and internationally, as outlined in Everett Rogers' 1962 classic, *Diffusion of Innovations*. Interdependent networks are almost inevitably necessary in the complex structures of international trade or imperial careers: their vulnerability to single points of failure was minimized not only by the intensity of Scottish networking, but by the determination – evident from early modern Europe onwards – of those networks to control supply chains, trading relationships and other potential points of failure in Scottish overseas markets. The inability to project the force necessary to achieve this result with security was a key element in the instability of the 1603–1707 monarchy, and led a large portion of the Scottish elite – though not Scotland's domestic society – to accept the Union as the price whereby British power could protect Scottish commerce, though religious motivations were far from absent. Scottish Presbyterianism too, however, was strongly linked to an austere and single-minded focus on personal and community success, which it did not originate but contributed to sustaining.

This history will also examine influences from the outside world which shaped Scotland: England, France (whose peak influence largely lies outside the period we are covering) and the Netherlands among others. It will consider the composite monarchy as a central concept in modelling its understanding of the longevity of the Scottish–British dual identity, beginning with the struggle for state rights within the Holy Roman Empire from 1618 to 1648. That very composite monarchy itself was arguably central to the success of Scots abroad, as the early engagement of Scottish elites with English opportunities reinforced these elites' abilities to blend into the expectations of a different culture while preserving their own. This was the source of the double-mindedness visible in the sympathies and practice of many of the Scottish imperial servants we shall meet, criticized as 'clannishness' when visible to outsiders. At the same time, as noted above, the strong institutions, high levels of education and the trading ports of eastern Scotland in particular were combined with a weak ability to project power overseas which drove networked careers with other European powers, temporarily reinforced after the Union by the Jacobites who opposed it.[10]

This will seek to be a bilateral history, not a history of Scots victimhood within the British Empire, but it will not shy away from the strong evidence that an increasingly introspective post-imperial Britain has undermined consent for the Union in Scotland or the extent to which eighteenth- and nineteenth-century Scottish participation in British overseas markets and the projection of British imperial power was instrumental as well as ideological. In addition, it will stress the continuing engagement of Scots with non-British European powers, not just in the pre-1707 era, but long after the Union. Recent modelling of the Scots diaspora has arguably underplayed this element in Scotland's continuing global relationships.

DIASPORA

The term 'Scots diaspora' is itself a long-established one and has been in common parlance for many years (and has a Wikipedia entry), but some remain uncomfortable with its use with respect to Scotland, because of its overtones of suffering and displacement, while many – though by no means all – Scots left Scotland for motives of opportunity and personal gain. However, the standard features of diaspora (dispersal, retained belief that the place from whence dispersed represents the true ideal, complex relationship with one's hosts and a mythology of community which can be fulfilled through ethnic associationalism) fit Scots abroad very well indeed. The only question that should remain is that regarding agency in the initial dispersal. The ambition of Scots to succeed outwith Scotland is downplayed where a passive view of a displaced and victimized population is preferred, which is part of the reason why the Scottish Clearances (a phrase we owe to Sir Tom Devine) have become so important in domestic accounts of displacement and loss. However one interprets the Clearances, there have been many reasons over many years for Scots to leave Scotland: religion, economic necessity, eviction, war, lack of appropriate opportunity and – of course – ambition. An intriguing mixture between push and pull factors in different proportions at different times is often evident. The picture is complex, but its complexity is core to the achievements of many Scots and the openness evident in many to transcultural identities. Had Scotland not been allied to France and deeply engaged in the Baltic trade before 1560, or not divided in 1560–1707 by impoverishing politics, deteriorating climate and too strong a body of educated citizens for the opportunities it offered, Scots would have gone abroad much less often before the Union. Clause IV of that Union offered Scots access to English markets overseas under the protection of the forces of the Crown, after over eighty years during which Scots' attempts to develop overseas colonies and trading stations had been frustrated by their own inability to project finance and force, as well as by the indifference and hostility of their British neighbours. Such resistance was manifested in legislation such as the Navigation Acts, whereby 'all cargoes bound for England' were to be 'carried into English ports by English ships'. In the following centuries, a 'noisy' and 'highly active' set of Scottish communities developed through the expanding British Empire, dominating professions in the 'maritime, missionary . . . medical, engineering and scientific' fields, with strong voices 'in the press, in publishing, and in other cultural forms that heightened their visibility'. As the historians Andrew Mackillop and Steve Murdoch put it: 'Scotland's imperial failure pre-1707 actually generated responses that assisted its success thereafter.' Scots relied – as we shall see – on 'transportable networks of political association and kinship' as well as commercial networks supportive of a 'highly opportunistic and flexible approach to expansion overseas', an approach which – Mackillop and Murdoch argue – had its genesis to some extent through the 'frontier context' of earlier Scottish military and administrative experience. Even Scots displaced through poverty, oppression or war could – if networked – find support in their exile abroad. And that network could, at its most basic, just be about being Scottish, for the 'link of common origin' was 'deployed far more often than might be expected' among strangers, while bonds of 'fictive kinship' through 'adoption, godparenting and fosterage' were also common. Indeed kinship, irrespective of social hierarchy, was a typical basis for trust, and was often itself tied to links to place of origin or regional allegiance. Place readily encompassed institutions, and the ancient burgh grammar schools of Edinburgh, Glasgow and Aberdeen and their slightly younger universities became powerful agencies for the educated and relatively privileged to foster power and patronage networks abroad.[11]

Scotland's highly developed institutions and professions in law, medicine, banking, education and the army, among others, created an associational network structure which rested on, reinforced and complemented longstanding kinship and geographical networks in a small country with strong regional, family and civic identities. In the nineteenth century, previously politically contested areas of Scottish culture (tartan, military piping, Scots language and literature) became the vehicles for a unified cultural narrative of the performance of Scotland abroad, a theatrical memory created by language, music and spectacle. This was the Scottish world created by Scottish Romanticism which – if it did not create a political nationalism as was the case elsewhere in Europe – nonetheless became the foundational story of Scotland in the world, and remains to this day key to the Scottish brand. The strongly developed education and culture of Scotland inflected literary genre, heroic history, a national story and cultural hybridity between both varieties of Scottish culture internally and Scottish and other cultures externally, which in combination transformed the performance of self in diaspora in ways that became historically distinct.

The career sojourners who repatriated wealth to Scotland in retirement as a matter of life planning may not deserve the term diaspora, but many Scots do, both because they were obliged to move to their host societies or because they wanted to stay there; even those who wanted to stay in Scotland often found the dice were loaded against them. To have your home burned to the ground because you cannot pay the rent is a different kind of experience from joining the army for the enlistment bounty or leaving because there was neither land nor opportunity at home, but both these latter were deeply intertwined with the economic conditions of smallholding and the risks of eviction that attended them in eras of landlord ambition and macro-economic challenge to their tenantry. This book will take the view that there is indeed a Scots diaspora, and that opportunities to leave all too often came accompanied with a contingent or absolute need to do so.[12] In the late 1990s, it was estimated that there were more than five times as many Scots by birth or descent in the world as lived in the country, and there are many more abroad from other nationalities who wish to be associated with Scotland.[13]

This history begins with the Thirty Years' War and its first major Scottish manifestation in the National Covenant of 1638, a statement of politico-religious nationalism which in championing Scotland's national rights paradoxically came later and enhanced its 1643 version to commit it to British political priorities. Internationally, the first chapter considers that the Thirty Years' War of 1618–48 is the right place to site the civil conflicts of the Three Kingdoms in the 1640s: neither the 'Covenant' nor the 'English Civil War' are events that can be understood fully from within the goldfish bowl of national historiography, for British exceptionalism is at work in separating the conflict between Archbishop Laud's (1573–1645) Anglican version of Catholic demands for orthodoxy and conformity (caesaropapism) and its opponents, from a Continental context. It is fully acknowledged that the book could have started at an earlier date, and throughout the text there will be glances back to the international engagements of a yet older Scotland, but the issues of sovereignty, empire and conflict arising from the country's entry into a composite monarchy crystallized in the seventeenth century. Scotland's story has often found itself occluded in a British context which can conceal more than it informs: to take only one example, the intensely Scottish and north-eastern network of Byron's contacts throughout Europe has been almost entirely written out of history by the restricted framework of understanding him as solely an Anglo-British poet, despite the availability of much evidence which finesses or indeed dislodges such a reading, and there are many other examples. In writing of Scotland as a global rather than an introspective entity, this book seeks to change the framework of how we understand Scotland in a much wider context than itself. In doing so it builds on the inspiring scholarly work of recent years.[14]

This book will have three super-themes: Conflict and Sovereignty (Chapters 1 and 2, which take us to 1760), Empire (Chapters 3 to 5) and Finding a Role (Chapters 6, 7 and Conclusion). All will be grounded in the concept of sovereignty and relationship: the paradoxical and powerful yet partial nature of Scotland's ability to project itself as an international actor. The great success enjoyed by many individuals and by the country and its culture in creating a global impact under the British flag after 1707 built on the structural strength which had come from within both Scottish society and its familial, geographical and institutional associations, and on earlier practice by Scots in the international sphere which was conducive to the subsequent extension of soft power on a transcultural basis.

Second order thematic questions to be addressed include Scotland's constitutional position (Chapters 1, 6 and 7); Scots in the Empire (Chapters 2, 3 and 5); the nature and reality of the Scots 'diaspora' (Chapters 3, 4 and 5); and the perception of Scotland in Romantic and romanticized terms (Chapters 4 and 7). At the dawn of the eighteenth century, political, military and religious conflict brought an end to the Scottish state and created the conditions for Scotland's administrative and commercial opportunities and military centrality within the British Empire, though modern histories have tended to over-emphasize these at the expense of Scotland's continuing links to Europe. This imperial Scotland only finally vanished little more than fifty years ago, ushering in a major change in Scottish society, even if poor language skills common among Anglophones in the wake of the British Empire and the rise of American power meant that if the European connexion offered by the European Union was a source of positive sentiment, it provided much less in the way of opportunity. Sixty years since, as Sir Walter Scott put it in a different context in *Waverley* (1814), modern Scotland began to emerge.

The first chapter shows a Scotland that was poorer in comparison to England due to conflict and climate change than it had been in the Middle Ages. It lacked silver and gold bullion and natural resources. It had – by contemporary standards – a highly educated population who had insufficient opportunity at home, and a reputation for exporting soldiers. It lacked the power to project its ambitions in global trade beyond its established strengths in sojourning or diasporic mercantile control within some European ports. Its institutions and overseas networking were highly developed in relation to its economy. It was a country religiously divided between Episcopalianism (favoured by the Crown and predominant in the north and east) and Presbyterianism (predominant in the south, centre and west). It was a state, but its sovereignty was compromised by the composite monarchy of Great Britain and Ireland, and by the mid seventeenth century it no longer sent or received foreign embassies, though it maintained both soft and some hard military power in Continental Europe.

Socially, Scotland was much more like Continental Europe in many respects than England, with a relatively large nobility as a proportion of the population (estimated at over 2 per cent in 1707); England was exceptional in the very small numbers of its nobility. In some other respects (for example in the legality of divorce and the provision of legal and medical aid and burgh pensions), Scotland too was unusual. It looked different: English visitors, as we shall see in Chapter 1, remarked on everything from its hygiene to its trees, its architecture to its gender roles. This identity came to find other means of expression as the years went on. The hybridization of Scottish with English society and social values in eighteenth- and nineteenth-century Scotland was arguably compensated by the creation of a powerful narrative of what was distinctive about Scottishness that was projected throughout the world. Moreover, the lessons learned by Scots in integrating into the new United Kingdom intensified the chameleon-like capability many had long evinced in operating in other countries both as Scots and as members of the receiving culture.[15]

Scotland's currency was the pound, but the Scottish and English versions of this unit (which had separated in the twelfth century) were very far from being in parity by the early seventeenth century. There were twelve Scots pounds (S£ in the text that follows) to the pound sterling in 1638, and although the exchange rate subsequently drifted out to 13:1 in the 1680s, 12:1 was the level at which it was standardized at the Union in 1707. The S£ continued as a unit of account into the nineteenth century, and terms such as 'bawbee' (S6d, an English halfpenny) into the twentieth. However due to a native shortage of bullion, other currencies also circulated freely in pre-Union Scotland, particularly in the burghs, where lists of exchange rates were published from the mediaeval period. This unstable, nominalist relationship with the specie of currency probably underpinned Scottish financial innovation, which rested on an infrastructure of experience of money as a flexible and relative entity rather than a 'sterling' one, and was driven by the domestic imperative of pursuing economic growth with inadequate supply and velocity of money. The 'elaboration of an agency/branch system, the invention of the cash credit (later to become the overdraft), the vigorous development of deposit-gathering reinforced by the payment of interest, the early adoption of joint-stock banking, experiments in exchange stabilisa- tion . . . the Savings Bank movement and the investment trust': all were Scottish-driven innovations which arguably grew from the combination of a highly educated population and a restricted bullion supply in an age when *fiat* currency – in so many ways John Law's (1675–1732) innovation, as we shall see in Chapter 2 – had not yet been invented.[16]

The Scotland of this study articulated itself distinctly in terms of its foun- dation myth and national story and its literary relationship to the classical and European generic and canonical traditions. It inflected and interpreted external influences – Dutch, French, English – towards its own specific conditions, and its people articulated themselves in national terms wherever they were in the world, performing identity in diaspora. This was a Scottish identity, for despite the lure of Romanticism and incessant Victorian racial- izing of British and global experience, Scotland was not a 'Highland' nation made up of a 'clan system' combined with a Germanic Lowland polity more akin to the English. This in itself was a story – now fading – which grew out of one particular strand of Enlightenment thinking, and which remains in popular consciousness to this day: its legacy can, to an extent, be seen in the category of the 'Highlands' as a concept where geographical, linguistic and ethnic grounds are blurred. This is the last redoubt of the racialized Scotland of the Victorian era, long left behind by genetics and a more integrated understanding of Scottish history and culture. 'Lowland' and 'Highland' are almost ineradicable categories in describing Scotland, but they obscure its history in a misleading simplification which presents geography as a short-hand for culture, ethnicity and language. In reality, matters were much more complicated.[17]

THE HIGHLANDS

In his magisterial book on *The Scottish Clearances* (2018), Sir Tom Devine gives an appraisal of the extent of the Highlands, though he does not quite call them that:

> Scottish Gaeldom . . . lay north and west of the Highland Boundary Fault . . . The core geographical region includes . . . Argyll, Ross and Cromarty, Sutherland and Inverness, but in earlier times, the western and northern districts of Aberdeenshire, Angus, Perthshire and Stirlingshire.[18]

Professor Devine is very careful, but one thing should strike us at once (and yet is all but always passed over): the 'Highlands' as defined here is a term which bisects counties, suggesting an incompatibility between Scottish civil administration and the culture of what it was administering. If one examines early maps of Scotland, it is these counties and/or their associated earldoms which are most frequently marked, rather than any internal ethno-cultural division that allegedly cuts across them: see, for example, the maps of Paolo Forlani[?], *Regno di Scotia*, Abraham Ortellius, *Scotiae tabula*, John Leslie, *Scotiae Regni Antiquissimi*, Gerhard Mercator, *Scotia Regnum*, and many others.

Much later, the historian Leah Leneman, in her *Living in Atholl* (1986) finds little disjunction between social behaviour in the 'Highland' and 'Lowland' parishes of the Duke of Atholl's estates, but does not draw the obvious inference that these foundational categories may themselves be inappropriate. As Charles Withers, now Scotland's Geographer Royal, put it many years ago, 'The Highlands have been created' as 'a sort of natural or anthropological curiosity', which later became 'a recreational commodity'.[19]

The categories of 'Highland' and 'Lowland' Scotland have prospered mightily from a lack of critical examination. Too often the 'Highlands' are equated with what Sir Tom Devine terms 'Gaeldom',

1. *Duo Vicecomitatus Aberdonia & Banfia*. By Robert Gordon (1580–1661) and Joan Blaeu (1596–1673), in the *Blaeu Atlas of Scotland* (1654). These are two Scottish counties in which a substantial proportion of the population spoke Gaelic in 1654 and parts of which are traditionally accounted the 'Highlands' by various commentators. Robert Gordon himself lived at Straloch Castle in Aberdeenshire, long owned by the family of Sir Reginald de Cheyne, who married the daughter of Freskin de Moray, Lord of Duffus and almost certainly a Gaelic speaker.

2. *A Description of the Highlands of Scotland* (1731). By Clement Lemprière (1683–1746), showing the clear bisection of several Scottish counties (including Aberdeen and Banff) by 'The Boundary of the Highlands'. Note that the indication of Scotland's mountainous regions excludes the area of high ground and clannish feuding now known as the Southern Uplands, while mountains make a marked appearance on the low-lying farmland of the Black Isle, north of Inverness. Though in previous centuries the Men of Galloway were held to be among the most ferocious of Scottish warriors, their place had now been usurped by the 'Highlanders'.

which as he correctly observes is a shifting entity. The historian Allan Macinnes likewise associates the 'Highlands' (including bisection of the counties of Aberdeenshire, Angus, Banffshire, Dunbartonshire, Kincardine, Nairnshire, Perthshire and Stirlingshire) as varying 'with the largely declining fortunes of the Gaelic language in the course of the eighteenth century': in other words, a geographically elastic entity which is nonetheless specifically defined. But the trouble even with this definition is that parts of Ayrshire and Galloway still spoke Gaelic into the eighteenth century, yet no one at all places these locations in the Highlands. The fact is that for a concept so bandied about in Scottish history and a place so frequently referenced, there are many disagreements about where the 'Highlands' are. James VI (r.1567–1625) himself distinguished between the western seaboard and the isles and Gaelic speakers who lived elsewhere. In 1639, Gilbert Blackhall defended the north-east against intruders from Lochaber with a 'Lowland' force which was armed in the same way as the men of Lochaber and who were in many cases Gaelic speakers.[20]

For General Wade, the Highlands had no precise county boundaries: various 'lines' had been drawn to suggest where they might start, but even these differed. In the 'Memoriall Anent the True State of the Highlands as to their Chieftenries' (1745), the Duke of Perth was at the same time described as of 'no Claned familie' while also being 'the head of a Considerable Number . . . of the Name of Drummond'. Forbes of Culloden (though he included other Dukes in a list of 'the clans') described the Murrays of Atholl as 'no Highland Family' while others describe them and their lands as 'Highland' and a 1715 *Explanation* of the risk posed by Jacobitism appears to render the whole of the country as tribally 'Highland'. In William Roy's 1747–52 military survey, the Highlands appear to include all of Scotland north of the Forth–Clyde line, and indeed Roy (unlike Lemprière, whose map was 'one of Wade's surveillance maps') tends to exaggerate mountain contours even south of Forth. In the wake of the 1745 Rising,

James Campbell wrote to the Duke of Argyll that 'Highlands is no certain description. The disarmed countys would do.' Campbell's problem was that which I have mentioned above, the disparity between the 'Highlands' and the fact that the counties of Scotland's civil administration had been formed without this 'Line' in mind. As indeed they had been. For British officers in Scotland such as James Wolfe, matters could be even more stark: for him 'Highlander' was a term extended to the Earl of Kilmarnock and the Irish brigade officer Brigadier Walter Stapleton. It was thus not just the 'disarmed countys' but opponents of the British Government as a whole who could receive the epithet of 'Highlander'. This was perhaps not surprising, since Charles Edward's Jacobite force termed itself (always in English) as 'the Highland army', a name meant to be evocative of northern valour rather than descriptive of geographical origin.[21]

If the 'Highlands' is a difficult concept then, can the 'Highlander' be made any more secure? The historian Allan Macinnes describes the clans as 'Anglian, Anglo-Norman and Flemish as well as Celtic and Norse-Gaelic in origin', which just about covers everyone living in early modern Scotland. But earlier writers had very different views of what Macinnes describes as 'the collective product of feudalism, kinship and local association', which again are concepts readily extensible to the plains as well as the hills of Scotland. Earlier commentators such as John of Fordoun (d. *c*.1384) are often quoted in support of the concept of Highlanders as 'wild Scots' but recent scholarship suggests that Fordoun inherited a particular formula of description rather than observing empirically and that 'the record does afford us ample means to question the existence of a . . . Scotland compartmentalised into Lowlands and Highlands by a "Highland line"'. 'Highlanders' were again identified as 'Wild Scots' by John Mair (1467–1550), and a narrative of Highland savagery and Scots civility took root some time during or after the end of the career of Alexander Stewart, the Wolf of Badenoch (1343–1405), and the Battle of Harlaw

(1411): in other words, it seems to have arisen in response to particular political circumstances. Yet Alasdair Mór mac an Rígh – the Wolf – was the son of Robert II, King of Scots, while at Harlaw, Dómhnall, Lord of the Isles, was in competition for the Earldom of Ross, also claimed by the House of Stewart, and was beaten off by one of its members, Alexander, the Earl of Mar. The politics of this classic 'Highland v Lowland' conflict were in fact over a great earldom under the Crown, and typically there are far more complex political questions which bisect perceived conflicts between these allegedly distinct cultures, both of which were in fact characterized to some extent by 'territorial associations, composed of a dominant kin-nexus and satellite family groups' in the countryside, with these groupings often becoming more intense as they became more remote from the political centre. Undoubtedly the balance between kinship and association and feudal practice varied between Scottish magnates and their followers, but this was a matter of emphasis rather than a disjunction. Remote lords were also Scotsmen 'under the Kings of Scotland', and this was normative.

In the eighteenth century, when the notion of 'the Highlands' became embedded as a concept in British discourse, it is noteworthy that the boundary of the area of Scotland that primarily spoke Gaelic (often from the late middle ages called 'Erse' (i.e. Irish), a term often but not always prejudicial but which undeniably reinforced notions of ethnocultural difference) mapped on almost exactly to what was *much* later (in the work of the English geologist George Barrow (1853–1932)) identified as the Highland Boundary Fault, itself a term of art framed by the expectations of history. In the Jacobite Rising of 1745 itself, the forces raised by the Jacobites in Aberdeen, Banffshire and Angus were described as 'one third . . . Highlanders', though many were the neighbours of the allegedly 'Low Country' men they fought alongside, while as long ago as the 1920s Sir Bruce Seton noted that witnesses could not reliably distinguish 'Lowland'

and 'Highland' Jacobite officers. Captain John Maclean, by all customary definitions a 'Highlander', left a diary of the campaign in English and was clearly interested in the Derbyshire textile industry. The great territorial lordships might still have been better at raising men in the north than in the south of Scotland, but Erskine, Forbes or Ogilvy, Drummond, Oliphant or Murray are hardly families fit for the Tír na nÓg of Gaelic romanticism, and indeed attempts to define great magnates like the Gordon earls of Huntly as having 'superiorities within Gaeldom' while not being Highland (though knowing Gaelic) are signs of the awkward definitions still commonplace with respect to 'Highland/Lowland' terminology. Lord Lovat, Chief of the Name of Fraser, was educated at Aberdeen Grammar School, as were some of the academic Gregory dynasty, cousins to Rob Roy, that archetypical 'Highlander', who was thus kin to several distinguished men among the urban Scottish professoriate. One of the major issues that any concept of 'the Highlands' has to deal with – but often does not – is the nature of 'Highland' social behaviour. Chiefs of the Name in the west Highlands, such as Cameron of Lochiel, mixed as easily in the ranks of European nobility as did those from the Scots-speaking areas of Scotland such as the Marquess of Montrose, Chief of the Name of Graham. Sir Alexander Grant, whom we will meet in Chapter 2, was born on Grant lands near the Spey, but moved easily in Scottish and wider society, eventually becoming a global tycoon in partnership with Richard Oswald, the Caithness-born brother of Glasgow tobacco merchants.[22]

It may be objected that Highland elites were one thing, rank and file another. Yet in the Jacobite Rising of 1745, many 'Lowlanders' were incorporated in 'Highland' regiments. The army as a whole was called 'Highland' because of the signification of true Scots patriotism attaching to the north, a cultural typology that can be traced back as far as the courts of James V and his daughter Queen Mary expressing patriotism through the 'aboriginal attire' associated with the north; but the army received its orders in English. Though Gaelic may have been used below company level, the surviving order books (from Ardsheal's and Ogilvie's regiments) do not suggest so, and private soldiers on occasion wrote fluently to their chiefs in English, for example in Glengarry's Regiment. Again and again, the term 'Highlands' or 'Highlander' is used unproblematically in many histories of Scotland and Britain, yet it is in reality a label which covers a complex and inconsistent tangle of ideological, linguistic, cultural and geographical assumptions of which we should be much more aware.

In 1784, the concept of the 'Highland Line' was introduced by the 'Wash Act' of Parliament 'as a convenient demarcation for the whisky-still taxation'. It was held to be:

> A certain line or boundary beginning at the east point of Loch Crinan, and proceeds from thence to Loch Gilpin . . . along the west coast of Loch Fyne to Inveraray and to the head of Loch Fyne from thence . . . to Arrochar . . . to Tarbet; from Tarbet . . . straight eastward on the north side of Loch Lomond, to Callandar . . . north eastward to Crieff . . . and to Ambleree [Amulrie] and Inver to Dunkeld; from thence along the foot or side of the Grampian Hills to Fettercairn . . . northward . . . to Kincardine O'Neil, Clatt, Huntly and Keith to Fochabers . . . westward by Elgin and Forres, to the coast on the river Findhorn, and any place in or part of the county of Elgin which lies southward of the said line . . .[23]

This precise definition itself owes not a little to the fortuitous coincidence between the area of the *Gàidhealtachd* as it stood in 1746, and the high ground of northern and western Scotland. Its very county crossing complexity and the tiny settlements held to be its border towns should give one pause for thought. Is Crieff in or out? Half in or half out? Do the inhabitants of Dunkeld speak Gaelic on alternative days of the week and does anyone south of the Findhorn in the county of Elgin need an interpreter to visit the county town? These are ridiculous questions, but they reveal how definitions of the 'Highlands' too often pass unquestioned. One thing the 'Highlands' initially benefited from under British legislation was lower whisky duty (equalized across Scotland in 1811 and across the UK as a whole only in 1858), but what constituted this area of Scotland was rendered even more problematic by the introduction of an 'Intermediate' zone in 1797, neither Lowland nor Highland, including areas such as southern Argyll and much of the counties of Aberdeen and Banff. British legislation also found the 'Highlands' problematic as a concept.[24]

Far from being a purely 'Highland' dress, the presence of tartan was noticed everywhere in early modern Scotland, though some observed that only 'the meaner sort of men' wore the plaid in the Lowlands. Was 'Highland' dress then a cultural or a class division? Or indeed can it be used to demarcate at all? In the study that follows we will meet tartan wearers in Edinburgh (estimated at 90 per cent of ladies in the city as late as 1747), major exports of plaid to Europe and the popularity of tartan among First Nations people in Canada, as well as an international community of Gaelic learners that dwarfs the number of speakers in Scotland, many of whom now in any case live in the central belt.

The 'Highlands' is a complicated concept, and will often deserve its inverted commas in the history that follows. This is not to suggest that it is an entirely meaningless one; but very often reflections on its social and cultural practices in our period identify what is visible in related form elsewhere in Scotland, while attempts to define difference by language run almost immediately into the problem of Gaelic's shifting footprint and its presence well outside high ground. The 'Highlands' is too often a shorthand for more complex questions of division and conflict which arise elsewhere.[25]

PART ONE

CONFLICT AND SOVEREIGNTY

1

A QUESTION OF SOVEREIGNTY

THE THIRTY YEARS' WAR AND THE 'WESTPHALIAN SYSTEM'

From 1618 to 1648, war raged across Europe on a scale of ferocity till then unknown. The Reformation and counter-Reformation conflicts which had endured since the sixteenth century, were extended and amplified in a Continent-wide struggle between the Habsburgs of Spain and the Holy Roman Empire against Bohemia, Catholic France and a range of northern European Protestant states including the Dutch Republic, for which the conflict was also a further episode in its long war of survival against Spain. The Thirty Years' War was as much one of ideology as territory, and when it ended eight million people had been killed or died as a consequence of the conditions of war: in the German states, the casualty rates would not be exceeded until the last months of the Second World War. In the words of the English political theorist James Harrington in 1656, Europe was 'Blown up'.[1]

The roots of the war were varied. Central to them was the attempt by Ferdinand II (1578–1637), King of Bohemia (1617) and Hungary (1618) and from 1619 Holy Roman Emperor, to impose Catholicism on the kingdoms and imperial states he governed. Early pressure in this sphere from the Empire before 1619 had led to the formation of the German Protestant Union (1608), which involved Pomerania, Brunswick and Saxony among other states, as opposed to the Catholic powers of the south; an adversarial Catholic League was founded in 1609. Matters came to a head when, following the election of Ferdinand II as Holy Roman Emperor in 1619, the powerful states of Bohemia and Hungary installed Protestant monarchs. In

Bohemia's case this was Frederick V (1596–1632), the Elector Palatine, who had married James VI's (1566–1625) daughter Elizabeth Stuart (1596–1662). Bohemian resistance was broken by Ferdinand's imperial forces at the Battle of White Mountain in 1620. Henceforward the interests of the Reformed German states had to be defended by the intervention of external Protestant powers: Denmark–Norway (1625), Sweden (1630) and later Catholic France (1635). In addition, following Dutch harrying of Spanish shipping on the high seas, Spain ended its twelve-year truce with the Dutch Republic in 1621, and entered the war on the side of its fellow Habsburgs in the Empire and their Catholic League allies. An initial attempt to secure peace via the 1629 Edict of Restitution proved to be too Catholic to be acceptable, and the war continued to rage. Denmark–Norway came out of the war in exchange for territorial concessions, only to be replaced within months in the Protestant interest by the more formidable Gustavus Adolphus of Sweden, whose victories paved the way for the 1633 Heilbronn League, which replaced the earlier German Protestant Union. Repeated external intervention, the presence of multiple borders between the more than 200 small states of Germany and the toxic mixture of religious passion and political opportunism intensified the bitterness of the war and its scale. Meanwhile Spain was less successful in the Netherlands than had been expected as 'The republic allied with France and assumed the offensive against a distracted Spanish Empire' which suffered a reverse at home through the short-lived establishment of the Catalan Republic in 1640–41 under French protection. The Dutch indeed part-financed the continuation of the war by the Protestant powers, supported by their increasingly powerful mercantile interests, such as the Vereenigde Oostindische Compaagnie (VOC), the Dutch East India Company, 'the world's first multinational corporation', founded in 1602, and geared to commercial as much as imperial exploitation. The VOC displaced the Portuguese in East Asia and encouraged the population of the East Indies 'to raise production of spices . . . to satisfy a world market'; eventually it controlled twenty-eight commercial agencies, stretching from Yemen to Japan, and 'provided financial services' to non-Dutch Europeans in its Asian markets.[2]

England's policy under Charles I (r.1625–49) was unfocused. His early parliaments had reservations concerning the king's military adventurism in

France and Spain from which he indeed gained little. The militant Protestant interest in France was defeated in 1628 following stupendously incompetent interventions by the Duke of Buckingham both against and for the Huguenot interest, following which 'Charles was forced to abandon the Huguenots, who were granted toleration' and Buckingham was assassinated by a disgruntled veteran. Spanish defeats in the Netherlands relieved England of any anxiety over a Habsburg threat close to home, and Charles continued to tinker round the edges of the Thirty Years' War. In response to a Swedish request, in 1630 the King granted James, 1st Duke of Hamilton (1606–49) the right to levy forces in support of Gustavus Adolphus's war effort, and in 1636–37 'signed a treaty with France that would have aligned England against the Habsburgs', but failed to back it by committing troops, unsurprisingly since Charles was short of funds.[3]

The Peace of Prague (1635) secured the terms of an end to the conflict in the Holy Roman Empire in agreeing that Catholicism could not be imposed on its states by force, but foreign powers continued to range in conflict over the imperial territories. The final peace eventually came in 1648, seven years after Spain, France and the Dutch Republic had begun to pursue it, and the conventional view is that this Peace of Westphalia was the first European peace achieved by the diplomatic system which embodied modern notions of national sovereignty. The series of Westphalian treaties agreed at (Lutheran/ Catholic) Osnabruck and (Catholic) Münster thus presaged the Congress of Vienna in 1815 and the development of the balance of power principle which collapsed with the First World War, only to make a reappearance in the concept of nuclear deterrence. More recently, scholars have sought to dismiss or downplay the claims that the Peace of Westphalia was an innovative settlement which defined the nature of the modern state. These claims include:

1. The right of a state to exclusive control over its territory;
2. The equal sovereignty of all states;
3. The consequent lack of any right to interfere in the domestic politics of any other state either by direct force or indirectly (such as letters of marque authorizing privateering and other state sponsored piracy, though these were not outlawed until the nineteenth century); and

4. All states (including the (usually small) imperial states of the Holy Roman Empire had the right to choose their own religion including Calvinism, initially returning to the ecclesiastical position of 1624, but subsequently with freedom to change, 'except in the Upper Palatinate and in the hereditary lands of the House of Austria, which were reserved for the Catholic faith'.[4]

Henry Kissinger has summarized the popular Western understanding of these so-called Westphalian principles of sovereignty thus:

> The Westphalian peace reflected a practical accommodation to reality, not a unique moral insight. It relied on a system of independent states refraining from interference in each other's domestic affairs and checking each other's ambition through a general equilibrium of power . . . each state was assigned the attribute of sovereign power over its territory. Each would acknowledge the domestic structures and religious vocations of its fellow states as realities and refrain from challenging their existence.[5]

Kissinger's summary is an elegant statement of conventional wisdom on Westphalia, but there is an implicit misunderstanding in it which arises from its framing within Anglo-American conceptions of sovereignty. While the 'general equilibrium of power' is a condition in foreign affairs which can only be maintained by major power blocs and their ability to offset each other, 'sovereign power over its territory' is a much more distributed concept, not an identical one (unless you are the United States or a similarly powerful entity, which is of course what Kissinger has in mind). Liechtenstein may technically have 'sovereign power over its territory', but it cannot project that power and thus is unable to participate in a 'general equilibrium of power' (and indeed its foreign and monetary policy are largely subordinate to Switzerland). The American commentator sees Westphalia through the prism of the United States, a state built – from the Monroe doctrine of 1823 to the Spanish-American war of 1898 – on the projection of power and highly resistant to its curtailment. Equality of sovereignty is always a fiction, though as the debate over Brexit in the United Kingdom has shown, it is one with a long history and legacy.

Kissinger's perspective has its roots in the Romantic nationalism of modern historiography. Its founding Saxon historian, Leopold von Ranke (1795–1886), was born in the Electorate of Saxony while the Holy Roman Empire yet survived, and died under an imperial and unified Germany. In many respects, his outlook as a historian reflected this process, and his 'influential conception of the Empire's history as the story of failed nation-building' (as opposed to the success of its Prussian inheritor) has arguably prejudiced our understanding of the Empire's complex confederal politics to this day. The Holy Roman Empire lacked a 'large, centralized infrastructure' which stood beyond individual kingdoms and peoples, and an era focused on the nation state has misunderstood it, as indeed it has arguably misunderstood its Habsburg successor, imperial Austria. The princes of the Empire's states exercised sovereign rights, but those were 'curtailed by imperial law and duty to the Empire'. This conditional sovereignty, called *superioritas territorialis* or *Landeshoheit*, was expanded by the Peace of Westphalia by extending rights previously held by Electors of the Empire (for the Emperor was elected) to a wider circle of princely rulers. The *superioritas* of the princes nonetheless remained constrained by the interest of the Empire, and 'The imperial princes identified their prestige and autonomy with the Empire's continued well-being.' It might be too much to say that the federalism of modern Germany has its roots in the Holy Roman Empire, but the limitations placed on state sovereignty by that Empire gave it a distinctive confederal flavour – with elements of composite monarchy – which does not seem entirely alien from the relationship of Prussia to the German Confederation in the nineteenth century or yet more recent German constitutional arrangements. Nor is the nature of the European Union itself entirely dissimilar: indeed, its legislation has on occasion been explicitly identified with that of the Holy Roman Empire.[6]

One of the reasons that that the Thirty Years' War took the path that it did – a reason core to its complex relationship to notions of sovereignty – arose from the fact that the composite monarchy was such a major feature of political organization in early modern Europe. Besides the examples given in the introduction, major players with this political structure included the Castilian–Aragonian–Portuguese (1580–1640) Iberian kingdom, the Polish-Lithuanian Commonwealth, the Kingdoms of England, Scotland and Ireland

and to some extent – though more complex – the Holy Roman Empire itself. English cartographical rhetoric, such as John Speed's *Theatre of the Empire of Great Britaine* (1612), presented the multiple kingdoms of the British Isles as an island parallel to the Holy Roman Empire, and could even be seen to present England's counties as a parallel to German states. Composite monarchies typically united different countries on a more or less federal to confederal basis under one crown (the Holy Roman Empire was the most confederal among such polities: confederation being closer than composite monarchy to the preservation of its constituent states as independent state actors internationally, as well as possessing entrenched domestic powers). The constituent kingdoms or imperial states of such monarchies typically possessed a degree of independence, albeit often – as we have seen – with foreign policy restrictions. If the composite kingdoms survived, the independent capacity of their weaker members tended to erode with time. From the eighteenth century onwards, the creation of fresh composite monarchies has been in decline, with the exception of their ill-fated renewal in the shape of Austria-Hungary from 1867 to 1918 and in the original foundation of the equally ill-fated Yugoslavia (1919–91) as the Kingdom of the Serbs, Croats and Slovenes. It was in fact the Austro-Hungarian model that Arthur Griffith (1871–1922) initially advanced as policy for Sinn Fein in Ireland in 1904, though Republicanism swiftly gained the ascendancy.[7]

The two major remaining survivals among the European composite monarchies of the early modern period are Spain – which no longer in practice considers itself to be a composite monarchy, though Catalans and others disagree – and the United Kingdom. Indeed, the United Kingdom alone has extended the model in the modern world. Her Majesty the Queen is also Queen of Antigua and Barbuda, Australia, Bahamas, Belize, Canada, Grenada, Jamaica, New Zealand, Papua New Guinea, St Kitts and Nevis, St Lucia, St Vincent and the Grenadines, the Solomon Islands and Tuvalu. These are now functionally independent states, but in an earlier stage of the then British Empire, dominions such as Australia and Canada existed in a confederal relationship with London, not entirely unlike the *Landeshoheit* of the imperial states of the Holy Roman Empire. As the extensive use of Dominion troops in both World Wars showed, these countries – though independent within the British Empire – did not in the last resort possess a foreign policy which could be exercised fully independently of its interests. From Australian participation in the Vietnam War in 1962–72 onwards, this was clearly no longer the case, although Governor General Sir John Kerr's dismissal of Gough Whitlam from office as prime minister on behalf of the Crown in 1975 was an outlier of the older politics.

Composite monarchies could be – though were not always – relatively stable where confessional differences were minimal; but where confessional differences were substantial between or within states in the post-Reformation era (as indeed they often were in the sixteenth and seventeenth centuries), the crown could find it challenging to maintain order. Henry VIII of England (r.1509–47) had boosted his status by creating the first multi-kingdom monarchy in the British Isles by fiat, elevating Ireland from a lordship to a kingdom by the Crown of Ireland Act of 1542, while further centralizing the dominant English polity by changing Wales's status through annexation legislation in 1536 and 1542. This legislation is now often misleadingly described as an Act of Union, a term more redolent of political correctness than historical accuracy: it was not used until the twentieth century, and Wales indeed was correctly termed as part of England under the Wales and Berwick Act of 1746 (20 Geo. II c. 42), a situation that remained unchanged until 1967. In 1542, Henry also renewed claims to feudal superiority over Scotland: these measures were linked to Henrician notions of 'empire' to set against the claims of the Papacy in the matter of the division between Orthodox Constantinople and Catholic Rome.[8] But it was with the accession of James VI of Scotland to the English throne in 1603 that the first true British composite monarchy was created. James indeed sought closer union with Scotland than the English parliament – which revived the ancient document of Magna Carta in defence of its position to claim the laws of the two countries were incompatible – would tolerate. The 1607 suggestion that the king might set up his seat at York (where the Council of the North met until 1641) was a compromise that pleased no one.[9] But outside the boundaries of the British kingdoms a tenuous iconography of unity could on occasion be seen in diplomacy and in the deployment of forces on the Continent to support the Protestant interest. The 'first known British-flagged army in history' was deployed on James's authority in 1610, and 'a Regiment of Britons' (the majority of whom were Scots, with 1,000 men under Colonel John Seton to protect James's daughter) 'arrived too late to participate in the battle of White Mountain' to support Protestant troops in 1620 after 'Scots nobles and gentry flocked to the defence of Elizabeth Stuart and her family'. Subsequently Sir Andrew Gray raised another 2,500 'Britons', of whom 1,500 were Scots.[10]

This was not untypical of other multi-kingdom arrangements: the limits of the weaker kingdom's sovereignty were first made visible on the international stage through foreign policy restrictions and joint actions with the superior partner. In Scotland's case this process was accelerated and intensified by the fact that 'The Scottish Parliament had never managed to secure much influence over foreign policy' from the Crown prior to 1603, and now the Crown was removed to London. Thus 'All Stuart diplomatic treaties and instructions' were 'issued in the names of the kings of Great Britain and Ireland' rather than that of any of their three kingdoms.[11] Indeed, perhaps the key structural reason for Portugal's ability to free itself from the Spanish crown after Philip II's annexation was the fact that it already possessed an overseas empire which was never properly incorporated into the multi-kingdom monarchy's foreign policy arrangements. When in 1581 the Cortes in Portugal 'gave legal sanction' to Philip's seizure of the Crown, it was 'agreed that the two colonial empires should remain separately administered entities'; for his part, Philip swore 'to appoint only Portuguese officials in those possessions' held by Portugal overseas. This legacy supported the persistence of Portugal as an independent state actor, and in the end helped to allow its resumption of full statehood.[12]

By contrast, diplomatic embassies from foreign powers to Scotland began to decline markedly from the 1620s, as the state's independence of action from the larger kingdom became increasingly compromised. In an era when the king was central to diplomacy, the fact that James and Charles I each visited Scotland only once after 1603 transmitted a very clear message about the importance and relevance of the country. The Union of the Crowns led to what Karin Bowie calls 'a cumulatively catastrophic reduction in consultation', which ultimately undermined the polity it had established. This became a source of anxiety by the reign of Charles I at least, if not even earlier. In 1630, the Scottish Privy Council 'commanded that the usage of Great Britain in treaties be avoided' and instead that the British Crown should engage itself 'under the name and style of Scotland, England, France and Ireland'. This idle claim to sovereignty over France was itself a treasured possession of the English crown for almost a quarter of a millennium after the loss of Calais, its last foothold, in 1558.[13]

Britain came late to its own front in the Thirty Years' War. It is of course conventional wisdom that it was never joined to this 'Continental' conflict on its own territory, despite contemporary references which aligned the two. The Bohemian Wenceslas Hollar (1607–77), who was to become 'scenographer, or designer of prospects' to Charles II, linked 'the war in the British Isles in the 1640s to events in Bohemia in the 1620s'. Hollar had experience of both environments, and thus had a good case to make, though, as we shall see, the very composition of the Scottish Army of the Covenant was yet more persuasive, embarrassing as it clearly is for British historians to consider the 1640s in terms of a European conflict. The bitter war in the British Isles – whether phrased in its ultimate solipsistic form as 'the English Civil War' or the more mildly introverted variant of the 'War of the Three Kingdoms' – is still typically seen as exceptionally British, in the popular historical mind at least. Yet its relationships to the wider conflict are compelling, both in the arena of confessionalism and that of centralization. After 1603, when he became King of England and Ireland, James's Scottish Government had displayed significantly centralizing tendencies in the north and west, seeking closer control of the western Gaelic-speaking areas and an end to their language in the Statutes of Iona (1609) and the Education Act (1616), while abolishing Norse law in Orkney and Shetland (1611). Under the Statutes, sureties were imposed on the *fine*, the gentry of the affected Gaelic-speaking families, and they were under an obligation to appear in Edinburgh on an annual basis.[14]

In England and indeed throughout the three kingdoms, Charles I and William Laud (Archbishop of Canterbury from 1633) sought – as did the Catholic powers of Europe – ecclesial conformity, a caesaropapist Anglican version of Catholic policy, including a greater role for the church in secular

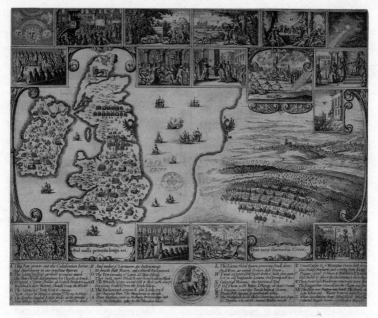

3. *A Comparison between the Bohemian and English Civil Wars* (1659).
By Wenceslas Hollar, showing a comparison between the wars in the
British Isles and in Europe in visual form.

government. Laud believed in the promotion of the clergy 'to places of greatest
honour and offices of the highest rank', and this had begun to transpire in
England in the 1630s, paving the way for a more central role for the Church in
supporting the Crown. Many associated this approach – exemplified in France
by Cardinal Richelieu (Armand Jean du Plessis, Duc de Richelieu (1585–
1642)) – with the growing influence of Henrietta Maria (1609–69), Charles's
French queen. In Scotland, Charles I insisted that his clergy should dress like
their English counterparts, and while Laud conceded a Scottish Prayer Book at
the request of the Scottish bishops instead of intruding the English liturgy, this
availed him little. Charles's vision of the 'public good' (which he saw as defined
by himself) demanded that 'the unity of the visible church had to be preserved
from public contest', and that required 'order and conformity' to a more
unitary form of religious practice throughout his kingdoms. All of the three

kingdoms, Catholic Ireland, Anglican England and Episcopalian/Calvinist Scotland were to converge towards a single form of high Anglicanism under the Crown. Here was a Protestant king, whose commitment to Protestantism many doubted, married to a queen from Richelieu's France, introducing centralizing religious policies redolent of the Habsburgs.[15]

Scottish soldiers had long served abroad in the armies of the country's European allies. In France, Scotland's greatest support had been given in the existential war against England after Agincourt (1415), where the Earl of Buchan's expeditionary force had secured a notable victory at Baugé over the Duke of Clarence in 1421. The Scots air 'Hey tutti taiti', was allegedly played at Bannockburn (1314) and by the Scottish forces serving with St Jeanne d'Arc at the crucial relief of Orléans in 1429. It remains a solemn march of the French armed forces, after being reset for military band performance a century ago by Léonce Chomel; in 2019, for example, it was played on the pipes at the funeral of Cédric de Pierrepont and Alain Bertoncello of Commando Hubert (killed in an operation to free hostages in Burkina Faso) attended by President Macron.

The Street of the Sword of Scotland in Orléans commemorates St Jeanne d'Arc's critical liberation, and some of the Scottish commanders, such as Patrick Ogilvy of Airlie, are also memorialized in the city; the Alliance France–Écosse has been responsible for some recent commemorations. St Jeanne herself was welcomed to Orléans by its Bishop, John Kirkmichael of Crail, while John Stewart of Darnley (1380–1429), Constable of France, who had led the first attempt to relieve Orléans, was buried in its cathedral. In the fifteenth century there were some 15,000 Scots resident in France (the Scots College in Paris was founded in 1333 and in Douai in 1592), and in later centuries it remained easy to settle since Scots 'received equality of treatment with French subjects in terms of inheritance' and were readily naturalized. When these rights were finally withdrawn at the dawn of the twentieth century, 'The French government declared that the terms of previous Franco-Scottish treaties remained valid for every Scot alive at the time of the Entente', that is, born before the Entente Cordiale of 1903–04.[16]

After the Scottish Reformation of 1560, Scottish military participation in the French army declined to the 100 or so men of the elite *Garde Écossaise*, the only one of the four *Garde* units 'allowed to remain constantly by the king'. On occasion, however, Scots recruitment on a larger scale continued to take place, for example to fight for Henri IV in 1589 or for France in the Thirty Years' War and in 1633 when Hepburn's (later Dumbarton's) Regiment in the French service was formed. Scots also continued to engage with mercantile activities and the professions in France. This was particularly true in French higher education, not least in the Huguenot colleges, every one of which had a Scottish principal at some time or another. In all, there were sixty-seven Scottish members of staff in the Huguenot academies in the century from 1580 to 1680, not far off half the total, including luminaries such as Zachary Boyd (1585–1633) and Aberdeen Grammar School boys Thomas Dempster (Historiographer Royal, 1579–1625), Walter Donaldson (b.1574) and Arthur Johnston (1579–1641). There were also well over a dozen Scots rectors of the University of Paris.[17] French architecture remained influential in Scotland, not only on the Netherbow port in Edinburgh (demolished in 1764), but also on Holyroodhouse, which echoed the Loire chateaux, and later in the work of Robert Adam (1728–92), influenced by Germain Boffrand (1667–1754) and others, while the vast tenement blocks of Edinburgh were built in conscious relation to those of Paris and other French cities.[18]

In military terms, the Reformation saw the recruitment of Scots soldiers in general switch to the Protestant states, with the Scots Brigade of the Dutch Republic (formed by 1603 and finally absorbed into domestic Dutch forces in 1782) among the most prominent units. More Scots were recruited from Gaelic-speaking areas into European theatres as the opportunities in Ireland dried up after the Flight of the Earls in 1607 and the completion of English conquest.[19] The Thirty Years' War saw this process reach its apogee. Between 1618 and 1648, almost 62,000 Scots were recruited for the Protestant allies and France, beside a much smaller number who fought with the Empire. In 1620, as we have seen above, Sir Andrew Gray and Colonel James Seaton raised 2,500 Scotsmen to fight for Bohemia, and in 1624 Gray recruited 4,000 more for the Protestant cause. Recruitment was carried out in support of Christian IV (r.1588–1648) of Denmark–Norway when he entered the war in 1625 (Charles I's own mother was a Danish princess), and by March 1627 13,500 Scots had enlisted under the nominal leadership of the Earl of

Nithsdale; the Scottish forces in Denmark flew the Saltire with a Danish flag in the corner. Christian's own forces were massively outnumbered by Scots in their own army (there were three times as many Scottish as native officers), and both Robert Scott and the Earl of Nithsdale rose to general officer rank. When Denmark–Norway left the war in 1629,[20] many of their Scots troops joined Gustavus Adolphus's Swedish forces, and by 1630 there were some 12,000 Scots in the Swedish service under the overall command of Sir James Spens of Wormiston (d.1632), who had planned to colonize the Isle of Lewis with Anglophone Scots in 1598. The next year between 6,000 and 8,000 more joined under Hamilton, the potential personal conflict between himself and Spens being resolved by Hamilton becoming 'General of British', while Spens was 'General of Scots'. Hamilton had received his licence to raise forces from Charles I as part of the king's limited and rather unfocused (but Anglo-British rather than Scottish) participation in the Thirty Years' War on its Continental fronts.[21]

Hamilton's 'British' were mostly Scots however. Between 1629 and 1660, Sweden commissioned 119 Scots colonels and lieutenant colonels, as well as being possessed of several Scottish generals, including David Drummond (1593–1638), James King (1589–1652) and Patrick Ruthven (c.1573–1650), and two field marshals, Sir Alexander Leslie, later Earl of Leven (1582–1661) and Robert Douglas (1611–62). Scots supplied over 100 governors or commanders to areas under Swedish power or the power of the Protestant cause, as in Augsburg (Thomas Kinnemond appointed governor in 1632), Bremen (William Legge, 1633), Frankfurt (Alexander Leslie, 1631), Kalmar (Patrick Traill, 1638), Munich (John Hepburn, 1632), Regensburg (Alexander Irving, 1633) and Riga (James Scott, 1632). By the end of the Thirty Years' War there were some thirty Scots in the Swedish nobility. Even before the conflict, there was a significant Scottish presence in the country's armed forces: 64 per cent of Swedish naval captains were Scottish by the late 1620s. By contrast, the Royal Navy's attempts to recruit in Scotland in 1626 were unsuccessful.[22]

To some extent, it is possible to view the strong Scottish participation in Swedish politics as a soft version of an independent Scottish foreign policy, with Sweden playing the role of 'allied state'. Scots were also highly active in Swedish trade and directed a number of companies there, while Scottish captains on Swedish trading vessels attempted to evade the terms of England's (then Britain's) Navigation Acts. Gothenburg, where John Spalding (*c.*1600–?) was President of Commerce 1658–67, was the core area of Scottish economic activity in Sweden. Spalding exported to destinations in the German states (where his brother Andrew was a merchant), Denmark, England, France, Norway, Spain and Portugal. Scots merchants, goldsmiths and silversmiths could be found in Stockholm. Later, Scottish capital was supplied to support the creation of the Swedish East India Company, and in the Jacobite era Gothenburg became the home of a 'smuggling trade' in 'Gothenburg tea' which evaded taxation: the 'godfathers' of this network were Scottish Jacobite exiles. Scottish born or descended families continued to be prominent in Sweden's major cities: men such as William Gibson of Arbroath (1783–1857) made a fortune from his Gothenburg base out of timber and iron exports during the Continental blockade of the Napoleonic wars, while his partner Alexander Keiller of Dundee (1804–74) went into shipping. As late as 1857 a Hamilton was Marshal of the Kingdom of Sweden, while William Franklin Thorburn (1820–1903) introduced curling into the country.[23]

There was also strong engagement with Denmark–Norway, with Scottish admirals such as Alexander Durham, Andrew Mowatt and John Cunningham (*c.*1575–1651) in the service of the Danish crown. Cunningham played a significant role in the domestic and international relations of his adopted country: his 1605 claim to Greenland for Denmark was contested by the British Crown, and he later went on to be virtually vice-regal governor of Finnmark. In all, Scotland provided thirty-five senior officers for the Denmark–Norway navy from 1580 to 1660, and twenty governors. Sweden tended to use Scots in war zones (highly effectively, Lumsden's Regiment alone capturing 'nine stands of colours' at 'the taking of Frankfurt in 1632'), and this echoed Denmark–Norway's use of men like Cunningham on the frontiers of the realm, a posting that denoted trust, resourcefulness and detachment from local politics. These qualities were also evident in the Scottish mercantile trade in both the Scandinavian kingdoms: almost half of Aberdeen's thirty trading vessels were in the Norway trade in 1712, and Scots in Bergen alone supplied 47 per cent of timber exports from the port to England in the seventeenth century. Scots rigging contractors, sailors and maintenance men supported the Swedish navy, while there were also the more typically peacetime professionals long associated with Scotland (where the first Chair of Medicine dates from 1505), with Jakob Robertson of Struan (1566–1652) acting as Physician to Queen Christina (1626–89). The Danish and Swedish armies were not the only Protestant and anti-Habsburg powers to benefit from Scottish recruitment either: Privy Council records note 2,800 recruitment warrants for the Netherlands, 10,000 for France and 1,500 for Bohemia. Intriguingly, there were also 800 for Habsburg Spain. In France, the Scottish military presence expanded back towards its mediaeval size with two further Scots regiments in the French service in addition to Hepburn's, the Régiment de Douglas and the Régiment d'Infanterie Écossais. Scots 'professionalism as soldiers coupled with their comradely clannishness made them attractive to potential employers', and their 'incredible fighting spirit' was also recognized in the 1618–48 conflict. It was to form the basis for the key role Scottish soldiers would come to play in the British Empire.[24]

By 1637, the Protestant war effort was coming home. Following the introduction of the Laudian Scottish Prayer Book to public worship, opposed by 'widespread petitioning', large parts of Scotland – both 'puritan' by inclination and to some degree further radicalized by years of European religious war – broke out in open resistance. Tolerating Episcopalian bishops who could not effectively dictate to local presbyteries was one thing; Charles and Laud's elevation of the episcopate to a central position in the demand for authority and conformity was another, particularly in central and southern Scotland where the Presbyterians were dominant. The National Covenant was drafted in opposition to the imposition of such religious innovations into Scotland, and was publicly adopted at Greyfriars Kirkyard in Edinburgh on 28 February 1638: it has obvious parallels with the resistance to the imposition of Catholicism in Bohemia, which are still perhaps too seldom addressed. The Covenant received wide support, except in the north and the universities (where only Edinburgh – more closely answerable to the civic authorities than the other ancients – was in full support). Conformity to the Covenant was demanded by the Scottish Parliament in 1640, thus ushering in a concept of Scotland as a 'confessional state' which was to be highly damaging in the years to come. While not explicitly outlawing Episcopacy, the Kirk that the

Covenant 'described as lawful was undoubtedly Presbyterian'. The National Covenant was an attempt both to resist the King and Archbishop Laud's demands for ecclesial conformity and also to express a notion of popular sovereignty in contradiction to the intrusion on rights of conscience and association by the Crown. This was a concept that built on a Scottish tradition which can arguably be traced back to the Declaration of Arbroath (1320) and more certainly to the thinking of George Buchanan (1506–82) and other sixteenth-century Presbyterians. Buchanan had argued (in his Dialogue of 1579) 'that the law was above the king, while his 1582 History attempted to show that the Scottish realm had been founded in ancient times on a principle of elective monarchy by which a king could be removed if he did not respect the law'. At the same time Dutch thinkers were making the same argument regarding Philip II of Spain's authority in the Netherlands, and mutual influence between Dutch and Scottish thought in this field is likely, as well as the Bohemian exemplar mentioned above. The Covenant followed a similar line to its Dutch comparators in that it 'argued for an inversion of authority by which those subscribing . . . were to determine the appropriate role of the church and the king', whose authority therefore was seen as depending on consent, not as a last but as a first resort. The Glasgow Declaration of 1639 further emphasised Presbyterian governance at the cost of royal authority. Covenanting control of the Scots Parliament in 1640/41 was used to pass legislation 'placing explicit statutory limits on royal power', while an 'explicit denunciation' was made regarding Episcopal government. The extension of civil powers to the clergy was also viewed as unlawful; this French-style development was causing concern in England also. Unsurprisingly, these actions only intensified the intransigence of the Crown.[25]

On the Continent, Cardinal Richelieu's government was concerned – given the ancient alliance between Scotland and France – at these rising tensions, and France made some moves to support the Covenanters, who were also largely successful in ensuring the neutrality of Denmark–Norway, despite a tendency towards explicit support of the Crown from the Danish king's side. Charles I's response to the challenge of the National Covenant in turn ensured that 'the Scottish crisis' 'emasculated England' as a major power, leading France to expose Charles' inability to support a Continental front in the war.[26] That front was in any case coming home, with '300 veteran officers from Swedish service' returning to Scotland in 1637–38. Many of them would soon find employment in a new conflict; and indeed there is evidence that what was to become the military centre of the Covenanting movement had already been preparing for such a venture.[27] Field Marshal Alexander Leslie himself returned to his homeland in 1638 to command the Army of the Covenant, where a large number of his men were veterans of the Swedish service and were far more formidable than their English opponents – or indeed later allies. Charles's own attempts to recruit from Scottish and English troops abroad do not seem to have been successful. The return of significant numbers of Scots veterans from the Swedish and other pro-Protestant foreign service in the Thirty Years' War thus enabled victory over the King's forces in the two brief 'Bishops' Wars' of 1638–41. Leslie (from 1641 Earl of Leven) did not forget the other theatres of the Thirty Years' War, however, intending to 'send out a full 10,000 men to Sweden to help finish the war once he reduced his army on their return from England in January 1647'.[28]

Charles' move to ally with Spain in return for troops to defeat the Covenanters in 1640 was potentially alike toxic and incompetent: hallmarks of his government. A prospective Dutch–Covenanter alliance loomed in response. In the short term, a fresh crisis in Ireland following a Rising on the Catholic side against the Anglican interest in 1641, brought some respite on the Scottish front as the Covenanters offered Charles men to suppress the Rising and protect the Presbyterian plantation of Ulster (where some 30,000 Scots had settled and were struggling to impose a Scottish micro-world in 'a hybrid society'). These troops were, however, to remain under Scottish command, which on occasion hindered joint operations. In England, Charles was forced to abandon his loyal supporter the Earl of Strafford to execution for treason on suspicion of creating an Irish army that could have been used to reduce England among other 'high crimes and misdemeanours'. Many in English metropolitan circles saw the Irish Rising as confirmation of their worst fears rather than a reason to rally to the Crown. (It is important to realize that, at this date, Ireland's population was probably more than a third of England's, so it was perceived as a real military threat; in 1700 Ireland, Scotland

and Wales put together had a population some 80 per cent of England's). The Catholic Remonstrance of March 1642 defended Irish Catholic interests against the Crown (while, like the Covenanters, protesting their loyalty to it). The Remonstrance was followed by the establishment of a quasi-independent Ireland outside Ulster, the Confederation, which defended 'Ireland's independence from the jurisdiction of Westminster' while maintaining loyalty to the Crown: the Confederation's political approach once again reflected the contemporary struggle for religious rights in the *Landeshoheit* states of the Holy Roman Empire. General Robert Monro (d.1680), a former Swedish colonel, landed in Ireland in April 1642 with a Scottish Covenanting army whose main goal was to protect the Ulster Scots, while Eoghan Ruadh Ó Néill (*c*.1585–1649), commander of one of the seven Irish regiments in the Spanish service, landed in Donegal to take command of the forces of the Confederation, which had requested money and arms from Spain. In England, fear that the King's drive for ecclesiastical conformity resembled that of the European Catholic powers and that he was willing to use Irish troops in support of his goals was rife, fed by domestic policy resentments and religious opposition to Laudianism. Open war followed in 1642: it was to lead to a death toll higher in percentage terms 'than the losses incurred during either the First or the Second World War'. There is nothing like religious conflict to bring out the best in people.[29]

In Scotland, following the military successes in defence of the Covenant, 'an imperialistic agenda ... gained momentum', which in the eyes of magnates like the Earl (later Marquess) of Montrose (1612–50) became an 'endeavour to export a particular form of religion to England and Ireland', despite the King having been forced to accept Presbyterianism in Scotland, a major goal of the supporters of the 1638 Covenant. Montrose, as a consequence, went over to the king's cause, though much of the heft of his initially successful army came from Sir Alasdair MacColla (1610–47), who was acting as a 'bridgehead' to Irish Catholic Confederation interests and was killed fighting for the Confederation at Knocknanuss.[30]

By the Solemn League and Covenant of 1643, the Scots Covenanters sought to extend their success by imposing Presbyterianism on the whole of the British Isles in a mirror image of the King's 1630s strategy:

The Reformation of Religion in the Kingdoms of England and Ireland, in Doctrine, Worship, Discipline and Government, according to the Word of God, and the example of the best Reformed Churches . . . shall endeavour to bring the Churches of God in the three Kingdoms, to the nearest conjunction and uniformity in Religion, Confession of Faith, Form of Church-government, Directory of Worship and Catechizing.

This would of course involve the 'extirpation of Popery, Prelacy [bishops]' and all other forms of opposition to the 'Common cause of Religion, Liberty, and Peace' promised by the imposition of Presbyterianism by these advocates of what would be Scotland's 'prominent role in the apocalyptic triumph of Christ over the kingdoms of Antichrist'.[31] What the Holy Roman Empire could not do in a war which had been raging for twenty-five years, the Army of the Covenant would deliver. The price of the Solemn League for Scotland was a form of closer religious and political association with England, but certainly not Union as it was understood post 1707: this was a measure rejected by many core Covenanters at the time and for years afterwards. The reward for the English Parliament was the military support of the most formidable fighting force in the islands in their struggle against the Crown, of which most Covenanters were, in some sense, supporters. Parliament gained this support not through a cast iron commitment to impose Presbyterianism but by a much more vague assent that effectively gained them extensive military support without agreeing to the changes sought by the Solemn Leaguers.

The lack of pragmatism of the Solemn Leaguers was not unique in the Europe of their era, but the incompetent scale of their ambition remains notable to this day. Other small states looked for domestic religious rights, not millenarian domination; the apocalyptic pretensions of the Solemn League have arguably been given a soft ride by some of Scotland's historians, but they were as staggering as they were inept. The League's short-term effects immensely benefited the English Parliamentary war effort, and it is a key paradox of the era that the most aggrandizing statement of Scottish nationality ever produced should in the end have been to the virtually sole benefit of English political interests and have led indirectly to Scotland's incorporation into the English-dominated Commonwealth polity of the 1650s.

In the shorter term, the Solemn League and Covenant brought Scotland into England's war on the Parliamentary side. At Marston Moor in 1644, the Scottish Army composed almost 60 per cent of the allied Army of Both Kingdoms opposed to the King. It was they who determined the final outcome, with the ability of Alexander Leslie's veterans to resist the Royalist cavalry being critical. This was the beginning of the end for King Charles, and it was a triumph largely delivered by Scottish troops, many of whom had seen war in the Continental theatres. Any political capital gained by the massive Scottish contribution to Parliament's victory was squandered in 1647–51 by a series of increasingly desperate deals with an equally desperate Charles I, then Charles II, to intrude even a temporary Presbyterianism on England, as (predictably) once the war had been won there was no interest in extending Scottish religious practice throughout England on the part of the Solemn Leaguers' allies. Far from delivering millennial Presbyterianism throughout the Empire of Great Britain, the Solemn League was merely to prove a useful tool in the establishment of a Cromwellian polity dominated by England.

In 1647, Charles engaged for a 'trial of Presbyterianism in England' in return for Scots help, but the so-called Engagers were fainthearts in Solemn League terms and such supporters of a temporary Presbyterian settlement were – together with the wide spectrum of certain Prelatists (Episcopalians and Anglicans) and quasi-Papists in Scotland – largely excluded from government and the army before Scotland went to war in support of Charles II in 1649–51, rendering Cromwell's victory all the more certain. For some more moderate voices, the Covenant had become an idol and the defeat of its once successful armies could therefore be read as a punishment for idolatry. As a consequence of his military victory, Cromwell's administration was able to incorporate Scotland and Ireland into a single Commonwealth and temporarily end the constitutional arrangements of the composite monarchy (though the Commonwealth retained the title of England, Scotland and Ireland rather than 'Britain') in 1652–54. Cromwellian Independents even entered into ministerial livings in Glasgow.[32] Suppression of disaffection was severe. One-fifth of Maclean townships were still lying waste more than twenty years after they lost 700 men in resisting on behalf of the Crown at

Inverkeithing in 1651, while the Macleod levies suffered such casualties at the battle of Worcester in the same year that it affected their military capacity and enthusiasm for decades. The suppression of the Earl of Glencairn's rising for the King in 1653–54 led to further devastation. Recalcitrant Scots were shipped out to the American colonies and the Caribbean in a foreshadowing of practice that would endure deep into the eighteenth century: 900 individuals to Virginia and 150 to New England in 1651; 6,000 to the American colonies and the Caribbean the following year. They were sold for about 365 kilogrammes of sugar in Barbados, and their working conditions appear to have been similar to those of enslaved African people, although the Scots could expect release and a smallholding within seven years in most circumstances: however, the climate in Barbados made surviving for this length of time challenging. Things were easier in the American colonies: although, in 1652, the Massachusetts Bay Militia Regulations lumped together 'Scotsmen, Negroes and Indians' as suspect categories in colonial society, the assimilation of the Scots was fairly rapid thereafter. Irishmen were also deported in significant numbers as Cromwell defeated the forces of the Confederation, with his soldiers killing thousands including many non-combatants at the sieges of Drogheda and Wexford.[33]

In the British kingdoms there was thus no equivalent of the Westphalian settlement. The preamble to the Act for the Settlement of Ireland in 1652 makes this chillingly clear:

> Whereas the Parliament of England, after the expense of much blood and treasure for suppression of the horrid rebellion in Ireland, have by the good hand of God upon their undertakings, brought that affair to such an issue, as that a total reducement and settlement of that nation may, with God's blessing, be speedily effected . . .[34]

For Cromwell's government, 'reducement and settlement' went together when dealing with nations other than England. Despite their incorporation into the new Commonwealth, neither Ireland nor Scotland were seen as integrated into being 'British' in any way. This was not entirely surprising as both countries were effectively composed of aliens, unknown in England.

Only 272 Scots were naturalized in England between 1509 and 1603, a quarter of the number of naturalized Frenchmen and women. There were only fifty Scots in London in 1567. The Commonwealth was a military import into unfamiliar lands.[35]

EUROPEAN SCOTLAND

Scots were found in greater numbers throughout Continental Europe than they were in London, and many more went into exile with Charles II (and some of those who remained behind went into exile when he returned). These Scots were part of what was already a long-established tradition of Scottish sojourning or exile abroad, where 'sojourning' indicates a period primarily dedicated to accumulating education, experience, expertise or capital, and 'exile' a political or religious displacement, sometimes a sojourn, sometimes more permanent. The extent of Scottish experience abroad was historically driven by three main factors: Scotland's relative overproduction of educated men and the inability of the country to offer scope for their ambition; the impossibility of expanding territorially because of a dispropor-tionately powerful neighbour; and the country's economy, which not only lacked bullion and required foreign currency to maintain monetary circula-tion, but also stood in need of a proactive trade policy. Scotland's exports of skins, fish and wool (high quality salmon from the rivers Dee and Don bore the ABDN (Aberdeen) kitemark on the barrels) were ill matched to its need for a greater variety of imports ('wine from France . . . consumer goods from the Netherlands, timber from Norway and rye and flax from Poland'), as well as brandy, Canary wine and citrus fruits in a trading network stretching from Scandinavia to the Mediterranean states.[36] As a consequence, Scots were especially active in the army, clerisy and in trade, whereby they often entered the markets from which they imported in order to engage with, if not control, the trade into Scotland from those countries. The near controlling interest in the Bergen timber trade, alluded to above, was matched by the high concentration of Scots merchants in cities such as Gdánsk/Danzig, which helped to enable huge import orders: 30,000 skins from one Aberdeen merchant in 1650, for example, and almost 70,000 metres of plaid the same year from Aberdeen to Gdánsk and Veere alone (see below). In the 1620s, 32 per cent of Scottish imports came from the Netherlands, 22 per cent from northern Germany and the Baltic, 22 per cent from England and 18 per cent from France. With the exception of England, these were all areas of high Scottish expatriate mercantile activity which sustained a network that incorporated both a breadth of engagement in other professions and a participation in the political power structures of the host nation, which extended far beyond the mercantile and military. By the sixteenth century, there were already notable Scottish expatriate merchants at Bordeaux, Bruges, Campveere, Copenhagen, Dieppe, Elsinore, Gdánsk and Malmö, among other locations.[37]

Besides France, already discussed, and the Netherlands, of which more shortly, Scots merchants were found in particularly strong concentrations in the vast Polish–Lithuanian Commonwealth composite monarchy. In Gdánsk there was a 'Little Scotland' or Scottish quarter (*Alt-Schottland*); in one small town in western Lithuania, Scots owned '64 per cent of all the properties' in the central district. Many areas of Poland still bear Scottish place names. Some 6,000 Scots merchants, mostly from the east coast, settled in the Polish part of the Commonwealth in all; they were mainly Protestant, particularly at Cracow/Kraków, and often perpetuated their wealth and community by intermarriage, even to the third generation and beyond. Contemporary estimates of the total number of Scots in the Polish–Lithuanian Commonwealth ranged as high as between 30,000 and 40,000, not all of whom were prosperous as the 1634 'ban on Scottish and Jewish peddling' indicated (there were also proclamations against Scottish pedlars in a variety of other locations, from Brandenburg (1558) to Norway (1667)). In terms of business, Scots often used the Baltic ports as export venues for goods from the Holy Roman Empire: men like Robert Blackhall supplying 'knives, candlesticks, pistols, mirrors, combs' and scissors from the German lands. These 'pedlars and merchants' were often viewed by the Poles with disdain or hostility, despite the Commonwealth's 'openness to foreign immigration'. The same criticisms were made of the Scots in Poland as were made in England in the eighteenth century: that they were 'hungry' and greedy. Indeed, the accusations of impoverishment and greed levelled at the Scots in Poland may have been – as they were elsewhere in later centuries – a sign of resentment and envy at the incomers' success. Certainly in the years following 1603, the Crown representatives in Poland tended to be Scots, reflecting the strength of the mercantile community there, which meant that 'Scottish diplomats . . . were best prepared to handle the British interests'. William Bruce (b.1560) was the first of these: an academic in France and Poland, with experience in the Holy Roman Empire and the Italian states, he was a typical elite European Scot, and became the first British Crown agent in Poland, where he held a professorship in Roman Law at the Zamość/Zamoyski Academy, in 1604–10.[38]

The Scottish community in Poland persisted long after Bruce's time, and it remained important in many Polish cities: the textile merchant Alexander Chalmers from Dyce was four times mayor of Warsaw between 1691 and 1703, and a plaque was unveiled in the city to honour him by Scottish minister Linda Fabiani in 2008. In later years, Poles showed enthusiasm for Macpherson's *Ossian* poetry (see Chapter 4), and Scots settled in the post-1815 Congress kingdom of Poland, which before its suppression by Russia 'imported Scottish engineers, managers and agricultural improvers with their families': some 1,000 Scots emigrated to Poland between 1806 and 1825 alone. A professional community had replaced a mercantile one, but the tradition of Polish–Scottish engagement persisted. One part of that tradition was that Polish-derived profits could be repatriated to Scotland, as was the case in support of Marischal College in Aberdeen at the turn of the eighteenth century and in the foundation of Robert Gordon's College in the city in 1732, supported by Gordon's profits from his business in the Commonwealth.[39]

Scots were frequently to be found throughout the other Baltic lands as well as elsewhere in Europe. Transnational activities were supported (as with the easy naturalization of Scots in France) by the theoretical entitlement of Scots to 'enjoy the same status as Danes and Norwegians' in Denmark-Norway under the 1589 Stuart–Oldenburg marriage alliance. Bergen (up to 10 per cent of whose population was Scottish), Stavanger and Trondheim were only three of the centres for Scots activity in the timber trade, and 'some 150 Scots became burgesses of Bergen between 1600 and 1660'. In

Sweden, there were dozens of Scots merchants active in Stockholm and Gothenburg, as we have already seen. Nor were all Scots merchants on the northern seas men: Elisabeth Kinnaird shipped from Amsterdam (where Sara Maclean and others were also merchants) to Stockholm, while Catherine Sinclair was active in Hamburg. Scots Catholics had national religious houses in France, Spain, the Papal States and elsewhere, while in the Holy Roman Empire they not only had their own religious foundations, but took over some former Irish ones too, which had originally been in the care of *Scoti*, as Irish monks were called in the early mediaeval period. Figures such as Ninian Winzet (1518–92), 'president of the German nation' at the Sorbonne, perpetuated Scottish Catholic as well as Protestant intellectual leadership. Alexander Kinghorn was professor of medicine in Copenhagen in 1513, while Adam Stewart was professor of philosophy at Leiden in 1645, themselves only part of a long trail of Scottish intellectual exports that reached back to Baldred Bisset at Bologna and Duns Scotus in Paris centuries before. Ratisbon, Würzburg and other Scottish Catholic religious houses continued in the German lands, Ratisbon in Regensburg in Bavaria surviving as a Scots abbey to the late date of 1862, long after its sister houses had been secularized.[40]

What was the country these Scots left like, and what were they like themselves? In 1561, Julius Caesar Scaliger observed that 'The Swedes, Norse, Greenlanders and Goths are bestial, and so are the Scots and Irish.' In Rotterdam (the most popular city for Scots settlement in the Netherlands), Scots were most noted for drinking (the alleged prelude to any deal with a Scots merchant) and public scolding: an intriguing observation since it suggests links with the traditional Scottish practices of 'flyting' (a public insults competition) and 'sherricking' (an – often public – scolding amounting to an accusation). Visitors from England to Scotland noted its strangeness, while inevitably comparing it with what was already familiar to them, sometimes to the advantage of the northern kingdom.[41] John Taylor, the Water Poet (1578–1653), visiting in 1618, described Stirling as like 'Windsor for situation, much more than Windsor in strength . . . much beyond Edenborough [sic] Castle in state and magnificence', while with some dismay noting of the Scottish capital that 'the gentlemens [sic] mansions and goodliest houses are obscurely founded'. Both James Howell in 1639 and Richard Franck in 1656 commented on the quality and low cost of French wine in Scotland (in contrast, dairy products were held inferior to those of England), while the strength of the country's castles and the scale of the Port of Leith, capital of Scotland's 'merchandize for treasure', were also remarked on. Glasgow, with its 'broad and pleasant' streets was compared to Oxford by John Roy in 1662, and generally preferred to Edinburgh by most, who found its urban layout more familiar than the capital's intense 'high and dirty' jumble of tall buildings and unfamiliar social practices, where 'most of the houses . . . are parted into divers tenements, so they have as many landlords as stories'. French visitors such as Jorevin de Rocheford[t] in the 1660s found themselves hosted by Francophone Scots with experience of the French service. Despite the widespread desire of nineteenth-century writers to divide 'the Highlands' in dress and culture from the rest of Scotland (addressed in the Introduction, and a tendency which is ameliorated rather than exhausted), visitors repeatedly note that men and women in the cities wore tartan plaid, which in any case (supplied from Kidderminster) had even become a fashion item in London in the seventeenth century in deference to the Stuarts. The prevalence of tartan in urban Scotland is remarked on, for example, by both Sir William Brereton in Edinburgh in 1636 and John Roy in 1662 ('When they go abroad none of them wear hats, but a party coloured blanket which they call a plaid.'). As late as 1747, James Ray noted that women in Edinburgh 'use the *Scots* Plaids about their Heads and Shoulders'. The fact that women were 'capable of estates and honours, and inherit both as well as the males' was noted, as was their retention of their maiden name on marriage. Thomas Morer, writing in 1689, divided Scotland along imagined ethnic lines in a way which foreshadowed the prejudices of the next two centuries, comparing Highlanders to ancient Britons and taking 'the Low-landers to be a medley of Picts, Scots, French, Saxons, and English'. Morer nonetheless notes the use of the plaid in the south among the 'meaner sort'; he also noted the lack of bullion to support an indigenous currency. The touchiness and arrogance of the Scots – particularly those of the *Gaidhealtachd* – was remarked on by some.[42]

Between 1676 and 1725, Scots were almost 6 per cent of all enrolled students in Dutch universities, with the vast majority studying either medicine or law. Sir James Dalrymple, 1st Viscount Stair (1619–95), author of the foundational *Institutions of the Law of Scotland* (1681), was enrolled as a student in exile at Leiden, regarded as a more progressive university than Utrecht, and a beacon in Dutch higher education. Dutch universities influenced Scottish legal developments and, even more so, medical developments, with Edinburgh's medical teaching modelled on Leiden's and eventually surpassing it. Curling and golf both arose as sports from the two-way exchange between Scotland and the Netherlands, with the Old Course at St Andrews dating from 1552, and a seven-hole golf course on Musselburgh Links dating from no later than 1672: the Royal & Ancient golf club at St Andrews evolved into the R&A (2004) and remains the global world governing body for golf outside the United States and Mexico. Dutch painting dominated Scotland's nascent art market, while Dutch-inspired land reclamation also influenced Scotland. Netherlandish architecture and design could be seen in church architecture, in the corbie stepped gables and pantiles (manufactured in Scotland by 1716) of the east coast ports, in the new country seats being built for the Scottish nobility in the late seventeenth century and in some striking urban architecture. Canongate Kirk, built for James VII in 1688, which serves a parish including Holyroodhouse and the Scottish Parliament, and which the Royal Family still attend when in Edinburgh, is a fine example of a Dutch gable built by James Smith (1645–1731), better known as an advocate of Palladianism. Dutch gardens and Dutch milling were alike influential. Scots served in the armies of the Dutch Republic (where there were three Scots regiments by 1628, termed the 'bulwark of the republic'), while Scots law and lawyers were strongly influenced by Dutch legal frameworks. Between 1660 and 1760, 40 per cent of those admitted to the Faculty of Advocates in Edinburgh had studied in the Netherlands.[43] From 1673, twenty Scots a year went to study accountancy in the Dutch merchant houses, which thus contributed towards the development of Scottish leadership in financial innovation in the British Empire in the century that followed. In their turn, Scots returned from the Netherlands to teach similar skills in Scotland, with commercial schools beginning to develop from the 1690s.[44]

4. Canongate Kirk, Canongate, Edinburgh, showing architect James Smith's prominent Dutch gable.

VEERE

A Scottish merchant Staple was founded at Veere (Campveere) in Zeeland in 1541 where, in the fifteenth, sixteenth and seventeenth centuries some 7 per cent of the population were Scots. From 1541, the post of Conservator of Scots Privileges in the Netherlands (who resided at the Scots House) was linked to the tax concessions the Scots community enjoyed in Veere. These diminished as the eighteenth century progressed, though the title itself was only absorbed into the role of the British Consul in 1847, almost fifty years after the Scottish Staple at Veere and any substantive role for its Conservator had effectively ceased to exist (in 1996 it moved back into the Scottish and political sphere when the title was awarded to the Scottish National Party

Member of the European (MEP) Parliament, Winnie Ewing). In the days before it was an honorary title, the Staple Conservator acted as a combination of diplomat and trade envoy, maintaining 'a working relationship with both the Convention of Royal Burghs and the Scottish Parliament, and . . . was assisted in his moral duties by the Staple minister', a Scots Kirk having been set up in Veere in 1614, and later as part of the Presbytery of Edinburgh. In critical times such as that of the Spanish–Dutch war, the Staple 'became one of the key diplomatic channels' for communication beyond the formal remit of the Crown's diplomatic network. A Scottish lawcourt was set up in Veere, and a Scottish Nation House established. Although Dutch tax changes in the eighteenth century progressively eroded the fiscal advantage of the Scots Staple, as late as the 1770s Scots are present in almost one in five of the 300 preserved documents of one Veere notary. In 1780, when Great Britain was on the verge of war with the Netherlands over their covert stance in the American War of Independence (a development which led to the incorporation of the Scots Brigade into the Dutch Army), the Scots of Veere were capable of adopting an independent foreign policy in drawing up 'a declaration of neutrality' with respect to the War.[45]

At Bruges, *Schottendyk* was the only wharf named after foreigners. In Rotterdam, where in the 1670s the Englishman Samuel Tucker noted that the Scots ships were 'more in number and better than the English', Scots 'worked in the [coal] trade as merchants, shipmasters, and mariners', facilitating coal imports (a coal ship came in at least once every three days from Scotland) in return for advantageous access to 'ironware . . . spices, drugs, brand, soap, and flax' from the local market. Thus the Scots gained access to this market by being 'prominent among the official brokers who regulated the trade for Rotterdam', utilizing their own institutions – such as the Scots Kirk, founded in 1643 – to support their mercantile networking in this increasingly important town, whose population matched Edinburgh's by

1700. Scots visited Rotterdam for recreational purposes, and there was a two-way flow between Scotland and the Netherlands, with Dutch communities in Stornoway as early as the 1630s. In the difficult years for Scottish Presbyterianism after 1660, there were dozens of ministers in the Netherlands, and the doctrinal squabbles which are such an enduring hobby of Scottish Presbyterianism were even reflected in the Scots communities abroad, with a 'Cameronian attack on the Rotterdam kirk in November 1683'. In the second half of the seventeenth century, Rotterdam and Veere dominated the Scots–Dutch trade, and many of those exiled by domestic political circumstances in Scotland apparently practised this trade without restriction. Rotterdam had developed its own *Beurs* (bourse, stock exchange) in 1598, its own *Kamer can Assurantie* (Chamber of Commerce) in 1604 and *Wisselbank* (Bank of Exchange) in 1635, twenty-six years after Amsterdam. The *Wisselbank* helped 'to resolve the practical problems created for merchants by the circulation of multiple currencies in the United Provinces', a situation which of course affected Scotland also.

Scots could purchase Dutch citizenship for around 3 per cent of the annual average wage, and Rotterdam was a key base for the triangular trading that underpinned the emerging slave trade. Scots women as well as men were partners in international business directed from Rotterdam, a sphere they often entered by merging their domestic and business arrangements. Lysbett Jans, who lived 'near the Rotterdam fishmarket at the sign of the thistle' was a Scotswoman (married to a Dutchman) named in a 1654 document relating to Dutch–Caribbean–Virginian international trading interests, for example. Scots were also serving directly in these. Scots colonists came to New York as part of Dutch settlement (they even joined the Swedish settlement on the Delaware) and joined the Dutch colonial service. In 1638, George and James Langland from Bo'ness 'shipped out on the *Zeelandia* in service of the Dutch East India Company' (VOC), while James Johnson captained the *Gouden Lyon/Walcheren* for the Dutch West India Company in the 1660s, and James Couper was a VOC Admiral twenty years later. Scots expatriate trading networks developed through such links, with frequent cross holdings: the bankruptcy of John Forbes, a director of the Royal Prussian East India Company, affected many Scottish merchants in Rotterdam. As at Veere, these ties endured. As late as the twentieth century Captain Rudolph MacLeod of the Royal Dutch Indian Army (KNIL), husband of the famous spy Mata Hari/Griet Zolle (1876–1917), was the direct descendant of generations of Scots in the Dutch service.[46]

Many of these Scots – like their Polish brethren – came from the east coast ports. In 1634, the Bo'ness Sailors Box had been established to support the numerous retired seamen of the Fife port, with a levy of S8d in the S£ for this early form of national insurance: it was to form part of a strategy of benevolent support for Scots nationals who operated abroad which went on to shape Scots societies in large parts of the British Empire – including London, where the Royal Scottish Corporation was incorporated in 1611 – and endures today. In Rotterdam, the Scots Kirk's deaconry 'kept starvation and unbearable hardship from the doors of many Scots' from these areas round the Firth of Forth and elsewhere. In 1697, the Scottish Seaman's Box of Rotterdam commenced operations, and in 1729 the Kirk opened a Scots orphanage. This commitment to charitable networking also extended to the repatriation of some capital to Scotland, a practice that was to continue influentially into the British imperial age. On the domestic front, anti-Dutch and anti-Highland propaganda often went together from the 1650s, while in the Anglo-Dutch conflicts of Charles II's reign, the presence of Scots in the Dutch naval forces helped Presbyterians to be seen as a potential fifth column in England's wars with the Netherlands.[47] By 1672, the Dutch marine 'employed as many as 1,500 Scots', and by the reign of Queen Anne 2,000, though there were also plenty in the English navy, both volunteers and pressed men in the Dutch Wars, as well as privateers operating under letters of marque. The Crown's use of the Royal Navy was similar to its foreign policy in that it coerced a nominally independent Scotland by extending use of pressing there, thus forcing them 'to fight in a conflict from which the Scots themselves had nothing to gain'.[48]

After 1660, though many Scots returned with Charles II (who had been supported in exile by subventions from Scots on the Continent), a number remained in the Netherlands and were joined by religious refugees from Scotland, usually Covenanters who tried 'to make the Scots Church in Rotterdam reflect their views'. They were not always otherwise introspective:

an example might be the family of John Livingston, a Covenanter exile whose sons variously migrated to the American colonies and returned to Scotland to become supporters of the Darien venture. This was not a surprising trajectory: Scottish resentment at the country's exclusion 'from the mercantile system defined by the [Navigation] Acts because it was held to be a potential rival to English commerce' was accentuated both by Ireland's inclusion in them 'as a docile dependency', and the Acts' hostility to the rivalry of the Dutch trade. Such antagonism also affected Scotland, which was deeply involved in Dutch commerce, and had led England into repeated wars with the Netherlands under Charles II. In 1673, James as Duke of Albany (later James VII and II), who was more sympathetic to Scotland than his brother, gave 'his personal backing . . . to a plan to create a Scots-Dutch trading network based on Albany' in what is now New York State. A Scots Charitable Society had been established at Boston in 1657, and the English Parliament took a relatively permissive attitude to Scots settling in New York, despite its Dutch connexions.[49]

It is arguable that the rise of Moderate Presbyterianism in Scotland (less intolerant, with more of a social and educational mission aligned to civic and national development) owes a great deal to Scots who returned from the more tolerant Netherlands with or in the wake of William III and II's invasion of England in 1688. One such was William Carstares (1649–1715), 'Cardinal' Carstares and 'the first of the Moderates', who became chaplain to the King in Scotland and was later Principal of the University of Edinburgh. Despite a misleadingly modest preferment at first, Carstares was King William's chief agent in Scotland; he had long been a key spy and agent for the Dutch government. Carstares' work for the Dutch interest against the British crown in the 1670s is almost certainly still underestimated. On landing with William's invasion force at Torbay, Carstares preached on the text 'In the name of the Lord I will destroy' from Psalm 118. James had few more serious enemies and it was Carstares who later worked behind the scenes to ensure 'that the Church of Scotland broadly supported the Act of Union'. A radical in opposition, a moderate in power, Carstares was one of the central routes through which a Dutch king gained control of the state apparatus in Great Britain. The Revolution of 1688 and the Bill of Rights, a core foundational document of parliamentary sovereignty in English constitutional mythology, can be seen differently from a Dutch perspective, where 'The revolution hastened the process by which important aspects of England's economy came to mirror those of the republic.'[50]

THE RESTORATION

At the Restoration, Charles II (r.1649/60–85) sought to reimpose Episcopacy in Scotland, though on a more moderate basis than Laud and his father had done. Scottish historiography has often been less than kind to his approach. But the data suggests that Charles's policy was not wholly without merit. In 1662, between 'less than a quarter' and about 'one-third' of the clergy of the Covenanting era were deposed from their livings, despite the return to Episcopacy, a much more inclusive outcome than that of the 'rabbling of the curates' in 1689–90 and the oppression of Episcopalianism that followed. In part, continuing hostility in historiography to Charles's ecclesiastical policy may descend from a now secularized version of a Presbyterian historiographical tradition which saw him as in breach of the Covenant, itself tied to a notion of Scottish sovereignty whereby 'covenanting and coronation oaths' were used 'to secure national interests in a regnal union'. The re-establishment of Episcopacy could thus be seen as the Crown using its prerogative to undermine the sovereignty of the Scottish state; yet Episcopalianism was hardly an imposition in a country where it was the confessional preference of a large proportion of the population, and a preponderance in the north, where around half the population lived. Nonetheless, ecclesiastical policy in Scotland was difficult. Without repression, there could be no settlement: and that was as true in 1690 as it had been in 1662. Charles's instincts were for toleration, as demonstrated by his December 1662 'attempt . . . to issue a Declaration of Indulgence suspending the operation of the penal laws against nonconformists and Catholics'. So heavily factionalized were his kingdoms however, that in the end he could only rule effectively by identifying with an Anglican–Episcopalian confessional state.[51]

Royal policy only turned to the repression of an irreconcilable minority after open rebellion broke out in 1666, when between 1,500 and 2,000

Covenanters – frustrated by the pressure on Scoto-Dutch trade by the conditions of the 1665–67 Anglo-Dutch war as well as by religious issues – protested about their grievances in arms and got as far as the Pentland Hills before being stopped by General Tam Dalyell (Sir Thomas Dalyell, 1st Bart (1615–85) and Scottish Crown forces at Rullion Green. Dalyell was reputed to have introduced the thumbscrews into Scotland from his time serving in Russia, and was brutal with the ringleaders. Nonetheless, a Declaration of Indulgence was issued in 1669 for 'such of the outed ministers who live peaceable and orderly', and some 42 of the 300 or so outed ministers were reinstated, followed by 89 more at the second Declaration of 1672. However, attacks continued on Episcopalian clergy and there were frequent military clashes close to the Scottish capital, ranging from firing on government troops in West Lothian in 1674 to the assassination of the Archbishop of St Andrews in 1679, an outrage followed by outright rebellion, defeated by Crown forces under the Duke of Monmouth at Bothwell Brig on 22 June.

Continuing disruption by militant Covenanters remained a threat, especially in the west, where documents such as the Sanquhar Declaration of June 1680 disowned 'Charles Stuart . . . as having any right, title to, or interest in the said crown of Scotland . . . forfeited several years since by his perjuring and breach of covenant'. It is hard to imagine any state today putting up with such a printed declaration from men who were often armed terrorists, but the final victory of Presbyterianism after 1689 mythologized the suffering of the Covenanters as a small price to pay for ensuring their access to power was cut off. Charles's response to such provocations – the 'Act anent the Test' passed by Holyrood in 1681 – was moderate enough in its demand to 'affirm and swear by this my solemn oath that the King's Majesty is the only Supream Governor of this Realme' (though 'Supream Governor' smacked of an Anglican formula to the Presbyterian mind). However, the form of words was often enforced in such a tyrannical fashion that it appeared to endorse the extremism it was designed to end. Dissident Presbyterians were sent to England's West Indian and American colonies, an intervention in Scottish jurisdiction which built on that practised by Cromwell after Dunbar. After 1689, the restored Presbyterian regime began the long-established and only recently challenged view of the Restoration era and its 'Killing Times' as the 'darkness before the dawn' of a truly Protestant Scotland. Even a modern historian who regards Charles II as the most religiously persecuting monarch that ever sat on the throne (a tall order when comparing his rule with the anti-Semitic pogroms enabled by England's mediaeval kings or the burnings and disembowellings practised by Henry VIII and his daughters), can find nothing worse to accuse the Covenanting demon John Graham of Claverhouse (1648–89) with than 'exacting free quarter, rifling the houses of suspects, and imposing excessive fines'. If this is 'brutality' in the context of the Thirty Years' War or indeed of Europe in the last hundred years, then the English language is short of vocabulary. There is no convincing evidence that Charles II 'ever exceeded his legal powers' in Scotland. Indeed, George III successfully resisted any moves to repeal the Test and Corporation Acts which obliged office holders to be Anglicans more than a century after the Restoration government introduced them. Covert statist history which implicitly exalts the 'Glorious' Revolution and demonizes the Stuart Crown is with us yet, it seems.[52]

For its part, Episcopalian Scotland was no mere nursery of quasi Catholic anti-Presbyterian bigotry: indeed some prominent Covenanters such as Andrew Cant (1584/90–1663) and Donald Cargill (1627–81) were educated in its heartlands. 'Scottish intellectual discourse was rendered cosmopolitan' in the seventeenth century, which deserves to be identified as the beginning of the Scottish Enlightenment.[53] Edinburgh, the capital and the originating city of that Enlightenment, was home to some 30,000 or 40,000 people in the early years of Charles II (*c.*54,000 including environs by 1690), with strong resemblances to French (and, increasingly, Dutch) cities in its model and urban layout. It was the second largest city in Great Britain.[54]

Edinburgh's highly integrated urban society rapidly took to the development of coffee house and tavern culture, as well as mounting major theatrical performances in Scotland for the first time since 1603. John Row's coffeehouse was the first to open in 1673, and by the turn of the century there were half a dozen important coffee-houses in the city: 'the Caledonia, the Royal Exchange, the Exchange, Donaldson's, McClurgs' and the German coffee-house, which became a location for both clubs and newspaper sales, as well as the sale of concert tickets, and even issued their own 'currency' tokens.[55] Schools developed rapidly in the capital, with the Merchant Maiden school for girls (today Mary Erskine's) opening in 1694, and its Trades Maiden counterpart in 1704. The first charity school opened in 1699, though hospital schools with a charitable function such as George Heriot's (1628) dated from earlier in the century.[56] Dutch and Huguenot immigrants brought fresh trades and skills, such as papermaking and japanning, and Edinburgh's European communities were as significant to its economy as were their counterparts in London, with the additional dimension that many Scottish trading and merchant houses and universities, lawyers and clergy themselves maintained bilateral links with the places of origin of Edinburgh's own economic migrants.[57]

THE SCOTTISH ENLIGHTENMENT AND THE SCOTTISH CAPITAL

The Enlightenment is a popular term, but also a vexed one. Many of the popularisers and defenders of the concept have over-simplified it as a ubiquitous attack on clerical authority or a set of ideas promoted and developed from and grounded in the thinking of one or more 'great men', often traditionally John Locke (1632–1704), more recently Baruch Spinoza (1632–77), with René Descartes (1596–1650) as a near-ubiquitous avatar. In the postcolonial era, defenders of minority identities – particularly in North America – have started to use 'Enlightenment' as a term which characterizes the assumption of superiority and entitlement by European colonial powers. Given such simplification and politicization, some recent historians are inclined to deny that there was an Enlightenment, and see the term as a post hoc colligation of various features which modern historiography would like to attribute to the eighteenth century. J.C.D. Clark is a prominent example of this trend. Other historians explore 'the sharper, almost insatiable appetite . . . for accumulating, systemising and publishing information' of the era without using the term

'Enlightenment' at all, as Linda Colley does in *The Gun, the Ship and the Pen* (2021).[58]

The Enlightenment has suffered as a concept by being popularized by scholars more interested in ideas than in historiography, with a decidedly philosophical tendency not to multiply entities beyond necessity (an insight attributed to William of Ockham (*c*.1287–1347), but also found in the work of Duns Scotus (1265–1308)). Unsurprisingly, the Enlightenment was more complicated than this and its associated ideas and practices were inflected in different (not necessarily 'good' or 'bad' ways) in different societies. The term 'Scottish Enlightenment' has been around for more than a century, but remains a rare example of the detailed characterization of Enlightenment in national terms (as opposed to the use of geography as a mere adjective).

The Enlightenment can be characterized in general as that set of practices which applied reason to knowledge. In the Scottish case, this took place in a context of material improvement, a dimension which was important precisely because of the country's relative poverty by the late seventeenth century: the interests of the Select Society (1754), founded to 'debate anything "apart from revealed religion and Jacobitism"' 'expanded from debates into the active encouragement of invention and enterprise in business', for example, as well as to the role of women in the professions.[59] At its most fundamental level, Enlightenment thinking in the British Isles and elsewhere is associated with measurement: the close division of the day by time and the widespread adoption of watches as personal time, particularly after the invention of the spring balance in 1675; the trend to standardize local weights and measures; the development in 1672–73 of an annual fashion season; the appearance of works such as Edward Cocker's *Arithmetick* (1677), which went through 130 editions; the creation of a consistently milled rather than an erratically hammered coinage (1662); the enabling of the mass production of glass (by

Ravenscroft (1674) and others) and ceramics, with further improved production techniques after 1750. In addition there were the related development of the housing and art markets, streetlighting, libraries, coach timetables, a postal service and civic regulation. These are the analogue predecessors of our digital cities in the modern era. Among these structures of standardization ideas which standardized – that is universalized – human thought developed as the interior mental counterpart to the taxonomical order being imposed on the exterior world of things. The key activities which mediated between the two involved clubs and societies based on shared interests in things or concepts.[60]

Edinburgh was in the forefront of this world. Its compact size (the core city measured only 900 metres by 450 metres, an area in which almost 30,000 people lived), wealth, dominant trading position and intermingled residential and commercial property mix supported innovation, as did its position as a seat of government and national professional institutions, both driven by a highly educated populace. Core Edinburgh had almost twice the number of professionals as London per capita at the time of the 1707 Union.[61] Between 1 p.m. and 3 p.m. in the first half of the eighteenth century, Edinburgh's citizens gathered for conversation at the Cross, and the capital's dark closes and high buildings drove extensive public sociability. Edinburgh also enjoyed good light and fire regulation, a key marker for innovation to this day, and transport links, with more sedan chairs than London per capita, and a numbered coach service. The city was also diverse (as was normative for major trading cities), with significant French and Dutch minorities engaged in developing jewellery, paper manufacture, japanning and other trades and with many of its domestic elite educated abroad. At home, Scotland's higher education sector 'cost perhaps a tenth of its English equivalent', and was more widely open, not least since the nobility were socially a much larger group than was the case south of the border, and their patronage reached more deeply into relatively humble levels of society. In addition, the Scottish university curriculum had moved strongly to embrace the scientific revolution and the relatively widespread reach of Scottish higher education served to spread Copernican and Cartesian ideas widely. The Scottish Parliament acted both to naturalize prominent members of the city's sojourning or diasporic communities and supported them directly, for example by granting a salary to a minister for the Huguenot community in 1690. The conditions of Edinburgh's urban life and business in the late seventeenth century would be expected to produce a 20 to 35 per cent premium in economic activity on current global smart city models.[62]

Bearing this out, Edinburgh was relatively wealthy, with almost 10 per cent of its households in 1694–95 estimated as having stock worth 10,000 merks (S£6,666 13s 4d) and above – a substantial sum, equivalent to over £100,000 at 2022 prices. The city was also diverse in terms of experience and gender as well as background and nationality, with 20–25 per cent of its merchants engaged in foreign trade and women burgesses recognized in the city trades. Women could divorce (there were even cheap fixed fees, as well as limited free advice from legal and medical professional bodies and the provision of pensions by the city) and wives could be named in causes for debt before the courts. In the early seventeenth century, as the historian Cathryn Spence's groundbreaking work has revealed, 36 per cent of burgh court debt cases involved a female creditor and 34 per cent a female debtor. Raising capital was important in a city with so much trading business. There were dozens of women merchants by the late seventeenth century and 400 exporters in total, a much higher ratio per capita than was the case in London. Eighty per cent of Dutch trade to the whole country came into the Forth (including the all important VOC 'Mocha' coffee imports from today's Yemen), and 63 per cent of Scotland's French wine imports came into Leith. In 1692, Edinburgh alone was responsible for 32 per cent of the tax rolls of

Scotland's royal burghs, in 1705, for 35 per cent, and in general it was between a third and two-fifths of the country's economy in the period covered by this chapter, despite only having under 5 per cent of Scotland's population.[63] In the 1660s, Edinburgh became (with Amsterdam and Paris) one of the first cities in Europe to adopt street lighting. Following the establishment of a Cleansing Committee in 1678, and the opening of its first water storage at the West Bow in 1685, the city moved rapidly to develop a public cleansing service, with twenty rubbish carts in place by 1687 and thirty 'muckmen' to clean and sweep the streets before 9 a.m.[64]

The first regular musical meetings occurred in 1695, and by 1710 there was a dancing assembly; it became one of the infrastructural organizations in which women played a major role, with 'lady directresses' dominating. Indeed, women could attend and vote in some clubs and also seem to have had clubs of their own in the eighteenth century, though William Alexander was probably closer to the experiences of many when he reflected in his *History of Women* (1779) that 'There is in the fate of women something exceedingly singular; they have at all periods, and almost in all countries, been, by our sex, constantly oppressed and adored.'[65]

Charitable performances and (on a strictly limited basis) the provision of some free legal services and, after the foundation of the Royal College of Physicians in 1681, free medical care, were combined with limited but still important pension provision. The historian Helen Dingwall estimates that between 3 and 4 per cent of Edinburgh's population 'received regular pensions' in an age when fewer than 1 in 6 reached the age of 60. The Dean of Guild Court regulated building practices on a consistent basis, while before 1708 the presence of the Privy Council and Parliament led to the usual attention to infrastructure, facilities and regulation that one finds in a city frequented by national politicians, the effect of which was magnified by Edinburgh's compact size. A postal service was founded in 1633 to communicate with London, supplemented by a Scots–Irish post in 1662. Newspapers flourished in large numbers (though often only for brief runs) after the 1650s, when Cromwellian propaganda had made Edinburgh readers aware of the power of the press and the need to find their own voice.[66]

Major libraries developed: as early as 1658, a library was established for the Royal High School, while what is now the National Library of Scotland was founded as The Advocates' Library in 1682, and there were huge private libraries in the hands of pioneering thinkers such as Andrew Fletcher of Saltoun (1653–1716), Archibald Pitcairne (1652–1713) and Sir Andrew Balfour (1630–94). In 1725, Allan Ramsay (1684–1758) founded what has been identified as the first subscription library in the British Isles in Edinburgh, and this was succeeded by the conversion to subscription libraries of smaller libraries in Scotland at Dunblane (1734, still in existence as Archbishop Leighton's Library), Dumfries (1736) and Kelso (1750), while at Ramsay's birthplace at Leadhills in Lanarkshire a library was created for the mineworkers in 1741 with the support of Sir James Stirling FRS, the mathematician who managed the mines as his Jacobitism barred him from official positions in the universities. In addition, free libraries began to be set up at Haddington (1729) and elsewhere. There were even libraries set up in inns. The result was that reading spread far beyond the clerical and secular elites who had monopolized it, crossing both class and gender boundaries. The Covenanter historian Robert Wodrow (1679–1734), who coined the phrase 'the Killing Times' for Charles II's ecclesiastical policies, was unsparing in his criticism of such developments, and in particular of 'all the villainous, profane and obscene books and plays . . . got down by Allan Ramsay, and lent out, for an easy price, to young boys, servant women of the better sort, and gentlemen'. Libraries in short opened up reading to those who some thought had no business with it, in particular women and children.[67]

The Edinburgh botanic garden was founded by Sir Robert Sibbald (1641–1722), Sir Andrew Balfour and others in 1670. Initially less than 150 square metres in size, by 1675 it had been extended to well over 5,000. The gardener, James Sutherland (1631–1719), was made 'Intendant of the Physic Garden by the Town Council' and it became integrated into the research – and, more importantly, the medical training – of the University, following the practice at Leiden, where the physic garden dated to 1587. This development – extended to other universities in Scotland – was later to become central, as we shall see, to the Scottish contribution to botany across the British Empire.[68]

Edinburgh's newspapers (which were to burgeon further after the removal of Scottish Privy Council censorship following the Council's abolition in 1708) were rooted in the city's dynamic printing and publishing industry: 237 out of Scotland's 243 imprints were published at Edinburgh in 1707. The capital's increasingly national newspapers were internationally focused and often viewed English foreign policy and 'the promiscuous Coppies of the Common *English News* Papers' and 'what they sometimes Falsely, and oftentimes Ignorantly are pleased to impose' with detachment.[69] In 1692, *The Present State of Europe, or, the Historical and Political Monthly Mercury* noted drily that 'England is in pursuit of Glory now upon a foreign Theatre, and therefore there is little to be expected from thence'. The strength of debate in the public prints in Edinburgh was brought home in the Union controversy of 1705–06, when 'hundreds of broadsheets and pamphlets of varying length and style . . . poured onto the streets of Edinburgh', many evincing sophisticated or original constitutional arguments. Despite aberrations like the narrowly passed condemnation of the freethinking Thomas Aikenhead as the 'Presbyterian Kirk determined to assert its authority' in the face of deteriorating economic conditions in 1697, the intellectual world of Scotland's capital was changing – and progressing – rapidly.[70]

Charles II's brother James's rule in Edinburgh as Duke of Albany 1679–82 has been characterized as 'a brief period of enlightened government' made possible by the Catholic heir's exile from the irrational hysteria of the aftermath of the 'Popish Plot' in England.[71] Both Charles and James carried out extensive building in the Scottish capital and supported civic redevelopment; indeed, what was eventually to become the New Town development was first envisioned under James. James created or supported many of the institutions which underpinned the Enlightenment: the Royal College of Physicians of Edinburgh (1681), the Edinburgh Merchant Company (1681), the Advocates' Library (1682) and the Order of the Thistle (1687), as well as the offices of Historiographer and Geographer Royal (1681–82). In the aftermath of Union, new institutions were developed to defend and preserve Edinburgh's capital status, such as Allan Ramsay's theatre (1736) and the Academy of St Luke, Scotland's first art school, in 1729. A large number of clubs and associations for improvement were formed, such as the Society for Endeavouring Reformation of Manners (1699), the Rankenian and Associated Critics Clubs (1716–17), the Honourable Society of Improvers in the Knowledge of Agriculture in Scotland (1723), the Society for the Improvement of Medical Knowledge (1731) and the Philosophical Society (1737). The University Medical School (where over three-quarters of students in the eighteenth century were not Scots) was founded by the support of the Royal College of Physicians of Edinburgh in 1726. Like the other Scottish universities, Edinburgh went on to benefit substantially from the addition to the student body of English and Irish dissenters, who were unable to attend Oxford and Cambridge because of their religious affiliations.[72]

Charles II's government commenced an expansion of the domestic Scottish economy (110 new burghs were founded between 1660 and 1707, with 'weekly and annual market centres' more than doubling), while at the same time excluding Scotland from the new overseas markets of the emergent English empire under the terms of the 1660/61 Navigation Act, which 'treated Scots as foreigners and banned their shipping from the colonies', directing 'that three-quarters of the crew of a ship trading with English colonies had to be of English nationality'. Scots likewise ceased to hold major court offices in England.[73] Britain – symbolized by Britannia, a new image created to commemorate the 1667 Anglo-Dutch Peace of Breda, with the Duchess of Richmond as the model – was to have control not only of foreign policy but also of trade policy, and Scotland was to be a domestic territorial state only.[74] The structural exclusion of Scotland as a co-sovereign participant in foreign relations, evident in much Crown policy since 1603, was to have momentous consequences. This was increasingly a relational era, with trade on the oceans via the company-states (East Indian Company (EIC), VOC and others) of the European powers being increasingly seen as globally significant determinants of national success in the projection of sovereignty (or its commercial analogue) overseas: these trading companies were themselves quasi state actors. How the sea could be legitimately exploited and who had the right to do so was a central question of sovereignty for the century, perhaps even more so than the question of domestic territorial authority over confessional rights. It surfaced in the Westphalian settlement in the agreements relating to privateers and letters of marque, key elements in the early modern state's use of private military resources to acquire or contest control of the seas.

The two positions on the question of sovereignty over the sea were *mare clausum* (the closed sea, under the jurisdictional control of maritime empires) and *mare liberum* (the free sea, open to all to trade). *Mare clausum* was championed by Spain and Portugal (Portugal claimed to be 'Lords of the Seas' in the Indian Ocean); *mare liberum* as a concept was most strongly associated with the Dutch, and as the seventeenth century progressed there was a degree of Scottish alignment with the Dutch position, which had its origins in the existential struggle for liberty against Spain and the role the VOC had played in that. By the late seventeenth century, the battle to gain a foothold in international trade in the face of English hostility led Scots to be increasingly seen as engaging in the 'unregulated use of maritime space in the Caribbean', and the shared intelligence networks between Scots merchants and buccaneers in the West Indies helped to underpin the Darien venture, which sought to plant a trading colony on the isthmus of Panama. This scheme depended on the concept of *mare liberum* in defiance of Spanish claims and its promotion of itself as a colony for trade rather than empire. William Paterson (1656–1719), the founder of the Bank of England, first promoted the Darien venture in the Netherlands in 1685, and we will return to it below.[75]

The controversy over sovereignty of the seas had its roots in Roman law, which, while not recognizing territorial jurisdiction over the ocean, saw the Mediterranean as *mare nostrum* ('our sea') and effectively operated a *mare clausum* policy regarding it. This could be seen as a circumstantial assumption deriving from the territory and history of the Roman Empire, thus suggesting that rights over the sea deriving from Roman law positions were uncertain in other contexts. The battle over their legality became a foundational one in international law, with its central role in the eighty-year war of independence between the Netherlands and Spain acting as an accelerant. Spain attempted to lay claim to the entire Pacific; and while the VOC captured its ships, Hugo Grotius (1583–1645), in his initially anonymous work on *mare liberum*, argued that the sea was like the air, there was no property in it, and each nation could trade with each upon it freely and that no 'state could make the sea an accessory to its realm'. The Netherlands was at that time under pressure not only from Spain but from England, where James I and VI was seeking to restrict Dutch fishing.[76] The controversy lives on the shape of the 'three mile limit' (first defined in 1702 and extended to 22 kilometres by the United Nations in 1982) and the concept of sovereignty over territorial waters, so much to the fore in the UK in the last stage of the Brexit negotiations in 2020.

The *mare clausum* position on sovereignty was attractive to imperial powers, and 'empire was a language of power'. England – which had tended to view 'the ocean' as 'the common property of everyone' under Elizabeth, at least where Spanish interests were concerned, moved towards a more imperial position in the seventeenth century, and indeed John Selden (1584–1654) originated the widespread use of *mare clausum* in his book of the same name published in 1635, though written somewhat earlier. Charles I's 102-gun flagship, the *Sovereign of the Seas* (1637; later *Royal Sovereign*), bore witness in its name to the instant appeal of Selden's formulation and its proclamation of English maritime power in the northern seas. *Sovereign* was the first English warship to have three full-length gun decks, and its figure-head was the Saxon King Edgar (r.959–75), an early overlord of all Great Britain who, according to English myth-history, was rowed down the Dee at Chester by eight subordinate kings in the year he was crowned King of all England in Bath (973). The playwright Thomas Heywood (*c.*1572–1641) was responsible for the decorations of *Sovereign* (including Cupid 'bestriding, and bridling a Lyon') and the legend on the stern, which proclaimed the imperial *mare clausum* in no uncertain terms: 'He who Seas; Windes, and Navies doth protect, Great Charles, thy great ship in her course direct.'[77]

It was however James VI and I who had earlier begun to move royal policy in the direction of *mare clausum*, building on his experience as king in Scotland. Scotland had had a longer tradition of support for *mare clausum* than England up to this date, not least because of its extensive coastline and relatively high dependence on fish: as early as the 1530s, James V (r.1513–42) had 'ordered his admiral to repel foreign competition in his fishing grounds'. James VI 'insisted that all his ships fly the Union flag', thus attempting to subject the Scottish to the English navy by royal prerogative, and in 1609 'tried to introduce Scottish concepts of territorial waters' to England. In the 1630s, the Scottish Privy Council attempted to set an exclusion zone of 45 kilometres for Dutch and 22.5 kilometres for English fishing. But as the seventeenth century wore on, the concept of *mare liberum*, the free sea, seems to have become more appealing in Scottish thought (perhaps because of the country's sheer inability to project the power required for any alternative, given its small fleet – only three ships by 1707 – and reliance on privateers) and this was associated with the country's ultimately unsuccessful struggles to become an imperial power. While England increasingly adopted a variant of Scotland's earlier attitude to the sea, Scotland itself moved closer to the Dutch view.[78]

In the wake of the Wars of Independence in the fourteenth century, Scotland had sought to demonstrate its sovereignty and 'fre Impire' (1469) through the adoption of the closed imperial crown on the coinage (1486) and subsequently in architecture (e.g. St Giles Cathedral in Edinburgh and King's College, Aberdeen) in a manner which was primarily defensive: a statement of absolute territorial sovereignty, and one which signalled the country's status as a European kingdom among equals. After 1603, as discussed above, the removal of the Crown had effectively degraded this status to a form of *landeshoheit/superioritas territorialis*, where domestic jurisdiction (itself under threat from religious imperialism) co-existed with a straitened and confined foreign policy and pressure on Scottish trade and rights over trade. Nor was English support for Scotland abroad forthcoming as compensation for English interference. While the Scots were encouraged to plant Ulster, where 'cheap and abundant land' was available at a time when the conversion of in-kind to cash rents in Scotland was placing increasing pressure on tenants at home, Scottish interests further west were not encouraged. By 1630, Ulster was home to some 16,000 Scots, while 'the first regular cross-Channel ferry service between Antrim and Wigtownshire' was established in 1622. The Plantation was successful, acting as an economic benefit to Glasgow's economy in particular through the 'stimulus of the Ulster market' to trade across the Irish sea. By 1672 there were an estimated 100,000 Scots there with 'Scotch-Irish' first recorded as a term to describe them in 1695. In the 1690s alone, some 50,000 Scots migrated to northern Ireland, the push and pull factors of domestic famine and Williamite conquest both serving to swell numbers. On the other hand, a 1617 grant of patent under the Great Seal of Scotland to James Cunningham, 7th Earl of Glencairn (1552–1630), to open a fishing enterprise off the Greenland coast and to 'establish a Scottish East India Company' was rescinded in 1618 in response to English pressure, in a pattern which was to be repeated.[79]

When Sir William Alexander, Earl of Stirling (*c*.1567–1640), sought to defend the rights King James had granted him in Nova Scotia in 1621 'from the St Croix to the St Laurence rivers' in terms of English precedent, English colonists in Canada used the same grounds to claim a right to trade independently of any Scottish authority. Sir William had persuaded James to allow him to set up a colony run by Scots Law, but turned to English precedents to support his case once the colony was up and running. They did not help him. Attempts to turn Cape Breton into New Galloway did not take root. When French forces fatally damaged the Scottish settlements there and at Port Royal a few years later, English power did nothing to protect them.

On 10 July 1631, Charles I ordered the Scots to abandon 'the Scottish fort' at Port Royal (built only two years earlier), conceding the Acadian territories to France under the Treaty of St-Germain-en-Laye in 1632. As the historian Sir Tom Devine notes, such responses 'confirmed that specifically Scottish interests were . . . likely to be sacrificed when broader issues of state were concerned'. Sir William Alexander was created Earl of Stirling in compensation, and the Nova Scotia baronetcies which had been sold to raise the money for the colony survived (the Earl kept on issuing them until 1637, when the last of his lands in North America were overrun by France), but they were all that remained of what was in many respects – though not in all – a distinctively Scottish colonial venture.[80]

A similar situation obtained in Scotland's early and more morally dubious engagement with Guinea in West Africa. In October 1634, Charles I granted 'a monopoly of trade between Scotland and Africa' to Patrick Maule of Panmure, Thomas Maxwell of Innerwick, Sir Thomas Thomson of Duddingston and Henry Alexander, the Earl of Stirling's son. The Guinea Company of Scotland was established with a 31-year grant, and in 1636 the *Golden Lion* and the *St Andrew* sailed for Africa. But Scotland could not project its own power elsewhere on the globe without relying on the power of another European state to protect it: it was 'a small country . . . with little military or naval muscle and few commodities vital to international trade'. The Portuguese captured the *St Andrew* en route back from Africa, killing the crew and seizing '£10,000 sterling' of gold, apparently fearing the ship was a Dutch vessel or engaged with the Dutch. Scotland did not re-enter these markets in its own right with any strength until the era of the Company of Scotland in the 1690s.[81]

While the Navigation Acts (1651, 1660, 1663, 1673) were suspended in wartime under Charles II, this legislation represented a formidable obstacle to Scots' ambitions to have greater control of the terms of trade, owing to their protectionist focus on English boats and 75 per cent English/colonial crews (12 Cha. 2 c.18). Scots used their commercial networks to evade the terms of the Acts, either through illegal trading or subterfuge: they had plenty of experience, having evaded their own country's export bans in the mediaeval period. Newfoundland, legally argued to be 'part of England' and not a colony, was used as a location 'with which the Scots were in fact allowed to trade openly', arousing the complaint of local English leaders, while Scots also employed 'English front-men in Scottish towns' to deal with imports. Scots' ships, such as the *Gift of God* from Dundee earlier in the century, also plied the Newfoundland trade to Continental ports. In 1681, the Surveyor-General of Customs described the 'Legerdemain jugles' of the Scots as follows:

> A ship would call in at some English port, take on a little coal or cargo of small bulk, proceed to Scotland where it woud [sic] load great quantities of linen and other Scottish goods and continue on her voyage to America with the clearing obtained at the English port.

This view was echoed by others. On arrival Scots would also benefit from the fact that they were popular in the colonies with some of the independent trading companies, such as the Hudson's Bay Company (HBC, 1670), where cheap and hardy Scots used to northern conditions – Orcadians in particular – were appealing employees for this remote and chilly corporate giant. Suggestions of compensating Scotland for its exclusion from the Navigation Acts by offering it the colonies of Dominica (1671) or St Vincent (1678) came to nothing, and instead the surrogate and underhand business developing between Scotland and the Americas 'helped the Glasgow merchants to get established in the tobacco and plantation trades' before the Union of 1707. The Navigation Acts also created a perverse incentive which worked against the development of shared British goals, as they encouraged Scots merchants and seamen to challenge English trade by incentivizing them to pursue their ambitions and develop their existing networks in the service of Continental powers. Consequently, Scots entered the services of other European states in order to create support networks for their own 'private mercantile syndicates'. This in its turn could be counter-productive to Scottish interests at home. The fact that the vast majority (up to 80 per cent) 'of the vessels engaged on the Dutch trade sailed to and from the Firth of Forth' only gave visible credence to 'the belief that to admit the Scots to the colonial trade would be tantamount to admitting the Dutch under a flag of convenience', a view apparently shared by the Portuguese. This was especially sensitive in the wake of the secret Treaty of Dover of 1670, which effectively placed Charles II on the side of France against the Dutch.[82] In Scotland, on the other hand, English wars with the Dutch were seen as damaging trade with Scotland's 'best customers'. When England took Nevis in the Caribbean from the Netherlands in 1664 there were already Scottish settlers on the island, and they were present in Dutch Curaçao as early as the 1630s. There were also Scots on the Swedish expedition to settle the Delaware in 1638, and Scots subscribers to the South Company of Sweden which supported – abortively – Swedish interests in the Americas. Scots could also be found in Portuguese and other colonial ventures.[83]

Despite the greater sympathy for the projection of Scottish power abroad evinced by James VII and II (r.1685–89, and effective viceroy resident in Scotland 1679–82) as part of his 'centralization and subordination of colonial interests to his own authority' in a manner which transcended the legislation of any of his kingdoms, Scotland continued to be a foreign power in terms of English legislation. James became progressively more opposed to a closer political union between Scotland and England during his life, and favoured instead 'internal freedom of trade for the three kingdoms and the colonies, an imperial trading system', while also seeking to keep Scotland in the mainstream of European mercantilism. He convinced the English Privy Council 'to allow Scots to share from the 1670s in the activities of the Royal Africa Company and Hudson Bay Company and to trade freely with New York', going on to support and endorse Scottish colonies in South Carolina (ironically some of the Scottish Rye House plotters of 1683 used the disguise of 'buying lands in Carolina' as a cover for their visits to London) and East New Jersey and granting a royal charter to the Edinburgh Merchant Company on 28 November 1681.[84]

Land grants to the Earl of Perth, James's Quaker friend Robert Barclay of Urie (1648–90) (whose son founded Barclays Bank), as well as to other settlers in East New Jersey in 1682 and to the emigrants who followed them, were handicapped by continuing limitations on the Scots' rights to trade. Naturally enough, there were attempts to circumvent the Navigation Acts and reinstate their own version of *mare liberum*. In August 1686 it was noted that 'many prohibited goods are imported at East New Jersey, the Governor being a

Scotsman'; the next month, the Scottish colony at Stuarts Town in South Carolina, founded two years earlier, was destroyed by Spanish forces. The colonists' – in the end there were some 700 in this 'colony within a colony' – insistence on using Scots law and the emigrant leader Lord Cardross's declaration 'that he was not subject to the authority of the Governor' had already gone down badly. The pattern was set whereby Scotland could not defend its embryo colonies abroad, and England would not. There were even efforts to exclude Scots from public office in the colonial sphere as a whole. Colonel Andrew Hamilton (d.1703), governor of East and West New Jersey in 1692–97, was (though later reinstated) deposed from office under an English act (c.22) of William III and II (r.1688–1702 in England, from 1689 in Scotland and 1691 in Ireland) which declared that 'no public post of trust or profit in the colonies could be held by any other than a natural born subject of England'. There were evidently first- and second-class citizens in the British composite monarchy. In 1699, the Governor of East New Jersey prohibited aid to 'Caledonia' (Darien). In 1702, New Jersey became a crown colony, and Scottish pretensions to its government ceased.[85]

THE DUTCH CONQUEST OR THE BRITISH REVOLUTION

In the meantime, King James had been deposed in a political cataclysm which resulted in major constitutional change. The birth of a Catholic heir to the throne on 10 June 1688 led to a number of Whig lords contacting James's nephew and son-in-law William of Orange to request his intervention. The Dutch king landed at Torbay on 5 November (15 November, New Style under the Gregorian calendar adopted in 1752) with a multinational army of about 15,000 (including many Catholics), and James's inability to act swiftly or with resolution – he may have suffered a nervous breakdown – led to an increasing pattern of desertion and in the end the collapse of the king's cause and the flight of the king. The English Parliament conferred the crown jointly on William and his wife, James's daughter Mary (1662–94). In Scotland, the Scottish Estates, inexpertly handled by James's ministers and threatened by a Whig mob, followed suit in early 1689, declaring in the Claim of Right using the language of the Sanquhar Declaration, that James had 'forfaulted the right to the Crown', a stronger statement than that made in England, implying that he had broken his contract with the Estates and the people of Scotland. John Grahame, Viscount Dundee (1648–89), made commander in chief in Scotland in almost James's last act as king, fought on and died in gaining victory for the Jacobite forces (supporters of James, 'Jacobus' in Latin) at Killiecrankie in July 1689. Dundee's successors continued to fight in Scotland with much more limited success, with the Bass Rock surrender in June 1694 marking the end of the Jacobite war (in Ireland, the war was far more bloody). On the way, events such as the massacre at Glencoe in February 1692 revealed the extent to which Scottish society was now divided: indeed, in both England and Scotland, 'The active supporters of William . . . were a minority.' In the same year, William had 1,000 Scots pressed to fight France and, by 1697, the British kingdoms were paying for 45 per cent of William's multinational army in Flanders and providing a quarter of its manpower. Some Scots units, like the Earl of Dumbarton's/Royal Scots (1678–79) and Scots Guards (1686), had already been placed on the English establishment. In Scotland where Hans William Bentinck, 1st Earl of Portland (1649–1709) was responsible for the Crown's business – aided by Carstares, who developed policy – the priority was 'securing Scotland's military commitment to the continental war'. As Scots were pressed into the Royal Navy, the refusal of that Navy to protect Scots merchant traffic effectively – and indeed stopping and seizing 'Scottish vessels on the pretence that they were bound for France' – escalated as a source of resentment in Scotland, leading early in the new century to outrages like the judicial murder of Captain Green, Master of the East India trader the *Worcester*, with two of his crew.[86]

Presbyterianism was re-established in Scotland in 1689–90, accompanied by the large-scale eviction of Episcopal clergy from their livings (initially 200–300, with 664 ejected by 1716) and purges of Episcopalians in public office; there were also attacks on clergy and pregnant women by the Presbyterian mobs 'rabbling' the Episcopalian ministers. King William, although he would have preferred to see Episcopacy remain established, consented to the establishment of its Presbyterian rival as the Episcopal Church remained loyal to James. Although Acts of the Scottish Parliament in

1693 and 1695 ameliorated the position of moderate Episcopalians, bringing almost 150 back into the fold in a mirror-image of Charles II's government's actions with regard to Presbyterians, it was not until the Greenshield case of 1711 and the ensuing Toleration Act of 1712 that Episcopalians – albeit briefly – regained liberty of worship if not their old established position. Their determined Jacobitism – reinforced after the Union – was to undermine any concessions.[87] The marginalization of Episcopalianism started to consolidate a change in the geographical balance of power within Scotland. The Claim of Right had tendentiously suggested 'that most people in Scotland preferred presbyterian church government', a claim obviously true only of the central belt and south of the country; equally for their part the Episcopalians argued that it was they who were 'predominant in the Nation'. At the end of the seventeenth century, Scotland had a population of a little over a million, half of whom lived north of the Tay. By comparison, England had some 4 million people, the Netherlands, Portugal, Sweden and Switzerland each between 1.2 million and 1.5 million people, Denmark 700,000, Norway 500,000 and Finland 400,000. The south-west of Scotland was dominated by radical Presbyterians, 'From the Forth to the Tay the adherents of Episcopacy and Presbyterianism were more equally divided; and . . . beyond the Tay the supporters of Episcopacy were much superior in number.'[88]

Scotland made one last large-scale attempt to project its power overseas, now hampered not only by the Navigation Acts, but also by English foreign policy entanglements, the growth of mercantilist and protectionist policies from France, one of Scotland's chief trading partners, and an unsympathetic Crown. Trade with England was easier, and was now on an upward curve, more than doubling to reach 50 per cent of Scots exports by the beginning of the eighteenth century. Scotland was therefore becoming increasingly dependent on domestic English markets. English ships began patrolling Scottish waters to curtail Scottish circumvention of London's trade frameworks. Following the Scottish Parliament's 'Act for Encouraging of Forraign Trade' in 1693, which built on James's strategy of the 1680s as Duke of Albany, 'The Company of Scotland Trading to Africa and the Indies' (1695) was established (see Plate 1), half of whose capital and half of whose directors were to come from within the kingdom of Scotland. Initially, the Company attracted significant English support, as 'powerful mercantile interests in London saw the opportunity to obtain separate legislation from the Scottish Parliament as an effective way of challenging, and if possible subverting, the monopolistic rights' of the East India Company (EIC). There was also unofficial EIC backing for the Bank of Scotland, also founded in 1695. The Bank claimed to be the 'first instance in Europe, and perhaps the world, of a joint-stock bank formed by private persons . . . solely dependent upon private capital', but whether or not this was the case, Scottish financial innovation was already out-capitalized by the changes in England which had led to the establishment of a bond market by 1692, when subscribers to loans could first transfer their title to a third party. It was this that was to help finance England's – then Britain's – global war efforts. By the Seven Years' War of 1756–63, 66 per cent of government revenue was devoted to servicing government debt.[89]

The Company of Scotland was widely subscribed. The central aim of the Company became the establishment of a permanent Scottish colonial trading *entrepôt* at Darien in modern Panama, on the isthmus between the Atlantic and Pacific oceans, to be called New Caledonia, although there were other developments, including an experimental voyage to East Asia. In July 1698, five emigrant ships sailed with 1,500 aboard from Edinburgh for Darien: the *Unicorn, St Andrew, Caledonia* (the 'three big ships'), *Endeavour* (which sank) and *Dolphin*; between 1,200 and 1,300 emigrants also left from the Clyde in the *Rising Sun, Hope, Hope of Bo'ness* and *Duke of Hamilton*. In the end, thirteen Company ships crossed the Atlantic.[90] Hopes were high, as a contemporary broadside makes clear, stressing as it does liberty and free trade, the values of *mare liberum*, as lying at the heart of Scotland's 'just and never-dying Fame':

To *SCOTLAND's* just and never-dying Fame
We'll in ASIA, AFRICA and AMERICA proclame
Liberty ! Liberty ! nay, to the shame
   Of all that went before us;
Wherever we plant, TRADE shall be free,
In three years time, I plainly foresee,
GOD BLESS THE SCOTTISH-COMPANY
   Shall be the *India – Chorus* . . .

... The *Muscovite, Tartar, Turk*, and the *Pope,*

The *Sophie, Mogul,* and *Morocco,* I hope,

To the Charm of our Land must yeild [sic] and give up,

   Their absolute Sway and Dominions:

Then the *Spaniards,* and *French,* and *Portugueze,*

Venetians . . . . and *Genoese,*

And the *English* themselves perhaps may please

   To alter their narrow Opinions.

   Trade's Release: OR, Courage *to the* SCOTCH-INDIAN-COMPANY[91]

The development of the Company took place against a background of severe famine in Scotland, which probably began with the harvest of 1694 and may have killed or exiled 15 per cent of Scotland's population in the years that followed. While 'Presbyterians viewed the famine as a providential judgement on a sinful nation', Episcopalians characterized it as 'King William's Ill Years', a punishment for overthrowing the House of Stuart in 1688–89. Compared to James, William's lack of interest in Scotland in areas from Empire to building projects was also likely to generate opposition.[92]

Scots pamphleteers writing in support of Darien portrayed it not as a colonial venture, but rather as the creation of 'a free and independent republic', with no right of conquest, in sympathy with local native leaders, who should be seen as 'independent rulers of their own domains' rather than the subordinates of a tyrannical Spain. Scots constitutional thinking, which already enjoyed a long tradition going back to the fourteenth century in the forms of the Declaration of Arbroath (1320), the contemporary *Regiam Majestatem*, the Declaration of the Clergy (1310) and the Blessed John of Duns' (Duns Scotus) *Ordinatio* (*c.*1300) stressed liberty and choice, together with the 'right to self-government'. Scotus had argued for the contractual nature of sovereignty, and this was to be a persistent feature of Scottish thought. This tradition was reinforced by the more contemporary natural law ideas of Samuel von Pufendorf (1632–94) and Hugo Grotius, including the foregrounding of *mare liberum*, and the primacy of trade over tyranny.[93]

NEW CALEDONIA

The Darien settlement was termed New Caledonia by the settlers, as an expression of their hope for the long-term success of the new Scottish power in Darien; James Byres writes of his passage in the *Rising Sun* for 'old *Darien* or *New Caledonia*'.[94] The name was not to disappear into history after the venture's ignominious defeat at the dawn of the eighteenth century, but was resurrected in a very different context, in an interesting example of the transformational continuities of Scottish cultural representation on a global stage.

Captain James Cook (1728–79) was the son of two Scottish emigrants to Yorkshire who had left their home country at about the time of the Jacobite Rising of 1715. Cook started his career as an ordinary seaman on the fourth rate *Eagle* of 60 guns in 1755, rapidly rising to be Master of the sixth-rate *Solebay* and then the fourth-rate *Pembroke* in 1757 (these terms for the size of warships have passed into our language more generally). Cook spent his early career patrolling the seas around Scotland, still suspected at this date of Jacobite disaffection.[95]

There were signs that Cook honoured his Scottish heritage, including his serving of haggis aboard the *Endeavour* on 9 March 1770 in celebration of a Scots officer's birthday; he may also have been influenced by the contemporary cult of Ossian, as the cultural theorist Nigel Leask has suggested.[96] The clearest evidence of the influence of Cook's Scottish heritage or more contemporary Scottish ideas was in the naming of New Caledonia in 1774. This collection of islands, in aggregate almost the size of Wales, is now part of *France d'outre-mer*, but its name (as Nouvelle-Calédonie) survives. In the eighteenth century, 'Caledonia' was not just a song by Dougie MacLean but a politically significant term. It was linked to the Darien project (the first New Caledonia) and the anti-Union rhetoric of 1705–07, where 'Caledonia'– deriving from Tacitus' *Agricola* and the resistance to imperial rule of the Caledonian champion Calgacus – was a clear sign of patriot sympathy. But in eighteenth-century rhetoric it also signified an iconic presentation of the Scottish nation as female, and often the victim of a predatory male, much as in the *Aisling* poetry of Ireland. In other words, Cook's use of Caledonia was – if not politically provocative in 1774 – at least patriotic and nostalgic.

In the nineteenth century, the islands became embroiled in the struggle for control of the Pacific, and were exploited for the supply of forced labour ('blackbirding') by Great Britain's Australian settlement and by France. Ever conscious of the importance of a ruler with his name to have an empire to match, Napoleon III ordered the annexation of the islands in 1853, following which they became a penal colony, to which Algerian nationalists and almost 5,000 Communards were deported in the late 1860s and early 1870s.

In the Second World War, New Caledonia held a referendum (1940) which confirmed its support for the Free French, and saw 'Pro-Vichy officials . . . interned'; the archipelago contributed to the Bataillon du Pacifique and became an important Allied base. More recently, in 2018, an independence referendum led to a narrow majority voting to remain with France by 57 to 43 on an 81 per cent turnout. In 2020, a second referendum was held, rejecting independence by 53 to 47 on an 86 per cent turnout. In aggregate these results fall very close to the result and turnout of the 2014 referendum in Old Caledonia, Scotland. A further referendum in New Caledonia is due to be held. A French film on New Caledonia was made in 2021 which explores the history of the territory and these issues.[97]

Almost as soon as the first Scots made landfall in New Caledonia in November 1698, they became an object of interest to the Spanish Crown, which viewed the Scottish venture as piracy, pure and simple: Don José Sarmento wrote to a fellow noble in March 1699 about the need to 'exterminate the Scottish pirates'. Early protection from Captain Long, a local English officer who had 'arrived a month before and put small groups of Englishmen ashore "to take possession for the King of Great Britain"' vanished with Long himself. Some captured Scots impersonated Englishmen and thus helped to drag England into their under-resourced imbroglio. The attempted engagement of state power to protect company interests by confusing the interests of state and company was a well-known tactic for company-states – the international corporations of which the East India Company was the most powerful – the last occasion being the Jameson Raid of 1895–96. The Company of Scotland did not however have the power nor did it evoke the sympathy to engage England. The king was irritated and 'issued an order forbidding the English to offer any form of support to or correspondence with the Scots'; his interest in close political union with Scotland began to increase. Despite some early successes by the settlers, Spanish power duly swept the colony away within a few months. Sentiment was bitter; George Ridpath (d.1726), a contemporary Scottish journalist, commented: 'Our Nation being so Unhappy, that those who Write or Act against it are Rewarded and Caressed; whereas those that Write or Act for it, must do it at their Perril!'[98]

Following the failure of Darien, subsequent Scottish legislation attempted to underline Scotland's sovereign independence in foreign policy and governance in what might be seen as an increasingly desperate fashion, where patriotic (and indeed often Jacobite) sentiment was in the ascendant. England's conduct was petitioned against and the Crown lost control of the Scottish Parliament. England's attempt to embed the Hanoverian Succession through the 1701 Act of Settlement was strongly resisted in the Scottish Estates, who were determined to display their sovereignty. The Act anent Peace and War of 1703 sought to protect Scotland's right to an independent foreign policy, while the Act of Security of 1704 sought to give Scotland the right to choose its own monarch and to have its 'conditions of government' recognized following the death of Queen Anne, and thus not bound by the terms of the English Act of Settlement, which settled the Crown on Sophia of Hanover and her son, the future George I. It was, in the historian Karin Bowie's words, 'designed to limit the royal prerogative and enhance the powers of the Scottish parliament'. These were attempts to improve Scotland's negotiating position within the composite monarchy, including pressure to end the country's exclusion from legitimate trade with England's colonies under the terms of the Navigation Acts. For its part, England had long been irritated by the power of Scotland's overseas trading networks, reinforced as they were by its own exclusionary legislation. The Darien failure had damaged Scottish commercial interests at home, but not to the same extent abroad. Now there was also a clear political and dynastic threat (itself also reinforced by the exclusionary assumption that Scotland would simply follow England's lead on the Act of Settlement). It was time to constrain Caledonian ambition.[99]

THE UNION

Both the Scottish Parliament's Acts, that of Security in particular, were seen as a threat south of the border, not only to the constitution, but to the War of the Spanish Succession (1702–13), where it was feared that Scots troops might be withdrawn from the theatre. The Act anent Peace and War had been in part born out of Scottish dislike of persistent hostilities against France: as George Lockhart of Carnwath (1682–1731) put it, Scotland was being 'brought into England's wars', while the Act of Security was also influenced by the war, as Queen Anne used 'the royal prerogative to involve her Scottish realm in the War of the Spanish Succession'. Although the queen continued to support 'distinctive avenues of Scottish service' abroad, and Scottish regiments might use the saltire, the incorporation of Scottish troops into a British Army reached a new high, with four Scots among Marlborough's thirteen staff and brigade commanders and five Scots regiments engaged with the Duke's forces. The limitations of Scotland's notional state sovereignty in a multi-kingdom monarchy where England was the only kingdom that counted was plain to see, but, as might have been predicted, the Scots Estates' attempts to test the limits of Scottish sovereignty met with a hostile response. The English Parliament introduced the Alien Act of 1705, which threatened to render all Scots in England aliens with their property subject to confiscation and Scots imports of 'cattle, linen and coal ... totally forbidden' if 'agreement on the succession ... as well as progress on the question of Union' was not achieved by Christmas. To make matters worse, in the same year Ireland was permitted by the English Parliament 'to export Irish linen directly to the American colonies', a preferential trading position in comparison with Scotland. The Royal Navy (which had already had some practice in having 'targeted Scottish shipping') was to be at liberty to forestall Scottish trade with France.[100]

Thus as a domestic territorial state, increasingly funnelling its customs' administration and bills of exchange through London markets with the associated administrative and transaction costs, Scotland was in an exposed position, with few options. The Scottish exchange in London, founded in 1673, had, as the historian Louis Cullen put it, 'some of the elements of a foreign exchange as well as an inland exchange'. The country was in other words an oddity within the Williamite composite monarchy and showed up the peculiar position Scotland had as a state within a state. This was a position which would officially be resolved by Scotland's incorporation into the united kingdoms of Great Britain by the Acts of Union, but as the very description of the new state in these plural terms suggested, the anomaly continued in more circumscribed form. To some extent then, Scotland after the Union was to remain a state within a state, but with this important addition: Scots could now engage as equals in domestic British and – more importantly – international imperial markets, with the price being the loss of political (though not institutional) autonomy. The Union might – as Andrew Fletcher of Saltoun (1653–1716) opined, leave Scotland 'under the miserable and languishing conditions of all places that depend upon a remote seat of government', but things were not much better immediately before the Union. The 'imperfect conjunction' of the Union of the Crowns had proven to be unstable in the context of the tumultuous constitutional and religious politics of the era. Federal or confederal arrangements – as favoured by some Jacobites and radical Presbyterians such as Fletcher – were alien to the English polity, a situation which has not changed in the ensuing centuries. It was control that was wanted, and no chance of French aid or a Stuart restoration. This certainly suited some Scots: the Williamite Presbyterians, who opposed both France and the Stuarts, were the backbone of support for the Union, while the Jacobites and many of the Covenanting Presbyterians – who disliked France and James but favoured Scottish liberties – were against it. Overall, all the indications are – as we shall see – that opponents of Union dwarfed its supporters in numbers, though not to quite the same extent in influence.[101]

In 1705, as the English ministry moved towards demanding an incorporating Union, some Scots questioned 'whether they would not be better served by becoming an eighth member of the United Provinces [the Netherlands]', with which there was increased talk of a confederal political arrangement. The Scots Privy Council authorized the *Haarlem Courant* (and indeed the *Paris Gazette*) to be translated and published to inform the public on the 'Dutch and French standpoints on the Treaty of Union'.[102] The constitutional issue was recognized as a major one, and underpinned a ferocious pamphlet war in 1705–06, by which time Union had been agreed in principle and its form was being determined by the largely biddable treaty commissioners, 'hand-picked' in accordance with the Crown's interest. Scots were very conscious of their constitutional history, both evidenced and fictive: of the six ancient Scottish worthies of learning who formed part of the pageant at the Scottish coronation of Charles I in 1633, four (Duns Scotus, William Elphinstone, Hector Boece and George Buchanan) had had a theoretical or practical engagement with Scotland's constitution.[103] Scotland was one of the mediaeval European kingdoms which had developed a concept of *communitas regni* (Community of the Realm) that allowed for the sharing of governmental responsibilities in time of crisis (England – for example in the Baronial Council of 1258 – was another). Like other kingdoms, such as Hungary, where King Stephen's doctrine of *unius linguae uniusque moris regnum imbecille et fragile est* ('weak and fragile is the kingdom based on a single language or set of customs') was a view nineteenth-century Hungarian nationalists and their successors would have done better to remember, Scotland was a realm of diverse languages and origins.[104]

SCOTTISH CONSTITUTIONAL THINKING

The Community of the Realm appeared as a concept after 1286, and its notion of the compatriot Scots under the banner of St Andrew seems to have underpinned a shift from the idea of a 'Kingdom of the Scots' towards that 'of the Scots as a wholly individual and distinct people' whatever their actual ethnic origins. The Declaration of Arbroath (1320) famously – while advancing Robert Bruce's right as a second Maccabeus who had liberated Scotland from foreign tyranny (as the latter had liberated Israel) – included a deposition clause which raised the possibility that the Scots could rid themselves of Bruce if he failed to stand up for their rights. Arbroath summed up the constitutional views expressed in earlier documents such as Canon Baldred Bisset's 1301 submission to the Curia, the 1310 Declaration of the Clergy and the Irish Remonstrance of 1317.[105] Most importantly, it echoed Duns Scotus' view that peoples should have the right to consent to their own governments and the form of those governments and have occasion to renew that consent, as argued in his *Ordinatio*. As a Scot, a major philosopher of freedom and one of the leading intellectuals of mediaeval Europe, Scotus (1265–1308) almost certainly had a direct influence on the development of political thought among his contemporaries. At the same time, the modernity of Arbroath should not be overstated, for it was at least as much an 'eloquent statement of regnal solidarity' as a constitutionally challenging document. The contemporary *Regiam Majestatem*, for example, later published by the Scottish Parliament in 1609, expressed the centrality of the Crown to the fundamental laws of Scotland in a manner derived from Anglo-Norman thinking.[106]

However, the Declaration endured: the language of Arbroath can be found in John Barbour's *Brus* of *c*.1375, was transcribed by Walter Bower (1385–1449) and appeared in *Liber Pluscardensis* (The Book of Pluscarden) in 1461. It was very likely alluded to in the writing of Hector Boece (1465–1536) and John Mair (1467–1550), may have influenced George Buchanan (1506–82) and was cited by Sir James Balfour (*c*.1600–1658) before 'an abbreviated text' was published in 1654, with further versions in 1680 and 1683. The concept of elective monarchy, present in Arbroath (which of course celebrates the choice of Bruce rather than Baliol as the representative of the *communitas regni*) resurfaces in Presbyterian thought in the sixteenth century, for example in the writing of George Buchanan in favour of deposition of monarchs and 'elective monarchy'. The contractual nature of monarchy was noted by the General Assembly of the Kirk of Scotland in both 1567 and 1649, and, in *Jus Populi Vindicatum* (1669), the 'future Lord Advocate James Steuart of Goodtrees defended violent popular resistance' against kings who had broken their 'compact' with the people. In 1689, Arbroath was republished in full in English for the first time as *A Letter from the Nobility, Barons and Commons of Scotland* because it was seen as a forerunner of the Scottish Parliament's Claim of Right which asserted the constitutional right to depose King James VII for misconduct in office. Arbroath was published fourteen times in all before 1760, being referred to in both the Darien pamphlets and several times in debates over the Union. In 1703, James Anderson wrote that 'A Claim of Right is no novelty in Scotland, but the principle and practice of our Fathers'. That Claim was arguably ultimately based on Arbroath, and in Chapter 3 we will be looking in more detail as to whether it went on to underpin the American Declaration of Independence.[107]

These foundational constitutional documents of Scotland came into play in full in the Union debates. While Arbroath had underpinned the Claim of Right, the Union removed the Scottish Parliament's ability to choose the Crown – the basis of the Act of Security – and allowed supporters of the Stuarts (who opposed the Union) to use the Declaration more freely than hitherto to support the Stuart monarchy: Patrick Abercromby (1656–1716), Alexander, Lord Forbes of Pitsligo (1678–1762) and Fr Thomas Innes (1662–1744) all seem to have used it in this context. The Duke of Atholl quoted directly from Arbroath in the Union debates, and the remonstrances against the Union from places such as Bothwell and Kilbride appeared to echo the Declaration too. As Karin Bowie has pointed out, a manifesto for an armed march on Edinburgh against the Union in 1706 reflects on Arbroath in the context of 'the publicly expressed mind of the nation' being against the

Union: Sir James Clerk of Penicuik (1676–1755), one of the Union Commissioners, thought 'not even one per cent' of the people of Scotland supported it. The Declaration had acquired a new constitutional life (see Plate 2).[108]

The Scottish Estates and the Union Commissioners were certainly not seen by many as legitimate representatives of the body politic. The Convention of Royal Burghs voted to oppose the Union and fifteen shires and twenty-two royal burghs petitioned against it among a total of eighty addresses opposing, with 'over 20,000 signatures, including those from middling to lower social ranks'; the Burgh Council of Ayr's unusual 'lukewarm endorsement' of the Union was countered by a petition of 1,000 names from the burgh itself.[109] Some Presbyterian critics thought that the legacy of the Covenants 'demanded the preservation of the Scottish realm and parliament and made an act of union with Anglican England impossible'; others made even more democratic arguments. James Hodges, for example, called for a 'National Assembly of Free-holders' including the 'Freeborn Fair Sex . . . All the Noble Ladies, and all the Bonnie Lasses' to vote on the measure. Popular engagement was seen as a 'Fundamental National Right'. Jacobites called for a 'Caledonian Commonwealth' with a federal, verging on confederal, relationship with England, which would limit monarchical power and ensure the right of the Estates, as there would be '[Scottish] parliamentary consent for state officers and foreign alliances'.[110] It was estimated that three-quarters of the anti-Union population favoured a return of the Stuarts. The times were dangerous and this was reflected in the concessions to the Presbyterian Kirk, whose establishment in the Kingdom of Scotland would be protected by the Union. Likewise the Crown Jewels (the 'Honours of Scotland') were to remain in the northern kingdom.[111]

In the end, however:

The making of the Union . . . rested on an assertion of untrammelled monarchical sovereignty, overtaking a form of constitutionalism that sought to impose statutory conditions on the monarch.[112]

The Union itself, as ratified by the Scottish Estates on 16 January 1707, was a strangely hybrid document, neither quite a law nor quite a treaty. Outside Scotland it is seldom cited as a foundational constitutional document. Scottish Unionists by and large historically believed that it was so; English ones were more prone to treat it as an ordinary Act of Parliament with some clauses that were better left alone than an international treaty. The Union was a treaty between two sovereign nations; it was also an act of both their parliaments, by which one of them extinguished its existence. It is therefore not surprising that interpretation of it varies on each side of the border.

The Union's key clauses were Article II, which enforced the Act of Settlement on Scotland; Articles IV, VI and VII, which addressed freedom of trade (particularly aimed at overseas markets) and a customs union, while Articles X to XIII and XVI to XVII invoke Westminster Parliamentary sovereignty over tax and the standardization of the currency and weights and measures (the latter was not fully effected until the Weights and Measures Act of 1824, operational from 1826). Articles XVIII and XIX preserve Scots Law but leave its regulation to the UK Parliament. Yet, despite the fact that there was to be one Kingdom, Great Britain (Article I), the Great Seal of Scotland was to be retained (Article XXIV) as a ' "Great Seal" for rights confined within that kingdom' [Scotland], which continued in respect of 'Officers, Grants, Commissions, and private Rights' and the Presbyterian Kirk. The Union simultaneously talks about 'that part of the United Kingdom now called Scotland' and the 'Kingdom of Scotland' which continues to subsist in respect of religious, legal, official and institutional rights as a separate jurisdiction. The doctrine of the Crown in Parliament does not seem to have finally crystallized until the 1719 Declaratory Act (6.Geo. I c.5), which 'declared the Irish Parliament subordinate' through the Crown acting in and through its Parliament and not alone – thirty years after the Bill of Rights in 1688 paved the way for the constitutional theory of parliamentary sovereignty. There was thus a separation between the rights of Crown and Parliament in 1688–1719, and the Royal Assent was not automatically given to parliamentary bills during this period. Indeed, Queen Anne's refusal to grant it in 1708 is the last time it was withheld.[113]

Distinctions between Crown and Parliamentary right were being drawn at least as late as the American conflict in the 1770s, and the Union with

Scotland belongs to the beginning of this constitutional era. It conceives of a United Kingdoms over which parliamentary rights are sovereign, while the Crown's own rights in the Kingdom of Scotland and patronage and protection of private right within Scotland are alike preserved in that kingdom, which thus endures albeit on even more constricted terms than previously. Those of the Union's clauses linked to the Crown tend to use language (such as 'for ever') which places them in a constitutional zone beyond the reach of Parliament: 'the permanency of the union seems to inhere in Crown rights over Scotland, the preservation of Scottish institutions hinges on Crown rights within Scotland'. More than three hundred years on, the Union remains an extraordinarily interesting document.[114]

The accusation that Scotland was 'bought and sold for English gold' in Burns' terms was a contemporary one: a poster appeared in late 1706 ironically suggesting that Scotland would be sold at public roup or auction at Scone (the ancient crowning place of her kings) on 1 May, with a reserve price of £400,000 sterling, that being the equivalent, or compensation offered to Scotland for her share of taking on the English national debt. English officers came north to 'supervise and reorganize the collection of taxes in Scotland'. They were met with passive resistance, but, although the collection of taxes was soon largely in the hands of Scots, 'brutal attacks on customs and excise officers and anyone who dared to assist them carrying out their duties were becoming everyday events.' A 'militant alliance' was in development between 'Jacobitism and the call for Scottish independence on the part of Scots who had been disappointed by the Union'. The development of this alliance in its various forms was to leave a deep mark on Scottish history for fifty years and on British history for much longer.[115]

2

CROWN AND NO KINGDOM, CHURCH AND NO STATE

SCOTLAND AT THE TIME OF THE UNION

Scotland in 1707 was a state unnaturally impoverished by almost seventy years of intermittent conflict and by the efforts made to give the country a place on the world stage. The country's resources had been overstretched by military expenditure and failed colonial schemes which expended capital while not bringing in material rewards, for, even if Darien did not bankrupt Scotland as is sometimes suggested, it severely constricted the amount of free capital available. These failures had disrupted the country's traditional elites, who were in any case increasingly divided on sectarian lines, although in Edinburgh the early development of a Moderate Presbyterianism, more adjusted to social and economic improvement than the Covenanting tradition, could render this division less marked than elsewhere. Many leading individuals of wealth and position had found themselves suddenly impoverished: the Company of Scotland had 3,000 shareholders, far more – and far, far more per capita from the Scottish population – than the East India Company (1,188) or the Bank of England (1,267). The effects of the Darien failure bit deep not only into elite society and Scottish self-confidence, but also into the pockets of the middling sort, for example the painter Thomas Warrender (1662–c.1715), a subscriber for £100 of Company stock. Many Scots blamed Darien's failure on England; the vast majority of Scots opposed the Union; and almost certainly, on the evidence we have, a majority of the population supported its overthrow by the restoration of King James 'VIII and III' (1688–1766), the claimant since 1701 to the thrones of England, Scotland and Ireland, and widely recognized on the Continent as the rightful heir to these titles. Jacobite activity to disrupt the Union had failed, but in 1708 France supported a Rising which petered out when the French admiral grew unnerved by the effectiveness of Royal Navy policing of the Scottish east coast and refused to put James ashore.[1]

The Great Britain which Scotland helped to create through the Union was already a highly centralized and centralizing state. England had centralized early by comparison to other European monarchies, and by the seventeenth and early eighteenth centuries was increasingly using the authority of Parliament – and the self-created myth of its sovereign rights, amplified into the doctrine of the Crown-in-Parliament in 1720 – to reduce all other sources and locations of power in the British Isles to itself. The Council of Wales and the Marches at Ludlow (where James VI and I had allowed cases to be brought in Welsh) was finally closed in 1694; the Scottish parliamentary Union was followed by the abolition of the Scottish Privy Council in 1708; Ireland was effectively reduced from a kingdom to a dependency in 1720; and the Church of England's bishops were rendered uniformly Whig by 1727. In 1752, even the Cornish Stannaries were abolished,[2] though British centralization of power in Westminster finally met its match in the American colonies.

For all that, Scotland remained very much a distinct and separate society, with large parts of its business and considerable internal patronage system usually controlled by a major magnate such as Archibald Campbell, Earl of Ilay and 3rd Duke of Argyll (1682–1761), or Henry Dundas, 1st Viscount Melville (1742–1811), who controlled thirty-four of the forty-five Scottish constituencies in 1790.[3] The country's national institutions – the Faculty of Advocates, the College of Justice, the Kirk, the schools (where the 1696 Education Act had recently reinforced some form of universal – if socially limited – provision),[4] universities and banks – all remained autonomous. The education system retained its independence under the Union because its roots lay to a great extent in its close historic relationship with the established church, one not finally breached until the nineteenth century. The Act of 1696 – building on the 1496 Act and its post-Reformation successors under Charles I's governments – gave presbyteries oversight of parish schools and allowed for such schools to be supported by both heritors and their tenants.[5] Scotland's separate legal system ensured that it remained a distinct jurisdiction, not merely a part of Britain, as was recognized in the ambivalence of the Union settlement; this not only created the Kingdom of Great Britain as an apparently unitary entity, but also retained the (it turns out enduring) concept of 'the united kingdoms', with a separate Scottish royal household and official patronage system. Moreover, for the first half of the eighteenth century at least, Scotland remained a highly militarized society, dangerous to the peace of Great Britain.

The Scottish nobility was a key part of that military tradition and formed a much larger proportion of Scottish than of English society. The nobility in Scotland was more akin as a proportion of the population to the 890,000 nobles in late nineteenth-century Russia or to the numbers of the nobility in France and Spain than was the case in England's unusually small blue-blooded elite. By contrast, in England the nobility proper were only a few hundred in a country of over 4 million, and the gentry numbered only 15,000, or 0.3 to 0.4 per cent of the population. Many people in Scotland could claim noble relations, and many more were interlinked with the nobility by family, geography, education or association. While the Union settlement deliberately minimized the influence of the Scottish aristocracy in Great Britain by allowing for only sixteen 'representative peers' to sit in the House of Lords, the Scottish nobility extended beyond the Lords of Parliament (the equivalent of the English baron, and a fifteenth-century creation) to the Scots barons (either holders of landed title or baronial office, such as Barons of the Exchequer) and Chiefs of the Name. Many Scots nobles at all levels did not hold widely distributed estates, as their English counterparts often did, but contiguous lands from which a 'fighting tail' (the feudal retinue who might go to war on their lord's command) might be raised. While Scottish histories continue to speak – as they have long done – of 'Highland chiefs' and 'Lowland lairds' as if they represented different social systems, all Scotland was in most respects a land-, kinship- and association-based society where the tenantry might be managed on more (the tacksman 'system') or less (the cash rent 'system') military lines. The Duke of Montrose was not a 'Lowland' magnate: he was Chief of the Name of Graham as surely as Argyle was Chief of the Name of Campbell, Atholl Chief of the Name of Murray and Cameron of Lochiel Chief of the Name of Cameron. The 'Highland' Frasers were originally Norman immigrants with a land grant from the Scottish crown, and Lord Lovat was Chief of the Name of Fraser, many of his tenantry taking his name over the years. That is not to say that there was no difference between the organization of landholdings in the Gaelic north-west and the Scots-speaking east coast (though there was precious little in the case of estates with both 'Lowland' and 'Highland' parishes, like those of the Dukes of Atholl), but we are looking instead at a continuum of family resemblance, not a disjunct or double system. Extended family and other links of background or situation were important across the country: Scotland was clannish from Edinburgh to Stornoway, but in different ways. Scotland was a *Guanxi* culture, where 'personal connection' and 'trust' were the foundations for business, and engagement was Dutch in its directness rather than oblique. Scotland was also, like Denmark and the Netherlands, a less hierarchical culture than England's, at least in the burghs, though this is not to say there were not strong social divisions, as was indeed the case elsewhere in northern Europe in the early modern period.[6]

The upper nobility was one of the few elements of Scottish society that integrated into Great Britain at an early stage. Intermarriage with English aristocrats had risen significantly after 1603, particularly after 1650, and a century later many of the children of such unions were no longer educated at the local school but at elite establishments, often in England. Lord William Douglas of the Queensberry family attended the High School of Glasgow as did William Johnstone, 2nd Earl of Annandale, while George Keith the Earl Marischal (1693–1778), his brother James Francis Edward Keith (1696–1758) and Lord Deskford, the Earl of Findlater's son, attended Aberdeen Grammar School, Lord George Murray (1694–1760) its counterpart at Perth, though Murray's son was at Eton. On the other hand, major landed families of the baronial but lesser nobility, such as the Clerks of Penicuik (Royal High School) or Hays of Leith Hall (Aberdeen Grammar School), continued to attend schools more locally into the nineteenth century. These families were important for the provision of patronage, and 'one of the springboards' to patronage 'was the existence of a dominant legal profession in Scotland'. The country's noble families, particularly the lesser nobility, thus unsurprisingly engaged in Scottish law, and many legal dynasties – the Dundases and the Hopes chief among them – stretched over centuries of senior office in the legal profession. Lord Hope (b.1938), Lord President of the Court of Session, Lord of Appeal in Ordinary in the House of Lords and then the first Deputy President of the Supreme Court, is the descendant of the King's Advocate (today Lord Advocate) of Charles I and other members of the same family, such as Charles Hope, Lord Granton, Lord President 1811–41. The Dundas legal and baronial dynasty stretches across centuries from Sir James Dundas, Lord Arniston (1620–79), through Robert Dundas, Robert Dundas the younger, Lord President (1685–1753), and a further Lord President and another Robert (1713–87). Yet another Robert Dundas (1758–1819), Chief Baron of the Court of Exchequer, declined the Lord President's office, while the controversial Henry Dundas, Viscount Melville (1742–1811), became Lord Advocate before embarking on his Cabinet career, which is now increasingly remembered for his role in managing Parliament with regard to delaying the abolition of the slave trade.[7]

The social status of the law was thus high in Scotland, higher than in England, and closer to the French concept of *noblesse de la robe*. Some 60 per cent of the lords of session were themselves drawn from the nobility, while over 40 per cent of advocates married into it. Through the Lyon King of Arms Act of 1672, the Lord Lyon controlled a public register of arms and bearings. The law thus guaranteed and recorded nobility, as well as being born to it, socialising in it and intermarrying with it. Like other Scottish professionals, the country's lawyers were also highly cosmopolitan: between 1690 and 1730, 658 Scots matriculated in law at Leiden, Groningen and Utrecht, and 40 per cent of Leiden's Scots law students between 1681 and 1730 became advocates at the Scottish bar. The story was similar, if to a lesser degree, in the other professions. Herman Boerhaave (1668–1738) alone taught 244 Scottish students in the Leiden medical school, while John Holland (c.1658–1721), who moved to the Netherlands in the 1670s, became important in the early development of the Bank of Scotland (1695); the Bank's first accountant, George Watson (1645–1723), whose legacy is the Edinburgh school that still bears his name, was trained in a merchant house in the Netherlands. Scotland's large nobility thus became to an extent fused at its lower end with the country's increasingly lucrative professions. Between 1690 and 1730, around a third of new advocates were the sons of peers and baronets. In the universities, the story could be a similar one. Charles Areskine, Regius Professor of Public Law at Edinburgh 1707–34, was in turn Solicitor General, Lord Advocate and Lord Tinwald; his successor in the Chair, William Kirkpatrick (1734–35), was the brother of Sir Thomas Kirkpatrick of Closeburn, while the mother of George Abercromby (1735–59), who succeeded Kirkpatrick, was a Duff of Braco, from the Earl of Fife's family. All three of these men were educated at Leiden, and Abercromby also studied at Groningen. Scotland was still replicating and extending its native elites, and these were further entrenched through the practice of preferring a son into a father's professorship and the associated growth of academic dynasties supported not only by relationship but also institutional association, such as the Gregorys, four of whom attended Aberdeen Grammar School.[8]

The Kirk was for its part far more than a Presbyterian version of the Church of England. It took its role as a national body seriously, refusing, for example, 'to set apart a solemn Day of Thanksgiving for the Union', though placed under considerable pressure to do so.[9] It exerted major levels of social control into the nineteenth century, and comprehended many of the intellectual and ideological debates of Scottish society, from the Enlightenment (where Kirk Moderates developed a notion of social Christianity, far from Continental anticlericalism) to landlordism. The greatest controversy of the latter was that of patronage – the right of lay nomination to Kirk livings – which finally split the Kirk in 1843 and caused multiple earlier and more minor secessions. The Patronage Act of 1712 gave landowners 'the legal right to appoint to vacant church offices in each parish', and took full effect in 1729, when the General Assembly ceased to veto such appointments. It caused a minor division and encouraged Cameronian and related Covenanting opinion to stay outside the Kirk: their Reformed Presbyterian tradition stood for a kirk which could only be established in a Covenanted state, and to this day retains adherents in Scotland and Northern Ireland.

However, the ascendancy of spiritual over temporal power favoured by the Covenanters and their interpretation of Knox, Melville and the spirit of

Scottish Reformation was not going to make a comeback in the Kirk, however much it and its heroes, heroines and *lieux de memoire* were honoured in Presbyterian cultural memory. Yet their spirit – and its glorification of resistance to the Crown – died hard. Opposition to the British constitution and especially to oaths of loyalty or conformity remained strong among Presbyterians in the eighteenth century. Oaths – for example the Burgess oath of 1747, taken in Edinburgh, Glasgow and Perth – were seen as 'approval of the establishment': it led to the creation of 'Burgher' and 'Anti-Burgher' congregations. The Burgess oath controversy caused a split even among the existing Seceder congregations, who had left in opposition to patronage in 1733. Hebronite Covenanters opposed the Union and the uncovenanted nature of the British Crown, while the Seceders 'made covenanting a condition of ministerial communion' in 1744; in 1745, a few of them seem even to have joined the Jacobite Rising, so strong was their dislike of the British constitution. By the 1770s, there were nearly 200 dissenting Presbyterian congregations in Scotland, including new dissenters and a few of the older Cameronians who opposed the Crown and the 'uncovenanted, Erastian, prelatic' British constitution. At the turn of the nineteenth century, the Auld Licht (evangelical) and New Licht (Moderate) divisions over doctrine divided both the Burghers and the Anti-Burghers. The largely New Licht United Presbyterian church (UP) followed from this division; while in the Disruption of 1843, the largest secession of all took place, when the Free Kirk split from the Kirk over the continuing sore of patronage. Before patronage was finally abolished in 1874, up to half of Scotland's parishes were in 'opposition to the appointment of ministers by lay patrons'. There was a gradual drift of UPs into the Free Kirk, most of whose more moderate members were back in the Kirk of Scotland by 1929, although both the Free Kirk and its conservative Free Presbyterian offshoot continue in existence.[10]

Scotland was also significantly different from England financially, culturally and agriculturally. Scotland had 6 million hectares of agricultural land to England's 9.9 million, and in the centuries before the deteriorating climate of the seventeenth century it had been closer in terms of productive value than it was by the time of the Union. The population in the north of Scotland put pressure on the land, and by 1650 there were only around 1.2 to 1.6 hectares of arable land per family, which was very low in European terms and aggravated by 'partible inheritance and the consequent subdivision of holdings'. By the late eighteenth century, the average was down to one hectare a head, and the hunger for land in the north – discussed further in Chapters 3 and 4 – was a significant motivating force. Extensive steps were already being taken in the 1670s and 80s to move towards larger-scale farms, not least in Borders sheep-farming, where twenty of the Buccleuch estates' farms had over 1,000 sheep in the 1680s. Farm rentals were 'augmented by sales of timber, fish, slate, linen and other produce', with some 30,000 cattle moving annually from their northern rearing to southern markets along the drove roads by the 1720s. By this time, cash rents for tenancies were becoming well established and had made progress in driving out rents in kind even in remoter areas: Harris and Skye rentals were already 50 per cent in cash by the 1680s. Nonetheless, demand for land remained high. Subtenants – particularly in the north and west – had historically rented their holdings via the tacksmen or tenants in chief, to whom they had owed a quasi-feudal obligation as part of their largely in kind rentals, and tacksmen consequently acted as the officer class in the 'fighting tail' or following of a Scottish feudal superior. In the case of the Chiefs of the Name of Campbell or Murray this might be 3,000 men or more, while the Chiefs of the Name of Cameron or Fraser (Lochiel and Lord Lovat) had around 1,200. Many 'Lowland' magnates could also raise hundreds or even on occasion thousands of men from their estates. In return for his role in the structural organization of this support, the tacksman took a margin from rents received, but this began to be eroded in the early eighteenth century: in 1710, Argyll offered leases directly to the highest bidder in Kintyre 'and then through his estates by 1737'. The British Government often found the Dukes of Argyll less than able to discharge their expected military duty in controlling Scottish dissent, and their commercial practices may have been one reason for this.[11]

Scotland had left the sterling area in 1367, but its currency had – typically of other European currencies – devalued against England's, so that by the time of Scotland's conversion to sterling in 1707 the exchange rate was between 13:1 and 12:1, the latter being the official conversion rate. Notwithstanding the creation of a single British currency (though the Irish pound had a slightly different value up to 1817), Scottish currency continued to circulate and the Scottish pound (S£) continued to be used as a unit of account, even appearing in legislation into the early nineteenth century. Similarly, imperial weights and measures were not standardized in Scotland until the nineteenth century as noted in Chapter 1, and the Dutch and the traditional trone measure 'continued in retail use in local markets': local practices were even more deeply rooted than they were south of the Border. In the age of Enlightenment and beyond, Scots literally measured, weighed and counted the world differently. Affectionate stories were buried in these simple facts and were themselves traces of Scots *mentalité*: for example the 'bawbee' (Scots 6d or an English halfpenny and long used to describe the latter when the former had vanished) was named for Alexander Crok of Sillebawby, Master of the Mint when the coin was first issued in 1538; the word only finally fell out of use in the late twentieth century.[12]

Women could inherit titles, and divorce was permissible, with almost 1,000 cases coming to court between 1684 and 1830, with women being 36 per cent of pursuers. At a time when divorce in England required an Act of Parliament, 'Uncontested divorces could cost less than £5', and action could be taken in cases of domestic violence, as when, in 1691, the Aulton (Old Aberdeen) burgh authorities 'commanded no brewer to sell drink to Thomas Read', who was guilty of 'stricking and abuseing his own wyff and familie'. Daughters of burgesses could inherit that status for transference to a husband, and there were female burgesses in the burghs. A woman's heritable (non-moveable) property was administered by her husband but not owned, and it would revert to her on widowhood, while her consent was required for its alienation. Women often acted as agents for their absent husbands, were a party to loans and otherwise displayed significant economic agency, married women being, for example, almost a quarter of executors. While women were also more economically engaged in England than conventional scholarship has always allowed, the distinctions in Scotland were significant. This was also true in the educational sphere: in Aberdeen, there was female education from 1598, and Catherine Forbes, Lady Rothiemay (1573–1652), gave S£1,000 in 1642 to set up a school for girls, which endured into the nineteenth century. In Edinburgh, the Merchant Maidens' Hospital, established in 1694 'for maintaining and educating poor young children of the female sex', endures today as Mary Erskine's.[13]

In cities such as Edinburgh (which was paying almost two-fifths of Scotland's taxes by the 1670s), the architecture was more redolent of the Continent than England, as 'Scottish townspeople habitually resided in stacked apartments above merchant's booths in the European manner, rank being defined by storey.'[14] And if urban and domestic architecture showed such features, the same was true of Scotland's grander statements of status in stone. As one French architectural historian puts it, Scotland's architecture was uniquely 'castellated. No other country, in either the first castle age or the second, was producing a similar architecture. The Scottish castellated style referenced other cultures but it was a brand of none . . . There was no single British architecture.' This native architecture continued to develop after 1707, with the creation of a culture of instant heritage which underpinned Romanticism and the picturesque, as 'Artificial ruins were used to confer a sense of continuous habitation.' Scottish architects also contributed extensively and distinctively to architecture beyond Scotland: Colen Campbell (1676–1729), the erstwhile advocate of noble family who designed Burlington House and Houghton Hall, is considered a founder of the Georgian style, while James Gibbs (1682–1754) was a Catholic Aberdonian Jacobite who left his mark across Whig and Tory England alike, from the Radcliffe Camera at Oxford and the extraordinary baroque church of St Michael and All Angels at Witley Court in Worcestershire, to the Senate House in Cambridge and St Bart's in London.[15]

In Scotland itself, the concept of a native poetry and music alike developed rapidly after the Union. Allan Ramsay (1684–1758; see plate 3) set out to make song and poetry in the Scots language respectable across the Anglophone world. Comparing Scots to Doric Greek (with English being implicitly Attic Greek), he presented the languages as equal variants, not in the hierarchical relationship of standard and dialect. Great classical authors had written in Doric Greek, which was the language of the pastoral poet Theocritus (fl. 300–260 BC), court poet in Egypt, itself the legendary birthplace of the Scots nation through 'Scota, the daughter of Pharaoh'. Doric was the language of Crete, Rhodes, Syracuse (the home of Archimedes) and above all Sparta, where Tsakonian Doric still survives in the Peloponnese. Doric was the tongue of Leonidas and the men who had stood against Persia at Thermopylae: if English Attic was civil and beautiful, Scottish Doric was pastoral, direct and brave. The eastern origins of pastoral (as they were supposed to be in the eighteenth century) fitted well with the legend of Scota, and since Scotland was already characterized as a pastoral landscape in many English ballads about the country and its inhabitants, Ramsay created a virtue of necessity and adopted an external caricature as a native identity. At the same time, in *The Tea-Table Miscellany* (1723–37) and elsewhere, he began the creation of a 'native' Scottish song tradition which was indebted to both Italianate settings and English songs from the London stage.[16]

The differences between the countries were noticed. While Daniel Defoe (1660–1729) might hope that the Union would lead to 'erecting manufactures' in Scotland 'under English direction', the reality was generally different.[17] Scotland was incorporated into Great Britain through outward conformity in encounter with English interests in and furth of Scotland, but there was a widespread awareness in England of Scottish difference and doubleness, with adherence to Anglo-British norms being widely suspected of harbouring latent and at times more explicit opposition. English prints – intended for an upper, and later a well-to-do middle-class, audience – presented a Scot as dressed in a blue bonnet and (increasingly in the first half of the eighteenth century) tartan, typically skinnier than an Englishman and often infected with lice and possessed of uncontrollable sexual urges, greed (sometimes this was conflated with anti-Semitic caricature) and disloyalty. Outwardly conformist though the Scots might be, the caricatures revealed anxiety about what lay within: clannishness, appetitive self-interest and an affection for absolutism and the Stuarts – treacherous qualities. The 1745 Rising fixed these stereotypes, and it provided a narrative of Scottish disloyalty and threat that can even be found in political cartoons aimed at nationalist Scotland today.[18]

Notwithstanding the relative lack of state control and intervention characteristic of the early modern era, the general population of Scotland did not much like integration into a state dominated by an old enemy who made them pay higher taxes. Despite temporary exemptions for Scottish 'salt,

5. 'Sawney in the Boghouse' by James Gillray (1756–1815). A late eighteenth-century version of a famous anti-Scottish image of 1745, which presented the Scotsman as so uneducated in basic cleanliness that he put his feet down the latrines while letting urine and excrement dribble between them on to the floor.

stamped paper, windows, coal and malt' after the Union, 'fiscal convergence' was the goal, and it was a process initiated rapidly, as Scotland experienced a four or five-fold increase in its overall tax burden. An attempt to 'extend the Malt Tax to Scotland in 1713 was so explosive that the Earl of Seafield's move to introduce a bill to dissolve the Union in the House of Lords failed by only four votes'. 'New and complicated procedures' made customs and excise seem even more intrusive, though only 3 per cent of collectors were English, so, despite widespread resistance to the new taxes, they were only a foreign imposition at second hand. Efforts to mitigate them via the Board of Trustees for Fisheries, Manufactures and Improvement (1727), 'funded partly in order to make . . . the extension of the malt tax to Scotland more palatable' and 'bounties on linens, fishing and whaling especially aimed at Scottish economic interests' represented an attempt to ameliorate the large increase in taxation, which was 'met with passive resistance and heightened smuggling'. Magistrates did not always 'support revenue officers in applying the law', while juries were 'reluctant to convict' on revenue offences. Nor was there a single fiscal or civil state in compensation: for example 'Scots crossing the border after 1707 remained formally excluded' from parochial relief, and were in effect migrants with no access to benefits. On the other hand, the special arrangements to support the Scottish economy recognized the country's 'differences and diversity' and there was widespread understanding that 'the state's legitimacy in Scotland depended on recognizing its different circumstances', while the specific measures to support Scottish industry had – not least in the case of linen – significant economic benefits. Moreover, while English levels of taxation came as a shock to Scotland, the country was a long way from paying its way per capita, despite its complaints.[19] The Duke of Newcastle (Thomas Pelham-Holles (1693–1768)) noted that 'The consequences for England would be fatal' if the spirit of 'that kingdom [Scotland] did not improve', and parts of Scotland were 'effectively ungovernable' because of resistance to taxes, while the Isle of Man, in the hands of the Dukes of Atholl until 1765, was widely used as a safe smuggling depot. Sir Tom Devine notes only 'up to 80%' of the taxes raised may have been spent in Scotland, though 'civil expenditure grew in importance after Culloden' (as did the more intensive collection of excise that supported it). It was no coincidence that, during the risings in favour of the Stuarts in the eighteenth century, the burghs occupied by the Jacobites were called on to pay taxes on the old Scots footing (see Plate 4).[20]

Smuggling became a politicized crime: as late as the 1740s, it was almost a quarter of the level of legal imports, its position doubtlessly improved by the fact that smugglers in Scotland (unlike in England) usually sold their goods for below market price, 'driven by cash flow issues'. Many of the east coast ports (such as Montrose) suffered from the shift away from Scotland's pre-Union markets, with a concomitant move to the western ports, though others such as Aberdeen (whose 30 ships in 1712 had grown to 150 in 1800) benefited. Smuggling was understood to offer some compensation to the eastern ports, though it was common enough in the west too. Rife with smuggling (also used as a conduit for Jacobite news, information and recruitment), the east coast ports were at the same time so short of cash that their smuggling crews had to accept a discounted price for the goods they brought in at such legal risk. Certain ships specialized in certain contraband: the *Charlotte* of Peterhead was a notorious carrier of spirits later in the century. It is estimated that between 1700 and 1722, over 50 per cent of Scotland's tobacco imports came via smuggling. The excise was seen as particularly confiscatory and unjust in the east, where economic decline fed a natural tendency to Jacobitism. Smugglers in England – as in Scotland – carried 'French agents' and Jacobite propaganda: one Kentish captain received 7,000 Jacobite medals in one 1699 shipment alone (see plate 5). The presence of Irish merchants in increasing numbers in French ports also served as a communication and recruitment link to the Irish brigades in the service of France. The 'export' of Scottish and Irish soldiers to France and elsewhere on the Continent in its turn 'served to rationalise hostile political attitudes' on the part of the British Government. There were substantial numbers of Irish and to a lesser extent Scottish troops in service in Continental armies (five Irish infantry regiments in the Spanish service alone, for example), and recruitment continued from the home countries well into the eighteenth century at a time when no Catholic could (officially at least) be recruited by the British Army.[21]

Food riots racked the east coast burghs in 1720, often connected to the increasing tendency for landowners to enclose common land in the cause of improvement, that is, improved in terms of fertility, yield and rents. This was not just a matter of greed or of making a show on the British stage. The creation of restrictive entails by the Scottish Parliament in 1685, where 'a succeeding owner could not break the line of inheritance' of an estate with sale or heavy indebtedness also 'prohibited', restricted room for manoeuvre. In northern and western Scotland as we have already seen, an increasing population put pressure on partible holdings, a pressure which only increased after 1745. In 1723, 'The Honourable Society of Improvers in the Knowledge of Agriculture in Scotland was established by a group of influential land-owners.' Improvement was thus not solely agricultural, and its processes led to a range of outcomes including the development of the first planned villages, such as at Inveraray (1742) on the Argyll estates: by the 1770s, these had become widespread. Long associated with 'progressive' British Whig politics, Improvement was in fact championed across the political divide: the notable Jacobite commander Brigadier William Mackintosh of Borlum (1658–1743) was the author of an *Essay on the Ways and Means for Inclosing* (1729), while Major General Alexander Robertson of Struan (1670–1749) 'ran an extensive commercial forestry operation and timber from his estates' Jacobite writers and 'whiggish improvers' alike often shared a discourse about land development. Figures such as Borlum and Struan were a long way from how the slippery term of 'Highlander' is often understood. However, in the longer run improvement came to be associated with the Union and Whig interest, not merely because of lazy narratives of progress, but also because 'The enforced enlistment of men into the Highland regiments of the British army formed an integral part of the business of estate improvement' in the years after the last major Jacobite Rising.[22]

The west coast of Scotland benefited to a greater extent than the east coast did from the Union, although there was also some new imperial trade in the east: for example John Burnett in Aberdeen was importing Virginia tobacco in the 1730s. But the scale in the west was far greater. By 1747, Glasgow had 50 per cent of British tobacco exports to France, rising to 60 per cent in 1751, and the French switch of the tobacco-purchasing monopoly from buying in England to buying in Glasgow led to rapid growth in 'the Clyde-Chesapeake tobacco trade'.[23] Yet although central and south-western Scotland seemed to benefit most from the new economic world of the Union in the short term, there were problems and protests here also. Concern over the importation of Irish cattle (a longstanding issue in western Scotland after the 1667 Importation Act (19 & 20 Cha. II c.12) kept Irish cattle out of England), as well as the enclosure of land in pursuit of English cattle markets, underpinned the significant agricultural protests in Galloway in 1724. This became the so-called 'Levellers' Revolt', when some 2,000 men – perhaps half of them armed – came out to protest against enclosure. Their religious background (the revolt was underpinned by Hebronite Covenanting support) only sharpened their distaste for the role that the farming of Irish cattle played in their protests, and the Jacobitism of some of their landlords may also have been a target. Six troops of cavalry and dragoons were deployed to secure order. There were also direct challenges from England to the

Scottish trades: for example in 1719–20 English weavers seeking to protect their own markets engaged in protests which further undermined an already failing industry north of the Border. The Duke of Roxburghe (John Ker (1680–1741)) warned of unrest in Scotland – indeed implicitly threatened it – if the British Government responded to the demands of the English weavers at Scotland's cost.[24]

JACOBITISM AND EUROPE

Jacobitism promised for many to be the answer to all these woes. Its goal was the restoration of the Stuart dynasty. In England this tended to manifest itself as clerical conservatism combined with xenophobia towards a Dutch, then German, monarchy with foreign policy considerations deriving from their Continental origins, later supported by disaffection arising from the exclusion of the Tories from office between 1714 and 1760. In Scotland and Ireland, matters stood differently. Support for the Jacobites was strongly tied to a range of national grievances and a desire to restore the Stuart composite monarchy in full, with strong national parliaments and inbuilt protection for Catholicism in Ireland and Episcopalianism in Scotland. William Forbes of Disblair's view of the necessity of 'a new Bannockburn' to liberate Scotland was not untypical of Scottish Jacobitism. Jacobitism was viewed very seriously by the authorities, but at the same time was often visible. Frequently on display through 'tartan, plaid, glasses, medallions, fans and feathers', its mute or musical symbolism (of which tartan was an increasingly important part, with its advertising and sales gaining prominence at times of Jacobite disquiet) put it beyond prosecution; treason legislation, which ultimately dated from the time of Edward III and which was extended to Scotland in 1708, almost always involved an act of spoken or written transgression. Tartan was most frequently used in acting 'as a rallying-centre . . . expressing social unity in a material form', one of the key reasons why it became such a target for the authorities, another being the uniforming of Jacobite armies in tartan, irrespective of their origin (see plate 6). White gloves and white handkerchiefs were also Jacobite symbols, and there were a significant number of Jacobite clubs from the time of the 1690s and the Greppa gatherings at Mistress Henderson's in Edinburgh, where at least one Jacobite club was still operational at the time of Robert Burns' visit to the capital in 1787. Of the twenty-one members of the Buck Club, who met 'weekly for supper in Parliament Close', sixteen fought in the Rising of 1745, while Magdalen Scott, Lady Bruce, 'provided open house for Jacobite refugees' in Leith Citadel.[25]

Other organizations, such as the Royal Company of Archers with their tartan uniform, also acted as Jacobite fronts. Closet pro-Jacobite publishing referenced Mary, Queen of Scots, William Wallace, Robert Bruce and the Wars of Independence.[26] There was a strongly anti-Union and also a confessional aspect to Jacobite support. In Scotland, the latter was not so much Catholic – though many Catholics supported the Jacobites and opposed the Union – as Episcopalian. The permanent exclusion of 'the Reformed Catholic Church in Scotland' from office, the extremely negative attitudes towards it held by Presbyterians, and the dominance of the central belt over the Episcopalian heartlands all had their part to play in this process of political alienation. By 1689–90, 'There was little in the eyes of Scotland's more extreme Presbyterians to distinguish Episcopalianism from Roman Catholicism', its 'sister in malignancy' towards which many Presbyterians were 'visceral, fundamental and unforgiving' in their loathing. This was not a healthy environment, and although a brief respite was gained with the Toleration legislation of 1712, its only longer-term benefits were to Anglicans ministering in Scotland rather than to the Scottish Episcopalian church.[27]

Possible covert quasi-Jacobite associations grew up in response, such as the 'Fund for Relief of Indigent Episcopal Clergy', which remained active until at least the mid 1750s. At the same time, 'Many Presbyterians were adherents of the exiled sovereign' on constitutional grounds, at least in the Rising of 1715. Scottish patriotism could be stronger than confessional identity. While many English Tories – contemporaries thought the majority – supported the Jacobites, particularly after 1714 when they were excluded from office, Scotland remained the military mainstay of the Stuart cause. As the end of Queen Anne's reign approached, there was public disquiet and pro-Stuart rioting in the Scottish burghs.[28]

Scotland's European networks continued to be important after the Union, not least because they were strongly reinforced by Jacobites in the first half of the eighteenth century, particularly in France, Spain, the Italian states and also in Russia, whose Orthodox ecclesiastical environment was more welcoming to Episcopalians than the Catholic powers. The establishment of the Jacobite Court in France and later Rome served as a source of patronage – via figures such as the Earl of Wintoun, Hay of Drummelzier and Andrew Lumisden – to Scots and other Jacobites abroad. Jacobite commanders, diplomats and artists were mobile across Europe: men such as the diplomat Sir William MacGregor, 2nd Bart (1698–1765), the soldier and administrator George Keith, 9th Earl Marischal (1692/3–1778), and the Austrian general James Lockhart (1727–90). Scots often benefited from easier passage abroad than Englishmen (and sometimes Irishmen) in early modern Europe. In 1704, the Spanish ambassador considered granting a passport to Scots and not English travellers, while in France, after the final defeat of James VII and II in Ireland and the ensuing Treaty of Limerick in 1691, the core of a first Jacobite army was formed at Lille. The English and later British Government forbade – it was a capital offence – recruitment into the service of the French armed forces, and occasionally put pressure on foreign countries and their agencies directly. In 1740, for example, James Steuart of Dalguise 'found that the Swedish East India Company had begun to dismiss the Scots in its service in direct response to concerns expressed by King George II'. The Swedish East India Company had been co-founded in 1731 by the Edinburgh man Colin Campbell (1686–1757), who also served as Sweden's first ambassador to China, and Scots Jacobites in Gothenburg had supported the Company, while the 'East Indian Asiatic Company' of Denmark 'provided opportunities for other Jacobite Scots such as the Browns of Colstoun, one of whose number became governor of the Danish Company's Indian settlement in 1773'. There seems to have been a pattern here of trying to replicate the company–state model which had failed at Darien in other relatively small northern kingdoms, despite the 'formidable barriers to entry' created by the major states. It is possible that the British authorities saw matters in this light also. There could be 'attempted curtailment of non-British patronage' elsewhere, although Scots in the service of sympathetic powers – such as the Netherlands – were viewed more positively by the Hanoverian state.[29]

The Russian Tsar Peter the Great (r.1682–1725) had a strong interest in the use of Scots in the military, not least Jacobite Scots. He was most likely influenced in this by his tutor, Colonel Paul Menzies, younger of Pitfodels (1637–94), who may well have left his royal master with an abiding taste for both Scottish educational distinction and martial valour. Peter appears to have personally recruited Henry Farquharson (c.1675–1739) from Aberdeen in 1698 to direct his first Naval Academy; his other Scottish commanders included Robert Bruce (1668–1720), Commandant of St Petersburg; General Alexander Gordon (1669–1752); Brigadier Count James Gordon (1668–1722); Admiral Thomas Gordon (1662–1741); Admiral James Kennedy (c.1694–1760); and Admiral Kenneth Sutherland, 3rd Lord Duffus (d.1732). Peter (like Louis XIV) also owned some of the symbols of Scottish military prowess, Caddell's famous Doune pistols, which had adopted Celtic designs by the 1740s.[30] Scottish soldiers were already highly respected in the Tsar's empire, where Episcopalian Royalists, such as William Drummond, 4th Lord Madderty and 1st Viscount Strathallan (c.1617–1688), Thomas Dalyell (1615–85), William Johnston, Charles Seton, 2nd Earl of Dunfermline (1608–73), and General Patrick Gordon of Auchleuchries, chief adviser to the Tsar (1635–99), had already held senior army commands in the seventeenth century.[31]

Some of the Jacobites in proximity to the Russian court, such as George Mackenzie in St Petersburg, were concealed under the guise of British diplomats: Mackenzie had originally been appointed in John Erskine, Earl of Mar's (1675–1732) interest and continued to act as his agent; Robert Erskine (1677–1718), Mar's first cousin, was the Tsar's chief physician and had 'overall responsibility for civilian and military medicine, the apothecaries, pharmacy, botanical gardens and so forth'. Erskine produced the 'earliest surviving Russian herbal' in 1709 and 'pioneered and superintended' the first Russian physic garden in 1714, based on the innovative garden development of Balfour and Sibbald in Edinburgh, discussed in Chapter 1. Erskine also purchased Archibald Pitcairne's (1652–1713) large private library for the Tsar and his own book collection 'formed a cornerstone of the Library of the Russian Academy of Sciences'. In 1714, Erskine became the 'first director of the Petersburg Kunstkammer and library'. The Jacobite court also had its own direct diplomatic representatives, such as Sir Henry Stirling of Ardoch (Erskine's nephew), Colonel Daniel O'Brien and Captain William Hay, while Jacobite noblemen in other foreign services also became ambassadors to St Petersburg, such as the Duke of Berwick, who represented the Crown of Spain from 1727 and himself became allegedly Grand Master of the Russian branch of the Jacobite secret society, the Order del Toboso, in which there was a strong crossover with Freemasonry and with the interests of the Earl of Mar. Subsequently many Scots followed in these footsteps. James Francis Edward Keith (1696–1758), the Earl Marischal's brother, came to Russia after the Jacobite Rising of 1715 bringing members of his own family with him, in classic Scottish style noting that 'If I am partial to my own kinsmen, it is because I know their nature.' Keith's associational networking was just as assiduous as his family patronage: he went on to be allegedly Master of the St Petersburg Freemasons (1732–34) and then provincial Grand Master of Russia in 1740, at the same time as his cousin John, the Earl of Kintore, took control of the English Grand Lodge. As a general officer in the Russian Army, Keith's innovations helped to bring it success, and he went on to govern Ukraine and Finland – where he was highly respected – in the 1740s.[32]

Scottish migration in the medical and certain other professions to Russia continued for many years, despite the opportunities opening up in the British Empire. To take only a few examples, C.S. Grieve (MB Edinburgh 1733) was City Physician of St Petersburg and Physician to the Empress Elizabeth (r.1741–62); John Grieve (1753–1805) was physician to Tsars Paul (r.1796–1801) and Alexander I (r.1801–25); Matthew Halliday (1732–1809) was director of the St Petersburg Inoculation Hospital, while John Rogerson (1741–1823) was 'Catherine's [r.1762–96] personal physician and a counsellor of state'. The court doctor Robert Lee (1793–1877) was a pioneer of the use of quinine against malaria, while Sir Alexander Crichton (1763–1856) was both Physician in Ordinary to Alexander I and head of Russia's civil medicine. Crichton's nephew, Sir Archibald William Crichton (1791–1866), was also a doctor to the Russian Court, while Sir James Wylie (1768–1854) was physician to three Tsars, Chief Medical Inspector of the Army and president of the Medico-Chirurgical Academy of St Petersburg.

Military commanders such as General Alexander Wilson (1776–1856) and General Robert Armstrong (1791–1864), Chief of the St Petersburg mint, continued to be appointed. There were also engineers such as Charles Baird (1766–1843), who built Russia's first steamship, *Yelizaveta*, and the leading architects Charles Cameron (d.1812), Adam Menelaws (1756–1831) and William Hastie (1754–1832), whose commissions included the royal residence of Tsarskoye Selo. In 1856, Murdoch Macpherson established the Baltic shipyard in which Russia's first armoured ships were built, an interesting task for a Scotsman to lead on given the recent Crimean War between the British Empire and its allies and its Russian counterpart.[33]

In their turn, a number of leading Russians became Scotophiles. Prince Alexander Yakovlevich Lobanov-Rostovsky (1788–1864) was a great enthusiast for Mary, Queen of Scots, and Vladimir Soloviev (1853–1900) was a protagonist of Gaelic. James Macpherson's (1736–96) *Ossian* – first translated into Russian in his own lifetime – was influential on the writing of both Alexander Pushkin (1799–1837) and Mikhail Lermontov (1814–41). Yekaterina Romanovna Vorontsova, Princess Dashkova (1743–1810) was an early tourist to Scotland, where her son became a student at the University of Edinburgh, where 'All who wish to perfect their knowledge of medicine come . . . to study', as did other Russians. As we shall see in the next chapters, Scotland's medical schools, and their overproduction of graduates with respect to domestic opportunities, were to make a substantial contribution to British imperial policy and practice. But it was not the only branch of Scottish education that was respected. As director of both the Imperial Academy of Arts and Sciences (later the Russian Academy) and the St Petersburg Academy of Sciences (the first woman in the world to head a national academy), Princess Dashkova secured honorary membership for the chemist Joseph Black and the historian William Robertson, to whom she committed her son's education.[34]

There were also religious connexions between Scotland and Russia. In 1717–21, Non-juring Anglicans – allies of the Scots Episcopalians – were involved in talks on the mutual recognition of their own and Orthodox communions based on their shared adoption of the ancient Usages (these were a series of Catholic/Orthodox ritual and liturgical practices, controversy over which divided the Episcopalian Church for a time: in some ways, their association with ecclesiastical rather than secular authority mirrored Presbyterian controversy over patronage). Peter the Great encouraged these conversations, and the Orthodox Church recognized Protestant baptism in 1718 and in 1721 permitted Orthodox–Episcopalian marriages if the children were raised Orthodox. As late as 1866, the year before the Episcopal Church of Scotland was formally incorporated in the Anglican Communion, Robert Eden, Bishop of Moray and Ross, was in Russia exploring the possibility of intercommunion between the churches. As a result of this relatively welcoming climate to Scots Episcopalians, Orthodox Russia was often seen as welcoming to Scots Jacobites. As the *Scots Magazine* put it proudly in 1739:

> At the head of the Russian fleet we find a GORDON; in the highest rank
> of the army a KEITH, and DOUGLAS, LESLEY, and many more, send
> their names from the extremities of that vast empire . . .[35]

James Francis Edward Keith left the Russian service due to internal intrigues in 1747 to be Frederick the Great's Field Marshal, serving together with fellow Jacobite officers such as Lord John Drummond, and becoming a Prussian folk hero by his death in battle at Hochkirk in 1758. Thomas Gordon's daughter married Sir Henry Stirling. It was a closely knit expatriate society, and other Scots rose to the highest ranks in the Russian service: in all, some twenty-five Scots served at general officer or admiral rank in the imperial Russian forces, even into and beyond the Crimean War; the last Scots generals in the Russian service appear to have been Robert Armstrong and Alexander Baillie (1800–1872). Many of these men sent their sons back to university or to their relatives for a time in Scotland, as did Samuel Greig (1735–88), a Russian admiral whose son – also an admiral – married the famous scientist Mary Somerville (1780–1872), and whose grandson was a Russian commander in the Crimean war. Young Greig's tutor in Russia was Adam Armstrong, himself the son-in-law of Robert Riccaltoun (1691–1769), a Kirk minister whose parish lay close by Mary Somerville's uncle's own living. It is thus clear that these Scots exiles also retained a strong network in their home country. There was often something of the sojourn about the European diaspora.[36]

6. The Palazzo del Re, home of the Jacobite court in exile at Rome from 1719.

From 1719, the Jacobite court was established in Rome at the Palazzo del Re, and with it a substantial Scottish community which endured for at least half a century. Scots in Rome such as David Wemyss, Lord Elcho (1721–87), gathered together – not least on St Andrew's Day, 30 November – to play and sing Scots songs (Elcho played them on the flute). The framing of exile and pining for home as a characteristic strain of Scots song seems to have become popular at this time: it left a lasting legacy, not least in 'Auld Lang Syne' with its images of wandering and overseas exile in the third and fourth stanzas. Scots formed an increasing proportion of the Jacobite king's household in the Court's years in Rome: Allan Cameron served as James's Master of Horse, James Edgar was the king's Secretary, while James Hay was Surgeon to the Household, James Irvine physician, James Murray Principal Physician and John Hay of Cromlix Secretary of State. Others, such as the Earls of Linlithgow and Southesk, Viscount Kilsyth, Viscount Kingston and Lord Forbes, spent some part of their exile near their king. The Stuart Court was home to a network of agents and also had its supporters among a large number of senior Jacobite officers in the forces of the Catholic or Orthodox powers, such as Colonel Livingston in the Venetian service and Generals James Wishart and James Lockhart in the Austrian service; Lockhart was also Chamberlain of Austria. In Spain and its Latin American colonies, the interests of Irish Jacobites predominated. The Stuart Court was central to the experience of British visitors to the Papal States in general; as well as granting passports into the States one of its roles 'was to help obtain a passport for any Grand Tourist who wanted to return home through France'. Indeed, 'At least one of the French ambassadors refused to give any passports without a recommendation from James III.' The Jacobite secretariat would often offer introductions to the Court or its members or military officers to sympathetic British travellers, a practice which still continued into the 1760s.[37]

Art was a key element to both the thematic propaganda and display and also the networks of the Jacobite court, which provided a stream of commissions for painters such as Antonio David (1698–1750) and Domenico Dupra (1689–1770). The artworks were then copied and distributed as propaganda portraits. Dependent on medals and reproduction artworks and engravings for propaganda purposes, and Scottish religious houses abroad for contacts and links, much of the overt connexion between Scotland and the Italian states took the form of trade in paintings and objects of *vertu*. Some of the Italian painters who worked for the Stuart court were themselves recommended to the court by Scottish artists: for example Francesco Trevisiani (1656–1746) was recommended by the Aberdeen painter John Alexander (1686–1767) to the Earl of Mar. Alexander had a partiality to Mary, Queen of Scots, and the developing genre of history painting had much to do with coded Jacobitical renditions of the Scottish past, often themselves commissioned by Jacobite or Jacobite-leaning patrons, such as Placido Constanzi's (1702–59) *Bannockburn* for the Earl Marischal and Gavin Hamilton's *The Abdication of Mary Queen of Scots* for James Boswell (1740–95). Many Scottish painters were drawn into Jacobite espionage networks through the art trade, conducted through Rome and Livorno (Leghorn), where the painter William Aikman's (1682–1731) brother John was among the active Scottish merchants. Andrew Hay (1690–1754) had been a pupil of the Edinburgh painter John de Medina, and went on to trade paintings and *objets d'art* to an elite Jacobite–Tory network: John Clephane (1705–58), son of the Jacobite Adjutant General in the 1715 Rising, supplied Scottish picture dealers in the Italian trade such as John Blackwood; William Duguid was 'a double agent in Italy while acting as a jeweller'. William Mosman (1700–71), a regular at the Jacobite masonic Lodge at Rome, acted as agent for the Jacobite art collector (and possible spy) Captain John Urquhart, who himself served in the Spanish army after fighting in the 1715 Rising. James Byres (1734–1817), son of a Jacobite exile, became a noted antiquarian and architectural visionary, while also acting as a facilitator for artists such as Gavin Hamilton, David Allan, Alexander Nasmyth and Henry Raeburn in Italy and possibly making donations to the Stuart household. Andrew Lumisden (1720–1801), who served at the top of the Jacobite secretariat for more than twenty years, was deeply engaged in a patronage network which included Alexander Runciman (1736–85) and many others, including a number of female artists such as Dundee woman Katherine Read (1723–78), who was the niece of the Jacobite officer Sir John Wedderburn and went on to a career as a painter in British India. Runciman himself – rather tellingly – converted from being a decorative to a history painter in Italy, before returning to paint an Ossianic cycle in Penicuik House in 1773. The painters Allan Ramsay (1713–84), who painted Prince Charles at Edinburgh, and Sir George Chalmers (c.1720–91) (who was John Alexander's son-in-law) both graced the environs of the Jacobite Court at one time or another, as did Robert Strange (1721–92), Lumisden's brother-in-law and the designer of the Jacobite banknotes of 1745 (see plate 7).[38]

Jacobite exiles or sojourners celebrated their own culture in the Papal states. Patrick Byres extolled the merits of Scottish scenery in Rome, 'preferring Loch Lomond and the valley of Stirling to Lake Nemi and the Campagna'. Material culture appears to have been produced in Scotland for these exiles abroad, such as a 1762 Dunfermline napkin with Scottish insignia on it and the legend 'C'est Les Armes d'Ecosse'. There were influences the other way too: Theodore von Neuhoff, elected King of Corsica in 1736, seems to have joined the Jacobite Rising in 1715 before entering the Spanish service and joining John Law in Paris: a web of connexion which arguably led to a linkage between Corsican patriotism and Jacobite intrigue which lasted until James Boswell's support for Pasquale Paoli in the 1760s and perhaps even beyond, as Napoleon's (the Corsican son of one of Paoli's officers) fascination with Celticism might indicate.[39]

Jacobitism was thus an international movement and made use of – indeed developed – international means of association. Freemasonry was a major mechanism of Jacobite networking. The Earl Marischal was a member of Frederick the Great's Masonic Lodge in Berlin, as well as 'Grand Master of the Jacobite-orientated Order of Saint Thomas of Acre', while the Jacobite exile Andrew Ramsay (1686–1743), Charles Edward's sometime tutor and an assiduous promoter of the national 'Scottish rite', was Grand Chancellor of French Masons from 1734 to 1743, where the Paris Lodge of St Thomas no.1 (named for St Thomas à Becket and the brutality of royal opposition to the Church) was founded by a group of seventeen Jacobite exiles in 1726. Among over 100 Lodges in France, only 7 or 8 seem to have been affiliated to the London Grand Lodge, while there were specific Lodges – such as 'Loge Irlandaise' no.37 at Toulouse – associated with the exiled Jacobite community. Irish Jacobite Lodges were also active in the army of the Kingdom of Naples among other places, while the Madrid Lodge was founded in 1728 by Philip, 1st Duke of Wharton (1698–1731), at that time in the service of King James. Jacobite diplomacy to Sweden and to a lesser extent Russia was dominated by these Masonic links, while the Jacobite Lodge at Rome at one time or another included figures such as William Mosman, John Murray of Broughton, Allan Ramsay junior, an 'ardent Jacobite', Alexander Cunynghame (later Dick of Prestonfield), the Earl of Wintoun and James Irvine, physician to James. Closer to home, Lodge Canongate Kilwinning no.2 in Edinburgh (apparently visited by the Lodge at Rome in 1738–39) played a significant role in the Jacobite world, and later attracted its sympathizers, such as James Boswell and Robert Burns (1759–96). These lodges were also a networking point for the professions: Canongate Kilwinning alone had sixty medical students in its membership in 1735–65. At the end of the 1760s, Boswell and John Dick's support for a subscription to the Corsican war effort in 1768–69 seems to have been mediated via Perthshire Masonic contacts in Scotland from the Drummond and Menzies families. The subscriptions were held at the bank of Andrew Drummond & Co, the younger brother of Major General William

Drummond, 4th Viscount Strathallan (*c.*1687/88–1746) who had fallen at Culloden leading a futile if heroic counter-attack with his Perthshire Horse.[40]

Jacobitism was thus closely woven into European society. The example of Georg Frederick Handel's (1685–1759) relationship to the House of Hanover was one of the grounds (although the immediate link probably lay in his patronage by Queen Marie of Poland) on which the Jacobite court adopted Giuseppe Domenico Scarlatti (1685–1757) as its chosen court composer in the event of a restoration, since Handel had joined George I in England in 1714. It appears that Handel himself was well aware of political alternatives, however, for 'Nine of Handel's operas from the period 1722–37 were settings of libretti previously performed in Rome . . . seven of which had been specifically dedicated to James III and Clementina.'[41]

Scottish and Irish soldiers in the service of Continental armies in this period are sometimes misunderstood as 'mercenaries'. The term has unfortunate modern connotations of brutality, irresponsibility and the improper substitution of financial reward for patriotic duty. Its use does not aid understanding. Firstly, in this era soldiering was not the mobilization of a nation, a total war fought on the basis of conscription, patriotism and common cause: this is a nineteenth- and twentieth-century norm. Armies were smaller and often volunteer forces: moreover composite monarchies necessarily drew on soldiers from different countries. Hanoverian Army troops were used as late as Waterloo by the British Army, for example, and perhaps less than one-third of Wellington's command on that day were actually British Army soldiers.

Secondly, Scottish and Irish Jacobites were not fighting for 'foreign' powers as they understood it, nor was loyalty to Great Britain a natural state of affairs for them. France or Sweden or Russia might well be instrumental in restoring the Stuart line and ending the Union, and these were the fundamental priorities of the Scots Jacobites, while their Irish counterparts saw France and Spain as the potential guarantors of a restoration of Catholic rights as well as the Stuart dynasty. Great Britain was, to them, a usurping power which had destroyed the constitutional settlement of their homelands and – affecting the Irish case in particular – a state which either prevented Catholics serving in its armed forces or severely limited their prospects if they were allowed to serve. Scottish and Irish soldiers fighting for France were no stranger than German Protestants fighting with Sweden in the 1630s against the Holy Roman Emperor, and rather less so than the International Brigades in the Spanish Civil War, whose political idealism exempts them (but not their early modern predecessors) in contemporary eyes from the stigma of mercenary motives. The term 'mercenary' is therefore not only presentist but also rests on a set of assumptions which normalize loyalty to Great Britain as natural for those who opposed it, who are deemed explicitly mercenary because they were implicitly unpatriotic. They were neither as we now understand these terms. On the other hand, they served abroad for a reason: the 'deep anti-French and anti-Catholic sentiments that pervaded both Scotland and England' rendered ultimate Jacobite success much more doubtful without 'foreign' aid, and the exclusion of Catholics from the armed forces effectively made a British military career impossible even for Hanoverian loyalists.[42]

In 1715, some 21,000 men, a vast multiple of the forces available to Montrose in fighting the Covenanters in 1645 or to Viscount Dundee in 1689, rose in Scotland to restore the Stuarts and end the Union, with a supporting force of some 1,000 from northern England. Given the risks of execution if caught, the extreme pressure of time and the lack of a recruiting and governmental infrastructure, it was a massive force which represented some two-thirds of the maximum fencible capacity of Scotland. Its commander John Erskine, 6th Earl of Mar, was a politician not a military leader, and could not cope with the scale of the forces at his disposal, but he was clear that 'His objective was to break the Union . . . fighting in the cause of Scotland's ancient liberties.' This was a hugely appealing message, reiterated in the commitment to 'retrieve the unhappy Consequences of the Union' in the Perth Proclamation of 1 November 1715. Mar had supported the Union in 1707, and though doubtless his patriotism was sharpened by his loss of office under George I's government, he does seem to have genuinely changed his mind and thereafter led on the issue with the zeal of a convert. Though both sides in the conflict 'used compulsion to mobilise men', there were thousands upon thousands of Jacobite volunteers.[43]

Mar's hesitant and poor leadership led him to divide his forces and not follow up his advantage at the battle of Sheriffmuir in November 1715.

There was no formal French support and James – who did not authorize Mar to raise his standard – only landed in Peterhead with the Rising in decline. A coronation – possibly to be followed by recalling the Scots Estates – was scheduled for Scone in January 1716 but did not take place. In any case, the King seemed almost a secondary consideration in Mar's propaganda. It was claimed on Mar's behalf that he:

> had treated and entered into a Correspondence with King James from whom he had all assurances imaginable that he would contribute towards the dissolution of the UNION . . . and SCOTLAND shall again be Restored to its ancient Rights and privileges . . . most of the Nobility and Gentry . . . Concur in their Zeal and Resolutions against the UNION . . . I pray God blesse all their honest designs with Successe and inspire al SCOTS-MEN to concur with them . . . [in] their DUTY to themselves . . . . & their POSTERITY.

The stress was clear, but Mar's Rising petered out before the spring.[44] Following its failure, there was a large influx of Jacobite exiles into France. There were 'as many as 2,000' Scots Jacobites in Avignon alone by the end of 1716, while by 1717–18 the Jacobite court at Urbino had a Scots duke, five earls and two viscounts, among many other men of rank. Scots exiles were offered hospitality by their fellow Jacobites in the Irish Brigades, who formed a major part of the French army and of French plans for a Stuart restoration.[45]

JOHN LAW OF LAURISTON, 1671–1729

John Law could be viewed as the patron saint of the modern Western economy, instead of which he is generally seen as something between a scoundrel and an adventurer. The Western state of today and the economic system which supports it rest on a mixture of fiat currency (money with no collateral value against gold, land or any other commodity or asset except itself) and immensely high levels of public debt, the interest payments on which are met by borrowing against a currency whose domestic value is guaranteed by the borrower, and some of whose purchasers (such as pension funds) are in some countries (the UK, for example) effectively forced by the state's law to buy the state's debt, which in recent years has typically come to pay a negative real interest rate. Fiat currency has immense convenience and allows for high levels of flexibility in the public finances, including spending in excess of the tax base: however, it is an instrument which works in the interest of the state and not the individual and is ultimately worth only what the credibility of the borrower can command.

John Law, born in 1671 in Parliament Close in the heart of Edinburgh, banker, economist and a major (if overlooked) figure of the European Enlightenment is arguably the founder of modern fiat currency in policy and practice. He came from a notable family of goldsmiths; one of his relatives went on to found Coutts & Co. His brother Andrew, sometime Deacon of the Edinburgh Goldsmiths, emigrated to New Caledonia in Darien, and died there. Law was a Scots patriot and the monetary schemes he was to introduce in France (and proposed elsewhere) were intended to enable the French state to prosper as the foremost power in Europe, no doubt at the expense of the British Empire; as Law said, '*J'avois formé le dessein de rétablir la France*' and to make it the financial capital of the world, the key in his view (and that of much modern scholarship) to military and imperial success in the era.[46]

Law was conscious of the lack of bullion in Scotland (a long-standing issue, which made Scots more open to the use of currency from abroad and thus more aware of the relative and symbolic nature of money),[47] and he believed that this shortfall in supply constrained the velocity of money in the economy and hindered economic growth. Law thus consistently championed the expansion of the money supply. His plans to use land as collateral for a monetary expansion received support in the Scottish Parliament but ultimately failed to be adopted in the politically tense and riven years leading up to Union.

In exile after killing a man in a duel, Law made a fortune at the gambling tables of Europe, and, after 1716, rose higher and higher in the councils of the Regent Orléans of France, who was saddled with unsustainable debts following the grandeur, opulence, ambition and waste of Louis XIV's (1638–1715) vanity and warmongering. Law's plan was to securitize French debt and to make the creditors of the state (often themselves annuitants who were engaged in state business) share the risks of empire-building through the *Compagnie d'Occident* (the Company of the West, frequently misleadingly nicknamed the Mississipi Company) of 1717, followed by the *Compagnie des Indes* of 1719. Law's System was to be a gigantic option on the investable nature of the French Empire, making of 'the whole nation . . . a body of traders'. Law correctly surmised that, without raising capital from the securitization of state debt, the trading potential of France's vast territories in North America would not be maximized, and France could not enjoy their benefit unless the French shared the risk for the benefits of the success they would both secure and enjoy. This was a form of thinking which may have been familiar from the days of the Company of Scotland, which his brother Andrew had supported, but expanded to colossal scale in the service of Europe's most powerful state. Coins and banknotes were to be '*signes de transmission*' only, tokens of the true wealth of the country, which lay in its 'labourers and traders'. In this, as in other ways, Law foreshadowed Adam Smith (1723–90), who, while critical of the outcome of Law's financial experiment, borrowed significantly from his great predecessor in *The Wealth of Nations*.[48]

In order to both pay off France's debt and simultaneously to capitalize its empire, Law both raised money too quickly and was guilty of 'incessant manipulations of the currency' in order to make new offers attractive and to diminish older liabilities, a classic tactic visible in a different context in more recent government framing of market conditions. Although he rose to the height of Controller General of the

French finances in 1720 (roughly Chancellor of the Exchequer in modern terminology), Law was ultimately over-exposed by the sheer volume of the potential liabilities, and – critically – the conservatism of the French nobility and rich mercantile class, who were unused to the fluctuations of fiat currency, even without the accelerants Law applied to them. It should be recognized, however, that modern states have done much the same as he did, though more cautiously and slowly. The 1971 abandonment of the Bretton Woods framework and its pegging of gold against the dollar helped to drive a fifty- to sixty-fold increase in the gold price, which was significantly, though not completely, reflected in the decline in the purchasing power of the dollar. In the UK, prices have risen fifteen-fold and the currency has more or less halved against the dollar since this monetary restructuring. Fiat currency and its instruments have depreciated in the hands of their users to the benefit of their issuers all over the world, and this outcome has been accompanied by major long-term inflation and escalating debt.[49]

Though Law had to flee from France without most of his wealth following the collapse of his system (he had converted many of his own paper assets to property investments!), he subsequently made a living once more from the gambling tables of Europe, taking over £11,000 in roulette and faro games in Venice, for example. His descendants continued to thrive in France despite their father's fall from office. Law's son Jacques-Alexandre was Marshal of France and Marquis de Lauriston, while his grandson was one of Napoleon's commanders and French ambassador to Russia. Jean Law, Law's great-nephew, 'became commander of artillery to the embattled Mogul emperor' and was later Governor General of French India. Far more recently, the broadcaster Billy Kay recalls meeting the nephew of Madame Elisabeth Law de Lauriston-Boubers (1899–1977), for thirty years head of the Bollinger champagne house. One thing united Law and his family: their commitment to France and French power, often in direct opposition to the interests of the British Empire. France did not understand John Law and Napoleon's ultimate sale of the Louisiana lands (including Arkansas, Iowa, Kansas, Missouri, Nebraska and Oklahoma, and some or most of Colorado, the Dakotas, Louisiana, Minnesota, New Mexico, Texas and Wyoming) to the United States for not much more than 3 halfpence per hectare in 1803, demonstrated that the inheritors of the Bourbon government likewise lacked the capacity or imagination to capitalize on their American lands, as Law had planned to do.[50]

Law was a Jacobite, probably through a combination of his Scots patriotism and his sense of obligation to the Duke of Ormonde, one of the leading Jacobite magnates, who had helped him escape a death sentence in England for duelling in 1694. When in office in France (and widely known to have views 'to the prejudice of England'), Law made substantial donations to the Jacobite cause, including over 300,000 livres (c.£22,500 at 1709 exchange rates) for the use of King James (whom Law was 'sincerely and truly disposed to serve') and 150,000 livres for Ormonde. It seems possible from Law's words and actions that he sought to develop a position of superiority for France which would underpin a Stuart restoration or at least curtail Britain's imperial ambitions. These kinds of motive appear to have been suspected by the British Government and its agents, but Law's impatience and the conservatism of the French elite undermined a project which would have enabled the French crown to compete with England's bond market and public finance innovations, themselves supported in no small part by the Dumfriesshire farmer's son John Paterson (1658–1719), the founder of the Bank of England, who had opposed Law's own economic plans in Scotland.[51]

Law was not the only important Jacobite economist: Sir James Steuart (1712–80), who studied in the Netherlands and met Ormonde at Avignon, Lord Elcho at Lyons and the Earl Marischal in Spain while on a Continental tour in the 1730s, later married Lord Elcho's sister. Jacobite ambassador to

France in 1745, in the years in exile that followed, Steuart planned both a universal system of weights and measures (1759) and 'a method . . . for establishing a gold standard' (1773). He also became a central figure in 'economic development and regional policy' through his *Principles of Political Oeconomy* (1767) and arguably a major advocate of the national champions thesis of limited protectionism in the interests of the state, a refinement of the French physiocrat tradition, which he had encountered through his acquaintance with Pierre-Paul Lemercier de La Rivière de Saint-Médard (1719–1801) at Angoulême.[52]

On the Atlantic and Indian oceans especially, there was a significant link between piracy and Jacobitism. This arose out of various factors. First, Jacobite trade, contraband by nature, intersected with pre-Union Scottish commercial networks overseas, and thus piracy could be seen as a kind of terrorist defence of *mare liberum* against the imperial powers. Secondly, there was a long tradition in English privateering of excessive actions which in the wrong political circumstances could shade into piracy; Queen Elizabeth I colluded in this by supporting covert war against Spain, and at a later date it was part of a more general inheritance of entrenched privateering in the Caribbean. This picture was now complicated both by the East India Company's increasing prominence and demands for monopoly rights and also by Jacobitism and the granting of authority to English and Scottish privateers by King James VII and II's court in exile at Saint-Germain. In 'September 1693, the French were officially notified' by the English government that privateers serving with Jacobite commissions would not be treated as legitimate, and, in 1698, English judges declared 'that letters of marque issued by James II were invalid, thus putting many privateers on the wrong side of the law'; a specific piracy act followed two years later. Henceforth, Scottish privateers such as William Kidd (*c.*1654/5–1701), who had switched his privateering allegiance from France to King William and then back again, and Alexander Dalziel (*c.*1660–1715), who sailed the *Agrippa* (the name of the admiral who had defeated Antony and Cleopatra and secured the supreme state power for Augustus) under King James's flag, were on the wrong side of the law. Indeed the very name of Dalziel's ship was suggestive of a restoration, as were others more obviously, with names such as *Royal*

James, King James, Ormonde, Queen Anne's Revenge and *New King James*: the historian E.T. Fox identifies fourteen of the forty-four known pirate ships of the era as having Jacobite names. Dalziel and other privateers (or pirates) were using Madagascar as a base to attack East India Company (EIC) ships – and indeed Indian ones – and to challenge the EIC monopoly. Again, in 1698, 'The colonial authorities, under pressure from the East India Company, began to cut off all trading connections to Madagascar.' The pirates and privateers (up to 1,000) on the island began discussions with the Company of Scotland 'to open a trade of African slaves to Brazil' in exchange 'for Scottish protection, pardon and nationality'. Scottish privateers themselves continued in a kind of half-life for a few years after the Union. As late as 1719, with the grant of the Governorship of Madagascar to the Jacobite William Morgan by the King of Sweden, there was a plan whereby Jacobite pirates would 'establish a colony in Madagascar under cover of the Swedish flag'. Pirates attacked British shipping in their Jacobite-named ships, seizing booty worth almost a quarter of a million sterling on the Guinea coast. In the Caribbean, Lord Archibald Hamilton (*c*.1673–1754), the (apparently Whig) governor of Jamaica from 1710 but also brother to the General Hamilton who served as a Jacobite army commander in 1715, may have had substantial 'financial and political involvement with the Jamaican privateers' while ostensibly resisting them, possibly with a view to creating an alternate 'rebel navy', and in the Atlantic as a whole a large proportion of pirates had Jacobite links. The politics of these was clear enough even when they were not operating under the authority of the Stuarts: in the event of a Jacobite restoration, 'They hoped to one day secure privateering commissions from the Stuart king.'[53]

Despite the forfeiture of some estates after 1715 and the dismissal of many Jacobite teachers, academics, magistrates and other officials, government progress in suppressing Jacobite patriotism in Scotland was slow. In 1726–38, General Wade's men built 40 bridges and 400 kilometres of road to make northern Scotland more accessible. However, many of the large estates – such as that of the Dukes of Atholl, Chiefs of the name of Murray – which were nominally held by those loyal to the British Government, were liable to supply the Jacobites with extensive forces in the event of a Rising. This occurred in

7. The memorial to the Black Watch (the 43rd, later the 'fighting 42nd') on the banks of the Tay at Aberfeldy, unveiled in 1887 opposite the site of its first mustering. A Victorian soldier at the base of the monument points out the extensive global list of battle honours. A Scottish warrior in eighteenth-century garb with a single feather – the symbolic clansman of ancestral valour – is at the top of the monument. Strangely, this figure is based on Pte Farquhar Shaw, executed for desertion in 1743 when the regiment mutinied in fear of being sent overseas.

1745 when the Duke's brother, William Murray, Marquess of Tullibardine (1689–1746), deprived of the ducal title after 1715, raised substantial forces from his ancestral lands. The creation and expansion of the Independent Highland Companies in 1724–25 on a professional basis, and as a fresh replacement for the then Earl of Atholl's 1667 'Watch' militia and its successors, to some extent occurred to counter this risk. The new Black Watch (*Am Freicadan Dubh*) was formed out of some of these companies and became the 43rd Highland regiment in response to the Spanish war of 1739, though they mutinied when it appeared they might be sent overseas four years later.[54]

SCOTLAND AND THE BRITISH EMPIRE

In the febrile circumstances of the second quarter of the eighteenth century, less insular and more aware British leaders such as Sir Robert Walpole (1676–1745) promoted Scottish opportunity within the trading and patronage networks of the first British Empire, in order to integrate the country more fully into 'these united kingdoms'. A 'well-defined patronage system was instituted by ministries, allowing a disproportionate number of Scots to fill positions in the East India Company and its shipping'. Walpole's 'steadfast aim was to maintain a United Kingdom' and 'All patronage was administered with this in mind . . . . London feared what the threat of Scottish patriotism and Jacobitism might do . . . so the Scottish dimension was boosted, and all manner of favours were used as sweeteners.' In important respects, this was to set the pattern for Scotland's disproportionate role in the British Empire, initiated as a quid pro quo for its domestic quiescence. Scotland's strong professional class – supported by both the infrastructure of high quality higher education and the sheer economic appeal that the professions had to a frequently impoverished nobility – took full advantage of a situation where these innate opportunities were combined with the overproduction of highly educated men in Scotland, the longstanding practice of Scottish sojourning abroad and the politicization of the patronage processes of the new British state.[55]

There were obstacles, however, not least the 'exclusion of Scotland as a country from the eastern Empire' ensured by the East India Company (EIC) following the founding of the Company of Scotland in 1695, an exclusion that persisted – and was indeed 'institutionalised' – after the Union. Only individual Scots could take part in the EIC, not 'the country itself or its institutions', and so these individual Scots had to be promoted through active English institutional and personal patronage. This had begun before Walpole's rise to power, with Scottish officers pursuing employment in the EIC after their demobilization following the Treaty of Utrecht in 1713; but it took Walpole's intervention to drive substantial change in pursuit of drawing 'some of the teeth of Jacobite disaffection'.[56]

Scots initially continued to combine such preferment with their own traditional European networks, and indeed the earlier model served as a template for the later, as Scottish imperial mercantilism was to adopt 'the same family and neighbourhood networks of recruitment as in the old continental centres'. The same pattern of creating commercial communities to control the export trade from other countries and, after the Union, to expand the re-export market from Scotland arising from such exports – was repeated and enhanced. Many elite Scots had careers which reflected both the institutional and associational frameworks inherited from the Scottish kingdom and those acquired by union in a British state. In 1712, Alexander Burnet, Master of the *Dragon*, was welcomed at the English (now British) possession of Gibraltar by his fellow Aberdonian Fordyce, who was 'commissary-general of transports'. On discovering their shared home town (and no doubt acquaintance), Fordyce secured Burnet a pass from the Governor of Tarragona, who helped to sell Burnet's fish and supplied a protective convoy; later, Burnet received custom from the Spanish Crown. Here, British power and Continental connexions alike served the interests of Scottish location-based networking. On a grander scale, in 1693 John Drummond (1675/6–1742), the son of George Drummond of Blair-Drummond and Elizabeth, daughter of Sir Gilbert Ramsay, went to Amsterdam to develop a mercantile career, but by 1702 he was an agent of the English government. In 1722, he became a director of the EIC, and in 1731 he was also Government Commissioner at Antwerp. It is possible that Drummond was utilizing his Low Country connexions (he was also involved in the VOC coffee trade) to pass intelligence about the VOC back to the EIC and the British Government. Meanwhile, he was very useful to his fellow countrymen, offering patronage to George Drummond, his kinsman and future Lord Provost of Edinburgh, to Sir Robert Clerk of Penicuik's friend Rankin and to a variety of young men from Jacobite families, including John Haliburton, for whom Drummond obtained a writership in Madras/Chennai. Incorporating the potentially disaffected in this way was profoundly useful to the new state. Between 1720 and 1757, Scots made up all the principal medical officers in Madras/Chennai, and by the 1770s and 1780s they were around half of the writers, officers and assistant surgeons in Bengal. The Indian service at this level may have lacked social prestige among the English elites, but it offered great opportunity for able, well connected but relatively impoverished Scots. Soon many of them were less impoverished, with Scots obtaining 60 per cent of free merchants' residence permits from the EIC, and coming to operate fourteen of Calcutta/Kolkata's thirty-eight merchant houses by the early nineteenth century. Scots also continued, however, to serve in Continental East India companies, such as Colin Campbell

(1686–1757), who, as well as being engaged in the founding of the Swedish East India Company, worked with the 'Habsburg Ostend Company' in 1720. Sweden later employed the Gothenburg-born Sir William Chambers (1723–96) on a series of missions to China in the 1740s. Scots such as these continued to keep their options open outside the nascent British Empire's patronage structures.[57]

If architects such as Colen Campbell (1676–1729) and James Gibbs (1682–1754) gained commissions in England, William Adam (1689–1748) reigned supreme in Scotland, where he had a dominant role in the design of institutional and residential buildings which reflected the country's new status as both national and British.[58] As the century progressed, the upper Scottish nobility became more integrated into a British aristocracy; they had often spent part of their education and formation outside Scotland, but England now gradually became a likelier destination than the Netherlands or France, and, while the Italian states retained an allure in their own right for artists and Jacobites, they and the Continent more generally were beginning to be seen through the prism of the English Grand Tour, itself established as a phenomenon in the wake of Richard Lassels' *Voyage to Italy* (1670); Lassels may have been the first to use the term. Noblemen such as Alexander Montgomerie, the 10th Earl of Eglinton (1723–69), who was educated at Winchester, gained contact with Italy in this way. The Tour largely depended – at least implicitly – on a particular vision of Italy as backward and in decline, a valuable lesson of the ruins of a great Empire undermined from within by Catholic luxury and weakness: a view of the fall of Rome most eloquently taken by Edward Gibbon (1737–94). Even those from more modest backgrounds in Scotland, such as the novelist and surgeon Tobias Smollett (1721–71), began to view Continental Europe through this new British prism, one far removed from those of the Scoto-Irish Jacobite merchants of Boulogne-sur-Mer, Bordeaux or Livorno. In his *Travels through France and Italy* (1766), Smollett noted that 'France is the general reservoir from which all the absurdities of false taste, luxury and extravagance have overflowed the kingdoms of Europe', while the inhabitants 'have no small resemblance to large baboons walking upright'. In Italy, he sneered that 'No Englishman above the degree of a painter or cicerone frequents any coffee-house in Rome', while the art of Catholic Italy 'can only serve to fill the mind with gloomy ideas, and to encourage a spirit of religious fanaticism'. Scot as Smollett is (and his Presbyterian disdain for the 'ignorant, petulant, rash, and profligate' among Grand Tourists still peeps through), his sense of British exceptionalism is strong, remarking that 'I do believe, in my conscience, that half a dozen English frigates would have been able to defeat both the contending fleets at the famous battle of Actium.' The nationality of the frigates is evidently more important than the presence of gunpowder. In the circumstances, the existence of the Rue Smollett in Nice is a tribute – given the area's mixed heritage – to French courtesy and Italian hospitality in the face of Smollett's arrant prejudice.[59]

Scots made rapid early progress in the American and Caribbean colonies and their associated trades, where they had already established a foothold under the 1626 settlement of James Hay, 1st Earl of Carlisle, and in larger numbers under the aegis of the Netherlands, which had successfully expanded in the Caribbean in the 1630s via the Westindische Compagnie (WIC). In 1641, Alexander Marshall and Malcolm MacFarlane were in Curaçao, and in the 1690s Robert Milne of Aberdeenshire left Scotland for the Netherlands and sailed for the West Indies two years later. There was a considerable Scots presence in Dutch Demerara, and later sugar and commodity firms such as Houston & Co (who were importing 15 per cent of Scottish sugar by the 1770s) built on the contacts Scots had developed in the Dutch empire to leverage their business. There was – as we have seen – concern among English administrators before the Union that Scots would use the Dutch Empire as a platform from which to extend their overseas trade. In 1695, Edward Randolph, the English Surveyor General of Customs in the Americas, feared that the Scots would set up 'in some West Indian island a staple for the exchange of European manufactures and colonial commodities' as the Dutch had done in Curaçao.[60]

Scots had also been imported to the Caribbean by England before 1707 as 'indentured servants' (twenty-six warrants were granted for voyages carrying Scots in this category between 1660 and 1685) and to suppress slave revolts (as requested by the Governor of Barbados in 1667). Scots had also come as traders and merchants seeking to subvert the Navigation Acts,

8. The Pineapple, the Earl of Dunmore's 1761 summerhouse celebrating Scotland's most exotic fruit.

and these merchants in their turn had Scots employees, such as Alexander Lindsay, factor in Barbados and St Kitts. While Irish indentured labourers (who were 'viewed with almost as much contempt as Africans') were some-times implicated in slave revolts (for example at Barbados in 1692), the same does not seem to have been true of Scots. Between 1650 and 1700, some 4,500 Scots went to the Caribbean as settlers or sojourners, and in the latter year many refugees from the failed colony at Darien went to Jamaica.[61] Colonel John Campbell, who left Darien in 1700, founded a western Jamaican Campbell landowning network with its 'heaviest concentration . . . in the county of Cornwall, particularly the parishes of Hanover and Westmoreland'. The network developed not only through personal contacts within the Campbell milieu, but also 'through letters of recommendation into the "interest" or circle of patronage' established by Campbell and others. This was interpreted as 'clannishness', not least because geography was a major driver: in 'Tobago the network was bounded by the towns of Elgin, Huntly and Banff'. North-eastern and Argyll Scots both settled extensively in Jamaica, where there were some 57 sugar plantations by 1670, 124 by the beginning of the eighteenth century and no fewer than 1,601 by 1786, by which time the number of slaves on the island had risen almost fivefold. Scots Masonic lodges were founded in the Caribbean to establish, reiterate and accelerate networking, and even a branch of the Fife sex club, The Beggar's Bennison, was established in Grenada. By 1754, 'A quarter of Jamaica's landholdings were in Scottish hands' and this proportion continued to rise. There was also extensive transatlantic patronage interest: the poet James Thomson (1700–48), for example, enjoyed his reward of being 'surveyor-general of customs for the Leeward Islands' at a distance, while his old (Scots) friend William Paterson took just over half the salary to perform the role on site.[62]

Scots arrived early in St Kitts, with James Chalmers, a merchant there, being entered as 'burgess and guild brother' of Ayr in 1665, and the first two governors there were also Scots, while the ubiquitous 'clannishness' of Scots not only in Jamaica but also in Antigua was remarked on. By 1750, '60 per cent of the doctors in Antigua were Scots or Scottish-trained', while 10 per cent of the Caribbean's Africa traders were Scots, who were thus closely integrated into the slave trade. Scots mobility to the Caribbean increased during the eighteenth century, with at least 12,000 and perhaps up to 20,000 Scots emigrating to or sojourning there in 1750–1800. In addition, some 600 Jacobites were transported to the Caribbean and some of the Jacobite Scottish Episcopal clergy fled to Jamaica after 1745. Jacobite arrivals (including women) were typically sold on the quayside at a few pounds each on their arrival; though they might be bought and freed by fellow Scots, not all were so lucky, perhaps including the MacDonalds transported to their historic rivals in Campbell-dominated Jamaica. Scots were also traded from home by their landlords, as Sir Alexander MacDonald of Sleat and Norman MacLeod of Berneray sought to do in 1739, when 100 people were kidnapped in Skye to be sold as 'indentured servants' in America, or by merchants; Aberdeen was known for the latter practice, with 'some 500 boys . . . abducted from Aberdeen and district in the years 1740–5'. While there is an understandable reluctance to classify these wretched people as 'slaves', that is apparently how poor whites were described by Africans on Barbados. In Scotland itself, the 'miners and salters' of Fife, still in serfdom in the later eighteenth century, supported David Spens' opposition to the 'legal action that aimed to return' him, as a Black resident of their county, to the West Indies as a slave in 1770. Attempts to treat poor white indentured labour as entirely different from enslavement are arguably as misplaced as attempts to equate it with African chattel slavery. While there appear to be no records of abducted or transported white people being thrown overboard or castrated or executed, theirs was still a miserable fate, for these people were frequently kidnapped and abducted and often sold, even if one day – if they survived – they might be free.[63]

Some Scots – like the serial killer Dr Lewis Hutchison (1733–73) of the Edinburgh Castle estate, hanged in Spanish Town, Jamaica – were brutal beyond the point even colonial society could tolerate. Up to half of the whites in Jamaica (where 90 per cent of the population were enslaved) and 80 per cent of those in Antigua were Scots by the latter part of the century, and they were generally successful: in Jamaica, Scots 'accounted for nearly 45% of all inventories at death . . . valued above £1,000' in the first half of the 1770s. By this period, Scots also formed at least one-third of the governing council in Dominica, Grenada and Tobago. It could nonetheless be hard to identify Scots in the Caribbean, as many came to describe them-selves as 'British': being 'Scottish' could be associated with being a sojourner, one who came to work for a time and repatriate assets, rather than someone committed to settlement. Many Scots were indeed sojourners, but one thing they found it hard to conceal was their networking and mutual support. As one Black commentator put it in 1780: 'England must be a large place and Scotland a small one; for Scots *Bacceros* [white men] . . . know one another, but English *Bacceros* do not.' The enslaved called shellfish 'Scotsmen' from 'the habits of these creatures in clinging one to the other'. English commen-tators bore them out, repeatedly noting that the Scots were 'clannish, ubi-quitous and doing very well for themselves'. Concentrations of interest such as this led to problems for the Scottish patronage network at home, where massive pressure grew from petitioning for place and office: the governorship of Barbados, for example, was worth £10,000 a year (by comparison, the richest Kirk livings were worth £140, the Principal of the University of Glasgow had £150 and a Lord of Session £700).[64]

While only ten slave ships left Scottish ports between 1717 and 1764 (eight from the Clyde and one each from Leith and Montrose), and no more than 4,500 slaves in total were shipped from Scotland from a Great British total of some 1.4 million in 1701–70, Scots were heavily implicated in chattel slavery, and not just at second-hand via their sugar (2 per cent of UK national income) and tobacco businesses, which continued to receive investment until at least the end of the eighteenth century. The huge duties on tobacco were remitted in their entirety by its re-export and those on sugar significantly so, and thus these trades proved irresistibly lucrative. Scots imperial traders were no better – or worse – than other imperial powers. While slaves were less visible in Scotland – England had c.15,000 in 1800, with 'perhaps fewer than one hundred' in Scotland – Scots provided some 40 per cent of surgeons on slavers, including men such as William Chiesley, Surgeon Major aboard the Africa Company's *Rising Sun,* and provided a substantial amount of capital to the Liverpool trade, where 'at least five Scots managed Liverpool slaving syndicates'. Robert Gordon from Moray ran a slave fleet in the Bristol trade, while Alexander Allardyce of Dunnottar was estimated to have sold as many slaves as the population of Aberdeen.[65]

In 1748, a Scots-dominated consortium, Grant, Oswald & Co (in which Caithness man Richard Oswald (1705–84) was the leading spirit) with experience of the plantation trade and enslavement, acquired a slaving 'trade castle' and associated outposts on the 6-hectare Bance Island 25 kilometres upstream from the mouth of the Sierra Leone river. Like other Europeans, their firm relied on a degree of 'permission from local leaders' to establish themselves in carrying on the slave trade: an African ruler would bring in 'the Africans that his men had captured' in return for manufactures, 'foodstuffs or luxury goods' greater than the value their prisoners could have contributed to their own local economies, and indeed African kings 'were the primary agents' and frequently set the price for their captives. It is important to note that slave traders had 'little control over supply', which arose principally from captives in 'local wars' and the economically marginal at risk in local famines. It has indeed been argued that 'Africans could have thrown

Europeans out at any stage' but chose not to, 'because local politics benefited from the trading relationship'; indeed '90% of those shipped to the New World were first enslaved by Africans and then sold to European buyers'. There were repeated profits to be made by selling and reselling, though the margin was in each case more misery than money. The paradox in Africa was that it was not the era of European colonial power on the African continent that saw the height of the slave trade, but an era of relative European weakness, where merchant houses provided a convenient way for African rulers to dispose of other Africans to those Europeans who were only too willing to buy them. An attempt by James Brydges, 1st Duke of Chandos (1673–1744) to switch the focus of the Royal African Company (RAC, 1672) from slavery to 'bilateral trade based on African commodities' in the 1720s was a failure. Both sides of the trade were too invested in their existing arrangements.[66]

Bance Island had not always been as profitable as this new consortium rendered it. It had been abandoned by the RAC in the 1720s, and George Fryer, a London slave trader, sold it on to Oswald and his partners. Following the collapse of the RAC, the African Trade Act of 1750, which opened up trade to private citizens more effectively than before, was well timed from the point of view of Grant, Oswald & Co. Their partners included the well-connected Sir Alexander Grant, 5th Bart (1705–82), who was a kinsman of Sir Archibald Grant of Monymusk and – helpfully – a friend of fellow Scot Robert Dinwoodie, the Lieutenant Governor of Virginia, the Duke of Argyll (who gave Grant an entrée into court circles) and the houses of Erskine, Findlater and Hopetoun. Oswald's connexions were not so good, though his brothers were 'eminent merchants' in Glasgow, importing 135 tonnes of tobacco every year by the 1730s. As a young businessman in the Chesapeake, Oswald's doctor was, however, this same Alexander Grant, and Oswald met his wife at Grant's house. Mary Ramsay was herself already a rich woman and the trustees of her tocher (dowry) were two more Scots, John Mill and Robert Scott. Scott was a childhood friend of the merchant James Murray and when Scott became a business partner of Oswald's, Oswald carried Murray's shipments to Scotland on commission. On Bance Island, dressed in tartan, Scots 'played golf by the slaving fort' their own capital had created: a visiting Swedish botanist noted 'African caddies, draped in loincloths of tartan design made from wool' (the wool itself came from near Glasgow). Large numbers of the white workers 'were close relatives' of the consortium partners. As often elsewhere in the British Empire, patriotic mummery both reinforced Scottish identity and networks abroad and in doing so rendered more secure and successful the brutal business these same Scots were pursuing.[67]

From Bance, 13,000 Africans were shipped into chattel slavery over the next thirty-six years. Oswald was, by the low standards of the age, moderately humane, demanding that Bance slaves were not branded and that families were kept together. Slavery was not the only business of the consortium. Oswald was an investor and a lender and both he and Grant became wealthy through providing supplies for the British Army in the global war of 1756–63, Grant, for example, having the contract 'to supply the Nova Scotia naval station with bread, beer, rum, beef, pork, pease, oatmeal, rice, butter, and cheese', while shipping 1,100 tonnes of sugar a year through another arm of his business in the 1760s. The scale of the company put a significant strain on Grant, Oswald & Co's fleet, whose vessels racked up long periods at sea and thus needed frequent replacement: the average age of their ships at sea seems to have been under eight years. The consortium became rich. What was also notable was the sheer scale of Scottish networking and its continuing ability to combine European and imperial contacts: Oswald had trading links in (among many other locations) Amsterdam, Antigua, Calcutta/Kolkata, Florida, Georgia, Grenada, Hamburg, Le Havre, Livorno, Nantes, Paris, Rotterdam, Rouen and Stralsund. His contacts took many forms: his wife's cousin Thomas Melville, for example, was able to provide many useful links during his 'tenure as Governor of Cape Coast Castle'.[68]

In North America, Scots – particularly ex-Jacobite soldiers – were central to the settlement of Georgia under the crypto-Jacobite James Oglethorpe (1696–1785), whose family were often explicit Jacobites and who himself had visited King James twice at Urbino in 1717–18. Oglethorpe founded the colony of Georgia in 1732, bringing in (then largely Jacobite) Freemasonry two years later, and appearing in Highland dress. John Mackintosh, nephew to the former Jacobite commander Brigadier William Mackintosh of Borlum, led the Clan Chattan (Mackintosh and Mackintosh dependents) settlers to

Georgia: in the end, some 260 sailed from Inverness. Other Jacobites such as Donald Cameron and Lachlan MacLachlan sent Jacobite veterans to help Oglethorpe fight off the Spanish, an activity possibly sweetened by the thought of revenge for Darien. Two hundred Mackintosh dependents had already been transported to Virginia and the neighbouring colony of South Carolina after the 1715 Rising, and Inverness merchants also recruited such Jacobites for the Georgia settlement. Scots were regarded both by others and by themselves as having the 'ability to negotiate satisfactorily with native peoples' due to a 'chameleon-like ability to adapt to local circumstances', and Oglethorpe certainly found it possible to ally with leading Native American nations. Lachlan MacGillivray (1718–99), one of Oglethorpe's Clan Chattan colonists, became the ancestor of a number of Native American/First Nations chiefs, as well as a successful plantation owner who 'functioned effectively in the Atlantic commercial world'. He married the Creek noblewoman Sehoy Marchand of the Wind Clan, and his son, Alexander MacGillivray (*Hoboi-Hili-Miko*, 'Good Child King', 1750–93), became a Creek chief who played off America against Spain: having 'heard about Culloden from his father and uncle', he 'tried to prevent the same thing happening to his own people'. MacGillivray's other descendants included William Weatherford (1781–1824) and Peter McQueen (*c*.1780–1820), who led the brutal American Indian attack on American settlers at Fort Mims in Alabama in 1813, the same year that Archibald MacDonald of Glencoe 'led a group of emigrants to the Red River settlement' and later married Koale Koa, the youngest daughter of a chief who had married his other daughters to Scottish traders. William Macintosh (1775–1825) (*Tustunnuggee Hutke*/White Warrior) likewise became a Creek chief, though an unsuccessful one, while Hugh Monroe (1798–1892) married the daughter of a Blackfeet Chief and John Macdonnel, son of a Jacobite exile, led dozens of raids in the service of Thayendanegea, the Mohawk military leader. Scots were four times as likely to marry Native Americans as other settlers, and men such as Alexander Cameron and John Macdonald lived among the First Nations. Macdonald's grandson was the most prominent among these Scottish-descended chiefs: John Ross (1790–1866), named *Guwisguwi* or 'White Bird', was the paramount Chief of the Cherokee who helped draft the ultimately unsuccessful

Cherokee Constitution, the first Native American constitutional document which defined the Cherokee as a nation. Later, Ross led his people on the Trail of Tears to Oklahoma and raised money for the west Highland potato famine through a 'Cherokee Relief Committee'. Until 'white women, Christian missionaries and Victorian and racist attitudes' reached North American trading communities, particularly 'in areas and eras where the fur and deerskin trades predominated, Scots and Indians coexisted and cohabited'. The prominence of Scots in the fur trade – growing rapidly in Canada in the 1770s – was an important part of this alignment.[69]

Families and cultures to a degree combined: Scots 'sent Scottish boys to live with Indian families and learn their languages and cultures' and also led mixed forces in battle. Scots such as John Stuart, David Taitt and James Grant evinced a preference for Native American societies over the 'thrusting commercialism that developed after 1763 on the American frontier'. By the nineteenth century, Native American/First Nations wearing of tartan was widespread, and this was not a one way process for, as the historian Colin Calloway remarks, 'Highlanders and Indians borrowed and adapted each other's clothing and style of dress.' Tartan shawls being a particular favourite among the Cree (who made a handsome mark-up from their trade with the Hudson's Bay Company (HBC)) in their signification of 'tradition and cultural persistence'. Blue bonnets and Glengarry caps were also widely worn among Native Americans, just as with their 'brother Scotchies'.[70]

Slavery was not initially permitted in Georgia, though this changed in 1743 after Oglethorpe's departure. In January 1739, eighteen Scots colonists from New Inverness in Darien county (a telling example of renaming) petitioned Oglethorpe – 'an abolitionist at heart' – against slavery, stating that it is 'shocking to human Nature, that any Race of Mankind and their Posterity should be sentenced to perpetual Slavery'. Their motives for doing so remain a matter of some controversy, but it is likely that some combination of humanitarianism, fear of Spain and the incompatibility of slave labour with their traditional social structures were all at play, and it has been argued that they were influenced in their thinking by Francis Hutcheson (1694–1746) the Irish-Scots philosopher who was to have such a profound effect on the American Revolution as we shall see in the next chapter.[71]

Elsewhere in the American colonies, Scots rose to early prominence. Robert Dinwiddie, the son of a Glasgow merchant and Lieutenant Governor of Virginia 1751–58 was, as we have seen, of considerable use to the Grant–Oswald syndicate in supporting their American contacts. Dinwoodie was also, as a former Bermuda merchant, an 'intimate friend of the governor of Bermuda, John Bruce Hope, a fellow Scot', and endeavoured to profit both by a 'reliance on Scottish ties' and the 'web of London contacts' he drew on to ensure metropolitan recognition. John Scott, the son of a Jacobite merchant, who emigrated to Charles Town, South Carolina, in 1748, went on to become British superintendent of Indian affairs in the south. In North Carolina, Gabriel Johnston presided over the colony for almost twenty years, from 1733 to 1752, and was able to facilitate the extensive Scottish Cape Fear settlement in the late 1730s. Being a man who 'sought his own success first and then that of his acquaintances and family' (his nephew Samuel became governor in 1769), Johnston attracted jealousy, being attacked for 'being too favorable to Scots and being a Jacobite sympathiser'. There may have been something to the accusations though, as Johnston allegedly received news of Culloden 'very coldly'. If this was the case, he was not alone. Although there was widespread support for the British Government and army in their conflict with the Jacobites in the American colonies, the Jacobites also had quite a number of supporters, particularly in the south.[72]

THE JACOBITE RISING OF 1745 AND THE END OF AN ERA OF CONFLICT

The Jacobite Rising of 1745 cut across this developing imperial era. It was the product of a number of factors: the dynamism of Prince Charles Stuart and of a number of his Scottish supporters; the changing power structures of the French Court; renewed war in Europe in the shape of the 1739–48 conflict over the Austrian succession; and the continuing weak economic conditions of much of Scotland, especially following the poor harvests of the early 1740s. The winters of 1738 and 1739 were both bad, and the price of oats had doubled by 1740, when there was an explosion of beggars in Edinburgh, as had been seen in the famine years of 1692–98. Then as now, relatively wealthy areas were a magnet for the displaced poor. Prices rose and wages fell: Glasgow's emerging tobacco trade held up (and Glasgow was – for both religious and economic reasons – unresponsive to Jacobitism in 1745), but masons' and labourers' wages halved, while both excise yields and (critically) higher quality linen production were down, by 33 per cent and 40 per cent respectively. Weak summer and winter temperatures persisted across Europe to 1745, and as in other cases where this occurred, marginal economies on the edge of Europe were among the most vulnerable. Scotland's 'harvest crisis' had consequences which included the potential maximizing of Jacobite support in the hope of ending a Union which was not delivering its promised benefits to Scotland; over a hundred years later the poor climate conditions, which caused potato famines in Ireland and Scotland, were also to play their part in the revolutionary convulsions of 1848 across Europe.[73]

The Scottish Associators (including James Drummond, the Duke of Perth; his brother Lord John; Simon Fraser, Lord Lovat and Chief of the Name of Fraser; Lord Linton, heir to the Earldom of Traquair; Donald Cameron of Lochiel, Chief of the Name of Cameron; and others), sought a Jacobite restoration and the end of the Union, seeing England as an 'other State'. On 23 December 1743, James 'VIII' declared against the 'pretended Union' by which Scotland, 'a Nation always famous for valour' was 'reduced to the condition of a Province'. When he landed in Montrose with Scottish and Irish troops in the French service in late 1745, Lord John Drummond took care to declare that he came 'to this Kingdom [Scotland] with Written orders, to make War against the King of ENGLAND' on behalf of Charles 'Regent of SCOTLAND'. Another declaration was made on behalf of Charles as 'Steward of Scotland' calling on Scots to 'fight for their freedom'. Charles issued a declaration against the Union in Edinburgh. As far as can be ascertained, the army he led never carried the Union flag in any form, though the saltire was prominent, and sympathizers south of the Border such as Beppy Byrom in Manchester were engaged to make saltires for the army.[74]

A serious French invasion attempt of 1744 was foiled by its slow development, vulnerability to espionage, leaks and poor weather, and when Charles Edward sailed in 1745 with some 200 Irish Brigade troops (the historian Daniel Szechi has recently established the number) and arms in the *Elisabeth* and *Du Teillay* (the latter ship had a history of use as a slaver by its owner, Antoine Welsh) it was an ostensibly private enterprise without the approval of the French court, though more probably it should be seen as a deniable special operation, not least because of the use of French regulars.[75] When his troops had to return to Brest after a sea fight with HMS *Lyon* of the Royal Navy, Charles pressed on without men or supplies, landing with 'the Seven Men of Moidart' on Eriskay on 23 July. For a while the position looked hopeless, but Charles's charisma and a belief in future French help began to turn the tide, and by the time the royal standard was raised among cries of 'King James the Eight . . . prosperity to Scotland and no Union' at Glenfinnan on 19 August, units of the nascent Jacobite army had already been victorious over British forces in two engagements: MacDonald of Keppoch's troops defeating a company of Colonel Swithenham and MacDonald of Tiendrish and his Glengarry men defeating the Royal Scots. On 3 September, thanks to General Wade's roads, the Jacobite army entered Dunkeld, and the next day Lord Ogilvy, Viscount Strathallan, Oliphant of Gask, the Duke of Perth and Lord George Murray joined the Prince.[76]

By 17 September Charles was able to enter Edinburgh unopposed, although the castle remained in government hands. Scots heralds proclaimed King James. Four days later came the victory at Prestonpans over the British Army in Scotland under Sir John Cope. Charles held 'Balls and Assemblies' at Holyrood Palace as Prince Regent, and the illusion of the restoration of the old Scots court was very pleasing to many. Some of the Jacobite leadership opined that they had 'risked their fortunes and their lives . . . to seat him on the throne of Scotland', but that 'they wished to have nothing to do with England'. The French envoy to Charles, Marquis d'Eguilles, told Lord Elcho 'that King Louis was happy to put James Stuart on the throne of Scotland', but 'it was all one to France whether George or James was King of England'. This was in keeping with a long eighteenth-century tradition in French foreign policy which sought to weaken the Union and/or Great Britain's hold over Ireland. English sources also feared that Charles would 'assemble the States in Parliament, when their first steps will be doubtless dissolving the Union, reviving the old alliance . . . & calling in a French army'. There was no doubt that this kind of thinking remained popular: even the establishment *Scots Magazine*, founded in 1739, noted that, 'in many things calculated for the good of *Great* Britain, *Scotland* is little more than nominally consider'd', and there was both disappointment at how little the Union was seen as a national partnership south of the border and how a Scottish perspective on international events was in danger of being lost. The Treaty of Fontainebleau on 24 October 1745 committed Louis XV to support the Jacobite effort. Voltaire was to write the manifesto for the French invasion force.[77]

Many Jacobite commanders did indeed want to reconvene the Scottish Parliament and raise an army that could resist invasion. But Charles, who carried the day by a single vote, wanted to invade England, in part perhaps because he feared the resources that George II, who had ascended the throne in 1727, might bring to bear against Scotland once Great Britain was under less pressure in the War of the Austrian Succession; in part also, both he and his father may have been aware of Charles I's error in not marching on London and have recalled Mar's dilatoriness in 1715. The financial power of the British state was certainly underestimated at the Jacobites' peril: Yorkshire alone raised enough in loyal subscriptions to George to have paid the Jacobite army for four months. Too few of Charles's Scottish commanders realized the degree of strategic urgency necessary to forestall the British fiscal-military state's immense ability to deploy money, troops and ships. In France, the Earl Marischal demanded 10,000 French troops and arms for 30,000 more men. He understood the scale of the challenge. Fortress Scotland was a delusion.[78]

After training and recruiting, Charles marched south in early November with 5,000 men and some 2,000 camp followers, less than half the peak total strength of his forces. Carlisle fell by mid November. In late November, Charles reached Manchester. On 3 December, the Duke of Devonshire withdrew from the defence of Derbyshire when the Jacobites entered Ashbourne. Just 1,000 to 1,500 regular soldiers and local militias lay between the 'Highland Army' (so-called to draw attention to its martial patriotism, long associated with the Scottish north, not because it was a Gaelic-speaking force) and London. Against Charles's fervent wishes, the Jacobite army turned back at Derby; no more than 1,000 men had joined the Jacobite cause in England, far fewer than expected (though indeed comparable to the numbers recruited for Charles II on the march to Worcester in 1651). Moreover, the French had not sent forces to England, whereas Franco-Scots and Irish forces had landed in Scotland under Major General Lord John Drummond, and Charles's commanders saw it as prudent to link up with them to consolidate the Jacobite position north of the border, where a second army was forming. Charles's commanders also seem to have found it hard to believe they were poised to enter London without fighting a major battle, though they were. France too was close to committing troops. The odds against success remained long at Derby, but retreat guaranteed defeat.

This was arguably a world-historical moment. The ensuing Jacobite defeat would set the stage for a range of innovations, from the changed and improved army regulations of 1748 to the incorporation of large numbers of Scots into the British Army, the creation of the martial myth of the Scottish soldier in the British Empire, and the critically effective deployment of such soldiers for the benefit of imperial campaigns from the Seven Years' War of 1756–63 onwards. It was in that war that the Irish and Scots Jacobites in the French service were defeated by British forces once and for all in India and Canada. It was also in the context of the tensions leading into that war that the depopulations and transportations favoured by Cumberland and his officers after Culloden, but seen as too extreme by the British Government, entered imperial practice with *le Grand Dérangement*, the expulsion of some 14,000 French Canadians from New Brunswick, Nova Scotia, north Maine and Prince Edward Island to sustain British control of these areas. This post-Culloden tradition left a long legacy, for the last British imperial depopulation on this model took place in 1968–73, with the removal of the Chagossians from British Indian Ocean Territory.

The Jacobite defeat thus crystallized aspects of the British Empire's policies abroad and greatly increased its ability to project military force. What might a Jacobite victory have secured? The maximalist case is that rapprochement rather than competition with France would have led to a bilateral world order (or indeed one dominated by France), where French strength in Canada would have forestalled the American Revolution by providing too great a military threat from a Catholic power to allow the colonies to risk pushing for their freedom, and that Great Britain would not have secured unalloyed success in India. France, unwearied by the great expense of a global war for hegemony, would have been more stable and wealthier in the 1780s, and Revolution would have been averted, and with it the rise of Bonapartism and the Napoleonic Wars, with their longer term consequences for the creation of German and Italian statehood. France's attempts under different governments to re-establish her global authority after the defeats of 1756–63 cost untold lives. A Jacobite victory might well have rendered many of these conflicts unnecessary and its consequences would have been global, not merely the reassertion of Scottish and Irish national rights within the multi-kingdom British polity. The maximalist case is fanciful to a degree, but had the Stuart interest prevailed there would have been international conse-quences. So much is clear: this was an international conflict, of which the Scottish question was but one dimension.

But the die was cast otherwise at Derby. The Jacobite army retreated, yet, even that December, it held off the British advance guard at Clifton and, in Scotland, Jacobite forces were victorious at the Battle of Inverurie. In January came another victory at Falkirk. By this time, there were nearly 14,000 Jacobites in arms. But the psychology of retreat without defeat is exception-ally difficult to manage. Under pressure from Lord George Murray and other Jacobite commanders – who saw no hope of final victory – Charles retreated north. In late February, the Jacobites lost access to the east coast ports through which France could supply troops. The end was now near. On the morning of 16 April, a failed night attack on the Duke of Cumberland's camp left the Jacobites outnumbered and disorganized as the British Army advanced, the death-rattle of its almost 250 kettledrums (a relatively new innovation) matching the skirl of the Jacobite pipes and announcing its threat from afar. The Battle of Culloden had begun. Outnumbering the Jacobites almost two to one, Cumberland ruthlessly pressed his advantage and, learning the lessons of Prestonpans, employed new tactics so that, even when the Jacobites broke the British line, the attack faltered under heavy fire, while the British cavalry, held back rather than being deployed too early as at earlier battles, destroyed the Jacobite flanks (the much vaunted revised bayonet drill adopted by Cumberland does not seem to have been particularly effective). Whole Jacobite regiments withdrew in good order when they saw the day was lost and were not pursued. But, instead, women, children and stragglers on the road to Inverness were cut down all the way into the town. Around 1,000 Jacobites died on the field, and 2,000 more people in the days that followed. Cumberland's actions, for all they were born of fear and anger, were atrocious war crimes and were regarded as such by a number of his English contemporaries.[79]

In the aftermath of the '45 Rebellion, William van Keppel, 2nd Earl of Albemarle (1702–54), supported the utter devastation of 'the recalcitrant districts' and the deportation of 'all their inhabitants to the colonies', but the British Government had less appetite for such measures in Scotland, although these were to become tools of imperial policy elsewhere. In the end, forty-one estates in Scotland were confiscated, with thirteen 'inalienably annexed and managed by the crown', and the majority of the rest sold off, sometimes to the friends, allies or even family members of the Jacobite leaders who had once owned them. Meanwhile the British Army employed the future Major General William Roy (1726–90), Paul Sandby (1731–1809), 'chief Draftsman of the fair Plan', and others to work on 'making what came to be known as the Great Map', a one inch to 1,000 yards (1:36000) map of Scotland, so that its inaccessible north and west in particular would present fewer obstacles to the British Army in the event of a new Rising. In later life, Sandby presented Scots Highlanders as primarily pastoral rather than agri-cultural, a representation of the country which was already familiar through its own literature, in the writing of Allan Ramsay and others, and presented their country as craggier and more louring, in tune with the contours of the Roy Map; this would contribute to the creation of the image of a primitive, Romantic Scotland we will be examining in Chapter 4. William Gilpin (1724–1804) and others responded to the world of Roy's map by 'enlarging "the scale of nature"' visually as the army mappers had done cartographi-cally. The tourist gaze was born (see plate 8).[80]

London and Liverpool merchants received £5 a head for transporting Jacobite soldiers for indentured labour for life in the colonies: in theory a permanent conditional enslavement, though in practice limited to seven years. Female Jacobites such as Anne and Flora Cameron, Isabel Chalmers,

Katherine McEwen and the eighteen-year-old Barbara Campbell were transported as well as men. Many were fortunately freed by a French privateer which landed over a hundred Jacobites in Martinique, including William Bell, a Berwickshire bookseller, George Keith an Aberdeen shoemaker from Glengarry's Regiment, Mary McDonald and the teenager Jane Mackintosh. In Scotland, recruitment continued for soldiers in the three Scottish regiments now in the French service, as well as the Irish Brigades.[81]

Jacobite disquiet continued for many years after Culloden, with the British Army occupying up to 400 garrisons and outposts across Scotland in the years after 1746. There were Jacobite handbills and protests in Edinburgh and disputes in burghs such as Perth and Stirling, where a party of soldiers singing loyal songs were attacked as 'English Bougars'. A man seized for wearing the trews at Killin was freed by a mob, and sheriff courts refused to convict those wearing Highland dress. Jacobite forces also remained active in the field: as late as the winter of 1748–49, five companies of foot were deployed to prevent raiding attacks in Aberdeenshire, Banff, Invernesshire and the Mearns. Ultimately, '*force majeure* was the . . . basis of Hanoverian rule' in northern Scotland at least, where the disaffected 'were to be cowed not only through the presence and proximity of soldiers, but also by the sight of the corpses of their heroes suspended in chains in their parishes of origin'. The prolonged occupation of the 1740s and 50s – in part so prolonged because the British Army appears to have had difficulty distinguishing between Jacobite and other civil disorder raised against the excise – may have introduced a number of intriguing cultural changes to Scotland. One of these was cricket, which was played by British troops during the 1745 Rising and afterwards, with soldiers recorded as playing it in occupied Perth in 1750. By the 1770s, it had begun to become a fashionable game in Scotland.[82]

Further research may show that the relatively long British Army occupation played a part in the better integration of Scotland into Great Britain evident by 1760. The incorporation of Scots troops into the British Army certainly played such a role, but it remained the case that the greater presence of Scots in England in the 1760s was not welcome and on occasion led even a staunch unionist like Henry Dundas (1742–1811) to threaten separation. Scots were still proud of their nation, but the first century after the Union showed they had to visibly participate in the shared norms of British public life to be accepted at home, however much they might promote or continue to profit by their own national networks abroad. In private or overseas, matters were different. But these were not separate worlds. We begin the next chapter with the major changes in Scotland and Great Britain as a whole, which formed the domestic counterweight to the expansion of the Scottish military presence overseas, beginning with the theatres of war in 1756–63.[83]

1. Minute Book of the Company of Scotland trading to Africa and the Indies: the Orientalist and exotic nature of this major colonialist venture is clearly visible. The top legend runs: 'Where the World Opens'.

2. The Union between Scotland and England. The images stress the Queen and her kingdoms: the iconography of a composite monarchy, not a unitary state.

3. Allan Ramsay (1684–1758), poet, patriot, cultural entrepreneur and champion of Scots language and song. The artist, William Aikman (1682–1731), was a cousin of Ramsay's close friend Sir John Clerk of Penicuik.

4. An anti-excise medal, portraying the Devil leading the Prime Minister Sir Robert Walpole (1676–1745) to hell in a noose: the heavy wear on this example clearly shows it was a popular token and not solely a collector's piece.

5. Jacobite jeton: a propaganda token for playing at cards. The equivalent of a chip in a modern casino, this example had a double portrait of James II and VII and his son (illustrated).

6. Edinburgh Tartan, 1713 pattern: Jacobite tartan in its distinctive sett, designed to irritate the authorities while evading prosecution. Prosecution for sedition or treason (under legislation which dated back to the reign of Edward III of England (r.1327–77)) relied on spoken or written language, and the Jacobites designed a complex symbolism to communicate without words to evade prosecution.

7. Portrait of Charles Edward Stuart, probably by Allan Ramsay (1713–84), the son of the poet, possibly painted at Holyrood, 1745. Recent research indicates the similarity of its frame to Edinburgh frames of *c.* 1750, thus reinforcing the provenance of this as the only painting of Charles Edward on campaign to be completed at the time, though doubts remain among some art historians.

8. *The Humorous Map of Scotland* from *Geographical Fun* (1869). Scotland was established as a country of pipes and tartan long before 1800, and the domestic image of the country remained, and to an extent remains, a caricature of its character and complexity.

9. *The Death of General Wolfe* (1770) by Benjamin West depicts the hero of the Plains of Abraham dying in the moment of victory over the French in Quebec in 1759. Simon Fraser, who commanded the 3rd Lovat battalion at Culloden (where Wolfe fought with the British Army) is depicted standing behind Wolfe, though he was not in fact there; the presence of the First Nations man contemplating Wolfe may suggest that, just as Fraser was once a lawless tribesman and is now a British officer, so in a future generation the Native American may enjoy the same opportunities.

10. Hugh Montgomery, 12th Earl of Eglinton (1739–1819), in front of a burning Cherokee village, by John Singleton Copley. The Scot as a ruthless and successful servant of empire.

11. The Glenfinnan Monument, blending Jacobite nostalgia with a tribute to the contribution of Scottish soldiers to the Napoleonic Wars. Commissioned by Alexander MacDonald and executed by James Gillespie Graham in 1815, the soldier at the top was added in 1835.

12. Dido Elizabeth Belle (1761–1804). Born illegitimate and into slavery, Dido was the daughter of the Scottish admiral Sir John Lindsay and great-niece to William Murray, 1st Earl of Mansfield, the Scottish nobleman who adopted her as a free gentlewoman and was responsible for the 1772 Mansfield Judgement which found slavery incompatible with English Common Law. The painting is now attributed to Fife man David Martin (1737–97), who studied under Allan Ramsay. Dido's dependent situation is reproduced in the experience of Fanny Price in *Mansfield Park* by Jane Austen.

13. *Am I Not a Man and a Brother?* This ceramic medallion was produced for Josiah Wedgwood (1730–95) in 1787 and distributed at abolitionist meetings. Its legend is a probable inspiration for Robert Burns' song of universal brotherhood, 'A Man's a Man', first published in 1795.

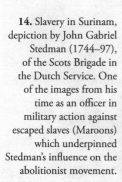

14. Slavery in Surinam, depiction by John Gabriel Stedman (1744–97), of the Scots Brigade in the Dutch Service. One of the images from his time as an officer in military action against escaped slaves (Maroons) which underpinned Stedman's influence on the abolitionist movement.

15. Anne-Louis Girodet (1767–1824), *Ossian Receiving the Ghosts of Fallen French Heroes*: this 1801 painting expresses the power of Ossianic Romanticism in the imagination of the Napoleonic Wars. Napoleon himself was an enthusiast for Ossian.

16. Arran Distillery Burns-branded whisky: typically over 90 per cent goes for export, with France the largest market for Burns malt whisky.

PART TWO
EMPIRE

3

THE FORCE OF SENTIMENT

BRITISH ARMY, GLOBAL WAR

One of the risks attendant on treating Jacobitism as marginal or as a side-show, as some historians still do, is that two major changes in Scotland's global presence in the British Empire depended on its defeat. Without the Rising of 1745 and its aftermath, the emergence of British military Scotland and Romantic Scotland in the global forms in which they rapidly became manifest and continued and continue to endure would not have occurred. The full incorporation of Scotland, particularly 'Highland' Scotland, into Britain's global military presence was the product of the necessity for, and the limited success achieved by, the British Army's initial occupation of Scotland in the years following 1746 and the British Government policy of confiscation and control with respect to local magnate power. The projection of Romantic Scotland as the dominant global image of the country arose from the creation of a taxonomy of glory, an embrace of both an imagined and empirical Scottish past, which was developed in the Jacobite era and subsequently became a vision of that era transformed by nostalgia, loss and transfiguration. From the elegy by Alasdair MacMhaighstir Alasdair (c.1698–1770) on the final collapse of MacDonald power in his own lifetime in *Birlinn Chlann Raghnaill* (Clanranald's Galley, c.1754) and James Macpherson's (1736–96) version of *Ossian* (1761–63), presented as the last of the bards of a heroic Gaelic Scotland, to Walter Scott's (1771–1832) *Redgauntlet* (1824), with its 'Cause' that is 'lost for ever', both Scotland's and that of the Stuarts, the Jacobite iconography of 'Highland' patriotism became the source material for Scotland's global brand. To a large extent this remains the case. These writers became the self-appointed masters of ceremonies for the obsequies of a lost world in which they or their families had often participated only a few years earlier. Alasdair was a captain in 1745 and Prince Charles's Gaelic tutor; Macpherson's cousin and collaborator, Lachlan, was a lieutenant in Cluny's regiment, where more than a dozen of Macpherson's relatives also served; Burns' grandfather was in all probability involved in the Rising of 1715, while Burns' acclamation as 'Caledonia's Bard' in Edinburgh in 1787 was made by the nephew of the Jacobite commander Lord Elcho. Scott's own father rode away as a boy with Murray of Broughton's Hussars in 1745 before being brought back home.[1]

For over a decade after Culloden, Scotland – the country as a whole rather than the 'Highlands' – was occupied by the British Army and 'largely garrisoned by non-Scottish regiments'. Jacobite disquiet continued for many years. Irish Brigade recruitment continued along the east coast by Scots in the French service. Episcopal chapels were destroyed and despoiled throughout Scotland's Episcopal heartlands and congregations either met in secret or sometimes attended Mass, for the far less numerous Catholics were less hard hit. Scotland's Episcopal Church continued to support the Jacobite cause officially until 1788. In Aberdeen on 14 November 1784, Samuel Seabury (1729–96), a Connecticut-born former medical student of the University of Edinburgh, was consecrated the first bishop of the American Episcopal Church, which thus became a daughter church of the Episcopal Church of Scotland. His inability as a citizen of the new United States to take an oath to King George III was no bar to a Jacobite church's bishop. Scottish Episcopalians did not formally join the Anglican Communion until 1867, though they revived in the Victorian era thanks to the support of W.E. Gladstone (1809–98), who took a lively interest in church appointments such as those of the Oxford Anglo-Catholic Scot Alexander Forbes (1817–75) to the bishopric of Brechin at the age of 30, which helped to embed high Anglican practice in the traditional Episcopalian heartland. Forbes (whose brother George was fittingly enough a scholar of Orthodoxy) was himself a great-great-great nephew of the Jacobite commander Alexander, Lord Forbes of Pitsligo (1678–1762), and wrote a Jacobite novella, *The Prisoners of Craigmacaire*.[2]

General James Wolfe (1727–59) was a regimental commander at Culloden and subsequently was commanding officer of the British forces in the garrisons of Perth then Inverness. In June 1751, he recommended the incorporation of disaffected Scots into the British army, not as an alternative to punishment, as had happened in 1746 and later, when 'many men were forcibly enlisted in the army as a punishment for flouting the ban' on tartan, but at scale. It would be 'no great mischief if they fall. How can you better employ a secret enemy than by making his end conducive to the common good?' Wolfe's views were by no means entirely new: in 1717, the Marquess of Breadalbane had suggested that using 'Highland' troops in the European theatre was a better solution than the 'trouble, expence and noise' of repressing them at home, while the 43rd (later 42nd) Foot, the Black Watch, had already been developed from the Independent Highland Companies, being formed into a regiment on 25 October 1739, with a first muster at Aberfeldy in May 1740. They won their first battle honours at Fontenoy, in a record that was to stretch across the globe. William, 2nd Viscount Barrington (1717–93), the Secretary at War, supported Wolfe's idea, and Thomas Pelham-Holles, Duke of Newcastle (1693–1768), prime minister 1754–56 and 1757–62, passed on this suggestion to William Pitt (1708–78), Paymaster General of the forces 1746–55, who in turn persuaded George II to approve the extensive recruitment of ex-Jacobites: 'I sought for merit wherever it was to be found. It is my boast that I was the first minister who looked for it; and I found it, in the mountains of the north', as Pitt later told the Commons, claiming the credit for himself.[3]

A necessary and perhaps sufficient condition for the decision to pursue widespread enlistment from former Jacobite areas was the fact that neither the Heritable Jurisdictions Act (20 Geo II c.43) nor any other legislation or military and administrative decision-making had succeeded in completely displacing local structures of social cohesion and control, which therefore could be seen as presenting a continuing threat. The Act of Attainder (19 Geo II c.26) identified Jacobites who could be deemed to be guilty of high treason without trial; the Disarming Act (19 Geo. II c.39) sought to disarm northern Scotland, while the Vesting Act (20 Geo II c.41) forfeited over forty Jacobite estates, fourteen of which came into the direct possession of the Crown under the Annexing Act (25 Geo. II c.41) five years later, although Commissioners for the forfeited estates were not appointed until 1755. All of these had an impact on society, and the chief impact came from the Heritable Jurisdictions Act. Yet even this Act – which attacked the foundations of hereditary sheriffdoms and rights of regality – if it extended 'the reach of government patronage' also had to recognize 'the continuing utility of local rule'. It was argued that without the preservation of baronial courts it would be impossible to manage estates effectively, and this was far from the only problem. It should be understood that at this time sheriff-substitutes did not have to be legally qualified, and thus, before the professionalization of 'the local monopolies that controlled the legal system', patronage networks could rule without professional restraint. Cumberland had declared that 'one half of the magistracy have been either aiders or abettors to the Rebellion, and the others dare not act for fear of offending the Chiefs or hanging their own cousins', and in consequence both General Humphrey Bland (1686–1763) and Andrew Fletcher, Lord Milton (1692–1766) and the Lord Justice Clerk until 1748, favoured army officers taking over as Justices of the Peace in the localities. They made little headway. Bland reported that 'In the Inverness region, no JP was willing to assist the army', and he was making similar complaints 'less than three years before the start of widespread recruiting in the Highlands in the winter of 1756–1757'. In such circumstances, the co-option of local elites was more likely – as Walpole had earlier found – to support a longstanding political settlement than continuing police actions and struggles between army officers and the civil authorities. One clear solution was to integrate key members of the elite into the army and let them export their unruly tenantry for service overseas.[4]

Such a process had – from the point of view of the British Government – additional benefits. Not only would a potentially hostile soldiery from Jacobite areas be sent abroad, but the power of the remaining landlords would be further undermined in a way which the Army occupation had not succeeded in completing. This did not just mean Jacobite landlords or those of doubtful loyalty. Lord President Forbes (1685–1747) had suggested dividing Jacobite estates 'amongst politically reliable favourites', and while Argyll and Lord Milton, supported by Lord Reay, had suggested that Jacobite estates should revert to the Crown, there were suspicions that Scottish magnates were looking to aggrandize themselves at the expense of their neighbours and in their own, rather than Great Britain's, self-interest. John Russell, the 4th Duke of Bedford (1710–71), First Lord of the Admiralty (1744–48) and Secretary of State for the Southern Department (1748–51), 'argued that to invest the Crown with Highland properties was an act of political chicanery designed merely to enhance the existing power of certain authoritarian Scottish magnates'. The chief among these was Argyll, to whom Henry Pelham (1694–1754, prime minister 1743–54 and Newcastle's brother) was determined not to concede too much power. Argyll's brother and predecessor had been suspected after 1715 of being too soft on the Jacobites, and in 1745–46 the house of Argyll also suffered in reputation, as its grandiose claims to authority over many dependents, despite in reality having little or no control, were impugned either in point of fact or of loyalty when these so-called dependents raised men for Charles. Nor was John Campbell, 4th Earl of Loudoun (1705–82), and his command entirely exempt, despite his conspicuous loyalty during the Rising. Although the British Government had recoiled from Cumberland's and others' demands that whole populations should be transported following Culloden (Newcastle had noted that these Scots, as well as other Britons, should have the protection of the law), it was proposed in 1748 that Loudoun's men – used in the garrisoning of Scotland – should be settled in Nova Scotia 'where their presence would counter . . . the French Acadians'. This deployment seems as much a dispersion of politically unreliable Scots as a reward. In 1749, another of Cumberland's senior officers, Colonel (later Lieutenant General) Edward Cornwallis (1713–76) was appointed governor of Nova Scotia, where he founded Halifax (on Mi'kmaq land) and adopted a policy of intense fortification and settlement designed to put pressure on the Acadian French inhabitants and their Mi'kmaq native allies. He then issued an extirpation order against the Mi'kmaq promising a reward for every First Nations man, woman or child destroyed (the production of their scalp to be evidence) or taken prisoner, in conduct reminiscent of his actions in Scotland against the domestic 'rebels and savages' after Culloden. In 1754 a new governor, Colonel (later Brigadier) Charles Lawrence, who had been wounded at

Fontenoy, ordered *Le Grand Dérangement* in Acadia (Nova Scotia, New Brunswick, Prince Edward Island and northern Maine) to expel the French-Canadian population in a manner which had been bruited, but not achieved, in Scotland a decade earlier. Thousands of 'peaceful farming people' were expelled, and 'mortality must have been heavy, for food supply was marginal'. Paradoxically, the Acadians left rich farmlands behind them which in their turn were often settled by veterans of the Scottish regiments. The Mi'kmaq once again fared even worse, with Wolfe observing that 'We cut them to pieces wherever we found them.'[5]

Loudoun was Commander-in-Chief of the British forces in North America and Governor General of Virginia in 1756–58 and thus in post during this process which, as one of Cumberland's commanders, he well knew had been advocated in Scotland. By then, the deportations proposed in the aftermath of Culloden had begun to be achieved by other means: the use of patronage to export Scottish young men of military age to fight for the British Empire within 'an exclusively overseas, imperial context', one in which commissions were used 'to engender loyalty' among the natural leaders of Scotland's conservative north, and to 'take advantage of the defeat of the Jacobites in 1746 to help Britain to victory over the French'. While tartan and loyalty to Chiefs of the Name was to be extirpated in the interests of domestic unity ('no man or boy . . . shall on any pretence whatsoever, wear or put on the clothes commonly called Highland Clothes . . . the plaid, philibeg, or little kilt, trowse, shoulder belts' as the 1746 Act of Proscription put it), both were to survive and indeed become prominent in the army serving over-seas. Lord Barrington had contributed to initiating this process by praising 'the martial ability of the Highlanders', and the premiss of 'Highland' valour which was to become so important in army mythology thus had its roots in British recruitment strategy. In their turn, landowners 'milked the glamorous and famed image of clanship in order to win profitable contracts from government for recruitment into their family regiments' while targeting enlistment among the 'cash crop' of the economically marginal on their own estates. The martial valour of these men was a good story, and like all good stories, not wholly true. The romance of the 'Highlands' was born out of the economic drivers of Scottish landlordism as much as it was from the pens of creative writers. The 'basic contradiction' to be found in the incorporation of Scottish landlordism into the British state was that the new social necessity of making 'a vain attempt to emulate the levels of display and consumerism of their peers elsewhere in Britain on the meagre surpluses of a poor peasantry' would change the very nature of Scottish landholding itself, and ruin the lives of many of its tenants. In the end what the abolition of heritable jurisdictions and the presence of British soldiers could not secure was achieved by the greater social integration of the landlord class into British society.[6]

The Royal Navy had played an important part in the war against the Jacobites, and after 1746 Murdoch Mackenzie (1712–97) was commissioned by the Admiralty 'to do a marine survey of the west coasts of Scotland and England and the whole of Ireland' to improve its reach. This was to be the naval equivalent of William Roy's (1726–90) more famous military map on land, which had – with Paul Sandby's (1731–1807) help – created 'graduations of tone' of 'no geometrical exactness' (as Roy himself admitted) in order to present Scotland as more 'Highland' than it actually was. Roy's mapping also emphasized an analogy between the Roman and British occupations of Scotland. Earlier in the Union era, the Navy had in general taken the Scottish naval officer Captain James Hamilton's advice that impressment should not be used in Scotland 'except in cases of absolute necessity' and thus there were no tenders sent to Scottish ports at times of crisis. Scots were thus 'under-represented on the lower decks of the Royal Navy and the press gang never really worked as a means of recruiting there'. The Navy thus continued to be seen as a predominantly English institution.[7]

Pressing in Scotland began actively in April 1756, with unmarried or landless men targeted; Captain John Fergusson, one of the most active (and brutal) officers in the Navy after Culloden, was the first to press his fellow Scots and this had an immediate impact on trade: by the end of 1756, 'shipping was almost at a standstill' in Aberdeen due to pressing of merchant seamen into the Royal Navy. The practice of 'widespread coercion' was extended to army recruitment also, for example on the Gordon lands and at Nairn in the 1750s, where there was extensive sharp practice, with recruiting agents often commencing recruitment before they had been authorized to do so. Local Justices of the Peace on occasion acted proactively 'in the safeguarding of local people who had enlisted in the army', particularly those recruits enlisted before beating orders had been received. On other occasions, local Justices of the Peace recommended against wearing tartan as a protection against forcible impressment into the army. It seems that Cumberland and Bland had had a point in their suspicion of the magistracy and its sympathies.[8]

Even with the proleptic and excessive use of recruiting powers in the localities, the British authorities were nonetheless surprised at how rapidly troops were raised initially, with Fraser of Lovat, for example, recruiting 1,100 men in the first three months of 1757, slightly more than he and his father had brought out in 1745–46. Tenants were 'expected to supply a family member' in the old manrent style, with £3 payable per recruit (this compares with bounties of £1 6s. to £2 8s. recorded for British army enlistment during posting in Scotland a few years earlier). The landlords might pay on this bounty in part, and otherwise 'used land on their estate as a substitute reward'. This led to the rise of crofting as the provision of land for veterans accelerated the subdivision of landholdings, even as it promoted an increase in links to the land among a people esteemed 'deeply rooted in the soil', and where 'land distribution' was an important part of the landlord's powers. The old system of *fear-taca,* which 'sub-rented land on the basis of providing the chief with manpower' via wadsetted (mortgaged) or tacked (leased) land held by tenants, was still operational in part, despite the rise of cash rents, but, backed by state power, the landlords increasingly had direct control in securing the margins on enlistment, at least while impressment provisions lasted (they expired by 1758). Subtenants demanded to hold land directly from the landlord in exchange for recruits, further undermining the tacksman system. Direct recruitment competed even further with the position of the tacksmen, and the newly raised soldiers also had 'tenurial ambitions'. The importance of *dùthchas* – the concept of land in which the tenantry held a hereditary cultural and ancestral right – incentivized local landholding as a goal for men who, especially if their landlords became their officers, could begin to elide their feudal and kinship-based loyalties into loyalty to those officers. In these ways, 'the immensely powerful rationales of land and contractual militarism' could be combined. In the meantime, surplus capital from 'the enforced enlistment of men into the Highland regiments of the

British army formed an integral part of the business of estate improvement.' The situation was, however, unstable, as it was associated with a rise in partible holdings and a crisis in the traditional pattern of landholding. As the global war of 1756–63 against France progressed, 'enlistment bounties' rose to between 3 and 5 guineas in excess of the government allowance as supply declined, and cash-strapped officers 'were forced to protect tenure and grant land as a substitute to monetary bounties', a process to which they very probably over-committed in order to integrate themselves and their tenants more fully into the armed forces and to maintain the local identity and control of recruitment. Returning ex-soldiers were 'upwardly mobile' (not least because they were on British incomes at a time when Scottish wages and prices were still lower) and the shortage of labourers caused by military recruitment combined with the injection of new money and ambition to raise costs and rents in the years following the end of the war. Lack of land led to population loss, which could be arrested by breaking up 'large tacks' of the increasingly redundant tacksman system; this was also under pressure as the tacksmen were now stressing their subtenants 'to improve production' so they themselves could meet the increasing rent demands that replaced the nominal rent they had once paid in return for the leadership and military role they had provided. The further subdivision of land arrested population loss, but at the long-term cost of unsustainability, and, although slowed down, the intensity of demand and the opportunities provided by Canada saw from 150 to 300 of the Frasers settle in Québec in 1763 and 21,000 hectares in Nova Scotia and Québec allocated to veterans later in the century. As the historian Sir Tom Devine notes, 'It was "'the very antithesis of the policy of land consolidation pursued throughout most of the Lowlands".'[9]

Pressed men from seven counties were allocated to George Perry's 55th Foot (almost half of whom were non-Scots), who were raising men at Stirling, while the burgh of Perth offered 1½ guineas (£1 11s. 6d.) to every man enlisting with Perry's or Lord John Murray's 42nd (The Black Watch). The Black Watch had not been used in the Jacobite Rising as it was regarded as untrustworthy following its mutiny in 1743 on rumours that it was to be sent to the graveyard of the West Indies (it was in fact intended for Flanders). It had been retained in England and then sent to Ireland in 1749–55, although Lord Murray had been in command of some detached companies in Scotland. Now it was thought the time was right to expand it and to use its service outwith Scotland as a template for other units. Murray (1711–87) was the Member of Parliament (MP) for Perthshire and half-brother to the Jacobite generals Tullibardine and Lord George Murray: a man of a Jacobite family was – as often in the early years of 'Highland' recruitment – seen as the right kind of leader for suspected and ex-Jacobites. Murray's 42nd arrived in New York in 1756, Perry's 55th in Nova Scotia in 1757. By this time, the 62nd (later 77th) Foot under Archibald Montgomery, 3rd Earl of Eglinton (1726–96), were recruiting at Stirling, incorporating an additional 1,500 primarily northern Scots, Camerons, Frasers and MacDonalds among others, following a warrant issued by Pitt on 4 January. On 3 September 1757, Montgomery's first detachments arrived at Charleston in South Carolina. Other troops being raised at Inverness by Simon Fraser, Master of Lovat and *de jure* Lord Lovat (1726–82), were initially ranked as the 62nd (later 63rd) Foot, but by 1758 had become the 78th (Highland) Foot, Fraser's Highlanders: these included MacDonells of Glengarry and Clanranald as well as Cameron troops. Barrington tellingly wrote to Cumberland that the new troops of The Black Watch, Montgomery's and Fraser's, 'should go to America as fast as the companies were raised, and none of them should remain in the Highlands'. Recommendation by the Duke of Argyll was to be sought for names of approved officers, and a pattern began to be reinforced whereby relatives, friends and fellow Scots supported and promoted each other in a new environment. This recruitment thus demonstrated the limits of British capacity to incorporate Jacobite Scotland over the decade since Culloden. Many of its inhabitants were judged to be only safe in the army and only safe out of Scotland. Indeed, the 2nd battalion of the Black Watch were only given arms on the day of their landing at Guadeloupe in 1759, and, despite considerable agitation from Scotland's elites, the country was not permitted to have a domestic militia, as indeed had been the case since 1715. This decision was not reversed until the era of the Napoleonic Wars, despite attempts to persuade the British authorities to permit recruitment of a Scottish militia in the 1750s and 1770s. The 'Highlanders' might be characterized as the epitome of Scottish disloyalty, but the country as a whole remained implicated. When ex-Jacobite officers such as General Allan MacLean of Torloisk (1725–98), Colonel of the 84th Foot (Royal Highland Emigrants), led his men into battle in North America wearing white cockades, the presence of some enduring suspicion was hardly surprising. In fact what was happening was the beginning of the recasting of Jacobitism as 'a usable past that could be employed in the context of the present', a story of misplaced but formidable loyalty now reassigned to British imperial service. In the end, eleven regiments were raised from northern Scotland for the Seven Years' War: four saw tours of duty in North America, four in the West Indies, three in Europe, one in India and one in Ireland. But even at the end of the war, other British regiments continued to garrison Scotland.[10]

Simon Fraser had commanded the 3rd Lovat battalion in 1746, and had arrived late on the day of Culloden. His rehabilitation was completed by the contribution of the 78th battalion to victory on the Plains of Abraham in 1759. General Wolfe died in the action and Benjamin West's (1738–1820) famous picture of *The Death of Wolfe* (1771; see plate 9) shows Simon Fraser standing behind the dying man while a First Nations Canadian contemplates the great general's last moments in solemn awe. The message is clear: the savage natives of Scotland have become tamed and successful martial partners in British glory; what they have become, you First Nations will one day be, and there is also probably an embedded reference to the story of Wolfe having sought to save the life of a Fraser officer on the field at Culloden. Simon Fraser was not in fact present at Wolfe's death: the painting is an ideological construct. West was to be well rewarded: he was made Historical Painter to the King in 1772 and President of the Royal Academy twenty years later.[11]

Typically, Scottish troops were regarded as having a unique relationship with First Nations/Native Americans. Even in the sixteenth century Algonquins and 'Picts' had been represented in a similar way, and in the campaigns of the eighteenth century the Black Watch were themselves described as 'a kind of Indians', while the Society in Scotland for Propagating Christian Knowledge (SSPCK) was sent on mission to the Native Americans as earlier they had been sent 'to bring social as well as spiritual reform to the Highlands and Islands'. Naturally, this did not stop Montgomery's 77th being used against the Cherokee, and Hugh Montgomery himself being painted standing in front of a burning Cherokee village (see plate 10). Nonetheless, both Native Americans and the Earl of Loudoun regarded the two peoples as highly similar. Scots could be found supporting a 'pan-Indian alliance', and Native American self-control appealed to figures such as Adam Smith. The wearing of tartan by Native Americans appears to have been commonplace.[12]

By 1758, Scottish 'Highlanders' were 17.5 per cent of the British Army in North America, though one must be a little cautious about such figures as the 'Highlander' was always an inexact category, and from an early date these regiments were not all homogeneous. However, Scots as a whole were almost 30 per cent of the British Army in North America in 1757, providing a major rank and file uplift to a force already strong in the higher ranks, with Scots having already 25 per cent of staff appointments and 20 per cent of colonelcies between 1714 and 1763, in an era when Scottish officers – though not rank and file to the same degree – had already been present in senior ranks in the British Army. The accession of manpower at lower ranks was now sizeable too, and the recruits required some acclimatization to standard British Army procedures. They paid dearly for their credibility in the manner of General Wolfe's initial recommendation for their use. The Black Watch suffered a casualty rate of almost 50 per cent (649 casualties including 25 officers) at Ticonderoga in 1758, while the 77th had a casualty rate of almost 60 per cent at Fort Duquesne in the same year; Fraser's 78th took not dissimilar losses on the Plains of Abraham. After the deployment of Scottish troops to the Caribbean theatre in 1761, some 60 per cent were lost the following year. By August 1763, of 2,000 who had been deployed in the West Indies, 'just 245 remained fit for duty'.[13]

As a consequence of the use of former Jacobites in the army, 'Some of those who accepted commissions in the new battalions had fought against their new employer', and under British colours now faced some of their former colleagues in arms. Chevalier Johnstone, Lord George Murray's *aide-de-camp* (ADC) in 1745–46 was now ADC to Louis-Joseph de Montcalm-Grozon, Marquis de Montcalm de Saint-Veran (1712–59). On the fall of Louisbourg in 1758, 'Johnstone had the chagrin of making a swift exit lest he was captured by precisely the regiments – Lee's, Warburton's and Lascelles' – whose surrender the Jacobites had accepted at Prestonpans.' On the other side of the equation,

Barrel's (now Duroure's) 4th (King's Own) regiment 'successfully combined with Highland levies in the Caribbean campaigns' despite the mauling it had received from these same areas and possibly the same men at Culloden.[14] Sometimes the new British soldiers had even seen French service, as was the case with Donald MacDonald, a Captain in the Écossois Royales in 1745, who fought with Wolfe at Québec with the same rank in Fraser's 78th. Indeed, quite a number of officers in the 78th were fluent in French, and General James Murray (1721–94), Governor of Québec 1760–68, was strongly sympathetic to the Francophones of North America.[15]

Some Scottish families – besides the Campbells in Jamaica – already had an interest in the lands their troops were now involved in defending. Cameron of Lochiel's family, for example, 'had interests in New Jersey land, colonial timber, and West Indian sugar plantations', while, by 1828, the majority of subscribers to a Gaelic dictionary were based in Jamaica. One of the falsities in the persistent emphasis on a Highland–Lowland subdivision of Scotland is that the benefit magnates and employees alike received from the Empire's major industries can be persistently underestimated: if Campbells and Camerons benefited from the West Indies, '62 per cent of all Scottish linen exports' went there by 1796 (to clothe slaves among other purposes), and 'The growth of the sugar refineries on the Clyde saw the population of Greenock rise from 2,000 in 1700 to 17,500 by 1801.' Yet if Gaelic-speaking Scotland was not simply a site of internal exploitation, it did suffer from it. Simon Fraser sought to rehabilitate his own family through the expenditure of his regiment's blood in both the Seven Years' and the American wars, and this was a feature of the officering and leadership of the 'Highland' regiments from the beginning. The landowning and officer class became deeply intertwined, with 26 per cent of the 'Highland' electorate holding officer rank by the latter part of the eighteenth century, while 'Between the regimentation of the 42nd, and the letters of service . . . to the . . . 93rd Sutherland Highlanders in 1799, 59 technically Highland units were created.' Their elite leaders were party to, and in some degree the promulgators of, what became the myth of Scottish martial valour in the British Empire while at the same time identifying with 'English Liberties' as lying at the core of their own values. These values seem to have been consolidated by the war of 1756–63, when the Magna Carta, the subject of William Blackstone's *The Great Charter* (1759), was 'put on ostentatious display' in London, while 'George III and some of his fellow aristocrats chose to have themselves painted . . . in close proximity to copies of Magna Carta.' In the king's case, this may have been an attempt to head off contemporary accusations of his high handedness. A Whig and parliamentary concept of British liberties was crystallizing through an imperial war in which Scots were for the first time participating at scale. This constitutionalism – combined with anti-Celtic racism then also gaining ground – could lead to dissociated views of personal and group identities. The Americans noticed British liberties did not apply to them, while in Scotland a growing British Whig consciousness contributed to a degree of dissociation between the country's past and present. Anne Grant (1755–1838) recorded 'Highlanders' disdain for the Highlands' in the early nineteenth century and the view that 'our Celtic ancestors were little better than ourang-outangs'; British incorporation and service had civilized them, and the type of the 'Hottentot Highlander' became an internal avatar of what the British Empire sought to achieve externally in the 'civilization' and incorporation of native peoples overseas. Culloden was frequently rhetorized as if it happened in another era, not in the current or previous generation, as public memory hastened to represent the Highlands as rescued from barbarism and oblivion through incorporation into the British polity. This was seen in texts such as George Kearsley's *The Virtuosi's Museum* (1779), which, through over 100 plates reworked by Paul Sandby, presented the incorporation of Scotland as a picturesque and primitive 'centre' of a unitary Britain, preserver of its spirit of ancestral liberty in the face of 'a metropolitan England softened by commerce and luxury'. Scottish history was reworked as a component of British destiny. When Friedrich Engels (1820–95) called the Highlanders 'a people without history', he was voicing the prejudices of the bourgeois Whig historiography which in another context he might well have excoriated. The internal native was exoticized and displaced. The accompanying step was to romanticize the Scot, in particular the 20–23 per cent of Scots who were Gaelic-speaking in 1755. Whereas Loudoun had not thought much of the Black Watch as a unit in North America, by the time that Major General David Stewart's

Sketches of the character, manners and present state of the Highlanders of Scotland appeared in 1822, the myth of the 'fighting 42nd' was embedded in the British Army (Stewart was himself a Black Watch officer), building on earlier celebration of Scottish 'warrior-heroes', as at Alexandria in 1801. The 42nd, the Cameron Highlanders, the 90th Perthshire volunteers and the 92nd Gordon Highlanders were all among the landing force at Aboukir Bay that year, and Seamus MacLagainn, chaplain of the Black Watch 1764–88, wrote a poem on Abercrombie's victory.[16]

Perceptions of Scottish bravery were thus further sharpened throughout the Napoleonic Wars, where Scots had provided up to 25 per cent of the officer corps and 36 per cent of the manpower of Britain's militia units, while the 42nd, 79th and 92nd Highlanders (as well as the 73rd) were again among the battle honours at Waterloo. By the early 1790s, bounty levels for Highland recruits had climbed from £21 to £30, such was the demand. Between 1793 and 1803, there were almost 4,000 men under arms from the MacDonald and the MacLeod estates on Skye and Raasay alone. The reputed martial valour of the (particularly 'Highland') Scottish soldier set them apart, and Stewart's study 'set the standard for histrionic interpretations of the Highland soldier into the twenty-first century'. Meanwhile the core northern counties involved most deeply in this myth found their economic progress compromised by their dependence on an economy both damaged and limited by the artificial rhetoric of Highland feudalism. The demilitarization of the 'Highlands' promised following Culloden had become their remilitarization in the interests of a global power. Even so, by the Napoleonic wars the majority of those serving in Highland regiments were not what could be called 'Highlanders', though the exotic dress of kilt and tartan – a core part of the mythos of the Scottish soldier –was retained on active service into the twentieth century (see plate 11).[17]

SCOTTISH AMERICANS AND AMERICAN SCOTS

British victory in the Seven Years' War opened up the prospect of extensive landed settlement not only in Scotland but also in North America for the subtenants and landless, or virtually landless, cottars who had fought in the conflict. Thousands of hectares of land were 'available for purchase and speculation', and of the 90,000 to 100,000 Scots who left for North America between 1700 and 1815, 'the majority' emigrated in the 1763–75 period. Areas of key settlement included Cape Fear valley in the Carolinas (initially settled from *The Thistle* in 1739), Georgia and the Mohawk and upper Hudson Valley, with between 10 and 15 per cent of the inhabitants of the Carolinas, Georgia and Virginia being Scots by 1790. Gaelic continued to be spoken in the Carolinas into the 1820s. The ex-soldiers of the 1760s were supplemented in the 1770s by 'farmers or artisans in the textile trades, which were then experiencing a serious depression', as the Scottish economy's historic overdependence on textiles adjusted in the face of new markets and rival manufactures, including duty-free Irish linen sales in England and the North American colonies. Despite the strength of Scots linen manufacture – in which Dundee was increasingly pre-eminent – the narrow base of Scottish exports was a sign of economic vulnerability, and Scots continued to go abroad as they had before the Union in order to establish control of import markets for domestic consumption or re-export. Scots sojourning or settling in North America thus acted as their predecessors had done, as a support network for Scottish business, above all the tobacco trade. By the early 1770s, 'Scots were reckoned to control over half the trade in the key areas of colonial tobacco production' and Glasgow's dominance in the trade in general and in re-export to some of Scotland's traditional markets (where the city had 60 per cent of the British tobacco export market to France by 1751) was noteworthy, if founded on the cruelties of slavery, as indeed was some of Scotland's success in textiles.[18]

Scots who came to North America at this period could often find a support network through the development of Scotland's unofficial embassies, the societal and associational nodes of the charitable and business networks, which sustained Scots abroad and were to reach their apogee in the years before 1914. Between 1707 and 1763, the Scots Charitable Society of Boston admitted 798 new members, all 'Scottsmen and the sons of Scottsmen', while the St Andrew's Society of Charleston had been founded in 1729 and that in Philadelphia twenty years later, followed by Savannah (1750), New York (1756, following an earlier 'Scots society' of 1744),

St John's New Brunswick (1798) and Buffalo (1806), by which time there were also three Scots associations in New York City. Other mutual benefit societies in North America included the Scots Club of Halifax (1768), the Scots Thistle Society of Philadelphia (1796) and the Caledonian Society of Lexington (1798). These organizations survived the American War of Independence, perhaps in part because some of their members supported it: in 1776, of the 109 members of the St Andrew's Society of Charleston, 77 sided with the colonists and only 32 with the Crown. Such societies thus continued to develop after 1783. By the time of the founding of the St Andrew's Society of Detroit in 1849, they were accompanied by a multi-plication of Burns Clubs, discussed in the next chapter. There was sometimes an openness about these organizations in keeping with Scottish engagement with Native American leadership, and on occasion Native Americans became members of these societies as early as the 1770s.[19]

The influence of Scottish emigrants and Scottish education was felt extensively in the emerging United States. Some 25 per cent of university-educated men coming to the American colonies had attended Edinburgh, Glasgow or one of the Aberdeen universities (King's or Marischal), and 'Before 1775 almost all the colonial medical profession was Scots or had been trained in Scottish universities.' Scottish influence was intensified given its disproportionate presence in certain specialist fields such as education. James Blair, a displaced Scots Episcopalian, became the first President of the College of William and Mary in 1693, remaining in post until 1751, and Scots continued to exercise a dominant influence in education in the Thirteen Colonies. Scottish teaching was 'much à la mode in Colonial Virginia' and, as Thomas Jefferson (1743–1826) noted, 'from that country [Scotland] we are surest of having sober attentive men'. Jefferson's own first teacher was William Douglas of Glencairn, and in his allusion to the 'rudiments of Latin and Greek', Jefferson may well have been referring to Thomas Ruddiman's *Rudiments of the Latin Tongue* (1732), at that time the predom-inant textbook (intriguingly, Ruddiman also published an edition of the Declaration of Arbroath). Jefferson subsequently received instruction from Dr William Small, the Scots professor of mathematics at William and Mary, who also taught 'Ethics, Rhetoric, and Belles Lettres', and had been a classmate of the poet James Macpherson (1736–96) at Aberdeen. James Madison (1751–1836) noted that 'All that I have been in life I owe largely to ... one man', his teacher Donald Robertson, while James Monroe's (1758–1831) school was run by Archibald Campbell. Elsewhere, Scots provided the Provost and Vice-Provost of the College of Philadelphia. The higher education curriculum in the Thirteen Colonies was heavily influenced by the Scottish undergraduate arts curriculum, a model which still remains visible in the generalism of the US undergraduate degree today. As Edgar Small, Provost of Penn, wrote in 1912, 'There is not the slightest doubt that the Scottish imprint upon American collegiate training is the only imprint worth talking about.' One of the clearest areas where this remains true is the prevalence of 'Speech' as a subject in US higher education, the legacy of the teaching of rhetoric in the Scottish universities of the Enlightenment, now abandoned by all, save in their student debating traditions. At Princeton, New York and Philadelphia (where Francis Alison had been his student), Francis Hutcheson's (1694–1746) moral philosophy was in the ascendant, and Thomas Reid's (1710–96) 'egalitarian epistemology ... humble empiricism, and ... communitarian morality' also found their followers, as did Henry Home, Lord Kames (1696–1782), who was a personal hero of Jefferson's and knew Benjamin Franklin (1706–90).

In 1759, Franklin visited Edinburgh and Glasgow, staying with Sir Alexander Dick, Allan Ramsay's friend, and meeting Hume, Kames (with whom Franklin also stayed in the Borders), Adam Ferguson, Joseph Black, William Cullen and Adam Smith. The polymathic Glasgow professor John Anderson (1726–96) was the guide on Franklin's tour of the 'Highlands', and worked with him subsequently. Franklin returned to Scotland in 1771, when Hume 'gave a large dinner party in his honour'. Later, Franklin also successfully applied to William Robertson for doctorates for some of his American friends. After Franklin's death, Anderson was touted as 'just the man to implement Washington's grand plan of a National University in the United States'. In the end, the university Anderson founded became Strathclyde, which supported the introduction of women into scientific higher education, and in the late 1790s they formed a substantial element of the student body. In this, as elsewhere, Anderson was a true Enlightenment figure, and it was this impetus in Scottish thought which had a profound influence on the development of the United States. To this day, the country is still strongly engaged with the stadial history of human society developed from classical, French and Neapolitan antecedents by Adam Smith, Anderson's colleague at Glasgow, and his successors. The idea that American governance represents a democratic ideal and the goal of all societies is deeply rooted in American culture and is evident in many spheres, from the 2003 Iraq war to the *Star Wars* franchise.[20]

Archie Turnbull in 1986 was perhaps the first to suggest that 'Thomas Jefferson modeled the Declaration of Independence on the 1320 Scottish Declaration of Arbroath', and later Edward Cowan and others have made the same case. Among the American patriots, James Wilson (1742–98), the founder of the Supreme Court, and John Witherspoon (1723–94), President of the College of New Jersey (now Princeton), were Scots signatories of the Declaration of Independence in 1776. Witherspoon – who derived the term 'Americanism' from the use of the term 'Scotticism' to describe the unwelcome elements of Scottish culture in English eyes – was himself a Scottish patriot who could not bear to hear 'anything in Congress which reflects badly on Scotland'. Witherspoon's grandfather had signed the 1643 Solemn League and Covenant, and he himself taught James Madison, Aaron Burr and nearly eighty future US senators and congressmen, besides other social leaders of the new republic. Witherspoon argued that Scotland 'has manifested the greatest Spirit for Liberty as a nation, in that their History is full of their calling kings to account & dethroning them when arbitrary and tyrannical'. The historian Ted Cowan at least is confident that he 'almost certainly knew of the Arbroath Declaration'. The founding father James Wilson, who hailed from Fife, went one step further and paraphrased the Declaration's paraphrase of Sallust's *Catiline*, speaking of 'Essential Liberty, which . . . we are determined not to lose, but with our lives'. Reprinted many times in the eighteenth century, it seems more than likely that some of the early leaders of the United States knew of the Declaration of Arbroath.[21]

That said, the dominant intellectual force underpinning the Declaration came from more recent Scottish history, which was more explicitly present in the citation of Scottish experience in the rhetoric of the American

Revolution. In 1774, Samuel Adams' 'radical circle invoked a "Solemn League and Covenant" to unite rural and metropolitan New England against British corruption', while in the July 1776 congressional debate on confederation, Witherspoon contrasted American constitutional plans with the incorporation of Scotland into a unitary state where it would not enjoy the rights of the US states. There is some evidence that the idea of states' rights and representation was supported by Scots who were reflecting on the relatively disadvantageous nature of the incorporating Union with England. It is certain that Scottish rhetoric and arguments concerning resistance to tyranny were central in the American Revolution, although the direct source of these was Enlightenment writing and its presence in the current curriculum of the colonial colleges, rather than the Declaration of Arbroath. Francis Hutcheson's coinage of the term 'the greatest happiness for the greatest number', and his view that 'whenever any invasion is made upon unalienable rights, there must arise either a perfect or external right to resistance' were among the underpinning ideas which led to the historian Garry Wills' view that 'the ideas expressed by Jefferson in 1776 . . . were not derived from Philadelphia or Paris, but from Aberdeen and Edinburgh and Glasgow'. Indeed, Hutcheson's 'Right to Resistance', itself arguably related to long-rehearsed debates about monarchical obligation to the community of the realm, is viewed by many recent scholars as central to the political rhetoric of the nascent United States. Hutcheson's terminology is certainly striking. In *A Short Introduction to Moral Philosophy* he writes that, 'If a mother country attempts anything oppressive toward a colony, and the colony is able to subsist as a sovereign state by itself . . . the colony is not bound to remain subject any longer.' Elsewhere, Hutcheson's sentiment that 'Large numbers of men cannot be bound to sacrifice their own and posterity's liberty and happiness to the ambitious views of the mother country' likewise proclaimed the centrality of the right of resistance to tyranny and arbitrary government which stretched back in Scottish thought through the Claim of Right, the National Covenant, George Buchanan and perhaps all the way back into the baronial shadows. In this context, one of the most fascinating aspects of the debate over the US constitution is that at a time when Scotland was increasingly adopting constitutional models based on English liberties into its domestic political discourse, it was Scottish ideas of the constitution that were so often to the fore across the Atlantic.[22]

Some prominent Scots rallied to the American cause. William Alexander, of the family of the Earl of Stirling and the son of a Jacobite exile, and Hugh Mercer, surgeon in Prince Charles's army in 1745 and killed in action at Stony Bridge in 1777, rose to general officer rank in the American forces, while General Lachlan McIntosh fought in the Continental Army with seven sons and grandsons. Chevalier John Paul (Jones) (1747–92), the son of a gardener in the Stewartry of Kirkcudbright, followed a well-worn path and joined the Russian Navy as Rear Admiral after he had 'captured and destroyed . . . British shipping from Bermuda to Nova Scotia' in the American cause, including an attempted attack on Leith in his native land. In Scotland itself, patriots like David Steuart Erskine, 11th Earl of Buchan (1742–1829), and James Boswell showed a positive interest in the American struggle.[23]

Not all Scots agreed of course, and Witherspoon's *Address to the Natives of Scotland Residing in America* (1776, 2nd edition, Glasgow, 1777) noted the failure of some Scots living in the American colonies to support their campaign for self-determination. Others with fewer native loyalties than Witherspoon were more explicit: Jefferson noted the threat from 'Scotch and foreign mercenaries . . . to invade and destroy us' and 'A free exportation to Scotchmen and Tories' was a popular toast. Six new 'Highland' regiments were added to the British Army in 1777–78 (though there were mutinies in all of them linked to posting abroad), and Alexander Wedderburn (1733–1805), Solicitor General and later 1st Earl of Rosslyn, was among the strong supporters of the war from the Scottish administration. In North America itself, Scots were associated with 'economic oppression and unacceptable ethnic clannishness in the tobacco country, and . . . political and military treachery everywhere'.[24]

This was indeed particularly the case with respect to the tobacco trade. Glasgow merchant contacts in the Chesapeake had been burgeoning since the 1740s and there were many Scots – notably in what were to become the southern states – with major financial interest in the status quo, such as Neil Jamieson of Norfolk, Virginia, partner in the Glassford, Gordon and Monteath business of Glasgow (Archibald McLauchlan's famous 1767

Glassford painting with its black servant on the margins depicts this family). Some 40 per cent of Scots in the Chesapeake were merchants and tobacco factors, and usually more than twenty ships a year sailed thither from Glasgow, with an additional one or two from Edinburgh. In the 1770s, Scots in the Chesapeake 'found themselves in a truly unenviable position' as 'demands for payment from Glasgow increasingly conflicted with the colonists' refusal to pay'. As a result, Scots began to leave in increasing numbers after 1774. Provincial legislatures, not least in the south, noted the prevalence of loyalist Scots and became hostile: in December 1776, Virginia gave merchants from Great Britain (many of whom in the Commonwealth were Scots) forty days 'to fight or leave the country'. Georgia's colonial assembly ruled in 1782 that 'No Scot was to be allowed to settle, or carry on any kind of trade' unless he was a patriot, and that those who were not could be 'imprisoned without bail and deported as soon as possible'. Such measures hardly induced enthusiasm for the American cause. American aggression and their own self-interest dictated loyalty to the Crown throughout most of the Scottish networks, as becoming American was now 'about the only way for a Scot' to succeed financially in the Chesapeake, and Scots were to claim 28 per cent of all postwar compensation. Scots sojourners who had 'become expert at manipulating the British colonial system to their own advantage' at the cost of their own national dependency now found themselves on the wrong side of a fight for national independence inspired in no small part by their country's own ideas. Scots with a stake in the colonial system and their networks thus often fought for it. Despite their defeat, it was a Scot who oversaw the close of the war. The chief British negotiator at the Peace of Paris in 1783 was none other than the Richard Oswald we have already met on Bance Island, who 'sat across the table from Benjamin Franklin during the peace negotiations'. Franklin thought Oswald a 'truly Good Man'. For his part, Oswald supported 'granting America unconditional independence'. It was a slaver who agreed the terms of American liberty – which would of course include the holding of slaves – and those who suffered so wretchedly contributed not a little to the £500,000 personal fortune (some £80 million at 2022 prices) left by Oswald from the profits of his global mercantile interests in 1784.[25]

In the Canadian provinces, there were signs of early dominance of Scots in commercial areas, not least the fur trade, which was still over 80 per cent run by Scots into the nineteenth century. Beaver pelts were central to the trade, and since First Nations people were also strongly engaged in it, 'Partnerships with Native women . . . made for contented traders and secured tight trading relationships'. Curling was introduced from Scotland in the Seven Years' War of 1756–63, while ice-hockey has been claimed to be a descendant of shinty. Scots were also heavily involved in two trades in particular: banking – John Richardson (1754–1831), the 'father of Canadian banking', was a Portsoy man who started in the military and the fur trade – and shipbuilding, developed by Christopher Scott (1762–1833), scion of a Greenock shipbuilders in New Brunswick. The workforces of both the North West Company, founded in Montréal in 1783 (the majority of merchants in the city were Scottish into the nineteenth century) and the late eighteenth-century Hudson's Bay Company (HBC, 1670) were predominantly Scottish, in the latter case as we saw in Chapter 2 overwhelmingly Orcadian. In 1800, 78 per cent of HBC employees were Orcadian, and a majority remained Scots with over 40 per cent from Orkney right through the 1824–70 period. In Nova Scotia, Sir Thomas Strange (1756–1841), Chief Justice 1789–97 thanks to his family's links to the Murray family of Lord Mansfield (he subsequently served sixteen years in the same role in the Madras Presidency), determinedly pursued an abolitionist agenda to make it difficult for colonists to retain control of their slaves.[26]

THE WEST INDIES

While Scots and Scottish education became prominent in North America and in determining the future direction of both the Canadian provinces and the Thirteen Colonies, Scots and their 'clannishness' were also becoming increasingly entrenched in the Caribbean. Place names such as Auchenbreck, Auchendown and Edinburgh Castle all reflected this influence, as did the seventeenth-century Scots (later Caledonian) Society and the Scottish influence on Jamaican Freemasonry. The 'red undergraduate gowns' of the University of the West Indies likewise later came to reflect Scottish practice.

Up to 20,000 Scots colonists and sojourners reinforced the numbers already in the Caribbean in the second half of the eighteenth century. Half of these came to Jamaica, where merchants, doctors, lawyers and estate managers made up some 70 per cent of the expatriate population. By 1754 'a quarter of Jamaica's landholdings were in Scottish hands' and this was only to increase after France ceded most of its West Indies territory to the British Empire in 1763. In that year, General Robert Melville (1723–1809), the son of a minister, a medical graduate and the inventor of the carronade gun, took over control of all the islands ceded by France: Dominica, the Grenadines, St Vincent and Tobago, with the exception of Grenada, where his control was intermittent. A British Army veteran of Culloden, Melville networked extensively through the Beggar's Benison sex club, which he brought to Grenada, becoming its Grand Master in the Tropics in 1764; it was evidently an alternative networking forum to the more conventional 'Scottish masonic lodges' on the traditionally British islands of Jamaica and St Kitts. Freemasonry in the Army and its impact on civil preferment was very likely a significant factor in imperial social mobility: the Royal Scots had their own lodges from 1732, and by 1756 over twenty regiments had joined them in the Craft. Military postings helped to drive Freemasonry's 'extensive role in colonial expansion in the Americas, the Caribbean and India'.[27]

Melville also founded the botanical garden at St Vincent in 1765. As an Edinburgh medical graduate, he had been exposed to the integration of botanical knowledge in the curriculum which – combined with the significant export of doctors from Scotland – was to prove so central in the development of botany in the British Empire (as indeed it did to the foundation of medical schools). Melville was a student of Glasgow and Edinburgh and enlisted his fellow Glasgow alumnus and contemporary, the surgeon George Young (c.1726–1803), to be the first superintendent of this garden. Young – quite possibly through the Melville connexion – became a correspondent with John Hope (1725–86), the Professor of Botany and Materia Medica (1760) at Edinburgh, being 'part of Hope's extensive global information exchange network stretching from Philadelphia to India'. This network was not a purely scientific one: Hope dreamed 'of diversifying the Scottish economy with cash crop transplants from different countries' and 'attempted to introduce ... Chinese tea ... and ... Chinese rhubarb'. One of his former students, William Roxburgh (1751–1815), a Madras/Chennai botanist, identified the potential of jute in the 1790s. This was to be a historic discovery which changed the Scottish and Indian economies, not least round Calcutta/Kolkata (where Robert Kyd from Angus had laid out the botanical garden in 1787): by 1914 there were 185,000 workers employed in the jute industry there. Thus the conflation between medicine, botany and commercialization led to a 'shift from botanical medicine to the manufacturing of plants such as cotton or jute', and indeed tea, where leading Scottish botanists in India such as 'John Forbes Rose, Hugh Falconer and William Jamieson' formed a dynasty at Saharanpur: the near 90 per cent in tea duty imposed by William Pitt in 1784 was no doubt a spur. By the nineteenth century, thanks to Scottish pioneers such as Charles Bruce (1793–1871), there were 800,000 hectares of tea production in Assam, a business in which medical botanists such as Archibald Campbell, the sixth of eleven children of the tacksman of Ardmore, remained prominent. The generalism of Scottish higher education promoted lateral thinking of this kind, and arguably that is the most grievous loss sustained by the system in the twentieth century. Contemporary research, for example Philip Tetlock and Dan Gardner's *Superforecasting: The Art and Science of Prediction* (2019), bears out the power of lateral thinking in the innovative diagnosis of future trends.[28]

After 1776, many Scots from the American colonies left for the West Indies, such as John Chisholm from Camden, South Carolina, who moved to Jamaica in 1782. Scots families in the Caribbean both married into families at home – George Ogilvy of Langley Park, Jamaica, married Barbara, the third daughter of James Dundas of that Ilk in Edinburgh in 1785 – and divided their career between the two locations: James Wordie (1799–1862) was successively minister in Kingston, Jamaica, and in Cupar in Fife. Sons sometimes came home to study and stayed, as did Andrew Watson, who studied at Marischal and became schoolmaster and minister in Tarland, or James and Robert Barrie, sons of a judge in the West Indies who came home to study in Glasgow. Scots also went to the Caribbean as indentured servants, forced to labour for their masters, as did Alexander Nichol, an Angus labourer indentured to Sir James Ogilvie on Antigua, or John Ross, a prisoner indentured for service on Jamaica with the Glasgow merchant John Ramsay.[29] It was not particularly uncommon for Scots in the Caribbean to send their children home to Scotland for schooling: some 8 or 9 per cent of pupils at Inverness Academy alone were from the Caribbean in 1804. Scots who married free women of colour often sent their children to Scots schools and these free women of colour themselves 'owned' significant numbers of the enslaved (5 per cent of the enslaved in Demerara, for example): the picture was a complex one.

Scottish culture was widespread in the West Indies, where the Scots increasingly 'presented themselves . . . as a distinctive national group'. Piping was adopted within Black communities, Scots words made their way into free Maroon culture, while Gaelic – often spoken by emigrants recruited to plantations owned by Gaelic-speaking landlords – also made its way into Jamaica. People of mixed Scots parentage played key roles in normalizing the contribution of the formerly enslaved to society. William Davidson (1781–1820), the son of a slave and the Attorney General of Jamaica, was sent to university in Aberdeen before being executed for his part in the Cato Street Conspiracy against the British Government in 1820: he sang 'Scots Wha Hae' as he was arrested. Robert Wedderburn (?1762–?1835), unacknowledged son of the Jacobite exile James Wedderburn (who died worth over £300,000) and the slave 'Rosanna', wrote *The Horrors of Slavery* in 1824, while Mary Seacole (née Grant) (1805–81), daughter of the Scottish officer James Grant and a free Jamaican woman of colour, imported her mother's tradition of medical expertise in nursing into the Crimea into the 1850s. Seacole achieved lasting fame for that contribution and for her (or her amanuenses) remarkably tolerant and good-natured *Wonderful Adventures of Mrs Seacole in Many Lands* (1857), which interestingly presented American racism as more endemic and bitter than its English equivalent. *Wonderful Adventures* certainly presents a comfortingly pro-British message: it must be remembered that it was produced and published with the aim of securing financial stability for its official author.[30]

Scottish capital – much of it the fruit of a slave economy – was also repatriated to Scotland for charitable purposes: in 1828 James Dick of Forres left £113,000 to support 'the salaries of parish teachers in the counties of

Aberdeen, Banff and Moray'. Dick wanted to see boys from his part of the country well prepared for King's and Marischal Colleges in Aberdeen so that they might receive an education that would give them the opportunity to succeed as he had done. In this respect, legacies and endowments frequently served as a central form of post-mortem networking with one's family, institutional or ecclesiastical association or geographical area, and this was to remain the case to some extent until the dissolution of the university bursary system in the 1980s.[31]

The 'vast majority' of Jamaican Scots were 'from middling and educated backgrounds', reflecting the Scottish education system's long-established capacity to produce more highly qualified Scots than the home economy had room for, and included younger sons such as George Munro, son to Sir Harry Munro of Foulis, who became a customs officer in Jamaica. Lawyers and estate managers were needed at scale for absentee landlords, while the threat to health in the Caribbean required doctors in plenty. Scots were up to a third of all white men in Jamaica, which itself was almost two-fifths of the total West Indian economy. As Lady Nugent observed in 1801, Scots are 'almost all the agents, attorneys, merchants, and shopkeepers . . . and really do deserve to thrive' in Jamaica. In Grenada, Scots 'possessed 40 per cent of all land planted in sugar and coffee'. There were a significant number of women among these landowning Scots.[32]

Slavery of course lay at the heart of the Caribbean economy. Governors were appointed in London and nominated their own councils, while 'white propertied inhabitants' elected island assemblies. Henry Dundas, 1st Viscount Melville (1742–1811) exercised a considerable influence in patronage across the Caribbean and this no doubt supported and was supported by the extensive presence of Scots throughout the governance of the region. The implications and consequences of Dundas's vast patronage network (the root of much of his power) for his equivocation over the pace of the abolition of slavery need to be borne in mind, as does his attempt to further expand that network by supporting aggressive action against France in the area in the 1790s. From the 1760s to the 1790s some 40 per cent of the council in Dominica and 27 per cent of the assembly were Scots; 39 per cent and 45 per cent respectively in Grenada; 23 per cent and 32 per cent in St Vincent;

and 62 per cent and 75 per cent in Tobago. Moreover, the British Caribbean was far from being a branch economy. As late as 1815, 17 per cent of British trade was with the Caribbean. Massive credit was extended by Scottish merchant firms to planters and traders, capital which was vulnerable in the event of insurrections by the enslaved in the West Indies, as it had been to colonial insurrection in North America. Men such as John Laing, Provost Marshal of Dominica, its governors Andrew Cochrane or Sir William Young, and James Campbell of Ornaig, commander of a native cavalry troop during the St Vincent and Grenada insurrection, helped keep order. Scots administrators often found themselves with a dilemma: as John Galt (1779–1839) put it, 'the right of the slave to liberty, is . . . universally admitted' but it is also 'correct and fair' to defend the rights of the planters. As the most powerful man in late eighteenth-century Scotland, Dundas lay at the heart of this paradox and thus on the wrong side of history.[33]

Inspired by the ideals of the French Revolution (which few Revolutionaries showed any interest in extending to non-white non-Europeans), Saint-Domingue (now Haiti) saw a major revolt of slaves, former slaves and their allies from French control in 1791, following the recognition of 'the constitutional basis of slavery' by the French Assembly on 15 May. Saint-Domingue was hugely important to the French economy, being the then kingdom's most profitable colony and 'the world's largest producer of sugar and coffee, along with significant amounts of cotton, indigo and cacao'. The island's sugar production required large quantities of slave labour and every year France imported thousands of slaves, many of whom died of yellow fever. The conditions were intolerable, and slave revolts an ever-present risk. François-Dominique Toussaint Louverture (c.1740–1803) emerged within a year as the leading figure of the revolution in Saint-Domingue. Though himself a slave owner on occasions, the radical nature of his movement was seen as a threat by the British Empire as well as France, and while it began to spread elsewhere in the West Indies, the British made the aim of seizing Saint-Domingue 'a key element in a wider strategy, adopted in 1793 by William Pitt and Henry Dundas: to conquer France's rich West Indian colonies, eradicate the French naval menace in the region and preserve the system of plantation slavery'. British forces accordingly seized Martinique, St Lucia and Guadeloupe, reinforcing slavery everywhere. Their commanders included many Scots. Dundas appointed Sir Ralph Abercrombie (1734–1801) – whose mother was a Dundas – as commander in chief, and he arrived in Barbados in March 1796. In the spring, Glasgow man John Moore (1761–1809) was largely responsible for taking St Lucia and reinstating slavery, albeit at some cost to his conscience, though at a much higher cost to the enslaved; John Knox played a significant role in taking St Vincent. In 1797, Brigadier General Thomas Maitland (1760–1824), son of the Earl of Lauderdale, landed in Saint-Domingue. Decimated by illness and outfoxed by Toussaint, he concluded a deal in July 1798, whereby Toussaint would refrain from attacking Jamaica (where Maitland's fellow Scots nobleman Alexander Lindsay, 6th Earl of Balcarres (1752–1825), was governor) in return for Great Britain withdrawing from Saint-Domingue. Two envoys on the island, Hugh Cathcart and Charles Douglas, reported back to Maitland and Balcarres on Toussaint's plans and actions; for his part, Toussaint continued to support – covertly at least – the liberation of Jamaica. Eventually his constitution, which was seen as a de facto declaration of independence, brought him down at the hands of Napoleon's forces, though the cost of their victory helped to ensure that the French leader sold his vast undeveloped American territories to the United States as the Louisiana purchase. The comparative neglect of Great Britain and the Scots' role in engaging with Toussaint's revolution perhaps tells its own tale about the embarrassing centrality of slavery to the West Indian economy.[34]

Scottish senior administrators like Ninian Home (1732–95), the Lieutenant Governor of Grenada, or Francis Humberston Mackenzie, Lord Seaforth (1754–1815), Governor of Barbados (1801–06), attempted to ameliorate the institution in which they were deeply implicated and which brought them personal benefit, with Seaforth pursuing a policy of making killing a slave a capital offence and allowing persons of colour to testify in court, but the Slaves Protection Act of 1805 did not undermine the entrenched economic injustice of chattel slavery. Home's similar paternalism in Grenada did him little good: he had after all purchased Paxton House in Berwickshire from the proceeds of his business as a planter. In 1795, a slave rebellion inspired by that of Saint-Domingue led to his murder. Home's attempts to reconcile Enlightenment ideas to the inherent injustice of the system on which his status rested mattered little to his captors, for whom his tyranny was no doubt more evident than his civility.[35]

By the time of Ninian Home's death, the abolition of slavery was moving towards the top of the political agenda. In Scotland, there was strong and rising support, tempered by the role linen exports played in clothing the large, enslaved labour force. The test cause (the Scottish legal term) brought by Joseph Knight against John Wedderburn of Ballindean (James's brother) regarding the legality of slavery in Scotland succeeded two earlier causes (Montgomery v. Sheddon (1756) and Dalrymple v. Spens and Henderson (1769–70)) which had never come to court because of the deaths of the complainer and defender respectively. It was another Scottish judge, William Murray, Lord Mansfield (1705–93), brother to the Jacobite Earl of Dunbar and himself accused of Jacobitism, who had found slavery unsupported in English common law in the Somersett judgment of 1772. Murray had himself adopted Dido Belle (1761–1804; see plate 12), his great-niece, who was the daughter of a slave and born into slavery, into his household as a member of his family in 1765: the film *Belle* (2013) is based on this. Joseph Knight's test cause went all the way to the Court of Session in 1777, and Henry Dundas, then Lord Advocate, defended Knight in the cause, which was couched in terms of a general denunciation of slavery. The outcome was recognized as being of national importance. Alexander Boswell, Lord Auchinleck (1705–82), said of Knight 'He is our brother, and he is a man, though not our colour' and that 'humanity and religion' as well as law forbade slavery, while Henry Home, Lord Kames (1696–1782), noted that the assembled judges were in session 'to enforce right, and not to enforce wrong'. The Knight cause reflected Scotland's legal and humane traditions powerfully, and three of the judges were significant Enlightenment thinkers in their own right: Kames, David Dalrymple, Lord Hailes (1726–92), who firmly backed Knight, and James Burnett, Lord Monboddo (1714–99). It must be remembered of course that while chattel slavery of white people was unknown in Europe, serfdom, which in certain circumstances allowed the labourer and his family to be bought and sold, was still in force until being abolished in British Hanover in the 1830s, the Austrian Empire in 1848, Prussia in 1850, Russia in 1861 and in Iceland as late as 1894.[36]

Scottish Enlightenment thinkers were divided on the issue of slavery, although a majority opposed it. Adam Smith strongly opposed enslavement (including 'domestic slavery'), while William Robertson (1721–93), possibly the world's first global historian in any modern sense, offered a comparative study of 'the simultaneous growth of the commercial and colonial systems' in the framework of a general undifferentiated humanity. Robertson noted the impact of Spain in the Caribbean including 'virtual annihilation of the Amerindian populations' and showed a persistent 'distrust of empire' in favour of 'independent states, inculcating civic virtues and bound together by networks of free trade'. For Robertson, Europeans acted 'in the pride of their superiority . . . to reduce' Africans to slavery. Robertson's anti-slavery analysis was utilized in the Knight cause. James Beattie (1735–1803) wrote passionately in *On the Lawfulness and Expediency of Slavery* (1778) that it was a matter of 'horror' that 'man, a rational and immortal being, should be treated on the same footing as a beast . . . or a piece of wood . . . merely because he is born in a certain country, or because he differs from us in the shape of his nose, the size of his lips, or the colour of his skin'. Beattie had a distaste for David Hume which seems to have been partly driven by a dislike for 'the latter's racism', as evidenced in his *Essay on National Character*; but, on the other hand, Hume also condemned slavery as 'more cruel and oppressive than any civil subjection whatsoever'. Lord Monboddo, although he extended the definition of Enlightenment humanity in the direction of the great apes, was rather more ineffective in the promotion of humane reform, supporting slavery in the Knight case because of the precedents for it in the ancient world. There was much inconsistency which an over-programmatic scholarship can lose sight of. Dundas both defended Knight with determination and yet later used his powers of parliamentary management to delay the possibility of action on abolition, and while James Boswell, 6th baron Auchinleck (1740–95), supported slavery in his uniquely fatuous *The Universal Empire of Love* (1791), he also passionately defended the rights of Samuel Johnson's heir, the ex-slave Francis Barber, from those who wished to defraud him and appears to have also supported Knight.[37]

In 1792, a tour of Scotland undertaken by the prominent abolitionist from Moffat, William Dickson (*c*.1751–1823), helped familiarize the Wedgwood 'Am I Not a Man and a Brother?' anti-slavery medallion in the country (see plate 13), and may have thus provided Burns with some of the language and imagery for 'A Man's a Man', first published three years later. There were well over 500 domestic petitions for the abolition of the slave trade in 1792, of which no fewer than 185 came from Scotland. Almost 11,000 signed in Edinburgh alone, a substantial proportion of the population, which stood at 93,000 in 1801 (of whom of course many were children). This was roughly three times Scotland's British population share per capita, and 'no Scottish petitions were sent to parliament opposing the abolition of the slave trade'. Scottish literature began to construct the worst excesses of slavery and racism as alien to true Scottish values. The critic Michael Morris has located this process as beginning perhaps with James Ramsay's *Essay on the Treatment and Conversion of African Slaves in the British Sugar Colonies* (1784), through John Ferrier's *The Prince of Angola* (1788), an adaptation of Southerne's *Oroonoko*, to texts such as Zachary Macaulay's *Negro Slavery* (1823). More explicitly Scots-language writing also appeared, such as Robert Burns' 'A Man's a Man' (1795) and Archibald MacLaren's *The Negro Slaves* of 1799 which gives 'Scottishness . . . a privileged role in the history of abolition', pitting Enlightenment hero McSympathy against English planters. MacLaren's text was underpinned in part by John Stedman's *Narrative of a Five Years' Expedition, Against the Revolted Negroes of Surinam* (1796), which provided a harrowing picture of the brutality experienced by Stedman in his service there with the Scots Brigade in the Dutch service in the 1770s. Stedman portrayed the Europeans as 'greater barbarians' than those they enslaved (see plate 14).[38] After 1833, when slavery was abolished throughout the British Empire (although several years of further indentured labour were prescribed for those freed), former Scottish slave owners of the Caribbean (rather than *in* the Caribbean, as 84 per cent of sugar estates were owned by absentees or minors) invested their money in coffee in Ceylon (Sri Lanka) where, though the workers might be paid, there was little freedom of labour and the margins remained handsome.[39]

INDIA

Scots – boosted by Walpole's earlier essays in patronage and desire 'to demonstrate the advantages of the Union' – also began to make major headway in British India with the East India Company (EIC) in the post-Culloden era, while continuing to be active in the EIC's Continental equivalents. In 1764, General Sir Hector Munro (1726–1805) became Commander-in-chief in British India, and in total over 2,000 Scots were recruited into the EIC between 1720 and 1780, not least under the controversial Governor and Governor-generalship of Warren Hastings in Bengal (1772–74) and India (1774–85), whose extended patronage to his 'Scotch guardians' was intended to maintain his position against critics in England. George Bogle (1746–81), son of a Glasgow tobacco lord, who undertook a historic mission to Tibet in 1774, acted as Hastings' private secretary, and like other such gatekeepers, was in an excellent position to support the benefiting of his fellow countrymen. Like many Scots in India, Bogle took an Asian woman (in his case Tibetan) as his partner: their three daughters returned to Scotland to be educated 'and married into the Ayrshire gentry'. Besides the support of gatekeepers like Bogle, Scottish opportunity in India also benefited from Dundas's relentless accumulation of patronage, which found new openings as 'King Harry' took on responsibility for the defence of India budget and later the Presidency of the Board of Control of the EIC, promising 'a steady stream of East India company appointments . . . in return for a guaranteed majority of Scottish votes in support of the government'. As the clergyman and wit Sydney Smith (1771–1845) sourly remarked, 'As long as he is in office . . . the Scotch may beget younger sons with the most perfect impunity. He sends them by loads to the East Indies, and all over the world.' Between 1790 and 1813, Scots continued to supply almost a quarter of new EIC officers.[40]

Scots had already provided more than one in five EIC officers in the ten years leading up to 1763. By 1760 'army patronage was a central agency' which helped to ensure Scottish interests in India; Scottish political culture also became gradually embedded in the subcontinent, though it often travelled under the radar as Scots frequently wished to participate in a 'British' identity which downplayed their disproportionately influential position. In Bengal between 1774 and 1785 at the height of the Hastings era, 47 per cent of EIC writer appointments went to Scots, 49 per cent of officer cadetships and 50 per cent of surgeon vacancies. A similar picture can be found elsewhere. In the 1780s, Scottish regiments were strongly engaged in India, where by 1762 Scots made up 21 per cent of commissioned officers in the Madras Presidency Army. In 1786, Sir Archibald Campbell of Inverneil (1739–91) became Governor of Madras. Sir Archibald, who had married the painter Allan Ramsay's daughter (he described Ramsay as 'the old Cadger . . . Rich and very Highly respected; a most Sensible, Pleasing Clever Old Man'), was not injurious to the Scottish cause in the Presidency. By 1800, Scots 'made up nearly 40 per cent of the medical establishment' in Madras (they later provided three of the first five directors of the Indian Medical Service), and had a strong position in the surveying service, where Colin Mackenzie became 'the first Surveyor-General of India' in the early nineteenth century. Almost half of the Council of Madras were Scots at one point, and they were generally 'prominent in activities like the armed forces and government contracting'. Specialist roles in the army could be especially remunerative: Captain Duncan MacLeod in the Engineers, for example, earned £1,800 a year, twelve times the salary of an infantry captain. Scots were adept at 'shaking the pagoda tree' in this way, and repatriating money following residence in India, although there was of course also a high mortality rate. However, the intensity of their networking, and its ability to exploit what the historian Andrew Mackillop has characterized as a predatory attack on Indian infrastructure and revenue systems, may have partially compensated, in that the process leading to the acquisition of private fortunes was itself often a shared enterprise.

The networks were very tightly drawn: a group of fewer than 200 Scots made enough capital in India to outstrip the reserves of their own domestic banking system. It was said that 'no man of any other nation can serve and survive in an Indian province, where the Chief is a Scot and where there is a Scot to be found', and if men served, women often benefited through the subsequent allocation of money earned in South Asia. Following the 1773 Regulating Act, which brought EIC activity partly under government control, Houses of Agency sprang up to channel business which was now circumscribed by regulation. In 1787, this situation was compounded when the new Governor General Charles Cornwallis's decrees 'ended all the private commercial activities of Company servants and stopped the privilege of sending funds home by bills of exchange'. This did not however bring daylight nabobbery to an end: Scots by this time were already 'almost 60 per cent' of the free merchants operating in Bengal, and were at the centre of the agency trade set up to circumvent EIC regulation. India thus remained 'the corn chest for Scotland' into the nineteenth century. There were 'some 214 Scottish-owned or controlled Houses of Agency between 1765 and 1834', with fourteen out of thirty-eight agencies in Calcutta/Kolkata alone controlled by Scots in 1813, the year in which Kirkman Finlay (1773–1842), one of the city's leading merchants, 'presented the Glasgow Chamber of Commerce's petition against the renewal of the East India Company's monopoly' to Parliament. Finlay's fellow High School of Glasgow alumni included Sir George Burns the future shipping magnate, James Ewing the sugar baron, Gilbert Hamilton, who had founded the Chamber of Commerce, John Hamilton the West Indies merchant who was five times Lord Provost, James Lumsden the co-founder of Clydesdale Bank, Charles Mackintosh the inventor of the raincoat and General Sir Thomas Monro, Governor of Madras, of whom more later.

Such professional and mercantile leadership was drawn from the minor baronial families and the middling sort (or 'middle class', as it increasingly came to be known in the eighteenth century) across Scotland: 90 per cent of Scots writers belonged to this group. However, even those below these strata could gain the opportunity to excel thanks to Scottish parochial school education (where the teaching day was longer than in England or France) and the bursary competitions of the universities, where, by 1800, 'Scotland had more places available in its five universities than any other country in Europe' per capita. This surplusage of talent continued to require opportunities abroad. Many Scots 'studied Indian languages to give them access to certain types of employment', and there was a recognition of the similarities between traditional Scots and Indian landholding systems, with the *sirkhar/zamindari* system being seen as similar to the Scots crown and its tenants-in-chief or chiefs of the name and tacksmen; Scots were however also engaged in reforming this system, as Alexander Read did in the Baramahal in the 1790s, to more closely resemble the new post-tacksman settlement of Scottish landholding, bypassing the *zamindar* class to deal directly with the *ryotwari* cultivators.[41]

Sir Thomas Munro, 1st Bart (1761–1827), Governor of the Madras Presidency at the same time as his acquaintance Mountstuart Elphinstone (1779–1859) was Governor of Bombay, was a typical successful Scottish figure of this era. Munro (whose grandson gave his name to the Munros, the 273 mountains in Scotland over 3,000 feet) was the son of a Virginia merchant who was ruined by the American War of Independence. Instead therefore of entering his father's business, Thomas joined the EIC as a cadet in 1779, serving in the years that followed under Sir Hector Munro of Novar and with John Munro of Teaninich (private secretary and interpreter to successive Commanders-in-chief in India and himself Quartermaster General at the age of 27 in 1802). It is not surprising in the circumstances of reporting to his namesake that young Thomas's career benefited (Thomas himself claimed to be a descendant of the Chief of the Name of Munro), no doubt aided by his investments in 'the indigo trade and other ventures'. Munro also showed significant sensitivity to Hindu practices including restoring the temple endowment at Mantrayalam, which continues to underpin his being 'still venerated as semi-divine in two temples in Andhra Pradesh'.[42]

Munro was one of the four officers who supervised Tipu Sahab's lands after the latter's defeat at Seringapatam in 1799 (see below), then lands formerly governed by the Nizam of Hyderabad, into which he formally introduced a British version of the *ryotwari* system, dealing directly with the cultivators of the land in respect of rents, which he then introduced in Madras/Chennai, shortly after taking up office as Governor. The system had the object of supporting 'numerous small and independent landholders' and allowing them to develop, as well as creating a transparent justice system. Rent 'in cash rather than kind was encouraged', reflecting the transition in the system of rents in Scotland in the previous century. Munro's preference for an increase in the number of small proprietors was again a reflection of contemporary Scottish trends. More controversial was his support for including Indians in governance, in direct contrast to the policy followed by Charles, 1st Marquess Cornwallis (1738–1805), as Governor General in 1786–93. Cornwallis's decision 'to exclude Indians from all senior positions in the army and administration' played its share in fostering a sense of haughty superiority with respect to British rule, as the historian David Gilmour has argued. By contrast, in his treatise 'On the Employment of Natives in the Public Service', Munro clearly stated that it was 'politically and morally wrong' to 'exclude Indians' from office, including high office. Munro's priority was 'to try to educate . . . Indian subjects so that one day they would be capable of governing themselves', and he told the EIC that they were 'not here to turn India into England or Scotland', but that they should 'work through . . . native systems' in preparation for the time when they should 'get out' of India. As someone who 'studied Persian and . . . local languages' and spoke Scots himself in private, Munro well knew what it was to inhabit two worlds. Shortly before dying of cholera in 1827, he is reputed to have seen 'near the temple of Veeranjaneya Swami . . . stretched between cliffs across the Papagni River, the Golden Garland of flowers which in the Ramayana had welcomed Rama after his victory over the demon king Ravana', a privileged vision which also 'presaged death'. Munro left over £150,000 (some £25 million at 2022 prices) and well symbolizes the combination of mystic, orientalist, innovative administrator and pragmatic, hardheaded man of action supported by and benefiting from the Scottish network in India.[43]

Speaking a number of native languages was a major benefit to an Indian career, so it was little surprise that Scots were prominent in this area. There was strong interest in Indian language and culture from a range of scholars including Alexander Hamilton (1762–1824), William Erskine (1773–1852), John Leyden (1775–1811), Alexander Murray (1775–1813) and Forbes Falconer (1805–53), and the value of such knowledge was recognized within the EIC. Alexander Dow (1735–79), the son of a Perthshire smuggler and a career EIC officer, learned Persian and published his *History of Hindustan* in 1772. William Robertson himself turned in his old age to India, publishing *An Historical Disquisition Concerning the Knowledge Which the Ancients Had of India* in 1791. Despite the by now extensive plundering of Indian assets by his fellow countrymen, Robertson was pro-Indian, and arguably saw Indian civilization as on a par with its European equivalent. As the historian Stewart Brown notes, Robertson observed that 'Europeans held up their own culture as a "standard of perfection" and viewed other peoples "with contempt"'. Robertson notes that, convinced of their superiority, 'Europeans thought themselves entitled . . . to exterminate' the natives of America. By contrast, the great Whig historian proclaimed 'the essential unity of humankind' and challenged 'the advance of imperialism', sticking firmly to the view – as we earlier saw in the American context – 'that the British and other European powers should content themselves with trade'.[44]

Serious intellectual and historical interest in India remained strong in succeeding generations, especially among those exposed to Robertsonian Enlightenment historiography through their education at the University of Edinburgh in particular. This has led to the argument – first broached by historian Jane Rendall in 1982 – that there was 'a distinctively Scottish school of East India Company administrators', of which Munro would be an obvious leading figure, as indeed were Elphinstone and his friend Major General Sir John Malcolm (1769–1833). Malcolm was one of seventeen children of an Eskdale tenant farmer, though his mother was better connected, and was related to the Elliotts of Minto, who subsequently opened up opportunities for him in India; in 1827 he succeeded Elphinstone as Governor of Bombay. Scots who studied India tended to be more sympathetic to 'the preservation of traditional Indian ways of doing things', and Elphinstone, Munro and Malcolm championed 'the need for indirect rule and the maintenance of indigenous social systems'. Elphinstone in particular was an opponent of his fellow Scot James Mill (1773–1836), whose *History of India* (1818), with its insistence on Hindu 'deceit' and 'perfidy', helped underpin the rise of Orientalist contempt in the British administration: Mill neither visited India nor possessed any of its languages.[45]

These Scottish administrators often brought their wealth and influence home (though Munro preferred 'the climate and country of India'), and in the tightly networked realm of Scottish society this new dimension had major effects, ones which were more geographically distributed than some of the wealth arising from the tobacco trade. As early as 1765, John Johnstone of Westerhall repatriated a fortune of at least £300,000 from India, and 25 per cent of Scottish civil servants in office in India between 1765 and 1774 returned with over £10,000, with more than one in ten bringing over £40,000 into Scotland. Many invested in industry or politics. In industry, advances in textile technology, such as bleaching for linen and the mechanization of spinning, though not weaving, which waited on Joseph-Marie Jacquard's major advance of 1804, were put to use in the development of new patterns reflective of Indian experience, both in carpets and particularly in Cashmere shawls produced in the textile capital of Paisley. In politics, by 1790 'over a quarter of Scottish constituencies were held by former EIC servants, a rate of political penetration unmatched anywhere' in the rest of the British Isles, while 'as late as 1844 . . . 23 per cent of civil servants' in India were Scots. John Galt's *The Last of the Lairds* (1826) and *The Member* (1832) deal with the influence of these 'nabobs' on Scottish and British society, while Walter Scott addressed imperialism in India obliquely in *Guy Mannering* (1815) and more directly in *The Surgeon's Daughter* (1826). Indian wealth – plundered, sequestered, gifted or otherwise acquired through business or bribery – made a significant impact on the Scottish economy.[46]

The victory of Major General Sir David Baird (1757–1829) of Haddingtonshire over the son of his former captor Sultan Fateh Ali Sahab Tipu (Tipu Sahab), Sultan of Mysore (1750–99), at Seringapatam in 1799 became one of the series of iconic Scottish victories in the era of the Napoleonic Wars. Combined with the highly military social leadership of (especially northern) Scottish society, it was clear that the Empire was disproportionately impacting – and as far as the elites were concerned, disproportionately benefiting – Scotland. This was a situation which in some respects was to continue deep into the twentieth century, and it was to be no coincidence that the decade the British Empire ended was the first decade in which Scottish nationalism achieved significant support (see Chapter 7). The Union succeeded primarily because of the opportunities it offered and the fact that these often did not stand in the way of Scots being visible abroad and organizing their own soft power networks. Scots might declare themselves British (or even English) on the international stage, but that did not mean they were integrated with their neighbours or wished to be so.[47]

COLLECTING, CULTIVATING AND EXPLORING

There were a number of fields in which Scots in the Empire early acquired a dominant or influential position, besides the established grounds of the military, medicine and law. One of these was missionary work, where by the nineteenth century men such as Alexander Duff (1806–78), John Wilson (1804–75) and John Anderson (1805–55) 'dominated missionary work in Calcutta, Bombay and Madras': kirks appeared in Bombay/Mumbai in 1814, in Calcutta/Kolkata and Madras/Chennai in 1818 and were soon also to be found in Colombo, Darjeeling, Penang, Singapore and Kuala Lumpur. At the Disruption of 1843, most of the kirks abroad remained with the Kirk of Scotland, but missionary activity moved largely into the hands of the Free Kirk, with a leavening of United Presbyterians. Scottish missionaries – like Scottish administrators – often learned Asian languages and contributed significantly to intercultural understanding. Some even converted in cultural terms themselves: Robert Morrison (1782–1834), who left for China in 1807, 'dressed in the Chinese fashion'. Others, such as James Legge (1815–70), who went on to be Professor of Chinese at Oxford, and John Ross (1842–1915), who translated the New Testament into Korean, made substantial contributions to spreading the Christian message abroad. David Livingstone (1813–73), the most famous of all Scottish missionaries and an inveterate opponent of the African slave trade, still enjoys a high reputation in Africa today: Livingstone and his role as one of the few white patrons 'of modern African nationalism' will be discussed in more detail in Chapter 5. For every Livingstone, however, there was more than one Alexander Duff, who argued that the massacres of the Indian Mutiny/Rebellion of 1857 'were the awful signs of God's displeasure for the failure to carry out Britain's responsibility to convert the Indian nation'.[48]

James Bruce of Kinnaird (1730–94) studied under the patronage of the Jacobite court's secretary Andrew Lumisden in 1762–63 before travelling through Africa in the person of an Arab doctor, El Hakim Yagoube, where he 'gained the trust of the Abyssinian court' (not least because of his linguistic abilities) and served as Gentleman of the Bedchamber and commander of the Emperor's household cavalry, before becoming the first European to identify the confluence of the Blue and White Niles. His vast *Travels* were published in 1785, by which time he had long retired to Kinnaird. The *Travels in the Interior Districts of Africa* (1796) of Mungo Park (1771–1806), the Selkirkshire man who was another of the Edinburgh-educated medical botanists, helped to emplace Africa in the Scottish imaginary. This was not yet a military or colonial interest, although the engagement of the Black Watch, the Cameron and Gordon Highlanders and the Perthshire volunteers in liberating Egypt from Napoleon was an initial stage of the mythologization of the Scottish soldier in Africa. General Sir Ralph Abercrombie and General Sir John Moore gave Scotland two commanding military martyrs in the Napoleonic Wars, while other successful figures such as Admiral Adam, 1st Viscount Duncan of Camperdown (1731–1804), also entered the public consciousness.[49]

Scottish gardeners and botanists had long had an international footprint, dating back at least to Robert Morison (1620–83), physician and gardener to the Duc d'Orléans, and mutual Franco-Scottish influence had played a significant role in the development of medicinal botany in Edinburgh, as we saw in Chapter 1. This was a two-way process. As the historian Douglas Hamilton puts it:

As the botanical gardens at Glasgow and Edinburgh were employed as teaching tools in medicine, and lectures in botany discussed the use of non-British plants, it is likely that West Indian knowledge filtered into the teaching of scientific subjects in Scotland by the latter part of the century.

Professor John Hope of Edinburgh – whom we have already met in the context of the Melville botanical garden in St Vincent – was 'instrumental in founding the Society for the Importation of Foreign Seeds and Plants' in 1763. Under Hope, 'Medical students were expected not merely to study the medicinal properties of plants but to develop an understanding of their cultivation in the botanic garden', and Hope, like other professors of medicine at Edinburgh after the medical school was founded with the support of the Royal College of Physicians in 1726, seems to have augmented his salary by engaging in business. The link between pharmacy and botany intensified in this context, and the 'relationship between health and the environment' came to receive attention it did not always gain elsewhere. Figures such as Alexander Garden (1730–91), scion of an Episcopalian and Jacobite family in Aberdeen, followed this botanical and medical route all his life, giving his name to the Gardenia. In addition, there was an extensive business in gardening more generally: manure was sold in the High Street of Edinburgh from 1725, and Robert Dickson's nursery, established near Hawick in 1728, was the first in Britain to grow and retail a large range of botanical produce. It was followed by others, such as the Perth Nursery of 1767. The Royal Caledonian Horticultural Society of Edinburgh (1809) likewise developed from eighteenth-century predecessors, and the Scottish garden business and Scottish gardens grew richer and more complex as plants often identified or secured by Scottish botanists abroad were sent home, such as the giant sequoia with an 11 metre girth at Cluny Gardens in Perthshire, introduced to Scotland by local collector John Matthew in 1853.[50]

Robert Brown (1773–1858) served as botanist to the 1801–05 Flinders expedition to Australia, while Charles Fraser (1788–1831) became the first supervisor of Sydney Botanic Garden, with Walter Hill (1819–1904) the first at Brisbane. Francis Buchanan 'took charge of the botanic garden at Madras in 1823 and brought back to Britain over 3,000 specimens of Indian plants', while Aberdonian Francis Masson (1741–1805), who sailed with Cook on HMS *Resolution*, sent back 500 plants from South Africa. James Drummond (1787–1863) had 'more than one hundred Western Australia plants . . . named after him', while James Hector and John Davidson were respectively responsible for the development of the botanic gardens at Wellington and Vancouver: Hector worked to preserve and expand New Zealand's declining forest areas. Closer to home, Andrew Carlisle noted in 1758 that 'most of the head gardeners of English noblemen were Scotch'; true to form, James Stuart, 3rd Earl of Bute (1713–92), Great Britain's first Scottish prime minister, 'established Kew Gardens as a centre of botanic knowledge'. Thomas Blackie, trained in Edinburgh, took over Kew and introduced the *jardin anglais* to France, while John Loudon (1783–1843) invented 'new ways of constructing iron-framed greenhouses which helped make possible the great public greenhouses of the mid Victorian period'. David Douglas (1799–1834) of the Douglas Fir, and Archibald Menzies (1754–1842), who 'introduced the Monkey Puzzle', are among other exponents of this field of expertise. Two features stood out in both these developments: the integration of botany into the medical curriculum, still evident in the gardens linked to three of the Scottish universities (Glasgow lost its rather splendid three hectares as part of the process that led to the move to the west end in 1870), and the boost Scottish practical gardening received internationally from its ability to address adverse climatic conditions.[51]

The botanical and zoological collections of Empire were, in their turn, central to the rapid advance of classificatory and taxonomical thinking, as intellectual models had to be modified to accommodate extensive new evidence. Scotland and Scots were to the fore in this process because of the broad curriculum of their universities and the creation of the major curricular connexions noted above. William Hunter (1718–83), whose collection formed the first public museum in Scotland (1807), was perhaps the first figure to arrange a collection ranging from the anatomical to the numismatic along taxonomical lines, definitively replacing the 'cabinet of curiosities' model of pre-Enlightenment collecting. But Hunter did not operate in a void. When he first came down from Glasgow to London in 1740, his fellow Scot and doctor James Douglas (1675–1742), Physician Extraordinary to Queen Caroline, gave Hunter his bearings and introductions. Hunter lived with the midwifery pioneer and fellow Lanarkshire man William Smellie (1697–1763) in Pall Mall and acted initially as his assistant, before becoming both one of the leading collectors of his day and a pioneer of modern surgery, from which he often earned over £1,000 a month. In Glasgow, John Anderson argued for the extension of the teaching collection model from its botanical base to a much broader spectrum of knowledge, and advocated a university teaching museum in 1765: eventually Hunter's collection, bequeathed on his death in 1783, would become the innovation sought by Anderson, while serving a wider public when it opened as Scotland's first public museum in

1807, with heating and ventilation specified by James Watt (1736–1819). At its entrance was a (now lost) bust of Francis Hutcheson (1694–1746), whose pioneering work on the emotional basis of morality and on colonial rights had so influenced the political conception of the fledgeling United States, and had also influenced Hunter and his network – including the painter Gavin Hamilton (1723–98). Hamilton's own pioneering and emotionally charged history genre painting of *The Abdication of Mary, Queen of Scots* (after 1765), done for James Boswell, is now in the possession of the Hunterian as a visual representation of the Hutchesonian alliance between politics and sentiment which was finding its historical outlet in the work of William Robertson and would feature centrally in the novels of Walter Scott. Hamilton was in contact with Lumisden at the Jacobite court, and Robert Strange (1721–92), the Jacobite engraver married to Lumisden's sister, also played a major role in supporting Hunter's collecting. Meanwhile, John Anderson had initially commissioned Watt to repair the model of the Newcomen steam engine held by the University of Glasgow in 1763, and subsequently discussed with him the limitations and possibilities of steam. Moreover, in his will Anderson had instructed the establishment of an inclusive higher education institution (Anderson's Institution, now the University of Strathclyde), which was to be 'the first regular institution in which the fair sex have been admitted . . . on the same footing as men'. Thomas Garnett (1766–1802), its first professor, taught almost 1,000 students in 1796–97, half of whom were women, and as late as 1840 there were 130 women registered in the Natural Philosophy (Physics) class. George Birkbeck (1776–1841), Professor of Natural Philosophy at Anderson's, went on to found in 1823 the London institution which still bears his name. This is only one microhistory of a Scottish intellectual network.[52]

The commanding position this network achieved in medicine (John Gregory (1724–73), Sir John Forbes (1767–1861), John Abercrombie (1780–1844), Neil Arnott (1788–1874) and Sir James Reid (1849–1923) were all physicians to the Crown from one provincial burgh grammar school alone), was mirrored in the universities more generally, with the ascendancy of classicists like Thomas Blackwell (1701–57) and philosophers such as James Beattie (1735–1803), David Fordyce, pioneer of student-centred education (1711–51), William Hamilton (1788–1856), Thomas Reid and Adam Smith. There was an intense ethos of professional localism, whereby the distinguished pupils of burgh schools went on to staff the local university and the major professions. In larger cities, such as Glasgow, they were somewhat less likely to seek their fortune in the British Empire than in smaller ones, in part perhaps because Glasgow itself was a large enough entrepôt for international businesses to be based there. Between one-third and two-fifths of the former pupils of Aberdeen Grammar School opted for imperial careers, whereas this seems to have been the case for only some 10 per cent of the distinguished former pupils of its Glasgow counterpart. But wherever able Scots of professional, or often more modest backgrounds, were schooled in Scotland, a more and more complex set of associational, geographical and educational networks sustained possibilities and opportunities that would have been far beyond the reach of their predecessors before the Union of 1707.[53]

4

SCOTTISH ROMANTICISM, TOURISM, CAPITALISM AND CLEARANCE

ROMANTICISM AND THE NATIONAL IMAGE

Like the Enlightenment, the Romantic era saw an international movement inflected in differing national forms. Enlightenment and Romanticism were intimately connected: in general the first sought universalizable principles of intellectual enquiry and human conduct; the second focused on the unique particularity of experience, whether personal, locational, national or emotional. Romanticism in these islands was not the opposite of Enlightenment, although it was in these senses its counterpart. It depended on the emotional basis – and thus particularity – of human vision and decision argued for by Francis Hutcheson (1694–1746), David Hume (1711–76) and other Enlightenment thinkers, and, in its reforming and identitarian moments, Romanticism drew both on the stadial historiography of the Scottish Enlightenment and – as the critic Cliff Siskin points out – on the rational ideal of System itself. While the Enlightenment tended to involve the application of reason to knowledge in a manner likely to result in a process leading towards the establishment or maintenance of universal truth claims, Romanticism frequently focused on the particularity of place and culture and its aesthetic, linguistic or social effects, but it often did so in a manner which relied on the systematization of human nature found in Enlightenment thought. Such thought itself arose out of technological developments of measurement, combined with a language of personalization and objects which sustained – and composed – personal moments and memory. Cocker's *Arithmetic*, with its recognizably modern problems, 'the spring balance which was to revolutionise watches' and make time personal, milled coinage and mass production in glass and ceramics and the earliest fashion magazines, such as *Le Mercure Galant*, all appeared in the 1660s and 1670s. The analogue data revolution of the Enlightenment was accompanied by the personalization of its processes, and Romanticism was a key outcome of this process.[1]

Scotland's Romanticism was nationally distinctive and remains so, for the legacy of Scotland's national Romanticism was the creation and then perpetuation of a national brand. There were two main reasons for this: the global influence of James Macpherson (1736–96), Robert Burns (1759–96), Sir Walter Scott (1771–1832) and George Gordon, Lord Byron (1788–1824), and the fact that the inaccessible landscapes of Scotland had once given rise to the greatest internal threat faced by the British Empire and were now – at least in popular accounts – the source of its external military power. These reasons were in their turn supported in the United Kingdom by the growth of internal tourism driven by the disruptions of the Revolutionary and Napoleonic wars on the Continent. All of these writers – but particularly Macpherson, Scott and Byron – drew on the confluence of Scottish landscape and militant masculinity which had already begun to emerge in the mapping of Roy and Sandby and the narrative surrounding the performance of Scottish troops in imperial war. Theirs was a magical landscape full of mighty men, a countryside as violent, sudden, torrential and dark as the moods and valour of its inhabitants. To many across the world Scotland remains this country of bagpipes and tartan, mountain and flood, castles, clans and conflict, whisky and golf, a territory simultaneously rural and organic, long associated with the supernatural. That Scotland is a product of Scottish Romanticism.[2]

In characterizing this (or indeed any other) national Romanticism, it is important to stress that the term 'Scottish' represents much more than an adjective. In general terms throughout Europe, both Enlightenment and Romanticism strongly bear the image of national cultures; indeed often they served to co-create them. Wordsworth's Lakes, the German stories of the Grimm brothers, the secret native Scotland of warlocks and dancing in *Tam o'Shanter* (1791) or the struggles of Italian patriotism against Spanish power in Manzoni's *I promessi sposi* (1827) all served to imagine and represent aspects of a national self. Many of the writers of this era became central to the creation of their respective national literatures: Burns in Scotland,

Mickiewicz in Poland, Pushkin in Russia, Goethe and Schiller in Germany. Such figures were often the subject of statuary, festivals or other large-scale public efforts to create *lieux de memoire*, places of public memory, which simultaneously celebrated the writer and the nation in a manner not entirely deriving from, but strongly influenced by, the role of the *fêtes révolutionnaires* in creating a shared sense of a national and Republican self through public monuments and festivals in the revolutionary France of the 1790s. Early examples of this included the return of Mozart's sons to Salzburg and the Mozart Monument of 1842, the return of Burns' sons to Ayr and the Ayr Festival of 1844 and the Beethoven Festival in Bonn, organized by Franz Liszt in 1845. Out of this movement towards the conflation of artist, place and nation came – on a lower register of national particularism – the phenomenon of literary tourism, the Burns Country, Scott Country and Wordsworth Country of the nineteenth- and twentieth-century tourist industry, as well as the idea of the folk tale and folksong and the enthusiasm for these forms by collectors who did much to create the modern idea of 'folk' literature while imagining they were preserving it.[3]

National culture is thus central to Romanticism. James Macpherson, born into a Jacobite family (over a dozen of whom, including his Gaelic scholar cousin Lachlan Macpherson, fought with the Prince in 1745), grew up in a world where Cluny, the Chief of his Name, was on the run till 1755, hiding on his own lands, chiefly in 'The Cage' high on Ben Alder. Just as the Jacobite officer Alasdair MacMhaighstir Alasdair (*c*.1698–1770) wrote a great elegy for the dying days of MacDonald power in *Birlinn Chlann Raghnaill* (Clanranald's Galley, 1754), so in *Fingal* (1761) and his other Ossian poetry, Macpherson produced a Scottish epic of defeat and loss in honour of Fingal (*Fionn mac Cumhaill*) ostensibly written by his son Ossian: later the followers of Fingal/Fionn, the Fianna, would give their names to the Fenians and activist Irish nationalism.

Macpherson's Ossian poems appeared to combine the unselfconsciousness of Homeric epic with the sensibilities of the Enlightenment, and as a consequence were instantly successful, being translated into French in 1774, Russian in 1777 and Polish in 1782, as well as into many other languages, and cited as early as 1767 as a language for Corsican nationalism. Friedrich Gottlieb

Klopstock (1724–1803) introduced Ossianic emotionalism into German verse, and Friedrich Wilhelm Rust (1739–96) first set *Ossian* to music, initiating a sequence of over 300 compositions. 'Nostalgia' first appeared as a term in English in the 1750s, and Macpherson amply catered for this emotion in his presentation of a remote martial past which was also a thinly disguised version of the recent political crisis that had convulsed Scotland. His polite representation of primal violence was the drawing room counterpart to the myth of the Scottish soldier's unique martial valour, and Macpherson was duly the subject of military enthusiasm. As the music historian James Porter notes, the Ossianic poems emerged into a Europe full of the 'military dead', given the estimated 800,000 to 1 million casualties of the 1756–63 war. These poems thus caught the need for a mood of mourning, nostalgia and military celebration. Napoleon – perhaps here drawing on his Corsican origins – was a great advocate of Macpherson's work, and had Jean-Auguste-Dominique-Ingres (1780–1867) paint the painting now known as *The Dream of Ossian* for the imperial bedchamber in 1811, while Anne-Louis Girodet's (1767–1824) painting *Ossian Receiving the Ghosts of Fallen French Heroes* (1805) was only one of the French artworks which rendered Macpherson's work (as later Scott's) an important part of the French imaginary during the Napoleonic Wars and restoration of the monarchy (see plate 15). On the other side of the great conflict which convulsed Romantic Europe, Field Marshal Alexander Vasdevich Suvorov (1729–1800) had the first Russian translation of Ossian dedicated to him, and was himself praised in Ossianic terms by the poet Gavrila Derzhavin (1743–1816). Field Marshals Akhsey Yermolov and Alexander Ivanovich Kutusov read *Fingal* 'to each other on the eve of the battle of Borodino' in 1812, in which Kutusov perished, while Ossianic poetry was also popular among the Russian Decembrists of 1825. Macpherson was not a 'forger' as he was dubbed by his contemporary enemies and by the careless critics of posterity, for he extended and did not invent a tradition. This extension was primarily one of sensibility and veiled contemporary reference. The epics of *Fingal* and *Temora* (1763) have a heroic and an elegiac quality which expressed Scottish distinctiveness while depoliticizing it through sentimentality and nostalgia, leavened with some imperial references which – to the rage of Irish commentators – turned Fingal from a shared Gaelic hero to a

Scottish one who prevailed in Ireland. *Fingal* contained more original tradi-
tional material than its successor *Temora*, but both epics and the ancillary
Ossian poetry produced by Macpherson became the epicentre of both a
culture war in the British Isles and a European enthusiasm for the authentic
voice of this *montagnard* (mountaineer) nation off the edge of the Continent.
Like the 'Swiss self-identification' with Albrecht von Haller's (1708–77)
Die Alpin (1729) and Johann Georg Zimmerman's (1728–95) *Von dem
Nationalstolze* (1758), Scotland's writers also used its landscape to express its
inhabitants' passion for liberty. Macpherson's Ossian poetry proved hugely
influential. Almost immediately, the example of *Ossian* led to imitative created
epics like the *De Hollandische nati* (The Dutch Nation, 1812) in the
Netherlands and the *Kalevala* (1835) in Finland, together with other similar
texts in Catalonia, Poland, Slovenia and elsewhere, besides their musical equivalents such as Wagner's *Ring Cycle* (1869–76). Macpherson wrote of the
nobility and warrior spirit of the ancient Caledonians in a manner which
chimed with the martial values of the emergent myth of the Highland soldier,
who seemed to be the descendant of the Scottish writer's Fingalian heroes.
Visitors came to see the country of Fingal, and new and old locations encouraged tourism. The so-called Fingal's Cave on Staffa was identified as such in
1774, while 'The Hermitage', built in 1757 in Perthshire, was renamed
'Ossian's Hall' from 1783, and the painter Alexander Runciman (1736–85)
decorated Penicuik House in Midlothian with a magnificent frieze of Ossianic
heroes after his return from Rome, where he was acquainted with the Jacobite
court. By 1784, a list was published in Perth of Fingalian wonders that it
would be possible to encounter on a day trip, while by the time of Felix
Mendelssohn's (1809–47) *Fingal's Cave* section in his Hebrides Overture of
1829, Ossian had become central to the realization of Scotland in the European
imagination. The name survives in both the context of Scotland's brand and
the more banal reference of mere location, as in Ossian Road in London N4,
Ossian Studios role-playing games, Ossian wines and the Ossian Rotary Club.[4]

Early on, language became very important to the Romantic concept of
nationality, not least as a result of the work of Johann Gottfried Herder
(1744–1803), who supported the development of German Romantic
nationalism by extolling the virtues of the German language as an expression

9. James Macpherson (1736–96), compiler of *Ossian*. Various artists.

of the German people, and linguistic nationalism of the Herderian type was later to be visible throughout Europe from the Czech lands to Ireland, perhaps most dangerously in Ernst Moritz Arndt's toxic song, *Was ist des Deutschen Vaterland* (1813). In Scotland, where Gaelic was in marked retreat, the phenomenon of national literary expression in this period often took the form of a hybrid language formed of a register stretched across both Scots and English. Scots, the speech of much of the country for many centuries, was strongly related to English, with little variation in grammar and syntax but substantial divergence in vocabulary (there are some 100,000 Scots words) and modes of expression. English tended to take more of its borrowed vocabulary from French and Latin through Norman French, whereas Scots took it directly from France; Norwegian influences were also strong in the language, and indeed in Shetland a form of Norwegian, Norn, was spoken until the nineteenth century.[5]

Scots was the perfect vehicle for the double identity of the country which grew up throughout the post-Culloden era as a private, local or domestic nation within a wider imperial and international British polity. Although there were attempts to eradicate Scots, it also had its defenders, and by the nineteenth century the language was generally accepted – thanks in no small part to its use by Burns and Scott – as a situationally appropriate vehicle for poetry or vernacular speech in prose fiction. Scots could be expressed intensively or left as the merest seasoning on standard English providing one was master of both: a variable register based on the national relationship to the English language could simultaneously reveal the self as 'English-speaking' in a metropolitan sense and at the same time present local variety best understood by insiders. The first writer to integrate Scots constructively into English (he was wont to use the term 'British' for this hybrid, but it did not catch on) was Allan Ramsay (c.1684–1758), who, as we saw in Chapter 2, originated the term 'Doric' to describe Scots as opposed to the English 'Attic': both variants of Greek, neither the superior of the other. Although Allan Ramsay himself was a Jacobite (his son, also Allan Ramsay, painted a portrait of Charles Edward at Holyrood in 1745 before going on to become court painter to George III), the use of Scots in tension or hybrid register with English in poetry or prose did not necessarily indicate profound political dissent, simply the preservation of a distinctive national voice within the Great Britain now rising to be a superpower.

Two men in particular put Scots on a global map: Robert Burns and Walter Scott. Burns first recited his poetry in Edinburgh in the drawing-room of Jane Gordon (1748/9–1812) Duchess of Gordon, who acted as one of his patrons, and was – as we shall see – central to the rehabilitation of tartan. Burns' poetry and song expressed a deep and universal humanity, born out of Enlightenment values of scepticism and sympathy, radical in tone and allusion but frequently indeterminate politically, comprehensive in expression and aspiration while rooted in the language and life of provincial Ayrshire farms and smallholdings. Burns was hugely more sophisticated as a major Romantic poet than his most ardent supporters often give him credit for, and while he had his own anxieties over farming and rents, he gave these universal voice at a time when in different parts of Scotland people were leaving the land for cities or else struggling to gain economic benefit from small landholdings. In large parts of the country land had been subdivided for wartime labour and returning soldiers in lieu of their bounty, which landlords often spent and did not reinvest. Burns' poetry not only used Scots as a national marker, but even – and this is still poorly understood – used different dialects of it within the same poem in order to convey different connotations or readings in tension with one another.[6] Both a poet and a collector and editor of Scottish song, Burns' work was first of all translated into German from 1795, where he appealed both as an Enlightenment radical and humanitarian and as a kind of one-stop shop for access to the authentic folk traditions of the peasantry which Herderian followers like the Grimm brothers were collecting in the German states. Here, Burns' anthem of universal brotherhood, 'A Man's A Man', first published in 1795 and itself probably influenced by the abolitionist William Dickson's popularization of the Wedgwood medallion during his 1792 tour of Scotland, may have influenced the revised text of Friedrich Schiller's 'Ode to Joy'. Now the tune of the Anthem of Europe, the 'Ode' was set by Beethoven in his Ninth Symphony in 1824 and, translated as *Trotz Alledem*, became a song of Austrian and German radicalism from 1848 to the present.[7]

'AULD LANG SYNE'

'Auld Lang Syne', now often accounted the second most widely used song globally after 'Happy Birthday to You', has a much longer history since it appeared in Robert Burns' version in 1796. Sung in benefit concerts and entr'actes from the beginning of the nineteenth century, it was also inscribed on a snuff box given to George IV on the occasion of the royal visit to Edinburgh in 1822 when the king also enjoyed a 'gala performance' of *Rob Roy Macgregor*, or 'Auld Lang Syne'. From 1818 at least, it was sung at Burns Suppers, first appearing in Philadelphia. The radical Andrew White, transported for his part in the 1820 Rising (discussed later in this chapter) referred to it as a New Year song as early as 1822. Used in political discussion in England from the 1817 Pitt dinner and in Continental opera, ballet and drama in the 1820s, by 1850 it had become – like 'Rule Britannia' and 'God Save the Queen' – a national song, performed on social occasions to express Scottish nationality on British ceremonial and imperial occasions. In the 1830s it was being sung by enslaved people in the Caribbean, and from at least 1852 was being played when British ships left port; by 1864 at the latest it was also used in ceremonies when 'regiments bade farewell to their old colours'. Used in the United States by Union troops in the Civil War and during Lincoln's funeral, and in British politics as a political anthem associated with W.E. Gladstone, it was also the subject of a statue erected in Central Park in the 1860s and provided a reference point in Victorian fiction and popular culture. In 1877, Alexander Graham Bell used it to demonstrate the telephone, and it was one of the first songs recorded for gramophone in 1890. In 1892, the Burns scholar James Dick termed it the 'most widely diffused song in the civilised world', and by this period it was regularly being played as a New Year song on both sides of the Atlantic. It subsequently became a song of the Scout movement, and was played at graduations in the US and Asia, where it was played at the British exit from Hong Kong in 1998, and can be heard signifying closing time in Japanese bars and supermarkets. 'Auld Lang Syne' is also played at funerals in Taiwan, as well as providing the closing ritual for millions who attend Burns Suppers worldwide, as it has done since at least 1890. Translated into many languages, it even made a brief appearance as the national anthem of the Maldives, as the Burns scholar Morag Grant informs us.

'Auld Lang Syne' was popularized as a New Year song for radio by Canadian musician Guy Lombardo at the Roosevelt Hotel in New York from 1929, and later emerged in transmuted form in the hands of Jimi Hendrix, Elvis Presley and Bruce Springsteen among many others. The song has made repeated appearances in American cinema, most often in a romantic context with a New Year reference – *Holiday*

(1938) is an early example. Such repeated uses in modern culture demonstrate 'Auld Lang Syne''s symbolic power, conveying overwhelming sentiment in a language not quite like English, where the characters do not always know what the words 'even mean' and sometimes say so. ('Old Long Since' is not an adequate translation and 'Old Long Ago' is not either; nor is it useable English. Scots allows for the use of a double intensifier, and 'syne' itself has multiple meanings, which allow the term to have an evocative ambiguity as well as a quality of positive nostalgia unavailable in short English words.) In films such as *When Harry Met Sally* (1989), *Sleepless in Seattle* (1993) and *Sex and the City* (2008) the song has played out as a moment of romantic climax and change, symbolized in the changing of the year. From *It's a Wonderful Life* (1946) onwards it has also been a Christmas song. Less positively, 'Auld Lang Syne' has been used to reference the loss of the antebellum South. The Cameron family in D.W. Griffiths' *Birth of a Nation* (1915) reflect the core Scottish martial values of bravery, chivalry and openhearted decency transplanted into a defence of white supremacy in the Confederate states before, during and after the Civil War. The 'Little Colonel' Cameron is presented in the film as the chief defender of racial politics against Black rights and miscegenation who keeps the world of 'Auld Lang Syne' alive in his bravery and resourcefulness in founding the Klan. The myth of the 'Celtic South', argued for in the historian James Michael Hill's *Celtic Warfare* (1986) and still widespread today, was deeply reinforced by Griffiths' film, originally to be titled *The Klansman*. Convivality, fraternal organizations (Grant argues that the crossing of arms which closes communal singing of the song derives from Masonic practice), social occasions and nostalgia for friends and the happy years spent with them are not always positive emotions, but Burns' version of this ancient – and in his day Jacobite – Scottish song in praise of a lost past (as all pasts are) is in many respects the signature tune of the Scottish brand (see plate 16).[8]

In the United States, Burns appealed as an advocate of liberal anti-monarchical America in opposition to the tyrannies of old Europe: Mark Twain (1835–1910) memorably described the American Civil War as a conflict between Scott (whose mediaevalism he satirized in *A Connecticut Yankee in King Arthur's Court* (1889)) and Burns, with Burns standing for the Union and Scott for the Confederacy. Burns was certainly used as a political symbol of reform in the United States from the early nineteenth century: 'A Man's A Man' became not only a song of Romantic brotherhood and German nationalism, but also, in the hands of Frederick Douglass (1817–95) and others, by building on its apparent reference to the Wedgwood anti-slavery medallion, became an anthem of the abolitionist movement in the United States. (Douglass, born Bailey, chose his own name in honour of Scott's *Lady of the Lake*.) The appropriation of the poet as standing for the best in American values was a persistent tradition: in 1925, the US Consul in Edinburgh, W.R. Bonney, described Burns' outlook as 'woven into the warp and woof of the Bill of Rights'. Burns made his appearance in regular US politics too, being (successfully) used as a basis for satire against John Quincy Adams by Andrew Jackson's supporters in the 1828 presidential election; the poem 'John Anderson, my jo' was also used by Lincoln's supporters in 1860, and was mocked in a Confederate version. In 1867, Lincoln's widow made a pilgrimage to the poet's birthplace: her husband, a great advocate of the poet, was caricatured in a kilt in *Vanity Fair* in 1861. Edinburgh erected the first statue to Lincoln outside the United States, and the first statue to Burns outside Scotland was erected in New York.[9]

If the United States tended to portray Burns as a revolutionary on the US model, in Canada he tended to be a representative of 'local and imperial' identity and a model for Canadian writing. The poet spread throughout the British Empire and its current and former colonies as a symbol of Scottishness and universal humanitarian values. St Andrew's Day dinners – for example at Pittsburgh in 1791 – began to celebrate him, and five years after his death the first Burns Supper, as we now understand the event, was held in his home town of Alloway. St Andrew's Day dinners were one of the roots of Burns Suppers; another were the Fox Dinners of 24 January for the Whig political hero Charles James Fox (1749–1806), whose birthday was very close to

Burns'. There were other related events in the patriotic and radical calendars in particular, such as the use of Burns toasts at a meeting in support of the Peterloo radical Henry Hunt in Paisley in 1822.[10] By the time of Burns' centenary in 1859 (which itself saw over 1,000 Burns Suppers globally, many addressed by the good and the great), there had already been thousands of recorded Burns dinners and events. Burns Clubs formed across the British Empire and were – unlike many St Andrew and Caledonian Societies of the time – 'generally open in their membership criteria to all ethnicities, which facilitated the dissemination of aspects of Scottishness throughout the Empire'. Today an estimated 9.5 million attend a Burns Supper every year in over 100 countries, with many more local and familial celebrations, and the Scottish haggis industry survives largely on this one event alone (see plate 17).[11]

Burns was intensely a poet both of locality and universality, a writer whose supreme mastery of evoked sentiment – Lincoln perceptively noted that 'Burns never touched sentiment without carrying it to its ultimate expression and leaving nothing further to be said' – allowed him to be claimed by radicals and conservatives, communists and freemasons alike.

10. Robert Burns' birthplace, Alloway near Ayr: an image of autochthonous, agricultural and pastoral Scotland which serves as a badge of authenticity and integrity of feeling and judgement to set against metropolitan sophistication.

His nature poetry (including the extraordinary transformation of folklore concerning birch and hawthorn into an analysis of erotic longing) and alignment of human and animal experience in 'To a Mouse' and elsewhere strongly influenced John Clare (1793–1864) and many of the later English Romantics. Burns presents Enlightenment ideas while interrogating them: the lines 'O wad some Pow're the giftie gie us/ *To see ourselves as others see us!*' for example, are a paraphrase of Adam Smith in his *Theory of Moral Sentiments* (1759, 6th edition 1790) placed in a comic context of greed and sexual desire; both these appetites are directed at a pretentious lady, whose appearance in the latest fashions bears witness to her invocation of both, rendered ridiculous by the louse who feeds off her, as the watching man would like to do. Burns puts his trust – following the affective morality championed by Hutcheson and Hume – in mutual affection which shows a forbearance for mutual self-interest:

> It's no in titles nor in rank;
> It's no in wealth like Lon'on Bank,
>   To purchase peace and rest.
> It's no in makin muckle, mair;
> It's no in books; it's no in Lear [learning],
>   To make us truly blest:
> If happiness hae not her seat
>   And centre in the breast,
> We may be wise, or rich, or great,
>   But never can be blest:
> Nae treasures nor pleasures
>   Could make us happy lang;
> The heart ay's the part ay
>   That makes us right or wrang. ('Epistle to Davie')

The importance of the 'heart', in so many ways the central organ of Scottish Enlightenment morality, is the foundation for Burns' global humanitarian appeal, acknowledged in the nineteenth century by nationalist language movements from Norway to the Czech Republic and in the twentieth and twenty-first by a vast range of figures from Sun Yat-Sen (1866–1925), leader of the Kuomintang and president of the Chinese Republic, who joined the Burns Club of London, to Maya Angelou (1928–2014) and Kofi Annan (1938–2018), who invoked the poet as a symbol of universal humanity in his 2004 Robert Burns Memorial Lecture to the United Nations.[12]

Scottish Romanticism was strongly oriented towards creating a national story which reflected a taxonomy of glory, a desire to celebrate a heroic past, not only in the writing, collection and adaptation of Macpherson, but also in Burns' claim to national bardic status.[13] Both were transcended by Sir Walter Scott's development of a narrative which glorified the history of Scotland in detail, accepting that the independence of the country was ended but also suggesting that certain issues remained unaddressed. Writing at the same time as figures such as Heinrich Lulen (1778–1847) and Leopold von Ranke (1795–1886), who were seeking to use history to 'demonstrate the emergence of national coherence', a 'fatherland' notion of history to parallel the contemporary development of the national epic (and one still with us as I suggest in the Introduction), Scott's very focus on Scotland was arguably radical in its continued case for the country as a real entity, albeit one imperilled by contemporary trends.[14]

Scott's poetry from *The Lady of the Lake* (1810) onwards became tourist travelogues of Scotland, designed to draw visitors to a country with a colourful (and apparently safely completed) past whose historical conditions could now best be witnessed in the environment and scenery which gave them birth. The visiting tourist could now access these more readily, for Scotland was – as Scott himself pointed out in *Waverley* (1814) – in the midst of extensive change, with major infrastructural developments, including the first stretch of the Forth and Clyde canal, completed in 1775, one among a range of projects designed to close the economic gap between Scotland and London, and paid for in part by more aggressive excise collection. Scotland's engineers, like Thomas Telford (1757–1834), whose 180-metre Menai Strait suspension bridge remains in use today, were at the centre of the developing infrastructure of Great Britain. But it was Scotland where the allure of the accessible 'primitive' in landscape and people was strongest, reinforced by painted panoramas, such as the 'Grand Moveable

Panorama of the Clyde' exhibited at Princes Street, Edinburgh, in 1809. The difficulty of travelling abroad in the Napoleonic wars, and the 'transport revolution initiated by the Commission for Highland Roads and Bridges after 1803, including new canal construction, and the rapid development of steam-boat transport', meant that the country was becoming newly accessible to mass tourism, and Scott's timing was impeccable. Moreover, the migration of many from the countryside to the rapidly industrializing heartlands of central – and especially west central – Scotland fed nostalgia for a rural past within the country, as well as seeming to mark a sharp dichotomy between that past and the present. Mass manufacturing in textiles built on English innovations such as John Kay's flying shuttle (1733), James Hargreaves' spinning jenny and Richard Arkwright's water frame (1764), the spinning mule (1779) and the power loom (1785) grew rapidly. The changes driven by these innovations affected lives and economies far beyond the 'central belt' of Glasgow and Edinburgh, though it reinforced their grip. In 1755, Perthshire and Aberdeenshire had been among the most populous counties in Scotland; between 1811 and 1851, 33,000 in Aberdeenshire alone lost jobs in textiles to the mills of the central belt, where lower labour costs and mass production drove the massification of business. Meanwhile, again building on innovation south of the border in the previous century, James Neilson's (1792–1865) 1828 'hot-blast process' 'made west central Scotland the lowest cost pig-iron producing region in the UK'. These transformations were – by the standards of the time – accomplished at electric speed. In 1839, '91 per cent of Scotland's cotton mills were in the Western Lowlands', mostly within 30 kilometres of Glasgow, and by 1848 Lanarkshire alone was producing almost eleven times as much pig iron as Scotland as a whole had in 1830. By 1851, Scotland 'was more industrialized than the rest of Britain', while displacing people internally and exporting them overseas in large numbers.[15]

Mass tourism in Scotland became industrial as well as historical. By the end of the eighteenth century, David Dale's (1739–1806) New Lanark mills, with their 'social regime' which supported a better developed and more motivated workforce, were themselves an international visitor attraction. In the 'Highlands', famous tourist accounts such as Thomas Pennant's (1769,

1772) and Samuel Johnson's (1775) had already built on a practice of visiting which had begun during the 1756–63 war with France, and the English poet Thomas Gray (1716–71) (who had enthused over the Swiss mountains in the 1730s) thought the 'beauty' and 'horror' of the 'ecstatic mountains' of northern Scotland compelling when he visited in 1765. Scotland was not the only beneficiary of the growing internal tourist market – somewhat incredibly, the Earl of Warwick's housekeeper 'left no less than £30,000 earned from tourists' tips' when she died in 1834. In the early days of great house tourism, the housekeeper guided the visitors (who were themselves generally respectable and well to do): this is the situation reflected in Jane Austen's *Pride and Prejudice* (1813), when Elizabeth Bennett visits Pemberley. On a more modest scale, tenants in what were to become known as the crofting counties began to sublet to holidaymakers in Scotland.[16]

Scott was not the first historical novelist, but he was the first to write within a paradigm of historical change. This had two features: the universalist historiographical models of Enlightenment stadial history, characterized in particular by William Robertson, perhaps the greatest influence on Scott; and the characteristically 'Romantic' particular characters and situations of a given landscape or place: the Solway in *Redgauntlet* (1824); Wolf's Crag in *The Bride of Lammermoor* (1819); Flora's enchanted glen in *Waverley*. All these kinds of location can be said to descend from the accentuated and politicized mapping and illustrating of Scotland from the Roy–Sandby era. The highly visualized *locus amoenus* – the particular place – provided the individual quality of Romantic character and scenery which, tinged with the *frisson* of fading threat, exists in Scott's writing in a fine balance with an Enlightenment conception of the universal processes of history. In this context, Scott often offered lightly disguised or open references to a location which could be visited (Hospitalfield in Arbroath as Monkbarns, Auchmithie as Mussel Craig in *The Antiquary*), most famously the Trossachs, where *The Lady of the Lake*, which sold 20,000 copies in its first year, 'triggered a rise in visitors to the locality'. Later *Rob Roy's* 'native heath' sustained the development of a 'Rob Roy country' in the neighbouring districts to accommodate spillover interest. The extensive development in Scotland of *locus amoenus* tourism based on Scott's novels or on the Burns Country was rapid, early and international: by 1900, there were over 3,000 American visitors alone to Scott's house at Abbotsford, still at that stage in family hands. In his (initially anonymous) novels from *Waverley* onwards, Scott outlined a highly coloured, chiaroscuro view of the Scottish and mediaeval pasts with oppositions and resolutions which underpinned progress and the development of modernity while suggesting that something of what had been lost was worth keeping, not least because it was so forcibly evoked in his writing. The suggestion was that by visiting these intensely realized locations one might be brought in contact with the fading charisma of their history, and learn something of their secrets. To the reader less influenced by an Enlightenment historiographical framework and British patriotism, Scott's pasts continued to pose questions to the present which were not answered: his Continental European readers often read him as more of a radical writer than his British ones did.[17] Some of Scott's questions were about justice (*The Two Drovers, The Highland Widow, Redgauntlet*), some about racism (*The Talisman, Ivanhoe, Guy Mannering*) and most were presented in a Scottish context. Scott offered powerfully comforting stories laced with just a hint – rather more than a hint in some stories – of disquiet and discomfort. The past was buried, but it was also in some sense alive. Lost Scotland was also revenant Scotland.[18]

Scott was inspiring across Europe and the world: his powerful visualizations, evident not only in the descriptive nature of his prose but in ancillary publications such as *Provincial Antiquities and Picturesque Scenery of Scotland* (1819–26), illustrated by J.M.W. Turner (1775–1851), inspired painter and writer alike in and beyond Scotland, particularly in the historical novel and associated genre painting. In France, Scott was seen as an opponent of revolution and a friend of the Royalist cause; in Italy and Hungary, as a moniker of national resistance against imperial power. Everywhere the stamp of his influence was felt in the great age of the novel, from Honoré de Balzac's *Les Chouans* (1829), Victor Hugo's *Notre-Dame de Paris* (1831), Stendhal's *La Chartreuse de Parme* (1839), William Thackeray's *Henry Esmond* (1853), Charles Dickens' *A Tale of Two Cities* (1859) and Leo Tolstoy's *War and Peace* (1865–69) via Gustave Flaubert's *Salammbô* (1862), and above all Alessandro Manzoni's *I promessi sposi* (1827) to George Eliot's *Middlemarch* (1871–2) and Thomas Hardy's *Mayor of Casterbridge* (1886), where a modernizing Scot provides the catalyst for change in an act of tribute to the master. In Scotland, Scott's Jacobite subject matter occupied a dominant place in the fiction of his successors, from R.L. Stevenson's *Kidnapped* (1886), *Catriona* (1893) and *Master of Ballantrae* (1889) to John Buchan's *A Lost Lady of Old Years* (1899) and *Midwinter* (1923). A substantial industry also grew up in Scott's homeland – sustained by figures like Cosmo Innes (1798–1874) – through the publications of the Bannatyne, Maitland and Spalding Clubs, to preserve Scottish history for future generations, an industry largely inspired by Walter Scott.[19] Scott was present in the great age of opera in the work of Rossini (*La donna del lago* (1819)), Donizetti (*Lucia di Lammermoor* (1835)) and Bizet (*La jolie fille de Perth* (1867)). In the American south, 'plantations, and even children' owed 'their first names to characters and places in Scott's novels' and in Roxburghshire 'Abbotsford . . . became a place of pilgrimage'.[20] In 1812, Scott's 'Hail to the Chief' was first played 'to honour the end of hostilities and the late George Washington', and has since become a signature tune of the US Presidency. Scott's modernizing agenda, which remains respectful of the past, was itself adopted almost

11. Ivanhoe Hotel in Sydney: another example of Scott's worldwide footprint.

Exhibited at the Edinburgh Exhibition, 1890.
Ran the 2 p.m. Scotch Express ex Euston from January, 1891, to August, 1899.
Has run 793,888 miles to end of Sept., 1904.

COMPOUND EXPRESS ENGINE "JEANIE DEANS".
BUILT 1890. DRIVING WHEELS 7FT DIAMETER.

12. The *Jeanie Deans* 2-4-0 locomotive, exhibited at the Edinburgh Exhibition in 1890 and on frequent express duty from London to Edinburgh from 1891 to 1899, travelling in the opposite direction to Scott's heroine in *The Heart of Midlothian*.

as a leitmotif for the Victorian era and the writer was often memorialized through the technological symbols of mobility and power, for example in Waverley Station in Edinburgh and the *Fair Maid* and *Talisman* express locomotives, or in *Rob Roy* (1818), 'the first cross-channel steamer'.[21]

THE DEERHOUND AND THE HUNT: SCOTT, LANDSEER AND LAND USE

The highly visual nature of Scott's prose and his introduction of iconic places (Loch Katrine) and animals (the Dandie Dinmont terrier) to his immediately vast audience's view of Scotland had a marked effect in transforming the way in which the country was seen externally and in some of its developments internally. Among other iconic features and animals, Scott popularized the Scottish Deerhound, which first appeared in his novels in the guise of the 'greyhounds' Bran and Buscar owned by the Jacobite Baron of Bradwardine in *Waverley*. The deer hunt, whether with hound or rifle, soon became a central part of how rural Scotland was viewed by the English gentry who came there in summer. It was popularized by Albert, the Prince Consort, among others (see Landseer, *Prince Albert at Balmoral* (1865–67)), and the provision of Scottish wildlife for royal sport soon began to underpin a wider interest in leisure pursuits of this kind among the British elite which are both celebrated and mocked in later fiction, such as John Buchan's *John MacNab* (1925). Scott owned deerhounds, which were associated with the Ossianic world of Fingal and the deer hunts of that Gaelic hero, and, from about 1825, Duncan McNeill (1793–1874), later Lord Colonsay, and Archibald his brother, later Keeper of the Registers of Scotland, instigated an extensive deerhound breeding programme as part of a revival in which many such dogs were named Bran, in honour of the greatest of Fionn/Fingal's hounds, and indeed of Bradwardine's dog in *Waverley*, as well as Buscar. Edwin Landseer (1802–73), who first visited Scotland in 1824, was commissioned to

13. Edwin Landseer, *Flood in the Highlands* (1845–60).

provide several frontispieces and vignettes for Scott's Waverley novels in 1828, when he had already acquired an emerging reputation as a painter of the rediscovered deerhounds including *A Deerhound* (1826), *Highlanders Returning from Deerstalking* (1827), *The Deerstalkers' Return* (1827) and *Dead Deer and Deerhounds* (1827). Landseer – an active deer hunter – based the scenes on a hunt he had been on in 1825 at Blair Atholl.

Landseer's *Deer and Deer Hounds in a Mountain Torrent* (1832; see plate 18) summed up the essence of the darkly violent side of Scott's Scotland for many in its colouration, bringing to life a range of the writer's references from *The Lady of the Lake* to *Waverley*, as is also the case in the chiaroscuro of paintings such as *Flood in the Highlands* (1845–60), where the dirk and broadsword recall a vanished and defeated Scottish past, the mountain torrent of Chapter 22 of *Waverley*. The deer, specifically the stag, had been used as a symbol of the Stuarts since the 1640s, and Landseer continued to depict deer and their hunting throughout his career, most notably in *The Monarch of the Glen* (1851; see plate 19). Landseer's deer offer a proto-Darwinian image of Scotland, with implicit reference to its Stuart past: magnificent history in a magnificent landscape, doomed to defeat by more adaptable forces (the reasons for the extinction of the giant Irish elk were a subject of actual controversy in the nineteenth century, and are possibly alluded to by Landseer; Darwin published *The Origin of Species* in 1859). This world, its colour and antiquity, was the world which had been depicted by Scott. *The Monarch of the Glen* was commissioned to hang in the Palace of Westminster: the symbolism could hardly have been more apt. Moreover, *The Monarch* was depicted with twelve antler points (a royal stag) whereas sixteen would be needed for a true monarch stag. In other words, the sovereignty the deer represents has been displaced: he is royal, but no longer a monarch, and such was the fate of the Stuarts. It is very unlikely that this was not deliberate on Landseer's part: as well as being a lifelong painter and hunter of stags he had illustrated a standard manual, his friend William Scrope's *The Art of Deer Stalking* (1838), which included at least one anecdote on the hounds of Fingal. Scrope was extensively advised by the McNeills.[22]

Meanwhile, the six deer forests which Scotland had had in 1811 expanded to forty by 1842 in the wake of a 'fall in sheep prices', and by 1895 there were 137, covering an astonishing 1.25 million hectares of the country, and putting pressure on alternate land use: whole forests were advertised for rent, as Glenfeshie was by the Duke of Gordon. In 1883, 16 per cent of crofting counties land was under deer. The Royal Commission (Highlands and Islands) (popularly 'The Deer Forest Commission') of 1892–95 'scheduled 1,782,785 acres [721,468 hectares] throughout the Highlands as suitable for occupation by crofters', including half the 28,000 hectares of forest on Lewis (which the impoverished locals had raided in the 1880s), but this made little difference: by 1911, an estimated 34 per cent of crofting counties land was under deer. The argument was made that 'If the low-lying, good land was given to crofters, there would be no place to winter the deer.'[23]

Thomas Duncan (1807–45), the Scots prodigy who painted the scenery for the first stage adaptation of Scott's *Rob Roy* in 1818, also depicted Scotland in the vein pioneered by Landseer, for example in *Bran, A Celebrated Scottish Deerhound*, painted for Duncan McNeill in 1842. Scott and Macpherson's *Ossian* combined to drive a new Scottish imaginary, one in which people were often symbolized with or as animals, as in William Skeoch Cumming's (1864–1929) tapestry *The Lord of the Hunt* (1912–24). Such imagery sustained the idea of Scotland as an unspoilt place where the relationship between the people and the land was close because of their jointly undeveloped nature. A sporting season in such surroundings allowed the visitor to re-enact the old ways and to get in touch with his – most often his – inner huntsman. As D.T. Thomson put it in *The Dogs of Scotland*

(1891), the deerhound 'still retains all the solid demeanour and haughty bearing of a Scottish chieftain of the olden time'. Other sports also fulfilled this role, of course: as early as the Game Act of 1772 (13 George III c.54), the relative challenge and inaccessibility of grouse had been reflected in the establishment of an early start to the shooting season – 12 August, rather than the autumn dates for partridge and pheasant. By the Victorian era, British elites were getting in touch with their inner primitive manliness through sporting summers in the 'Highlands'. Rewilding – for example through the reintroduction of the locally extinct capercaillie from Sweden in 1837 – reinforced the idea of rural northern Scotland as an ancient unspoilt place, a view still visible in contemporary conservation debates.[24]

The Romanticization of Scotland thus took many forms. The presentation of the country nationally and internationally as 'Highland' not only partook of a long historiographical and ideological tradition of the 'patriot north', where northern Scots were the truest to Scotland, but also built on a number of substantial eighteenth-century innovations in cultural practice and representation, not least the association of tartan, the pipes and Highland landscapes with the sublimity, beauty and ruin of the Jacobite cause. Scott did not invent these connexions; rather he re-presented them. Romantic Scotland thus preserved the bravery and grandeur of the defeated politics of its native dynasty and sovereignty in a displaced and fossilized form.[25]

Scottish literature, in many respects created as a separate imaginary entity from English writing in the century following the Union, provided a paradigmatical example for North America of 'a literature that was not English, even if it used the English language as its medium of expression'.[26] Scott was especially useful in this context, as the long and often pejorative comparison of Highlanders to Native Americans in history and propaganda proved a useful basis for creating a literature of the frontier utilizing the structural framework he provided. James Fenimore Cooper's (1789–1851) *The Last of the Mohicans* (1826) used Scott's approach to ethno-cultural conflict in an

American context in presenting Native Americans as a tragic race, while John Richardson's (1796–1852) *Wacousta* (1832) and *The Canadian Brothers* (1840) ensured that a key strand in Canadian literature rested on the sturdy cultural shoulders of Scottish Romanticism in general, and Walter Scott in particular, again drawing on the longstanding association of Scottish 'Highlanders' with Native Americans. Scots in general and 'Highlanders' in particular were held to have a special linkage of sympathy with 'primitive' peoples in the Empire. Sometimes this was sentimental, sometimes seriously political: Scottish and Irish fratriotism, the espousing of the causes of other small or oppressed nations as a version of one's own nationality, was a major feature of the Romantic and Victorian eras in Scotland.[27]

Fratriotism is a concept which I explore in more detail in my book on *Scottish and Irish Romanticism* (2008, 2011). It was a common feature of Scottish and Irish identities in the imperial era, arising from conflicting loyalties generated by inclusion in a state with which one does not fully identify. In Ireland it was widespread; in Scotland it was most clearly seen among the descendants of Jacobite families and students of the more radical Enlightenment thinkers. While fratriotism as a concept identifies a definitive strain of behaviour and outlook, it is not to be taken as the view of the majority or a collective exculpation for the vices of colonialism, though it has certainly been misrepresented as such by some scholars. It is most definitely not any 'innate predisposition for solidarity' among Celtic subalterns; on the other hand, it is a sufficiently important theme to deserve attention. The Native American Scottish chiefs we have already encountered in Chapter 2, for example, emphasize that the Scottish diaspora might behave very differently from some of their British counterparts in engaging with their host communities, particularly in areas such as the fur trade, where there was greater economic equality in native and colonial exchange. Fratriotism's primary expressions were sympathy and engagement with the peoples of empire who were not either Scottish or Irish: the transmutation of the first into the third person in articulating political disquiet or cultural dissonance.

Fratriotism grew to maturity in the Romantic era and persisted into the twentieth century. James Boswell's (1740–95) Corsican patriotism was an early example: there were almost a company's worth of Scots volunteers fighting for Corsica at Ponte Nuovo in 1769 and Boswell raised a subscription for the supply of Corsican artillery from the Carron ironworks. Later examples include Joseph Hume's (1777–1855) Greek nationalism, Octavian Hume's (1829–1912) co-founding of the Indian National Congress, William Lyon Mackenzie's (1795–1861) Canadian rising of 1837 and Thomas Cochrane's (1775–1860) leadership of the navies of Chile, Brazil and Greece in their struggles for independence. Cochrane, welcomed to Valparaiso as Admiral of Chile by its Hispano-Irish founding father Bernardo O'Higgins (1778–1842) with a St Andrew's Day dinner apparently bedecked with Royal Stuart tartan, was toasted by contemporary radicals as the great contributor to 'the speedy and permanent establishment of liberty in South America'. An 1826 political cartoon, *This Engine Was Erected by John Bull*, shows him as swathed from head to foot in tartan; his nationality was perfectly understood, and his reputed greed for money was associated with it. Cochrane continued to be celebrated in Latin America: George Lawson (1832–1904) was commissioned to execute his statue in Valparaiso in 1874, and even today Cochrane features as a branding icon for Chilean wine.[28]

Not all such figures were altruistic, as Cochrane's reputation indicates. General Sir Gregor MacGregor (1786–1845) exceeded them all. A Venezuelan patriot who gained Native American support and received the 'Medal of the Order of Libertadores' from Simón Bolívar (1783–1830), MacGregor subsequently turned into a confidence trickster, raising £200,000 for land purchase in the non-existent country of Poyais. Others made their lives in their new countries: Captain Robertson of the Chilean Navy was granted the island of Mocha by the Chilean government. John and William Robertson from Kelso projected and financed the Monte Grande Colony in Argentina, 30 kilometres from Buenos Aires, and 'Between 1806 and 1824, twenty-nine Scottish merchants had established themselves in Buenos Aires and twelve of them also owned important tracts of land.'

One of the most interesting cases of the Scot abroad adopting other nationalities is that of George Gordon, Lord Byron (1788–1824), who, despite being in his own words 'half a Scot by birth, and bred/A whole one', is usually characterized and discussed with hardly any reference to Scotland at all. While Byron was a hybrid figure, this is misleading. Initially educated at Aberdeen Grammar School, characterized by Lady Caroline Lamb as a Scot, an enthusiast for Bruce and Wallace who wore tartan habitually in his Greek campaign and networked with Scots throughout Europe, Byron was described by his first biographer, Sir Cosmo Gordon, as born in Aberdeenshire and a hardy 'Highlander', 'allowed to expand his lungs and strengthen his limbs upon the mountains of the North . . . upon mountains that had never been permanently trod by the foot of a conqueror'. Although this is only partially accurate (Byron was not born in Scotland, but came there as an infant), it is significant that Byron's own identification with Scotland markedly intensified in his campaign for the liberation of Greece, where a disproportionate number of his closest friends and associates had strong Scottish connexions, particularly with regard to north-eastern Scotland, which through his Gordon links remained central to the Byronic network throughout his life. Thomas Gordon (1788–1841), formerly of the British and Russian armies, raised funds for the Greek struggle and served in the campaign, ultimately as director-general of the Greek army; he was himself a distant relative of Byron's, being the son of Charles Gordon of Buthlaw in Aberdeenshire. Lord Charles Murray (1799–1821), scion of the house of Atholl, was killed in the Greek cause. With the support of Joseph Hume and others, Thomas Cochrane – whom Byron admired and who may even have inspired him to go to Greece – had been appointed to the Greek naval command, and appointed Major Urquhart and other officers to support him. Byron, who had already presented the Albanian Suliotes in the guise of Eastern European Scots in a manner which may have inspired Scott in *Waverley*, was recommended to go to Greece by another Scot, James Hamilton Browne. There, he found that the British resident in Cephalonia was Charles James Napier (1782–1853), the grandson of Lord Napier of Merchistoun, nephew of the Duke of Lennox and great-nephew of the Earl of Elgin. Napier had begun his career as aide-de-camp to Sir James Duff, who was related to Byron (Byron was cousin to Mary Duff, his godfather was Robert Duff of Fetteresso and his grandmother was Margaret Duff Gordon). Napier – who made 'wha wadna fecht for Charlie' the marching song of the first regiment he commanded – was appointed to Greece by Sir Thomas

Maitland (1760–1824), son of the Earl of Lauderdale, who had opposed war with Tipu Sultan and whom we met in Chapter 3 in the context of Toussaint Louverture's black republic on Saint-Domingue, which Maitland thought 'should be abandoned to its native population'. Two streets in Colombo, Sri Lanka – where he was the lover of a local dancing girl, Lovina, while Governor of Ceylon – are named after Maitland. Napier himself later published *Colonization* (1835), an attack on the abuse of native peoples from Australia to Ireland. When Byron arrived in Greece, Napier also contacted Sir Frederick Adam, Deputy (later Lord High) Commissioner of the Ionian islands, who was the son of the Rt Hon William Adam of Blair-Adam and Eleanora Elphinstone: Eleanora was the aunt of Byron's friend Margaret Mercer Elphinstone and the sister of Cochrane's first patron, Viscount Keith. Margaret's mother was a Jacobite Mercer of Aldie and her great-great uncle was George Keith, the last Earl Marischal. Byron gifted her an Albanian 'kilt' costume, probably in honour of these connexions and his perceived link between 'Highland' and patriot Scotland and Albania. In the last year of his life, Byron also grew close to George Finlay, brought up in Dunoon by his uncle Kirkman Finlay (1773–1842), Lord Provost of Glasgow in 1812, and who described the Greeks as 'Scottish chieftains' in his *History of the Greek Revolution* (1832). There were many other Scots linked to the Greek cause's network and to Byron.[29]

Thus both in the British Empire and throughout Europe, a Scottish brand was emerging in the Romantic era. In Europe the impact of James Macpherson's Ossian poetry on figures as diverse as Napoleon and Goethe was succeeded by Robert Burns' role as both the voice of the people and an advocate of progressive radical values. Meanwhile, Sir Walter Scott provided the basis for much of the mediaeval revival and his historical novel format was replayed from France to Russia by novelists engaging with their own histories. Although the influence of Burns endured longest, that of Scott was even more pronounced in the nineteenth century. 'Waverley Streets' appeared in New South Wales, British Columbia, Palo Alto (Steve Jobs lived at 2101), Perth in Australia, Winnipeg and many other global locations. Scottish societies abroad continued and continue to promote a view of the home country strongly dependent on Scottish Romanticism, which thus became foundational to the global visibility of Scotland up to the present day. Scottish tourism rapidly embraced both the country's new global writers and the colours, landscapes and customs associated with them. By 1820, early steam boats on the Clyde (the site of the first commercial voyage by steamboat) were being given names such as *Rob Roy, Robert Bruce, Fingal, Oscar* and *Robert Burns*.[30] Scotland became associated with sublime landscapes, tartan, Highlanders, folk culture, the supernatural, a history of ruin, conflict and tragedy rife with lost causes, both political and personal (as represented in Scott's *The Bride of Lammermoor* (1819), which became Donizetti's *Lucia di Lammermoor* in 1835). Byron put it clearly:

'Shades of the dead! have I not heard your voices
    Rise on the night-rolling breath of the gale?'
Surely, the soul of the hero rejoices,
    And rides on the wind, o'er his own Highland vale!
Round Loch na Garr, while the stormy mist gathers,
    Winter presides in his cold icy car:
Clouds, there, encircle the forms of my Fathers;
    They dwell in the tempests of dark Loch na Garr.

'Ill starr'd, though brave, did no visions foreboding
    Tell you that fate had forsaken your cause?'
Ah! were you destined to die at Culloden,
    Victory crown'd not your fall with applause:
Still were you happy, in death's earthy slumber,
    You rest with your clan, in the caves of Braemar;
The Pibroch resounds, to the piper's loud number,
    Your deeds, on the echoes of dark Loch na Garr.

George Gordon Byron, 'Lachin Y Gair'

Conjuring up an Ossianic heroic ancestry, realized in wild landscape and chiaroscuro colours, the heroes of Scotland are both defeated in a specific history and yet will always be remembered and celebrated in the martial music and song of their own land: such are Byron's Scots in particular, and the overwhelming image of Romantic Scotland in general. Within Scotland's sublime landscapes, the past is entombed and yet alive. Highlanders, mountains, ruin, conflict and tragedy stalk these brief stanzas.

TARTAN

No sign of Scottishness was more visible than tartan. For decades following the Jacobite Risings tartan, the uniform of the Jacobite armies and the symbol of their sympathizers both in Scotland and England, had been legal to wear in public only in the British Army. What had become in the wake of Union 'a truly political textile' was now being co-opted for British rather than Scottish patriotism. By 1778, the Highland Society of London was agitating for a repeal of the legislation against tartan and this finally arrived in 1782. Jane Duchess of Gordon, Burns' patron and the 'Tartan Belle', helped to popularize tartan in London society at her Scottish dances and elsewhere, while adding to its British military mystique by supporting the raising of the Gordon Highlanders in 1793–94 by allegedly giving each volunteer the opportunity to take the King's shilling from between her lips in a kiss. By now, William Wilson and Sons of Bannockburn 'had begun a significant trade in civilian patterns' in tartan. Tartan still signified the military tradition and valour of Scotland, northern Scotland in particular, but now this tradition was the emblem of a diaspora of courage, the service of Scots in the British Army and for the British Crown. Prince George (the future George IV) wore tartan at a masquerade ball in 1789 for the first time, and by the time of the royal visit to Edinburgh in 1822, tartan had become the badge of Hanoverian as once of Stuart loyalty to the Crown. Walter Scott and Major General David Stewart of Garth (1772–1829) masterminded the King's visit; as we have already seen in Chapter 3, Stewart published his mythologizing history of Highland valour in the same year. Tartan was associated with ethnicity, loyalty and the all-conquering British military in the wake of Waterloo; sometimes, as in Alasdair Macdonell of Glengarry's (1773–1828) Society of True Highlanders (1815) it was a badge of identity which was exclusive and signified 'purity' of ancestry; sometimes as with Stewart of Garth's Celtic Society (1820), of which Scott was the first president, it was more inclusive. In the Glenfinnan Monument by James Gillespie Graham (1815), tartan monumentalism reconciled the brave Jacobite past with the brave British present and the Highland warriors common to both: though it ostensibly commemorated the raising of the Jacobite standard in 1745, the Glenfinnan Monument's cylindricality (modelled on Trajan's victory column) implicitly invoked British triumph in the Napoleonic Wars.

Tartan was also a magnet of fashionable status in France, having appeared in Paris under the Duchess of Gordon's influence on *bon ton* and in the dress of Scottish soldiers after Waterloo, a source of fascination as was clear from the contemporary print *Le Prétexte*, which showed French women manoeuvring to see what Scotsmen wore under their kilts. In September 1822, '*La Belle Assemblée* proclaimed that "The prevailing colour this month is tartan".' This was followed by other recommendations, and in 1826 in Paris women were 'advised to adopt highland bonnets and plaid dresses' (see plate 20). Depictions of tartan had already appeared far beyond Europe in the eighteenth century, including on Qing porcelain.[31]

By the 1780s, the Highland Society of London had begun to link Highland dress to social prestige, and in 1815 began to make a register of chiefs' tartans. Wilsons of Bannockburn had been producing family setts since the 1790s (family tartans of some kind date back to the sixteenth century); by 1819, their Pattern Book represented this more formally, and in 1822 Glengarry's True Highlanders wrote a guide to formal Highland dress for 'Chieftains and Men of Unquestionable Family'. The association of tartan and family reached a peak in the factitious *Vestiarum Scoticum* (1842) and *Costume of the Clans* (1845), both suitably by the 'Sobieski Stuarts', two brothers who claimed direct descent from the main Stuart line. Tartan – once a badge of association, loyalty, status and location as well as of family – was now often utilized as a visible sign of Scottish bloodline, a kind of ethnic badge of local identity within the British Empire, one which had come to prominence through military service, and which by the middle of the nineteenth century became a global phenomenon. Both its ethnicity and its militarism were stressed: Englishmen who wore it in Scotland in season were often mocked for such a shallow pretence of 'going native' in *Punch* and elsewhere, though the Royal Family were exempt from this both by status and their own Scottish blood-lines. Evening dress based on the kilt, with its polished buttons and epaulettes, reflected its military associations. Specialist 'Scottish shops opened in London during the 1830s' with a range of accessories to complement the new fashionability of Scottishness, and the medi-aeval militarism of the 1839 Eglinton Tournament added tartan to its celebration of Scottian mediaevalism. The 'Scotch suit' for Victorian schoolboys turned tartan into a fashion item for elite English children (though not adults) and mourning tartan developed after the death of Prince Albert in 1861, while the appearance of variant setts ('ancient', 'hunting' and so on) with different colourways kept sales busy even from clients of the same name and family.[32]

Queen Victoria and Prince Albert's first visit to Scotland with the Prime Minister Sir Robert Peel (1788–1850) in September 1842 set the seal on tartan's status, and the building of a new Scots baronial castle at Balmoral, which was decorated extensively in tartan, institu-tionalized it a decade later. In 1842, 'Lord Glenlyon's Highlanders, with halberds' came to guard the Queen outside Dunkeld, while the Marquess of Breadalbane (who had been responsible for reintroducing the capercaillie in 1837) presented over 100 of his retainers in 'kilts, plaids, coats of green cloth, hose, blue bonnets', armed with consciously antique targes and Lochaber axes, and the Duke of Atholl performed a similar kind of Scottian mummery for Royal delight. By the middle of the nineteenth century, tartan was accompanied as a global phenomenon by the spread of many other cultural practices associated with the presentation of Scotland as 'Highland' and Romantic: 'piping, and Gaelic language' were two other causes promoted by the Highland Society of London, for example. The first Highland Games in Scotland appears to have arisen from a Highland Society meeting at Falkirk (hardly the most 'Highland' of destinations) in 1781, and by the early nineteenth century – certainly before the royal visit to Edinburgh in 1822 – such societies and events were spreading throughout the colonies.

The Gathering/Game phenomenon was presented as a kind of festival of equality, where landlord, tenant, 'crofter and shepherd' could meet on equal terms once a year. Some attributed it to the immemorial past, but the Victorians were most talented at inventing tradition, and we should be very cautious at crediting the Gatherings as more than a picturesque device to assert unchanging antiquity at a time of rapid economic dislocation. Breadalbane followed his 1842 entertainments with his first Highland Gathering the next year, and games of a similar kind spread through the country, with the Royal Family taking a prominent role in attending some of the most high profile of them, such as the Lonach Gathering, which evolved from the 'Lonach Highland and Friendly Society' of 1832. Royal attendance at the Lonach was a practice which endured. The 1848 Braemar Gathering under the patronage of Queen Victoria probably accelerated the growth of such practices throughout Scotland, where in the next half century Gatherings spread from Pitlochry to Assynt. These events grew to great size, with 51,000 spectators at Cowal in 1910. Highland Gatherings also took off in the British Empire. The Glengarry Highland Scots Gathering in Canada of 1819 was followed by the New York Highland Society Games in 1836. The Highland Society of Antigonish, founded in 1861, claimed to have been celebrating Highland Games since 1763, while by the late nineteenth century the Games were spread by the rapid rise in 'Highland' societies: the American Order of the Scottish Clans, founded at St Louis in 1878, grew to have 250 branches, and a number of individual clan societies followed. The Grandfather Mountain games and gathering, with 30,000 attendees one of the largest Highland Games in the world in recent times, was founded in 1956. It traces its foundational values to the Braemar Gathering, and the first games were held on the anniversary of the raising of the Jacobite standard at Glenfinnan on 19 August 1745.[33]

THE CLEARANCES AND RADICALISM

The Scotland into which its Romantic writers provided a window was becoming more and more different from its emerging global brand with every decade. The decline of the tacksman class saw the idea of 'heritable trusteeship' in landholding in the 'Highland' estates – comprehended under the Gaelic term *dùthchas* – come under increasing threat, even while the appetite for land which the concept naturally supported remained undiminished. The wars which recruited thousands of men from northern Scotland in 1756–63 and 1793–1815 had often depended – as we saw in Chapter 3 – on small grants of land in lieu of part of the enlistment bounty, and many landless men returned as veterans to these smallholdings, crofts carved out of marginal land or the holdings of displaced subtenants. By 1820, smaller crofts predominated over communal land use, with the limited living such smallholdings gave supplemented by fishing or kelp, a seaweed algae that could be burnt to produce soda ash, used in glass and soap manufacture. High levels of sometimes temporary migration to towns increased population instability. The foundation of the Highland and Agricultural Society of Scotland in 1784 led to an ever greater focus on economic improvement, which was more and more necessary, as the population of northern and western Scotland continued to rise beyond the limit of sustainability. Moreover, as the nobility became ever more integrated into British society, the need for them to secure higher rents in a world of partible and ever reducing landholding could only increase, driven also by population pressure and land grants to the military veterans so necessary for sustaining the myth of martial valour. Landlords who resisted this process, like Norman, Chief of the Name of Macleod (1754–1801), became increasingly rare; incidentally and perhaps not entirely coincidentally, MacLeod was also a strong abolitionist. Before the Reform Act of 1832 in particular, landowners also secured their grip upon Scotland's tiny electorate 'by splitting superiorities among kinsmen, associates and clients' to produce fictitious votes in their interest, thus further destabilizing the system. Since the 1770s, it had become increasingly difficult to accommodate cottars with a 'smallholding in return for supplying labour' and estate villages were needed to accommodate them in their new roles of 'tradesmen or day labourers'. From both above and below, economic pressure was being exerted on the remains of traditional landholding practice. As Chris Whatley remarks, 'In 1829–30, as Felix Mendelssohn conceived and composed his "Hebrides" overture . . . Lochiel was completing the process of "wholesale evictions" which he had begun in 1824. The clash of cultures could scarcely have been more jarring.'[34]

The economic downturn which followed the conclusion of the Napoleonic wars in 1815 'saw the winding down of the old Highland cattle economy, as well as the failure of the newer kelp and fishing industries' which had been taken up by many following the initial clearances to the coast in the Sutherland Clearances of 1794–1820, as flock-masters sought access to land for their sheep which could command a higher rent. Troops were used to suppress protests against sheep farming in Ross and Sutherland, though in places like Argyll, where there was sufficient 'pasturage for livestock', the Campbell family experienced far less difficulty. The notorious brutality of the Sutherlands' factor Patrick Sellars (tried and acquitted for culpable homicide in 1814) helped to give the process of Clearance an irreversibly bad name, and this was accentuated by the 'instant transformation' demanded of the economic behaviour of the tenantry, and the fact that the townships which took in the evicted became more economically vulnerable themselves as a consequence. The return of demobbed soldiers and the fact that most evicted families were re-accommodated on the Sutherland estates only increased the pressure. Moreover, kelp production, on which many of the evicted were engaged, peaked in 1810 and both kelp and wool, the produce of the new industry and the old, went on to decline in value after 1815, as the 'wartime interruption of trade' abated and cheaper imported kelp became available. Grain prices surged during the Napoleonic wars, but from a peak prices almost halved between 1813 and 1830, and many hereditary families were forced to sell their lands, which were 'acquired by a new wealthy elite'. Further evictions and population loss were clearly predicated by these economic pressures and social changes. Although some writers, such as John MacCulloch, justified aggressive landlord policies, others, such as Stewart of Garth, opposed them, but by the time he wrote 15,000 had already been cleared in Sutherland alone. Agricultural discontent naturally followed on from these developments, although it was not so aggressive or so immediate as that found in England or especially Ireland, owing to a variety of reasons including longstanding trust for the landowners and the nexus between military service and farming, which had only intensified in the first generations of 'Highland' recruitment into the British Army.[35]

The 'Highland Clearances' ('Highland Clearing' was a term first used by William Skene in 1848 and Alexander Mackenzie's *The History of the Highland Clearances* (1883) later crystallized the term at a crucial historical moment) were themselves not one but a sequence of events whose effects were intensified by the economic disruption of adjunct or replacement industries like kelp. The MacDonald of Glengarry and Sutherland Clearances were only an early phase in a process which lasted almost a century, where the initial process of partible smallholding leading to impoverishment became replaced with larger shooting estates, and deer rather than sheep became the norm in changing land use. Although the evictions and betrayal by the landlords loom large in cultural memory, and there was indeed an intention on the part of some landlords to thin the numbers of their tenantry, the principal reason for leaving Scotland was 'the inevitable pressure of

14. The gentlemen's toilet in the Lios Mor/ Lismore public house, Dumbarton Road, Glasgow, displays a distinctive practice in cultural memory with regard to the Sutherland Clearances, as well as evidencing a fusion of Scottish and Irish identities with regard to landlord oppression.

This urinal is dedicated to three men who participated in the Scottish Highland Clearances.

These men took part in what is now recognised as a form of Central Government endorsed ethnic cleansing.

Through their greed and bigotry, they and others have been instrumental in destroying a centuries old Scottish Highland way of life.

PLEASE FEEL FREE TO PAY THEM THE RESPECT THEY ARE DUE

COLONEL FEL

In more recent times this man continued the Highland Clearances process on the Island of Lismore through enforced evictions of the indigenous population.

population on severely restricted resources', which is not to say that forced economic migrancy is not itself often a miserable process. Structural stress, the perception of such stress, opportunities and invitations to leave and the positive permissibility of emigration all played a role, as did adverse climate impacts. In the 1780s and 1805–20 in particular, 'cold years' occurred, with several volcanic eruptions impacting the climate, chiefly that of Tambora in 1815, which provided the 'year without a summer' that followed on from a sequence of cold summers. Failing harvests were important, as well as grasping landlords. Poor health and epidemic outbreaks were common: in 1818, 25 per cent of the population of Glasgow caught typhus and one in eight of them died, while a global cholera pandemic broke out between 1817 and 1824.[36]

Despite emigration, the continuing expansion of the population and the presence of multiple smallholdings intensified economic vulnerability.

Rent arrears – all too frequent in such circumstances – were then used to justify forced expulsion, while potato famine struck Gaelic-speaking Scotland as well as Ireland in the late 1840s. British civil servants – in many cases sympathetic to the 'racial science' of books such as Robert Knox's *The Races of Men* (1850), which divided 'Saxon' Lowlanders from 'Celtic' Highlanders – were given to blame economic failure on native indolence and inadequacy. The collapse of the kelp industry speeded up population loss from locations like Tiree, while between 1841 and 1861 populations almost halved in many areas, with almost 90 per cent being displaced from Knoydart. In 1848–51 alone, 3,000 tenants and cottars left Gordon lands for Québec. The Duke of Argyll commented that 'I wish to send out those whom we would be obliged to feed if they stayed at home.' Such attitudes have been credited for the 'paucity of recruits' raised for the Crimean War in 1854–56. As the economic benefit of sheep receded, more and more land was used for seasonal sporting leisure, especially the high status deer hunt, 'the deer that have taken over our ploughing-land' in the words of John McRae, leader of the Lochcarron Land League. Public disorder in support of 'historical rights' began on the Braes near Portree in Skye in 1883 and endured in the Hebrides into the 1890s. The Highland Land Law Reform Association (*Dionnasg an Fhearainn,* based on the Irish Land League) secured the election of five MPs in the crofting interest in the 1885 general election, and 'the crofters' agitation allowed the [newly established] Scottish Office to bargain effectively with the Home Office for the transfer of sole responsibility for law and order'. In the end, the Napier Commission of 1883–84 gave rise to the Crofters' Holdings (Scotland) Act of 1886 (modelled on the earlier Irish Land Acts), which established fair rents, security of tenure and compensation for improvement. Almost 9,000 applications 'to fix fair rents' were made to the Crofters' Commission in its first year of application, a demand so overwhelming that only one in four cases was dealt with: the average rent reduction decided upon between 1886 and 1892 was between 20 and 30 per cent. As we have seen above, the Royal 'Deer Forest Commission' followed in the 1890s, though its findings – staggering as they were in terms of the claims for the amount of crofting land under deer – were not acted upon to the same extent.[37]

15. The ballroom at Mar Lodge, Linn of Dee: the charnel house décor, dedicated to the deer hunt, was not uncommon in Scotland and is here only remarkable in its scale and intensity.

RACISM AND SCOTLAND

As Colin Kidd observes, 'Scottish intellectuals were to the forefront in the rise of racial science in nineteenth-century Britain.'[38] Edinburgh man John Pinkerton's (1758–1826) *Dissertation on the Origin and Progress of the Scythians or Goths* (1787) was a key text in reinforcing the anti-Celtic racism which disfigured British society from the late eighteenth to the late twentieth centuries, but its lineaments had already begun to emerge in the narratives which had arisen to accommodate midland, southern and eastern Scotland more readily into a British narrative. Writers such as David Hume had begun the process of presenting Lowland Scotland as a fit partner for future Union given its Anglo-Saxon character in contrast to the 'Celtic' Highlands, though other writers such as James Macpherson had identified the cultural differences between 'Highland' and 'Lowland' as historically accidental developments of an essentially unitary people.[39] Despite Macpherson's attempted recuperation of Gaelic Scotland, however, there was an emergent alignment in much Enlightenment thought between the ability of Scots to integrate into the new broader state and the degree of their Germanicity; even liberals like John Millar (1735–1801) were given to projecting English historical models of German liberty onto Scotland, and a wish to adopt a shared past of 'British liberty' supported this on a more popular level.

The 'innate laziness' of the Gael (similar accusations were made against former slaves and their descendants in the Caribbean by Scots such as the racist Thomas Carlyle (1795–1881)) was contrasted with Saxon industry, and civil servants such as Sir Charles Trevelyan (1807–86) thought of the west Highland potato famine as an opportunity to promote Celtic exodus and German immigration. Trevelyan's (a Cornish/Welsh name of course) contempt for 'Celts' was evident in his remarks on Ireland and the Irish, and he is still held accountable for the exacerbation of the Irish Famine by many to this day. In 1851, he co-founded the Highland and Island Emigration Society and later went on to be Governor of Madras. He had left office when the first of a series of great droughts struck India in 1876, but the country – like Ireland – was arguably to be a 'utilitarian laboratory' in the hands of men with a similar outlook. The terrible food shortages he witnessed helped lead Allan Octavian Hume (1829–1912), son of the Greek patriot Joseph, to recommend the founding of what became the Congress movement in 1885. In their turn, Indian nationalists expressed support for the Irish Land League, and compared British Government policies in both countries openly. Subsequent Indian famines were likewise arguably unaddressed. Victor Bruce, 9th Earl of Elgin and 13th of Kincardine (1849–1917), Viceroy 1894–99, spent a fortune (estimated at £20 million, some £3 billion today) on the

1897 Diamond Jubilee celebrations while up to some 10 to 11 million people in the subcontinent starved. The reach of Anglo-Saxonism and its assumptions of the superiority of the Germanic quest for liberty had many indirect victims, even if its hands were less immediately bloody than were those of the racist regimes of the twentieth century.[40]

Outside the 'Highland' counties, smaller landholders – 'bonnet lairds' – in the south, and those reclaiming marginal land in the north-east, fared better than those in the north and west, with many innovations, such as those of Hugh Watson of Keillor, who 'pioneered the Aberdeen-Angus breed', or James Kilpatrick of Kilmarnock's development of the Clydesdale breed supporting the development of a robust rural economy. Rural discontent of the kind found in contemporary Ireland and England in the 'Captain Swing' and 'Captain Rock' protests was largely absent, perhaps in part due to the 6- or 12-month feeing system, which placed rural labour in many of these counties on a more secure footing than the daily or weekly hire faced by English agricultural workers. The economically challenged and volatile practice of day labouring was much more marginal in Scotland, although – possibly due to their intensely socialized isolation – there were signs of openness to radical ideas among the bothymen of the north-east, the only agricultural group to respond positively to Chartism in Scotland. Agriculture in this part of Scotland also benefited from surplus labour from the north and west: one study suggests that 'In the 1840s most highland families had at least one member engaged in seasonal work in lowland Scotland.' James Matheson of the Jardine Matheson empire even offered 'free transport aboard his private yacht, *Mary Jane*, for seasonal migrant workers' from his land 'travelling to the labour markets of southern Scotland in 1847' during the west Highland famine. (Matheson also assisted emigration from whole uneconomic townships and to individuals two or more years behind in their rent).[41]

Although the French Revolutionary era did not create the kind of political impact in Scotland that some hoped for at the time and sympathetic scholars can still be prone to allege occurred, certain social changes fed radical pressures. Scotland had 'as many as 70,000 Highlanders' serving in the British Army between 1793 and 1808 and discharged soldiers – often crippled – presented a significant social problem, while weavers were at the forefront of Scottish urban radicalism, as the industry attracted more people in the context of unstable and often falling textile prices, thus exerting strong downward pressure on wages with the resulting economic discontent. As a consequence, radical groups such as the United Scotsmen and various reform societies emerged from 1792 to 1820. There were repeated if generally isolated events of public disorder: the King's Birthday Riots in Edinburgh in 1792; the planting of liberty trees in Perth and Dundee; and above all the 'extensive and serious' riots in response to the 1797 Militia Act, which effectively imposed conscription in a modern form for the first time in Scotland, after decades of refusing the country even a volunteer militia. Despite its provisions for local service and the concession of a £10 buyout (itself economically divisive) the militia ballot was especially unpopular. There were thirty casualties in the worst rioting, at Tranent. While Scotland had nothing to show on the scale of Joseph Fouché's (1759–1820) savage police actions in France, the first regular police force in the United Kingdom was established in Glasgow on 30 June 1800, with the addition of special constables, of whom there were 300 by 1816. In addition, Government spies were widespread, and in a manner reminiscent of the Jacobite era, 'exaggerated the threat of insurrection'. In reality there was little organized response to provocative French claims that Scotland was 'nothing but a dependent colony of the English government' (itself in keeping with the divide and rule tactics of the Bourbons towards Great Britain), though opposition to militia recruitment does seem to have fed United Scotsmen sympathies. Nonetheless, this should not be exaggerated: defensive and volunteer militia (again, as with regular regiments, strongly local in identity, make-up and leadership) were raised on a similar scale to England despite a much smaller population.[42]

A more national politics can be seen in the cases of a few of the radical elite, but the extent of loyalism and the degree to which sentiments of reform operated within a British context should not be underplayed, though there were those who played on British fears of radicalism to help contain local grievances, as when Sir Hector Munro of Novar (1726–1805) requested military support to suppress what was nothing more than hostility to his 'introduction of sheep farming'. Nonetheless, there were a few radicals who might deserve to be called nationalists, such as Basil William Douglas-Hamilton, Lord Daer (1764–94), Thomas Muir (1765–99) and possibly David Erskine, 11th Earl of Buchan (1742–1829). There is little evidence that these men represented a significant body of opinion, though similar sentiments were not unknown: in 1792, James Thomson Callender opined that 'To England we were for many centuries a hostile, and we are still considered by them as a foreign, and in effect a conquered nation.' Whether Scottish or British politics were involved, there was a continuing consciousness of the country's history, with 10,000 on a Covenanting march in Ayrshire in 1815, and 15,000 assembling for the 500th anniversary of Bannockburn the previous year, though these could be seen in the context of a wider discourse of British liberties, which in turn allowed William Wallace to be co-opted by English radicals. However, the increasing centralization of Great Britain in the Napoleonic era was seen by some patriotic Scots as a dilution of the Union settlement; tellingly, this could be seen to have commenced with the English system of Lords Lieutenant being intruded into Scotland in 1794, with these new appointments subsequently being central to the raising of the militia. This process continued. In 1823, separate Irish and Scottish revenue commissioners were abolished; in 1827, the management of Scottish civil society by local magnates was effectively ended by George Canning (1770–1827) and there were a number of further centralizing measures. The 'High Court of Admiralty of Scotland ceased to exist' from 1830 and the Scottish Board of Customs and Excise followed in 1843, together with the Scottish Mint and the Scottish Household; in 1852–89 the blue books of annual statistical accounts ceased to treat Scotland as a separate entity. These changes began to open the way for the development of organizations such as the National Association for the Vindication of Scottish Rights (NAVSR) (1853), and limited domestic agitation for recognition of the Union as a partnership.[43]

It is nonetheless important not to project modern left-wing nationalist sentiment back into the Romantic era. While leading Enlightenment figures such as Thomas Reid (1710–96), John Millar, Dugald Stewart (1753–1828) and Robert Burns might be associated with support for the French revolutionary cause, the associated reform societies went into retreat in the early 1790s. The beginning of war with France and the permission for Scotland to raise its first militia since the Union appealed to far more Scots than the nostrums of revolutionary violence and the modernizing destruction of tradition espoused by the radicals, despite the opposition to the terms of the Militia Act. Jacobinism was a minor pursuit, with intermittent support from economically disadvantaged groups (its 'intellectual progressivism' is one reason why the academy still overemphasises it by comparison with contemporary loyalism and earlier Jacobitism, as many professors are on the lookout for their political and intellectual predecessors). What radicalism there was remained generally of a much more British than Scottish colour: the Hampden Clubs formed in Scotland after 1815 and other developments of a similar kind spoke to the language of English radicalism and the Whig tradition, not to Scottish-specific concerns. Nonetheless, in the era of the rise of modern Scottish nationalism there have been persisting attempts to exaggerate the Scottish patriotic dimension of the so-called Rising of 1820, a general strike combined with a nugatory attempt at an armed rising, which took place in the context of the Peterloo massacre and the escalating radicalism of Britain in general over the preceding year. In Scotland Peterloo was compared to Glencoe, with white scarfs worn in Ayr in mourning, referencing Henry Hunt's famous white hat. Henry Addington, Lord Sidmouth (1757–1844), Home Secretary 1812–22, introduced the Six Acts in 1819, which included the Training Prevention, Seizure of Arms and Seditious Meetings Acts: widespread disquiet was clearly expected, and it occurred in the Cato Street conspiracy and in Scotland. There was a memorial rally for Peterloo at Paisley on 11 September 1819, and in spring 1820 a provisional government was declared, making reference to Magna Carta and the Bill of Rights: entirely English Whig points of reference. This was 'the Scottish Insurrection of 1820'. A general strike across the Ayr, Dumbarton, Lanark, Renfrew and Stirling areas followed on 3 April involving some 50,000 to 60,000 people, arms were reported for sale in Balfron and there was a march to Carron Ironworks to get more, which led to the 'Battle of Bonnymuir', a brief engagement between some thirty radicals and a similar number of Hussars and Yeomanry. Among the leaders, only the ex-United Scotsman James Wilson (1760–1820) with his 'Scotland Free or a Desart' banner, seems to have reflected Scottish national rather than British political and economic differences. Together with John Baird and Andrew Hardie, engaged at Bonnymuir, Wilson was executed. Although large crowds attended the executions, in the late 1840s – the high watermark of British Chartism with its radical calls for annual parliaments and further substantive political change following the great Reform Act of 1832 – the Baird and Hardie Club had only twenty members. Matters changed decisively in the era of Winnie Ewing's Scottish National Party victory at the 1967 Hamilton by-election, with Peter Beresford Ellis and Seamus Mac a'Ghobhainn's *The Scottish Insurrection of 1820* (1970) and Frank Sherry's *The Rising of 1820* (1968, with a foreword by Winnie Ewing) situating the Rising as an avatar of left-wing nationalism. Theorists of the composure of cultural memory will find it an interesting study. When it came to actual practical progressive measures like Catholic emancipation (1829), 'twice as many Scots petitioned against it as for it'. The 'narrow and intransigent Scottish *ancient regime*' was still popular.[44]

Nonetheless, there was significant industrial unrest, even if it was normally without national focus. The 'real wages of Glasgow weavers had . . . fallen by half between 1815 and 1818' and fell further in 1819: this made the trade an obvious flashpoint for discontent. On one occasion in 1819, the 7th and 10th Hussars, detachments of the 6th and 13th Foot, 'a battalion of the Rifle Brigade, ten field pieces' and 500 Yeomanry were assembled in the city (a much greater force than was needed at Bonnymuir), and, as late as 1825, the 13th Foot found itself attacked in the Saltmarket. Caps of liberty were worn in Glasgow in 1819, but this was also the year of the foundation of the Union Societies in the city, where Scots, Irish and English national airs were played. The Scots national air of choice was 'Scots Wha Hae': evidence of the growing influence of Burns and his writing in Scottish self-definition within the Union.[45]

If discontent in the towns was important, it was so to the extent that Scotland was rapidly urbanizing. In the 1750s, 51 per cent of Scotland's population lived north of the Tay, and some 37 per cent in the central lowlands. By 1821, this balance had begun to change rapidly, with an additional major shift to the west. Scotland's population was less than twice what it had been in 1750, but Glasgow was over five times the size and Aberdeen almost three times the size, while Paisley had grown seven-fold. The country was industrializing rapidly, with 25 per cent of pig-iron output and 25 per cent of the wool output of Great Britain and Ireland by the early to mid nineteenth century. Ayrshireman William Murdoch's (1754–1839) invention of gas lighting, Alloway man Charles Tennant's (1768–1838) production of chemical bleach in powder form and Glasgow inventor James Beaumont Nelson's 'hot blast' furnace all made a substantial contribution to the rapidly rising Scottish dominance of heavy industry, built on the shoulders of the iconic James Watt (1736–1819) as well as on English inventions and technological developments. In 1812, Henry Bell's (1767–1830) *Comet* was the 'first successful river steamboat in Europe', and helped to lay the foundations for the Scottish dominance of British imperial trade and commercial steam transport, which will be discussed in the next chapter. Not only was Scotland a major supplier of industrial and scientific innovation: it also framed public discourse through a wide range of publishers from Black to Macmillan and the central magazines of the period, *Blackwood's* and *The Edinburgh Review* as well as the radical *Morning Chronicle*, edited in London by Aberdeen man James Pirie/Perry (1756–1821).[46]

The invention of actuarial tables by the ministers Robert Wallace (1697–1771) and Alexander Webster (1707–84) and the establishment of the Scottish Ministers' Widows Fund (1748) as the first recognizably modern pension fund have been described as 'a milestone in financial history' by the historian Niall Ferguson. Likewise the 'invention of graphs' by William Playfair (1759–1823) in 1786 helped to transform the presentation of numerical information. Just as, from fiat currency to the overdraft, Scottish financial innovation in the Bank of England had characterized the eighteenth century, so Scottish banks – despite an attack on their note-issuing rights in 1826, repelled by Scott in the *Letters of Malachi Malagrowther* – continued to occupy a dominant position, being 'better able to mobilise capital and considerably more responsive to the needs of industrialisation' than their English counterparts. They were supported by business networking, with Gilbert Hamilton

(1744–1803) founding the first Chamber of Commerce in Glasgow in 1783. In 1818, legislation was put in place to prohibit 'the circulation of Scottish notes in England' as their use in northern England had become so frequent. Scottish banks supplied finance to the Lancashire and Yorkshire railway and many large textile and chemical employers in England were Scots. Scottish banks opened branches in England, and by the Victorian era it could also be remarked that 'Three quarters of the foreign and colonial Investment Companies are of Scottish origin. If not actually located in Scotland, they have been hatched by Scotchmen and Work on Scottish models.' Their success reflected the increasing economic success of Scotland, which between 1860 and 1914 was contributing more than its per capita share of UK taxes.[47]

These developments were supported by the continuing increase of students at Scottish universities, which ran counter to a general Western tendency for student numbers to decline in the long eighteenth century. There were other significant social changes, not least the rising social mission of the Kirk following on from the social theology of eighteenth-century Moderatism, and the early signs of a triumph in the major population centres for a socially responsible Presbyterianism over a theologically pure one. Despite widespread petitioning against Catholic emancipation in the 1820s, it was supported by prominent Presbyterian ministers such as Professor Thomas Chalmers (1780–1847), who later gave his name to Port Chalmers in New Zealand and became the first Moderator of the Free Kirk, following the Disruption of 1843. The Reform Act of 1832, which enfranchised a larger proportion of the middling ranks in society, had a disproportionate effect on Scotland in particular, given its historically small and tightly controlled electorate. There was a major shift in political sympathy towards the Whigs and later the Liberal Party. The focus on personal integrity, conscience, duty and success in Scottish Presbyterianism marched well with free trade liberalism: its wastefulness was in general confined to the fissiparous nature of Presbyterianism itself, with the misallocation of capital all too evident in the building of Kirk, Free Kirk and United Presbyterian church buildings to rival each other in relatively small towns.[48]

Although the population of the north and the west was still rising (80 per cent in the Western Isles and 53 per cent across the west generally, with a tripling of numbers in hotspots like Tiree before subsequent depopulation), there was now substantial 'Highland' migration into the bigger towns and cities, particularly in the west: 29 per cent of the population of Greenock in 1801 were deemed to have been born in the 'Highland' counties (as we have seen, the 'Highlands' as a concept cut across counties and no such demarcation existed). Irish immigration too was beginning to increase. Nonetheless, the vast expansion in business and industry in Dundee (which overtook Hull as Britain's premier flax port in 1826) and the central belt led to a heavy dependence on child labour as the 'conscripted shock troops of a somewhat tardy Scottish industrial army', ameliorated by innovative developments such as the provisions made at New Lanark, at the heart of the mill industry (by 1839, Lanark and Renfrew housed 175 of Scotland's 192 mills).[49]

Emigration out of Scotland continued to increase in the context of a rapidly rising population. It is still a live question how much of it was driven by ambition and how much by desperation. *The Scotsman* in 1817 clearly took the former position in arguing that 'political feelings induce many to emigrate, who have no reason to complain of their worldly circumstances', an association of the colonies and the United States with liberty and the pursuit of personal well-being and independence. Similarly, projects such as the abortive Topo settlement near the coast in Venezuela, supported by James Mackintosh MP (1765–1832), Chair of the Colombian Society for Agricultural and Other Purposes (1824), drew in artisans, weavers and ex-servicemen desirous of bettering themselves, via an old school Inverness network. When the land proved to be poorer than advertised, the settlers were rescued and resettled in Canada by John Galt (1779–1839), without clearance from the Canada Company, of which Galt was secretary, and became founding members of the settlement at Guelph. These settlers were supported by a network on their departure to Venezuela and on their arrival in Canada, though crucially not in Venezuela itself. On the other hand, there were many poor emigrants without such networks. In Canada, many Scottish merchant houses in 'Montreal, Halifax and Quebec commonly subscribed substantial sums to assist indigent passengers on arrival'. While too much historical interpretation can be erected on single texts such as the globally resonant 'The Canadian Boat Song', printed in *Blackwood's Edinburgh*

Magazine in 1829 and possibly written by one of its staffers, it remains the case that, while settlements such as the 800 Catholics who left Barra for Antigonish in 1802 or the similar numbers who went with the Earl of Selkirk to Prince Edward Island the following year were looking for a better life, others were being forced to seek one. This was surely the case with the 300 cleared from Rum to Cape Breton in 1825, the 1,681 shipped from Barra and South Uist to Québec in 1851 in sardine-like conditions and the 7,000 orphans sent from Quarrier's homes into service in Canada after 1871. As ever, the picture was mixed. One consistent feature can be seen, and it was one deeply engrained in northern Scottish tradition: the importance of acquiring land. The 'benefits of owning land in Canada were touted ceaselessly in the Scottish press' on the grounds of cost and opportunity, with the repeated assurance that good farms could be bought 'for the equivalent of a year's rent at home'. Family recommendations and geographical and kin networks also played a major role. The long tradition of settling Scottish soldiers in Canada helped to smooth the way in providing an infrastructure for the nature and development of such networks, and Scots in general clustered together, as at Bon Accord in Ontario. The stage was set for the Scottish world of the high Victorian empire.[50]

THE CANADIAN BOAT SONG

Listen to me, as when ye heard our father
Sing long ago, the song of other shores-
Listen to me, and then in chorus gather
All your deep voices, as ye pull your oars:

CHORUS.
Fair these broad meads – these hoary woods are grand;
But we are exiles from our fathers' land.

From the lone shieling of the misty island
Mountains divide us, and the waste of seas-

Yet still the blood is strong, the heart is Highland,
And we in dreams behold the Hebrides:

Fair these broad meads – these hoary woods are grand;
But we are exiles from our fathers' land.

We ne'er shall tread the fancy-haunted valley,
Where 'tween the dark hills creeps the small clear stream,
In arms around the patriarch banner rally,
Nor see the moon on royal tombstones gleam:

Fair these broad meads – these hoary woods are grand;
But we are exiles from our fathers' land.

When the bold kindred, in the time long-vanishd,
Conquer'd the soil and fortified the keep-
No seer foretold the children would be banish'd,
That a degenerate Lord might boast his sheep:

Fair these broad meads – these hoary woods are grand;
But we are exiles from our fathers' land.

Come foreign rage – let Discord burst in slaughter!
O then for clansman true, and stern claymore-
The hearts that would have given their blood like water,
Beat heavily beyond the Atlantic roar:

Fair these broad meads – these hoary woods are grand;
But we are exiles from our fathers' land.

The image of martial valour and betrayal by a native elite who
should rely on it and honour it have passed into the cultural memory

of the era of the Clearances. Seldom can one anonymous poem or song have had such an effect in summarizing a historical memory which expresses the complex underlying issues of the era in such simple terms. 'The Canadian Boat Song' first appeared in *Blackwood's Magazine* in the 'Noctes Ambrosianae' column in 1829, and continues to be assigned to a variety of different authors. It is a very good story, and therefore – acknowledging Dr Johnson – not wholly true. However, it expresses in fiction what was believed to be a real experience. In that sense, it is central to the expression and impact of Scottish Romanticism.

5

THE SCOTTISH WORLD

SINEWS OF EMPIRE

The Victorian era saw the maturation of the second British Empire following the loss of the American colonies. But in addition to territory, the ascendancy established by Great Britain in transport and other forms of technology provided a British infrastructure for world commerce and military power which extended far beyond even the huge areas under Great Britain's direct control. If the eighteenth century's 'sinews of power', to borrow John Brewer's famous phrase, were dependent on the financial infrastructure of the British state, the nineteenth century's sinews were those of technological leadership. The transport and communication revolution brought – in Constantin Pecqueur's words in 1839 – 'changes in material innovations' which produced 'changes in the cultural sphere', what Marx was eighteen years later to term the 'annihilation of space by time' through the railways, steamships and telegraphy. An age in many ways analogous to the modern era of globalization emerged, where innovation vastly changed the geopolitical and commercial landscape: money and people and their habits moved with greater velocity and precision than ever before between globally facing cities, exchanging raw materials for manufactured goods in hitherto unimaginable quantities at hitherto unknown speeds. Global trade quadrupled and Calcutta/Kolkata's opium exports rose tenfold, while by 1900 jute was 'nearly 40 per cent' of its export trade. As the historian John Darwin puts it, there were 'fleets of steamers for goods, migrants and mail; lines of rail to prise open remote interiors for occupation and trade' pushed into and between great port cities, the 'beachheads' and 'great agents of steam globalization' creating 'new kinds of exchange and new zones of commerce' through which travelled power, violence and the more progressive 'libertarian message of the European Enlightenment'. This was the infrastructure on which the Scottish world was built.[1]

Rail was central to this, as was the control of the seas for the transport of men and *materiél*, goods and passengers. The rapid technological development of steam transport by sea and land and the innovative margin in these areas possessed by the British Empire provided the arterial infrastructure and initial commercial ascendancy of the early and mid Victorian era. Scottish science, enterprise and international networking stood at the centre of these developments: William Symington and the steamboat (1788); Richard Trevithick and the steam locomotive made possible by the partnership of James Watt and Matthew Boulton (1802); John Loudon McAdam and tarmac (1806); James Chalmers and the adhesive stamp (1834); Kirkpatrick Macmillan and the bicycle (1839), followed by Robert Thomson and John Boyd Dunlop and the development of the pneumatic tyre; James Nasmyth and the steam hammer (1839); Alexander Bain and the synchronizable electric clock (1840) and 'chemical telegraph' (fax) (1846); James Young Simpson and chloroform (1847); Alexander Wood and the hypodermic syringe (1853); James Harrison and the refrigerator, following William Cullen's earlier work in the 1750s (1856); Joseph Lister and antiseptic procedure (1865–67); Alexander Graham Bell and the telephone (1876). These advances were due to a variety of domestic factors, but general education – and the instrumental nature of education in the application of reason to knowledge in a context of material improvement called for by the Scottish Enlightenment – played a major role. John Anderson's 1763 request to Watt 'to repair the University's model of a Newcomen engine' and Joseph Black's (1728–99) attempt to devise a bleaching process for linen that was reliable and non-soluble were alike evidence of the power of an Enlightenment 'network . . . of professors, industrialists, financiers and aristocrats who were involved in complementary ways in developing industry'.[2]

The century that followed showed that this connectivity in Scottish education from apprenticeships to aristocracy continued to be highly effective. Sir James Dewar (1847–1932) began as a laboratory assistant to Professor

J.D. Forbes; James 'Paraffin' Young (1811–83) was a Professor at Anderson's College in Glasgow (now the University of Strathclyde) and also on the business side opened the first oil refinery near Bathgate in 1850; James Blyth (1839–1906) was Freeland Professor of Natural Philosophy at Anderson's and developed the first wind turbine in Scotland in 1887; William Thomson, Lord Kelvin's (1824–1907) business interests included directorships of the Atlantic Telegraph Company (whose business was made possible by his science) and the Kodak Company among others, while he continued to hold his Glasgow professorship. Sir John Pender (1816–96), a former pupil of the High School of Glasgow who supervised the laying of the transatlantic cable which Kelvin pioneered, founded thirty-two telegraph businesses, including what was to become Cable and Wireless. By 1890, nearly 'two-thirds of the telegraph lines in the world were owned by British companies'.[3]

SCOTTISH EDUCATION

There were – it has been claimed – four key elements in Scottish education at school and university levels which differentiated it on the international stage: it was more socially open; it was largely public in nature, with a very small private school sector (under 2 per cent as late as 1967); it was broad and externally connected; and it was driven by a passion for ideas, linked to the instrumental role philosophy played throughout the university curriculum. From the first Education Act of 1496 – designed to support the consistent schooling of the nobility – to the 1696 Act, the Scottish Parliament had exerted a keen interest in educational matters. Scottish burgh schools, initially run by the Church, and often of ancient date, with those at Aberdeen (no later than 1418, possibly 1257), Ayr (1233), Dundee (1239), Edinburgh (1128), Glasgow (1124), Lanark (1183) and Stirling (1129) among the oldest, were adopted by the secular authorities after the Reformation. While these were supplemented by the Merchant Company/Hospital Schools (George Heriot's (1628), Hutchesons' Grammar School (1641), The Merchant Maiden (now Mary Erskine's,

1694), Robert Gordon's College (1732) and others), and the imitation English public schools such as the later Fettes (1870) and Glenalmond (1847), the burgh grammar schools retained high status. It was only in the mid eighteenth century that the scions of the upper nobility in Scotland definitively moved away to be educated in English private (public) schools. Even so, the burgh schools continued to attract the able members of an elite and even foreign pupils, sometimes of part Scottish ancestry, such as Siang Hye Eu and Cornelius Agnew Suvoong, who both attended Aberdeen Grammar School in the late nineteenth century before returning to pursue successful professional careers in East Asia. The burgh grammar schools were in no sense déclassé, as their English equivalents might have been: the Orléanist princes in exile attended the Royal High School in Edinburgh, for example.

The school system seems to have driven high literacy rates, which reached 85 per cent in the mid Victorian era, compared to 70 per cent in England and 25 per cent in Italy, and there was some significant innovation in education for those suffering from disabilities: 'Braidwood's school for the deaf and dumb', established in Edinburgh in 1760, was 'the first . . . in Great Britain'. Bursaries and relatively low fees made higher education accessible, and there were both very young (William Thomson, Lord Kelvin, went to university at ten) and mature students who had saved for a higher education in the classes. Unlike Oxbridge, education at St Andrews (1411), Glasgow (1451), King's (1495), Marischal (1560) or Edinburgh (1583) was not a rite of passage for a demographic cohort of elite young men. Rather the universities – like the burgh schools, but even more so – were also seen as part of the institutional fabric of the country, which indeed in large part was created by their products, men such as Robert Adam (1728–92, Royal High School and University of Edinburgh), William Burn (1789–1870, Royal High School) and Robert Lorimer (1864–1929, Edinburgh Academy and University) among them.

Some who had never attended the Scots universities, such as the Dunfermline-born steel magnate Andrew Carnegie (1835–1918), left fortunes to benefit them.[4]

The Scottish higher education system gave its model to the United States, Canada, Australia and elsewhere: today, university provision in the United States is truer to the history of Scottish higher education than Scotland is itself, both in its generalism and in the provision of professional subjects such as law as a second rather than a first degree. In the eighteenth and nineteenth centuries, when Scotland enjoyed a lead through the development of its native higher education tradition rather than being a ruletaker from an increasingly centralized British system, its strong focus on links between business and study, and later in some universities between study and industry, were important in driving innovation. When the first four professors of medicine at the University of Edinburgh were appointed in 1726, they engaged in external business, and – as has been discussed earlier – the crossover between medicine, botany and pharmacy in the curriculum and outside business interests drove major international developments far outside the realm of medicine itself. Similarly at Glasgow in the eighteenth and nineteenth centuries, professorial assistants, demonstrators and instrument makers provided a link between physics and engineering as subjects, and their applicability in industry. As we have already seen, John Anderson's college, founded at his death in 1796, pioneered higher education for women, while the gifted doctor James McCune Smith (1813–65), denied entry to Columbia on the grounds of his race, crossed the Atlantic to Glasgow, where he passed out at the top of his class and subsequently became a campaigner for women's suffrage, prominent abolitionist and a co-founder of the 'National Council of Colored People' in New York in 1853.[5]

Scientific innovation in its turn supported entrepreneurial development. Practical innovations came readily from scientific thought – as with James Young Simpson's (1811–70) development of chloroform as an anaesthetic – because of an already familiar environment which located university, professional and commercial life in social and civic adjacency, supported by networks of association, institution, location and relation. These networks pooled individual social capital – in the sense described by Pierre Bourdieu (1930–2002) – in profoundly effective ways. Medicine was a key area for this, with developments such as psychiatric nurse training and the first hospital X-ray unit (1896) reflecting this combination of conception, innovation and application: the core nexus of what made Scottish higher education globally significant. The natural sciences and engineering also benefited from this to a disproportionate extent: the infant James Clerk Maxwell's (1831–79) desire to know 'what's the go of it?' displayed precisely this mixture of theory and practice in embryo. When the Royal Society of Edinburgh (1783), the country's national academy, took an official photograph of its Fellows in 1903, William Thomson, Lord Kelvin and Joseph, 1st Baron Lister (1827–1912), the antiseptic pioneer who had been successively Professor of Surgery at Glasgow and Edinburgh, stood at the front, aptly symbolizing the strength of medicine and the natural sciences in the nineteenth-century Scottish academy and society. Though no Scotsman, Lister's ability to work across infirmary and university practice in Scotland was critical to the development of his work. Later figures such as John Logie Baird (1888–1946), John MacLeod (1876–1935), the discoverer of insulin, and Robert Watson Watt (1892–1973), the inventor of radar, came from the same marriage of scientific theory and its applications.[6]

As we have already seen, Scottish botanists, ranging from those with practical garden experience to beneficiaries of the joint botanical and medical university curricula which 'connected medicine with knowledge about botany, climate and geology', played a major role in understanding, depicting, collecting and resettling the flora of global British power. Figures such as David Douglas (1799–1834, of the 'Douglas Fir'), Robert Fortune (1812–80), Francis Masson

(1741–1805), Archibald Menzies of Aberfeldy, who introduced the Monkey Puzzle, William Paterson (1755–1810, Lieutenant Governor of New South Wales), Hugh Cleghorn (1820–95), 'who catalogued forest products for the 1851 Great Exhibition and endowed a chair of forestry at Edinburgh University', and Sir Joseph Hooker (1817–1911) at Kew were central to these developments. These men's contributions frequently sustained British economic power, for example in the case of Fortune's contribution to the tea industry. Douglas began as an apprentice gardener on the Scone estate, Robert Fortune at a Berwickshire nursery, while Masson had worked at Kew. Aberdonians Hugh Falconer (1808–65), Sir George King (1840–1909) and Sir David Prain (1857–1944) superintended the Royal Botanic Gardens at Calcutta/Kolkata or were professors of botany there; Prain went on to direct Kew, and King to direct the botanical survey of India. All three attended the University of Aberdeen and both King and Prain went to Aberdeen Grammar School; unsurprisingly King mentored Prain, helping him to gain openings in India and in Kolkata. Forestry experts such as Alexander Gibson (1800–67) from Stracathro and Hugh Cleghorn transformed the landscape from India to New Zealand, and were among the first to believe 'that there was a direct relationship between deforestation, climatic change and environmental degradation', a case which convinced government and helped to lead to the establishment of the Indian Forest Department in 1864. Sir Charles Lyell (1797–1875) from Angus built on James Hutton's *Theory of the Earth* (1785–88) to develop modern geology, while Sir Roderick Murchison (1792–1871) from Tarradale, 'the immensely influential president of the Royal Geographical Society . . . produced global, overarching theories of the formation of the earth and of geological zones'. Murchison commissioned one of Landseer's great paintings, *Rent Day in the Wilderness* (1855–68), 'to celebrate the exploits of his forebear' Colonel Murchison's defence of the Marquess of Seaforth's estates after the failure of the 1715 Jacobite Rising and the Marquess's exile. In Anderson's College, Professor James Blyth (1839–1906) created the first wind turbine to light his holiday home in Kincardineshire. These figures frequently worked across disciplinary boundaries, as encouraged by a Scottish university curriculum which still fully reflected its own national traditions, and further supported by works such as James Brown's *The Forester* (1847), which 'provided practical advice on how to create and manage a forest in the Scottish landscape based on scientific principles'. Brown, who was forester on the Dundas estate at Arniston, became the first president of the Scottish Arboricultural Society. The holistic education and openness to international ideas of Scottish botanists was widely recognized. When 'Sandford Fleming, born in Kirkcaldy, embarked upon his great survey of the route of the trans-Canada railway in the mid 1870s, he took with him a historian and a naturalist to complement his own extensive interests in the natural world.'[7]

It is of course possible to be nostalgic and a cheerleader for Scottish higher education in the nineteenth century and to decry the major changes that came upon it in that era, as George Davie famously did

16. Edwin Landseer, *Rent Day in the Wilderness* (1855–1868),
celebrating Sir Roderick Murchison's Jacobite ancestry.

in *The Democratic Intellect* (1961), which recognizes the important role philosophy played in the historic Scottish curriculum. Its practice not only prepared students in the art of thinking, but also served as an adjunct to the hard-headed pragmatism of public policy and administration, in the shape of the 'Scotch philosophy' of 'Common Sense' and later Utilitarianism: philosophers such as Thomas Reid (1710–96) were for a long time influential in French and American education. This central role of philosophical thinking certainly began to diminish under the gradual pressure of conformity to British specialization. Yet it is fair to note that the introduction of new subjects and new systems of governance by the British Government in the Victorian era may have made the Scottish universities more competitive and dynamic, although figures such as Francis, Lord Jeffrey (1773–1850), editor of the *Edinburgh Review*, and Henry, 1st Baron Brougham (1778–1868), the Lord Chancellor, were robust defenders of the traditional system. Indeed, the production of top Mathematics Wranglers at Cambridge such as Thomas Barker, George Chrystal, William Mollison, George Slessor and James Stirling, who all came from one burgh school at a time when almost all their fellows would study at the Scottish universities, hardly suggests that Scottish school education was wanting. Overall it is hard to resist the conclusion that Scotland's education and in particular its higher education did not entirely benefit from the process of Anglicization, which increased in the late nineteenth and early twentieth centuries, such as the school boards of 1872 with their arguable bureaucratization of distinctive missions. Things may not have improved in the later twentieth century: in the 1960s and 70s some might argue – although largely not in Scotland – that the great burgh grammar schools were undermined, destroyed or driven into the private sector in pursuit of a British model of homogenized comprehensive schools which England never fully implemented and later abandoned. These are still controversial areas, but what is beyond doubt is that, in the two centuries after Culloden, Scotland's intellectual elites made a disproportionate contribution to British power, innovation and dynamism which has never been surpassed. The Scottish higher education system made its way across the world, and Scots such as James McGill (1744–1813) founded what are today major international universities. Those who would not attribute Scottish success and the imitation of the national system of education in any way to the country's distinctive approach would be reaching a different conclusion from that demonstrated by evidence, including the evidence for greater participation from socially disadvantaged groups. But if Scottish policy today still values education, it is less clear that it values innovation and excellence, and it was these – combined with the nationally typical striving for mutual advantage – that made the Scottish world which is the subject of this chapter.[8]

William Symington (1762–1831) developed a steamboat on commission from Patrick Miller of Dalswinton (1731–1815), who has some claim to be the inventor of the paddle wheel. There had been other attempts to use steam on water, but, like the pre-Watt steam engine, these had not undergone focussed development. The Symington–Miller partnership (which also included James Taylor) 'designed and sailed a twin-hulled paddle boat on Loch Dalswinton' on a test run on which Robert Burns was a passenger in 1788. The Forth and Clyde canal employed Symington to experiment with steam power in 1800, and in 1801 a boat had initial trials on the River Carron. On 4 January 1803, the 17-metre *Charlotte Dundas,* with a central paddlewheel, made its first trip on the Forth and Clyde canal. There was resistance to the technology, but Henry Bell (1767–1830) introduced the first passenger steam service in Europe in 1812 (Robert Fulton's *Claremont* on the Hudson, 'powered by a Boulton and Watt engine', ran five years earlier) with the 30-tonne *Comet* (see plate 21). The *Comet's* boiler was built by David Napier (1790–1869), and the Napier family's innovative engineering was to underpin much of the success of Scottish shipbuilding in the century that followed. By 1814, the Rothesay service was able to travel at six knots and by 1840 twice that. Steamboats prospered on internal routes: their greater capacity drove tourism and lowered prices, just as they were later to open up interior waterways commercially in the colonies, far from Great Britain. The 'new wave of tourism powered by steamboat' was in its turn celebrated in visual imagery, such as John Knox's (1776–1845) *First Steamboat on the Clyde* (1820); the rapid changes of scenery achieved by such transit methods were akin to Knox's own panoramas. By 1826, between 60 and 70 pleasure trips were advertised from Glasgow, and by 1850 some 20,000 people left the city on Fair Saturday in July to travel from the Broomielaw on the Clyde to the coast in thirty-five steamers. While an inside seat on a coach from Stirling to Callander (16 kilometres) cost 4s. 6d. (£35 today), a cabin from Stirling to Edinburgh (65 kilometres) on a steamboat cost 1s. 6d. plus a pier charge. Mass travel and mass tourism were not solely the prerogative of the railways.[9]

In 1837, James MacQueen (1778–1870), an erstwhile sugar plantation manager in Grenada and later part-owner of the *Glasgow Courier* and contributor to *Blackwood's Commercial Reports*, 'presented a preliminary plan for a global imperial network of mail shipping lines to the Post Office and especially to the Admiralty'. In 1838, MacQueen's plans were published as *A General Plan for a Mail Communication by Steam between Great Britain and the Eastern and Western Parts of the World*, and proposed to Francis Baring, Secretary to the Treasury, as a scheme 'to bind the Colonies together'. The strategic goal of such a service would not only be mail delivery, but was intended to provide merchant naval domination of the seas to match the Royal Navy's on the military side. MacQueen saw the establishment of what was to become the Royal Mail Steam Packet Company (RMSP) as a means to gain British pre-eminence in commerce over the United States and other foreign powers, and planned to extend the service as far as China and Australia. He pointed out that mercantile and naval military domination could not only work in tandem, but that one could unobtrusively sustain the other, for commercial shipping could carry substantial quantities of military *matériel* to support Great Britain while attracting less attention than naval reinforcements. It was increasingly clear that steam would provide substantially enhanced capacity for carrying cargo with the potential of making the British Empire 'masters of the ocean' and gaining 'access into every country, and to every land'. In 1839, MacQueen secured the support of the West India Committee of London merchants and former plantation owners. John Irving MP (1766–1845), 'of the influential merchant banking firm of Reid, Irving and Company', founded by fellow Dumfriesshire man Sir Thomas Reid (1762–1824) on the basis of a firm set up by their mutual relative John Rae, was a strong supporter, given his interests in Central American silver. On 26 September, Queen Victoria granted a Royal Charter to the 'Royal Mail Steam-Packet Company' and MacQueen – though he subsequently lost position and favour – became its first General Superintendent. In April 1840, RMSP contracts for its steamer fleet were awarded: seven to Scotland, principally the rapidly developing Clyde yards, seven to England. The power of Scottish networking was in full view, and surly comments on the 'Scotch aristocracy' recalled the days of Bute in the 1760s. Among the RMSP partners, former High School of Glasgow pupil Sir George Burns (1795–1890) became a partner in 1839, going on to own 107 steamers with his brother James. Between 1840 and 1880, UK steam horsepower (Watt's measure) rose from 620,000 to 7.6 million: globally, only the United States, with the demand for steam on its long rivers, had more. British steam was not alone however: by the 1840s, the Austrian Royal and Imperial Steamboat Company was transporting 'over 200,000 passengers on the Danube every year'.[10]

In these early years of Queen Victoria's reign, other similar developments were afoot which would help reinforce Great Britain's 'sovereignty of the seas', and present a global light-touch *mare clausum* to protect and project the nature of British power, with heavy investment of Scottish capital and business leadership. From 1822, Brodie McGhie Wilcox (1786–1862) and Shetlander Arthur Anderson (1792–1868), both later Liberal MPs, developed extensive business with Spain and Portugal. Their business later became the Peninsular Steam Navigation Company (1830) and then the Peninsular & Oriental Steam Company (P&O). The founding Minute of the firm as P&O was taken on 23 April 1840, in the same month as the RMSP contracts were awarded. P&O were soon sailing through the Mediterranean and

Alexandria, 'with an overland passage to Suez and onward to Ceylon, Madras and Calcutta'. In 1828, it took five months to reach India from Great Britain; by 1848 it was five weeks, and this dropped further to three after the opening of the Suez canal in 1869. By the middle of the 1840s, P&O 'were implementing plans for eastward extensions to China and contemplating future services to Australia'. P&O then entered the opium trade in 1847, shipping almost 60,000 chests a year; fittingly enough, Sir James Matheson (1796–1878) (of Jardine & Matheson – see below) became the chairman of P&O in 1851, and the company took the view 'that there should always be one man on the board who had some personal experience of the opium trade'. Their long voyages and need for cargo space created a demand for technically innovative ships, and the company 'cultivated face-to-face connections with Clyde contractors', such as Tod & MacGregor and Caird & Company. Meanwhile, Professor William Thomson's work at the University of Glasgow was perfecting underwater telegraphy, leading to the laying of the Atlantic Cable in 1858. Thomson's lab assistants were put to work on small practical research projects which would enhance steam technology, and these were shared with his students in the virtuous circle between business, industry, research and education typical of Scottish universities at the time. Thomson was knighted in 1866, became a peer in 1892 (the first scientist ever to be ennobled) and a Privy Counsellor in 1902, eventually being buried next to Isaac Newton in Westminster Abbey. Meanwhile P&O continued its Scottish connexion in the person of Sir Thomas Sutherland (1834–1922), the son of a housepainter who attended Aberdeen Grammar School and won through to higher education at Marischal, Aberdeen's second university which merged with King's in 1860. Sutherland ran the P&O business in Hong Kong (after 1842 the prime receiving port for China-destined opium), becoming Managing Director then Chair of P&O from 1872 to 1914. He remained close to John Caird and his Greenock yards, from which P&O ordered eighty steamers between 1870 and 1914; in 1900, half of the P&O fleet was registered at Greenock. For sixteen of these years (1884–1900), Sutherland – who also co-founded HSBC – was Liberal MP for Greenock, and thus his home constituency did excellent business. Our age might identify a conflict of interest, as indeed we might in noting that, in serving as MP for Ross and

Cromarty in 1847–68, James Matheson represented the interests of 'his own properties' in Parliament. Such things were then routine, and at least had the advantage of being in plain sight.[11]

Cunard from its foundation was a to be 'a private partnership that relied heavily on a few investors'. In 1839, the Canadian Samuel Cunard (1787–1865) entered into a contract with Robert Napier (1791–1876), David's cousin, to supply ships. In his turn, Napier helped 'to unlock the capital of Glasgow's wealthiest merchants'. A consortium of thirty-three Glasgow businessmen provided the necessary capital for the establishment of what was soon to become the Cunard passenger line, with *Caledonia* being launched in 1840, and the *Persia* and *Scotia* coming to provide a fast and reliable service across the Atlantic. Napier's technical expertise helped to supply the 'largest and most powerful steamer afloat' in the shape of the *Persia* in 1856, though this was temporarily overshadowed by *The Great Eastern* (1858), built by Scottish engineer John Scott Russell (1808–82), who had developed a steam-driven car in the 1830s, in collaboration with Brunel. Clearly Napier's and other Clyde yards had the applied research and production scale necessary to occupy a dominant global position, sustained by Scottish capital and the intensity of national networking at home and overseas. By 1913–14, 44 per cent of 'total world investment' was British (nearly half the country's annual savings were held abroad), and the per capita Scottish contribution was far above the average, with firms such as Scottish Widows (1815) and Standard Life (1825) investing millions overseas. One-third of global securities 'were being traded in London', while 'nearly half the world's foreign capital . . . derived from Britain or was remitted through London'. As the *North American Review* remarked, under Cunard, P&O and RMSP 'The Atlantic, the Mediterranean . . . and the waters of the East had . . . been taken possession of . . . as though they had all been included in her [Great Britain's] rightful domain.'[12] Over '80 per cent of the world's goods were carried on British ships' and many – and often most – of those were Scottish; British 'domination of the seas' guaranteed near monopolies in certain markets, for example in 'cotton sales to Latin America'. From the *James Watt* to the *Lord of the Isles* (1853) and the *Scotia*, the names of the ships which exerted this dominance carried the signs of their origin, and the owners and chairs of these great companies fed a stream of orders on the Clyde while establishing new businesses, such as the British & African Steam Navigation Company, founded at Glasgow in 1869. Up to and including the *Queen Elizabeth 2* (1967), 99 of Cunard's 134 ships were built in Scotland.[13]

This revolution in steam transport – even today, '90% of world trade moves by sea' – rendered other improvements in the mechanization of manufacturing or the navigation of inland waters geometrical in their effects in the promotion of rapid and increasingly frictionless trade, which in its turn was controlled by the countries that held a technological lead. The final abandonment of the Navigation Acts in 1849–51 cleared the way for the internationalization of British seaborne commerce, and by 1899 'all but 2 per cent of the world's manufactured exports' came from a few Western countries. Standardization of prices by telegram and the creation for the first time of 'regularity and certainty in the transit times of people, goods and mail' revolutionized business. Further, the projection of steam on the river systems and, thanks to Islay man Alexander MacDougall's (1845–1923) whaleback ships, on the Great Lakes, fed into the sea at the prosperous ports of the world helping to spread development beyond the ocean-facing entrepôts of the coast. Steam's appetite for coal led to the use of coal gas for industrial and domestic purposes, while on land 'railways reduced the cost of overland transport' as much as 13-fold. By 1913, over 40 per cent of British overseas investment supported the 'construction and operation of overseas railways'.[14]

THERMOPYLAE

If the west coast shipyards in Scotland pioneered the latest steamship technology, the last Indian summer of sail was supported by the technical expertise of the country's east coast yards, including the 'Aberdeen Bow' devised by Alexander Hall & Co in 1839. The Bow increased the speed and sailing performance of schooners and then clippers, a class of swift sailing ships developed from schooners which combined speed with size. The clipper rose to prominence in the second quarter of the nineteenth century with increasing demand for the rapid transport of China tea to Western markets following the First Opium War of 1840–42 (see below), when Hong Kong island came into British hands and five ports opened to British commercial trade in China. Following the Aberdeen proto clipper *Scottish Maid* in 1839, the first clippers proper were developed in the late 1840s and Jardine Matheson's search for the latest technology played a role. George Thomson of Pitmedden (1804–95), like Sutherland at P&O an Aberdeen Grammar School boy, founded the Aberdeen White Star Line in 1825 (later taken over by Cunard), and was deeply engaged in the tea trade from 1848, for which clippers were a key mode of transport, sometimes as a cover for the opium trade. These ships were widely regarded as 'essential to the commercial intelligence of the India-China trade', and the Jardine Matheson clipper fleet was 'larger than the navies of some small nations'.[15]

The composite clipper had an iron frame covered with wood, and it was these that became the fastest unpowered full-size ships ever built. In 1860, 'registered sailing ship tonnage' was still 'ten times that of steam', and was still four-fold greater ten years later, as sail enjoyed a brief Indian summer dependent on onboard mechanization and no need to refuel. These sailing ships were not so much survivors as examples of fusion between new and old technologies. *Thermopylae*, built in 1868 for George Thomson by Walter Hood & Co – a major supplier to the White Star Line and clipper specialists since the construction of *Kosciusko* for Thomson in 1862 – was just over 64 metres long and 11 metres in the beam, but only just over 6 metres deep, weighing less than 1,000 tonnes gross and displacing 2,000 tonnes. Her hull was sheathed in copper. She carried a figurehead of Leonidas, King of Sparta, who fell defending Greece from Persian invasion at Thermopylae in 480 BC. Despite symbolizing the defence of the West, *Thermopylae* like other clippers was intended to convey produce from East Asia.

Her maiden voyage to Melbourne in just over 60 days remains the fastest trip ever made to Australia by sail, and her 'record day's run' was well over 600 kilometres, though Donald McKay's American-built clippers gained other records (including the incredible 861 kilometres in 24 hours achieved by *Sovereign of the Seas*). The *Melbourne Argus* commented (13 January 1869):

> The splendid and almost unprecedentedly rapid passage made by the new clipper ship *Thermopylae*, from London to this port, has created more than ordinary interest in nautical and commercial circles ... It seemed almost impossible, and certainly never entered into the calculations of the most sanguine, that a voyage to the antipodes could be accomplished by a sailing-ship in fifty-nine days, the period taken by the *Thermopylae* to within sight of the Australian coast ... She is in every respect a fine specimen of naval architecture, a model of symmetry and beauty; her sweeping lines and exquisite proportions, her graceful outline and general compactness, conveying an idea of perfection.

In 1869, *Cutty Sark* (named from Robert Burns' *Tam o' Shanter*, and designed by Bernard Linton from Inverbervie in Kincardineshire) was built in Dumbarton, specifically to outrun *Thermopylae*. In the fiercely contested China tea run, *Thermopylae* initially had the edge, though *Cutty Sark* was to prevail in later years. In 1872, *Thermopylae* raced *Cutty Sark* on the Shanghai–London tea run, finishing nine days ahead after falling behind, thanks to her rival's loss of her rudder off the South African coast. With the rise of steam, spurred by the new Suez canal, on the China run from the 1870s, *Thermopylae* was first of all moved to the Australian wool export trade and then sold for the Vancouver–Asia trade in 1890, crossing the Pacific in a record twenty-nine days. In 1895 she was sold as a training ship to the Portuguese Navy, being disposed of by torpedo in 1907. The wreck was located in 2003.[16]

The sinews of international transport boosted migration and population mobility as well as cargo, and also provided a huge uplift to growth: the annual growth in world trade more than quadrupled from under 1 per cent to over 4 per cent between 1820 and 1870. Scotland benefited from the technology it did so much to pioneer. From a position where the country had 73 per cent of the rest of Great Britain's production per capita in 1815, and had persistently lower wages in consequence of its poorer economy (around 60 to 70 per cent of British averages in many cases), matters altered to such an extent that the Scottish economy had overtaken England and Wales in per capita terms by the middle of the century. The Great Exhibition of 1851 – itself developed from the Jacobin idea of a 'universal exhibition', the earlier exhibitions of 1845 in Berne and Madrid and immediately from the 1849 Exposition in Paris – attracted 6 million visitors to its displays of British and global innovation. The chef Alexis Soyer (1810–58) brought cuisines from across the globe to feed these vast visitor numbers in his Symposium of All Nations. Scotland contributed everything from tartan and steam tractors to the 'first self-acting fountain pen', invented by R.W. Thomson (1822–73) two years before, and Alexander Shanks' (1801–45) lawnmower. One of the legacies of the Exhibition was the aim of promoting 'regional' industrial museums: the one founded in Scotland in 1854 eventually became the National Museum of Scotland.[17]

Scottish capital, imported from the Empire in the long eighteenth century, was now increasingly exported, not least by virtue of the fact that, by 1912, Scots had a controlling interest in one in eight of the world's biggest shipping lines. James Wilson (1805–60), a Scottish businessman and founder of the Chartered Bank of India, Australia and China, established *The Economist* newspaper in 1843 to campaign for free trade and support the globalization of Scottish and other capital; the campaign bore fruit in 1849 with the repeal of the Navigation Acts, a major boost to free trade. Abram Lyle of Greenock (1820–91) used his shipping interests to spread the market for his golden syrup. In the United States, 75 per cent of ranch investment came from Scotland, and 'Scottish mortgage finance also played a key role in the development of US agriculture'. The investment trust movement helped to support the provision of international capital from a wider demographic base in Scottish society than the 0.33 per cent (*c.*14,000 individuals) of the super-networked elite who enjoyed 25 per cent of the national income on the back of their kin- and association-based pooling of social capital. This was more a class than a patriarchy: in 1913, Scottish women 'held 21 per cent of overseas investments'. Our abandonment of class for gender and identity-based analyses of social exclusion can miss some important facets of history. Such women took an active role too: Betsy Miller of Ayr (1793–1864) was 'the first woman to be registered with Lloyds as a ship captain', while Jane Waterston (1843–1932), originally a teacher in the Cape Colony opposed to 'distinction of race, colour or sect' and to the 'tinselly, slovenly kind of stuff that used to be thought enough for a girl's schoolroom', eventually became a doctor and Fellow of the Royal College of Physicians of Ireland while developing the public health service in Cape Town. Matilda Chaplain (1846–83), one of the Edinburgh Seven, the first female medical students in the United Kingdom, went on to open a midwifery school in Japan.[18]

There was intensive Scottish investment not only in the US, but also in Canada, Australia, India and Ceylon. In Glasgow, Sir John Muir (1828–1903), educated at the city's High School and University, became Lord Provost in 1889, having been Vice-President of the previous year's Great Exhibition, where he ran the 'India and Ceylon section' in view of his near £5 million (£700 million at 2022 prices) assets in tea, some of which was no doubt served by Joseph Lyons at the Exhibition's 'Bishops Palace Temperance Café'. The Scots contribution to imperial investment overall ran at 'about 60 per cent above the British average'. Scotland was home to up to two-thirds of all British investment in the US stock market, and by 1914 had 12 per cent 'of all British foreign lending'. The rigid probity attributed to Scots in money matters – damaged to the point of destruction in the financial crisis of 2008 – dates from this era. It was portrayed in the domestic economy by Samuel Smiles' (1812–1904) *Self-Help* (1859), which embodied the ideology of a secular Presbyterianism in its view that poverty was the result of irresponsibility and lack of probity and effort: 250,000 copies were sold in Smiles' own lifetime. One of eleven children from a Haddington family, Smiles moved from being a doctor's apprentice to being a medical student at Edinburgh, then a Chartist, a newspaper editor and a famous writer. For him, those who lived at the expense of others were enemies to society. To many today, he would seem on the far right; in the 1840s, he was a radical who favoured nationalizing the railways and criticized an unreconstructed free market, while having a ruthless attitude to those who had opportunities of which – in his view – they did not take advantage.[19]

From the early nineteenth century, the Indian pattern shawls manufactured in Paisley and the associated Paisley pattern grew to have a dominant position in international markets, while Coats of Paisley controlled 'no less than 80% of world thread-making capacity in the early twentieth century'. In Glasgow, Templeton was the largest carpet manufacturer in Great Britain, while in the 1880s, almost 100 million litres of whisky a year were being 'charged for duty', a level of business not too far off today's. Glasgow innovations, such as former High School pupil Charles Mackintosh's (1766– 1843) eponymous raincoat, changed everyday lives extensively, and by 1820 Glasgow was being described as the Second City of the Empire – the term was apparently first used in Edinburgh. In Dundee, the city's rapid development as 'Juteopolis' in succession to its earlier linen boom depended on the vast importation of raw jute, over 140,000 tonnes of which was being landed annually by the 1870s. Indian-style chairs and designs and Chinese-style ceramics – particularly the latter – were manufactured in large numbers for export, with techniques and designs likely to have been exchanged between the Scottish and Indian industries, for example through successive Scottish directors of the India Museum and widespread collecting of Indian craft textiles. Architects such as Alexander 'Greek' Thomson (1817–75) injected an eclectic mixture of Greek and Egyptian influences into Scotland's domestic architecture. This architecture in turn developed a new flavour in the work of William Burn and others, in which a baronial Gothic celebrating the country's past martial traditions was recrudescent, for example in Burns' fellow Royal High School former pupil David Bryce's (1803–76) remodelling of the Duke of Atholl's seat at Blair in 1869. In most of the industrial centres though, the combination of highly priced land and the demands of feudal duties meant that Scottish builders in search of profit maximized the number of households in each building', and even after slum clearances almost half of Scots households lived in only one or two rooms. These areas of high density were convenient sources for a large industrial workforce.

Such a workforce was not only active in ship or locomotive building, or decorative textiles and ceramics. Michael Nairn's linoleum factory in Kirkcaldy achieved as dominant a position in floor coverings internationally as Dundee did in jute: as the *Art Journal* put it in 1862, 'The Scottish firm is without any real rival whatever.' Nairn's was indeed promoted in these terms internationally, being very much advertised as Scottish rather than British in France, for example. Nairn's son, Sir Michael Nairn (1838–1915), succeeded his father at the head of the firm and was awarded a baronetcy in 1904.[20]

Domestic heavy industry grew to vast proportions, as 'the bulk of Scottish heavy industrial output was basic and destined for export'. Some 20 per cent of the population of Scotland lived in industrial centres in 1801; a century later, this had risen almost to half. Yet, despite becoming 'one of the most urbanised societies in Europe', Scottish levels of emigration sat alongside – if not quite equal to – largely rural societies such as Ireland or Norway. Although between a quarter and a third of Scottish migrants returned to Scotland and are thus more properly described as sojourners, huge numbers left the country for good. Net emigration was some 900,000 between 1860 and 1914, with surges in movement to Australia and New Zealand (40 to 50 per cent of migrants in the 1850s and 60s, many supported by assisted emigration packages), the USA (75 per cent of migrants in the 1880s and 1890s) and Canada (over 50 per cent of migrants from 1900 to 1914). Apart from the Clearances, one of the other reasons for this may have been 'the limitation of the service and professional sector in the Scottish economy' which 'restrained the spread of prosperity'. Only Edinburgh achieved substantial growth in services between 1850 and 1900, and the latter part of this period began to shadow the industrial decline which characterized so much of Scotland's twentieth-century story. Concentrated heavy industry was prone to both boom and bust: while shipbuilding gave rise to 100,000 jobs in the imperial heyday from 1881 to 1921, textiles lost 40,000 jobs.

Some of Scotland's innovative developments domestically in the Victorian era did not have the extent of their potential recognized for many years: at Stirling, Howietoun (1873) was the 'first commercial fish farm in the world', and the 'first large-scale hydro plant at Foyers' in 1896 followed on from the pioneering development of hydroelectric power at Niagara in 1881. The arable and grazing economy – located on the east coast from the Black Isle to the Borders and in Ayrshire and Galloway – for its part came under pressure from the increasing popularity of deerstalking, with 'absurd numbers' of deer having 'devastating effects on young trees and other vegetation'. The heir to the throne, Edward, Duke of Rothesay (Edward VII, 1841–1910), had shot his first stag on 21 September 1858 at Balmoral, where Queen Victoria had established a royal residence in response to the advice of Banffshire man and Aberdeen University graduate Sir James Clark (1788–1870), her doctor, who suggested Deeside as just the place to address her and her husband's rheumatism. The fact that the Prince Consort's doctor, Sir John Forbes (1787–1861), was another Aberdeen man was also no doubt useful. Having first arrived in Edinburgh in 1847 on the *Trident* of the General Steam Navigation Company, the Queen visited Aberdeen in 1848 (where White Star Line magnate George Thomson, then Lord Provost, received her), and attended her first Braemar Gathering on 12 September 1850. The establishment of a royal residence at Balmoral and the representation of Albert's keen if not always expert engagement in blood sports drove the prestige of Scotland and of a sporting season in Scotland, a country Albert liked for its similarity to the Swiss and Alpine landscapes he knew from the Continent. The increase in sporting use of Scotland's land led to the presence of large numbers of game birds and the eradication of their predators, as the Scottish wildcat went into serious retreat in the face of farming and gamekeeping hostility. Balmoral was, however, more than a sporting estate – it was also a place of positive political engagement which benefited Scotland's reputation. The prospective marriage of the Princess Royal was advanced by the visit of Friedrich of Prussia there in the 1850s, and the Royal Family entertained often powerful foreign royalty – for example Tsar Nicholas and the Empress Alexandra in 1896 – rendering Balmoral a locale of government and interstate discussions far from London.[21]

SOUTH AND EAST ASIA

Notwithstanding the later competition from P&O, Jardine Matheson & Co, trading in Canton with a fleet under a version of the Saltire Flag from the early 1830s, was the central player in the opium trade until it distanced itself from the business in the 1860s. Opium culture was strong in China, which saw increasing domestic production despite imperial opposition, with opium becoming the major crop in the Wei valley after 1870. The vast commercial empire of Jardine Matheson was founded by William Jardine (1784–1843), known to the Cantonese as 'the Iron-Headed Rat', one of seven children born to a Dumfriesshire farmer, and his partner Sir James Matheson (1796–1878), the Sutherland-born son of an army officer and trader. Both men were educated at the University of Edinburgh, an opportunity which in Jardine's case could hardly have opened up for him anywhere else in Europe. The opium trade was used as a way of 'offsetting the costs' of the tea trade by Jardine and others, and opposed by the Chinese authorities as a threat to their hegemony and the historic trade surplus they had built up with Europe in the eighteenth century. For their part, Jardine Matheson promoted the trade and their other business interests via corporate hospitality such as the 'splendid dinner' William Jardine gave in Canton in 1835. Attempts to use William, 9th Lord Napier of Merchiston (1786–1834) ('the Barbarian Eye' to the Chinese and the chief superintendent of trade from China to the British Empire), to further their commercial interests was not altogether successful. However, Napier seems to have been the first to suggest seizing Hong Kong and came to the view that Chinese interference in the freedom of trade would need to be met by force. For their part, the Chinese launched a counterstrike, initially by boarding British ships 'in international waters' and confiscating and destroying their opium, as part of Viceroy Lin Zexu's moves against the covert trade in 1838–39, which led to the seizure of 20,000 chests of the drug and a ban on trade with Great Britain. Inevitably such actions led to conflict with the British Empire (which Jardine did more than a little to engineer) in which commercial concessions were won – including at Shanghai – and Hong Kong Island ceded to Great Britain (1841). Subsequently both Jardine and later Matheson entered Parliament.[22]

Although Benjamin Disraeli in his novel *Sybil* (1845) described Jardine as a 'dreadful man! A Scotchman richer than Croesus, one McDruggy fresh from Canton with a million of opium in each pocket', opium was much more socially acceptable than it subsequently became. It was both widely available and widely legal to use in the nineteenth century with prominent British users including S.T. Coleridge and Thomas De Quincey. As the

17. An opium pipe and cabinet, nineteenth-century decorative *chinoiserie* for Western décor.

historian Sir Tom Devine notes, laudanum (opium mixed with alcohol or water) 'was the most popular analgesic of the age'. It was completely unregulated until 1868 (indeed being sold in 'tobacco shops in Hong Kong') and as late as 1895, the *British Medical Journal* argued that 'drinkers had no right to criticise opium users'. As the historian Richard Grace notes, 'until the beginnings of the public health movement in the 1830s, there was virtually no established distinction between medical and non-medical uses of opium' and the drug's reputation was relatively 'anodyne', while 'respected medical professionals endorsed the use of opium preparations for calming very young children'. It is thus only doubtfully appropriate to frame Jardine Matheson's commercial activities in a crude presentist framework of drug-trafficking and cartels, and to do so risks simply reiterating Chinese imperial propaganda from the Victorian period. Opium was politics, an extension of European power, and Hong Kong would not have developed as a British colony without it: indeed, the British victory in the First Opium War enabled Jardine Matheson to move from Macao to Hong Kong, where they pursued a 'systematic recruitment of Scots' (they had been incorporating their family in the business from the 1820s, with William's nephew David trading in dye, textiles, tea, timber (and opium) via Jardine, Skinner & Co. at Mumbai/Bombay). The move enabled the company to benefit not only from a new base, but also from the advantageous tariff position of the Treaty Ports in general following the end of the war in 1842. Hong Kong was a colony in which Scots remained prominent, being seen as providing almost two-fifths of the impact on trade, banking, finance, business and policy even in the last half-century of the colony's existence. In 1997, when Great Britain withdrew from Hong Kong, the Black Watch was the last regiment in place and 'Will Ye No Come Back Again' was their farewell song to Chris Patten as governor, just as 'Auld Lang Syne' had been played on the retreat of the British Army from India fifty years before. The 'Scottish descendants of William Jardine' still control Jardine Matheson, and the conduct of the Chinese authorities in Hong Kong should give pause to any who seek to view the former colony – the indirect product of the opium trade – as a colonial victim of British power. The legacy of Jardine Matheson, who engaged in relieving famine in China in the years after they stopped selling its inhabitants drugs, was a complicated one. Today the company's revenues normally exceed US$50 billion and almost all its profits still derive from East Asia.[23]

In India, although Gilbert Elliott, 1st Earl of Minto (1751–1814), became the first Governor General/Viceroy in 1807 and Victor Hope, Marquess of Linlithgow, was the last Scot to fill that office in 1936, Scottish influence was perhaps less prominent by the late Victoria era than it had been a century before: indeed, three successive viceroys in the late nineteenth century all derived from one Oxford college alone. The introduction of an examination for entry to the Indian Civil Service (ICS) in place of patronage relationships in the 1850s doubly damaged Scottish opportunity by being framed in terms favourable to the Oxbridge curriculum and by compromising the northern kingdom's disproportionately active patronage network, while the East India Company, its remaining reputation severely damaged by the Mutiny/Rising of 1857, was finally wound up in 1874. Nonetheless, many Scots rose to high office in India throughout the nineteenth and twentieth centuries, and the position in the ICS was to an extent recovered, with Scottish burgh grammar school boys, for example, obtaining more ICS roles than many English public schools such as Radley, Stowe and Sherborne, between 1900 and 1945. Scots continued to be found throughout the 'agency houses in the Presidency capitals' and were 'prominent in the factories of Bombay and Kanpur', while new businesses emerged. Scots also came to dominate the 'tea plantations of the south': Francis Mackenzie Gillanders established the oldest Calcutta/Kolkata tea agency in 1819, with the support of his uncle John Gladstone, a major slave owner and the father of the prime minister. Later Andrew Yule & Co was founded in the same city – Yule's brother George went on to be President of the Indian National Congress in 1888, by which time John Jackson's 'first steam-powered tea roller' had long begun its work with the 'Scottish Assam Tea Company'. Following the development of the tea business in Ceylon/Sri Lanka by James Taylor of Auchenblae (1835–92) and his cousin Peter Moir, by 1875 'half of Ceylon's plantation mangers were from Aberdeenshire or Kincardineshire'. Taylor worked with fellow Scot Sir Thomas Lipton (1848–1931) on the development of the Ceylonese tea market and Scots too led the Planters' Association of Ceylon (1854). Scots dominated the business, with many plantations enjoying Scottish names such as Culloden and Lochnagar, though the largely imported Tamil work-force often endured poor conditions amounting to indentured labour (Indian indentured labour, called a 'new system of slavery', tellingly supplied over 400,000 people to the Caribbean alone). Lipton himself cornered 10 per cent of the tea trade, following his potent move to 'vertical integration' of his tea empire through matching brand marketing to his control of raw supplies. By the beginning of the twentieth century, '400,000 Tamils were employed in 1,600 tea plantations' on Ceylon. By 1930 there were almost 200,000 hectares of Ceylon under tea, and the island exported 250,000 tonnes of the beverage annually. In June 2019, a commemorative statue of James Taylor, designed by Sarath Chandrajeewa, was unveiled in his home town of Auchenblae.[24]

Former slave owners – who tended to leave the Caribbean after emancipation – invested in coffee as well as tea, helped by the environment created for them by James Mackenzie (1784–1843), who supported the developments which made 'Ceylon's coffee plantation industry viable', and did much to 'shape the evolution of colonial society in Ceylon'. Technological innovations such as the Aberdonian William Clerihew's (1811–70) coffee drier drove further success for these businesses. Around half of the leaders of the coffee industry in Ceylon were Scots, who also took up influential positions in 'journalism . . . law, brokerage, manufacturing and banking'. Scots were some 20 to 30 per cent of settlers or sojourners from the British Isles, and Ceylon itself was described as a 'Scotch colony' at a St Andrew's Day dinner in 1887. Today, the Kirk of Scotland at Colombo is the last left in Asia, and the Caledonian Society of Sri Lanka's 'annual Burns Night attracts more than 200' people.[25]

By 1900 there were 450 jute wallahs from Dundee managing mills near Calcutta/Kolkata alone, employing 184,000 Indians. St Andrew's Day dinners were 'common affairs' and the sociable networking traffic of Scots and their associated charitable establishments continued, with money being raised 'in support of Scottish Women's Hospitals' and other home charities. Perhaps the central claim which has been advanced by historians is that – prior to the introduction of the ICS exams – there was a 'Scottish school' of Indian governance centring on Sir Gilbert Elliott, 1st Earl of Minto (1751– 1814), Mountstuart Elphinstone (1779–1859), Sir Thomas Munro (1761– 1827) (discussed in Chapter 3), John Leyden (1775–1811) and others, who set out to preserve what they could of what was identified as the 'fallen greatness' of India. This group (Elphinstone, Minto and Leyden were all educated in Edinburgh) tended to share the experience of being educated by Dugald Stewart (1753–1828) and other leading figures of the stadialist interpretation of history, and it is argued that their influence in governance was followed by a generation of leading Scottish orientalists. Among these were Sir William Muir (1819–1905), Lieutenant Governor of the North Western Provinces and later Principal of the University of Edinburgh, 'by far the most distinguished scholar of his day' in the field of Islamic studies, and John Muir, Principal of the Victoria College at Benares (1844–54), who established the chair of Sanskrit at Edinburgh. Others in this group included Glasgow man Sir John Cumming (1868–1958), Principal of the School of

Oriental and African Studies, and Forbes Falconer (1805–53), Professor of Oriental Languages at University College London.[26]

Whether or not one subscribes to the notion of a 'Scottish school' in Indian governance as opposed to the undeniably liberal opinions of some of the country's leading Scottish administrators, it is clear that not all Scots belonged to such a school or even sympathized with it. James Broun-Ramsay, 1st Marquess of Dalhousie (1812–60), Governor General from 1848–56, appropriated the Koh-i-Noor diamond among other achievements, and was blamed for inciting the Indian Mutiny/Rising through his high-handedness, arrogance and policy of annexation, whereby Great Britain became the residuary legatee of all native principalities that were left without an heir. Later in the century, Victor Bruce, 9th Earl of Elgin (1850–1917), as Viceroy of India from 1894–99 both presided over a colossal famine in which millions died and spent a colossal amount on the Queen's Diamond Jubilee celebrations, about 1s. 6d. for every man, woman and child in India.[27]

The insurrection Dalhousie may have indirectly contributed to was combated in its turn by Field Marshal Colin Campbell, Lord Clyde (1792–1863), one of the Victorian Empire's most significant and distinguished commanders. Born the son of a Glasgow cabinetmaker and educated – like Sir Thomas Munro and General Sir John Moore before him – at the city's High School, Campbell fought with distinction in the Peninsular War (1812) and the First Opium War (1839–42). At Balaclava in 1854, the Thin Red Line of his Highland Brigade repulsed the Russians, a significant moment in the Crimea overshadowed by the futile display of gentry ethos on show from the Charge of the Light Brigade in the same engagement, which came to be naturally preferred in its tragic performativity of the cult of the amateur. In the existential threat to British rule posed in India in 1857, however, a professional was needed. Lord Palmerston – who as Foreign Secretary had had full oversight of Campbell's efficacy in the conflict with China in 1839–42 – turned to him to save India for the Crown almost at once. On 11 July 1857, two months after conflict had broken out, Campbell became Commander-in-chief, relieving Lucknow and defeating the Indian forces at Cawnpore/Kanpur; the Black Watch and the 93rd Sutherland Highlanders, who had fought in his Highland Brigade and in the Thin Red

Line at the Crimea, gained fifteen Victoria Crosses between them at Lucknow alone. From his earliest engagements on, Campbell was noted for his immense personal bravery – he led the forlorn hope at San Sebastián in 1813, and was wounded twice – and his efficiency. Although the postcolonial era remains much more sympathetic to British military interventions in Europe than in the British Empire, there is little understanding how these were connected as, for example, Russia's threat to Persia which helped ensure that the British Empire entered the First World War. Campbell, although no progressive, was no reactionary either, and deserves to be considered alongside Wellington or Nelson. Though not their equal, it is important to consider why Nelson, who fought in the West Indies and was aggressively pro-slavery, remains a less controversial – and publicly more venerated – figure. The geopolitical significance of India may be one reason.[28] Indian historical opinion today tends to blame Campbell's inferiors for the atrocities carried out by the British Army in the conflict of 1857–58, while the Bollywood film *Mangal Pandey: The Rising* (2005) has as one of its central characters the sympathetic Scots officer Captain Gordon, apparently modelled in part on Sergeant Major Robert Gordon, who fought with the Indian insurgents at Delhi. The Scottish fratriot tradition was also exemplified by Allan Octavian Hume's co-founding of the Congress Party. Not only George Yule (1829–92), former president of the Indian Chamber of Commerce and now head of Yule & Co at Kolkata, but also Sir William Wedderburn, 4th Bart (1838–1918), a member of a Scottish dynasty of civil servants in India, served as President of Congress, in Wedderburn's case twice.[29]

Though Campbell and a few others set the seal on their military reputations in India, it would be misleading to focus on British India as beset by militancy and unrest as a whole, though there was plenty on the frontiers, as the over-promoted Major General William Elphinstone (1782–1842) found when his command was destroyed, captured or enslaved in Afghanistan, together with thousands of camp-followers, in his indecisive and incompetent retreat from Kabul. As the nephew of Admiral George Elphinstone, Viscount Keith and a former aide-de-camp to George IV, Elphinstone, whose career looked to have stalled at a colonelcy, was promoted to general officer rank at the age of 59, just in time to demonstrate at the expense of thousands of lives that networking and connexions did not always coincide with merit. Many Indian Army officers went through their careers without any combat experience, and at moments like this such lack of experience could show.[30]

Sir Charles Dilke, 2nd Bart (1843–1911), the radical Liberal statesman, noted in his best-selling *Greater Britain* (1868) that:

> The Bombay merchants are all Scotch . . . from Canada to Ceylon, from Dunedin to Bombay, for every Englishman that you meet . . . you will find ten Scotchmen. It is strange, indeed, that Scotland has not become the popular name for the United Kingdom.[31]

Dilke's advocacy of 'Greater Britain' was taken up in Sir John Seeley's (1834–95) *Expansion of England* (1883), but, whereas Dilke saw the kinship of the Anglophone world as having the potential and reflecting the need to renew Britain's antiquated governance through Crown, Lords and Commons, Seeley's version was arguably more complacent. Its preference for stressing British military power over trading expansion in the acquisition of Empire, combined with the cult of amateurish but effortless superiority evident in Seeley's own contention that the British Empire had been acquired in 'a fit of absence of mind', implicitly endorsed Anglo-Saxon military and politico-cultural ascendancy without examining the sources of their currency with sufficient thoroughness.[32]

Scots did much to supply infrastructure and the infrastructure of business in South and East Asia, from Robert Home, who designed carriages, barges and furniture at Lucknow, to Bell of Glasgow's ceramic exports, with even Port Blair on the Andaman Islands sporting an 'Aberdeen Bazaar'. The Indian love of gold was catered for by Edinburgh goldsmiths Hamilton & Co., who established a branch in Calcutta/Kolkata in 1815. In Scotland itself, panoramas of India were popular. Some of the Indian princes responded in kind: Raja Sri Sham Singh Bahadir, who reigned in Chamba State from 1873 to 1904, subsidized 'an imposing Scottish Presbyterian Church'. Sir William Mackinnon (1823–93), a former grocer from Campbeltown, founded the Mackinnon Mackenzie Company in tandem with his old friend and fellow townsman Robert Mackenzie in 1847. This was later formed into the Calcutta and Burmah Steam Navigation Company in 1856, and eventually absorbed into P&O under Mackinnon's successor James Lyle Mackay, 1st Earl of Inchcape (1852–1932), an Arbroath man who became Chair of P&O and the founder of Inchcape plc. Inchcape's remark that 'there is no scope in Scotland for the energy, the brains, the initiative and the ambition of all the youth of the country' stands in a long line of international and globalizing rhetoric. Although the numbers of Scots in East Asia were small (some 2,000–2,500 by the 1850s) and the Scots there were mostly sojourners rather than migrants, networks were correspondingly tightly drawn across a highly focused professional and mercantile elite. In Singapore, which became a British colony in 1819, twelve of the first seventeen trading partnerships formed were either wholly or predominantly run by Scots. William Farquhar (1774–1839) from Aberdeenshire became resident and commandant at Malacca in 1813 and at Singapore (in succession to the legendary Raffles) in 1819. Farquhar 'spoke Malay and married a French Malaccan woman'. Like many Scots, he entertained a lively curiosity about the culture with which he was engaging, and, in a vein familiar elsewhere, Farquhar's 'survey of the flora and fauna of the Malay Peninsula led him to commission a magnificent set of paintings by Chinese artists which are the pride of Singapore museum'. Farquhar was succeeded by Dr John Crawfurd (1783–1868), an Islay man who was likewise a devotee of 'Malay languages and culture', and who published a grammar and dictionary of Malay.[33]

St Andrew's Day dinners were established in Singapore from 1837, becoming 'the focal point for . . . Scottish residents in the city', and remaining central to the social calendar into the twentieth century: for example, in 1908, Sir Arthur Young (1854–1938), the then Colonial Secretary of the Straits Settlement, was in the Chair. Young went on to be Governor of the Straits Settlements and British High Commissioner in Malaya in 1911, the year after 1,000 people attended the St Andrew's Ball in Singapore. One custom of these balls was the sending of fraternal greetings from other St Andrew's Day celebrations, and as the historian Tanja Bueltmann points out, at one ball at Singapore there were greetings from Bangkok, Colombo, Hong

Kong, Jakarta, Kobe, Kuala Lumpur, Malacca, Penang, Shanghai, Tientsin and many others, while one celebration in Hong Kong saw the message 'Scotland Forever' wired to fellow bodies in China, India, Japan, Malaya and the Philippines as well as Singapore. In keeping with their role in maintaining the sinews of Empire, Scottish naval officers sent similar messages. St Andrew's Societies were also founded at Jakarta (1838), Shanghai (1865), Hong Kong (1881), Kuala Lumpur (1885), Bangkok (1890) and many other East Asian locations, while the St Andrew's Burns dinner at Shanghai in 1902 attracted 600 diners. Haggis – as at Raffles Hotel in Singapore in 1908 – could be specially imported for these events, some of which were even larger: there were up to 1,500 at 'the Caledonian Ball' in Shanghai, and it was the major event in the city's calendar.[34]

In Burma/Myanmar, the Rangoon Oil Company (later Burmah Oil) was founded by David Sime Cargill (1826–1904) in Glasgow in 1886, later becoming the parent company for BP. In Malaya (Malaysia), the Irrawaddy Flotilla Company (1865), managed by the Glasgow shippers Patrick Henderson & Co., operated the 'largest fleet of river boats in the world, carrying 9 million passengers and over a million tons of freight a year', while by 1913 the Scottish firm of Guthrie & Co alone 'owned more than 25 per cent of the land in the colony possessed by British Agency Houses'. Guthrie's continued to be 'operated through a network of friends and relations' in Scotland (mainly north-eastern Scotland) until the 1950s. By the time of the 1901 census, Scots were over 25 per cent of Britons in Hong Kong, a sizeable proportion rendered even more effective by relentless networking. Between 1886 and 1911, a quarter of Clyde-built tonnage was destined for southern and eastern Asian use, while in the half-century before the outbreak of the First World War, no fewer than seventy-six Scottish investment trusts 'had interest in Asian tea and rubber plantations', with the major insurers, Scottish Widows, Standard Life and Scottish Amicable (initially the West of Scotland Life Insurance Company (1826)) all having a multinational footprint including substantial exposure to South and East Asian markets.[35]

The intensity and power of Scottish networking, further socialized and supported abroad through St Andrew's Societies, Burns Clubs and other organizations, was widely recognized in the era. The proverbial 'clannishness' of Scots was both apparent and commented on: there were over a thousand Scottish societies throughout Britain and its Empire at their peak in the late Victorian period, acting as 'sites of memory; networks of sociability ... carriers of civility, which potentially linked immigrants directly to the power structures of society'. According to *Freeman's Journal*, the true Scot 'thinks and acts for his countrymen', and such associations were as likely to be established in England as New Zealand. Initially many were set up with the aim of providing help and support to indigent Scots, supporting immigrants or sojourners through direct – if normally small-scale – financial relief. This was the shape of the early London and Boston (1657) societies: the Scots Charitable Society of Boston – modelled on the 1611 Royal Scottish Corporation of London – is the 'oldest charitable society still in existence in the United States today'. As the Scots community grew, Caledonian societies, which were more predominantly social than charitable, developed, together with a range of activities such as Highland Games and Burns Suppers either arranged via such societies or through standalone organizations devoted to a single kind of activity. In Montréal in 1904, there were 1,400 Caledonian Society and 400 St Andrew's Society members, while in Alberta the Caledonian Society of MacLeod was dedicated to promoting 'a taste and love for Scottish Music, History, and Poetry'. As befitted their philanthropic status, St Andrew's Societies tended to be more socially elite: financial support required wealthy backers. The events they organized were sometimes substantial, involving up to 2,000 people, and were deeply redolent of Romantic Scotland. At the 1879 Waverley Ball at Shanghai, guests dressed as characters from Scott's novels, while at the 1921 St Andrew's Ball, as reported in the *North China Daily Herald* for 3 December, clan shields hung on the walls together with Lochaber axes and quotes from Burns and Scott, while 'Each of the big windows framed a Stewart-tartaned piper illuminated by hidden lights in settings of heather and greenery.'[36]

The spread of Scottish culture – and with it, soft power – was thus an important part of these developments. David Kennedy (1825–86) carried out a world tour singing Burns and other Scottish songs in 1872–76: for his daughter Marjory Kennedy-Fraser (1857–1930), herself a popularizer of Gaelic song, her father's ambition was 'to sing the songs of Scotland to the exiled Scots throughout the world'. Kennedy – whose Burns tour was part of a complex branding of Burns and Wallace as Scottish icons for consumption in the British colonial world in the era – was not alone in this desire to spread Scottish culture among the Scottish diaspora to maintain their links with the old country. James Scott Skinner, a Banchory fiddler, toured the US and Canada in 1893, and Scottish comic Neil Kenyon 'played Australia, Singapore, New Guinea, Java, Sumatra, Timor, Egypt, and Algeria in 1910', while Harry Lauder's (1870–1950) stage Scotsman – popular in India and elsewhere – was only the most prominent aspect of an internationally visible music hall tradition. The military use of Scottish music, enshrined in a War Office order of 11 February 1854, led to the formation of Scottish pipe bands throughout the Empire and the United States, with the first World Pipe Band Championships held at Cowal in 1897. The Caledonian and St Andrew's societies which were formed were not unique – there were German and English expatriate societies in places like Singapore and Hong Kong – but Scots seem to have invested more in them socially and professionally as they had to take the place of embassies, trade missions and the other structures of an absent national system of governance.[37]

Glover House in Nagasaki 'is reckoned to attract over 2 million visitors a year' who come, among other reasons, to honour the memory of the man who was involved in the establishment of the Meiji regime, 'sold the Japanese Imperial Navy its first grand ships', was 'the country's first major industrialist in the European sense', was 'involved in the project to create Japan's first mint', and 'founded the first modern domestic brewing company, which later became Kirin' in 1885, as well as playing a founding role in the firm which is now Mitsubishi. Thomas Blake Glover (1838–1911), the fifth of eight children of the chief coastguard in Fraserburgh, was not educated – as his elder brothers were – at Aberdeen Grammar School, as his father could not afford it. Supported by a naval and shipbuilding network – and possibly also Masonic – Glover became a shipping clerk in 1856 and travelled with Jardine Matheson in 1859 to Japan, where Edinburgh man Kenneth Ross Mackenzie, who managed to be appointed French Consul as well as working for Jardine Matheson, was an early mentor. Nagasaki was now one of three Treaty Ports in the hesitant opening of the Japanese economy. In

Shanghai, Glover had heard rumours of Commodore Perry's 1853 visit to the hitherto partly closed society, and he now went there himself. He was not the first Scot to do so: Ranald MacDonald, son of the Archibald MacDonald of Glencoe, who had founded the Red River settlement in Canada and his wife Koale Koa, had become 'the first teacher of English in Japan' after a period of imprisonment as an alien in Nagasaki. Glover was to be much more fortunate. Assessing that the social trend in Japan was towards openness and modernization, Glover – who was personable, engaging and took the trouble to try to speak some Japanese, unlike even British diplomats at the time – engaged in a wide range of business deals for Jardine Matheson, and developed his own on the side, as was permitted. In 1861, Glover's associate James Mitchell opened the Aberdeen yard at Nagasaki; Glover's own 'first independent business venture' was 'in the export of Japanese tea' (by 1863 he employed 1,000 packers), and he was later involved in silk and coal. In the conflict between the regional lords and the Shogun, Glover supplied both sides with arms, which deflected attention from his increasing interest and confidence in a Meiji victory.[38]

Glover picked the winning side, even running the risk of alienating the British authorities in order to do so, and by January 1868 the Shogunate was overthrown. Thus when Meiji Japan, boosted by the 'development fund' it had gained from 'monies taken from erstwhile samurai . . . in exchange for government pensions', 'became the first Asian state to pursue a strategy of rapid modernisation . . . Scotland was likely to be one of the advanced economies of the West to which it looked for expertise, advice and ideas.' Viscount Yamao Yōzō (1837–1917) sought to develop engineering skills in the country on behalf of the Emperor, and sought the advice of Hugh Matheson (1821–98), senior partner in Matheson & Co (closely associated with Jardine Matheson) and founding president of Rio Tinto (RTZ). Matheson had enabled five Japanese students (the 'Choshu Five', who later rose to the highest positions in Japan, including Itō Hirobumi (1841–1909), who became prime minister) to study in the West. They were smuggled out of Japan on a Jardine Matheson ship in 1863 with Glover's support and some of them were met off the boat in Southampton by his brother James Glover: Linda Colley interestingly describes the process by saying the Five 'smuggled themselves in disguise on to a merchant ship' and 'attached themselves to University College London', thus providing another example of the invisible Scot in British history by depriving this transcultural experience of mutual agency. In fact the enrolment in London was far from a self-generated miracle. Four of the students went to University College to study under Arthur Williamson (1824–1904), the son of an Elgin clerk, to whom Matheson personally introduced them. The fifth, Yamao Yōzō, went to work in Napier's shipbuilding yard in Glasgow and thence to Anderson's College, being deeply influenced by that 'useful learning' instrumentalism which as we have seen characterized Scottish education in general and which was embedded in Anderson's foundational bequest. Yōzō returned to found the Imperial College of Engineering. Naturally Matheson's advice was sought in its development.[39]

In supporting the foundation of the Imperial College, Matheson turned to Lewis Gordon (1815–76), a fellow Royal High School former pupil and later Professor of Civil Engineering at Glasgow, for advice. Both Matheson and Gordon had had fathers in the legal profession in Edinburgh, and were doubtless connected on many levels. Gordon recommended William Rankine (1820–72), who had succeeded him in the Glasgow chair: both Rankine (1850) and Gordon (1855) had been proposed for Fellowship of the Royal Society of Edinburgh by James Forbes (1809–69), Professor of Natural Philosophy (Physics) at Edinburgh. Rankine in turn recommended his student Henry Dyer (1848–1918) to be Principal and Professor of Engineering at Japan's new 'Imperial College of Engineering', which Dyer headed from 1873, basing its curriculum on what he and Yōzō had experienced at Anderson's College (now the University of Strathclyde). Fourteen of Dyer's twenty-two British staff came from Scotland, and William Thomson, Lord Kelvin, had a key role in this patronage network: for example Sir James Alfred Ewing (1855–1935), one of the Tokyo professors who later became Director of Naval Education, had worked with Thomson and his Edinburgh professor Fleeming Jenkin (1833–85) on the laying of telegraph cables in Brazil in his student vacation. Other Scots such as Richard Brunton (1841–1911) from Fetteresso imported Scottish design into Japanese lighthouses through his influence and supervision of the contract to the Stevenson family of Edinburgh to build them. In 1882 Dyer received the Order of the Rising

Sun from the Emperor, then returned to Scotland having had a transformational impact on engineering in Japan. Dyer was now a married man, having married while in Japan: the fact that his wife was Marie Ferguson, daughter of Duncan Ferguson of Glasgow, was another indicator of the intensity of Scottish networking in what was still a largely closed society, although Scottish–Japanese intermarriage was also typical. Places opened up for Scots in Japan to meet, as Glover's younger brother Alfred founded a St Andrew's Society in Nagasaki in 1886. Other Scots of distinction were resident in Japan, including Henry Faulds (1843–1930), whose application of finger-printing to criminal investigation, first adopted in Argentina in 1891, became a global template. Dyer spent the rest of his life in educational governance in Scotland and acting as an unofficial advocate for Japan and its government, language and culture. Glover did much the same, though he never satisfactorily resettled in Scotland. Instead, he helped to fulfil the order for Japan's first three new warships (*Satsuma* (1864), *Ho Sho Maru* (1868) and *Jho Sho Maru* (1869)) by a process of procurement typical of Scotland's world: he secured the contract with Alexander Hall & Son of Aberdeen with his brother Charles's Aberdeen firm acting as agents. Charles and James Glover had founded a shipbroking business in Aberdeen after Jim returned from visiting Thomas in Japan in 1865, no doubt to facilitate further contracts. Glover also sent students to Aberdeen, and – like Dyer – promoted Japanese relations with Europe in general and Scotland in particular.[40]

Japanese influence on Scotland was strong in its turn. In 1878, there was a major cultural exchange between Glasgow and Japan, with some 1,150 items being sent from the Pacific power to the Scottish city, many of which were displayed at the Corporation Art Galleries, in what was to be one of a series of exhibitions. Some of the Glasgow Boys school of painting visited Japan to absorb its artistic techniques, while Japanese art was also influential on the Glasgow Style of Charles Rennie Mackintosh (1868–1928), Margaret Macdonald Mackintosh (1864–1933) and others, and thus on the foundation of architectural modernism's Glasgow dimension. Quintessentially 'Celtic' paintings such as George Henry (1858–1943) and E.A. Hornel's (1864–1933) *Druids Bringing in the Mistletoe* (1890) also show the impact of Japanese art. Hornel had trained in Antwerp under Charles Verlat (1824–90), whom

Vincent Van Gogh – himself interested in *japonaiserie* – also wanted to have as a teacher. Van Gogh shared a flat with the Glasgow art dealer Alexander Reid (1854–1928), who had been responsible for staging the 1889 exhibition of Katsushika Hokusai's (1760–1849) prints in Glasgow (a decade after the city had exchanged gifts with the Meiji government) and was to become 'Hornel's supporter and dealer'. Henry and Hornel made an extended visit to Japan in 1893–94, funded by the shipping magnate and art collector Sir William Burrell (1861–1958). Hornel – who visited Japan again in 1924 – also made visits to Burma/Myanmar, Ceylon/Sri Lanka and Australia in the British Empire. But it was Japan that 'would completely change his way of seeing the world and his way of working'. While Hornel could be accused of seeking the 'sensuous embodiment of an unwesternized Japan, frozen in happy communion with nature and feudal mores untouched by civilization', it was the relatively new technology of photography that underpinned his images of Japanese women and the development of his depiction of face and hands. During his visit, Hornel's fellow Scot William Kinnimond Burton (1856–99), the Historiographer Royal, John Hill Burton's son and a professor at the Imperial College of Engineering, was responsible for organizing the *Exhibition of Foreign Photographs* for the Photographic Society of Japan: a sign of the domestic interest in the technology.[41]

Hornel was influenced by the Japanese garden, which had more of an impact as an imported style in Scotland than any other garden type had had since before 1707: sharing a rocky landscape and often damp climate, Scotland proved an accommodating location for Japanese garden styles. Charles Anstruther-Thomson (1855–1925), George Bullough (1870–1939), Osgood Mackenzie (1842–1912) and John Henry Dixon (1838–1926) all created notable Japanese gardens in Scotland, and the Japanese style was also influential on institutional gardens, such as the Cruickshank botanical garden at the University of Aberdeen. One of the most accessible survivors is the (now restored) garden created by Isabella ('Ella') Christie of Cowden (1861–1949), who brought Takai Haidu from the Royal School of Garden Design at Nagoya to lay out a garden over almost three hectares in Clackmannanshire, which has been dubbed 'the best garden in the Western world' by at least one Japanese expert (see plate 22). In 1911, the Scottish

National Exhibition at Glasgow featured a Japanese tea garden next to its mock Highland village, *An Clachan*.[42]

In 1888, Archibald Barr (1855–1931) and William Stroud designed an optical rangefinder, which, despite initial scepticism, was eventually adopted by the Royal Navy. Stroud was a Bristol man and Barr was from Paisley, spending time as a lab assistant to Lord Kelvin's brother and benefiting from the confluence of practical technological development and the theoretical curriculum. In 1890, Barr accepted the Regius Chair in Engineering at Glasgow, and, in 1893, the initial partnership of Barr & Stroud was set up in the city, becoming Barr & Stroud Ltd in 1913, in a tribute to the porosity between higher education and business in Scotland. With their confidence in Scottish engineering, the Japanese ordered Barr & Stroud rangefinders for their navy. In the critical conflict at the Tsushima Strait in May 1905, Barr & Stroud's latest model 1903 FA3 Rangefinder enabled Admiral Tōgō and the Japanese fleet to hit Russian warships at a distance of 5,500 metres and win an overwhelming victory. The *Osiyabya* gained the unenviable distinction of becoming the first modern battleship sunk by gunfire alone, and the Russian navy lost eleven battleships in all. Thus ended the Russo-Japanese War, which recalibrated Western expectations of the power of Japan. In the aftermath of that victory, Glover was photographed beside the Meiji veteran Tōgō, the only westerner in a picture of silent tribute to the mighty role he had played in the making of modern Japan. Glover's son, Tomisaburo (1870–1945), like his father, spent his life in Nagasaki and committed suicide in the wake of the dropping of the atom bomb on the city in 1945. Fortunately, Glover House survives. Barr & Stroud is now part of Thales UK, which still evinces its historic connexion, as optronic periscopes are still supplied from Glasgow to the Japanese Self-Defence Force.[43]

CANADA AND THE AMERICAS

From the time of Sir Alexander Mackenzie (1764–1820), the first man 'to make an overland crossing of the North American continent' onwards, Scottish travellers and businessmen had been particularly active in Canada. As early as 1800, Scottish exports to Nova Scotia were running at five times the imports, and 'the years after 1804 saw the beginning of the golden age of the New Brunswick timber trade, and the apogee of Scottish mercantile influence', as the exclusion of British fur traders from the United States south of the Great Lakes after the Treaty of Paris (1783) served to drive expansion in Canada. The withdrawal of British forces from their Great Lakes outposts in the 1790s was a continuation of this process. Timber and fur were dominant in this first phase of Canadian development, and Scottish fur traders integrated closely with many First Nations peoples as some of their French predecessors had done; it was through 'the fur trade that Canada took on its character resembling a Scotland of North America'. Tartan was also used as a visible sign of Scottishness and a Scottish workforce, and new association tartans were created in Canada, as the cloth became used for networking and as a public symbol of trust. First Nations chiefs received tartan as a gift, and their people wore it. At Fort Vancouver alone in 1849, 1,438 yards of MacDuff, 1,119 of Clanranald and 965 of Royal Stuart, Argyll and Ancient MacGregor were sold – some two miles (3,200 metres) of tartan. There was a strong preference in tartan sales and wear for red tartans, with their long-standing connotations of status and authority. In terms of that authority, Scots were already prominent, with General Sir Gordon Drummond (1772–1854) and George Ramsay, 9th Earl of Dalhousie (1770–1838), who was educated at the Royal High School and the University of Edinburgh, both serving as Governor General. In William Lyon Mackenzie (1795–1861), the Dundee-born son of a weaver, Canada found a revolutionary whose failed 1837 insurrection was intended to extend the US model of governance to the Upper Canadian territories.[44]

For many British Canadians however, the United States was more of a threat than an opportunity. US forces had invaded in 1812, and there was serious concern that in the wake of the American Civil War the victorious Union would pose a threat to Canada. The Confederation of 1867, the foundation of the modern Canadian polity, was the response: eight of the ten 'Fathers of Confederation' were 'born in Scotland or of recent Scottish extraction'. The aftermath of this new political settlement saw the militarily weak company-state of the Hudson's Bay Company (HBC) sell its land to Canada – in preference to a US offer – to enable a more secure response to US aggression or settlement on British territory. Under the Rupert's Land Act of 1868, these former HBC Northwest Territories became incorporated in the British Empire.[45]

Scots went on to dominate Canada's early political development. Glaswegian Sir John Macdonald (1815–91) was Canada's first prime minister and in office for nineteen of the twenty-four years following Confederation, while Alexander Mackenzie (1822–92), a stonemason from Logierait in Perthshire, became Canada's second prime minister. Macdonald's attitudes to First Nations Canadians have caused significant unease in recent years, and in August 2018 his statue was temporarily removed from the British Columbia state capital of Victoria: seen both as a national founding father and a colonial tyrant who represents an obstacle to reconciliation between indigenous peoples and other Canadians, Macdonald's reputation as a Victorian statesman now comes a remote second to his role in contemporary culture wars. Lyon Mackenzie's grandson, William Lyon Mackenzie King (1874–1950), was to be the dominant political figure in Canada from the 1920s to the 1940s, serving as prime minister for all but five years in the 1921–48 period. Some 20 to 25 per cent of British Isles emigration to Canada was Scottish in 1871–1921 (including experiments such as the New Kincardine colony), and Scots remained prominent in Canada, with immigration offices being set up in Glasgow (1880) and Aberdeen (1907), and farm employment for emigrants being guaranteed by the Canadian government in 1927. The North British Society, the 'earliest Scottish association in Canada was established in 1768 in Halifax' and others followed including a society in New Brunswick in 1798, the Glengarry Highland Society of Ontario (1819) and the St Andrew's Society of Montréal (1834). Other organizations included the Gaelic Society of Canada, founded by Alexander Fraser (1860–1936), and the 'Sons of Scotland' (Toronto, 1876), which utilized a Lodge system modelled on Freemasonry. Scots societies in Canada – such as the St Andrew's Society of Guelph, which donated £20 to relieve 'unemployed cotton spinners' in Glasgow – both supported immigrants into the country and offered help to Scots in Scotland. Ontario had a number of Highland Games events as early as 1819; by the 1870s, there were 15,000 attending the major Games at Toronto.[46]

En route to the coast, the Canadian Pacific Railway Company (1881) promoted emigration through the Emigrants' Information Office and elsewhere, as large-scale settlement in western Canada was a driver of its traffic. The Company was envisaged by Sir John Macdonald's government and John Galt's son, Sir Alexander Tilloch Galt (1817–93). An initial contract was granted to Sir Alexander's cousin Sir Hugh Allan (1810–82), an Ayrshire tycoon whose giant Allan Line was one of the leading shipping companies in international steam transit, but the bribery associated with this contract (the Pacific Scandal) removed Macdonald from government: Scottish networking had for once gone too far. When Macdonald returned to office in 1878, Donald Smith, 1st Baron Strathcona and Mount Royal (1820–1914), the son of a Forres saddler, who had risen to prominence in the HBC, became the major sleeping partner and funder of the railway's development. Smith later became Chair of Burmah and Anglo-Persian Oil. Smith's cousin and business partner George Stephen, 1st Baron Mount Stephen (1829–1921), the son of a Dufftown joiner, was also involved, as were the finances of John Kennedy (1830–1909), the fifth-born in a family of nine children in Blantyre, who became President of the St Andrew's Society of New York in 1884. Others engaged included Duncan Macintyre (1834–94) of Callander, Richard Angus (1831–1922), the son of a Bathgate grocer, and the Canadians James Hill and Norman Kittson. The steam transit of Canada by land effectively displaced the fruitless efforts to find a clear sea passage to the north, which had led to two expeditions by Sir John Ross (1777–1859) and a third unsuccessful rescue mission to find Sir John Franklin and the crew of the *Terror*.[47]

In the United States, Scottish emigrants continued to make a major impact, such as John Muir (1838–1914), the founder of the National Parks movement; Allan Pinkerton (1819–84), Gorbals-born cooper and Chartist, the founder of the detective agency and head of Union intelligence in the Civil War; David Dunbar Buick (1854–1929), the carmaker from Arbroath; and Peter Henderson (1822–90), the 'father of horticulture and ornamental gardening'. Scottish societies developed rapidly in their traditional format. The New York Caledonian Club was founded in 1856, that of Chicago in 1865, San Francisco in 1866 and the North American United Caledonian

Association in 1870, while the Illinois St Andrew Society was established in Chicago in 1846, a year before the first Burns Club was founded in New York. The Highland Society of New York developed Highland Games in 1836, and a 'traditional games' event at Boston followed in 1853, with Philadelphia (1858) and Newark (1861) in its wake. Scottish naming for settlements, places and customs was perhaps adopted more widely in the United States than anywhere else in the world: there are seventeen Aberdeens alone. Curling appeared from Canada (whither Scottish soldiers had brought it a century earlier) in the 1860s, and pipe bands followed at Buffalo (1890), Pittsburgh (1900) and elsewhere. Scottish interest newspapers also appeared, including the *Scottish Patriot, Scotsman, Boston Scotsman* and, the most successful, the *Scottish-American Journal*, which ran from 1857 to 1919. A monthly special interest journal, the *Caledonian*, flourished from 1901 into the 1920s.[48]

The Civil War of 1861–65 was a traumatic conflict and also finally transformative of the United States, signalling what has been called 'the final demise of a core constituent of the western arm of the old eighteenth-century British world economy'. The first southern state to secede was South Carolina in December 1860, where the possible secession of the state from the Union was discussed on the premises of the St Andrew's Society of Charleston, already rich with memories of the constitutional history of the United States. Mark Twain famously argued in *Life on the Mississipi* (1883) that Sir Walter Scott's 'sham grandeurs, sham gauds. And sham chivalries of a . . . worthless long-vanished society' had inspired the mythology of the South, and the idea that the 'Highland Charge' underpinned elements of Confederate battle tactics is stubbornly present in much later writing such as James Michael Hill's *Celtic Warfare* (1986). Whatever validity such views have, the end of the Civil War seems to have given a major fillip to performative Highlandism in the shape of an increase in the number of Highland Games, with large-scale events in Boston, Brooklyn, Detroit and elsewhere achieving major audiences in the 1870s, with some '80 Scottish associations holding annual Games' by 1875. The 'foundation of the Order of Scottish clans' was established at St Louis, Missouri, in 1878, and Clan Society lodges developed throughout the country, with some 200 to 250 branches and 'a combined membership of well over 20,000 by 1900'. The idea that the more sinister – but not perhaps entirely unrelated – Ku Klux Klan had been 'formed by emigrant Scots cavalry officers within the Confederate army' was a persistent one. Thomas Dixon's *The Clansman* (1905) – which underpins D.W. Griffiths' strikingly bigoted *Birth of a Nation* (1915) – promoted this approach through its title and the centrality of the Camerons to his story of the Klan, but in reality the organization was founded by ex-officers from Tennessee with other names who claimed Scottish ancestry, and adopted the trappings of Scottish Romanticism – including the 'Klan' name and the use of Burns' 'To a Louse' in initiation ceremonies. The traditional Scottish recruitment symbol of the 'Crostarie' or Fiery Cross was also used to symbolize the movement.[49]

More positively, many of the Scottish societies developed a mission supportive of Scottish culture, such as the St Andrew's Society of Philadelphia, which resolved 'to establish a Library of Scottish Literature' in late February 1910, while a 'Scottish Old People's Home' was founded in Illinois in 1901. There were also women's societies, such as Daughters of Scotia (1895), which had 14,000 members by 1921. Scottish cultural heroes were widely honoured: Robert Burns was commemorated by a statue by Sir John Steell (1804–91) in Central Park, while a statue of William Wallace was erected in Baltimore in 1893. While St Andrew's and Caledonian societies had separate missions, there was cross-associational benevolence and support after events such as the Chicago Fire of 1871, in which '90 per cent of the St Andrew's Society of Illinois's members ... lost their homes'. In its turn, Scotland became the home of the loots and fruits of political struggle in the United States. On his visit to Glasgow in 1891, William Cody's (Buffalo Bill) fellow 'performers sold a ghost shirt to Kelvingrove Museum where it remained for over a century before repatriation'.[50]

Freestanding Scots colonies also took root outside the British Empire, as they had done in Continental Europe in former days. Despite the failure of some Scottish ventures, such as the colony in Topo in Venezuela, others such as the Scots merchant colony at Buenos Aires thrived. Scots expatriates had been present in Buenos Aires as early as the 1730s, and by the 1820s there were several active merchant houses. A Kirk of Scotland congregation was founded in 1828, and in 1835 St Andrews in Buenos Aires became the first Kirk in Latin America; St Andrew's Scots School followed in 1838. Later in the nineteenth century, a fresh influx of Scots with shepherding and farming experience settled in Patagonia, and Scots contributed extensively to the development of football in Argentina, while Sir Archibald Williamson, the son of Stephen Williamson, whom we will meet later in the context of Easter Island, became one of a number of prominent Scots businessmen in the country as director of the Central Argentine Railway. Scots customs, games and associations were also to be found elsewhere, for example the 1842 shinty match at Montevideo in Uruguay, a country where Duncan Stewart Agell (1833–1923), the son of a Perthshire father, was briefly President in 1894.[51]

AFRICA

In 1795, following the French victory over the Netherlands, George Keith Elphinstone (1746–1832), Admiral of the Red, and General Sir James Henry Craig (1748–1812) were sent to take Cape Colony in the name of the House of Orange to remove it from potential French control. If it was to be 'liberated' by two Scots, it was also defended by one: Colonel Robert Gordon (1743–95), son of a general in the Scots Brigade in the Dutch service, who was defeated and committed suicide. Returned to the Netherlands in 1802, the Cape Colony was recaptured by another Scottish commander, Sir David Baird, in 1806. It was clear that successful retention of the Cape would require colonists from Great Britain, and in 1808, the view was circulating that colonizing the Cape with Highland Scots would enable them to share their understanding of the transition from a tribal to a commercial society with the Xhosa, and encourage them to follow the same path. By 1820, Scots were 10 per cent of Cape settlers (rising to 14 per cent by 1910), and a 'Highland' identity was retained there which was made manifest in later military developments such as the creation of Scottish units in the South African armed forces. Scots became prominent in radical journalism in South Africa, with figures like Thomas Pringle (1789–1834) and John Fairbairn (1794–1864), both possibly influenced by Dugald Stewart's radical lectures at Edinburgh, reaching prominent positions. Pringle, who was himself disabled, 'often sheltered abused blacks', learnt native languages and disliked terms of racist abuse, becoming Secretary of the Anti-Slavery Society in 1826. He was joint editor of *Blackwood's* then of Constable's *Edinburgh Magazine*, and while on the South African scene he and Fairbairn – who supported colour-blind policies and was also 'a passionate abolitionist' – collaborated on the *South African Journal*. Their South African Literary Society was 'declared to be illegal', and Pringle and his literary allies, the 'Scotch Independents', were 'anathema' to the British authorities and seen as 'dangerous to the running of the colony'. Other radical journalists like the New Lanark-born David Dale Buchanan (1819–74) followed, and the wider Scots diaspora 'consciously bridged the literary, press, scientific and commercial worlds', helping 'to create an alliance between the professional and mercantile elites'. Figures such as Sir Donald Currie (1825–1909), the third of ten children from Greenock, began a steamer service from Britain to South Africa. The first South African Caledonian Society was founded in 1870–71 and four more by the end of the next decade. A Highland Society was formed at Port Elizabeth, a *Comunn Gaidhealach* at Natal and a Caledonian Society at Cape Town, and there were other sectional societies, such as the 'Aberdeen, Banff and Kincardine Society of Cape Town'. By 1905, 'there were over forty Highland and Caledonian societies in South Africa', while the Scottish soldier's contribution to the Boer War was widely honoured, even though it was that conflict which first saw the 'distinctive weaponry and items of dress', as well as the traditional organization of the Scottish regiments, compromised by the demands of modern warfare. In 1911, Scots were 20 per cent of the UK-born in South Africa, and they reached figures of up to 50 per cent of the settler population in neighbouring colonies such as Nyasaland.[52]

Throughout Africa, Scottish missionary and liberal opinion made a strong impact. Here too, Scottish botanists and plant hunters such as Francis Masson (1741–1805) and William Paterson (1755–1810) were early pioneers and what was to become Malawi was largely dominated by Scots colonists, while in East Africa, a tradition of 'Scotchi' dancing grew up, with African dancers 'dressed in kilts and later using bagpipes'. The inevitable crowd of St Andrew's and Caledonian Societies developed from the 1860s at Bulawayo, Gwelo, Nairobi (where dinners could attract between 12 and 15 per cent of the European population) and Zanzibar. The events associated with these societies became a forum for policy discussions, as well as being a popular highlight. Burns Suppers and musical events were popular from Nairobi to Johannesburg, and Scottish culture was widely promoted: the Salisbury Caledonian Society offered prizes for Scottish history and poetry and funded a bursary to pursue the study of the 'glorious history' of Scotland. When the British East Africa Company was established in 1888, its directors were almost exclusively Scottish.[53]

David Livingstone (1813–73), the son of a Blantyre weaver, must always stand at the heart of the Scottish engagement with Africa in this period. Like Glover in Japan, Livingstone was adept at winning trust among those of very different background to himself, a fact which was put down – even at the time – to his Scottishness. Livingstone's central purpose was not so much evangelization or medicine in their own right, but rather the creation of what he called in 1857 'an open path for commerce and Christianity'. By the latter, he meant not only the traditional set of emotional inclinations, faith and moral values typical of his era, but something more: the end of the slave trade, where slaves 'were transported across the Sahara by Muslim merchants'. Like others of his era, Livingstone saw the Pax Britannica as central to achieving this goal: indeed, the 'temporary weakening of British imperialism' in Africa has been seen as the cause of an increase in Arab–Swahili slave trading and it was the Royal Navy's 'pressure on the Sultan of Zanzibar to halt the selling of slaves in Arabia and South Asia in the 1870s' which helped to undermine the African trade. This process was supported by Livingstone's close links to fellow physician and Angus man Sir John Kirk (1832–1922), who accompanied Livingstone between 1858 and 1863 before becoming vice consul at Zanzibar, where Kirk took up the struggle to control the Arab slave trade, which was 'still growing strongly'. Egypt, for example, only banned 'the importation and sale of enslaved white people' in 1856 and black people some twenty years later, and the Marquess and Marchioness of Aberdeen played a small role in heightening consciousness over the miseries of slavery in that country. The struggle against slavery has been a longstanding passion of that family, from George Hamilton-Gordon, the 4th Earl's Aberdeen Act of 1845, which gave the Royal Navy power to stop and search Brazilian slavers, to the current Marquess of Aberdeen and Temair's strong support of the 2015 Modern Slavery Act. For his part, Kirk played a major role in the Treaty between Great Britain and Zanzibar for the Suppression of the Slave Trade in 1873. In this sense, Livingstone was both the opponent of slavery and the 'gatekeeper of colonialism', since his positive view of British imperialism as a force for good played its part in encouraging the scramble for Africa at the end of the century. Nevertheless, Africa does not by and large hold Livingstone responsible. Kenneth Kaunda (who described him as 'the first freedom fighter') and other African leaders have played on the benefits of Livingstone's legacy and invoked his memory across the continent, while some would 'gladly say he was a saint'. Churches are named after him, and both Blantyre in Malawi and Livingstonia in Zambia memorialise him. In 1973, the centenary of Livingstone's death was commemorated in dozens of countries across Africa (thirty-four issued stamps) at a level quite beyond that of his enduring reputation in Scotland.[54]

From the 1880s, students of African descent or African origin began to enter the Scottish universities in numbers. Some had come much earlier, such as William Ferguson from Jamaica, subsequently governor of Sierra Leone, to Edinburgh Medical School in 1809; James McCune Smith to Glasgow in 1837 and James Africanus Beale Horton (1835–1883), a Sierra Leone man who graduated with an MD at Edinburgh in 1859. Horton rose to Surgeon Major in the British Army before returning to Africa to found the Commercial Bank of Sierra Leone. Other students included the Trinidadians John Baptist Philip and John Alexander (1873–1924), who was a delegate to the first Pan-African Congress in London in 1900, William Meyer, Christopher Davis of Barbados, the Jamaican Theophilus Scholes (1854–1937) and Tiyo Soga (1829–71), who sent his sons to Dollar Academy. Andrew Watson, a man of colour born in British Guiana in 1856 became, via his Orcadian father, a Scottish football international and the winner (with Queen's Park) of three Scottish Cups, while Peter McLagan (1823–1900), MP for Bathgate 1865–93, a suffragist and supporter of a restored Scottish Secretaryship, who established the Scottish Chamber of

Agriculture in 1864 and was the longest-serving Scottish MP of Queen Victoria's reign, was the son of a black mother and a planter father.

On the – to most – remote island of Tristan da Cunha, William Glass of Kelso (1786–1853) became the island's first governor after founding the town which is still the island's main settlement, Edinburgh of the Seven Seas, the most remote capital city on earth. Scottish traditions there remained strong, with first footing being recorded at New Year as late as 1961, the year in which volcanic activity forced a temporary abandonment of the island.[55]

THE KIRK OF SCOTLAND

The Kirk of Scotland and its offshoots and divisions – indeed Scottish nonconformity in general besides the adherents of the established Kirk – played an important role in creating an infrastructure for Scottish identity throughout the British Empire and indeed beyond, and thus made 'a huge contribution to the forging of Scottish identity overseas'. Imperial-focused missionary societies developed from the 1790s, and the East India Company supported the development of Presbyterian kirks at Bombay/Mumbai (1814) and Calcutta/Kolkata (1818), while kirks were also founded from Australia to Cape Town in the first quarter of the nineteenth century and later. James Laidlaw Maxwell (1836–1921) founded the first Presbyterian Church in Taiwan in 1865 (though Maxwell was a Scot, this was a technically English Presbyterian foundation). Missionaries such as Dugald Christie (1855–1936) in China made significant contributions to medicine and education. While the Kirk operated at a structural disadvantage to the Church of England, which was much more central to the development of what Sir John Seeley would come to identify as 'Britishness as a concept occupying the whole world', it nonetheless played an important role in some areas of the Empire, and indeed outside; imperialist grandiosity and theological solipsism helped support the development of a significant minority of ministers who considered the possibility of converting Levantine Jews 'in order to create a new Christian Israel' in the years following 1838. Glasgow missionary William Wingate (1808–99) among others was a lifelong enthusiast for the conversion of the Jews. Accordingly, the Kirk established itself in Jerusalem (where it still remains in a more respectful and eirenic context), Tiberias and (more briefly) via missions at Damascus, Aleppo and Beirut. The division of the Kirk caused by the Disruption of 1843 saw between 400 and 500 ministers leave under charismatic leadership such as that of Thomas Guthrie (1803–73), the advocate of the 'Ragged Schools' movement in Scotland, but also led to the Kirk proper becoming dominant in the overseas mission field. The Free Kirk, however, won over all the missionaries in more radical areas like Bengal and was strongly engaged in the development of settlements such as Dunedin in New Zealand.

Free Kirk thinking – as was evident in Hugh Miller's (1802–59) *The Witness* and elsewhere – could express reservations about the British imperial mission. Domestically, the Free Kirk was seen as being more likely to be on the side of the tenantry in Highland estates (part in any case of its anti-patronage ethos), while the Tory Party suffered electorally by its association with landowners, whose patronage rights in the Kirk – long a sore point in its domestic politics – had helped to precipitate the final split in 1843. There were further splits – the Free Presbyterian Kirk split from the Free Kirk in 1893 – but none of these had as marked an effect. There was, however, arguably a drag on the Scottish economy through the erection of multiple churches between 1843 and 1847 (the United Presbyterians (UP) formed in the later year, largely from earlier seceders) and from 1900 to 1929 (the year of the merger of the UPs and the Free Kirk and the merger of both of these – in large part – with the Kirk of Scotland respectively). Scottish towns are often rather oversupplied with church buildings as a consequence, many of which have been or will be sold off for other purposes.

Although the work of individual women in the Kirk has been cele-brated, such as the Aberdonian weaver Mary Slessor (1848–1915), who went as a missionary to West Africa in 1876 and is associated with extraordinarily brave actions such as an attack on infanticide, the role of women in the mission field remains underexplored, despite representing 60 per cent of Kirk missionaries by 1890. The structural role of women in the Kirk of Scotland abroad for generations before they could enter the ministry remains an interesting feature of Scotland's world in the Victorian era. They were often highly effective in the field, with Slessor, for example, becoming renowned for 'her lack of pretension' and openness to African experience.[56]

THE PACIFIC, OCEANIA AND ANTARCTICA

In the Pacific, from the mid Victorian period up to 1953, when Chile declined to renew the lease, Scottish business interests, predominantly those of Williamson, Balfour and Company, founded by two Fife men, Dundee High School pupil and St Andrews graduate Alexander Balfour (1824–86) and Stephen Williamson (1827–1903) of Cellardyke, changed one of the most remote territories of the world through commercial development:

Scottish entrepreneurs transformed Easter Island from a subsistence economy to a commercial wool-producing ranch. In doing so, they created in eastern Polynesia the landscape, economy and socio-political system of a nineteenth-century Scottish estate.

The development of the Easter Island landscape from the 1860s onwards, in terms of the land use for sheep practised by Scottish landlords in Scotland a generation before, was one of the most far-flung examples of the Scottish world, which had a major presence throughout the Pacific, from Easter Island to Honolulu. Captain Russell Elliott – a member of the Elliotts of Minto family – introduced a constitution to Pitcairn Island in 1838 which incorporated universal suffrage, while the Reverend John Dunmore Lang (1799–1878) proposed a US-style constitution for Australia, rather as his compatriot Mackenzie had in Canada: fratriotism in action. In the more conservative society of Hawaii, Archibald Scott Cleghorn (1835–1910) set up a dry goods store in Honolulu and married into the Hawaiian royal family, though his daughter did not inherit the throne due to the US take-over in 1893, acknowledged to be illegal under the Clinton administration a century later. On 27 September that year, arguably Scotland's most famous Pacific expatriate, Robert Louis Stevenson (1850–1894), addressed the Scottish Thistle Club of Honolulu, founded in 1891 to foster Scottish music and writing under the chieftainship of . . . Archibald Scott Cleghorn. In 1995, the Western Samoa rugby team, playing at Inverleith, knocked on the author's door in Howard Place, Edinburgh, and asked very respectfully to be photographed in the sitting room next to the room in which Stevenson was born. The memory of that anti-colonial writer (nonetheless served at dinner at his great house in Vailima by Samoans wearing tartan) remained strong a century after his death.[57]

In 1766, John Callender published his *Terra Australis Cognita*, which emphasised 'the value of the distant lands and Britain's role as natural leader of expansion in the region'. Four years later, the *Endeavour*'s botanical artist Sydney Parkinson (1745–71) was 'a likely contender for the first Scot to set foot on Australian soil', and his 600 drawings and 269 paintings indicate how the continent caught his imagination. From the beginnings of British colonization in the 1780s, Scots 'were readily identifiable as a distinct ethnic and colonial group' in Australia. General Lachlan Macquarie (1761–1824), the Hebridean son of a joiner, the nephew of Allan MacLean, the ex-Jacobite Canadian general and a veteran of the war against Tipu Sultan, educated at the Royal High School in Edinburgh, became Governor of New South Wales in 1809–10 – a territory where Scots settlers tended to concentrate, and which was to become dominant in the wool industry. Macquarie's determi-nation to integrate transported criminals into society in New South Wales helped to build up a developing civil society in Australia. His enlightened policies of public works, medical care, job placement and probationary 'tickets of leave' helped give hope to many transports: it was particularly the case that English convicts were exiled from their homeland and families for what we would now consider trivial offences. Macquarie's land grants created 'a broadly based society' and he even moved to include ex-convicts in the government of the new country, which he first officially termed 'Australia' (a name first proposed by Matthew Flinders (1774–1814)) in 1817: 'Governor Macquarie recommends Australia be used as the official name for the island continent, instead of New Holland', as it was reported at the time. Macquarie saw his colony as a place of sanctuary and refuge, sponsored extensive exploration of the Australian interior and laid out the street plan of modern Sydney, which he viewed as a major Georgian city. Needless to say, he was not universally popular and there was an enquiry into his governorship in 1817, which he survived, though it contributed to his final resignation in 1820–21. Macquarie was followed by another Scot, though one with perhaps a more reliable establishment pedigree, Major General Sir Thomas Makdougall Brisbane, 1st Bart (1773–1860), though he too ran into local difficulties. Although Macquarie can be held responsible for authorizing armed resistance (albeit with clear rules of engagement) to aboriginal attacks on settler lands, he also founded the Native Institution in Parramatta to educate Aboriginal children, admittedly in a more Eurocentric manner than we now find comfortable. Nonetheless, assessed as an Enlightenment man taking the difficult decisions of government rather than measured against a scale of values he would never have understood, Macquarie remains a man ahead of his time: uncomfortably so for many of his contemporaries. His tomb on Mull is the sole site in Scotland maintained by the National Trust of Australia: its inscription reads 'The Father of Australia'.[58]

Macquarie's example in Australia was followed by a number of Scots, with Alexander Maconochie (1787–1866), Professor of Geography at University College, London, producing a 'report on the penal system in Australia for the Society for the Improvement of Prison Discipline' in 1837, which favoured 'early release by rehabilitation'. Sir James Stirling (1791–1865), who became governor of Western Australia in 1828 and whose reputation is still stained by the Pinjarra attack/battle/massacre of 1834, named Perth and led the way on much other Scottish place-naming, as well as promoting Enlightenment ideas more generally. The Scots Kirk in Sydney was begun in 1824, and the first Caledonian Society organized there in 1829; it was followed by others in Victoria (1858), Ballarat and Bendigo and the federated South Australian Caledonian Society, which had different branches, in 1881. St Andrew's Societies developed at Melbourne (1842) and Adelaide (1847), while there were other associations such as Geelong's *An Comunn Na Feinne* (The Society of Fingalians/Fenians, 1856) and Maryborough Highland Society (1857). The Scottish societies in Australia were 'designed specifically to counteract the apparent and growing dominance of English influences in Australia', to 'regulate and control Scottish sport' and 'establish scholarships for children of Scottish descent'. By the 1890s, there were Scottish societies in 'almost all the Australian states'. This process continued: a federal Scottish Union was founded 'to give order to the multiplication' of Scottish societies in 1905, and a further seventeen new Scottish societies were formed in Victoria alone between 1906 and 1910. Andrew Fisher (1862–1928), a former Ayrshire miner, became the first Labour prime minister in the world in Australia in 1908, and went on to serve on two further occasions.[59]

Beginning with Robert Campbell in 1798, Scots came to establish businesses, with the Australian Company of Edinburgh and Leith being founded in 1822, followed by firms such as the North British Australasian Company (Sydney, 1839) and the Scottish Australian Investment Company (1840), which 'sought the contributions of small investors across Scotland'. Some emigrants had extraordinary career reach: Aberdeen man Alexander Dawson (1849–1913) was professor of English at the University of Otago in New Zealand, a barrister at Melbourne and a director of mining companies, while being a dairy farmer and stock breeder. Scottish business 'made a disproportionate contribution to capital foundation' and was 'a formative influence on the evolution of the banking system' in Australia, as it had been in Canada. By 1839 Melbourne – where David Syme developed 'the *Age* newspaper' – was regarded as 'almost altogether a Scotch settlement', and a St Andrew Society (1846) and Scotch College (1851) duly followed in the city, while Scots settlement was also heavily concentrated in other areas, and Scottish baronial-style architecture began to appear, such as Ercildoune near Ballarat (1859) and Overnewton Castle at Keilor, built in the same year. In the decades following 1860, some 12 to 15 per cent of UK-born Australians were Scots (with concentrations of up to 40 per cent at Portland Bay), but, as was the case elsewhere, their networking capacity helped ensure that they made an impact out of proportion to their numbers. On visiting Australia in 1873, Anthony Trollope noted that 'in the colonies those who make money are generally Scotchmen', and this was in no small part due to the assiduity of Scots networking through their associational societies. These were not always ethnoculturally exclusive: *An Comunn* at least involved Aboriginal peoples in its activities.[60]

Clearance was not absent from Scottish activity in Australia as in Scotland. Massacres of Aboriginal peoples – notably at Warrigal Creek in 1843, where 50–150 were killed in reprisal for the murder of Ronald Macallister near Port Albert – were intermittent occurrences. Angus Macmillan from Skye led what was called the 'Highland Brigade' of some twenty colonists to attack native people at several locations with the aim of extirpating all the Aborigines in the area. Scottish networking could lead not only to mutual benefit, but to savage reprisals against those who hurt or killed a Scot. While some Aboriginal people were singing 'Bonnie Highland Laddie' in 1840, others were being poisoned by arsenic by those same 'bonnie Highland laddies' in 1842. Origin in Gaelic Scotland was no guarantee of virtue. On the other hand, there were also figures such as Archibald Meston of Aberdeen, who 'migrated to Sydney in 1859' and whose 1894 report formed the basis of the Aboriginals Protection Act of 1897; James Dawson, a West Lothian man who was 'an early agitator for Aboriginal land rights'; Gideon Lang (1819–1880), who 'stressed the responsibility of the settlers to the Aborigines'; and John Murray (1851–1916), Premier of Victoria, who was 'a consistent defender of the Aborigine people'.[61]

New Zealand advertised itself as 'THE FIRST SCOTCH COLONY' to potential Glasgow emigrants in 1839–40, and indeed George Rennie MP 'suggested a Scottish settlement' in more formal terms for New Zealand in 1842. By 1861, despite the difficulty of immigration from November to May owing to the condition of the seas, one-third of the population of New Zealand was Scots-born. Scots were 20 to 30 per cent of British Isles immigrants between 1800 and 1945 (a higher proportion than anywhere else except Canada), while the Scots population of Otago – the core zone – peaked at 55 per cent in 1881. Thomas Bryden was 'responsible for the first shipment of frozen meat from New Zealand to London' following the innovative ideas of James Harrison (1816–95), the son of a Dunbartonshire fisherman and former student of Anderson's College, who 'saw the potential for refrigeration' for the long-distance transport of meat as early as 1850. Mauchline man Thomas Burns (1796–1871), Robert Burns' nephew, played a leading role in the foundation of Otago, where 'two-thirds of the early . . . migrants were Free Church Presbyterians'. Dunedin itself, loosely based on the Edinburgh New Town in its initial layout and initially called 'New Edinburgh', was 'established as a Free Church Settlement in 1848', and the campaign for Dunedin's High School for girls and for higher education for women at Otago was led by Coupar Angus woman Learmonth Dalrymple (1827–1906), herself educated at Madras College in St Andrews. The first headmistress when it opened in 1871 was Edinburgh woman Margaret Gordon Burn (1825–1918). Both 'politicians and entrepreneurs born in Scotland led New Zealand to become a nation of smallholders', and Scots were over-represented in New Zealand's farming communities, having 'about half the farms of more than 40 hectares'; by 1892, Scots were also '40% of those owning more than 4,000 hectares'. They were also dominant in some agricultural sectors, such as the 'New Zealand and Australia Land Company', machinery and the ever-present gardening or botany. George Mathewson established 'Dunedin's leading nursery', James Geike laid out the city's botanic gardens, Andrew Duncan engaged with the development of the 'civic botanical gardens' at Christchurch, while Sir Thomas Mackenzie, the son of an Edinburgh gardener, championed national park development. Sir James Wilson, who owned some 27,400 hectares in North Island, 'founded the New Zealand Forestry League in 1916 and advocated the replanting of native forests'.[62]

In 1873, the 'Scottish farmer and grape-grower, David Herd, planted the first vineyard' in Marlborough: by 2012, wine accounted for 72 per cent of New Zealand's exports. In 1884, the Shetlander Sir Robert Stout (1844–1930), a Dunedin MP, became prime minister of New Zealand, and nine years later women won the right to vote, in what was their first achievement of suffrage in a modern western democracy. Secondary education was more modelled on Scottish burgh grammar schools than on the English public school system, while numerous companies were founded throughout the country with Scottish capital. There were also dedicated newspapers, including the *New Zealand Scot* (1912–33) and the *Scotia Pacific.*[63]

As ever, Scottish cultural associations and events accompanied these developments, and indeed – as usual – 'Scots spearheaded associationalism', with its inevitable 'patronage and employment opportunities' in New Zealand, beginning with the Otago Caledonian Society of 1862. Unlike North America, where 'benevolence and philanthropy' was the predominant mode of Scottish associationalism, New Zealand activity focused on 'sports and entertainment', although there were other special interest groups, sometimes dominated by women, such as the Dunedin Gaelic Society (1881) and the New Plymouth Scottish Women's Club (1936). Gaelic indeed continued to be spoken in pockets in nineteenth-century New Zealand. By 1900, there were 'some 100 Caledonian societies in New Zealand', as well as Burns Clubs, such as the 1891 foundation at Dunedin which, as the novelist Liam McIlvanney notes, was attracting 2,000 people to its Halloween celebrations as late as the 1950s. Caledonian Games, the number of which reached almost twenty-five at their peak in the 1880s, were the central major public event. On New Year's Day 1888 – a more clement season in New Zealand than in the homeland – 7 per cent of the entire population of the colony, some 45,000 people, either 'participated in, or more generally were spectators at, Caledonian Games'. The Games movement was instrumental in 'the development of field athletics' in New Zealand, while the first national pipe band contest was founded in Christchurch in 1907; by 1953, there were 100 pipe bands in New Zealand.[64]

In the southern seas, after Sir James Clark Ross (1800–62) had claimed Antarctica for the Queen in 1841, William Speirs Bruce (1867–1921), who was born in England but devoted much of his life to his father's native Scotland, led the Scottish Antarctic Expedition of 1902–04 with an all-Scottish crew in the *Scotia.* Bruce surveyed the South Orkney Islands, located 600 kilometres north of Antarctica and almost 850 kilometres southwest of South Georgia, to which he 'would not lay claim . . . without a Government mandate'. He did consider the possibility – an interesting reflection on the continuing power of Scottish national identity within the Empire – of 'claiming them for Scotland' but feared it would not have been recognized. Unable to carry on a planned attempt on the South Pole due to a lack of financial support (the generosity of his backers at Coats of Paisley, co-founded by former Paisley Grammar School pupil Sir Peter Coats of Auchendrane (1808–90) would only reach so far), Bruce established a meteorological station on South Orkney. His crew flew the Scottish Lion over their observatory there until it was transferred to Argentina in 1904. Bruce's photograph of Gilbert Kerr in full regalia playing the pipes to a penguin has become a minor icon of the expedition. Bruce's passion to see Scotland on a more equal footing with other nations, and his insistence on categorizing his ventures as 'Scottish', may have led to some unwillingness among potential funders to support further ventures. Later he advised the ill-fated Robert Falcon Scott (1868–1912) that his Antarctic supply dumps were too far apart, and attempted the commercial development of Spitsbergen, but this project was critically interrupted by the First World War. The 1907 Shackleton expedition which followed Bruce was also financed from Scotland by Sir William Beardmore (1856–1936); Sir Jameson Adams (1880–1962) from Aberdeen was its deputy leader.[65]

EUROPE AND THE MEDITERRANEAN

One of the largest (if not the largest) destinations for Scottish migrants was the rest of the United Kingdom, whither almost 750,000 Scots migrated between 1841 and 1931 (Ireland was of course part of the United Kingdom for the vast bulk of this period). Among British prime ministers, W.E. Gladstone (1809–98) was the son of the Scots merchant Sir John Gladstone (who had more than 2,500 enslaved people working for him, prior to receiving over £100,000 compensation for their being freed in 1834), and the Earl of Rosebery, Arthur Balfour and Sir Henry Campbell-Bannerman were all Scots-born, while Ulster Scot Bonar Law (1858–1923), whose perspective on the Irish Question was derived more from his tribal sympathies than any statesmanship, was educated at the High School of Glasgow, as was

Campbell-Bannerman.[66] In the imperial capital, among the exponents of a tradition of Scottish-designed buildings and infrastructure were Robert Mylne (1733–1811) (Blackfriars Bridge), Sir George Washington Brown (1853–1939) (St Paul's Bridge), Sir William Arrol (1839–1913) (Tower Bridge) and John Rennie (1761–1821) (Waterloo Bridge and a huge range of English infrastructure). This heritage had begun with James Gibbs (1682–1754), Sir William Chambers (1723–96) and Thomas Telford (1757–1834). Just as the sinews of imperial power were being constructed by sea and rail, so Britain's roads were transformed by John Loudon McAdam (1756–1836), who in 1816 invented the macadamization process, which underpinned what would become 'tarmac[adam]', the single greatest advance in road technology in the Christian era. In 1820, McAdam was made Surveyor General of Metropolitan Roads. Four years later, James Braidwood (1800–61), the tenth child of an Edinburgh cabinetmaker and a pupil at the Royal High School, founded the first municipal fire service in the United Kingdom, if not the globe, in Edinburgh, subsequently becoming director of what was to become the London Fire Brigade.[67]

London was and remained a key destination for Scots (there were 110,000 Londoners who were Scots-born in 2001), and Scottish associations accompanied Scotsmen and women as night follows day. The Highland Society of London was founded in 1778 with the aim of preserving 'the Martial Spirits, Language, Dress, Music and Antiquities of the Ancient Caledonians'. In 1815, the Royal Caledonian Asylum was established for 'supporting the descendants of Scottish military men who had died or fallen on hard times'. Many regional Scottish societies also flourished in London, such as the Morayshire Club (1813), the Orkney and Shetland Society (1819), the Liddesdale Benevolent Society (1872) and the Aberdeen, Banff and Kincardine Society (1884). By 1888, there were almost thirty Scottish associations in London with between 4,000 and 5,000 members, and in 1891 the Caledonian Club was established in Belgravia. Scots played a leading role in Fleet Street, and famously the young John, 1st Baron Reith (1889–1971), mentioned in his application to be general manager of the BBC in 1922 that 'I am an Aberdonian and it is probable you knew my family.' The 'you' in question was Reith's fellow Aberdonian Sir William Noble, 'chair of the

THE ALL-CONQUERING SCOT.

Old Scotsman (to his son, who has just returned from a business trip to London). "WEEL, LADDIE, AND WHAT DAE YE THINK O' THE ENGLISH NOO?"

Son. "OH, I DIDN'T HAVE MUCH OF A CHANCE TO STUDY THEM. YOU SEE, I ONLY HAD TO DO WITH THE HEADS OF DEPARTMENTS!"

18. *The All-Conquering Scot, Punch.* Dilke's view of the prominence of Scots in the empire was widely held.

Broadcasting Committee'. Reith's father, George Reith (1842–1919), was an Aberdeen Grammar School former pupil and had been Moderator of the Free Kirk's General Assembly in 1909. It was this kind of relationship which led T.W.H. Crosland in *The Unspeakable Scot* (1902) to comment that 'At the present moment England is virtually being run by the Scotch' and Lord Birkenhead to note more charitably that 'Scotland is renowned as the home of the most ambitious race in the world.' Some Scots hoovered up offices at a ferocious rate, such as Sir William McGregor (1846–1919), a former farm labourer and son of a Towie crofter, who secured four imperial governorships among other honours. These ambitions could extend to taking on the mantle of other cultures, even English culture itself: quintessential expressions of English childhood, rural ideality and derring-do such as *The Wind in the Willows* (1908) by Edinburgh author Kenneth Grahame (1859–1932), or *Treasure Island* (1883) by Robert Louis Stevenson, were both written by Scots. These authors proved particularly adept at caricaturing a particular kind of Englishman, such as in Mr Toad of Toad Hall, without giving offence, as indeed J.M. Barrie (1860–1937) also did in *Peter Pan* (1904). Grahame was Secretary to the Bank of England, just the kind of employment one might expect for a London Scot.[68]

In Great Britain as a whole, in the second half of the eighteenth century, '90 per cent of British doctors had graduated from Scottish universities', setting in train a rich seam of fiction, soap opera and caricature which extended from Elizabeth Gaskell's (1810–65) last novel *Wives and Daughters* and George Eliot's *Middlemarch* (1872), to *Dr Finlay's Casebook* (BBC, 1962–71), based on a 1935 novel by A.J. Cronin. Scots Presbyterian churches had been established in England as early as 1566, and from 1603 the Kirk was permanently represented in London, with St Columba's in Pont Street opening in 1884. Scots societies were founded in the English provinces (for example at Norwich in 1775) to 'supply the defect in the English law, with regard to the natives of Scotland, who are by these laws, in common with natives of all other nations, deemed foreigners or strangers', not being entitled to parish relief. Following the development of Burns Suppers in the early nineteenth century, Burns Clubs grew up throughout England, such as those at Newcastle (1864), Sunderland (1897) and Darlington (1906). Burns was seen – both in England and internationally, through musical tours such as David Kennedy's – as representing 'the journey of the ordinary Scot', and thus the ordinary man, through the world and through life.[69]

Although the focus on Scots abroad after 1707 has overwhelmingly concentrated on their presence in the British Empire in recent years, emigration to and sojourning in Continental Europe continued, not least in Poland and Russia, which continued to attract a trickle of Scottish emigrants or sojourners into the mid nineteenth century. Scottish travellers – such as Andrew Archibald Paton (1811–74), who visited Belgrade in 1840 – often remained as curious about other countries as those countries were about them. Paton, who walked from Naples to Vienna in 1836, became acting British consul general in Serbia three years later, but his interest in Continental Europe reached far beyond that expected of a diplomat. Paton's books, including *Highlands and Islands of the Adriatic* (1849), reflected both that curiosity and the Scottish habit of identifying their own landscape as the template for those they found on their travels.[70]

European influence continued in Scottish architecture right up to the First World War, with the Glasgow Necropolis (1832) being 'modelled on Père Lachaise' in Paris, opened in 1804, while the grand middle-class suburb of Hyndland in Scotland's largest city, built from 1885, continued to echo the models of nineteenth-century practice in France and Belgium in its tenemented apartments. In developing the National Museum of Antiquities, which he directed from 1869, Joseph Anderson (1832–1916) made comparative visits across Europe. It was noteworthy that, in focusing on Scotland's national status in his presentation of the collection, Anderson both dissolved the British context in which museums had been conceived after the Great Exhibition, and used European rather than Anglo-imperial comparators to formulate his curatorial approach. Likewise Scots, such as the Free Kirk Moderator Thomas Guthrie, continued to study at Continental universities, though the practice was not so common as it had been in the preceding century.[71]

In its turn, Scotland influenced Europe, not only through the Romantic writers discussed in the previous chapter (Ferdinand Freiligrath's (1810–76) *Trotz Alledem* translation of Burns' 'A Man's a Man' became a signature tune for the revolutionary year of 1848, for example) but also as an inspiration to the European nationalism absent in Scotland itself. In the aftermath of that tumultuous year – driven by serious crop failures which had their domestic counterparts in the Irish and west Highland potato famine – the Hungarian patriot Lajos Kossuth (1802–94) and the Italian patriot Giuseppe Garibaldi (1807–82) alike toured Scotland. There was – in the critic Kirstie Blair's words – a 'prevalent idea that Scotland was better placed to understand and sympathise with European revolutionary nationalism' than other parts of the British Empire, with the possible exception of Ireland. Kossuth, Garibaldi and the founder of Young Italy, Giuseppe Mazzini (1805–72), all agreed that Glasgow was a 'stronghold' of radicalism, and Garibaldi received almost two and a half times as much money in support of his cause from Glasgow as he did from the whole of England.

These European nationalists in their turn supported the building of the Wallace Monument, a mid century expression of Scottish patriotism planned from 1856 and opened on the Abbey Craig in Stirling in 1869. Statues of Wallace had been used to represent Scottish patriotism since the Earl of

19. The 1814 statue of Wallace at Dryburgh, commissioned by the 11th Earl of Buchan (1742–1829), bearing the legend 'Great Patriot Hero! Ill-Requited Chief!'

Buchan's 1814 statue of the 'Great Patriot Hero, Ill-Requited Chief' at Dryburgh in the Scottish Borders. Now at the peak of Empire the creation of the national Wallace Monument at Stirling was indicative of the continuing power of Scottish patriotism and its awareness of its history, not least the Wars of Independence fought by William Wallace (*c.*1270–1305) and Robert I Bruce (1274–1329), from which the Declaration of Arbroath had been born. Garibaldi wrote that 'William Wallace, Scotland's noblest hero, sheds as bright a glory on his valourous nation, as ever was shed upon their country by the greatest men of Greece and Rome', while to Mazzini, 'Wallace stands forth from the dim twilight of the past as one of the High Prophets of Nationality to us all: Honour him; worship his memory; teach his name and deeds to your children.' Had the rejected design for the memorial by Noel Paton (1821–1901) been accepted (at what was later deemed an inquorate meeting) its image of the Scottish lion crushing the English serpent would have been exceptionally controversial. However, the fact that it could be conceived at all and

20. The rejected Paton design for the Wallace Monument.

advanced as appropriate reveals something of the double mindedness of Scottish patriotism within the British Empire, designed in its numerous overseas associations to promote the interests of Scots at the expense of everyone else. Garibaldi formed a 'Scottish volunteer company' in Italy with 'distinctive Scottish dress' accompanied with 'tartan shirts and bonnets topped with a Scottish thistle' to emphasize the mountaineers' love of liberty. He also donated to the Monument, which implicitly represented Wallace as a man of the mountains by virtue of its eminent situation on the Abbey Craig. Some of Garibaldi's officers went on to fight for the US Confederacy, which itself received significant aid in breaking the blockade from ships sailing from Glasgow. While historians of the era such as Graeme Morton describe the sentiments underpinning monuments of the kind built on the Abbey Craig as 'Unionist-Nationalism', this excellent term perhaps does not quite cover all bases. Paton's design was stronger meat than this, and was avoided as such. However, the fact that it was seriously considered is itself an interesting indication that there were situations and contexts which could arouse patriotic fervour in Scotland.[72]

21. The Wallace Monument, Abbey Craig, Stirling.

Multiple cultural connexions with Europe also continued to develop. The polymath Patrick Geddes (1854–1932) founded a Franco-Scottish society in 1895, which held its first meeting at the New Sorbonne in Paris (chaired by Louis Pasteur), at which a drawing by John Duncan (1866–1945) of *Jehanne d'Arc et sa Garde Ecossaise* was given to all attendees. Duncan himself owed a 'stylistic debt to the French mural artist Puvis de Chavannes', while Geddes was deeply influenced by Belgian, Breton and French practice, and was engaged with the Paris exhibition of 1900, as well as founding the Collège des Écossais, Montpellier in 1924. The site was chosen by the botanist in Geddes because it was the location of the first *Jardin des Plantes* in France, opened in 1593 as part of the medical faculty there, a link that Scotland had come to make its own. Likewise, as the cultural historian Michael Shaw has pointed out, *La Jeune Belgique* movement was very influential on Scottish art. This cosmopolitan openness to international influence was reflected in Andrew Lang's (1844–1912) historic collection of Fairy Books, which for perhaps the first time moved away from the Grimm model of fairy stories as a kind of national anthropology of *volkisch* essence to envisioning them as a global tapestry of mythology: Lang found room for Arabian, Japanese, German and many other stories in his historic collections, and indeed relatively few Scottish ones are included.[73]

SCOTLAND

Scots enjoyed the possession of national profile, projection and self-promoting soft power across the globe, supported by their country's outstanding achievements and the infrastructure of the British Empire. The quid pro quo for this liberty – the liberty to seek to control colonial place, position and opportunity in their own interests and (to be frank) against the interests of other subjects of the United Kingdom – was the expectation of loyalty to the Crown and the Union, which was almost always forthcoming. Indeed Scots, sensible of the great benefits the Union had brought their country between 1760 and 1914, were often in the vanguard of British loyalism. There was nonetheless a paradox. In Scotland itself there was at times an uneasy sense that the country's institutions and distinctive cultural life, no longer left to the remote management of Scottish magnates, were under threat from British legislation that neither knew of them nor cared about them: that, in short, Scotland was overlooked and worse, inadvertently damaged by legislation that took no account of its national circumstances. This response was visible from Sir Walter Scott's *Letters of Malachi Malagrowther* (1826) in defence of the Scots banking system to the establishment of the National Association for the Vindication of Scottish Rights (NAVSR, 1853), which objected to the use of the term 'England' (which, confusingly, many Scots were content to accept in the Empire, though much less so at home) for 'Great Britain'. Although NAVSR, which at one time boasted 1,000 members, faded away in the jingoism of the Crimean War, the issue of giving Scotland its proper name did not. There were repeated controversies over what may seem tokenistic issues, such as the flying of the Scottish quarterings (two Lions Rampant) by the Crown in Scotland or the fact that the St George's Cross of England dominated in naval ensigns, which continued to generate complaint into the era of the First World War. The

22. *Sandy MacPartington and the 'English' Flood.* Humorous 1898 *Punch* cartoon which reflects Scottish sensitivity to the use of non-inclusive language in the Union.

SANDY MACPARTINGTON AND THE "ENGLISH" FLOOD.

[A petition signed by 104,388 Scottish people has been presented to the QUEEN against the use of the words "England" and "English" as representing Great Britain.—See *Standard*, December 30.]

historical novelist James Grant (1822–87) went further, and argued that Scotland was 'disgraced and demoralised', her Highlands 'depopulated', her laws 'violated' and her institutions 'subverted' within the Union. From the 1880s, the term 'North Britain' for Scotland came under increasing pressure and had largely disappeared by the First World War, despite survivors like the North British Hotel in Edinburgh (now the Balmoral) which lasted until the end of the twentieth century.[74]

The industrial exhibitions of the nineteenth century, beginning with the Great Exhibition of 1851, combined leading edge technology and innovation with a Romantic sense of the national self, visible throughout Europe. At the 1867 Paris World Fair, Austria and Russia represented the values of their nations through idealized depictions of village life, while the 1879 'Parade of the City of Vienna' reflected the historicized civic values already celebrated in a German context in Richard Wagner's *Die Meistersinger von*

Nürnberg, first staged in Munich in 1868. While costumed processions and parades of this kind were common throughout Great Britain, those in Scotland tended to represent national history rather than local identities. However, the pattern was broadly similar. The reconstruction of 'Old London' in 1884 was followed by 'Old Edinburgh' at the International Exhibition of Industry, Science and Art in the Scottish capital in 1886, the reconstructed 'Bishop's Castle' at the Glasgow International Exhibition (1888), and by Alt Wien (1892), Vieux Bruxelles (1897) and many more. Romantic historicism (as seen also in the Wallace Monument) underpinned national self-definition as a modern, innovative and technological force, but the era of the Great Exhibitions and historical pageants demonstrated this as a Scottish, not a British, nationality. The 1888 Glasgow International Exhibition foregrounded Scottish culture and history, a *catalogue raisonée* of which appeared in the large and handsome volume *Scottish National Memorials* in 1890. The 1901 exhibition in Glasgow attracted 11.5 million visitors and left an enduring legacy in the shape of Kelvingrove Museum and Art Gallery, while that of 1911 foregrounded the 'cultural achievements' of the country. There had been some earlier stirrings of celebrating these: for example the campaign for the return of Mons Meg to Edinburgh in the 1820s and the development of a national museum from the 'Scottish Industrial Museum' conceived in the wake of the Great Exhibition (and visited by over 90,000 in 1862–63 alone), but now this process intensified. The view of John Hill Burton (1809–81), from 1867 Historiographer Royal, that Scotland was 'built on the achievement of Lowland Teutonic Scots and hindered by Celtic Highlanders' began to be challenged. Some Scottish historians, such as William Burns (1809–76) (a key supporter of the Wallace Monument) in *The Scottish Wars of Independence* (1874) and W.F. Skene (1809–92) in *Celtic Scotland* (1880), began to push back against this dominant post-Enlightenment historiographical discourse which racialized Scottish history into Teuton and Celt and presented the Celts as inferior. Skene presented a collectivist and ideal Highland society which modernity had ejected from a kind of golden age. Such approaches defended Scotland's ability to present itself in terms of Romantic national unity, and they were beginning to be manifested in its wider culture also. At Edinburgh in 1886 a limited reconstruction of the mediaeval and early modern city was accompanied by exhibitions of shipbuilding, jewellery, potteries, mines, quarries and Scottish design (the 'Artisan Section') as well as two halls for 'Foreign Exhibits', while at the 1888 Glasgow exhibition there was a vast show of the whole conspectus of Scottish history. In terms of specifically Gaelic culture, *An Clachan* (The Village) was a hugely popular exhibition at the Scottish National Exhibition of 1911 and the Empire Exhibition of 1938 (see plate 23): it was both native and traditional and also part of the exotica of Empire, as were the 'Indian craftsmen and shop workers' at the 1888 Glasgow exhibition and the 'Senegalese village' at the Scottish National Exhibition of 1908, which imported '70 natives of French Senegal' for the purpose.[75]

In these and other respects, Scottish identity was reinforced in a number of ways in Scotland in the 1880s. The pioneering work of William Burn had already embodied what was to become known as the Scottish baronial style – presenting a distinctive national perspective on the revisitation of the past – in buildings such as Helen's Tower (1848) and Balintore Castle (1859). The restoration of the Mercat Cross in Edinburgh (removed in 1756) in 1866–85 was of a piece with these developments. Sir Robert Rowand Anderson (1834–1921) went yet further in transplanting the baronial into the heart of the capital city. His Scottish National Portrait Gallery (1885) challenged the surrounding Georgian New Town's environment of Hanoverian names and Unionist identity with its vernacular baronial design, as did William Hole's (1846–1917) internal frieze of national history, which was added in 1897–98. Consciousness of that history was increasing, with visitors to the Wallace Monument averaging 36,000 a year from 1897 to 1901. Jacobite material was increasingly prominent in the major exhibitions of the era. New cultural and historical societies developed, such as the Gaelic Society of Inverness (1871), Scottish Text Society (1882), Scottish Historical Society (1886), the Royal Scottish Geographical Society (1886), the Royal Scottish National Orchestra (1895), the Scottish Trades Union Congress (1897) and *An Comunn Gaidhealach* (1899). Perhaps the new national institutions with the strongest impact on Scottish culture were the Scottish Football Association and League (SFA, 1885; SFL, 1890), which – after an era when Scottish sides had competed in the English FA Cup – guaranteed

23. The restored
Edinburgh Cross, 1885.

Scotland an autonomous national football culture which continues to occupy a central role for many people in their sense of self.[76]

In company with the development of the understanding of a distinctive Scottish history and literature (a Chair in these subjects was founded at Glasgow in 1913 endowed from the receipts of the 1911 exhibition, and a Scottish History chair was founded at Edinburgh in 1901), David McGibbon posited 'The Characteristics of a Scottish National Architecture' at the 1889 Congress of the 'National Association for the Advancement of Art and its Application to Industry' (1889), while Patrick Geddes promoted a 'Scottish Renascence' of 'cultural rebirth' in *The Evergreen* (1895–7). This journal was named in honour of Allan Ramsay's encapsulation – or invention – of a distinctive Scottish vernacular tradition in his 1724 poetry collection of the same name. Geddes promoted the revival of vernacular style in the Old Town of Edinburgh in his redevelopment of Ramsay's house on Castlehill as

Ramsay Garden in 1892–94, part of the expression of a 'synthesis of Arts and Crafts aesthetic philosophy and tenement living' both 'traditional in ethos and modernist in application'. For Geddes, 'Celticity was allied racially to a renewed cultural alliance of Scotland, Wales, Ireland, Cornwall and Brittany' such as was represented in the contemporary pan-Celtic Congresses. Geddes directed the 1907 Edinburgh Congress, as well as bringing out a new *Poems of Ossian* on the centenary of James Macpherson's death in 1896. While these Congresses themselves were largely cultural and pictorial, with a contemporary liking for pageant and fancy dress highly evident, not least at Caernarfon in 1904, there was a political substrate to pan-Celticism, represented by figures like the Irish Home Ruler and land reformer Michael Davitt (1846–1906), and his political engagement in the crofting cause. Both Ireland and Scotland 'had small tenants who employed a rhetorical version of their own history of oppression to good political effect', and there were close engagements between the Irish and Highland Land Leagues in the last quarter of the nineteenth century.[77]

Ramsay Garden itself was decorated in Celtic form by the artist John Duncan, who included an image of the Admirable Crichton, the Scottish Renaissance polymath who was symbolic of the country's European links and heritage (and who, like Geddes himself, was a former pupil of Perth Grammar School). Kirriemuir weaver's son Sir James Barrie (1860–1937) named his 1902 play *The Admirable Crichton*: in it, the modern version of the Scottish polymath is reduced to being a butler in a London household full of airheaded gentry, notable only for their incapacity and snobbery. When they become marooned on an island, Crichton takes over and manages everything from governance to civil engineering (a metaphor for Scots in the Empire). Crichton dominates in the colonial setting of the central acts and is marginal back in Britain. The implication for Scotland's status was clear, though as so often Barrie's deep social critiques of the cultural marginalization of Scotland and the vacuity and sexism of society (*What Every Woman Knows* (1908), *Dear Brutus* (1917), *Mary Rose* (1920)) were accepted by their audience as simple comedies of manners on account of their detached tone: it is sadly fitting in this context that Barrie's *Quality Street* (1901) has only passed into public consciousness as the name of a brand of chocolates.

George Shaw Aitken (1836–1921) restored Lady Stair's house in Edinburgh as a city museum in the 1890s, and at St Giles the architect Robert Lorimer (1864–1929), who had learnt 'the value of national identity in modern design' from Rowand Anderson, designed the Thistle Chapel in 1909–11 as a symbol of that Scottish royal order, instituted by James VII in 1687. The Scottish National Exhibition at Edinburgh in 1908 included a National Pageant of Scotland's 'Allegory, Myth and History' with John Duncan's representations of a joint Scottish and Irish Celtic past. The renewal of Celticism in Scottish art which, influenced by *japonaiserie* and the strong links between Glasgow in particular and Japan, was manifest also in the work of the 'Glasgow Boys' artistic group and 'The Four': Charles Rennie Mackintosh (1868–1928); Margaret Macdonald Mackintosh (1864–1933); Herbert McNair (1868–1955); and Frances Macdonald McNair (1878–1921). Mackintosh and Macdonald, like Geddes himself, were also engaged with Continental practice, not least the design dynamism of the Austro-Hungarian capital of Vienna, where they exhibited in 1901. Macdonald's work was influential on the leading Vienna secessionist Gustav Klimt (1862–1918). Other artists, such as Jessie M. King (1875–1949) and Marion Wilson (1869–1956), also manifested similar styles.[78]

Although much of this national historicism was cultural, there was a political dimension too. The Highland Land Law Reform Association (Land League), developed in 1882–83 in both Edinburgh and London, refocused attention on issues of Highland land use as agricultural disturbances occurred on Skye and elsewhere (now mostly remembered through the Battle of the Braes) in response to failures in fishing and the potato crop. In 1885, the election of five MPs of the Crofting Party indicated the emergence of a peculiarly Scottish politics for the first time in the modern democratic era. The acceptance by the 1884 Napier Commission of theories concerning ancient communal Celtic traditions in landholding outlined by Skene in *Celtic Scotland* became manifest in a Celtic revivalism in the 1890s and the subsequent development of a 'Celtic Communism', which saw Celtic society not as savage or disorganized, but collectivist and ideal. Writers and theorists from John Stuart Blackie (1809–95) to Peter Kropotkin (1842–1921) responded to this Romantic fantasy. Blackie, a professor at the University of Edinburgh and a champion of Highland land rights, became chair of the new Scottish Home Rule Association (SHRA, 1886), established shortly after the restoration of the Scottish Secretaryship in 1885 by the Marquess of Salisbury following a mass meeting in Edinburgh. This restoration initiated the first stirrings of administrative devolution, although unsurprisingly the Home Office 'conducted a rearguard action'. Scotland also enjoyed notable patriotic leadership among senior figures such as Archibald Primrose, 5th Earl of Rosebery (1847–1929), who was sympathetic to Home Rule in an imperial context. Political divisions over the 1886 Irish Home Rule Bill both reinforced Unionism and opened up a debate about 'Home Rule All Round' in response to fears of 'national assimilation' to England (the terms used by Charles Waddie, author of *How Scotland Lost Her Parliament and What Came of It* (1891)). Indeed, Ireland was – not for the first or last time – a divisive factor in Scottish politics, because the SHRA saw Home Rule as privileging Ireland at Scotland's expense. This led to some paradoxical relationships, as Liberal Unionists (who contributed to a Unionist majority in Scotland as late as 1955) could hold office in the SHRA. There were other related organizations, such as the Liberal Young Scots Society (which had fifty-eight branches by 1914) and the Scottish Patriotic Association, as well as a Scottish branch of the Gaelic League, established by the prominent Irish cultural nationalist and later President of the Free State Douglas Hyde (1860–1949) in 1896. The Liberal leader W.E. Gladstone 'hinted at the possibility of altering the relationships between the three kingdoms', and 'serious consideration' was given to the possibility of Home Rule 'all round', with significant support from Scottish MPs for the 1913 Home Rule Bill. There was little interest from England, however, and the constitutionalist A.V. Dicey (1835–1922) warned in 1886 that federal parliaments would dilute the sovereignty of Parliament and devolved ones would distribute it unequally. However, a new language of Scottish nationality was beginning to be articulated by politicians like R.B. Cunninghame Graham (1852–1936), Liberal MP and first President of the Scottish Labour Party, who in his maiden speech in the House of Commons in 1887 attacked the Royal Family and British oppression in Burma and Egypt. In 1906, Graham – who in the 1920s became the first explicit nationalist elected to any position on that ticket – argued that the days of the multi-kingdom monarchy where power was disproportionately allocated were coming to an end, as 'Hungary, Poland and Ireland, with Bohemia and Macedonia, all mortally detest their union with great oppressive states.' Nor was there any British exceptionalism to this rule: 'Conscience', Graham noted, 'is a British product, and once across the English Channel it withers and dies' – there was one rule for England, and another for what it perceived as lesser nations. For Graham, the future lay with such small states.[79]

Antiquarian culturalism and politics could go together, as it had in the case of Skene's influence on land reform. In a related but politically distinct context, the Australian Scot and neo-Jacobite Theodore Napier (1858–1924) initiated the first stirrings of a recognizably modern Scottish Nationalist position in his journal *The Fiery Cross* (1901–12) and elsewhere, and developed the annual anniversary pilgrimage to Bannockburn, which attracted 15,000 by 1912 and continues to this day. A range of other short-lived and limited circulation patriotic publications marked the turn of the new century, including a number of explicitly neo-Jacobite papers (of which, though its range was broader, *The Fiery Cross* was one). Even figures of the distinction of James McNeill Whistler (1834–1903) and Andrew Lang engaged with the neo-Jacobite movement, though only its antiquarian rather than activist wing. There was a definite connexion between neo-Jacobitism and the growth of a modern Scottish national politics. Ruaridh Erskine of Mar (1869–1960), co-founder of the more activist Legitimist Jacobite League in 1891, went on to co-found the Scots National League (1921) whose newspaper, *The Scots Independent* (1926), is still published.[80]

In London, the *London Scotsman* was founded in 1888, and ten years later was arguing over whether Scotland was or was not a net contributor to the UK Exchequer, a debate which is with us yet. St Andrew's societies began to speak of the 'vindication of Scottish rights within the British union' and to encourage the study of Scottish history and literature. At the heart of the era of high empire in Britain and on the threshold of the age of Jingo (from the 1877–78 song, 'We don't want to fight, but by *Jingo* if we do/We've got the ships, we've got the men, we've got the money too . . . The Russians shall not have Constantinople'), certain limited but visible elements of Scottish society were beginning to articulate themselves distinctly once again.[81]

THE PATH TO WAR

Scottish identity in the British Empire had a foundational tie to militarism. As we saw in Chapter 3, the myth of particularly Highland martial valour had led to these soldiers being viewed as the most dynamic manifestation of British military power. This narrative was sustained by the formation of a 'Highland Brigade' in conflicts such as the Crimea (42nd Black Watch, 79th Queen's Own Cameron Highlanders, 93rd Sutherland Highlanders) and the Boer War (2nd Seaforths, 2nd Black Watch, 1st Argyll & Sutherland Highlanders and 1st Highland Light Infantry). The 'Highland warrior' was 'drawn from a remote, austere and unspoiled landscape', a domestic colonial, a picturesque mountaineer. He was increasingly seen in the Victorian era as synecdochal for all Scottish soldiers. From 1881, the War Office imposed forms of Highland dress and semi-Highland accoutrements upon the Lowland

24. Celtic Cross Memorial to the 78th Highlanders, the Ross-shire Buffs, who died suppressing the Indian Mutiny/The Great Rebellion, 1857–58.

regiments, namely tartan trews, kilted pipers (where pipe bands did not exist), doublet and basket-hilted broadswords.[82]

This focus on the visual and performative representation of the Scottish military may have been a response to the actual declining significance of Scots in the British Army: 13.6 per cent of its strength in 1850, by 1866 this had fallen to just over 8 per cent. Clear efforts to bolster the image of the Scottish soldier followed. W.E. Gladstone's Midlothian speeches of 1879–80 compared 'the mountain clans' of Scotland to the 'high-spirited and warlike people' of Afghanistan that the British Empire had struggled to prevail against on more than one occasion. At Tel-el-Kebir in 1882, there was a media campaign to build up the significance of Scotland's military contribution in the traditional style, and indeed – as so often – Scottish casualties at that engagement appear to have been disproportionate. Scottish recruitment, however, did not improve as a proportion of British forces and after 1902 the distinctive visibility of Scottish troops and their national dress were largely incorporated – not without protest – into British khaki.[83]

Before this, in the new patriot era of the 1880s, Scots were not only at their most visible as 'Highland' troops in the British Army, but identifiable Scottish military units also began to grow overseas, thus sustaining the diminishing position of the Scottish soldier outside its home in the domestic British military. The military/social Highland Guards – later the 79th New York Highlanders – had been formed in the United States as early as 1855, and this kind of development grew in Great Britain's current colonies in the last part of the nineteenth century. Units 'such as the New South Wales Scottish Rifles, the 48th Highlanders of Canada and the Cape Town Highlanders' were established, with Scottish companies also coming into being in the Hong Kong, Tianjin, Singapore and Malay states' volunteer forces, as well as in Calcutta/Kolkata and Shanghai. A 'Transvaal Scottish' unit was also established, while the formation of the 'Scottish Horse' was supported by the Johannesburg Caledonian Society in 1900–01. In New Zealand 'at least fifteen Scottish units' were established in the half-century up to 1910, while, in 1912, there was controversy concerning whether Australian regiments should be 'kilted', with this in the end being restricted to limited occasions. In 1910, fifty years after the first Scottish units had developed in Canada, Vancouver 'saw the creation of the 72nd Highlanders' (later the Seaforths); 'the 79th Highlanders' (later the Queen's Own Cameron Highlanders) were established at Winnipeg, while the Victoria Scottish Regiment was founded in 1898. In the First World War, Canadian recruitment was couched in terms of 'a specifically Scottish patriotism' and 'Scottishness and military Scottishness were . . . acceptable identities within Canadian nationalism.' The *Royal Highlanders of Canada* recruiting poster displayed this as did the *British Commonwealth in Arms* poster, which depicted Canadian and South African recruits in kilts. Only Canada and South Africa sent explicitly Scottish units to the front. The Caledonian Society of Otago also supplied its local battalion with the instruments for a pipe band and units ranging from the New South Wales Scottish Rifles to the Tyneside Scottish associated themselves with the country's martial tradition. After 1918, there was 'an explosion of Canadian units that elected to become Scottish or Highland'. In the end there were to be six Scottish regiments formed in Australia, four Scottish battalions in the South African forces and the 1st Armoured in New Zealand.[84] The uniforming which signified the Highland or Scottish soldier before the twentieth century thus composed a globally recognized performativity.

The combination of Scotland's immensely strong imaginary, the potency and determination of its kin, locality, burgh grammar school and university alumni, its continued production of relatively poor but well-educated, eager and networked people keen to take advantage of imperial markets, and the layered national self-promoting networks in such markets, from charitable grants to society balls, combined with a legendary and highly visible military presence, all served to make the long nineteenth century the era of the Scottish world. In 1981, Christopher Harvie published the first edition of his history of Scotland since 1914, called *No Gods and Precious Few Heroes*. It was an apt title, for the First World War was to usher in a long period of slow decline and slower readjustment to Scotland's place in the world, or increasingly the lack of one.[85]

17. Burns Night Udo Mushaira, Edinburgh 2020. The power of the global Burns movement to transform the poet's humanitarian message into a wide range of cultural referents and expressions is an extraordinary part of its strength. The Mushaira is a form of north Indian/Pakistani ceilidh associated with the Muslim community in Hyderabad, where poets gather together to recite their works.

18. Edwin Landseer, *Deer and Deerhounds in a Mountain Torrent* (1832). The revived deerhound breed is portrayed both as an expression of Scotland's brutal landscape and as an agent of the hunter's pursuit of sovereignty over it.

19. Edwin Landseer, *The Monarch of the Glen* (1850). This iconic painting depicts the 'royal' (12-point antlered, but not a 16-point 'monarch') stag of Scotland as a symbol both of that kingdom's dignity and of the subjugation of its royal line to another line of monarchs. Prince Albert was a keen deer hunter and he and Queen Victoria adopted Balmoral as their Scottish residence in 1852. The Stuarts had been identified as hunted deer in an iconographic tradition that dated back to John Denham's *Cooper's Hill* (1642).

20. *La nouvelle mode ou l'Écossais à Paris*: tartan becomes fashionable in France after the end of the Napoleonic Wars.

21. Henry Bell's *Comet*, the first European steamboat passenger service on the Clyde, 1812–20.

22. Cowden Japanese Garden, Clackmannanshire, created with the advice of Taki Handa originally from the Royal School of Garden Design at Nagoya: it is known as Shá Raku En, 'the place of pleasure and delight'.

23. Members of the Royal Family visit the post office at *An Clachan*, Empire Exhibition 1938. This strong state endorsement of Scottish distinctiveness was to become increasingly a thing of the past after 1945.

24. The Scottish Avenue, Empire Exhibition 1938. The central position of Scotland in the British Empire is manifest in the architecture of an exhibition which drew some 12.8 million visitors.

25. The Scottish Parliament: frontage. Designed by Catalan architect Enric Miralles (1955–2000), it opened in 2004.

26. Queensberry House. This 1681 building, the townhouse of the Duke of Queensberry who was one of the most prominent supporters of the Union of 1707, now provides office space for the Presiding Officer (Speaker) and senior officials of the Scottish Parliament. The house is reputed to be haunted by the servant allegedly roasted alive by Queensberry's son, the Earl of Drumlanrig, in 1707.

27. Statue of Donald Dewar (1937–2000), first First Minister of Scotland, by Kenny Mackay, located in Buchanan Street, Glasgow. The line 'There shall be a Scottish Parliament' opened Dewar's 1998 Scotland Act.

28. *Choosing Scotland's Future: A National Conversation* (2007); this Scottish Executive document opened the campaign for independence from within government.

29. *Robert the Bruce, King of Scots 1306–1329*, sculpture by Alan Beattie Heriot (2011): this contemporary celebration of the remote Scottish past is located in Broad Street, Aberdeen and supported by the City Council.

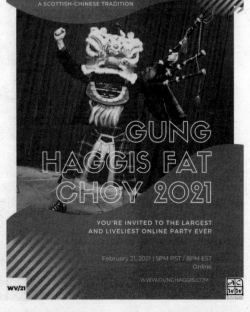

A SCOTTISH-CHINESE TRADITION

GUNG HAGGIS FAT CHOY 2021

YOU'RE INVITED TO THE LARGEST AND LIVELIEST ONLINE PARTY EVER

February 21, 2021 | 5PM PST / 8PM EST
Online

WWW.GUNGHAGGIS.COM

WV/21

30. Gung Haggis Fat Choy: the hybrid celebration of Scotland's Burns Night and the Chinese New Year in Vancouver pioneered by Todd Wong in 1993. It has since spread to Seattle and other locations.

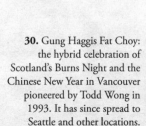

31. Alexander McQueen (1969–2010) for Givenchy, 1999/2000 collection. McQueen's alignment of tartan with edginess, rebellion and victimhood in his classic collections *Highland Rape* (1995) and *The Widows of Culloden* (2006) injected historical depth into the rebirth of tartan as a rebel cloth in the punk era.

32. *Punk: Chaos to Couture* exhibition, New York 2013. Tartan has retained its staying power in the language of design while continuing to represent Scotland as an international brand globally.

PART THREE

FINDING A ROLE

6

WAR AND SUPPLY
SCOTLAND AND THE BRITISH EMPIRE,
1914–67

PUBLIC MEMORY AND COLLECTIVE ACTION

About half of all male Scots aged under 45 served in the First World War. The scale of the sacrifice of the Scottish regiments has long been argued to have been disproportionate, notwithstanding the presence of Scottish commanding officers, most notably the controversial Douglas, 1st Earl Haig of Bemersyde (1861–1928). The National War Memorial in Edinburgh presents Scotland as having 13 per cent of British dead, 25 per cent higher than its population share, and there are higher estimates. Whether or not this was the case, and distinguished historians have recently expressed caution, there was a determination in the wake of the conflict to create a special *lieu de memoire* – a location of public memory – for the contribution of Scotland to the war. Sir Robert Lorimer (1864–1929) was commissioned to design the 'Scottish National War Memorial', fundraising for which was launched at Bannockburn in 1922 on the anniversary of the battle in a tribute to the martial history of a specifically Scottish nation. Lorimer was an architect with an established record of expressing national identity in stone, and the intention behind the Memorial was that the 'Scottish dead had to be honoured in Scottish terms', set in the context of a national and 'collective military tradition' reaching back centuries. Scotland's contribution to the war and its sacrifices were thus expressed in unequivocally national terms in the Memorial which opened at Edinburgh Castle in July 1927.[1]

While the 'homes fit for heroes' (Lloyd George's phrase) rhetoric of the postwar era was in general not acted upon, there was a positive exception in Scotland. Following the report of the Royal Commission on Scottish

Housing (1917), public housing provision commenced on a scale which both outpaced private building and also drove up the quality of the overall housing stock. Between the wars, public housing was 67 per cent of all housing development in Scotland, but only 25 per cent in England and Wales, in an attempt to correct a situation which by 1911 had seen six times as many Scots living in one or two-roomed accommodation as was the case south of the border; even by the late 1920s, Edinburgh was only slightly better than Sunderland on overcrowding indicators. A new climate of social welfarism seemed to become incipiently present in a country which had both been changed and damaged – even more than the rest of the UK – by the immense scale of the conflict it had gone through. In 1914, Scotland's percentage of UK output had been 20 per cent ahead of its population share, and in the heavy industries that supplied the sinews of both Empire and war it had been higher than this, though US locomotive and German steel production were already putting it under pressure before the war began. In order to secure the support of Scottish heavy industry most effectively, the British Government had intervened in the Scottish economy in wartime as never before. The Munitions Act of 1915 was only one example of central government direction which rapidly eroded the autonomy, innovation and enterprise of Victorian Scottish business, as well as lessening differentials in status and thus feeding labour unrest. Clyde ship production escalated to meet merchant shipping losses; overcapacity was created that could not be sustained in peacetime. The cordite factory at Gretna alone had almost 30,000 workers, many times the population of this small border town. At the same time this overcapacity was unable to compensate for the damage to other sectors of the Scottish economy, such as textile and coal exports, caused by the war: coal exports declined 75 per cent in 1914–18. One of the longer-term consequences of the levels of political interference with enterprise was a closer association between Scottish business and government, operating in an incipient climate of social welfarism in a context of economic upheaval. There was substantial charitable giving to support wounded and disadvantaged veterans, through initiatives such as 'The Harry Lauder Million Pound Fund' (1917), which the entertainer had set up following the death of his son, Captain John Lauder. This kind of welfare began to extend to civilian society as its different, but related, economic casualties mounted. In 1913, less than 2 per cent of insured workers were unemployed in Scotland, compared with almost 9 per cent in London, but this state of affairs did not long survive the war. In areas like the coal industry, hard-hit in its export markets, there was an especially 'tight partnership between the state and owners' which would in time lay the basis for nationalization of the industry at a UK level after 1945. More immediately, this 'partnership' meant that Scottish industry was more closely tied to British Government priorities: enterprise and agility were circumscribed, and this – combined with the sharp downturn in surplus capital and overseas investment opportunities consequent on the conflict – meant that the Scottish economy could not so readily compensate for the bias of 'imperial' and infrastructure expenditure towards London and the south-east. As the British economy shrank back from overseas investment towards a pattern of domestically owned wealth and rentier income secured on the government stock issued to cover the much swollen national debt, offering enhanced real interest rates as wages fell and prices halved from 1918–32, Scotland doubly lost out in its freedom in both domestic and overseas enterprise, both alike resting on overlapping networks. At the same time, mass production innovations in the United States helped to stifle developments such as the emergent Scottish car industry before it could reach critical mass, while the inheritance of state-directed overcapacity helped to focus attention on inherited strengths rather than new emergent industries: to take one example, civil aircraft carried only 6,000 passengers in 1930, but 1.2 million by 1938. Between 1932 and 1938, 1,400 new 'manufacturing plants' with over 25 employees were formed in greater London, but only 200 in Scotland and Wales combined. Traditional regional industries also suffered, with a major impact on the fishing industry, which had supported almost 9,000 jobs in Aberdeen alone in 1900 and two-thirds of the Scottish trawler fleet. Like the heavy industries, fishing was to be of declining importance to Scotland's economy while also being part of the mythology of what was 'real' or important to that economy.[2]

Even in the years before the First World War, the make-up of Scottish society itself was changing. Large-scale Irish immigration (by 1851, 7 per cent of the Scottish population had been born in Ireland), particularly from

Donegal and predominantly into west central Scotland, had combined in the great metropolis of Glasgow with internal population movement from the *Gàidhealtachd* and back-migration of Ulster Scots from Northern Ireland to create the unique – and divided – character of greater Glasgow which still endures. In the years before the First World War, Glasgow, like Liverpool, became a second home for Irish nationalism, with branches of the Irish National and Gaelic Leagues being founded, as well as the 'Rapparrees Hurling Club' (1901), to say nothing of the much larger and enduring Celtic Football Club (1888). Padraig Pearse visited the city in 1899 and 1902, and soon there were no fewer than seventeen branches of the Gaelic League in west central Scotland, which in turn supported the development of Gaelic Athletic Clubs and twelve Cumann (branches) of Sinn Féin, the largest of which had at least 200 members; by 1918, there were 80 branches of Sinn Féin in Scotland. Glasgow Irish were involved in the Irish War of Independence in 1918–21 on the nationalist side, and there was a strong reaction, manifested in the infamous 1923 Church and Nation report of the Kirk of Scotland, which included a section on 'The Menace of the Irish Race to our Scottish Nationality'. By contrast, Dundee, which had extensive Irish Catholic migration but little back-migration from the Protestant north of Ireland, experienced much less in the way of sectarianism, and Aberdeen – with a small native Catholic population and little immigration – had next to none.[3]

By 1911, there were 'almost 400,000 people' living in Scotland who had not been born there, including significant Italian migration from the 1880s onwards. Scotland was not unusual in this: indeed 'in 1961, Italians made up one-quarter of the foreign migrant labour force in Britain', free to work in many roles before the UK joined the European Economic Community that they would later be barred from in the wake of Brexit. Although the vast majority of these incomers came from England and Ireland, some 25,000 people came from Continental Europe. Scotland also had a significant Jewish population, which reached 20,000 by 1939, three-quarters of whom lived in Glasgow, mainly on the south side of the city, where movement from the Gorbals (where 90 per cent of Scotland's Jewish population lived in the early twentieth century) had already started towards the suburbs of Giffnock and Newton Mearns. By the Second World War, there were also small Asian communities, with Chinese seamen in Glasgow, a couple of Chinese restaurants in Edinburgh and an Indian community of around 400.[4]

Scottish emigration more than made up for such immigration. Scotland's net population was largely stagnating, in no small part due to its industrial overcapacity in the heavy industry with which much of the industrialized world was catching up by 1900, and which was afterwards yet further expanded beyond its sustainable capacity by the demands of imperial and war production. The attempt to correct these imbalances through centralized planning arguably only compounded the problem: as the historian Richard Finlay notes, 'The reality of the Scottish economy . . . was that it was in the hands of a narrow oligarchy . . . a cartel in all but name.' Top-down planning – not for the first or last time – brought little net economic benefit while not protecting economic casualties either. Between 1911 and 1980, almost a quarter of those born in Scotland emigrated, and while in 1911 Scotland's population was 86 per cent that of Sweden's, a century later this proportion had dropped to 56 per cent; likewise the Republic of Ireland's population rose from 60 per cent to 90 per cent of Scotland's in the twentieth century, despite the tradition of high emigration from Ireland. By 1991, Scotland's population was lower than it had been in 1961, and only 5 per cent higher than it had been in 1931, though its relative position has stabilized over the last generation, as the return of political power to Scotland has helped to arrest the conditions of economic decline. In 1911, Sweden had only 53 per cent of Scotland's GDP per capita: by 1970, this had reached 255 per cent, but by 2017 the ratio had shifted significantly in Scotland's favour. Within the United Kingdom, Scotland had moved from around 90 per cent of the UK GDP per capita average to parity.[5]

The 1920s in particular saw heavy emigration from Scotland, with 390,000 leaving between 1921 and 1931, 85 per cent to the rest of the UK; in all, between 1825 and 1938, almost 3 million 'left Scotland to search for a new life overseas'. There was a growing perception that the Scottish economy was becoming less autonomous, which was also evident in much comment of the period, while between 1924 and 1937, as the GDP of the United Kingdom rose by 2.2 per cent per annum, Scotland's rose only by 0.4 per cent. In 1923, the Scottish railway companies, among the country's biggest domestic organizations, were merged into the LMS and LNER networks, of which the first letter in both cases stood for 'London' (London, Midland and Scottish Railway, and London North Eastern Railway). Imperial Chemical Industries (ICI) became much less dependent on Scottish capital, and in 1929 the British Linen, Clydesdale and North of Scotland banks were taken over by Lloyds, Barclays and the Midland. Significant elements of Scottish steel manufacturing moved to Corby in Northamptonshire, taking a good part of their workforce with them. Overcapacity developed to sustain the war effort in 1914–18 was hit doubly hard by the Depression, as 'Scotland's industrial structure was heavily skewed towards "traditional" industries such as coal, iron and steel, shipbuilding, engineering and textiles.' These industries employed 42 per cent of the labour force in 1924, but only 27 per cent by 1939. Between 1929 and 1931 alone, 'coal production dropped by about a quarter, iron by three-quarters and steel by over a half'. The human cost of this transition was inevitably horrific. In 1929, 25 per cent of world shipping was built on the Clyde; by 1932, 52 per cent of shipbuilding workers were unemployed. Overall unemployment reached 28 per cent compared to 16 per cent in the UK as a whole and income per capita fell significantly – up to 13 per cent – below the UK average. A lesser but still significant decline affected Scottish higher education, with university places contracting 5 per cent in the interwar years, compared with a near 19 per cent gain in available places in England. Moreover, the international derangement of 'the mechanisms of credit and capital' caused by the massive indebtedness of the British Empire and other great powers after 1918 disturbed, as noted above, the optimal operation of Scottish overseas economic networks to an extent which is arguably still not fully recognized. The social disruption and decay that post 1918 social changes initiated in Glasgow in particular were charted in the novel *No Mean City* (1935) by H. Kingsley Long and Alexander McCarthy, the themes and title of which were reprised for a new era of industrial deracination in the early series of *Taggart* from 1983, which adopted as its theme tune 'No Mean City' by Mike Moran and sung by Maggie Bell. For many suffering the same conditions in Europe, 'The only escape from economic inequality would be to seize more resources by predation or war', and this is what happened in 1939.[6]

In these declining interwar conditions, modern Scottish nationalism began to take root, although more in terms of a vanguardist discourse than as a genuine popular movement: for the time being, it remained marginal in its political appeal. While pro-Soviet leftists such as John Maclean (1879–1923) have produced a degree of romantic nationalist nostalgia, the viewpoint such people represented was always the fringe of a fringe except occasionally at times of labour unrest (such as that on Clydeside in 1915–16 in the wake of the Munitions Act). Maclean was regarded as a useful potential ally by the infant USSR, which later commemorated him through a street name and a stamp. The Red Flag unveiled in George Square in Glasgow in January 1919 was more of a provocation than the 'Bolshevist rising' feared by Robert Munro (1868–1955), the Scottish Secretary and others in the British Government, though their anxiety was perhaps understandable. On 1 May that year, Maclean, John Wheatley (1869–1930) and the Irish Citizen Army leader Countess Markievicz MP (1868–1927, the first woman ever elected to Parliament) spoke to 100,000 in Glasgow with the Irish Soldiers' Song sung alongside the Red Flag. But Maclean's prophecy of Glasgow as 'a revolutionary storm-centre' was to prove an empty one.[7]

If Maclean's politics lay at the extreme, even the moderate Scottish Home Rule Association (SHRA), reformed in September 1918, was hardly mainstream, although its 'principal architect' the distinguished businessman Roland Muirhead (1868–1964), a former member of the Young Scots Society, took a leading role in this avowedly moderate organization, geared to 'requesting a Scottish Parliament from the British state'. The Labour and in particular the Independent Labour Party – home to figures of stature such as Tom Johnston, Jim Larkin, James Maxton, Edwin Muir and John Wheatley – had sympathies with Scottish and Irish home rule, but these did not emerge as priorities for the wider Labour movement. In particular, the Labour Party kept its distance from the SHRA, despite the leadership of Ramsay MacDonald (1866–1937), 'the illegitimate son of a ploughboy and a serving girl' from Lossiemouth, who rose to be prime minister on two occasions. Muirhead went on to become the first chair of the National Party of Scotland (NPS) in 1928, subsequently chairing the Scottish National Party (SNP) from 1936 to 1950. Tom Johnston (1881–1965), Secretary of

State for Scotland in the Second World War, and himself engaged with the SHRA, respected Muirhead as a great patriot.[8]

At the same time, other organizations grew up which took a stronger and explicitly nationalist line, such as the Scots National League (1920), founded by William Gillies/Liam MacGille Losa (1865–1932), the son of a City merchant, and Ruaraidh Erskine of Mar (1869–1960), the neo-Jacobite scion of the Earls of Buchan, possibly in association with the celebration of the 600th anniversary of the Declaration of Arbroath, in which Maclean too was involved. Erskine was a pan-Celticist who supported a future federation of the Celtic nations and founded *Guth na Bliadhna* (Voice of the Year), a constitutionally radical magazine which was published in Glasgow from 1904 to 1925. For his part, MacGille Losa had a longstanding background of Gaelic activism, and had founded *Comunn nan Albannach* in 1912. The background of most SNL members – who probably did not exceed 1,000 – was in Land League politics leavened with 'Gaelic romantics', and there was a broad streak of sympathy with Irish Republicanism, which was not characteristic of the SHRA. The SNL effectively agitated for a Celtic state and promoted abstentionism in the place of the British participatory agenda of the SHRA; they were also notably anti-imperial in their support for colonial liberation movements. The SNL's newspaper, *The Scots Independent* (1926), still survives (unlike contemporaries such as *The Scots Observer* (1926–34)), but the organization amalgamated with the more moderate SHRA and others in 1928 to form the National Party of Scotland (NPS). A more right-wing and pro-Empire (as well as largely anti-Catholic and anti-Irish immigration) Scottish (Self-Government) Party was founded in 1930, and after the exclusion of some of the more radical SNL contingent from the NPS, the Scottish Party and the NPS amalgamated to form the Scottish National Party (SNP) in 1934. This was subsequent to the 1933 Kilmarnock by-election in which the Scottish Party president Sir Alexander McEwen (the Calcutta/Kolkata born son of the Scots Recorder of Rangoon) took 17 per cent of the vote when the NPS stood aside to give him a clear run. Although the party won its first seat at a wartime by-election in Motherwell in 1945, it was not until Winnie Ewing's 1967 Hamilton victory that it began to break through as a major Scottish political force.[9]

This lay in the future. But for the first time since the eighteenth century, the 1920s and 1930s saw the emergence of a significant group of Scottish intellectuals and patriots who wanted major change to the Union arrangements, including prominent international figures such as R.B. Cunninghame Graham (1854–1936), whom we have already met in Chapter 5. A co-founder of the SHRA in 1886, Graham was to become – after a lifetime of radical campaigning – the first president of the SNP. An impressive political figure, Graham is largely written out of socialist or radical history because of his Scottish nationalism. He was also able – unlike lone wolf radical nationalists such as Wendy Wood (Gwendoline Meacham, 1892–1981) and Hugh MacDiarmid (the pen name of Christopher Grieve, 1892–1978) – to work within organizational parameters and to participate in movements other than those he thought himself certain to lead.

If the relationship between government and business in Scotland was appearing increasingly synergetic in a manner which constricted wider economic flexibility, constructive collective action enabled a new generation of Scottish thinking and cultural organizations to develop. Scottish suffragists (who favoured peaceful campaigning) had set up the Edinburgh National Society for Women's Suffrage in 1867, and, after the development of the Suffragette movement (which favoured direct action) in the form of the Women's Political and Social Union, established in Manchester in 1903, Scottish branches developed and a Scottish HQ was established in 1908. Scottish suffragettes – like their English sisters – set fire to buildings and committed acts of petty vandalism in protest at the exclusion of women from the democratic process, an injustice partially addressed in 1918. In the years after the war, figures such as A.S. Neill (1883–1971) and Marie Stopes (1880–1958) continued the campaign of emancipation by making original contributions in championing liberation for children and women, the internal subalterns of British society, in an increasingly activist and campaigning fashion, while more conservative campaigning sought to preserve Scottish history and society as distinctive entities. Institutions such as the National Library of Scotland (1925), the National Trust for Scotland (1931) and the Saltire Society (1936) developed a campaigning vision for the preservation and promotion of a distinctive Scottish culture, heritage and history.[10]

25. *Punch* cartoon on the 1938 Empire Exhibition displaying Scottish national identity.

NORTHWARD HO!

British policy responded to changing circumstances in Scotland with developments in administrative devolution through the establishment of the Scottish National Development Council (1931) and the Scottish Economic Committee, as well as the Special Areas Legislation of 1934 and 1937. Walter Elliot (1888–1958), a sympathetic Undersecretary (1926–29) then Secretary of State for Scotland (1936–38), whose phrase 'democratic intellectualism' seems to have inspired the far more radical George Davie, modernized Scottish local government and supported the creation of a recognizably modern Scottish civil service; some 94 per cent of its staff were based at St Andrew's House in Edinburgh after it opened in 1936. Elliot also supported a number of Scottish soft power initiatives, such as Films of Scotland (1938) and above all the £11 million (some £800 million today) 1938 Empire Exhibition, which was intended to boost the Scottish economy and to provide a window to the world not only for the Empire, but also for Scotland the brand (see plate 24). The Exhibition, held at

Bellahouston Park on the south side of Glasgow rather than the traditional west end location, drew a record 12.6 million visitors to a striking juxtaposition of technological modernity in the Tait Tower and historical iconography in the Scottish national pavilion and the ever popular *An Clachan*, with its hint of Gaelic internal exotica providing a domestic counterpart to overseas local imperial identities. Elliot's approach to supporting Scottish pride, visibility and employment in an administratively devolved context were early indicators of what by the Second World War would become an incipient 'regional' strategy, with the development of the Scottish Council on Industry and the North of Scotland Hydro Electricity Board in 1943, following on from earlier hydroelectric developments dating back to the 1920s. The emerging 'British' narrative of the Second World War was to begin to change Scotland's national status in the 1940s, when the term 'region' to describe the country first became current and when the Beveridge Report of 1942 'proposed UK-wide solutions' in a context of dwindling attention to Scotland's specific circumstances. The decades preceding the War were still rich in the national iconography of Scotland within the Union, from the first journey of *The Flying Scotsman* in 1923 through to the Empire Exhibition, the Rose and Thistle designs of the LNER Coronation Class observation cars, and the introduction of the Scottish shilling in 1937 in honour of George VI's Queen, Elizabeth.[11]

THE SECOND WORLD WAR AND ITS LEGACY

The Second World War was many things, most of them terrible. Among all these, it was also the beginning of the last chapter in the long history of the foregrounding of Scottish militarism throughout the British Army. Its position began to draw to a final close with the commencement of the disbanding of the Scottish regiments as the British Empire retired west of Suez in the 1960s. In 1940, the Highland Division was left to fight a rearguard defensive action, 'uselessly sacrificed' according to one of their officers, as British troops were evacuated from Dunkirk, and some 10,000 of them were taken prisoner. Nonetheless, despite some industrial unrest not now usually dwelt on in accounts of the conflict, Scottish support for the war was always strong. This was true even among nationalists. Notwithstanding opposition to conscription by a group on the radical wing of the SNP spearheaded by figures such as Arthur Donaldson (1901–93) and Douglas Young (1913–73), there was broad support for the war, the advent of which had postponed the 1939 Scottish Convention on a 'comprehensive programme of recon-struction' for Scotland. The Convention represented a form of political organization which was to endure rather than disappear.[12]

On 17 September 1939, up to a million Red Army soldiers entered Poland on two fronts, subsequently holding joint victory parades with Third Reich commanders. Many of the defeated Polish forces regrouped abroad. Following the arrival of almost 20,000 Polish troops at British ports in the summer of 1940, this exiled army was largely deployed in Scotland. Two Polish brigades were formed in Fife and Angus, while the 'staff college of the Polish Army in exile, an engineering school' and 'the training estab-lishment for the Independent Polish Para Brigade near Leven' were located in Scotland. The Poles initially received a warm welcome which subsequently faded under the twin pressures of British pro-Soviet propaganda and Scottish anti-Catholic sectarianism. Disgracefully, the trade unions, the Labour Party, the BBC and the *Daily Express* united with the pro-Soviet *bien pensant* Left to attack the Poles for their anti-Communism. In 1946 Protestant Action condemned the 'foreign papists', whom it was thought should go home, despite the fact that the Western Allies' settlement with Stalin had sold out the country the British Empire had allegedly gone to war to defend in September 1939 to one of the powers that had invaded it. The reward of the Poles who had risked their lives in Poland and for the British Empire and France was to be handed over to their invaders, with some of the country's territory permanently incorporated into the USSR. Despite the 1947 Resettlement Act, which gave Poles 'and their families the right to stay and settle in the UK', the 1951 census recorded just under 11,000 Polish born in Scotland, a third of the figure in the year the Act was passed; with leading trade union figures rejecting foreign labour, this was hardly surprising. Meanwhile, Polish consulates and embassies were infiltrated with Soviet agents, and in some cases directly staffed by Russians. Those Poles who remained in Scotland benefited from supportive organizations such as the Scottish–Polish Society (1941), the Polish Catholic Mission in Scotland (1948) and later the Scottish Polish Cultural Association (1970), which promoted mutual understanding as rosy delusions about the intentions of the USSR began finally to fade.[13]

Although the Clydebank Blitz of 13/14 March 1941 saw enormous damage inflicted by the 260 German bombers engaged, leaving almost the entire population of the town homeless (55,000 in Clydebank and surrounding areas altogether), Scotland in aggregate suffered less from German bombing than some English cities. It became a training and garrison country, where Polish and Free French forces were accommodated and there was a training ground for Free French commandos. In total, some 250,000 men of all national backgrounds were trained at the Commando Combined Training Centre at Inveraray (Commando basic training was in Achnacarry). Scotland also played its role in defence of Great Britain in 1940 in the person of Hugh, Lord Dowding (1882–1970), and in the development of special forces at home and abroad, with Sir Archibald David Stirling (1915–90) founding the Special Air Service (SAS) in North Africa in 1941. The Free French used the symbol of the Cross of Lorraine, possibly to evoke the memory of St Jeanne d'Arc (canonized in 1920), whose Scottish guard had been a part of the relief of Orléans hundreds of years before. Charles de Gaulle (1890–1970), the Free French leader and future president, was more than aware of the symbolism of the Auld Alliance: his uncle had been a noted pan-Celticist and de Gaulle himself refused to land in France in 1944 until a Scottish staff officer could be found to escort him. In 1942, he described Scotland as France's 'oldest alliance in the world', noting that 'There were always men of Scotland to fight side by side with the men of France'. The quotation is now on the Free French house in the Edinburgh New Town, bought by the Free French when de Gaulle visited and now the official residence of the Consul General of France.[14]

Scottish troops were engaged in Burma (including Chindit operations), Italy, North Africa, Norway, Singapore and elsewhere, with '40,000 or more Scots' engaged in the Normandy campaign in 1944. The Royal Scots even made it to Madagascar, and, in 1940, the Scots Greys 'carried out what was probably the last cavalry charge by the British Army' in Palestine. One Scottish chaplain, William McGhie (1914-58), who served in Aden, Belgium, Burma, Ceylon, France, Germany, India and the Netherlands, became a friend of Sir Alexander Bustamente (1884–1977) in Jamaica in the 1950s, and probably suggested the saltire design for the Jamaican national flag that was adopted at independence in 1962, when Bustamente became Jamaica's first Prime Minister. This was to be both the last era of the Scottish world and the first of Scotland's regionalization within the United Kingdom. Many of the earlier generations of Nationalists had themselves been global Scots who had served the British Empire and, as in earlier eras, this experience could radicalize them. One of these, Willie McRae (1923–85), who died in mysterious circumstances, competed unsuccessfully for the leadership of the SNP in 1969. The son of a Falkirk electrician, McRae had served as an officer in the Seaforth Highlanders and Lieutenant Commander in the Royal Indian Navy, becoming ADC to Lord Mountbatten, the last viceroy. McRae also supported the Indian independence movement and appears to have been a friend of Gandhi. Later an adviser on maritime law to Israel (which planted 3,000 trees in his honour) and Emeritus Professor at the University of Haifa, McRae was both a traditional global Scot and to become a new and radical critic of post-imperial Britain.[15]

During the 1939–45 conflict, Scotland was fortunate in its Secretary of State, Tom Johnston, who, despite his political differences with Churchill, was trusted by the Prime Minister to run Scotland more or less unquestioned from 1941. The Scottish Office had been definitively moved to Edinburgh, and Elliot's civil servants were busy there at St Andrew's House. Johnston was a patriot, and a supporter in some degree of home rule, and was strongly in favour of increasing administrative devolution. In 1941 he suggested that Scottish MPs should meet in Edinburgh and have access to Scottish civil servants, and that Scottish legislation, if approved by this group, should be rubber-stamped by Westminster. He also suggested a Council of State of former Scottish Secretaries. Like many ideas that in their time would have served to ease constitutional tensions, this was met with the passive-aggressive intransigence characteristic of the British Governmental approach to constitutional change (or even window-dressing), but Johnston nonetheless made a significant difference. Presenting himself 'as a defender of Scottish national interests', he secured 13.5 per cent of all war contracts for Scotland, and his legacy included the development of hydroelectric power (Johnston stepped back from politics to run the Hydro Board in 1945), the Scottish Tourist Board (STB), which he went on to chair, and the Scottish Council for Development and Industry (SCDI), both established in 1946. Johnston intended the STB 'to persuade exiled Scots to return and visit their homeland', an approach later formalized in events in the 1950s, and which had its legacy in Jack (now Lord) MacConnell's support as First Minister for the first formal Homecoming celebration of 2009. Johnston's tenure as Secretary of State could have marked the beginning of a period of transition between Scotland's role as a local British nation in the Empire and a national partner with its own distinct political arrangements in the post-imperial United Kingdom. That this was not the case owed something to the lack of a wider distribution of colleagues with Johnston's personality and vision, but more to another set of circumstances.[16]

The legacy of the Second World War came quickly to be understood and remembered as a supreme national – not imperial – effort, evident in the focus on the war in Europe rather than in East Asia or North Africa (a focus which has only increased with time), the existential mythologizing of the Battle of Britain and the Labour Party's 1945 election campaign, which was based on extending the collectivities of wartime emergency into a programme for peacetime. There was a worthy drive to ensure that all the survivors of 1945 would benefit, and that 'homes fit for heroes' would not be the empty promise it had begun to be seen as in the years after 1918: the transference of a wartime national effort to a peacetime one was key to Labour's appeal in 1945. The 1945–51 Labour Government was to be the only Labour administration which retains the relatively unalloyed affection of Labour activists, and it had many achievements to its credit, though these were secured at the cost of a centralized bureaucracy, high expenditure rather than industrial renewal and the prolongation of rationing for political reasons. The 1945–51 era also laid the basis for the development of what was to be a new British narrative, one which increasingly excluded Scotland. In the twenty-five years that followed the end of the war, the decline and end of Empire left only one coherent narrative for Britishness: the supreme resistance of 1939–45, with the gigantic contributions of the US and the USSR (and indeed the British Empire) increasingly driven to the margins. The Battle of Britain was always a better story than the fall of Singapore. The central story was one of intro-spective solidarity, 'Britain' at one and alone simultaneously, a spirit miracu-lously prolonged in the social changes of the era of Bevan and Attlee. The collocation of virtue and necessity in this national narrative of *contra mundum* sovereign solitude ('When Britain Stood Alone') resurfaced with vigour in the era of Brexit, but from the start, the closer integration of Scotland into a unitary and homogenous British narrative after the Second World War was damaging to the constitutional integrity it professed to protect, long before the European Union became an issue. Even the war-dead in 1939–45 became recorded as 'British' rather than 'British Empire'; after India insisted in 1949 that the Commonwealth should not be the 'British Commonwealth', the new nation of insular Britain could more easily rhetorically separate itself from its wider histories. The 1945 Labour manifesto used 'Britain' and 'British' twenty-six times, with no reference to the constituent nations. After 1945, nationalization and the creation of more 'British' public sector jobs in the National Health Service (although the Scottish NHS was separately established), the BBC and elsewhere, regulated centrally from London and often recruited directly to London, compounded the conditions brought about by the loss of Empire and incipient globalization through a tendency to export headquarters' functions to England and to diminish the influence of Scottish networks. As the 1950 Conservative general election manifesto put it, 'Until the Socialist Government be removed neither Scotland nor Wales will be able to strike away the fetters of centralization and be free to develop their own way of life.' Little changed when the Tories did regain power the following year.[17]

Although Empire Day and its associated jingoism was never popular in Scotland, the country's attachment to the British Empire remained strong, even if, as there had always been, there was a sense of the instrumental about it. The Empire was good for Scotland, and so Scotland supported the Empire; but there was often a sense of emotional detachment in this relationship. This can be seen not only in the very Scottish – not British – manifestations of patriotism throughout the Empire, from military units to St Andrew's Societies, but also in the sense found among some Scottish imperial servants (noted in Chapters 4 and 5) that the Empire itself was a great game. This view found its voice in this era in the greatest writer from this group, John Buchan, 1st Viscount Tweedsmuir (1875–1940). The son of a Free Kirk minister, educated at Hutcheson's Grammar School, the University of Glasgow and Brasenose College, Oxford, Buchan spent his life in the service of the British Empire, concluding his career as Governor General of Canada. Yet his fictions of an Empire under threat or in crisis told a more complex story than was evident in the novels of his English contemporaries on the same topic, such as those of Dennis Wheatley (1897–1977). *Prester John* (1910) took a negative view of the English (but not the Scots) in South Africa and evoked – while not endorsing – the struggle for black majority rights; *The Power-House* (1916) meditated on the fragility of all human civilization, while *John Macnab* (1925) conjured up an underlying passion for anti-landowner lawlessness among senior Scottish figures in the British Government. 'No Man's Land' (1899) and *Witch Wood* (1927) evoke Scottish history as repressed by sectarianism and wider British conflicts and opportunities, while *A Prince of the Captivity* (1933) is a Zionist novel which presents Scotland and Israel as parallel cases of longing and displacement. Just as the hero Adam's life is saved by his Jewish handler at the cost of his own life in the First World War, so Adam sacrifices himself to a thinly veiled Third Reich at the end of the novel. Finally, in the posthumous *Sick Heart River* (1941), Buchan's dying hero Leithen first pursues a French Canadian who has abandoned life in the United States to find himself in his homeland, then sacrifices himself for a First Nations people. Buchan evokes Scotland in displacements and struggles throughout the globe. His support for Zionism in the Commons led to his inclusion on Hitler's hit list, and it is a sign of the magnitude of the continued misunderstanding of Buchan that he is still characterized in some quarters as an anti-Semite, despite being inscribed in Israel's Golden Book for his work for the Jewish National Fund. In a speech at Shoreditch Town Hall on 9 May 1934, Buchan made his sympathies clear:

> I have been an enthusiast for the Zionist cause ever since twenty years ago when I talked it over with my old friend Lord Balfour . . . The Scottish race has many affinities with yours . . . and is very sympathetic to Jewish aspirations. The Old Testament is in our blood, as it is in yours. In one

thing we have been more fortunate than you. We have never lost our Jerusalem as the centre of our terrestrial loyalty. I rejoice to think that you are now recovering it. Zionism is a great act of justice and reparation for the centuries of cruelty and wrong. For Britain it is a solemn obligation of honour. We have pledged that no obstacle other than economic necessity shall impede the returning Jewish pilgrims. Palestine is not a museum of antiquities, but in the fullest sense a Homeland for the present inhabitants of the country and for your ancient race.

As passionate about Scotland as he was about a Jewish homeland, Buchan's global imperial Unionism was the counterpart to what he was, on occasion, not shy of describing as 'Scottish Nationalism'. It was a political position hallowed by the era of Scotland's world, and it was soon to appear very out of date.[18]

The continuing key roles that Scots played in the British Empire (in 1937, the governors of Canada, India, Australia and South Africa were all Scots, as Andrew Dewar Gibb (1888–1974), the right-wing nationalist, remarked) initially served both to marginalize and to create internal stresses for the incipient national movement. In the Second World War, the SNP emphasized the importance of self-determination for small nations, but a group on the radical wing of the party opposed conscription as it had been opposed in Ireland in 1914–18. In 1942, the party split between moderates under John MacCormick's (1904–61) Scottish Union – later Scottish Convention – movement, who were prepared at that point to accept a federal United Kingdom, and the anti-war ultras, who enjoyed more electoral support than public memory now acknowledges. In 1944, the anti-conscription candidate Douglas Young won 41 per cent of the vote in the Kirkcaldy by-election (in the First World War no anti-war candidate had registered above 22 per cent in Scotland), and some areas of Scotland had very strong acceptance rates for application for exemption from military service on the grounds of conscientious objection. Although Young and his allies lost the battle (one of the key by-election issues was the 'conscription of female labour to work in factories in the Midlands'), their stand in some sense won the war within the SNP between home rule federalists (normally the position taken by MacCormick, who 'wanted to convert the Scottish establishment' to this less threatening option) and supporters of a restored Scottish state, who were in the ascendant by the end of the war and remained so. In 1945, Dr Robert McIntyre (1913–98) briefly won Motherwell for the SNP at a by-election in the relatively advantageous circumstances of the wartime truce between the major parties.[19]

The 1945–51 Labour government published a White Paper on Scottish Affairs in 1948, which appeared to follow on from Johnston's wartime arrangements by suggesting 'a degree of administrative devolution for parliamentary business, economic affairs, the machinery of government and nationalized industries', perhaps a belated recognition that Labour's policy of public ownership had the effect of centralizing control of these industries in London, as with the nationalization of the Bank of England (1946) and the creation of a National Coal Board (1947), National Health Service (1948) and British Railways (1948). However, these very premisses indicated the central contradiction of Labour's approach, which understood Britain in terms of unity not diversity. Scotland appears to have been first formally described as a 'region' in Second World War planning documents, and the 1945–51 Labour Government gave few signs of comprehending the country as a different kind of entity from the West Midlands. Initiatives such as the Clyde Valley Plan of 1946 simply intruded English planning formats into Scotland. Robert McIntyre, now the SNP leader, attacked 'the joint concentration of economic and political power' being presided over by Labour in 1949. Many of these developments appear to have come about as much by accident as design, being a consequence of a political programme based primarily on social class, and a concept of British national solidarity founded on common interests rooted in social justice and equality of provision rather than culture or difference, which was – broadly speaking – the traditional imperial model. The moment of change for Scotland as a local nationality within empire can arguably be seen in the move from the 1938 Empire Exhibition's Scottish Pavilion to the presentation of 'The Land and the People' of Britain in the 1951 Festival of Britain, which (although Tom Johnston represented Scottish interests on the steering committee) 'sought to portray Britain as a cohesive singular nation, with diverse cultures, but existing as a seamless whole, one of whose symbols was a common language'.[20] In other words, Britain and Britishness were to be presented not as a globally hybrid identity, but as a Romantic national culture realized within its borders by a commonality it had never possessed. *An Clachan*, 'the village', so popular in 1911 and 1938, seems to have disappeared; there was no Gaelic and no subtitling for the Welsh Folk Museum event either in the Festival in the summer of 1951. Instead of the United Kingdom's multiple nationalities acting as an exemplar for the diversity of overseas Britishness, the Festival began a narrative where everything came home. Compared to the Empire Exhibitions, it was very introspective and, following the arrival in June 1948 of HMS *Empire Windrush* from Jamaica with 492 West Indian passengers, it initiated a vision of British internal diversity based round immigration into Britain, not nationalities within Britain. Multiculturalism began to be about the Empire coming home, not reflecting home in the Empire. The red, white and blue star of the Festival replaced the

26. Festival of Britain poster, 1951: the elision of local nationalities compared to the 1938 Empire Exhibition is striking.

346

multiple flags of Empire, and the traditional historical pageantry of the old Empire Exhibitions – the saltire had been visible at the centre of one of the 1924 posters for the Wembley exhibition – was marginalized. Devolution was limited to two travelling exhibitions and the Festival closed with the singing of 'Jerusalem', with its definitive reference to England. Modern Britishness was under construction; 8.5 million people visited the Festival in its various incarnations, only some 67 per cent of the visitor numbers in Glasgow (not London) in 1938, and less than a third of the numbers at Wembley in 1924–25. Like the previous London exhibition, the Festival was commemorated by its own stamps – unlike the Glasgow event.[21]

NEW BRITAIN AND OLD SCOTLAND

These developments were recognized at the time, even if they were not widely understood. John MacCormick played a significant role in identifying and resisting these changes, notably through the 1949–52 Covenant movement when, following the establishment of a 600-strong Scottish Convention in 1947–48, MacCormick and his allies secured 1.7 million signatures in support of Scottish Home Rule. Although ignored by Westminster, the Covenant was supported by a series of plebiscites in Scotland extending over more than a decade, beginning in Glasgow in 1950. The postwar period was barren ground for the SNP electorally, but MacCormick's moderate initiatives reached a substantial constituency who were clearly dissatisfied with the current political settlement in Scotland. MacCormick tried to build a coalition which went beyond the SNP, and, although ultimately he was unsuccessful, he contributed to the beginnings of change in the political climate. In 1950, the removal of the Stone of Destiny from Westminster to Scotland by a group led by Ian Hamilton QC (b.1925) was only the most prominent and well-publicized of a series of tokenistic activist gestures of resistance, which included assaults on a postbox bearing the legend 'E II R' in Edinburgh (as Elizabeth was only the first Queen of that name in Scotland) a couple of years later. Initially defaced, the postbox 'on the junction of Gilmerton Road and Walter Scott Avenue', was attacked with a sledgehammer then blown apart; on 13 February 1953, a Lion Rampant was 'laid on its remains'. New postboxes in Scotland henceforth bore the simple legend 'E R'. It was on a similar, apparently token, question of the regal title that MacCormick went to court in 1953, which on appeal before the Lord President, Thomas, Lord Cooper (1892–1956) was partially upheld, gaining a recognition of the principle of Scottish popular sovereignty as set against the claimed unlimited sovereignty of English parliamentary doctrine. Cooper's judgment remains instructive and, when it was given, ushered in a new interest in the Union as a legal document in academic circles and a more widespread belief in a Scottish tradition of popular sovereignty:

> The principle of the unlimited Sovereignty of Parliament is a distinctly English principle which has no counterpart in Scottish Constitutional law . . . I have difficulty in seeing why it should have been supposed that the Parliament of Great Britain must inherit all the peculiar characteristics of the English Parliament but none of the Scottish Parliament, as if all that happened in 1707 was that Scottish representatives were admitted to the Parliament of England. That was not what was done.

Cooper, 1st baron Culross, was himself a scholar of the Declaration of Arbroath and may indeed have been influenced by the historian Agnes Mure Mackenzie's (1891–1955) contrast between the concentrated and 'unrestrained' sovereignty of Westminster and the more communal and co-operative Scottish tradition which she had identified. But he was no Scottish nationalist. Cooper had been a Unionist MP from 1935–41, though he belonged to the strongly patriot tradition which helped to make Scottish Unionism so appealing to a broad swathe of the Scottish electorate. Thus, ironically, it was a former Unionist MP who was responsible for the judgment which has influenced the constitutional thinking of the SNP and other advocates of Scottish popular sovereignty ever since.[22]

After their return to power in October 1951, the Tories and their Scottish Unionist allies (the Conservative Party did not at this time stand in Scotland) planning authority on roads and bridges devolved to the Scottish Office, and a number of new national organizations and institutions such as Scottish Television (STV, 1955) and Scottish Opera (1962) were founded:

however, the overall current of centralization continued to flow strongly. Scottish culture – long a Unionist strongpoint – was in fact to be better funded under the 1964–70 Labour Government, with the country's share of the Arts Council budget rising from 6 per cent in 1963 to almost 11.5 per cent by 1970.[23] There were nonetheless many continuing issues in the governmental conception of Scottish policy which seem to have had their roots in the postwar reframing of Great Britain and British identity addressed above. One of the key problems with the regionalizing of Scotland in policy terms was that the country had its own regions and that there was significant disparity between them, but this was only haltingly recognized. Whereas the Toothill Report of 1961 was alert to the need to 'fine-tune' regional distinctions within Scotland, the 1964 Scottish Development Area introduced by the incoming Labour government (following the promises of *Signposts for Scotland* (1962)) appeared to restore centralist and homogenizing policies, relieved only by the creation of the Highlands and Islands Development Board (HIDB) in the following year. However, earlier initiatives commenced under Macmillan's administration to support the flagging Scottish economy, such as the car plant at Linwood (1963), the Fort William pulp and paper mill (1964), and later the Invergordon aluminium smelter (1968) all ultimately foundered on the British branch economy model inherent in centralist planning assumptions. Senior management, research and development and marketing among other central functions remained remote and undevolved, while supply chains could also be partial and inadequate. Without a stake in leadership and innovation, the long-term fate of branch developments was always likely to be closure. From a dynamic entrepreneurial powerhouse in 1900, Scotland was becoming a comparatively impoverished branch line of the British economy, a marginality aptly symbolized by the Beeching railway cuts of 1963–65, though these at least were ameliorated by increased real spending on road infrastructure, with the Forth Road Bridge opening in 1964 and the Tay Bridge two years later. Urban planning did not go so well: Glasgow's population dropped 25 per cent in the thirty years after 1950 and none of the New Towns developed in the era to accommodate its 'overspill' met their population targets. By 1961, Scotland's GDP per capita had sunk to only 86 per cent of the UK average.[24]

Scottish emigration overseas increased markedly in the final ages of empire, and in proportional terms accelerated, as Scotland's natural increase in population was declining: between 1861 and 1931, 'Net migration was 43 per cent of the natural increase in population; from 1951 to 1981, it was 102 per cent.' Of the 608,000 who left Scotland between 1951 and 1971, 299,000 – almost half, went to overseas destinations. Many were supported by the 1922 Empire Settlement Act (1922), which supported over 400,000 assisted passages by 1936. Australia, Canada and New Zealand were dominant, especially in the aftermath of the 1952 McCarran–Walter Act in the United States, which severely limited immigration among those whose skills were not in demand. Canada's introduction of a 'points-based immigration system in 1967' was to have an effect later in this period, and from the early 1970s emigration to Commonwealth countries in general became more difficult. By this time, it was clear that rising immigration into the UK was not proportionately matched by levels of immigration into Scotland, and this contributed – given continuing substantial emigration, still over 100,000 in the 1980s – to population stagnation and the absence of dynamism from some parts of the economy.[25]

The representation of Scotland to itself was also becoming an increasing issue. While Scottish newspapers, which had played a significant part in protecting and promoting regional, national and even linguistic identity since the Victorian period, as William Donaldson demonstrated in the 1980s, continued to dominate the Scottish market, the situation was otherwise with the electronic media. The British Broadcasting Corporation (BBC) had become one of the incipient organizations of a new British centralism in the 1920s and 1930s and even in these early days the National Party of Scotland had pressured them to put on more Scottish programmes. This position had become entrenched during the Second World War, by which time, in the historian Christopher Harvie's view, the 'puritanical parochialism' of its public sector broadcasting had become a byword. The BBC typically spent far less than its licence fee revenue from the nations and regions outside London, and Scotland was no exception to this. Moreover, BBC representation of Scotland to itself dwelt on the couthy and stereotypical, while the structure of news and current affairs was very much based round national (London) and regional (lesser, subordinate and local, 'where you are') news: there was no place for a 'four nations' agenda, and to a significant extent this structure endures. This was especially true in Northern Ireland, where poor understanding of the province was – and is – intensified rather than dissipated by the mass media. Radio Scotland was not founded until 1978, and as a consequence it was left to the independent companies, STV and Grampian (Border oddly straddled both Scotland and England, and even more oddly still does in the devolutionary era) to articulate a sense of Scottishness, though STV was always hampered in comparison to Granada or Thames by more limited advertising revenue. It was not only Scotland that suffered: programming about European or developing countries was also marginal as UK public broadcasting fostered an introspective sense of self-celebration in compensation for a fading empire.[26]

The final decline of the Empire, resisted by many during the 1950s, was inescapable by the 1959–63 Macmillan government. The 1959 Conservative manifesto called for a 'free market' in Western Europe, and Macmillan's administration made the first British application to join the European Economic Community. It was vetoed by a sceptical de Gaulle, a disappointment inadequately compensated for by Great Britain clinging 'desperately to the United States' as 'the sustainer of Britain as a nuclear weapons power', while altogether failing to accept the compromised autonomy of Britain's nuclear deterrent by comparison with France's *Force de frappe/Force de dissuasion*. The dissolution of the British Empire had a profound effect, for it had long provided – as we have seen – disproportionate opportunities for Scots abroad, and was strongly engaged with at home; almost three in five Scottish school history textbooks discussed the Empire, and almost a quarter of Scottish Leaving Certificate history questions addressed it in one way or another. It is not always now well understood that the independence of India was not the end of Empire, and it was not even seen by many contemporaries in the major political parties as the beginning of the end. That was one reason why the 1956 debacle at Suez was politically possible: the extent of diminishing British power was not realized. Harold Macmillan's (1894–1986) Winds of Change speech to the South African parliament on 3 February 1960 is a convenient marker for the beginning of a widespread political understanding that the beginning of the end had come, just as the end of the Mediterranean fleet, the withdrawal west of Suez and the monetary devaluation of 1967 could be seen as marking a symbolic end. Almost twenty-five colonies became independent in this period, with eighteen achieving this outcome between the beginning of 1960 and the end of 1964. South Africa left the Commonwealth (1961) and Rhodesia unilaterally declared independence (1965). The global projection, power and significance of Great Britain was drawing to an end, and with it the opportunities Scots had won by the Union of 1707. There was a widespread view – strong in Scotland – that the decolonization had been too rapid. Scots tended to dislike the jingoism of Empire, and the 'snobbish, aloof, and pretentious' English administrators in the colonies, but this did not mean they were anti-imperial. Rather, as the historian Bryan Glass points out, Scottish administrators in the last days of Empire such as Jock Donaldson in Tanganyika/Tanzania thought that the English had done a great deal to inflame the colonies against Great Britain, and that those sent out 'were the worst of the empire'. This may have been to an extent a delusive attitude, but there was frustration that ameliorative and developmental change such as was promoted by the Scottish Council for African Questions (1952) had deteriorated into a Gadarene rush for the exit: ironically perhaps it was a Colonial Secretary of Scottish descent, Iain Macleod (1913–70), who accelerated the pace of withdrawal in the face of opposition from organizations such as the League of Empire Loyalists (1954–67). The opposition to the Central African Federation (CAF) by Edinburgh alumni Julius Nyerere (later President of Tanzania) and Hastings Banda (later President of Malawi), who spoke out against the CAF in Edinburgh, likewise evidenced frustration at the tendency of British bureaucrats to draw 'lines in the sand' irrespective of local views.[27]

In the aftermath of the major rush to decolonization that precipitated the foreign policy retreat 'west of Suez', being Scottish and British suddenly became an exceptional claim for status, not a general recognition of it; being 'Australian and British' or 'Canadian and British' were becoming anachronistic or at best nostalgic terms, and 'Scottish and British' thus seemed increasingly exceptionalist. Meanwhile, a post-imperial and artificially unified 'Britain' was constructed in the narratives of its public memory as a new version of the state, now presented not as a global entity but an island standing alone, forged in the common sacrifices of the Second World War. This imaginary took many years to come to fruition, but it involved a major cultural shift away from recognizing the once centrally cherished myth of Scotland's national martial contribution to the British Empire, all the more bitterly made manifest in the slow erosion of the Scottish regiments from the late 1960s. After the Second World War, the emphasis on Scottish militarism often came chiefly from dubious sources, such as the use of South African Scottish units as a core icon of the 'white military tradition' by the apartheid regime. But it was not only the Scots who suffered. British military memory became 'disparaging . . . to the many Canadians, Indians, East, West and South Africans, Australians, New Zealanders, Americans, Poles, Czechs, Fijians, West Indians, Nepalese, Malaysians and others' who had fought for it and its Empire. Typically, British public memory and representation of the World Wars moved gradually from the 1960s onwards to occlude Imperial and Commonwealth forces (the Canadian film industry responded rather irritably to this with *Passchendaele* (2006)) and Scottish troops – still very visible in major films such as *The Charge of the Light Brigade* (1969) and *Waterloo* (1970) – began to fade from view in all historic representations of Britain at war. Such representations, no longer focused on the Empire or its contribution, laid more and more stress on British conflict with European powers, a conflict in which the British Army was often represented as both English and without imperial or external European allies: the Polish pilots of *The Battle of Britain* (1970) have long disappeared from representations of that struggle. In representing the World Wars, Britain no more stands shoulder to shoulder with France (there were 1 million Free French forces in the European theatre alone in 1944–45) than it does with India. Bernard, 1st Viscount Montgomery of Alamein (1887–1976), the General Officer Commanding the British Eighth Army at El Alamein, did not forget to cite the French contribution to victory, but memory of it has now largely disappeared, as has the consciousness that the Eighth Army in North Africa included two Indian and two Anzac divisions. The proposed 'Franco-British Union' of 1940 – proposed by Churchill and talked down by the architects

of Vichy – is a long way from the use of the Second World War in Brexit rhetoric. German diplomats have complained in recent years about the now unceasing educational and media focus on the Nazis as the defining representation of German culture and society in the UK. It is a strange week on the television schedules in Britain when there are not ten or twenty programmes on the Nazis or set in the Second World War, and the litany of cultural memorialization in schools again frames Germany in this way. In 2021, the Commonwealth War Graves Commission Report on Historical Inequalities in Commemoration noted the lack of recognition given to imperial forces.[28]

The continuing decline in Scotland's protected domestic sphere was thus combined with this loss of imperial opportunity and recognition. The creation of a unified British social and economic policy on an unprecedented scale after 1945, combined with the slow emergence of globalization and the opportunities for domination it offered to US business and brands, started to undermine Scotland's social and cultural autonomy within, as much as the loss of empire curtailed its opportunities without. The slow decline of the influence of the Kirk on domestic social mores reinforced this process, and ongoing secularization involved significant changes in Scottish society. Christmas only became a public holiday in Scotland in 1958, and it was still a normal working day in parts of the country into the following decade, while as late as the 1970s head teachers were removing Christmas trees as pagan symbols. In 1960, almost 70 per cent of Scots over fourteen were claimed as Kirk members, three times the proportion that the Church of England enjoyed south of the Border; by 2001, while 42 per cent still regarded themselves as members of the Kirk, the reality was that only 16 per cent were so in any meaningful sense, and this number has halved again. Not all of the changes resulting from this were secular ones, for Catholicism – despite its own problems – became proportionately stronger in Scotland in the later twentieth century.[29]

Piecemeal administrative devolution could not address the core issue revealed in both UK national policy and the external context of imperial decline: that the Union bargain which exchanged limited sovereignty as an international political actor for the global projection of soft power and the autonomy of critical native institutions was no longer holding. The Tories and Unionists recognized the need to respond to the concept of 'more control of Scottish affairs by Scots', but, while the 1954 Royal Commission on Scottish Affairs might seek to prioritise 'Scottish needs and the Scottish point of view', Scots could see the institutions which had supported these collapsing round them. By the 1960s, almost all of the 200 Scottish trade unions in existence in 1900 had disappeared, and the country's stock exchanges were following them out of existence: Scottish stock exchanges were amalgamated into a national Scottish Stock Exchange in 1964, but this too had disappeared by 1973. In 1962, the appearance in schools of the 'O' grade, a transparently tartanized O-level in partial replacement for the old Leaving Certificate, began an Anglicization process in Scottish school education which was only halted – though not reversed – by strong professional resistance in the 1960s and 1970s. In 1962 likewise, the University of Edinburgh became the first university in Scotland to join a UK-wide central clearing system, a process which by 1985 included all of Scotland's universities. Calling centralized planning 'Scottish' rather than 'British' helped neither its efficacy nor its authenticity, and, although such window-dressing sufficed for a time, that time was borrowed.[30]

A brief window of success for Scotland's heavy industries had followed the Second World War, as most of Europe and East Asia were rebuilding their damaged and disrupted economies. In 1950, this Indian summer saw the Clyde launch a third of global ship tonnage; by 1960, 'the year of the celebratory but also elegiac film *Seawards the Great Ships*', it was 5 per cent, and by the end of that decade had halved again. Nationalized industries were subsidized and began to perform a social rather than an economic mission: in the period from 1955 to 1965, the Scottish deficit within the National Coal Board was £136 million, some £3.5 billion at 2022 prices. At the same time, the loss of Scottish control of private industry was also accelerating. Between 1937 and 1950, some 235 firms from the rest of the UK were established in Scotland, thus diluting the politics of local control which were so central to Scottish Unionism. Building societies, hitherto very marginal in Scotland, began to push banks out of the deposit market, while Scotland's historic strengths in life and general assurance began their slow decline which led to the disappearance of all Scottish control by the 1990s. The social problems associated with the relentless decline of labour intensive heavy industry were exacerbated by the concentration of population in west central Scotland which had resulted from the development of that very industry. Policy initiatives tended to try to address the issue by offering piecemeal reinforcement to local strengths, such as the motor plants at Linwood and Bathgate and the steel strip mill at Ravenscraig near Motherwell. These created an artificial planned market structure – which never worked as intended – where Scotland had once demonstrated economic dynamism driven by individual enterprise. Nationalization and the globalization of capital were drawing power to the centre, and when regional policy used taxpayers' money to reverse the consequences of this agglomeration of power, it repatriated largely manufacturing and assembly jobs, for they were cheaper than senior management, headquarters and research and development jobs, presenting better headlines for their political initiators in terms of the number of jobs created. By the 1990s, Scotland had less than half of the UK private sector's research and development spend, measured on a per capita basis.[31]

The 1945–67 period also marked the last phase of Scottish Unionism proper as the country's leading electoral force. At the 1955 general election, the Unionists and their allies (including Liberal and other Unionists) won thirty-six of Scotland's seventy-one seats, and, although they were not quite so successful in 1959 in terms of seats, they again returned some half of the popular vote. In 1965, the Unionists merged with the Conservative Party of England and Wales to form the Conservative and Unionist party, an organization which from the 1966 election onwards (when it won twenty seats) was never as successful as its predecessor, a distinctly Scottish party which included centre as well as right-wing views in its support for Scotland within the Union. Much misunderstanding continues to surround this: while some Scottish Tories such as Murdo Fraser (Member of the Scottish Parliament, 2001–, deputy leader, 2005–11) seem to understand the bifurcated tradition they inherit, the *canard* that in 1955 the Conservatives had a majority in Scotland is frequently repeated to this day.[32]

On the nationalist side, John MacCormick's approach had always included reaching out to Home Rule activists in other parties, not least the

Liberals, given their longstanding interest in federalism, but attempts to form electoral pacts between the Liberals and the SNP in the 1960s did not meet with success. MacCormick early diagnosed that one of the key issues facing modern Britain would be its narrow and centralist definition in what, in 1955, he called 'the new and spurious and artificial nationalism of Greater London'. MacCormick was prescient, but, even at the end of his life in 1961, the signs of the centralization of the concept of Britishness in the face of the decline of Empire were visible. As the Empire declined and international Britishness with it, the demand that Britishness in Great Britain should be a unitary entity rose, reinforced by the increase in central planning and the decline in Scottish industries and institutions. The centrality of Unionism in general and the Unionist party in particular to the patriotic defence of Scotland's history, culture and institutions was weakened: if the Unionists were failing to defend Scotland's national distinctiveness in the Empire – and they were not even a Scottish party after their 1965 amalgamation with the Conservatives – then there was political room for a party which defended the old Unionist ground in a new era. Intermittently downgraded from a nation to the new term 'region', no longer an imperial partner or dominant force in the administrative, industrial and financial sinews of a disappearing Empire, provincialized by centralist planning, in industrial decline and losing ground in emerging global markets, its institutions diluted by change, Scotland's status was in decline on every front. The SNP gave Scots an opportunity to demonstrate dissatisfaction and difference. On 2 November 1967, Glasgow solicitor Winnie Ewing won the Hamilton by-election from Labour with a colossal swing of 38 per cent, the fourth largest UK swing of all time, with the Conservative Party losing more than half their votes at a time when they were in opposition in Westminster. Winnie Ewing always demonstrated a talent for the arresting phrase, and she campaigned to 'Put Scotland Back on the Map', while her acceptance speech included the sentence (later the title of her autobiography) 'Stop the world, Scotland wants to get on'. The message could not have been clearer. Sixty years since, the world was full of Scotland and its significance; in the late 1960s nearly all that had gone. Scotland had aligned with Britishness at home (while preserving its domestic industries and institutions), while often presenting itself as distinct abroad.

27. Winnie Ewing election poster 1967: reintegrating Scotland into the global community.

Now both its domestic autonomy and its international visibility were under threat. Although Winnie Ewing lost Hamilton in 1970, the SNP won their first seat at a general election, outpolled the Liberals and have subsequently never ceased to be a major force in Scottish politics, as well as steadily redefining Scotland's politics as primarily constitutional. The SNP's supporters in Scotland have in general never been as passionate for the establishment of a separate Scottish state as the political party they support has, though in recent years there have been signs that this is changing, in part as a consequence of the lack of understanding among Unionists of the elements driving that support and of the need to assert Scottish distinctiveness. The constitutional instability of Scotland as it has gradually developed over the last fifty years is in many ways a product of the postwar reconceptualization of Great Britain as an entity which has no other constituent nations than itself and the loss of the instrumental benefits which Scotland gained from the centuries of compromise which preceded the end of empire in 1967–68.[33]

7

WEST OF SUEZ TO OUT OF EUROPE, 1967–

END OF EMPIRE

In June 1967, Great Britain disbanded its Mediterranean fleet, which had been in existence since its English predecessor was established in 1654. On 2 November 1967, Winnie Ewing won Hamilton for the SNP with a pledge to put Scotland back on the global map. Two weeks later, the Chancellor of the Exchequer – following the 1966 sterling crisis – signalled a new phase in the UK's economic and political weakness by recommending a 14 per cent devaluation of the pound against the US dollar to the Cabinet. This was implemented on 18 November and led to James Callaghan's resignation as Chancellor. The ensuing exchange rate (US$2.40 to the pound) almost halved again in the next half century. On 27 November 1967 Charles de Gaulle vetoed United Kingdom membership of the EEC for the second time. He continued to hold his 1963 view that 'transformations' were needed in the 'Atlanticist impulses' of the UK towards 'the growth of a more European frame of mind', also noting the 'extraordinary insistence and haste' of the UK negotiations, which he attributed to 'the great economic, financial, monetary and social difficulties with which Britain is at grips'. Prime Minister Harold Wilson (1916–95) may have claimed stability for 'the pound in your pocket', but not for the first or last time, others could see things more clearly.[1]

On 30 November 1967, Great Britain withdrew from Aden, following four years of Arab nationalist unrest, which had seen some of the last Scottish military action framed in terms of the martial myth of national valour, when Lieutenant Colonel Colin Campbell Mitchell's ('Mad Mitch', 1925–96) 1st Argyll and Sutherland Highlanders (the 91st and 93rd) retook the Crater district of Aden in Operation Stirling Castle in January that year with a theatrical display of pipes and drums playing 'Monymusk', and no casualties. In January 1968, Harold Wilson and his Secretary of State for Defence, Denis Healey (1917–2015), announced the withdrawal of British troops from bases in the Persian Gulf, Indian Ocean and East Asia east of Aden, popularly 'east of Suez'. Despite the retention of small units in Singapore (until 1971), Hong Kong (1997) and elsewhere, or more recent shows of force such as HMS *Queen Elizabeth*'s appearance in the South China sea under the 'Global Britain' brand, this was a watershed moment. These months marked the beginning of the final end of Empire: the United States took over some of British bases in the Atlantic, the Gulf, the Indian Ocean and East Asia. In August 1969, the Unionist government of Northern Ireland requested the deployment of British troops under Operation Banner to reinforce the Royal Ulster Constabulary and to assert the authority of the British Government in Northern Ireland in the face of extensive civil rights protest and rioting, including the declaration of Free Derry in the 'Battle of the Bogside', which began on 12 August. Two days later, the British Army was in the city, although they did not enter the Free Derry zone. The first conflict of the Empire (a claim to empire was first made by Henry VIII on the creation of the Kingdom of Ireland in 1541) was also to be one of the last. In the 1970s as in the 1650s, the plantation of Ulster had to be defended by troops from the neighbouring island, with over 20,000 deployed at the peak of the Troubles.[2]

There were many more peaceful signs of the transition from Empire in these years which were also in their own way evidence of weakness. On 14 February 1966, Australia abandoned the pound for its own dollar, followed by New Zealand the next year. South Africa had already introduced the rand in 1961 and Fiji abandoned the pound in 1969: the 'Commonwealth sterling area' was in serious decline, accentuated by the 1967 devaluation, which led to an acceleration in an already established diversification in locally held assets away from sterling. The United Kingdom itself announced the decimalization of the pound in 1966, and by 1968 this process had become irreversible. In that same year, the SNP secured over 100 seats in the Scottish council elections and the British Government began to take the prospective electoral threat from Scotland seriously, although at this stage it was seen more in terms of discontent with the balance of power between central and local government, a misunderstanding on the Labour Party's behalf which was to dog its decision-making all the way to the implementation of devolution in 1999 and beyond.[3]

DEVOLUTION NOT REVOLUTION

The discovery of oil off the Scottish coast at the end of the 1960s was not a political gamechanger (despite the campaign which dominated SNP electoral politics over the next decade), but it was an economic one for the UK, which benefited from around £170 billion in inflow from oil revenues by 2006. Substantial as these were over time, they made a particular political impact in the 1980s when they reached (at 2022 prices) around £27.5 billion in 1982–83, rising to some £77 billion in 1984–86. These peak income points made a significant difference to Mrs Thatcher's Conservative Government, giving it far more room for fiscal manoeuvre than it would otherwise have had, and helping to ensure its return to office with substantial majorities in 1983 and 1987. The omission of the effects of oil revenues from many accounts of the Thatcher years is a classic example of metropolitan mindset history, where nothing that does not happen in south-east England or abroad can have any material impact on the fortunes of a government. Apart, briefly, from the Liberal Party in the 1970s, no UK political party suggested that Scotland should directly benefit from the oil in its waters, although such arrangements (for example in Alabama, Alberta, North Dakota and Texas) are evident at levels subsidiary to national government elsewhere. Nor was there a UK sovereign wealth fund, such as underpins Norway's social ambitions and support for pensions. The money was simply spent, with the sole exception of Shetland Council, whose access tax on oil companies was used to support public services via the Shetland Islands Council Charitable Trust (now the Shetland Islands Trust), whose reserves have reached well over £300 million. Thus a tiny local administration planned more securely than the British Government.[4]

Although the performance of the SNP in the 1970 general election (where it polled 11 per cent) had fallen short of the political threat the party had seemed to carry after Hamilton, the British Government continued to work via a Royal Commission on the Constitution, headed first by Lord Crowther (1907–72) then by James Shaw, Lord Kilbrandon (1906–89), to address the issue of Scottish governance. A specific Conservative Party report also appeared in 1970, which recommended some tinkering with the review of the committee and report stages of Scottish bills. The Kilbrandon Commission took a long time to report, and in 1972 the veteran nationalist Wendy Wood (1892–1981) declared that she would fast to the death to pressurise the Prime Minister, Edward Heath (1916–2005), to act on the support for 'legislative devolution' he had given at the 'Declaration of Perth' at the Scottish Conservative and Unionist conference in 1968. Wood was appeased by the promise of a Green Paper after the Royal Commission had reported: the very definition of long grass, even down to its colour. The Kilbrandon Commission eventually concluded its work in late 1973, recommending a Scottish Assembly with unspecified powers, the nature of which were a source of disagreement among the Commission's members. By now an additional complicating factor was the European Economic Community (EEC, now the EU), which the United Kingdom had joined on 1 January 1973, its membership endorsed in a 1975 referendum. The Scottish nationalists were in general opposed to the EEC at this time (although there was a long tradition of pro-European thought in the party, dating back to Marian McNeill (1885–1973) and William Power (1873–1951)), seeing it as heralding a process where powers migrated yet further from Scotland, and Lord Crowther-Hunt and Professor Alan Peacock on the Kilbrandon Commission indeed took the view that 'it did not make sense' for powers which would migrate to Brussels to be devolved.[5]

The SNP, under the leadership of Billy Wolfe (1924–2010), who did much to change it into a social democratic party from the uneven collection of eccentrics, leftists and romantics leavened by a few forward thinkers that it had once tended towards, launched their *It's Scotland's Oil* campaign in 1973. Although it is one of the best-known political campaigns of the twentieth century in the British Isles, there is very little evidence, despite the strong polling for the SNP in the 1974 general elections which followed, with 22 per cent of the vote and seven seats in February and 30 per cent and eleven in October, that it had very much direct effect on the party's electoral support. However, the victory of Margo MacDonald in the Govan by-election in November 1973, eight days after Kilbrandon had reported, lent a sense of electoral urgency to the Scottish constitutional question which was only deepened by the 1974 results. These – combined with a weak Labour government – led first to the Scotland and Wales Bill, which proposed a Scottish Assembly with no tax powers whose legislation could be vetoed by the Secretary of State for Scotland, and then to a Scotland Bill in 1977. This continued to grant 'quasi-Viceregal powers' to the Secretary of State, and was inconsistent in terms of what powers were devolved. A referendum was first conceded to endorse the Bill, followed on amendment by a clause that 40 per cent of the electoral roll should vote in favour with an opt out for Orkney and Shetland if they voted against. This legislative mess was the basis of the referendum held on 1 March 1979. The result saw victory for the 'Yes' side by a majority of 52 to 48, but the 40 per cent hurdle was not reached given that turnout was under 65 per cent. The immediate outcome was an increase in the rate of decline in support for the SNP, whose membership dropped from 28,000 in 1979 to less than half that by the mid 1980s, giving it little more than £100,000 in annual income. Yet, despite this appearance of fresh acquiescence in British politics, in the longer term Scotland became increasingly detached. Support for outright independence, as low as 14 per cent in 1979, more than doubled in the ensuing decade and subsequently increased further. Although the Conservative governments of 1979–97 watered down their policies in Scotland (with the signal exception of the Poll Tax or Community Charge, which they introduced a year earlier in Scotland, granting the SNP an opportunity they duly took advantage of), they were still widely resented as illegitimate. Mrs Thatcher's deindustrialization policies led to real hatred for her government in west central Scotland in particular, and there was evidence of the adoption of radical politics elsewhere as a form of protest at home – not least in the strength of the anti-apartheid movement in Glasgow and the renaming of St George's Place as Nelson Mandela Place in 1986, five years after the imprisoned ANC leader had been granted the freedom of the city by the Labour administration. In the view of many, Mrs Thatcher 'instinctively rejected, or could not comprehend, that a distinct political system existed in Scotland', and 'Her government . . . had no sense of the historical partnership terms of the Union.' She had always been less popular north of the Border, and in 1990 even '56% of Conservative supporters thought the party was mainly an English party with little relevance to Scotland'. In 1979, there had been a small swing to Labour in Scotland in stark contrast to the rest of Great Britain, and Scotland's electoral behaviour was increasingly diverging from England's, as the political scientist William Miller percipiently argued in *The End of British Politics?* (1981). The initial beneficiaries were the Labour Party, who swept aside ill-advised attempts to outflank it from the left by the Nationalists, but in the end, as independence began to replace devolution as a priority, the electorate turned to the SNP.[6]

Socially, Scotland had significant differences from England. The development of the New Towns such as Cumbernauld and East Kilbride had a disproportionate impact on population movement compared to their English peers, and the aspirational but grounded lower-middle-class experience of such towns and their hesitant modernity is brilliantly captured in the 1981 film *Gregory's Girl*, which portrays a new generation of Scots moving into the strange worlds of secularism and gender equality. The SNP had strong traction from this group in the 1970s, but largely lost them to Labour in the following decade. In England, this social group often turned towards the Tories, but there were factors in Scotland – partly a matter of cultural heritage, partly environmental – which reinforced a tendency to social solidarity, even among the 'urban overspill' from Glasgow into the New Towns. One of these was home ownership: in 1981, on the threshold of the enabling of council house sales by the Conservative Government, 55 per cent of Scots lived in public housing compared to only 32 per cent elsewhere in the UK, and some 75 per cent of Scottish houses built from 1950 to 1980 (even higher than the proportion in the interwar era) were public housing. Scottish egalitarianism, again most marked in west central Scotland, can be exaggerated, but it was nonetheless a factor. Although working-class social groups were of similar sizes in Scotland and England, middle-class identity was 'unpopular' in Scotland, particularly in the west. It was seen as pretentious and even non-national. Social equality is a key – perhaps the key – area where Scottish social attitudes diverge strongly from those elsewhere in the UK. Despite the rise in prosperity between 1980 and 2000 (central heating up from 53 to 93 per cent of homes, freezers from 41 to 96 per cent, higher education participation from 18 to over 40 per cent, the highest in the UK), Scotland did not swing noticeably to the right, whereas in England the same developments made life much more difficult for Labour, except in its Blairite incarnation.[7]

In the 1980s, with the Labour Party enjoying an Indian summer of anti-Thatcherite social solidarity in Scotland, there was nonetheless a discernible move towards stronger expressions of cultural nationalism. From the 1930s onwards, Scottish writing had shown signs of becoming increasingly introspective. The panoramas of John Buchan (1875–1940), Arthur Conan Doyle (1859–1930), R.L. Stevenson (1850–94) or even James Barrie (1860–1937) were often – not always, Naomi Mitchison (1897–1999) being an exception – replaced by fictions that tried to make sense of the flagging national trajectory in the wake of the First World War. These included books such as Lewis Grassic Gibbon's *Scots Quair* (1932), Nan Shepherd's *The Weatherhouse* (1930), Neil Gunn's *Highland River* (1937) and *The Serpent* (1943), Fionn MacColla's *The Albannach* (1932) and Willa Muir's *Imagined Corners* (1930). In poetry, Christopher Grieve's (Hugh MacDiarmid) (1892–1978) use of Scots – for example in *A Drunk Man Looks at the Thistle* (1926) – pointed in similar directions, albeit in a more internationalist context. Other globally minded poets such as Edwin Muir (1887–1959) felt uncomfortable with the increasingly limited focus of the pre-war 'Scots Renaissance': he and his wife Willa promoted Scotland and Scottish interests internationally through the national writers' group Scottish PEN, which MacDiarmid and Neil Gunn had played a leading role in founding in 1927. In the post-1945 era, novels such as Muriel Spark's (1918–2006) *The Prime of Miss Jean Brodie* (1961) and Robin Jenkins' (1912–2005) *The Cone Gatherers* (1955) in their differing ways continued to reflect a simultaneous sense of narrowness, corruption and decay in the national life and its cultures. In the Thatcherite era and its immediate aftermath, Irvine Welsh's (b.1958) *Trainspotting* (1993), James Kelman's (b.1946) *The Busconductor Hines* (1984), Iain Banks' (1954–2013) *The Wasp Factory* (1984) and Alasdair Gray's (1934–2019) *Lanark* (1981) were among the prominent novels which intensified this sense of bleak hopelessness. Gray's Glasgow/Unthank is a surrealist version of Joyce's Dublin in *Dubliners* and *Portrait of the Artist*: a place with its own culture and identity, yet one rendered unreal by the framing and social construction of British society, which demands that real things always happen somewhere else. Despite their often gruesome pessimism, by the end of the 1980s it was becoming clear that a 'Matter of Scotland' was emerging, a national story focused on legacies, problems and the present, largely urban by contrast with its 1930s predecessors, and far from the histories of Scott's Sixty Years Since or even deeper ventures in time. There still existed within this new framework writing which ran the worlds of history and contemporaneity together: John McGrath's (1935–2002) *The Cheviot, The Stag, and the Black, Black Oil* (1973) and Liz Lochhead's (b.1947) *Mary Queen of Scots Got Her Head Chopped Off* (1987) being outstanding examples. But there was an increasing desire to see Scottish life in a contemporary national frame, even if that framing was partial and incomplete. This incompleteness was sometimes born out of sentiment: Roy Williamson (1936–90) of The Corries' 'Flower of Scotland' (1966) was an anthem which suffused the 1970s and still remains an important part of Scottish culture, but its yoking of nostalgia for Bannockburn and promise of contemporary national renewal has not found universal acceptance.

That sentiment was even more powerfully present in the way in which Scotland was represented internationally. Hollywood and other anglophone studios tended – and tend – to focus on Romantic and Jacobite Scotland, with the pawky or fey natives of *Whisky Galore* (1949), the eternally preserved (and, beyond its location, irrelevant) *Brigadoon* (1954) and the tragic Jacobites of *Bonnie Prince Charlie* (1948) and *Kidnapped* (1971), giving way to the epic romances and historical spectaculars of *Highlander* (1986), *Rob Roy* (1994 – itself a successor to the 1953 *Highland Rogue*), *Braveheart* (1995) and *Mary Queen of Scots* (2018), where Saoirse Ronan appears to be in the Highlands every time she steps outside the front door of her dark and dirty palace. Generically, as the dramatist Ian Brown points out, the Scottish epic has become very close to the pioneer or Western film, as indeed James Fenimore Cooper and Thomas Richardson (see Chapter 4) saw long ago: *The Patriot* (2000) almost appears to be a remake of *Braveheart*. Angry men who are tough fighters and fine swordsmen dominate many of the classics of the genre, and the immortal Romantic north of the tousy and flawed *Highlander* has such a pull that this persiflage of cliché has become a cult film. *Brave* (2012) knowingly revisits some of these conventions in its portrayal of 'a land of tradition' with sublime landscapes, ancient monuments and a patriarchal society in order to satirize, but also, arguably, to celebrate them. Even where these stereotypes are absent, others are usually inscribed to replace them: so the portrayal of a Scots doctor in the service of Idi Amin in *The Last King of Scotland* (2006) presents the Scot as a medic, ambitious, opportunist, unscrupulous, not a racist but determinedly on the make – and we have seen many of such in the preceding pages. A wild and Romantic landscape and people and a violent Romantic past – Chapter 22 of Scott's *Waverley* in a nutshell – remain characteristic in whole or part of non-Scottish representations of Scotland in a huge range of otherwise diverse cinema, from Hitchcock's *39 Steps* (1935) to Neil Marshall's *Dog Soldiers* (2002). The references to James Bond's Scottish ancestry via the torrent of cliché released in *Skyfall* (2012), with its remote castle, Catholic(?) chapel, secret passage, ancient retainer and air of broken-down Romantic irrelevance, took this pattern of reference to new depths; it remains the case, however, that George Lazenby's Bond in *On Her Majesty's Secret Service* (1967) is the only one to don the kilt, Sean

Connery never going near it. In recent years, there have been signs of an attempt to respond more thoughtfully to the intensely marketable international stereotypes of Scotland in work such as Netflix's highly popular *Outlaw King* (2018) and the more philosophical and introspective *Robert the Bruce* (2019). Both films seek to present a more thoughtful, multifaceted Bruce than Scottish blockbusters usually permit themselves, with – it must be admitted – mixed success, especially in the latter case. On the other hand, the far more influential *Outlander* series – with 30 million sales of the books and a TV series running since 2014 – remains securely encamped in the traditional imaginary with its magical tartanry, and has been responsible in recent years for a major positive impact on Scottish tourism.[8]

While Romantic, Jacobite and historic Scotland hold sway in the international imaginary of the country, the representation of contemporary Scotland domestically in TV and cinema has tended more towards the small town or urban wasteland model. *River City* (2002–), *Rab C. Nesbitt* (1988–99, 2008–14), *Taggart* (1983–2010), *Shallow Grave* (1994), *Red Road* (2006), *Filth* (2013) and *Trainspotting/ T2 Trainspotting* (1996, 2017) reflect the latter; *Dr Finlay's Casebook* (1962–71), *Sutherland's Law* (1973–76), *Local Hero* (1983) and *Machair* (1992–98) the former. *Tutti Frutti* (1987) rather cleverly encompassed both worlds, which helps to render it a modern classic. Scotland remains largely differentiated from Great Britain via the imaginary under which many of its nineteenth-century social and economic leaders camouflaged their own ambition: a highly distinct but also limited brand, internationally Romantic with a domestic contemporaneity which is pawky or bleak.[9]

Gaelic writing and the Gaelic language played a slowly but increasingly recognized role within the development of Scottish self-representation, and not always at secondhand, as in the Anglophone fictions of Neil Gunn (1891–1973) or Fionn MacColla (Thomas Douglas MacDonald, 1906–75). Beginning with major collections of Alasdair MacMhaighstir Alasdair's and other eighteenth century poetry in the 1920s and 30s, a contemporary tradition in Gaelic writing emerged in which Somhairle MacGill-Eain (1911–96) was the dominant figure in creating a modern Gaelic poetry which conjoined history, landscape and radical politics. Institutionally, the rapid decline of

Gaelic – still spoken across 40 per cent of Scotland in 1891 – began to be addressed by a range of organizations in the postwar era. The *Historical Dictionary of Scots Gaelic* was founded in 1966 and the Gaelic Books Council three years later. Gaelic-medium higher education was developed at Sabhal Mòr Ostaig in Skye from 1973, and education more generally via Comunn na Gàidhlig (1984) and successive developments such as the Meek Report (2002), Bòrd na Gàidhlig (2003) and the Gaelic Language Act (2005). From 1989 Gaelic broadcasting benefited from dedicated funding, backed by a legal obligation under the 1991 Broadcasting Act, and in 2008, following a £12 million investment from the Scottish Government, BBC Alba was launched as the first dedicated Gaelic-language TV channel, reaching an average audience of 530,000 by 2011 and increasing both tolerance and appreciation of the Gaelic language. Bilingual obligations on public bodies in the context of a National Gaelic Language Plan have followed in more recent years, together with a steady growth in Gaelic-medium education, with specialist units in primary schools gradually expanding into full-scale secondary school provision. Gaelic publishing and children's playgroups took root, and Gaelic units in schools began over time to develop into the dedicated provision of fully Gaelic schools: in 2021, there were at least 137 nurseries and primary or secondary schools offering some Gaelic-medium education. Gaelic rock emerged with bands such as Runrig (1973) and Gaelic traditional music in general became more prominent. The Scots language, competence in which was the subject of a question for the first time in the 2011 census, also found its defenders. The *Scottish National Dictionary*, founded in 1931, was initially completed in 1976, and the appearance of W.L. Lorimer's *New Testament in Scots* (1983) was a further sign of the slow growth of a Scots publishing industry and provision of resources to schools. Scottish history, largely exiled from the curriculum since the 1950s and 60s, began to return in the late 1980s: in 1995–97 the distinguished historian Chris Whatley championed it when he chaired the Scottish Consultative Committee on the curriculum. Following the introduction of 'Scottish Studies' into the school curriculum in 2011–12 (the author convened the National Champions Group in support of this development), Scots Language Officers were initially put in place across Scotland.

The study of at least some Scottish literature in schools became obligatory at Higher level, and, while universities remained the primary places for the study of Scotland, they too benefited from an increasing awareness of the international appeal of the country and its culture. The International Association for the Study of Scottish Literatures was launched by the author in 2014 and the main journal in the field, *Studies in Scottish Literature,* edited from South Carolina, had achieved almost half a million article downloads worldwide.[10]

The long dominance of the Conservative Party in government and its perceived intransigence towards Scotland helped to renew interest in the devolution project, particularly in the era of the introduction of the Poll Tax and fresh indications of support for the SNP. Civic Scotland – the members of its institutions, professions and public sector – turned increasingly towards the idea of a devolution which would acknowledge Scotland's historic national status, and be delivered painlessly by an incoming Labour Government. The Claim of Right (1988) self-consciously mimicked the language of the Scottish Parliament of three centuries earlier – and perhaps also the Declaration of Arbroath – in claiming sovereignty for the Scottish people, and the Constitutional Convention, established in 1989 (its terminology following on from the 1947 MacCormick Convention), set itself the task of developing a workable system of Scottish governance; it was chaired by Canon Kenyon Wright (1932–2017), who invoked the Arbroath Declaration. The SNP – despite being wooed by the sovereigntist language included in the Claim at the apparent 'insistence of the Liberal Democrats' – withdrew from the Convention almost at once. From their point of view, the party had been damaged by its support for Labour's messy devolution bill in the 1970s, and it was not about to involve itself again in being a cheerleader for whatever a Labour-dominated Convention might establish. Determined to retain its freedom of manoeuvre, the SNP launched its own internationalist *Scotland in Europe* strategy in 1989, aligning itself strongly with the European Union: it was rewarded by achieving 26 per cent of the vote in the European elections that year, and a stunning 34 per cent in 1994, despite the controversy over the Maastricht Treaty and closer European political and economic integration. In that year, a poll showed that support for a joint Scottish and European identity 'to some degree' was the identified preference of 64 per cent of SNP, 55 per cent of Labour and between 25 and 30 per cent of Conservative and Liberal Democrat voters.[11]

There was a strong rhetoric of Scottish national status and the importance of Scottish consent to British governance in the Claim of Right and the Convention. In 1989, the vast majority of Scotland's MPs supported the Claim, which stated that the Convention stood in support of 'the sovereign right of the Scottish people to determine the form of Government best suited to their needs, and do hereby declare and pledge that in all our actions and deliberations their interests shall be paramount'. Following the establishment of the Edinburgh Parliament in 1997–99, Labour (in office in London and Holyrood) failed – except for Henry McLeish's brief term in office in 2000–01 – to act as if they truly considered Scotland to be a national entity in the terms outlined in the 1988–89 documents which they had supported

28. *A Claim of Right for Scotland.* Although a document produced by a body simply calling for a Scottish parliamentary body within the UK, it invoked claims of Scottish national and popular sovereignty.

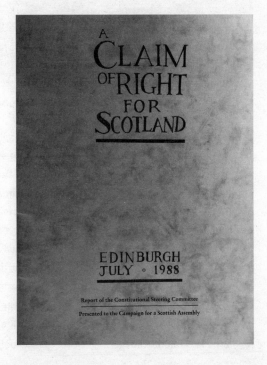

A CLAIM OF RIGHT FOR SCOTLAND

We, gathered as the Scottish Constitutional Convention do hereby acknowledge and assert the sovereign right of the Scottish people to determine the form of government best suited to their needs, and do hereby declare and pledge that in all our actions and deliberations, their interests shall be paramount.

We further declare and pledge that our actions and deliberations shall be directed to the following ends:

To agree a scheme for an Assembly or Parliament for Scotland.

To mobilise Scottish opinion and secure the approval of the Scottish people for that scheme.

To assert the right of the Scottish people to secure the implementation of that scheme.

29. *A Claim of Right for Scotland* signatories.

in opposition. Section 4 of the 1988 Claim, 'The English Constitution – An Illusion of Democracy', and Section 3, 'The Present – and the Future Being Forced Upon Us', read particularly hollowly in the Brexit era.

When the SNP committed to Independence in Europe as a policy, it began to commission background research on Scotland's future development in the EU as an independent state. Among the figures in the foreground of the SNP's EU engagement was Sir Neil MacCormick (1941–2009), Regius Professor of Public Law at Edinburgh and later an MEP (1999–2004). A major theorist of the development of shared sovereignty via an overlapping 'pluralistic . . . multiplicity of legal orders', MacCormick helped draft the Constitutional Treaty of the European Union which, though agreed by eighteen member states, was not in the end finally ratified and was replaced by the Treaty of Lisbon. Other key figures were Professor Christopher Harvie (b.1944, Professor of British and Irish Studies at Tübingen, and Member of the Scottish Parliament, 2007–11), and Winnie Ewing (b.1929) herself, MEP 1975–99 and one of the key architects of the ERASMUS scheme and its successors, which promoted educational and later workplace exchanges throughout the European Union, and whose latest incarnation will triple the size of a vastly successful programme.[12]

In 1997, the incoming Labour Government insisted on a referendum on the devolution settlement. Though this was to be by simple majority, the return of Labour to power in Westminster saw a withdrawal from the Scottish sovereigntist language of the Claim of Right to a more customary emphasis on the complete sovereignty of London. The Secretary of State for Scotland, Donald Dewar (1937–2000; see plate 27), who was to become Scotland's first First Minister in 1999, was nonetheless a man of shrewdness and high ability who understood constitutional precedent. Following a resounding referendum result (74 to 26 in favour, 64 to 36 in favour of tax-varying powers), in which there were 'Yes' votes in every area on the first question and 'No' on the second only from Galloway and Orkney, Dewar's Scotland Act of 1998 was introduced. It harked back both to the Government of Ireland Act of 1920 and ultimately to Gladstone's Secret Memorandum no. 3 of 1885 in that it stipulated reserved, rather than devolved, powers and was thus much cleaner than the 1970s legislation. A First Minister would lead a Scottish Executive in the parliament: only the downgrade to 'Executive' from 'Government' remained from the 1970s, though this was changed de facto by the 2007 SNP administration and de jure by Westminster in 2012. There would be 129 members, 73 elected 'first past the post' from the existing Scottish constituencies plus the division of Orkney from Shetland, with 56 elected proportionately on a list system from different regions across the country, with the aim of creating a rough overall proportionality: it would be theoretically possible, but in practice very difficult, to win an overall majority. This was an important concession by Labour, even if it was predicated on an enduring Labour–Liberal Democrat coalition, which was not quite how matters turned out after a time. Foreign affairs, defence, macroeconomic policy, social security and the constitution headed the list of reserved powers, to which devolutionary sceptics in Labour secured the addition of broadcasting, drugs, firearms and equal opportunities, as well as abortion and related issues and monopolies and mergers. There was scope for intergovernmental co-operation, though this was always stronger in theory than it was to be in practice.[13]

The first elections to the new parliament took place in May 1999. It was initially to be held in the General Assembly hall of the Kirk of Scotland, going on tour when the General Assembly itself met. In the meantime a new parliament building was to be erected at Holyrood, chosen as a compromise between the Unionist Fountainbridge and Nationalist Calton Hill sites, it is as central as the second but hidden away from the skyline like the first (see plates 25 and 26). To the surprise of the Labour Party, the SNP raced to an early lead in the polls before falling back on election day, partly as a result of its leader Alex Salmond's condemnation of NATO's armed intervention in Kosovo, which bore witness to the SNP's continuing refusal to stay focused on domestic matters, and its ambition to be the vanguard of a new form of Scottish internationalism. Nonetheless, the SNP won thirty-five seats on 28 per cent of the overall vote and became the official opposition to the Labour–Liberal Democrat coalition which formed shortly after the election, emerging almost seamlessly from the discussions of the Constitutional Convention. The triumph of the ill-defined centre-left political consensus of the Convention was, however, to be short-lived. The SNP's strong showing reflected underlying changes in Scottish society which were to have a major impact in the years to come, although these were ignored by a Scottish commentariat who were themselves usually signed up to the Convention's outlook on the world, which could best be described as 'Conventional'.[14]

There was a division between how the British Government saw the Scottish Parliament – as a local democratic forum which Labour could use as a platform in the event of a future Tory government – and how the Scottish Parliament and the people of Scotland saw it.

From the beginning, and long before the Nationalists came to power in 2007, the Scottish Parliament saw itself not as a substate regional government, but as a national parliament 'reconvened' as Winnie Ewing, with her gift for historic quotation, described it in the first session after the 1999 election. The institution's view of itself seemed to be shared by the electorate. In a major *Economist* poll that same year, 46 per cent of Scots thought that their parliament would be the most important element in Scotland's governance in twenty years' time, with 31 per cent opting for the European Union and only 8 per cent for Westminster.[15] This was very far from the ranking of priorities in the minds of the Blair government and its successors, and slowly but surely this began to cause problems for Labour in Scotland. Dewar was perhaps to an extent aware of this risk. At the official opening of the Scottish Parliament in July 1999, Dewar (now First Minister) gave a speech which echoed that of the Irish Party leader Charles Parnell at Cork in 1885:

> This is more than our politics and our laws. This is about who we are, how we carry ourselves . . . Walter Scott wrote that only a man with soul so dead could have no sense, no feel of his native land. For me, for any Scot, today is a proud moment: a new stage on a journey begun long ago and which has no end.[16]

This so clearly referenced Parnell ('We cannot ask the British constitution for more than the restitution of Grattan's parliament, but no man has the right to fix the boundary of a nation. No man has the right to say to his country, "Thus far shalt thou go and no further", and we have never attempted to fix the "ne plus ultra" to the progress of Ireland's nationhood, and we never shall'), suggesting that devolution was a process which might be expected to develop, not a terminus. The fact that Dewar had pressed at Westminster for a devolutionary model very similar to Gladstone's Irish model lent constitutional weight to the comparison. Most importantly, it was a statement of Scottish nationality, a 'we' that transcended the constitutional arrangements of substate government. In the wake of the 1998 Good Friday Agreement and the establishment – at least notionally – of the Council of the Isles or the British–Irish Council, Dewar visited the Republic of Ireland. He was received with protocol more befitting a national leader than the leader of a regional assembly, enjoying, for example, direct talks with the Taoiseach, Bertie Ahern, and calling on Mary McAleese, the President. But the British–Irish Council was only one of the instruments of post-devolutionary governance that the British Government – wedded to the absolutist notion of parliamentary sovereignty dating back to 1688 – failed to take seriously and allowed to wither on the vine. Fundamentally, the Council was about consultation; and consultation with lesser powers – and even sometimes with peers – was something the British Parliament and Government find constitutionally difficult, as the repeated emphasis on 'sovereignty' in the Brexit negotiations made clear.[17]

Donald Dewar died in 2000. His successor, Henry McLeish, understood the way the wind would blow and sought to rechristen the Scottish Executive the Scottish Government and to present his Labour–Liberal administration in more national terms. This was unwelcome to many Labour MPs who, post-devolution, had relatively little to do in terms of domestic bread and butter issues. In McLeish's own words, a 'small but damaging cabal' formed against him, and a relatively small-scale infringement of the rules governing the sub-letting of his constituency office made its way to the media and conveniently brought him down. The succeeding administration of Jack McConnell (2001–07) seemed, to some, to bear out McLeish's own view that one of the problems of devolution in practice was that 'for Scots, the will of London still seems to prevail'. If so, karma was about to intervene. Intervention from the London Labour Government in the 2007 Scottish elections almost certainly contributed to McConnell's defeat by a single seat, and in a historic change in Scottish politics, he stood aside for the SNP, refusing attempts by the London leadership to persuade him to stitch together a coalition to frustrate the nationalist victory.[18]

One industry which failed to prosper in post-devolution Scotland was the media. Scotland had historically had a strong domestic press, partly due to the late delivery of English papers, which in some cases were only available in the afternoon as late as the 1960s. There were some titles with globally leading penetration, as was the case of *The Sunday Post* from D.C. Thomson of Dundee, publishers of *The Beano* (1938–) and *The Dandy* (1937–2012), which at its peak circulation of 1.14 million was read by 79 per cent of Scots. The quality titles – *The Herald* and particularly *The Scotsman* – had long been sympathetic to devolution. In 1999, they had 179,000 sales between them, with the biggest Scottish regional paper, the Aberdeen-based *Press and Journal*, reaching 102,000. By contrast, *The Times, Telegraph* and *Guardian* combined sold 66,000 in Scotland. In the tabloid market, the situation was similar, with sales of the *Daily Record* at 651,000. Increasing confidence in change in Scotland led to the launch of *Scotland on Sunday* (1989) and *The Sunday Herald* (1999), and there was even an attempt to launch a financial paper, *Business AM*, in the aftermath of devolution in 1999, though it lasted only a few years.[19]

While newspapers in general went into decline in the twenty-first century, the Scottish papers suffered particularly badly. This was in part due to the creation of more complete Scottish editions of English papers which diluted their unique coverage, and in part perhaps due to the disinclination of the Scottish press to continue to articulate Scotland, Scottish society and aspirations as they had once done. Instead they frequently adopted a tone of captious complaint and negativity as they saw themselves replaced by the Holyrood Parliament as the premier guardian of a Scottish public sphere. By the end of 2019, *The Scotsman* had a circulation of little more than 14,000, of which 20 per cent were distributed free, and *The Herald* 22,000; by the end of 2021, *The Scotsman* was barely shifting 5,000 copies a day for cash. The *Press and Journal*, less easy to replicate given its regional focus, had held on to rather more of its readers, with a circulation of 39,500. The *Daily Record* was just over the 100,000 mark, while *The Sunday Post* was at 68,000. *The National* (2014) and *Sunday National*, papers committed to independence, had just over 12,000 subscribers by early 2021, with a smaller number of casual purchasers. Advertising revenue was falling rapidly and was not returning through open access to digital content, while it was unproven that data harvesting would be acceptable as the price of access to sites which – compared with UK rivals like the *Daily Mail*'s digital offer – could be perceived as low value. In addition, the non-devolution of broadcasting in 1999 created a gradual gulf between the Scottish public sphere and the BBC over the following twenty years, with an increasing price paid in failing trust between public sector broadcasting and its audiences in Scotland. Hesitant steps to diversify the BBC's 'British' mission have been taken behind the curve of much public opinion, with the concession of a Scottish news programme occurring twenty years after the campaign for its post-devolution development. In the meantime, the broadcasting landscape had changed enormously and the average viewer of terrestrial BBC TV news is now over sixty. By the second decade of the twenty-first century, Scotland was a country where public debate and political sympathies were increasingly out of step with the printed and electronic media: in 2015, 'Just 48% of people in Scotland thought the BBC . . . good at representing their life in news and current affairs content.' Tribalism and conspiracy theory grew at the edges of society in consequence. Although these remained largely confined to activists, they were nourished by a wider climate of distrust.[20]

Under the SNP from 2007, the underlying belief that the devolved government was a restoration of Scotland's national parliament became more explicit. This was recognized in the language of further extensions to Scotland's devolved powers in the years that followed. The 2009 Commission on devolution under Sir Kenneth Calman (b.1941), set up to examine the further devolution of powers after the nationalist victory and the opening of the SNP's 'National Conversation' on independence, explicitly stated that 'The United Kingdom has never been a unitary state' (1.169). Calman also acknowledged both the Acts of Union of the Scottish and English Parliaments as foundational constitutional documents of the United Kingdom, thus clearly contradicting the notion of unlimited Westminster sovereignty, which is described in the Commission report as only a 'convention' (1.171). The report likewise confirmed that the 'UK has always had a territorial constitution' with 'more than one legal jurisdiction' (1.172), and pointed out (2.5 ff) that many post-Union institutions had a distinctively Scottish cast, thus renewing as well as preserving elements of domestic sovereignty. In stating that 'The UK is . . . a State of different unions . . . each . . . has its own history, dynamic and likely path of future development', Calman's conclusions reconstituted the Scottish Parliament as a state actor. The Commission recommended that that parliament should reach agreement with Westminster on the terms of the British social union (Recommendation 2.1), which itself is presented both as a given and as something to be continually negotiated, as 'the balance between . . . distinctive and shared elements' of sovereignty have been historically 'determined . . . by what the Scottish people have aspired to' (Summary 12). The Calman Report, though it recommended only further powers for the Scottish Parliament, and not independence, to a degree acknowledged it as a state actor, operating on behalf of the Scottish people, not simply as a branch of Westminster government. The idea that devolution compromised Westminster sovereignty was one which was not simply floated by the Calman Commission, but was already in circulation. Lord Steyn's 2005 judgment in R (Jackson) v. Attorney General that 'The supremacy of Parliament . . . is a construct of the common law' and that the 1998 Scotland Act settlement 'points to a divided sovereignty' was supported in the same case by Lord Hope's insistence on the gradual qualification of a 'parliamentary sovereignty . . . no longer, if it ever was, absolute'. Of course, where the Commons has diminished the power of the Crown and the Lords, and the patronage of the Executive has much greater power than was once the case in the Commons, Parliament did and does not necessarily agree. This was made clear by the 2019 case on the Prime Minister's prorogation of Parliament, brought by Gina Miller in England and the SNP MP Joanna Cherry QC in Scotland, and successful at the Supreme Court of the UK. The Calman Report led to additional devolved powers, but the constitutional grounds on which it argued for them were of little interest to the British Government, though they were consonant with the contemporary language of respect for the Scottish Parliament and Government espoused by the Conservative–Liberal Democrat coalition under the premiership of David Cameron after 2010.[21]

THE INDEPENDENCE REFERENDUM

In their first term in office, the SNP under Alex Salmond had started a 'National Conversation' as a prelude to a further referendum on the creation of a separate Scottish state (see plate 28). In 2011, they won an overall majority in a Scottish general election with 45 per cent of the vote, and proceeded to legislate for such a referendum. This was a remarkable political sea-change. The British Government consented to the referendum under the terms of the Edinburgh Agreement of 15 October 2012: this agreed that the vote would be beyond legal challenge, could be legislated for at Holyrood, would be conducted so as to command confidence among its stakeholders and that all parties would respect the result. Cameron was a liberal Prime Minister, but he also – in common with most of the British political class – expected a resounding victory for the Union that would shut up the nationalists for a long time to come. Although support for independence was somewhat volatile, as late as October 2013 the Scotsman was reporting polling putting independence at 25 per cent, although this figure was 36 per cent excluding 'don't knows'.[22]

The 'Yes' campaign's multiple sectoral groups, strong engagement across civil society, optimistic and hopeful (if sometimes imprecise and utopian) message and innovative use of social media were all very effective.[23] The 'Better Together' (no) campaign, led by Alistair Darling, the former Labour Chancellor, focused on the dangers and risks of independence, particularly with regard to currency, the economy, pensions, EU membership and oil revenues, as well as some less plausible golden oldies, like the status of Orkney and Shetland, where 82 per cent of the inhabitants by now self-identified as Scots. Better Together's economic arguments and the EU case among, in particular, non-UK EU citizens resident in Scotland, were tactically effective if strategically less so, for the campaign for the Union also accelerated already evident damage to the Labour Party by making it a spokesperson for a political position held most strongly by the Conservatives. A substantial proportion of Labour voters supported independence, but this position did not receive any recognition from the party. When Wendy Alexander, its Scottish leader, had supported an independence referendum in May 2008, she was immediately contradicted by Gordon Brown as Prime Minister, and within a month was no longer leading the Labour Party in the Scottish Parliament. Now Labour doubled down on that uncompromising position, while the Better Together campaign as a whole overlooked the number of soft or persuadable Yes voters by failing to come up with anything resembling a coherent development of the status quo until the very last minute.[24]

Partly as a consequence, in September 2014, Scotland almost surprised the British Government. The independence referendum saw an 85 per cent turnout (almost a complete turnout, given the vagaries and duplications of the electoral register) across Scotland. The result was far closer than David Cameron had expected when he agreed the referendum, and, by the time the votes were counted, the Better Together side was anxious, with late polling for the first time suggesting the possibility of a victory for Yes. In the end 45 per cent voted Yes to complete sovereign status and the creation of an independent Scottish state under the British Crown. Three of Scotland's thirty-two local authorities registered a Yes vote, including the cities of Glasgow – the largest in the country – and Dundee. A majority of Scots-born voted Yes as did a majority of all those aged under 55, irrespective of origin, while there appears to have been a majority Yes vote from the Scots Asian community, though the strong support for the SNP by 55,000 Polish Scots ('15 per cent of all those born outside the UK') in 2011, when 41 per cent backed the nationalists, was not replicated: ironically many of them feared the risk of loss of EU membership.[25]

The vote was nonetheless seen as a vindication by the British Government, not as a warning. Some small concessions on devolutionary powers – some of which were promised the week before the result to head off a still tighter

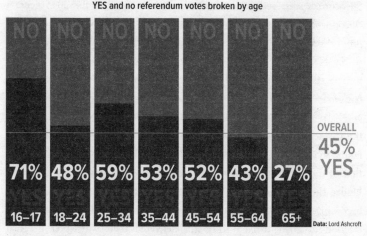

WHAT ARE THE CHANCES YOU VOTED YES TO SCOTTISH INDEPENDENCE?
YES and no referendum votes broken by age

NO	NO	NO	NO	NO	NO	NO	
71%	48%	59%	53%	52%	43%	27%	OVERALL 45% YES
16–17	18–24	25–34	35–44	45–54	55–64	65+	Data: Lord Ashcroft

30. Voter demographics in the 2014 Scottish independence referendum.

outcome as part of a UK cross-party Vow – were a compromise offer to Scottish opinion following a further Commission on devolution, the Smith Commission. The Vow set out three points: that the Scottish Parliament would be constitutionally permanent (a very doubtful promise given British constitutional reliance on the absolute sovereignty of parliament, and the consequent commitment to the idea of the inability of any parliament to bind its successors); that the present pattern of funding would continue; and that extensive new powers would be devolved. Fewer powers than expected were in the end devolved, and nationalists looked on the Vow as not having been implemented. The lukewarm response of the British Government to the Vow following the victory of the No side was accompanied by an emphasis on restricting Scottish MPs' right to vote on English issues. This was announced the morning after the result when Cameron rather gracelessly responded to his victory by proclaiming that in future there would be 'English Votes for English Laws' at Westminster from which Scots MPs would be excluded (this measure was reversed in 2021, being seen by post-Brexit Conservatives as an acknowledgement of the multi-national nature of the Union, and thus incompatible with centralizing moves such as the Internal Market Act). Aided by other factors, these developments combined to support consolidation of the Yes vote, which led to 56 of the 59 Scottish seats at Westminster falling to the SNP at the 2015 general election, in which the party recorded half the Scottish vote. A significant proportion of the SNP's success derived from Labour Yes voters moving over to the Nationalists. Not only has it proven hard for the Labour Party to retrieve this support, but also the number of Yes voters in their own ranks has grown back from its low 2015 base, suggesting a fresh fissuring of their vote is possible. In addition, strong Labour Unionists began to defect to the Conservatives in Scotland, as Labour paid the price on two fronts for failing to differentiate their constitutional offer in the 2014 campaign from that of the Tory Government they were supposed to be in opposition to. Under the fresh leadership of Anas Sarwar, Labour retrieved what was becoming a very weak position to achieve 22 per cent in the Scottish general election of 2021, though this still delivered their worst-ever Scottish Parliamentary result.[26]

OUT OF EUROPE

In 2016, Scotland once again demonstrated how far it was a different country from England. In the referendum on leaving the European Union that June, 32 out of 32 of Scotland's local authority areas voted 'Remain', some by swingeing majorities, for example the capital Edinburgh, where the margin for Remain was almost three to one (74 to 26). The vote in Scotland was completely ignored by the British Government and by both the main UK opposition parties. UK-wide, the nature and scale of the vote indicated a preference for a continued UK presence in the single market or a deal which retained those benefits. Such had been widely promised by the 'Leave' campaign, and, while many Leave voters wanted a total severance from the EU and its institutions – which was closer to the eventual outcome – polling showed some 20 to 30 per cent of the Leave vote favoured an EEA type of solution, which would retain access to the single market. In Scotland, the frustration of the democratic vote did not lead directly to increased support for independence. The extent to which the Remain vote depended on Unionist support and the significant proportion of nationalists voting Leave both served to undermine the Scottish First Minister Nicola Sturgeon's call in 2017 for a fresh independence referendum, and saw a recovery in the Unionist vote in Scotland, with the Conservative Party being the main bene-ficiary. Around 10 per cent of SNP voters in north-east Scotland migrated directly to the Conservatives in the 2017 general election: these seem to have been mainly Leave voters driven by irritation at the poor fishing deal the UK had from the EU, one hardly improved by the eventual Brexit settlement. There was some constituency for European Free Trade Association/European Economic Area (EFTA/EEA) membership in Scotland, particularly in the north-east, and the SNP themselves had espoused the merits of a Norway-style economy and relationship before independence in Europe was adopted as a policy in 1989. However, the fact that even Scotland's Tories were on the whole moderate in their views towards the EU did not help them when the absolute nature of the British negotiating position became ever clearer, with the Scottish Government and other devolved administrations excluded from any meaningful influence. In particular, the Sewel Convention, which

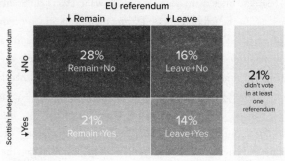

How did Scots vote at the independence and EU referendums?

EU referendum

↓ Remain   ↓ Leave

Scottish independence referendum

↓ No

28%
Remain+No

16%
Leave+No

21%
didn't vote
in at least
one
referendum

↓ Yes

21%
Remain+Yes

14%
Leave+Yes

You**GOV**® | yougov.com   3,166 Scottish adults surveyed between
August 29 and December 16, 2016

31. The relationship between the 2014 and 2016 votes in Scotland: it is important to note that, depending on the outcome of a vote, a proportion of people tend to retrospectively adjust their recollections as to how they voted. This table shows how a substantial crossover between the Yes and Leave votes in these two referendums made it initially difficult for the Scottish National Party to align remaining in the European Union with independence.

allowed for the British Parliament to legislate in devolved areas only with Holyrood's consent, was overridden. The SNP began to gain votes once again, and accelerated in the 2019 general election, held on the Withdrawal Agreement. The Conservative Party demanded complete loyalty to the agreement from its candidates less than a year before it whipped its MPs to vote to breach it through the Internal Market Act. Scandinavian-style semi-detachedness from the European project has got some traction in Scotland; xenophobic self-congratulation about the wonders of being British, not so much.

Faced with an extreme vision of Brexit, it was no surprise that the Scottish vote began to drift back towards the SNP, moving it from strong to exceptional levels of support, evident in the 2019 European elections and 2020 polling. In the final UK European election, the Brexit Party topped the poll in the whole of England and Wales, barring London; the SNP topped the poll in every Scottish local authority area. Twenty-five per cent of those who voted Labour in Scotland in the UK general election of 2019 reported that

Brexit had pushed them towards Scottish independence. Such figures were reflected in the fact that support for independence and for the SNP rose to over 50 per cent in the final year before the 2021 Scottish elections, which the SNP proposed to fight on an explicit mandate for independence. The Scottish Government's approach to the Covid-19 pandemic also won it support, but this was blunted by the British Government's decisive vaccine acquisition strategy. Nonetheless Scots remained much more likely to trust their own government on the issue, with polling in Scotland in late 2021 showing approval levels of two-thirds for the Scottish Government's handling of the pandemic, with the British Government's approval ratings in the same sphere at barely more than a quarter: a somewhat ironic disjunction since there was a strongly four-nations articulation in the response to Covid-19, however Scotland and Wales might trumpet their areas of divergence. Meanwhile, the British Government's Internal Market Act (2020 c.27) enabled the British Government to bypass the Scottish Parliament and to fund in devolved policy areas directly, even in contradiction to existing Scottish Government priorities. This would undermine devolved policy-making in areas such as energy and food standards in pursuit of the creation of a seamless UK (or more properly British) market. In the 2021 election in Scotland, the SNP came very close to an overall majority with 48 per cent of the constituency vote, and the divided nature of the Scottish electorate was visible in the fact that 49 per cent of the constituency vote and just over 50 per cent of the list vote went to pro-independence parties, including the clamorous but ineffective Alba Party, founded by Alex Salmond, to give what was termed a 'supermajority' in favour of independence, but largely attractive to impatient activists, conspiracy theorists and those with a grievance against the current SNP leadership. Some 70 per cent of Alba voters (as contrasted with 48 per cent of SNP and 35 per cent of Scottish Green voters) wanted an independence referendum within twelve months of the election, while '49 per cent of voters' viewed the constitution as the most important issue, compared with education at 28 per cent, health at 27 per cent, the economy at 16 per cent and Covid-19 on 15 per cent. The re-elected SNP thus held a mandate – in collaboration with the Greens – to hold a legal referendum, but one which did not take place too soon. The strongly procedural element of this approach began to look rather thread-bare to many: it was difficult to see *what* an independent Scotland would make better and *how* it would do it. If Alba was not the answer, there was still a question.[27]

PROCESS AND PROCEDURE; RISKS AND OPPORTUNITIES

As was the case in 2012–2014, the route to put a Scottish independence referendum beyond legal challenge remains the Section 30 order which transfers UK powers to enable Holyrood to legislate competently in the area of the constitution, which was reserved under the terms of the 1998 Scotland Act and its successors. Possible alternative routes have been suggested: given the obsession with the doctrine of parliamentary sovereignty, the consulta-tive nature of referendums in the UK system has been seen by some to open the door for Holyrood to hold a consultative referendum. This would – the argument runs – be non-binding and hence not outwith Scottish parliamen-tary competence: the 1994 Strathclyde Regional Council water referendum which successfully resisted water privatization in Scotland is seen as an exem-plar. It is all but certain though that the British Government would chal-lenge this approach in the courts, and it is probably unlikely that a finessed position of this kind would survive the ensuing legal process in a manner which would allow its implementation.[28]

For its part, the SNP has been circumspect, particularly in the context of the 2017 Catalan Referendum, as the Scottish Government are aware of the risks of a Spanish veto on EU membership if a referendum is carried without ultimate British Government consent to its process. However, some of the party's MPs and MSPs and many in the wider Yes movement, which prior to the pandemic could put marches of 100,000 people on the streets of Scotland's major cities, a multiple of previous march numbers, are impatient. The 2010 International Court of Justice (ICJ) decision which recognized Kosovo's seces-sion from Serbia has in the past been seen by some nationalist theorists as having 'shifted the balance towards an inherent right of self-determination'. On the other hand, the situation which has developed in Catalonia points in the other direction, having been inflamed by the Spanish Constitutional Court's 2010 intervention to strike out – partly or wholly – fourteen of the agreed provisions of Catalan nationality arising under the terms and result of the legitimate 2006 referendum on the Statute of Autonomy, including the use of the term 'nation'. There is understandable caution in some quarters about making the issue of Scottish independence into a 'playground for lawyers'. Under the leadership of Alex Salmond, who visited Catalonia in 2008, the Scottish Government was very positive towards the Catalan case (indeed the Scottish Parliament itself had been the design of a Catalan architect), and the 'symbolic referenda' in Catalan municipalities were closely observed. But after the 2017 Catalan Referendum, though prominent Scottish lawyer Aamer Anwar was to the fore in defending against extradition Clara Ponsati, the former Councillor for Education in the Generalitat who also held an academic post at St Andrews, the Scottish Government itself was notably circumspect. A similar process occurred earlier in the case of Québec, once prominent as a Scottish comparator and then marginal and in the last ten years much less heard of. In part this is due to a greater focus on Europe, in part to the fact that provincial powers within the federal state of Canada and the – albeit unofficial – recognition of the Québécois as a 'nation' by the federal House of Commons of Canada in 2006 have lowered nationalist pressures. It may well be argued that if a federal or federal to confederal structure had been introduced in Ireland in the 1880s or Scotland a century later, a similar process might have been observed in the British archipelago. But the obsession with Westminster's absolute sovereignty, which dates back to the 1688–1720 period and is so evident in the Brexit process, combined with the additional accelerant of the governmental trend of seeking to absorb powers into the executive, has seen to it that the kind of processes seen in Canada are unthinkable in a UK context.[29]

If Scotland were to become independent following concession of a referendum by a Westminster government exhausted by the issue and the continuing lack of support for British parties in Scotland, or by rising support for independence, or through a process arising from a successful court action, or otherwise, what would this new Scotland be, and where would it stand in the world? In 2019, Scotland's GDP stood at £180.4 billion, £33,200 per capita for a population of 5.4 million. Scottish productivity, about 10 per cent lower than the UK average in 2008, was within 1 per cent of that average ten years later, with Scottish productivity rising more than twice as fast as its UK equivalent; gross median weekly earnings were now in line with the UK average. In that sense, Scotland has – despite low levels of private sector spending on research and development – begun to address one of the 'three key, deeply persistent and interrelated problems' of the UK economy identified by the historian Peter Hennessey: low productivity, lack of technical skills and an inability to commercialize innovation successfully. Indeed in the latter two areas also, the Scottish Government's close links with universities, awareness of their economic impact (£11 for every £1 spent), excellence in research (three in the global top 100, 2 per cent of world's most highly cited research outputs equalling almost thirty times the country's share of world population) and high per capita level of spinout companies (19 per cent of the UK total) all bode well. Goods exports are growing more strongly than elsewhere in the UK, which receives some 60 per cent of Scottish trade, about 10 per cent more than was the case just before the Union. The Netherlands was Scotland's largest export market in the EU-27 in 2016, followed by France, which mirrors exactly the situation in 1700. Scotland's largest industries are energy (oil, gas and renewables, 9 per cent of GDP), financial services (7 per cent of GDP, per capita as high as England), tourism (up to 5 per cent of GDP) and food and drink; strengths in these areas are widely spread geographically. Scotland exported almost £6 billion in food and drink and between £3 billion and £4 billion in both professional services and oil and chemicals in 2018–19, while almost 180,000 are employed in the digital and creative economies. Naturally Brexit will disrupt this pattern: to what extent and in what directions remains to be seen.

Energy	101,000 jobs	£16.2 billion (bn) Gross Value Added (GVA)
Financial Services	247,000 jobs (9.5 per cent of employment)	£15.7bn GVA
Engineering	126,000 jobs (4.8 per cent)	£8.1bn GVA
Construction	149,000 jobs (5.7 per cent)	£7.9bn GVA

Digital	97,000 jobs (3.7 per cent)	£6.6bn GVA
Creative Industries	77,000 jobs (3 per cent)	£4.4bn GVA
Tourism	218,000 jobs (8.3 per cent)	£4.1bn GVA
Food and Drink	44,000 jobs (1.7 per cent)	£3.6bn GVA
Life Sciences	40,000 jobs (1.5 per cent)	£2.4bn GVA
Chemicals	11,000 jobs	£1.3bn GVA
Textiles	8,000 jobs	£321 million GVA
Fishing	4,860 jobs	£301 million GVA

Renewables were accounted to be 90 per cent of gross electricity production in 2019, up from 59 per cent four years earlier. A figure of 100 per cent was anticipated for 2020, and the final number was only slightly adrift of this, all but completely meeting the massively ambitious targets set by Alex Salmond's administration a decade earlier, which had led to Scotland 'gaining recognition as a leader on climate change' as early as the Conference of the Parties (COP15) at Copenhagen in 2009, the year the largest windfarm in the UK opened at Whitelee. Scottish Government policy in this area has been particularly effective by comparison with the reception granted innovative technology elsewhere: the 'Salter Duck' was invented at Edinburgh to harness wavepower by Stephen Salter (b.1938), whose invention failed to receive investment after the cost of its energy production was misstated by the UK's Department of Energy by a factor of ten, leading to 'false information' being given to the EU authorities.[30]

New industries such as gaming in Dundee (*Grand Theft Auto* is one of its most famous products, while *Lemmings* has sold 15 million games worldwide), and Jim McFarlane's specialist Endira cycle-clothing in Livingston offer innovation and diversity, while Scottish engineering continued to innovate in the 2002 Falkirk Wheel and elsewhere. Scotland also retains a comparatively affordable housing market, with strong supply and weak population growth both serving to sustain the possibility of high levels of internal mobility.[31] But all is not of course sweetness and light: Scotland's higher public spending gives it a greater deficit than the rest of the UK, its small and medium-sized enterprises are less attuned to export, and, although roughly as well off as England in GDP per capita, a small but not insignificant part of that derives from the attribution of highly volatile oil and gas revenues. Scotland has a claim to the lion's share of the North Sea fields which rests 'on the 1982 UN Convention of the Law of the Sea', but the social and economic role of oil – and its political acceptability – are weakening all the time, and the cost of extraction from the North Sea renders low oil prices uneconomic for the industry.[32]

In addition, Scotland has major internal inequalities, which extend far beyond the fact that a few hundred people own half its land: the country remains one of the most feudal globally. The average salary is the highest in the UK outside the south-east (and long-term saving, as reflected in Individual Savings Accounts (ISAs), is higher than anywhere outside the south of England), and generally lower house prices and more free and good quality public services compensate for a higher tax bill on medium and upper incomes. However, average pay in different locations in Scotland varied in 2018 by over 30 per cent, a significantly larger gap than exists between the poorest and richest areas of England, excluding London. In addition, while growth is strong in the major cities (Glasgow was twice the Scottish average in 2019, and Edinburgh, Glasgow and Stirling are predicted to be the Gross Value Added (GVA) growth leaders in 2020–24), many other areas are very weak indeed, contributing to an anaemic overall growth rate and many locations of poor opportunity and endemic poverty. Enterprise in Scotland can be very unevenly spread. In 1996, the proportion of VAT-registered businesses per 10,000 population varied from over 400 in Aberdeenshire and 250 in Edinburgh to between 125 and 130 in North Lanarkshire and West Dunbartonshire.[33]

Identity politics is central to the development of state consent in the case of new polities, which is one of the weaknesses of a purely instrumental reading of independence. As long ago as 1999, *The Economist* found that only 49 per cent of Scots identified with the Union flag, while 72 per cent primarily identified as Scottish rather than British. Four times as many English as Scots identified with the Stars and Stripes of the United States, and there was little interest south of the border in the European flag.[34] By

2001, 80 per cent of Scots identified as Scottish and only 27 per cent as British (compared to 57 per cent in England), and in 2005 only 14 per cent of Scots chose a British identity in a forced choice between Scottish and British, compared with 25 per cent in 1992. Movement at the extremes of identity has been relatively rapid. Between 1992 and 2000 alone, the proportion of Scots declining any British identity even when free to admit it, doubled. Though 64 per cent expressed some pride in Great Britain in 2007, only 23 per cent expressed a strong pride, little more than half the English total. There were parallel – though much milder – rises in the declaration of English identity south of the Border. The rise in Scottish nationality was also borne witness to in a major shift from those opting for class as a primary determinant of identity over nationality (54 per cent in 1979 opted for class not Scotland, but by 1999 this was down to 35 per cent). Some of this may have been due to a stronger association of nationality with class values brought about by Mrs Thatcher's government, which was widely hated in Scotland: in 1999, 61 per cent of Scots favoured redistributing income and wealth, but only 36 per cent in England, while in 2010 – after thirteen years of Labour government – 40 per cent of Scots favoured 'increasing taxation and government spending', compared to 30 per cent in England. In effect, class was becoming nation: Scotland as a concept was becoming the national manifestation of continuing support for the 1945–79 British social democratic model, but the Labour Party, so long associated with that model, was no longer trusted to run it in Scotland's best interests because of its relentless British centralism, which was increasingly visible to the Scots electorate. According to recent research, Scots remain the most dissatisfied substate country in Europe in respect of the division between their domestic and Westminster powers. Thus, although the Scottish Social Attitudes Survey regularly shows that Scotland does not diverge from the UK average substantially in many key areas, those where it does, notably redistributive economic policies and governance, are increasingly critical to political behaviour. In the 2020 Scottish Social Attitudes survey, 73 per cent believed the Scottish Government should have most influence over how Scotland is governed, with only 15 per cent opposing. Moreover, it is Scotland's own government which enjoys credibility as a government: an October 2020 Progress Scotland poll indicated that the Scottish Government leads the British Government in public approval by 21 points for authoritativeness, 37 points for competence and effectiveness, 51 points for empathy and understanding and 52 points for good communications. This is only the latest stage in what has been a long process.[35] Royalism, very much in evidence in Scotland during the Queen's Silver Jubilee in 1977, appears also to be in relatively rapid if muted decline, with only 50 per cent now in support of keeping the royal family. Street parties to celebrate the royal calendar had never been popular in Scotland – not just because of the weather – and were almost non-existent for the Diamond Jubilee in 2012 and the weddings of the sons of Prince Charles, Duke of Rothesay. In Scotland, 55 per cent are not proud of the Queen, compared with 17 per cent in England, and 15 per cent are proud, compared with 50 per cent south of the border.[36]

Scottish nationalism is a much more unusual creature than conventional historians of nationalism might suppose. It is closer in many respects to the political development of New Zealand or other former dominions than to ethno-cultural nationalism of a more familiar European type. It is also not riven between left and right to the extent one might expect, particularly in the world after 2008. Michael Russell, who in *Grasping the Thistle* (2006) expressed a strong concern over 'the potential of our economy to be dragged down by excessive public expenditure' served in the Cabinet of both SNP First Ministers, where he was associated with strongly reformist moves in land reform and local democracy. In 2014, Alex Salmond, who had by this stage presided over a seven year freeze in local council tax rates in cash terms, presented a vision for a Scotland which was a modern European state, immigration-friendly, Scandi-lite in tax and social policy and at the cutting edge in the knowledge economy and renewable energy. In 2016, the somewhat more left leaning Nicola Sturgeon established the Sustainable Growth Commission under the chairing of Andrew Wilson, with the following remit:

To assess projections for Scotland's economy and public finances, consider the implications for our economy and finances under different potential governance scenarios, and make recommendations for policy on:

392

- Measures to boost economic growth and improve Scotland's public finances – both now in the aftermath of the EU referendum and in the context of independence.
- The potential for and best use of savings from UK programmes in the event of independence, such as Trident.
- The range of transitional cost and benefits associated with independence and arrangements for dealing with future revenue windfalls, including future North Sea revenues.

In addition, the Commission was asked to take account of the recommendations of the 2013 Fiscal Commission reports, and the outcome of the EU referendum, and consider the most appropriate monetary policy arrangements to underpin a programme for sustainable growth in an independent Scotland.[37]

The Wilson Commission's findings proved to be too fiscally conservative for the utopian Yes left, who range from those with Socialist views to the left of Corbynite Labour to the verges of Occupy type street activism. Indeed, tension between Yes movement activists and the SNP leadership has become increasingly evident since 2014. Many supporters of independence and the EU are not prepared for the kind of policies needed to secure alignment with EU deficit rules to allow Scotland to rejoin the bloc after independence. To this extent, identity politics have frequently trumped serious attempts to provide a route map to a sustainable independent Scottish economy. There are real questions as to how far such an economy could diverge from England on issues of taxation and spending, especially with much lower levels of state consent than those pertaining in the Republic of Ireland, which despite longstanding dependence on England diverged in economic policy because of the level of mutual hostility through which independence was achieved, which itself brought other problems. Ireland has switched to much fuller integration into the EU economy and much lower levels of dependence on the UK, but this process took a long time, and there are questions about how patient a Scottish electorate would be post-independence, given the mixture of pre-1979 British social democracy and utopian Scandinavianism which characterize the views of many in the Yes movement. The question is not can an independent Scotland survive and thrive, but how long it would take to do so, given the transformative expectations of its supporters. Outside the EU or EEA, it would not thrive at all except as a dependency of London: opposition to EU membership among some nationalists was particularly bizarre in this context. Besides the potential for greater economic autonomy, one of the important benefits of the EU, in particular for small nations, is that its institutions, opportunities and programmes act as a counterweight to introspection and provincialism. Not that these are limited to small states: on 28 June 2019, Lord Digby Jones, a former director general of the Confederation of British Industry (CBI) and British Government minister, claimed that Ireland did '90% of its trade . . . with the UK', when the most recent figures indicated that the numbers were 11 per cent in goods and 6 per cent in services. The EU has enabled Ireland to reorient its economy away from the UK market, and an independent Scotland would need to be in the EU or be content to depend on the UK single market and presumably the provisions of the Internal Market Act (IMA), which the parties in Scotland's devolved parliament have already objected to. Any attempt to abrogate the IMA would surely be met with the threat of tariffs, which would also be keeping Scotland out of European markets: reorientation towards the single market might be economically challenging to certain sectors in the face of British tariffs, but Ireland has shown it is more than possible, and – unlike Brexit – it offers a trajectory of realignment and economic growth. By contrast, an independent Scotland outside the EU would not be economically independent or have the capacity to be so, and membership solely of the EEA would bring nearly all the disruption attendant on independence as a European state with only some of the benefits.[38]

However, while this may be an obvious analysis, it is one which is at odds with the bulk of electoral support for a Scottish state. The broadest support for an independent Scotland comes from those who see it as combining a modernized version of the 1945–79 British social and welfare compact with the creation of a state freed from the lumber of chauvinist and ceremonial exceptionalism that marks out Great Britain more clearly with every passing year, and which was crystallized in the referendum of 2016. This position, with its reliance on a degree of nostalgia for the postwar social democrat consensus (now identified more in 'Scottish' national than in British class terms) and a distaste for the increasingly shrill voice of British nationalism, is a key reason in its turn for the key weakness of Scottish nationalism, its relatively impoverished levels of state consent, that is, belief in an independent state which makes its own decisions without undue reference to the internal arrangements of other states. This can be seen in many areas, from the debate over the Scottish currency following independence to the political impossibility (for example) of an independent Scotland instituting fees for practices which are free in England, as the Republic of Ireland does with GP visits. Scottish Government policy can be more generous with public expenditure and taxpayers' money than England, but almost never less so: that is not the approach of a different country so much as it is a one-way demonstration of moral conscience. It can be read as a nationalist version of a Labour unionist position: the UK is valuable because Scotland offers an egalitarian leaven to the English class system and nativist Toryism, so it is the conscience of Britain and should not leave it. This is not an argument for less generous social policies: but any country which compares itself to a neighbouring one with the sole view of outperforming them in 'moral' terms is not really thinking like an embryonic state. The Scottish Government has always (even prior to 2007) had a tendency to differentiate itself from England by making more things free: but is this a rational grounding for the challenging transition to an independent economic policy that follows statehood?

This weakness can be centrally seen with respect to the currency issue. Affection for sterling – a weakening, if historic, currency – among Yes voters was exploited by Better Together in 2014 by the dubious claim that England would 'prevent' Scotland using the pound, while current proposals for an independent currency – the merk? the dolour? the bawbee? – seem naïve in the context of the likely reaction of international financial markets to the dissolution of the UK and the scale of Scotland's initial budget deficit. Moreover, a very substantial part of an independent Scotland's assets would be held in sterling and everything from financial services to cross-border pension schemes would be subject to prolonged squabble and negotiation, not to mention the taxing friction of exchange rates, all of which in its turn would be destabilizing to an embryonic floating currency. The economist Sir John Kay has raised the issues of the prolonged nature of currency transitions, the legacy of claims on cross border assets (for example between the Czech Republic and Slovakia) and the challenge of small countries running an independent monetary policy successfully, while the case of Jersey (where sterling circulates but where the government hardly utilizes financial instruments beyond the printing of banknotes) is surely not a suitable exemplar for an independent Scotland. There is relatively little sign these issues have been thoroughly addressed as part of the consideration of any transition to independence, and rather more that a substantial proportion of the Yes coalition are not interested in hearing the answers.

Attempts to close a Scottish trade deficit in a new currency might well fuel inflation and increase taxes, driving high earners, industry and innovation south of the border. The euro, the obvious solution to Scotland's currency question – which moves away from sterling while preserving stability in the face of exchange rate friction and disruption – is also the least popular answer to it, which tells the interested onlooker something about the levels of public consent for an independent Scotland in Europe as opposed to an idealized Britain recreated north of the Tweed. There is much pro-European sentiment in Scotland, but much less understanding of European economics, governance, integration and policy development. Although the SNP administration supported the euro more robustly in the past, the 2008 financial crisis changed that approach, which itself indicated the 'Britishness' of much Scottish nationalism, as the UK is the only European state where the euro has been widely expected to fail since its introduction. That this idealized 'North Britain' bears some relation to the Attlee–Wilson era in Great Britain can arguably be seen in the extent to which the administration and public sector provision of Scotland remains strongly rooted in the world of officials and organizations who prioritise internal stakeholders and the producer interest, a world born in its present form in the 1930s with the increasing power of the 'permanent official' and consolidated after 1945. The SNP has at present won the argument about who runs the Labour state, but a Labour state it remains, and what political observers from Christopher Harvie to Tom Nairn have identified as a 'restrictive', 'mediocre' and 'secretive bureaucracy', and a 'pickle jar' of limited horizons and experience (in contrast with the widespread European and global experience of earlier elites charted in this book) continues to predominate in many Scottish organizations and institutions, although matters are slowly improving. Much opportunity remains in the development of stronger and more integrated branding in culture, tourism and domestic produce and in the development of a wider set of small and medium-sized enterprise engagement in export markets, which is beginning. Exports are on a rising curve, and Scotland's economy overall is matching the UK average, as it has not done for many years, while in certain areas, such as renewable energy and space, the country is in a highly competitive position internationally.[39]

The historic volatility of the SNP vote – by contrast, for example, with the Irish Party vote in 1885–1918 – provides plenty of evidence for the relatively thin nature of support for an independent state over the last fifty years, though again this may be changing. Many Scots have historically hoped for an intermediate position: a modernized and federal (maybe with some confederalism thrown in) United Kingdom. Many of these have now lost faith in the ability of the UK to change into a modern state, and this is yet another sphere where the Brexit referendum has played out. Contemporary Scotland increasingly echoes Dean Acheson's speech at West Point in December 1962, when he said:

> Britain's attempt to play a separate power role – that is, a role apart from Europe, a role based on a 'special relationship' with the United States, a role based on being the head of a Commonwealth which has no political structure or unity or strength and enjoys a fragile and precarious economic relationship – this role is about played out.[40]

Harold Macmillan responded at the time by objecting that Acheson 'seems wholly to misunderstand the Commonwealth in world affairs', but even sixty years since Enoch Powell (1912–98), Macmillan's Health Minister, saw the Commonwealth as 'a gigantic farce' of 'expensive and delusory souvenirs' of a vanished imperial past, 'a valueless psychological comfort blanket'. Reading Acheson sixty years later, his words seem as prophetic, accurate and ignored as ever.[41]

NEW SCOTS AND SCOTTISH GOVERNANCE

While the godfather of Brexit, Enoch Powell, may have seen the loss of Britain's global role as an opportunity to locate 'at the heart of a vanished empire . . . the sap still rising from her ancient roots, to melt the spring, England herself', this autarkic vision has had little currency in post-imperial Scotland. From its establishment in 1999, the Scottish Executive/Government sought to profile the country abroad for trade and other purposes. Donald Dewar's administration set up effectively the first Scotland House in Brussels, in succession to the Scotland Europa representation introduced by the UK Conservative government in 1992. It was followed by 'an office in the UK Embassy in Washington DC' opened by McLeish's administration in 2001 and one in Beijing under Jack (Lord) McConnell. Further offices followed under the SNP governments in Berlin, Dublin, London, Ottawa and Paris, with new developments in Copenhagen and Warsaw planned at the time of writing. The hubs act as locations for events boosting Scottish trade, culture or research and providing a space for diplomatic exchange. Hub activities also take place in a wider strategic context. In 2019–20, the Scottish Government launched a joint strategic review with the Irish Government, designed to stocktake existing collaborative activity and to plan for future collaborative activity between Ireland and Scotland in the years 2020–25, which was launched by Michael Russell, the Cabinet Secretary for the Constitution, Europe and External Affairs, in October 2020. A smaller scale exercise on Franco-Scottish research links was completed in 2021.[42]

In 2001, the Global Scot programme was set up by the Scottish Executive, 'focused on growing the economy and Scotland's global connections'. Although it was cited as an example of 'best practice' by the World Bank Institute, it arguably never received the support it needed to develop its potential. It did, however, begin to intensify relationships with some of the Scottish diaspora, who often – if not always – tended to retain a positive image of their home country. Already under Labour–Liberal Democrat leadership the vision of Scotland projecting itself as a 'small but vibrant, soft power nation' was evident: as McConnell put it in 2018, 'I wanted to be proactive outside Scotland. I wanted the Scottish Parliament and Scottish

Government to be engaged.' This engagement took shape in other forms besides that of overseas paradiplomacy, itself not simply an expression of nationalism, but also of the importance of Holyrood's responsibility for 'trade and its international components'. Direct international aid in engagement with Malawi, and later with other African and Asian countries (the current International Development Fund is £10 million annually) was important to the McConnell administration, as was a recognition that Scotland needed immigration: Scottish population growth, which had lagged England's since 1800, had now stagnated altogether. While persuading some of the diaspora home permanently or – via Homecoming 2009 – temporarily was part of the agenda of encouraging immigration, a stronger element came through McConnell's Fresh Talent initiative, launched in 2004, which enabled overseas students to work in Scotland for an initial two years after graduation. As this was a power reserved to the British Government, it required McConnell's Labour-led administration in Scotland to reach agreement with the UK Home Office. After the SNP came to power in 2007, UK immigration rules changed, and the Fresh Talent scheme did not survive. Nonetheless, the Scottish Government continued to prioritize immigration as a benefit to the national economy, and it formed part of the independence case in 2014.[43]

The positive language surrounding immigration in Scotland to an extent reflects social attitudes. In 2015, 40 per cent of Scots thought immigration improved the country, and such antipathy as there was to the new wave of immigrants from eastern Europe was often confined to the young and those on lower incomes. Scots opposition to immigration was substantially lower than south of the border, and there tended to be a net positive view of immigrants among those expressing an opinion, while Scots were only just over two-thirds as likely as those in England to view cultural conflict between Islam and western society as a serious issue. Nor was immigration to Scottish society itself a recent phenomenon: Scottish society had been diversifying since the 1960s and 1970s, though some groups, such as West Indians, remained significantly under-represented in terms of the UK average. In 1955, 'A group of young Pakistanis founded the Pakistan Social and Cultural Society in Glasgow', the first Sikh Gurdwara opened in Edinburgh in 1958, and by 2011 there were 82,000 Scots of South Asian origin and almost 34,000 Chinese born in Scotland, some 40 per cent of these being students. There is a strong concentration of so-called BAME communities (all individual people of course, no matter how convenient collective labels may be to policy) in Glasgow, with Pollokshields as a whole having by far the highest concentration – mainly South Asian – in Scotland, and other parts of the south of the city home to the majority of Scotland's Roma and Jewish populations. For their part, immigrant communities on the whole, though not universally, have found Scotland a good place to live in, and Scottish Muslims tended to be more pro-Scottish than was the case with parallel dual identities south of the Border. In Scotland, the community of Pakistani origin identifies as Scots (31 per cent) or mixed (Pakistani/British Scottish, 56 per cent) far more often than they identify as Pakistani (13 per cent), and is at least as likely to support Scottish independence as are the general population. Of residents of Scotland born outside the UK, 43 per cent identified as more Scottish than British, and a further 25 per cent as equally Scottish and British. In fact, although those born outside the UK were less likely to support independence (often at that time on EU membership concerns) than the Scots-born in 2014, they were much more likely to support it than those born in the UK outside Scotland. Almost two-fifths of those born overseas intended to vote SNP, and almost as many (48 per cent) as Scots (51 per cent) thought Scotland was materially disadvantaged by the Union. There is also strong evidence of engagement with Scottish culture. Many individual acts of racism and hate notwithstanding, there is significant evidence for historian Enda Delaney's conclusion that in Scotland, 'There is no doubt that immigration has not become a political issue as in other countries and that immigrants themselves say that they have experienced relatively little hostility or racial prejudice.' Much may hang on that 'relatively': still it is something as is, in a related context, the conclusion that 'The relative absence of popular prejudice towards the Jewish population remains a defining feature of Scotland's past that differentiates it from other parts of the UK.' In the first half of 2021, there were 1,300 anti-Semitic incidents recorded across the UK, of which 22 were in Scotland.[44]

There are of course other tensions here besides internal ones. In particular, the extent to which adaptation to Britain and Britishness as a recognized international – and hence multicultural – identity has been important to minorities coming to the UK from Commonwealth countries has often been at odds with the developing picture of multiculturalism in Scotland. As noted in Chapter 6, the representation of 'black Britons' as part of a new national, rather than an old international, community dates back to the Festival of Britain in 1951, and the very notion of 'black Britain' is, as Joseph Jackson argues, a key part of 'the refashioning of the Union state-nation'. In this context, there is a continuing tension between the use of 'black British literature' to promote the new post-imperial version of 'British state nationalism' and the idea of the Black or Asian Scot as a 'new Scot', often with a very different political outlook on the nature of that state. It is thus an intriguing feature of modern Scotland across the board that groups who settle there from a non-UK ethno-cultural background are much more likely to adapt to the country's political culture than those who settle there from England or Wales.[45]

THE WORLD'S SCOTLAND

Scotland itself has been gradually moving from what Carol Craig identified in 2003 as a crisis of confidence to a much more inclusive and positive sense of self in recent years, though national backbiting, provincialism and self-hatred are by no means extinct, and have indeed received recent reinforcement from the tribalism which is the counterpart of populism, and which is increasingly prevalent throughout Europe, as the political adoption of simple solutions for complex problems finds its natural expression in demonizing those whose 'fault' everything is, be they migrants, bankers or governments.[46] Nonetheless, the trajectory in Scotland has been on the whole a positive one, and democracy in the country has not succumbed to populist nostrums, even if some of its supporters have. As this process of regaining self-confidence has gradually intensified, it has been accompanied by a greater awareness, though still not one which is widely spread, thanks in part to its absence from mass media, of the country's history and international links. Sir Tom Devine's *History of the Scottish Nation 1700–2000*

(1999) briefly outsold J.K. Rowling at the height of the Harry Potter craze, so avid are the appetites of many Scots to be educated in a history which most of them never encountered in school, though that situation is improving. It nonetheless remains the case that there is an imperfect under-standing of the position Scotland occupies in the eyes of the world, one not always best served by Scottish commentators who have sometimes had a tendency to scorn the popular and inevitably clichéd portrayals of Scottishness evident in both the Scottish diaspora and in the way in which Scotland is broadly seen and celebrated internationally. The consumption of a country's history is inevitably accompanied – both internally and externally – with tasty side orders of simplification, stereotyping, cliché, mythology and inven-tion. These are central to its marketing to internal and external audiences. It is the job of the historian both to hold them to account and to understand the role their appeal plays in the brand image of the country concerned else-where in the world: once again, as indicated in the Introduction, national histories are always improved by understanding their relational qualities and inner dynamic rather than through the crude jingo of exceptionalism by which *we* disguises its *me*.

In pursuit of a better understanding of how Scotland is regarded, the Scottish Government began to commission an annual report on the coun-try's national brand recognition via the Anholt-GfK Roper (now Anholt Ipsos) Nation Brands Index of fifty countries carried out annually since 2008. Scotland's position in the Anholt–GfK Roper measure tends to come in at around 15th to 17th, a position of relative strength underpinned by a very strong set of primarily cultural images. It is particularly noteworthy that much of the image of Scotland abroad is reflective of a national reputation which was created in the period from 1740–1860. This provides underpin-ning strengths, but also a number of limitations.

The Index measures perceptions in seven areas: Exports, Governance, Culture, People, Tourism, Immigration and Investment. Scotland ranks highly for Governance (it was 13th in 2020) with particular subsidiary strengths in trustworthiness and reliability and often in peace and security, arising from a strong belief in the country's fairmindedness, humanitarian values and devel-oped justice system. This ranking may also reflect Scotland's engagement with

NGOs and its 'soft power' interventions elsewhere in the world, as well as its development of regional policies such as the 2019 Arctic Policy Framework. There is also a high ranking (12th in 2020) for Tourism, but the country's innovation in science and technology is normally ranked outside the top twenty globally, despite a history of colossal achievement and the current reality of Scotland being the second or third most highly cited jurisdiction in the world per capita. There is thus poor understanding internationally of Scotland's significance in modernity and technology (see plate 29).

In general terms, Scotland's rankings reflect its international visibility, which was in 2018 highest in the United States, the Commonwealth, Russia, Poland and East Asia, and lowest in its erstwhile ally France, where only 43 per cent recognize Scotland as being possessed of a distinct national culture. This culture is seen by those who think they recognize it as being old-fashioned in its social and industrial organization, rural, humanitarian and Romantic. Agriculture, food and crafts all gain high recognition within the perception of Scottish culture, while museums, music and sports are also all seen as important. Ranked in 15th place for the 'people' category, Scots are seen as fascinating, hard-working, exciting, honest, educational, skilful and developing: all very nineteenth-century stereotypes, while the country was ranked 7th in the world for national beauty, in keeping with its Romantic appeal; in more modern terms, it was ranked 10th for environmental protection. The typical Scot, therefore, seems to be someone who is smart, works hard on the farm to produce good food, before attending a fun ceilidh in the evening and is out on the mountains before visiting a museum or castle at the weekend. In 2019, the British Council also produced a report on Scotland's soft power, which echoed the Anholt–GfK Roper survey in some areas, while contradicting it in others – possibly partly as a result of the very different way the two surveys were framed. However, Scotland is not assessed by either as a place of scientific innovation but as more of a historic brand. In recent years, while the overall rating of the country has tended to decline slightly, evidence of its increasing international profile is visible in rising awareness of Scotland's national brand in China and India, as well as – politics notwithstanding – the rest of the UK. Familiarity with Scotland rose from 61 per cent to 67 per cent between 2018 and 2020, while favourability towards the country also increased internationally – and among Scots. Interestingly, despite a relatively low ranking of 22nd for exports, business people tended to rank Scotland higher than any other group. Nonetheless, the national brand remains primarily cultural and historic, rather than scientific and progressive.[47]

There are other indicators of this historic inheritance of the Scottish brand. One of these is translation. Scotland prides itself on its intellectual influence across the world. As of 2005, Adam Smith had been translated 262 times and David Hume on 461 occasions. But these figures are dwarfed by the writers and memorialists of the Romantic Scotland addressed in Chapter 4: Burns with 3,100 translations, Scott with 2,900 and Stevenson with 3,500. This gives Scottish literature a global reach which is often unsuspected at home. However, the global influence of these writers once again reinforces the more traditional elements of the Scottish brand, as it was distributed throughout the world through Burns, Caledonian and St Andrew's Societies. These societies remain globally strong today, with a geographical reach which includes the presence of such societies in Bermuda, China, Ghana, Indonesia, Japan, Kenya, Nigeria, Peru, Saudi Arabia, South Korea, South Sudan, Tanzania, Uganda and many more. Burns Suppers are held in over a hundred countries worldwide, and have in recent years taken place in Antarctica, Svalbard, Kilimanjaro and other exceptional locations. Burns is presented in a vast range of guises, from hipster to Che Guavara, while his flexibility as a writer of universal sentiment is reflected in the number of hybrid or fusion Burns Suppers that take place, such as the Yak and Yeti Burns Night in Nepal or Gung Haggis Fat Choi in Vancouver, Toronto, California and elsewhere. The 'primary marketing image' of the Gung Haggis phenomenon is 'a kilted Scottish piper wearing a large Chinese lion mask': the event itself has become a brand (see plate 30).[48] More recently, Scotland's location as a haven of international memory for Romantic and historic tradition extends to Scottish Gaelic, which is now taught in Canada, the Czech Republic, Germany, Sweden and the United States, among other countries. Since adding Gaelic to its repertoire, the online language learning facility Duolingo has seen a community of some 600,000 learners develop, one-third of them from the United States. In 2021, the search engine Firefox introduced a Scots language browser.[49]

32. Khartoum Caledonian Society Burns Supper.

TARTAN REBORN

If Scottish politics rarely finds its way outside Scotland except in the generally rather Romanticized attitudes towards the country's history and future, one of the interesting – if oblique – exceptions to this has been in the route to the revival of tartan since the 1970s. This revival was first seen outside Scotland at scale in the stage performances of Noddy Holder and Slade, Rod Stewart and the Bay City Rollers in that decade (although Bill Haley and His Comets had introduced tartan to pop in the 1950s). Following the trial of the 'Tartan Army' extremist nationalists in 1975–76 and alongside the increasing adoption of tartan by the Scottish supporters of 'Ally's Army' in Scotland's ill-fated football World Cup adventure in Argentina in 1978 ('Ally's' in reference to the manager, Alistair MacLeod (1931–2004)), the singer Andy Cameron (b.1940) released a song, 'Ally's Tartan Army' (1977), which adopted the tune of an Irish rebel song ('God Save Ireland', commemorating three Fenian activists hanged in Manchester in 1867) in its chorus. While 'Ally' disappeared from the scene, the term 'Tartan Army' endured as a description of Scottish football supporters, whose tartan outfits tended to get more extreme as the years progressed, not least to mark them out from England supporters, increasingly seen as badly behaved abroad from the Heysel disaster of 1985 onwards. Ironically perhaps, the Tartan Army's international peaceableness was sometimes celebrated as latent masculine aggression in the Scottish press, as the *Daily Record* did in 2009 in contrasting them with 'the chinless wonders of the All England Tennis and Croquet Club . . . crying into their Pimms'.[50]

Tartan's restricted international use as a sign of aristocratic heritage, for example as practised by the Duke of Windsor (Edward VIII, 1895–1972) on the Riviera, where he played the bagpipes and sweltered in 'the Balmoral tartan with dagger and jabot', became hugely changed in a short space of time. Contemporaneously with its use in pop and football came its adoption by punk. Vivienne Westwood's (b.1941) repurposing of tartan's clichéd association with the military, the professions, the traditionalist diaspora and nationalist or unionist eccentrics into a statement of radical chic associated with her counterculturalism in the 1970s and 80s (even her shop assistants at Seditionaries were uniformed in it at one point) marked a major shift back into the international mainstream for the Scottish cloth, which Westwood incorporated as a unitary symbol of rebellion, masquerade and historical collage. Through punk, tartan made 'anarchy, alienation and indeed sedition wearable', and this return to its eighteenth-century status as a sartorial disruptor, a rebel cloth, began to be marked in Scotland also. Tartan was no longer centrally a symbol of eccentricity, but had once again begun to develop, most obviously at weddings, but also elsewhere, into a form of social bond, a collective statement of self. New Scots were included in such statements: the Sikh tartan dates from 1999 (based on one used earlier in the British Army), the 'Chinese Scottish' and 'Polish' tartans appeared in 2006 and the Spirit of Pakistan in 2013. From being a badge of family and bloodline for almost two centuries, tartan had returned to its early modern roots as a textile of group loyalty and political and geographical association.

International representations of Scotland combined this sense of national belonging with the counter-cultural revival of the tartan as a rebel cloth pioneered by Westwood. As the fashion historian Jonathan Faiers remarks, '*Braveheart*'s tartans could be seen as a response to the so-called "grunge" look of the early 1990s.' Early references to Royal Stuart in Westwood's 1980s designs had become much more diverse, variegated and modern by the following decade, when a further transformative envisioning of tartan occurred in Alexander McQueen's (1969–2010) *Highland Rape* collection of 1995–96, which was followed by his *Widows of Culloden* (2006–07) and other references to Scottish experience: collections which expressed, in McQueen's own words 'England's rape of Scotland'. The shrouds, suggestively ripped clothes, and partial revisiting of tartanry in the first full collection were returned to, in greater complexity, in the second. In *Widows of Culloden*, torn eighteenth-century dresses, sporting tweeds with fantastical dead bird hats in ironic homage to Victorian Highlandism, fighter plane and antler hats, black-stained clothing and tartan culottes, all symbolically commented on the destruction, misprision and exploitative reinterpretation of Scotland for a global audience, the occasional appearance of a Sam Browne belt providing a visual hint of Irish Republicanism. Tartan has continued to be a powerful fashion signifier into the twenty-first century: the sale of an alleged plaid of Charles Edward Stuart in 1999 seems to have been a catalyst for referencing it in numerous designs, including a coat by Marc Jacobs for Louis Vuitton in the 2004–05 season. More recently,

Bronson van Wyck's interior designs have shown a marked interest in tartan and saltire décor utilizing Prince Charles's tartan and multiple references to the Victorian use/misuse of tartan excess, revisited with both celebration and mild irony, while the tartan look was once again in for the 2020–21 season, with Dior, Gucci, Westwood and others revisiting this apparently timeless rebel cloth (see plates 31 and 32).[51]

CELEBRATING AND PERFORMING

The Scottish Government has long sought to establish ongoing contact with those of Scottish heritage abroad. The Homecoming event of 2009, revisited in 2014, was a modern reinterpretation of the clan gatherings of the 1950s, and indeed even replicated them in the Clan Gathering march up the Royal Mile on 30 July 2009. More than 300 events took place across Scotland, primarily referencing the 250th birthday of Robert Burns, with additional whisky, golf, minds and innovation, and culture and heritage themes. The promotional video featured a range of Scottish celebrities singing Dougie MacLean's 1977 anthem of loss and hoped for return, *Caledonia,* which had featured in a successful Tennent's Lager advertising campaign in the previous decade. Though there was some – typically Scottish – distaste for the apparent kitchness of some of the events, Homecoming was judged a success, with £54 million generated in Scotland, 95,000 new visitors and '£154 million of positive global media coverage'. In 2010, a 'diaspora engagement plan' was developed in the wake of Homecoming, but success here has been mixed in comparison with the Irish model, following on from the relatively unsophisticated and unsuccessful Scotland Funds initiative of 2005–08.[52]

Famously, there are dozens of Aberdeens, Edinburghs, Hamiltons and other towns and cities named after a Scottish original throughout the world. In 2006, the size of the overall Scottish diaspora was estimated at between 40 and 80 million, but this is a grossly optimal figure, and one of the reasons why this history has sought in general to confine itself to those from Scotland or with a strong association with the country. Many accounts of the exploits of 'Scots' abroad depend on the unexamined premiss that bloodline is more relevant than acculturation. This premiss is worth examining, for its implications are often not very positive: whatever one thinks of nationalism, purely ethnic and genetic definitions of it are almost ubiquitously poisonous when combined with political power. Sentiment can be a product of distance lending enchantment to the view, and, while there were 350,000 Scots born in the United States in 1930, there were fewer than half that number in 1970, while the numbers reporting Scottish or 'Scots-Irish' ancestry remained very strong, with 10.1 million in 1980, 11 million in 1990, 9.2 million in 2000 and 8.7 million in 2010. In 1980, a vanishingly small proportion of this group identified as Scots-Irish, while in 1990 the majority did, and such huge fluctuations may indicate the emergence of the category into more public discourse, as well as the unstable influence of sentiment. The numbers reporting as 'Scottish' have remained more consistent, at 5.4 million in 1990 and 5.5 million in 2010. In other words, the number of Americans reporting Scottish ancestry is approximately the same as the population of Scotland itself. In Canada, almost as many, 4.8 million, claimed Scottish ancestry in the 2016 census, some 14 per cent of the population. In the same year, 2 million Australians claimed Scottish ancestry, far more than the 40,000 of Scots birth or reported ancestry in New Zealand in 2013, itself a major underestimate, which shows how unstable a concept ancestry or heritage can be. It is wise to treat numbers for the Scottish diaspora with care in the absence of any corresponding activity which consistently maintains a Scottish identity furth of Scotland. Scottish clubs and societies in Australia (where there are around a dozen) and New Zealand, in common with those elsewhere, are increasingly for heritage and association Scots rather than first generation immigrants, a process which has been under way for a century. Scots associationalism nonetheless continues to flourish, with dozens of Scots Clubs and 'Highland dance schools'. Occasional historic political gestures also still take place in the contemporary era, such as the replacement of 'Cumberland Street' with 'Culloden Road' on Dunedin street signs, though these – as in the idea of Scottishness traditionally supported by organizations such as the Caledonian Society of Melbourne – remain strongly linked to a Romantic image of Scotland, visible in other cultural practices, such as the dipping of bonnets in the Well of the Dead at Culloden by North American visitors to the site.[53]

North America remains the central location for Scottish diasporic activity, as has been the case for many years, though even here there have been major cycles of change. Scottish newspapers, Caledonian Games and other celebrations dwindled in the United States between the 1920s and 1950s, but, at the latter end of this period, a growing 'interest in heritage and family history' drove re-engagement with Scotland. Long before the Homecoming celebrations of 2009, Dame Flora, Chief of the Name of MacLeod, 'visited America in 1953 and made her famous plea to the diaspora to "Come back to Scotland"'. Although this call went largely unheeded, there was an increase in activity. The American Scottish Foundation was established in 1956 'to champion the relationship between the people of Scotland and the United States' and Scottish Heritage USA (SHUSA) was founded in 1965, with a brief which extended from supporting heritage in Scotland financially to bringing invited speakers on lecture tours. In 1974, the Council of Scottish Clans and Associations (COSCA) was founded as a coalition of groups including the Association of St Andrew's Societies, the American-Scottish Foundation, Caledonian Foundation USA, the Association of Scottish Games and Festivals, SHUSA and later the 'Living Legacy of Scotland', founded to present 'educational displays and productions for public events, for schools, museums and libraries'. *An Comunn Gàidhealach Ameireaganach* (the American Scottish Gaelic Society (ACGA)) was founded in 1980 (albeit membership is in the low hundreds), and there is also a Scottish Gaelic Foundation of the USA as well as at least one Canadian society among over 300 or so North American societies. The Association of Scottish Games and Festivals was founded in 1981, as was the Scottish American Military Society. Over 150 Highland dancing schools were founded in the US with nearly 300 in Canada by 2005, when there were also 150 Scottish clan and family associations in the United States.[54]

Pipe bands and especially Highland Games have been central to the performativity of Scottishness in North America, with over 200 active clan societies and 125 pipe bands reported in the last decade of the twentieth century. While there were only some 75 Highland Games in the US in the 1980s, by 2000 there were 205, with only Delaware, North Dakota and Wyoming without one among the continental states. These sometimes took place alongside Celtic Festivals, which can either be Scottish, Irish or generic in character. Across the United States, Celtic Festivals USA lists over 100 Scottish festivals, 80 Irish and almost 60 mixed. The peaks are in California (13 festivals, 7 Scottish), Colorado (10, 3 Scottish), Florida (14, 5 Scottish), New York (17 festivals, 3 Scottish), North Carolina (10, of which 8 are Scottish) and Pennsylvania (13, of which 5 are Scottish). Peculiarities include the Aztec Highland Games in New Mexico, the Covenanter Scottish Festival and Highland Games in Pennsylvania and, in a marginal tribute to other Celticisms, the Welsh festival in Idaho and its Cornish equivalent in Wisconsin.[55]

Visual renditions of Scottish performativity reach across ethnic communities in North America, for example through the use of tartan by some Québécois, while other 'Scottish' American traditions, such as the 'kirking of the Tartan' – first developed from a 1943 sermon by Dr Peter Marshall at New York Avenue Presbyterian Church in Washington DC – inspired a communal practice in the United States which reinforced an articulation with the memorialisation of ethnic roots at a time of global crisis. Tartan has remained important. The development of 6 April as Tartan Day (first ratified in Nova Scotia in 1987, followed by Ontario, Saskatchewan and New Brunswick in the early 1990s, then Tennessee (1996) and North Carolina (1997)) was intended as an inclusive celebration of Scottish ancestry and its contribution to North America. In 1998, Senator Trent Lott (b.1941), Senator for Mississipi 1989–2007, introduced US Senate Resolution 155, which formally entered Tartan Day in the US calendar on 6 April, the date (or rather the day, since the Julian calendar in use in 1320 has long been replaced by its Gregorian equivalent) of the Declaration of Arbroath. Senator Lott's text ran as follows:

> Whereas April 6 has a special significance for all Americans, and especially those Americans of Scottish descent, because the Declaration of Arbroath, the Scottish Declaration of Independence, was signed on April 6, 1320 and the American Declaration of Independence was modelled on that inspirational document;

Whereas this resolution honors the major role that Scottish Americans played in the founding of this Nation, such as the fact that almost half of the signers of the Declaration of Independence were of Scottish descent, the Governors in 9 of the original 13 States were of Scottish ancestry, Scottish Americans successfully helped shape this country in its formative years and guide this Nation through its most troubled times;

Whereas this resolution recognizes the monumental achievements and invaluable contributions made by Scottish Americans that have led to America's pre-eminence in the fields of science, technology, medicine, government, politics, economics, architecture, literature, media, and visual and performing arts;

Whereas this resolution commends the more than 200 organizations throughout the United States that honor Scottish heritage, tradition, and culture, representing the hundreds of thousands of Americans of Scottish descent, residing in every State, who already have made the observance of Tartan Day on April 6 a success;

Whereas these numerous individuals, clans, societies, clubs, and fraternal organizations do not let the great contributions of the Scottish people go unnoticed:

Now, therefore, be it Resolved, That the Senate designates April 6 of each year as 'National Tartan Day'.[56]

The result of this Resolution has been a themed Scotland Week (the name sought by the Scottish Government) in New York, which has attracted mixed reviews in Scotland that reflect a continuing distaste for nostalgic flummery among elements in the country's intelligentsia, despite the increasing popularity of tartan in Scotland itself. Performativity is very marked in these celebrations, as in the element of nineteenth century pageantry in the New York Tartan Day Parade or in the 'Scottish Village' opened by actor Alan Cumming at Grand Central Station in 2005–07, which carried echoes of the imperial localism of *An Clachan* from Empire exhibitions gone by.[57]

For a long time, American Scottish societies were seen as orthogonal to today's Scotland, and unrealistically nostalgic and detached from the realities of the country as it now is: this was most seriously the case in the South, where a large minority of Americans identifying as of Scottish ancestry or heritage live. The right-wing nature of US society in these states and the undoubted investment in Scottishness as a form of 'respectable' white cultural identity has led over the last thirty years to a number of journalists making 'a genre out of articles that simplistically link the Scottish heritage movement in the United States to a white supremacist conspiracy': this is, though not entirely without foundation as this book has indicated, a reductive and negative frame in which to view the complex nature of diasporic relationships. Canadian Scottish societies (CASSOC, Clans and Scottish Societies of Canada) and activities tend to be articulated with today's Scotland, not least on the music scene. The Scottish Society of Ottawa promotes Dougie Maclean's *Caledonia* on the landing page of its website and also promotes the dot.scot domain name. Canadian Scottishness has also received extensive political support, not least from Angus MacDonald, premier of Nova Scotia 1933–54, who while promoting statues of Burns and Scott, and a 'lone sheiling' on Cape Breton Island opened by Dame Flora Macleod, also introduced Glasgow Corporation lamp-posts to the province. Of late, however, American Scottish societies, such as the St Andrew's Society of San Francisco, have been engaging far more closely with contemporary Scotland and the central questions of its future economic and cultural development. The increasing connectivity with the diaspora being developed through the Scottish Government's hubs appears to have played a role here.[58]

Nostalgic and romanticized perceptions of Scotland and practices relating to it among those identifying with Scottish heritage abroad are part of a division which grew up between domestic Scottish society in the aftermath of the Second World War, when the lurid and nostalgic antics of rich Scots and those of Scottish heritage abroad, which might have been welcomed by the Scots-born themselves a few decades earlier, now seemed increasingly remote from a country impacted by imperial decline and metropolitan centralism. The costumed theatricality of Scots abroad was very much part of the social calendar in 1900, and Harry Lauder was popular in Scotland and abroad in 1925. But fifty years later there was a gulf, as post-imperial Scotland became increasingly dissociated from a past which England still embraced. It was no longer Scotland's world, but the world's Scotland.

Although this situation began to change with a renewed emphasis on theatricality in Scotland (in 1975 tartan was rare at weddings, twenty years later it was all but mandatory), a relationship with the diaspora – in contrast to the situation in Ireland a century ago – has proved difficult to develop, both because of the introspection and indeed exceptionalism of Scottish politics, and also due to the diaspora's complex and differentiated hybrid identities which need to be engaged with rather than presumed upon. Research carried out in the 1990s indicated that North Americans of Scottish heritage usually remember their families as having left Scotland for reasons of economic betterment even if historically they were cleared off the land, while those of Irish heritage recollect displacement and oppression even if their ancestors left for economic betterment. Victimhood, which tends towards unifying the political views of a diaspora, is not often found in the Scottish diaspora or in those who adhere to it, and indeed there is sometimes a degree of self-congratulation to the extent that it is not unknown for American Scots to be of the view that all the most able Scots have already left the country, however much they may invoke it in performative memory. This view is not of course incompatible with the general view of the Scotland brand as lacking in technology and innovation. For many, Scotland is what it used to be, not what it has become. Nonetheless, a fascination with the place remains, with Scottish societies and especially pipe band culture found far outside the former Dominions, while almost two dozen Bollywood films 'have used Scottish locations' in recent years.[59]

One of the most intriguing examples of Scottish performativity which is largely separate from that of the context of diaspora is that located in Continental Europe. As the commentator David Hesse notes, 'Playing Scotsmen is an international phenomenon', and although there is no Scottish diaspora or heritage community in Europe to speak of (with the exception of very small groups such as the inhabitants of one Italian town who claim to be the descendants of sixteenth-century Scottish *condottieri*), Europe is home to a wide range of celebratory Scottish activity, from the Scottish Festival at Salzburg to the Alba Festival in Grasse. The *Schotse Beurs* (Scots Fair) in Ghent, in common with other Scots Festivals, attracts over 10,000 visitors a year, and Scotfest in Tilburg twice that (and 35,000 visitors in 2010), making it the largest of its kind in Europe. In 2010 there were over 130 Highland Gatherings (overwhelmingly concentrated in Austria, Germany and the Low Countries) and some 230 drum and pipe bands in Continental Europe. All the pipe bands seem to date from after the foundation of the Scottish (later Royal Scottish) Pipe Band Association in Glasgow in 1930, and bagpipe manufacture is important business, with 'the Pakistani town of Sialkot' being 'one of the world's top manufacturers'. 'Highland Cathedral', for some a candidate for a future Scottish national anthem, was originally 'composed by two Germans . . . for a Highland Games held in Germany in 1982', while Highland Games in France can sometimes involve bizarre fusion events, such as the tossing of a giant champagne cork. In South Tyrol, the Games can be seen as representing the traditional symbolism of the mountaineer as friend to liberty, while European Scottish pipe bands also serve as a focal point for the revival of local folk and popular music traditions. Scottish shops, restaurants – for example in Bratislava – and tourist mementoes can be found throughout central Europe. More recent kinds of 'Games' can be seen also: for example Pontremoli and Apicana in Tuscany field 'Celtic' and 'Rangers' sides in the Italian amateur leagues. Nor are these a matter of names only: 'Celtic', for example, is seen as 'a tradition of starting small and achieving bigger things with the right ambition', a set of values which are perceived as 'Scottish'.[60] Scottish Country Dancing is also widespread, with some sixty Scottish dance societies, including the Royal Scottish Country Dance societies of Paris and Lyon, the Munich Caledonians, the Budapest Scottish Dance Club and the Schiehallion Dance School of St Petersburg. In the Netherlands, the Amsterdam Scottish Country Dance Group and the Den Haag Clansmen meet weekly, while Germany is the European head-quarters of Scottish dancing, with some twenty societies.[61]

The Scottishness promoted by the festivals and pipe bands, and to an extent the other societies, is one which is strongly male and draws on the tradition of martial valour outlined in Chapter 3: the 'Scots of Europe' are indeed in general 'Scotsmen from the past', (white) (male) representatives of autoch-thonous chivalry, valour and nation formation. Whether or not European celebrations of Scottishness are part of a 'white ethnic revival' as Hesse suggests (and they hardly partake of the politics associated with such revivals in

North America), the image of Scotland presented is Romantic and historic. Historical re-enactment groups such as Montgomerie's Highlanders from the Czech Republic underline this association with Romantic military Scotland. In France, the Alliance France-Ecosse (1995) 'was founded . . . to produce an inventory of all the Scottish sites of memory in France', while the Scots Heritage Club of the Netherlands undertakes tasks such as the upkeep of Lord George Murray's grave: Murray was a Jacobite Lieutenant General in 1745. Some of the celebrations hark even further back: the Fêtes Franco-Ecossaises at Aubigny-sur-Nere (1990) are a modern promotional tool for the town which bring thousands every year in commemoration of John Stewart of Darnley (c.1380–1429), who 'prepared the way' for St Jeanne d'Arc at Orléans and fell trying to liberate the city from English rule. Stewart's descendants lived in Aubigny until the seventeenth century, and an Aubigny tartan was registered with the Scottish Tartans Authority after it was established in 1996.[62]

CONCLUSION

Scotland is one of the oldest nations in Europe. Its territory is fundamentally unchanged since the fifteenth century, and its southern border with England has barely altered – with the exception of Berwick and a few square kilometres of 'debatable' land – since 1237. By contrast, the states of the European Union often date from the nineteenth and twentieth centuries (the Baltic States, Belgium, Bulgaria, Croatia, Cyprus, the Czech Republic, Finland, Germany, Greece, Ireland, Italy, Luxembourg, Malta, Poland (in its current form), Romania, Slovakia, Slovenia); or have seen major changes to their borders in this period (Austria, Denmark, France, Hungary). Indeed, only Portugal and Sweden in the entire European Union have maintained anything resembling Scotland's duration of territorial integrity, though the Netherlands and Spain are closer to it than most. Even the state of which Scotland is an essential component – the 'United Kingdoms' established by the 1707 Union, now the 'United Kingdom' (the 'United States' changed from plural to singular in a similar way) – has seen a major change to its borders through the establishment of the Irish Free State (1922) and then Republic (1949). In this kind of context, Scotland's survival as a national entity is itself worthy of comment: the majority of European states in being when this history begins have not survived, and most of them have no remaining institutions, jurisdictions or national identity, all of which are central to the Scotland of the last few centuries. Huge movements of population have taken place across Europe, not least in the mass displacement of ethno-cultural Germans from the former lands of imperial Germany and Austria after 1945. By contrast, though there are many new Scots, Scottish families with Scottish roots in Scotland going back generations or centuries remain typical.[1]

In such a situation, it may appear surprising to some that Scottish nationality is not universally acknowledged, but while its visibility has become very much more marked in recent years, it is also widely ignored or unknown. This is due to at least three reasons. First, the way history is remembered frames our experience and the composite monarchy model – a very important part of a United Kingdom with separate institutions and jurisdictions – is now marginal in global statehood, having been central, in Europe at least, when this book began. In the years of an imperial Parliament with Britishness as an international and not simply a national identity, aspects of the old composite model survived better than they were to do in more recent generations. Chapter 7 charted the marginalization of Scotland within the promotion of a unitary 'British' home identity from the 1940s on, but this is not the only issue. Other states have systems of governance which find it easier to accommodate a centralized and unitary outlook than the more accurate alternative: for example France, where the long tradition of a single unified Republic frames an understanding which tends to reflect itself in viewing other states. Despite their long shared histories, the existence of a distinctive Scottish national culture is least understood in France as a consequence of the nature of France itself, although there are many individual advocates of Scotland there. In a different context, Germany, while understanding composite states better through the prism of its own history, often sees Scotland as a type of constituent federal state like its own, as was evident in the visit of the then Bavarian Minister of Education, Ludwig Spaenle, which I helped to host at Glasgow in 2012. States with a surviving composite monarchy model they do not always wish to acknowledge – such as Spain – are suspicious of Scottish nationality for other reasons which also arise from the framing of national selfhood.

Secondly, despite the relatively recent formation of the vast majority of the states of the European Union (and indeed of the world), there is – as the historian Susan Reynolds pointed out many years ago – a strange tendency to treat countries which exist now as states as if they have always existed, and to treat countries without states as potentially or actually illegitimate entities. There are practical reasons for doing this of course in the interests of political stability, but this viewpoint extends far beyond the practical into the ideological and quasi-religious. A form of political Darwinism seems to operate, in which states which no longer exist as states were always destined to dissolution and those existing now were always the only authentic states destined to exist. This is related to the intensely national framing of history mentioned in the Introduction: historians of states formed within living memory can write 'national' histories of them as if they had always existed, while changing borders can lead to exclusions. The Irish Question may have loomed large in late Victorian England, but it is a much smaller part of most of today's histories of the United Kingdom in that era because Ireland left that union. It thus suits many Irish historians to minimize the Britishness of their state, and it suits many British ones too. Meanwhile, theorists of nationalism often posit nationalism as the quality of agitating for changing borders, not of the use of force to maintain them. This outlook – aligned as it often is with policy – can have serious consequences. The European Union arguably failed to understand in 1991 that the collapse of Yugoslavia (originally founded as the continent's most recent composite monarchy less than a lifetime before) was a sign of the unsustainability of the state in the face of competing nationalisms, and the residual Yugoslav government in Belgrade (arguably in fact a Serbian nationalist government, covertly supporting ethno-cultural war) was initially granted too much credence because Yugoslavia was perceived as the 'real' country in an unexamined and apparently uncritical way. Since the Austrian government had identified Serbian deniable special operations as a key source of the threat posed by that state in 1914, it is almost incredible that in the same century major politicians treated similar activities as if they were designed to preserve the 'real' state of Yugoslavia rather than to promote a narrower agenda, but those who do not know history are indeed condemned to repeat it.[2]

This brings us to the third reason for the relative lack of understanding of Scottish nationality: our modern and partial view of the nature of sovereignty as defined by the Westphalian peace of 1648, the place where this book began. Just as Henry Kissinger in Chapter 1 characterizes the Westphalian settlement as a 'winner takes all' formula fitted for big states, power blocs and exclusive notions of sovereignty, so President Woodrow Wilson's view of nationality in the lands of Austria–Hungary and the German Empire in

1918–20 provided in its simplistic formulae at least some of the infrastructure for the Second World War and a lifetime of population expulsion and ethnic cleansing. It is hard to see how the composite monarchy of the Habsburgs – had it survived – could have delivered more human suffering in aggregate than its successors did, and senior Austrian administrators undoubtedly understood the minorities of the Empire better than Wilson and the Allies. The last generations of imperial Austria's increasingly cosmopolitan society provided some of the greatest artists and thinkers of the twentieth century: Sigmund Freud (1856–1939), two of whose sons fought for imperial Austria in 1914–18, F.A. Hayek (1899–1992) of the imperial Austrian artillery, the German-speaking Bohemian (and now adopted Czech) Franz Kafka (1883–1924), who was barred from joining the Austrian forces on medical grounds, Gustav Klimt (1862–1918) and Ludwig Wittgenstein (1889–1951), an officer and decorated imperial war hero in the First World War. Many of these people became refugees in the political climate that developed after the end of the Monarchy.[3]

Like the Holy Roman Empire at the start of this history, the composite monarchy of the last Habsburgs has not fared well in the historical memory of the states who defeated or replaced it, but whatever its qualities and flaws it and other composite monarchies were more attuned to the limited and shared sovereignty of the Westphalian settlement than those who claim that sovereignty is indivisible and limitless and who will, as a consequence, tend to be disappointed with the outcomes of political decisions based – like Brexit – on this assumption. By contrast, weak states such as Liechtenstein (where the Swiss franc circulates and the authorities have a responsibility to implement Swiss monetary policy), Montenegro (with a currency pegged to the euro) or Bosnia–Herzegovina (where the euro circulates) compromise in major areas of sovereignty, while those with even less sovereignty (Catalunya, Flanders, Québec) often champion supranational institutions and currency unions as part of their claims to sovereignty. The power of the euro comes from a version of a composite settlement which benefits even smaller states more than their own floating currency might, as Greece's determination to remain in the euro in 2010–12 demonstrated. Shared sovereignty is not only, to some extent or another, the manifest norm of international organizations and trading blocs: it is the aspiration of some while its very existence is denied by others. Its nature and role in the development of the Scottish governance, institutions and networks over the last four centuries have been central to this book. And it has been a concern of Scottish thinkers, writers and politicians for even longer than this: from Duns Scotus and Baldred Bisset to John Mair, George Buchanan and Andrew Fletcher and on to the debates round constitutions from the United States to the Pitcairn Islands and more recently the European constitution, Scots have been centrally involved in determining questions of sovereignty and governance, as this history has shown. This tradition almost certainly has its roots in the nature of the Scottish experience itself, which has long had a vested interest in questions of sovereignty and its limits. In an interdependent world, the questions it raises and the opportunities Scotland and Scots have enjoyed in the context of their answers alike deserve our attention.[4]

In this context, where next for Scotland? For many years – and even in the context of the 2014 Referendum – 'the option of devolving more powers to the Scottish Parliament . . . continued to be the most popular one' among the Scottish electorate, who favoured the universal or near universal control of domestic affairs over separate statehood: a classic composite position, but one very much at odds with the British polity and its Parliament's understanding of its own history and therefore ultimately politically irrelevant. This support for a federalist settlement verging at times into confederalism – always at risk of being viewed through a British lens as Scottish exceptionalism – has become increasingly marginal in the polarization of Scottish politics since 2014 and still more given the different but related polarization of Brexit. It retains some support, however, especially among those who have not thought through the constitutional implications of leaving the European Union in terms of a commitment at UK level to the indivisibility of sovereignty in governance, legislation and sentiment. Emotions run high, and support for 'indyref 2' or 'our precious Union' is increasingly expressed in forms as passionate as they are limited. On the part of the Scottish Government, the transition to independence is as yet undeveloped as a concept, as is a dataset of comparative evidence and the issue of the need for budgetary alignment with the EU. On one level this is easy to understand because so many of the supporters of independence take an overly rosy view of the initial financial capacity of a Scottish state, when even larger countries have restricted ability to run an independent monetary policy and currency transitions can take decades. For their part, the advocates of Union have little to offer beyond nostalgia and negativity; whereas their predecessors were frequently Scottish patriots, today the denigration of Scotland and everything Scottish is the default language of those who stress – but thus fail to demonstrate – its importance to the United Kingdom.[5]

For its part, in opposing Scottish independence the United Kingdom Government has sought to weaponize one of the statements made in the 2014 referendum – that it was a once in a generation opportunity – by claiming that this amounted to a formal promise not to seek to hold another referendum for a long time. Moreover, the 2012 Edinburgh Agreement was only reached because the British Government thought the Yes option would lose heavily. There would be no such optimism this time, with high figures for Yes and up to 75 per cent of those domiciled in Scotland indicating they would vote Yes if Scotland would gain economically. This is itself an interesting paradox: there is a desire for Scotland to grow economically, but a lack of will to support policies that might help it do so, a potential contradiction usually elided by insistence that Scotland's disproportionate wealth is siphoned off by the British Government. This contestation – and its mirror image, the view that British Government expenditure in Scotland is funded by non-Scottish taxpayers and is in effect a gift to an ungrateful nation – are both highly partial. In support of the latter argument, the current Conservative government is bringing more overt British Government activity and politics into Scotland, with a view to integrating Scotland to a greater degree and weakening the SNP. Maintaining visible central government activity was a key element of Castilian practice in Catalonia: it was not notably successful. But the British Government is probably gambling on the relatively weak and shallow nature of Scottish nationalism historically. This weakness is perhaps borne witness to in the fact that, despite having large majorities of Scottish seats at Westminster since 2015, the SNP have eschewed the kind of parliamentary spoiling tactics pursued by Parnell's Irish Party, carried on in the face of the substantial Unionist majority in the 1886

Parliament. If a referendum is postponed beyond the 2024 lifespan of the current British Government, much then depends on the level of activity and support in persisting in opposition to the British Government's strategy and the nerve of those implementing it. Disruptive parliamentary tactics would become more likely, and civil disobedience must be a possibility; on the other hand, the Yes movement may lose heart. As the 2024 UK general election approached, the Labour Party would doubtless emphasise its commitment to a 'federal UK' which Scots would get only if they voted Labour. By that time, however, levels of trust for the British Government and political system will probably have attenuated further: the unprecedented extension of government control over daily life in the Covid-19 pandemic combined with the apparently not entirely consistent observation of the rules prescribed for the citizenry by politicians themselves may well accelerate the increasing distrust of the British political system. Any pro- and post-Brexit British parliamentary party (which currently includes Labour and even technically the Liberal Democrats) would have difficulty persuading the Scottish electorate that they would in reality cede power within a federal structure, even if there was some inclination to believe them, for the core Brexit argument is that sovereignty is indivisible. The initial constitutional outcome in the next few years will thus depend on the extent of Scotland's lack of trust in any British Government, the extent to which there has been active and visible demonstration of that in public opinion, actions and institutions, and the outcome of Brexit. There is a widespread view – very fully supported by evidence – that Brexit can only cause serious long-term economic damage, but also a view passionately held by its ideologues that it offers opportunities. To achieve the latter outcome Brexit Britain needs to become more like Singapore; but it is very much the case that while the UK can imagine itself as a freebooting imperial power it is in reality a European state with high levels of social spending and a demand for more. The need for extensive increases in taxes is far more often found in political discourse than the desire for the opposite: the economy, never particularly efficient and supported by major infrastructure spending in the south-east which continues to make the UK one of the most unequal countries internally in the West, has long-standing problems which Brexit will only intensify. Infrastructure spending in London in 2017–21 was almost £2,000 per capita, compared to £600 in the second most benefited area in England, the North-West, and a mere £200 or so in Yorkshire. Scottish independence is one question for our era, but another is the economy and internal balance of the United Kingdom as a whole, with its 'joint concentration of economic and political power' in the south-east currently seen as an exemplar for 'levelling up' not redistribution: Burnley must be as wealthy as Bloomsbury, but at no cost to the latter. The political response can only be to raise debt or taxes in a climate of increasing rage where many believe the rich are defrauding the country rather than seeking to understand the reasons for the decreasing tax base which they, in many cases, themselves voted for. Faced with less stark challenges, ten UK prime ministers in succession decided that membership of the European Union was the best solution for a global Britain. Placed beyond that choice, what happens next is a question not only for Scotland to answer.[6]

NOTES

INTRODUCTION

1. Arthur Hermann, *How the Scots Invented the Modern World: The True Story of How Western Europe's Poorest Nation Created Our Modern World and Everything in It* (New York: Crown Publishing, 2001).

2. Sebastian Conrad, *What is Global History?* (Princeton: Princeton University Press, 2017 [2016]), 6; John Darwin, *After Tamerlane: The Rise and Fall of Global Empires, 1400–2000* (London: Penguin, 2008 [2007]); Vincent Morley, *The Popular Mind in Eighteenth-Century Ireland* (Cork: Cork University Press, 2017), 310. The current history 'culture wars' in post-Brexit England are discussed in Margot Finn, 'Material Turns in British History', *Transactions of the Royal Historical Society* XXXI (2021), 1–21 (see 6, 9).

3. Lynn Hunt, *Writing History in the Global Era* (London and New York: Norton, 2014), 5.

4. This is the moniker of the Scottish Studies Global Research theme, founded at the University of Glasgow by the present author in 2010, which has received over £20 million in grant income for its various projects; Richard J. Evans, *The Pursuit of Power: Europe 1815–1914* (London: Penguin, 2017 [2016]), xvi.

5. E.H. Dance, 'Bias in History Teaching and Textbooks', in Otto-Ernst Schuddehopf et al., *History Teaching and History Textbook Revision* (Strasbourg: Centre for Cultural Co-operation of the Council of Europe, 1967), 73 ff; H.T. Lambrick, *Sir Charles Napier and Sind* (Oxford: Clarendon Press, 1952), 32; Richard Holmes, *Sahib* (London: HarperCollins, 2006 [2005]), 60.

6. Conrad, *What is Global History?* (2017), 89; David McCrone, *Understanding Scotland: The Sociology of a Stateless Nation* (London and New York: Routledge, 1992).

7. Ted Cowan, quoted in Jim Hewitson, *Far Off in Sunlit Places: Stories of the Scots in Australia and New Zealand* (Edinburgh: Canongate, 1998), 5; Andrew Mackillop, ' "The More Mischief, the Better for Us": Scots and Irish Officer and Predatory Imper ialism in South Asia, *c.*1740–*c.*1820', unpublished paper, Scottish Centre for War Studies and Conflict Archaeology, 24 March 2021. These arguments are more fully developed in Mackillop's *Human Capital and Empire* (Manchester: Manchester University Press, 2021).

8. Morley, *Popular Mind* (2017), 283.

9. Sir John Seeley, *The Expansion of England* (1883); Murray Pittock, 'Scottish Sovereignty and the Union of 1707: Then and Now', *National Identities* 14:1 (2012), 11–21; Sir John Elliott, 'A Europe of Composite Monarchies', *Past and Present* 137 (1992), 48–71.

10. Joep Leerssen (ed.), 'Belgium: Background: Historical Context', in Joep Leerssen (ed.), *The Encyclopedia of Romantic Nationalism in Europe*, 2 vols., (Amsterdam: Amsterdam University Press, 2018), II: 688–89.

11. John Mackenzie, 'Foreword', in Andrew Mackillop and Steve Murdoch (eds), *Military Governors and Imperial Frontiers c.1600–1800: A Study of Scotland and Empires* (Leiden: Brill, 2003), xiii–xxi (xv–xvi); Mackillop and Murdoch, idem, 'Introduction', xxv–li (li);

Steve Murdoch, *Network North: Scottish Kin, Commercial and Covert Associations in Northern Europe 1603–1746* (Leiden: Brill, 2006), 6, 7, 27, 39, 49; Peter Frankopan, *The Silk Roads: A New History of the World* (London: Bloomsbury, 2016 [2015]), 267; Murray Pittock, 'What is a National Culture?', in *Litteraria Pragensia* 19:38 (2009) (Scotland in Europe Special Number), 30–47; see also Murray Pittock, *Scottish and Irish Romanticism* (Oxford: Oxford University Press, 2011 [2008]; Duncan Sim, *American Scots: The Scottish Diaspora and the USA* (Edinburgh: Dunedin Academic Press, 2011), x.

12. Tanja Bueltmann, Andrew Hinson and Graeme Morton, *The Scottish Diaspora* (Edinburgh: Edinburgh University Press, 2013), 17–18, 23; Tanja Bueltmann, *Clubbing Together: Ethnicity, Civility and Formal Sociability in the Scottish Diaspora to 1930* (Liverpool: Liverpool University Press, 2014), 9; Pittock, *Scottish and Irish Romanticism* (2011).

13. Duncan A. Bruce, *The Mark of the Scots* (New Jersey: Birch Lane Press, 1997 [1996]), 3; David Hesse, *Warrior Dreams: Playing Scotsmen in Mainland Europe* (Manchester: Manchester University Press, 2014).

14. See for example Murray Pittock, 'Byron's Networks and Scottish Romanticism', *The Byron Journal* 37:1 (2009), 5–14.

15. See Murray Pittock, *Enlightenment in a Smart City: Edinburgh's Civic Development, 1660–1750* (Edinburgh: Edinburgh University Press, 2019), 20–21, 62 and passim; Bruce Lenman, *Enlightenment and Change: Scotland 1746–1832* (Edinburgh: Edinburgh University Press, 2009), 21.

16. Murray Pittock, 'John Law's Theory of Money and its Roots in Scottish Culture', *Proceedings of the Society of Antiquaries in Scotland* 133 (2003), 391–403; Sydney Checkland, *Scottish Banking: A History, 1695–1973* (Glasgow and London, 1975), xvii.

17. Hesse, *Warrior Dreams* (2014), 37–39; Pittock, *Scottish and Irish Romanticism* (2011). See for example Tim Harris, *Restoration: Charles II and his Kingdoms* (London: Penguin, 2006 [2005]), xviii ('Although there was a significant Gaelic culture . . . Lowland Scots, of Anglo-Saxon extraction . . . dominated the government of the country'). Compare https://www.medievalists.net/2019/09/genetic-map-of-scotland-revealed/ and Edmund Gilbert et al., 'The Genetic Landscape of Scotland and the Isles', *Proceedings of the National Academy of Sciences of the United States of America* [*PNAS*] (2019), 116 (38), 19064-70.

18. T.M. Devine, *The Scottish Clearances: A History of the Dispossessed 1600–1900* (London: Penguin, 2019 [2018]), 18.

19. National Library of Scotland Maps EMS s.6.a, Smith.b.09.07, Marischal 1, 2, 4, 5 and passim. See Charles Withers, 'The Historical Creation of the Scottish Highlands', in Ian Donnachie and Christopher Whatley (eds), *The Manufacture of Scottish History* (Edinburgh: Polygon, 1992), 143–56 (143, 146, 154); Leah Leneman, *Living in Atholl: A Social History of the Estates, 1685–1785* (Edinburgh: Edinburgh University Press, 1986).

20. Alison Cathcart, 'Crisis of Identity: Clan Chattan's Response to Government Policy in the Scottish Highlands, *c.*1580–1609', in Steve Murdoch and Andrew Mackillop (eds), *Fighting for Identity* (Leiden: Brill, 2002), 163–84 (164); Allan I. Macinnes, *Clanship, Commerce and the House of Stuart* (East Linton: Tuckwell Press, 1996), 24.

21. National Library of Scotland, Saltoun Papers, MS 16681 f. 121; Murray Pittock, *Scottish Nationality* (Basingstoke: Palgrave Macmillan, 2001), 67–68; Murray Pittock, *Culloden* (Oxford: Oxford University Press, 2016), 121; Carolyn Anderson and Chris Fleet, *Scotland: Defending the Nation* (Edinburgh: Birlinn/National Library of Scotland, 2018), 83, 97; Patrick Mileham, *The Scottish Regiments 1633–1996* (New York: Sarpedon, 1996 [1988]), 12.

22. Colin G. Calloway, *White People, Indians, and Highlanders: Tribal People and Colonial Encounters in Scotland and America* (2008), 15–16, 61; Murray Pittock, *The Myth of the Jacobite Clans: The Jacobite Army in 1745* (Edinburgh: Edinburgh University Press, 2009), 31–38; Macinnes, *Clanship*, ix, 1, 38, 55; Martin McGregor, 'Gaelic Barbarity

and Scottish Identity in the Later Middle Ages', in Dauvit Broun and Martin MacGregor (eds), *Mìorun Mòr nan Gall, 'The Great Ill-will of the Lowlander'? Lowland Perceptions of the Highlands, Medieval and Modern* (Glasgow: Centre for Scottish and Celtic Studies, 2009 [2007]), 7–48 (7, 9, 17, 37).

23. Michael Brander, *The Emigrant Scots* (London: Constable, 1982), 3; MacGregor in *Mìorun Mòr nan Gall* (2009), 48.

24. Julian Hoppit, *The Dreadful Monster and its Poor Relations: Taxing and Spending in the United Kingdom, 1707–2021* (London: Allen Lane, 2021), 72–73, 75.

25. Pittock, *Enlightenment in a Smart City* (2019), 166; Maria Hayward, *Stuart Style: Monarchy, Dress and the Scottish Male Elite* (New Haven and London: Yale University Press, 2020), 26.

CHAPTER 1: A QUESTION OF SOVEREIGNTY

1. Quoted in Alan Ereira, *The Nine Lives of John Ogilby* (Richmond: Duckworth, 2019 [2016]), 5.

2. Dagomar Degroot, *The Frigid Golden Age: Climate Change, the Little Ice Age, and the Dutch Republic, 1560–1720* (Cambridge: Cambridge University Press, 2018), 53–54, 86, 154–55, 186; Norman Davies, *Beneath Another Sky* (London: Penguin, 2017), 549; G.J. Bryant, *The Emergence of British Power in India 1600–1784* (Woodbridge: Boydell Press, 2013), 17; Peter H. Wilson, *The Holy Roman Empire* (London: Allen Lane, 2016), 124–26; John Darwin, *Unlocking the World: Port Cities and Globalization in the Age of Steam 1830–1930* (London: Allen Unwin, 2020), 46; Niall Ferguson, *The Ascent of Money* (London: Penguin, 2009 [2008]), 136.

3. Andreas Osiander, 'Sovereignty, International Relations and the Westphalian Myth', *International Organization* 55:2 (2001), 251–87 (254–66); Kevin Sharpe, *The Personal Rule of Charles I* (New Haven and London: Yale University Press, 1992), 8, 65–69, 79, 510; Jerry Brotton, *The Sale of the Late King's Goods: Charles I and His Art Collection* (London: Pan Macmillan, 2017 [2006]), 207.

4. Norman Davies, *Europe: A History* (London: Pimlico, 1997), 565; Degroot, *Frigid Golden Age* (2018), 194.

5. Henry Kissinger, *World Order* (London: Allen Lane, 2015 [2014]), 3.

6. Wilson, *Holy Roman Empire* (2016), 7–9, 127, 235, 279, 280, 283, 377, 441, 664; Darwin, *Unlocking the World* (2020), 17; Philip Allott, quoted in Peter Gatrell, *The Unsettling of Europe* (London: Penguin, 2020[2019]), 322.

7. C.R. Boxer, *The Portuguese Seaborne Empire 1415–1825* (London: Hutchinson, 1969), 108; Arthur Griffith, *The Resurrection of Hungary: A Parallel for Ireland* (Dublin: UCD Press, 2003 (1904)); Jane Ohlmeyer, 'Introduction', in Ohlmeyer (ed.), *Political Thought in Seventeenth-Century Ireland* (Cambridge: Cambridge University Press, 2000), 1–31 (9).

8. The Crown of Ireland Act 1542 (33 Hen. 8 c.1) and the Wales Act 1536 (27 Hen. 8 c.26) and the Laws in Wales Act 1542 (34 & 35 Hen. 8. c.26); David Armitage, *The Ideological Origins of the British Empire* (Cambridge: Cambridge University Press, 2004 [2000]), 37, 42, 62.

9. Sir John Baker, *The Reinvention of Magna Carta 1216–1616* (Cambridge: Cambridge University Press, 2017), 343; Murray Pittock, *Jacobitism* (Basingstoke: Macmillan, 1998), 13.

10. Steve Murdoch, '"It Started Off in Fyfe, It Ended Up in Tears": Scotland and the Thirty Years War, 1618–1648', *History Scotland* 20:2 (2020), 24–29 (25); Steve Murdoch, 'James VI and the Formation of a Scottish–British Military Identity', in Murdoch and Andrew Mackillop (eds), *Fighting for Identity: Scottish Military Experience, c.1550–1900* (Leiden: Brill, 2002), 3–31 (19–20); Murdoch, 'Introduction', in Murdoch (ed.), *Scotland and the Thirty Years' War, 1618–1648* (Leiden: Brill, 2001), 1–23 (3).

11. T.M. Devine, *Scotland's Empire 1600–1815* (London: Allen Lane, 2003), 3; Murdoch and Mackillop, *Fighting for Identity* (2002), 4, 24.

12. David Armitage, 'Making the Empire British: Scotland in the Atlantic World, 1542–1707', *Past and Present* 155 (1997), 34–63 (62); Boxer, *Portuguese Seaborne Empire* (1969), 108.

13. Steve Murdoch, 'Anglo-Scottish Culture Clash? Scottish Identities and Britishness, *c*.1520–1750', *Cycnos* 25:2 (2008), 245–66 (256); Steve Murdoch, 'James VI and the Formation of a Scottish-British Military Identity', in Murdoch and Mackillop, *Fighting for Identity* (2002), 3–31 (30); Karen Bowie, ' "A Legal Limited Monarchy": Scottish Constitutionalism in the Union of Crowns, 1603–1707', *Journal of the Scottish Historical Society* 35:2 (2015), 131–54 (138).

14. Gordon Donaldson, *Scottish Historical Documents* (Edinburgh and London: Scottish Academic Press, 1974), 177–78; T.M. Devine, *The Clearances* (London: Allen Lane, 2018), 40; Murdoch, *Scotland and the Thirty Years' War* (2001), 7.

15. Donaldson, *Scottish Historical Documents* (1974), 188–89; Sharpe, *Charles I* (1992), 194–95, 282, 410, 538, 732, 785; Liza Picard, *Restoration London* (London: Weidenfeld & Nicolson, 2003 [1997]), 25.

16. See for example https://www.youtube.com/watch?v=eEsDynBjxII. There are many recordings of this tune; Jonas Berg and Bo Lagercrantz, *Scots in Sweden*, with an introduction by Eric Linklater (Edinburgh, 1962), 7; Christopher Smout, 'The Culture of Migration: Scots as Europeans 1500–1800', *History Workshop Journal* 40 (1995), 108–17 (108); Siobhan Talbott, *Conflict, Commerce and Franco-Scottish Relations, 1560–1713* (London: Pickering and Chatto, 2014), 29, 31; Billy Kay, *The Scottish World: A Journey into the Scottish Diaspora* (Edinburgh and London: Mainstream, 2006), 80, 84.

17. Marie-Claude Tucker, 'Scottish Masters in Huguenot Academies', *History of Universities* XXIX/2 (2016), 42–68 (65–67): Marie-Claude Tucker, 'Scottish Philosophy Teachers at the French Protestant Academies in the Seventeenth Century', in Alexander Broadie (ed.), *Scottish Philosophy in the Seventeenth Century*, The Oxford History of Scottish Philosophy (Oxford: Oxford University Press, 2020), 50–72 (53–54, 57, 61); Philip Long and Joanna Norman (eds), *The Story of Scottish Design* (London: Thames & Hudson/V & A, 2018), 18–19; Matthew Glazier, 'Scots in the French and Dutch Armies during the Thirty Years' War', in Murdoch, *Scotland and the Thirty Years' War* (2001), 117–41 (118); Patrick Mileham, *The Scottish Regiments 1633–1996* (New York: Sarpedon, 1996 [1988]), 11, 66.

18. Clarisse Godard Desmarest, 'Architecture, patrimoine et nation: enjeux identitaires en Écosse', l'Habilitation a Diriger des Recherches (Paris: Sorbonne, 2020), 57, 59, 81.

19. Devine, *Clearances* (2018), 39.

20. Steve Murdoch, 'Scotland, Europe and the English "Missing Link" ', *History Compass* 5:3 (2007), 890–913 (891–94); Douglas Catterall, *Community Without Borders: Scots Migrants at the Changing Face of Power in the Dutch Republic, c.1600–1700* (London: Brill, 2002), 31; Alexia Grosjean, *An Unofficial Alliance: Scotland and Sweden, 1569–1654* (Leiden: Brill, 2003), 4. 59; Murdoch and Mackillop, *Fighting for Identity* (2002), fig. 3; Calloway, *White People, Indians and Highlanders* (Oxford: Oxford University Press, 2008), 91. Christian IV left the war by the Peace of Lübeck, which traded territory for a Danish exit from the conflict.

21. Sharpe, *Charles I* (1992); Steve Murdoch, 'James VI', in Murdoch and Mackillop, *Fighting for Identity* (2002), 22.

22. Grosjean, *An Unofficial Alliance* (2003), 107, 132, 215; Dauvit Horsbroch, ' "Tae See Ourselves as Ithers See Us": Scottish Military Identity from the Covenant to Victoria', in Murdoch and Mackillop, *Fighting for Identity* (2002), 105–29 (109); Brian Lavery, *Shield of Empire: The Royal Navy and Scotland* (Edinburgh: Birlinn, 2007), 3.

23. Alexia Grosjean, 'A Century of Scottish Governorship in the Swedish Empire, 1574–1700', in Murdoch and Mackillop, *Fighting for Identity* (2002), 53–78 (53–54, 56, 57, 60–61, 70–72); Grosjean, *An Unofficial Alliance* (2003), 4, 7, 39; Steve Murdoch, *Network North: Scottish Kin, Commercial and Covert Associations in Northern Europe 1603–1746* (Leiden: Brill, 2006), 211, 215; Berg and Lagercrantz, *Scots in Sweden* (1962), 7, 25–26, 45, 52, 54–55, 60; Les Wilson, *Putting the Tea in Britain: The Scots*

Who Made Our National Drink (Edinburgh: Birlinn, 2021), 41; Berg and Lagercrantz, *Scots in Sweden* (1962), 70–75; Victoria E. Clark, *The Port of Aberdeen* (Aberdeen: D. Wyllie & Son, 1921), 104.

24. Murdoch and Mackillop, *Fighting for Identity* (2002), xxiii; Steve Murdoch, 'Scotsmen on the Danish–Norwegian Frontiers, *c.*1580–1660', in Andrew Mackillop and Steve Murdoch (eds), *Military Governors and Imperial Frontiers c.1600–1800: A Study of Scotland and Empires* (Leiden: Brill, 2003), 1–28 (1, 5–7, 26); Rune Hagen, 'At the Edge of Civilisation: John Cunningham, Lensman of Finnmark, 1619–51', idem, 29–51 (29, 33, 50); Nina Østby Pedersen, 'Scottish Immigration to Bergen in the Sixteenth and Seventeenth Centuries', in A. Grosjean and S. Murdoch, *Scottish Communities Abroad* (Leiden: Brill, 2005), 134–67 (163); Glazier, 'Scots in the French and Dutch Armies', 123; Paul Dukes, 'New Perspectives: Alexander Leslie and the Smolensk War, 1632–4', 173–89 (187); Hartmutt Ruffer and Kathrin Zickermann, 'German Reactions to the Scots in the Holy Roman Empire During the Thirty Years' War', 271–91 (291), all in Murdoch, *Scotland and the Thirty Years' War* (2001); Smout, 'Culture of Migration' (1995), 111; Andrew Mackillop, ' "As Hewers of Wood, and Drawers of Water?" Scotland as an Emigrant Nation, *c.*1600–*c.*1800', in Angela McCarthy and John M. Mackenzie (eds), *Global Migrations: The Scottish Diaspora since 1600* (Edinburgh: Edinburgh University Press, 2016), 23–45 (27); T.M. Devine, *To the Ends of the Earth: Scotland's Global Diaspora* (London: Allen Lane, 2011), 25; Clark, *Port of Aberdeen* (1921), 67–68.

25. Laura A.M. Stewart, *Rethinking the Scottish Revolution: Covenanted Scotland, 1637–1651* (Oxford: Oxford Universty Press, 2018 [2016]), 29, 85, 87, 126; Scott Spurlock, 'Problems with Religion as Identity: The Case of Mid-Stuart Ireland and Scotland', *Journal of Irish and Scottish Studies* 6:2 (2013), 1–30 (17); Karen Bowie, 'Cultural, British and Global Turns in the History of Early Modern Scotland', *Scottish Historical Review* 92 (234) (2013), 38–48 (40); Bowie, 'Legal Limited Monarchy' (2015), 135, 141; Bowie, *Public Opinion in Early Modern Scotland* (Cambridge: Cambridge University Press, 2020), 52; Salvatore Cipriano, 'The Scottish Universities and Opposition to the National Covenant, 1638', *Scottish Historical Review* XCVII:1 (2018), 12–37 (14–15).

26. Sharpe, *Charles I* (1992), 535, 896.

27. Mackillop, 'Hewers of Wood', in McCarthy and Mackenzie, *Global Migrations* (2016), 28. Steve Murdoch has done significant recent work focusing on Scottish military preparedness abroad for action at home in the 1630s: see Steve Murdoch, '*Nicrina ad Heroas Anglos:* An Overview of the British and the Thirty Years' War', in S. Jones (ed.), *Britain Turned Germany: The Thirty Years' War and its Impact on the British Isles 1638–1660'* (Warwick: Helion & Co., 2019), 15–36.

28. Murdoch, 'Scotland, Europe' (2007), 894; 'Scotland and the Thirty Years' War' (2020), 27–29; *Network North* (2006), 41–42.

29. Óscar Reico Morales, *Ireland and the Spanish Empire, 1600–1825* (Dublin: Four Courts, 2010), 114–16, 135–36; Edward M. Furgol, 'The Secret History of the Bishops' Wars: Part 2', *History Scotland* (September/October 2020), 48–53 (51, 53); Horsbroch, in Murdoch and Mackillop, *Fighting for Identity* (2002), 110; Murray Pittock, *Celtic Identity and the British Image* (Manchester: Manchester University Press, 1999), 19; Nicholas Canny, 'The Origins of Empire and an Introduction', in Nicholas Canny (ed.), *The Origins of Empire: The Oxford History of the British Empire* (Oxford: Oxford University Press, 2000 [1988]), 1–33 (13–15)); Allan I. Macinnes, 'Covenanting Ideology in Seventeenth-century Scotland' in Ohlmeyer, *Political Thought in Seventeenth-Century Ireland* (2000), 191–224 (210); Brotton, *Sale of the Late King's Goods* (2017), 199.

30. Scott Spurlock, 'Problems with Religion as Identity: The Case of Mid-Stuart Ireland and Scotland', *Journal of Irish and Scottish Studies* 6:2 (2013), 1–30 (18–19); Macinnes, 'Covenanting Ideology' in Ohlmeyer, *Political Thought in Seventeenth-Century Ireland* (2000), 213.aa

31. Donaldson, *Scottish Historical Documents* (1974), 208–09; Spurlock, 'Problems with Religion as Identity' (2013), 20.

32. Donaldson, *Scottish Historical Documents* (1974), 214–226; Spurlock (2013), 'Problems with Religion as Identity' 21–25 offers a more detailed guide to the shifting definitions of Presbyterian royalism in this period.

33. Devine, *Scottish Empire* (2003), 28–29; David Dobson, *Scottish Emigration to Colonial America, 1607–1785* (Athens and London: University of Georgia Press, 1994), 36; Andrew Mackillop, *'More Fruitful than the Soil': Army, Empire and the Scottish Highlands, 1715–1815* (East Linton: Tuckwell Press, 2000), 8.

34. Commonwealth and Protectorate iv. 82–5.

35. Dobson, *Scottish Emigration* (1994), 9.

36. Smout, 'Culture of Migration' (1995), 109; Clark, *Port of Aberdeen* (1921), 17, 34–35, 67–68, 75.

37. Devine, *Scottish Empire* (2003), 8; T.M. Devine and Philipp R. Rossner, 'Scots in the Atlantic Economy, 1600–1800', in John Mackenzie and T.M. Devine (eds), *Scotland and the British Empire* (Oxford: Oxford University Press, 2011), 30–53 (31); Clark, *Port of Aberdeen* (1921), 41.

38. Devine and Rossner in Mackenzie and Devine, *Scotland and the British Empire* (2011), 32; Anna Tryc-Bromley, 'Foreword', ix–x (ix); T.M. Devine and David Hesse, 'Introduction', 1–6 (2); Neal Ascherson, ' "Brothers and Sisters for a' that": Rediscovering the Polish-Scottish Relationship', 7–17 (9); Waldemar Kowalski, 'The Reasons for the Immigration of Scots to the Polish Commonwealth in the Early Modern Period as Outlined in Contemporary Opinions and Historiography', 38–50 (40–41); Anna Kalinowski, ' "Pardon me my Lord, that I wrytte to your honour in Scottish": William Bruce as the First Stuart diplomatic agent in the Polish-Lithuanian Commonwealth', 51–61 (51–53, 58); Peter P. Bajer, 'Scots in the Cracow Reformed Parish in the Seventeenth Century', 62–90 (60, 73, 75, 82); David Worthington, ' "Men of Noe Credit? Scottish Highlanders in Poland-Lithuania, *c.*1500–1800', 91–108 (92–93), all in T.M. Devine and David Hesse (eds), *Scotland and Poland: Historical Encounters, 1500–2010* (Edinburgh: John Donald, 2011); Waldemar Kowalski, 'The Placement of Urbanised Scots in the Polish Crown during the Sixteenth and Seventeenth Centuries', in Grosjean and Murdoch (eds), *Scottish Communities Abroad in the Early Modern Period*, 53–103 (55–58, 63); Murdoch, *Network North* (2006), 131; Michael Broun Ayre, 'Prosperity, Calamity and Survival in the Grand Duchy of Lithuania', *History Scotland* 21:1 (2021), 16–19 (16–17).

39. Devine and Rossner in Mackenzie and Devine, *Scotland and the British Empire* (2011), 32; Anna Tryc-Bromley, 'Foreword', x; Neal Ascherson, ' "Brothers and Sisters for a' that": Rediscovering the Polish-Scottish Relationship', 9–11 in Devine and Hesse, *Scotland and Poland* (2011); Mona K. McLeod, *Agents of Change: Scots in Poland, 1860–1918* (East Linton: Tuckwell Press, 2000), 51, 71, 79.

40. Smout, 'Culture of Migration' (1995), 109, 111; Murdoch, 'Anglo-Scottish Culture Clash' (2008), 264; Murdoch, 'Scotland, Europe' (2007), 895, 897–98; Devine, *Scottish Empire* (2003), 10, 12; Ginny Gardner, *The Scottish Exile Community in the Netherlands, 1660–1690* (East Linton: Tuckwell Press, 2004), 3; Long and Norman, *Scottish Design* (2018), 22; Alexia Grosjean and Steve Murdoch, 'The Scottish Community in Seventeenth-Century Gothenburg', in Grosjean and Murdoch (eds), *Scottish Communities Abroad* (2005), 191–223 (210); Mark Dilworth, *The Scots in Franconia* (Edinburgh and London: Scottish Academic Press, 1974), 23, 63, 65, 267, 269; Michael Brander, *The Emigrant Scots* (London: Constable, 1982), 21.

41. Joep Leerssen, *National Thought in Europe: A Cultural History* (Amsterdam: Amsterdam University Press, 2006), 56; Catterall, *Community without Borders* (2002), 27, 61–62.

42. P. Hume Brown (ed.), *Early Travellers in Scotland* (Edinburgh: The Mercat Press, 1978 [1891]), 110, 118, 140, 160, 191–93, 206, 214, 221, 228, 231, 237, 256, 260–61, 268, 271, 272, 276, 277, 279, 289; James Ray, *A Journey Through Part of England and Scotland Along With the Army Under the Command of His Royal Highness the Duke of Cumberland* (London: Osborne, 1747), 95; Carolyn Anderson and Chris Fleet, *Scotland: Defending*

the Nation (Edinburgh: Birlinn/National Library of Scotland, 2018), 35, 43; Picard, *Restoration London* (2003), 43.

43. Smout, 'Culture of Migration' (1995), 113; Mackillop, 'Hewers of Wood' in McCarthy and Mackenzie, *Global Migrations* (2016), 29; Laurent Jaffro, 'James Dalrymple, 1st Viscount of Stair, on Legal Normativity', in Broadie, *Scottish Philosophy in the Seventeenth Century* (2020), 140–57; Alexander Fleming and Roger Mason, 'Introduction', 1–6 (4); Alexander Fleming et al., 'Flemish Migration II: Merchants and Craftsmen', 55–67 (60); Matthew Price, 'Towns and Churches', 85–100 (88, 99–100); Robin Bargmann, 'Sport and Recreation', 113–29 (119–20, 129), all in Fleming and Mason (eds), *Scotland and the Flemish People* (Edinburgh: John Donald, 2019).

44. Richard Savile, *Bank of Scotland: A History 1695–1995* (Edinburgh: Edinburgh University Press, 1996), 10; Lindy Moore, 'Urban Schooling in Seventeenth- and Eighteenth-Century Scotland', in Robert Anderson, Mark Freeman and Lindsay Paterson (eds), *The Edinburgh History of Education in Scotland* (Edinburgh: Edinburgh University Press, 2015), 79–96 (91); Gardner, *The Scottish Exile Community in the Netherlands* (2004), 3, 26, 117, 118, 122, 210–11; T.M. Devine, 'The Merchant Class of the Larger Scottish Towns in the Seventeenth and Early Eighteenth Centuries', in George Gordon and Brian Dicks (eds), *Scottish Urban History* (Aberdeen: Aberdeen University Press, 1983), 92–111 (96).

45. Peter Blom, 'In Search of Scotland in a Zeelandic Town: Sources for Scottish History in the Records of Veere', http://www.fdca.org.uk/veere/veere_13.pdf; John Davidson and Alexander Gray, *The Scottish Staple at Veere* (London: Longmans, Green & Co., 1969), 211, 253, 262, 266; Esther Mijers, ' "Addicted to Puritanism": Philosophical and Theological Relations between Scotland and the United Provinces in the First Half of the Seventeenth Century', *History of Universities* XXIX/2 (2016), 69–95 (73–74); Andrew L. Drummond and James Bulloch, *The Scottish Church 1688–1843: The Age of the Moderates* (Edinburgh: Saint Andrew Press, 1973), 6; Murdoch, *Network North* (2006), 149; Stephen Gethins, *Nation to Nation: Scotland's Place in the World* (Edinburgh: Luath Press, 2021), 30.

46. Catterall, *Community without Borders* (2002), 19, 25–27,33, 39, 43, 64, 109, 116, 141, 344–45, 347; W. Steven, *The History of the Scottish Church, Rotterdam* (Edinburgh, 1832); Grosjean and Murdoch, *Scottish Communities Abroad* (2005), 'Introduction', 1–24 (5, 7); also David Dobson 'Seventeenth-Century Scottish Communities in the Americas', 105–32 (125–27); Andrew R. Little, 'A Comparative Study of Scottish Service in the English and Dutch Maritime Communities, *c.*1650–*c.*1707', 333–74 (333); Thomas O'Connor, Sölvi Sogner and Lex Heerma van Voss, 'Scottish Communities Abroad: Some Concluding Remarks', 375–93 (375), all in Grosjean and Murdoch; Joachim Miggelbrink, 'The End of the Scots-Dutch Brigade', in Murdoch and Mackillop, *Fighting for Identity* (2002), 83–103 (83); Murdoch, *Network North* (2006), 168; Ferguson, *Ascent of Money* (2009), 49.

47. Richard L. Greaves, 'Conformity and Security in Scotland and Ireland, 1660–85', in Elizabethanne Boran and Crawford Gribben (eds), *Enforcing Reformation in Ireland and Scotland, 1550–1700* (Aldershot: Ashgate, 2006), 228–50 (231).

48. Catterall, *Community without Borders* (2002), 34, 343; Devine, *Scottish Empire* (2003), 35; Mackillop, 'Hewers of Wood' (2016), 23–45 (32); Steve Murdoch, *The Terror of the Seas? Scottish Maritime Warfare 1513–1713* (Leiden: Brill, 2010), 255 ff, 278; Tim Harris, *Restoration: Charles II and his Kingdoms* (London: Penguin, 2006 [2005]), 111.

49. Catterall, *Community without Borders* (2002), 75, 344; Devine, *Scottish Empire* (2003), 37; Dobson, *Scottish Emigration* (1994), 41, 44; Degroot, *Frigid Golden Age* (2018), 196, 198; Armitage, *Ideological Origins of the British Empire* (2004), 149–50; Worthington in Devine and Hesse, *Scots in Poland* (2011), 97.

50. Roger L. Emerson, *Academic Patronage in the Scottish Enlightenment: Glasgow, Edinburgh and St Andrews Universities* (Edinburgh: Edinburgh University Press, 2008), 231; Mijers, 'Addicted to Puritanism' (2016), 69; Drummond and Bulloch, *Scottish Church* (1973),

21–22; Gardner, *Scottish Exile Community in the Netherlands* (2004), 129, 194, 204; Degroot, *Frigid Golden Age* (2018), 245 on the Dutch perspective of the Revolution.

51. Bowie, 'Legal Limited Monarchy' (2015), 154; see also Bowie and Alasdair Raffe, 'Politics, the People, and Extra-Institutional Participation in Scotland, c.1603–1712', *Journal of British Studies* 56 (2017), 797–815; Harris, *Restoration* (2006), 63, 114.

52. Smout (1995), 111; Spurlock, 'Religion as Identity' (2013), 27; Donaldson, *Scottish Historical Documents* (1974), 226, 235–36, 241–43; Greaves, 'Conformity and Security in Scotland and Ireland, 1660–85' (2006), 232–34, 244; Clare Jackson, *Restoration Scotland, 1660–1690* (Woodbridge: The Boydell Press, 2003), 2–3; Gardner, *Scottish Exile Community in the Netherlands* (2004), 130; David Dobson 'Seventeenth-century Scottish Communities in the Americas', in Grosjean and Murdoch, *Scottish Communities Abroad* (2005), 105–32 (116); Harris, *Restoration* (2006), 118–22, 331, 337, 347–48, 374; Jeremy Black, *George III: Majesty and Madness* (London: Allen Lane, 2020), 76.

53. Jackson, *Restoration Scotland* (2003), 31.

54. I.D. Whyte, 'Scottish and Irish Urbanisation in the Seventeenth and Eighteenth Centuries: A Comparative Perspective', in S.J. Connolly, R.A. Houston and R.J. Morris (eds), *Conflict, Identity and Economic Development: Ireland and Scotland, 1600–1939* (Preston: Carnegie Publishing, 1995), 14–28 (24).

55. Bill Findlay, 'Beginnings to 1700', in Bill Findlay (ed.), *A History of Scottish Theatre* (Edinburgh: Polygon, 1998), 1–79; Janet Starkey, 'Food for Thought: Coffee, Coffee-Houses and le bon gout in Edinburgh during the Scottish Enlightenment', *Book of the Old Edinburgh Club* ns no. 14 (2018), 23–44 (29, 32–34, 39).

56. Moore, 'Urban Schooling in Seventeenth- and Eighteenth-century Scotland', in Anderson, Freeman and Paterson (eds), *The Edinburgh History of Education in Scotland* (2015), 87–88; James Scotland, *The History of Scottish Education*, 2 vols, (University of London Press Ltd, 1969), 93.

57. William Cowan, *The Holyrood Press 1686–1688* (Edinburgh: Privately Printed, 1904), 3; Brotton, *Sale of the Late King's Goods* (2017), 29.

58. Linda Colley, *The Gun, the Ship and the Pen* (London: Profile Books, 2021), 61. For a much more detailed examination of this question and the nature of Enlightenment, see Murray Pittock, *Enlightenment in a Smart City: Civic Development in Edinburgh, 1660–1750* (Edinburgh: Edinburgh University Press, 2019), in particular Chapter 1.

59. Jennifer Macleod, 'The Edinburgh Musical Society: Its Membership and Repertoire 1728–1797', unpublished PhD (University of Edinburgh, 2001), 14; Janet Starkey, 'Food for Thought' (2018), 40.

60. Michael Nairn, 'Peter Lole on Jacobite Glass and the Jacobite Clubs', *The Jacobite* 159 (2019), 6–15 (6–7); Picard, *Restoration London* (2003), 112, 115, 192.

61. R.A. Houston, *Social Change in the Age of Enlightenment: Edinburgh, 1660–1760* (Oxford: Clarendon Press, 1994), 105; Helen Dingwall, *Late Seventeenth-century Edinburgh: A Demographic Study* (Aldershot: Scolar Press, 1994), 9, 121.

62. Edward Glaeser, *Triumph of a City: How Urban Spaces Make Us Human* (London: Pan, 2012 [2011]), 8, 64; Pittock, *Enlightenment* (2019), 19, 60–65, 90–97; Bruce Lenman, *Enlightenment and Change: Scotland 1746–1832* (Edinburgh: Edinburgh University Press, 2009), 255; David Dobson, *Huguenot and Scots Links 1575–1775* (Baltimore, Maryland: Clearfield, 2005), 54; *Proceedings of the Huguenot Society of London*, Volumes 18 and 19 (London, 1947–58); Steven J. Reid, 'On the Edge of Reason: The Scottish Universities in between Reformation and Enlightenment, 1560–1660', in Broadie, *Scottish Philosophy in the Seventeenth Century* (2020), 33–49 (46); Darwin, *Unlocking the World* (2020), 35–36; Starkey, 'Food for Thought' (2018), 36.

63. Savile, *Bank of Scotland* (1996), 11; Dingwall, *Late Seventeenth-century Edinburgh* (1994), 20, 175, 205; Sir John D. Marwick, *Edinburgh Guilds and Crafts* (Edinburgh: Scottish Burgh Records Society, 1909), 196–97; Murray Pittock, *Enlightenment in a Smart City: Edinburgh's Civic Development, 1660-1750* (Edinburgh: Edinburgh University Press, 2019), 42, 66; Cathryn Spence, *Women, Credit and Debt in Early Modern Scotland*

(Manchester: Manchester University Press, 2016), 14, 38, 60, 62–63; Devine in Gordon and Dicks, *Scottish Urban History* (1983), 93; Starkey, 'Food for Thought' (2018), 25.

64. Rab Houston, 'Fire and Faith: Edinburgh's Environment, 1660–1760', *Book of the Old Edinburgh Club* New Series 3 (1994), 25–36 (33); D. Bell, *Edinburgh Old Town* (Edinburgh: Thalis Publishing, 2008), 20; see also Michael Graham, *The Blasphemies of Thomas Aikenhead* (Edinburgh: Edinburgh University Press, 2013 [2008]), 11; Thomas Ferguson, *The Dawn of Scottish Social Welfare: A Survey from Medieval Time to 1863* (London and Edinburgh: Thomas Nelson, 1948), 138–39.

65. William Alexander, *The History of Women* (Philadelphia: J.H. Dobelbower, 1796 [1779]), 110; the opening of Chapter V.

66. Macleod, 'Edinburgh Musical Society' (2001), 22; Dingwall, *Late Seventeenth-century Edinburgh* (1994), 247, 256–57, 268; Pittock, *Enlightenment* (2019), 65; *Caledonian Mercury* 5 February 1740; Hugo Arnot, *The History of Edinburgh* (Edinburgh: West Port Books, 1998 [1779]), 316–17; R. Scott Spurlock, 'Cromwell's Edinburgh Press and the Development of Print Culture in Scotland', *Scottish Historical Review* XC:2 (2011), 179–203 (197).

67. K.A. Manley, *Books, Borrowers, and Shareholders: Scottish Circulating and Subscription Libraries Before 1825* (Edinburgh: Edinburgh Bibliographical Society/National Library of Scotland, 2012), 7–9, 11–12, 14–15, 17–19, 28; J.B. Barclay, *The Tounis Scule* (Edinburgh: Royal High School Club, 1974), 40; Lenman, *Enlightenment and Change* (2009), 65; Annie Tindley, 'Setting the Standards for Scholarship', *History Scotland* (September/October 2020), 61; Allan Kennedy, 'The Killing Time', *History Scotland* (September/October 2020), 59.

68. Emerson, *Academic Patronage* (2008), 273–74; A.D. Boney, *The Lost Gardens of Glasgow University* (Bromley: Christopher Helm, 1988), 30.

69. *The Scots Post-Man, or The New Edinburgh Gazette*, 7 September 1708; Stephen W. Brown and Warren McDougall, 'Introduction', in *History of the Book in Scotland*, Volume 2 (Edinburgh: Edinburgh University Press, 2011), 1–22 (14).

70. Houston, *Social Change in the Age of Enlightenment* (1994), 112; Robert T. Skinner, *A Notable Family of Scots Printers* (Edinburgh: Printed Privately for T & A Constable, 1927), 1; W.J. Coupland, *The Edinburgh Periodical Press*, 2 vols (Stirling: Eneas Mackery, 1908); *The Present State of Europe: Or, the Historical and Political Monthly Mercury* III (1692), 110; Christopher A. Whatley (with Derek Patrick), *The Scots and the Union* (Edinburgh: Edinburgh University Press, 2006), 7; Graham, *Aikenhead* (2013 [2008]), 4.

71. Morrice McCrae, *Physicians and Society: A History of the Royal College of Physicians of Edinburgh* (Edinburgh: John Donald, 2007), 6; Murdoch, *Network North* (2006), 135.

72. Arnot, *History of Edinburgh* (1998 [1779]), 171; Pittock, *Enlightenment* (2019), 45, 52, 112, 197; also Pittock, *Inventing and Resisting Britain: Cultural Identities in Britain and Ireland, 1685–1789* (Basingstoke: Macmillan, 1997), 105; Aonghus MacKechnie, 'The Earl of Perth's Chapel of 1688 at Drummond Castle and the Roman Catholic Architecture of James VII', *Architectural Heritage* XXV (2014), 107–31 (110, 115, 117).

73. Donaldson, *Scottish Historical Documents* (1974), 237; Devine, *Scottish Empire* (2003), 4, 32; Pittock, *Inventing and Resisting* (1997), 7; Christopher A. Whatley, *Scottish Society 1707–1830* (Manchester: Manchester University Press, 2000), 19; Harris, *Restoration* (2006), 131.

74. James Anderson Winn, *Queen Anne: Patroness of Arts* (Oxford: Oxford University Press, 2014), 22. This form of constitutional settlement was revisited in the British arrangements with the Trucial States in 1892, which preserved the domestic authority of the Emirates while assuring British control over the Persian Gulf.

75. Bryant, *Emergence of British Power in India* (2013), 21; David Armitage, 'The Political Economy of Great Britain and Ireland after the Glorious Revolution', in Jane Ohlmeyer, *Political Thought in Seventeenth-century Ireland* (2000), 221–41 (236); Oliver Finnegan, ' "Saints turned freebooters": The Darien Venture, Piracy and the Nationalisation of Maritime Space, 1695–1702', unpublished paper, 2nd World Congress of Scottish Literatures, Vancouver, 23 June 2017.

76. Armitage, 'Making the Empire British' (1997), 52; Murdoch, *Terror of the Seas?* (2010), 22.

77. Charles E. Orrer Jr, *An Archaeology of the English Atlantic World, 1600–1700* (Cambridge: Cambridge University Press, 2018), 214–15; Davies, *Beneath Another Sky* (2017), 445; Murdoch, *The Terror of the Seas?* (2010), 24.

78. Armitage, 'Making the Empire British' (1997), 52–55; Murdoch, *Terror of the Seas?* (2010), 20–23; Lavery, *Shield of Empire* (2007), 23, 26.

79. Ian Charles Cargill Graham, *Colonists from Scotland: Emigration to North America, 1707–1783* (Port Washington NY and London: Kennikat Press, 1972 [1956]), 18–19; Devine, *Scottish Empire* (2003), 1, 3, 22–24, 147; Devine and Rossner in Mackenzie and Devine, *Scotland and the British Empire* (2011), 33; Dobson, *Scottish Emigration* (1994), 26; Allan Kennedy, 'Scotland's Colony of Nova Scotia', *History Scotland* (July/August 2019), 27; Patrick Fitzgerald, 'Scottish Migration to Ireland in the Seventeenth Century', in Grosjean and Murdoch (eds), *Scottish Communities Abroad* (2005), 27–52 (28–29); Brander, *The Emigrant Scots* (1982), 28.

80. Armitage, 'Making the Empire British' (1997), 38, 50; George Pratt Insh, *Scottish Colonial Schemes 1620–1686* (Glasgow: Maclehose, Jackson & Co., 1922), 3, 49, 85, 92–93; Dobson, *Scottish Emigration* (1994), 19; Devine, *Scottish Empire* (2003), 3; Douglas Hill, *Great Emigrations: The Scots to Canada* (London: Gentry Books, 1972), 5–6; David Dobson, 'Seventeenth-Century Scottish Communities in the Americas' in Grosjean and Murdoch, *Scottish Communities Abroad* (2005), 105–32 (107, 113–14).

81. Robin Law, 'The First Scottish Guinea Company, 1634–9', *Scottish Historical Review* LXXVI: 2 (1998), 185–202 (185–87, 191, 197–99); Devine, *Scottish Empire* (2003), 2, 30.

82. Devine, *Scottish Empire* (2003), 4, 7, 32–33; T.C. Smout, *Scottish Trade on the Eve of Union 1600–1707* (Edinburgh and London: Oliver & Boyd, 1963), 188, 196; Douglas Hamilton, *Scotland, the Caribbean and the Atlantic World, 1750–1820* (Manchester: Manchester University Press, 2005), 2; Ereira, *George Ogilby* (2019[2016]), 307; Law, 'First Scottish Guinea Company' (1998), 189; Graham, *Colonists from Scotland* (1972), 13; David S. Macmillan, 'Scottish Enterprise and Influences in Canada, 1620–1900' in R.A. Cage (ed.), *The Scots Abroad: Labour, Capital, Enterprise, 1750–1914* (London: Croom Helm, 1985), 46–79 (50–51); Dobson in Grosjean and Murdoch (eds), *Scottish Communities Abroad* (2005), 106; Clark, *Port of Aberdeen* (1921), 2, 8, 11, 37.

83. Dobson, *Scottish Emigration* (1994), 21–22, 26, 39, 41; Devine, *Scottish Empire* (2003), 1; Smout, *Scottish Trade on the Eve of Union* (1963), 18; Murdoch, *Network North* (2006), 208–11.

84. Alastair Mann, *James VII: Duke and King of Scots, 1633–1701* (Edinburgh: John Donald, 2014), 127–29; Saville, *Bank of Scotland* (1996), 11; Whatley, *Scottish Society 1707–1830* (2000), 30; Steve Pincus, 'Reconfiguring the British Empire', *William and Mary Quarterly* 69:1 (2012), 63–70 (65); Harris, *Restoration* (2006), 312.

85. Insh, *Scottish Colonial Schemes* (1922), 4, 118–19, 145, 149, 151, 163, 179–81, 185, 210; Devine, *Scottish Empire* (2003), 38; William R. Brock with C. Helen Brock, *Scotus Americanus* (Edinburgh: Edinburgh University Press, 1982), 5–7; Ned C. Landsman, 'The Middle Colonies: New Opportunities for Settlement, 1660–1700', in Canny (ed.), *The Origins of Empire* (2000), 351–74 (358).

86. Pittock, *Jacobitism* (1998), 15, 19–24, 30; David Onnekink, 'The Earl of Portland and Scotland (1689–1699): a Re-evaluation of Williamite Policy', *Scottish Historical Review* LXXXV:2 (2006), 231–49 (232, 238, 248); Murdoch, *Terror of the Seas?* (2010), 322; N.A.M. Rodger, *The Command of the Ocean: A Naval History of Britain 1649–1715* (London: Penguin/National Maritime Museum, 2006 [2004]), 140; Tim Harris, *Revolution: The Great Crisis of the British Monarchy, 1685–1720* (London: Penguin, 2007[2006]), 274, 393; Mileham, *Scottish Regiments* (1996), 11, 42–43; Claim of Right Act 1689 c. 28.

87. Jeffrey Stephen, *Defending the Revolution: The Church of Scotland 1689–1716* (Farnham: Ashgate, 2013), 165, 170–71, 180; Kieran German, 'The Scots Episcopalians after Disestablishment, 1689–1723', in *Institutional Change and Stability* (2009) 49–62 (54–56); Harris, *Revolution* (2007), 65, 376, 378, 415.

88. George Grub, *An Ecclesiastical History of Scotland*, 4 vols (Edinburgh: Edmonston and Douglas, 1861), III:316; Morgan Kelly and Cormac O´Gráda, 'The Waning of the Little Ice Age: Climate Change in Early Modern Europe', *Journal of Interdisciplinary History* XLIV:3 (2014), 301–25 (319); Boxer, *The Portuguese Seaborne Empire* (1969), 114; Bowie, *Public Opinion in Early Modern Scotland* (2020), 185; Harris, *Revolution* (2007), 416.

89. Pittock, *Inventing and Resisting* (1997), 67, 73, 83.

90. James Byers, *A Letter to a Friend at Edinburgh From Roterdam* (Edinburgh, 1702), 16–17; Devine, *Scottish Empire* (2003), 29, 31, 34, 40–41, 45–47; Dobson, *Scottish Emigration* (1994), 78–79; Savile, *Bank of Scotland* (1996), 9; Alan Cameron, *Bank of Scotland 1695–1995: A Very Singular Institution* (Edinburgh and London: Mainstream, 1995), 18; Eric J. Graham, *Seawolves: Pirates and the Scots* (Edinburgh: Birlinn, 2005), 144.

91. National Library of Scotland Rosebery MS Ry III.a.10 no. 83, stanzas 11 and 13.

92. Allan Macinnes, *Union and Empire* (Cambridge: Cambridge University Press, 2007), 217–18; Tom McInally, *The Sixth Scottish University: The Scots Colleges Abroad: 1575 to 1799* (Leiden and Boston: Brill, 2012), 77.

93. Bridget McPhail, 'Through a Glass Darkly: Scots and Indians Converge at Darien', *Eighteenth-Century Life* 18 (1994), 129–47 (134–38, 143); Hector L. MacQueen, '*Regiam Majestatem*, Scots Law and National Identity', *Scottish Historical Review* LXXIV:1 (1995), 1–25 (3).

94. Byers, *Letter to a Friend* (1702), 4.

95. John McAteer and Nigel Rigby, *Captain Cook and the Pacific: Art, Exploration and Empire* (London and New York: Yale Unversity Press, 2017), 25; Orrer (2018), 214. At the time of Darien, a first-rate ship was some 50m long and carried 96 to 110 guns; a second-rate was of similar size carrying 84 to 90; a third-rate was some 47 metres and carried 64 to 80, and smaller fourth- (48 to 60), fifth- (26 to 44) and sixth- (16 to 24) rates made up the ranks of naval power.

96. Sydney Parkinson, *Journal of a Voyage to the South Seas* (London: Stanfield Parkinson, 1773), 122; Geoffrey Lachassagne, *Caledonia*, Petit à Petit & Kepler, 2021. I am indebted to Nigel Leask for the suggestion regarding *Ossian*.

97. Davies, *Beneath Another Sky* (2017), 464; Richard Evans, *The Pursuit of Power: Europe 1815–1914* (London: Penguin, 2017 [2016]), 272, 637, 640. For New Caledonia film, see Lachassagne (2021), *Caledonia*, Petit à Petit prod. & Kepler22 prod.

98. Julie Orr, 'Captain Robert Pincarton', *History Scotland* (July/August 2019), 16–21 (17–20); Finnegan, 'Saints Turned Freebooters' (2017); George Ridpath, *Scotland's Grievance Relating to Darien, &c* (Edinburgh, 1700).

99. Bowie, 'Legal Limited Monarchy' (2015), 149–52; Bowie, 'A 1706 Manifesto for an Armed Rising against Incorporating Union', *Scottish Historical Review* XCIV:2 (2015), 237–67 (239).

100. Whatley, *Scottish Society 1707–1830* (2000), 40–41; Talbott, *Conflict, Commerce and Franco-Scottish Relations* (2014), 146; Bowie, 'Legal Limited Monarchy' (2015), 150; Murdoch and Mackillop (eds), *Fighting for Identity* (2002), xli–xliii; Thomas A. Fischer, *The Scots in Germany* (Edinburgh: Otto Schulze & Co., 1902), 118–19; Mileham, *Scottish Regiments* (1996) Plate 8 for Scottish forces carrying saltires at Blenheim.

101. Christopher A. Whatley with Derek J. Patrick, *The Scots and the Union* (Edinburgh: Edinburgh University Press, 2006) remains the leading study of the beliefs and outlook of the Union's core supporters; Smout, *Scottish Trade on the Eve of Union* (1963), 262; L.M. Cullen, 'The Scottish Exchange in London, 1673–1778', in Connolly, Houston and Morris, *Conflict, Identity and Economic Development* (1995), 29–44 (29); Pittock, *Scottish Nationality*, 53–54; John A. Robertson (ed.), *Fletcher of Saltoun: Political Works* (Cambridge: Cambridge University Press, 1997), 213–14; Colin Kidd, 'Protestantism, Constitutionalism and British Identity under the Later Stuarts' in Ben Bradshaw and Peter Roberts (eds), *British Consciousness and Identity: The Making of Britain,*

1533–1707 (Cambridge: Cambridge University Press, 1998), 321–42 (331); Lindsay Paterson, *The Autonomy of Modern Scotland* (Edinburgh: Edinburgh University Press, 1994) was one of the first to argue for the continuing quasi-statehood of Scotland.

102. Macinnes, *Union and Empire* (2007), 202, 238.

103. John Jackson, *The History of the Scottish Stage* (Edinburgh: Peter Hill, 1793), 7; Bowie, 'A 1706 Manifesto' (2015), 240.

104. Susan Reynolds, *Kingdoms and Communities in Western Europe 900–1300*, 2nd ed. (Oxford: Oxford University Press, 1997 [1984]), 257, 262, 270.

105. Dauvit Broun, 'Defining Scotland and the Scots before the Wars of Independence', 4–17 (5–6, 11); Fiona Watson, 'The Enigmatic Lion: Scotland, Kingship and National Identity in the Wars of Independence', 18–37 (22, 31); Edward J. Cowan, 'Identity, Freedom and the Declaration of Arbroath', 38–68 (40–42), all in Dauvit Broun; R.J. Finlay and Michael Lynch (eds), *Image and Identity: The Making and Re-making of Scotland Through the Ages* (Edinburgh: John Donald, 1998).

106. MacQueen, '*Regiam Majestatem*' (1995), 1–25.

107. Murray Pittock, 'The Declaration of Arbroath in Scottish Political Thought, 1689–1789', in Klaus Peter Müller (ed.), *Scotland and Arbroath 1320–2020* (Frankfurt: Peter Lang, 2020), 165–80; see also Edward J. Cowan, 'Declaring Arbroath', 13–31 (14, 15, 29) and Grant G. Simpson, 'The Declaration of Arbroath: What Significance When?', 108–15 (112–13), both in Geoffrey Barrow (ed.), *The Declaration of Arbroath: History, Significance, Setting* (Edinburgh: Society of Antiquaries of Scotland, 2003); Bowie, 'Legal Limited Monarchy' (2015), 131, 143–46; Archie Turnbull, in David Daiches, Peter and Jean Jones (eds), *The Scottish Enlightenment, 1730–90: A Hotbed of Genius* (Edinburgh: Edinburgh University Press, 1986), 144; Reynolds, *Kingdoms and Communities* (1997), 274.

108. Karin Bowie, unpublished paper on the Declaration of Arbroath, Newbattle, 20 May 2021, referencing National Library of Scotland Wodrow Q73 f. 285; Bowie, *Public Opinion in Early Modern Scotland* (2020), 237; Pittock, 'Declaration of Arbroath' (2020); Cairns Craig, 'Constituting Scotland', *Irish Review* 28 (2001), 1–27 (2).

109. Karen Bowie, *Scottish Public Opinion and the Anglo-Scottish Union 1699–1707* (Woodbridge: Boydell and Brewer/Royal Historical Society, 2007), 115; Karen Bowie, *Addresses Against Incorporating Union, 1706–1707* (Edinburgh: Scottish History Society, 2018); Bowie, *Public Opinion in Early Modern Scotland* (2020), 237.

110. Bowie, 'Legal Limited Monarchy' (2015), 152–53; 'A 1706 Manifesto' (2015), 237; *Public Opinion in Early Modern Scotland* (2020), 212, 233.

111. Pittock, *Jacobitism* (1998), 32; Whatley with Patrick, *The Scots and the Union* (2006), 11.

112. Bowie, 'Legal Limited Monarchy' (2015), 153.

113. Murray Pittock, 'Scottish Sovereignty and the Union of 1707: Then and Now', *National Identities* 14:1 (2012), 11–21 (12–14); Julian Hoppit, *The Dreadful Monster and its Poor Relations: Taxing and Spending in the United Kingdom, 1707–1821* (London: Allen Lane, 2021), 104.

114. Pittock, 'Scottish sovereignty' (2012); Black, *George III* (2020), 46.

115. Whatley with Patrick, *Scots and the Union* (2006), 12, 14–15.

CHAPTER 2: CROWN AND NO KINGDOM, CHURCH AND NO STATE

1. Murray Pittock, *Enlightenment in a Smart City: Edinburgh's Civic Development, 1660–1750* (Edinburgh: Edinburgh University Press, 2019), 51. For the 1708 Rising and further details on the political climate of the time, see John Gibson, *Playing the Scottish Card* (Edinburgh: Edinburgh University Press, 1988) and Daniel Szechi, *Britain's Lost Revolution? Jacobite Scotland and French Grand Strategy 1701–8* (Manchester: Manchester University Press, 2015); Wolfgang Behringer, *A Cultural History of Climate* (London: Polity, 2010 [*Kulturgeschichte des Klimas,* 2006]).

2. Murray Pittock, *Inventing and Resisting Britain* (Basingstoke: Macmillan, 1997), 13–15, 54, 100; Norman Davies, *Beneath Another Sky: A Global Journey into History* (London: Penguin, 2018 [2017]), 46.

3. T.M Devine, *Scotland's Empire 1600–1815* (London: Allen Lane, 2003), 236; Roger L. Emerson, *An Enlightened Duke: The Life of Archibald Campbell (1682–1761) Earl of Ilay 3rd Duke of Argyll* (Kilkerran: humming earth, 2013).

4. Gordon Donaldson, *Scottish Constitutional Documents* (Edinburgh: Scottish Academic Press, 1974), 263.

5. Donald J. Withrington, 'Church and State in Scottish Education Before 1872', in Heather Holmes (ed.), *Institutions of Scotland: Education*, Volume 11 of Scottish Life and Society (East Linton: Tuckwell Press, 2000), 47–64 (52).

6. Pittock, *Enlightenment* (2019), 20; cf. Erin Meyer, *The Culture Map* (New York: Public Affairs, 2015 [2014]), 125, 166, 171; Richard Evans, *The Pursuit of Power: Europe 1815–1914* (London: Penguin, 2017 [2016]), 278.

7. George McGilvary, *East India Patronage and the British State: The Scottish Elite and Politics in the Eighteenth Century* (London and New York: Tauris, 2008), 203.

8. Pittock, *Enlightenment* (2019), 64–65, 96–97, 115. The four Gregorys at Aberdeen Grammar School were James Gregory FRS (1638–75), David Gregory FRS (1659–1708), John Gregory FRS (1724–73) and James Gregory FRSE (1753–1821).

9. *Remarks and Collections of Thomas Hearne,* Volume II, ed. C.E. Doble (Oxford: Clarendon Press, 1886), 12.

10. T.M Devine, *The Scottish Clearances* (London: Penguin, 2019 [2018], 124, 136; Colin Kidd, 'Conditional Britons: The Scots Covenanting Tradition and the Eighteenth-Century British State', *English Historical Review* 117 (2002), 1147–76 (1149, 1152, 1157–59, 1162, 1163, 1165); Henry R. Sefton, 'Presbyterianism', in Holmes, *Education* (2000), 127–42 (133).

11. Robert A Dodgshon, 'Everyday Structures, Rhythms and Spaces of the Scottish Countryside', in Elizabeth Foster and Christopher A. Whatley (eds), *A History of Everyday Life in Scotland, 1600 to 1800* (Edinburgh: Edinburgh University Press, 2010), 27–50 (37); Devine, *Scottish Clearances* (2019), 42–45; Robert I. Frost, '"The Penury of these Malignant Rogues": Comparing the Rural Economies of the Scottish Highlands and the Polish-Lithuanian Commonwealth in the Early Modern Period', in T.M. Devine and David Hesse (eds), *Scotland and Poland: Historical Encounters, 1500–2010* (Edinburgh: John Donald, 2012 [2011]), 109–31 (120, 128); Elizabeth Gemmell and Nicholas Mayhew, *Changing Values in Medieval Scotland: A Study of Prices, Money, and Weights and Measures* (Cambridge: Cambridge University Press, 1995), 8–9, 380.

12. Gemmill and Mayhew, *Changing Values* (1995), 19, 24, 382; R.D. Connor and A.D.C. Simpson, *Weights and Measures in Scotland: A European Perspective* (Edinburgh and East Linton: National Museums of Scotland and Tuckwell Press, 2004), 409; Julian Hoppit, 'Reforming Britain's Weights and Measures, 1660–1824', *English Historical Review* 108 (426) (1993), 82–104; Evans, *Pursuit of Power* (2017), 376.

13. Leah Leneman, *Alienated Affections: The Scottish Experience of Divorce and Separation, 1684–1830* (Edinburgh: Edinburgh University Press, 1998), 13, 15–16; Murray Pittock, 'Contrasting Cultures: Town and Country', in, Patricia Dennison, David Ditchburn and Michael Lynch (eds), *Aberdeen: A New History* (East Linton: Tuckwell Press, 2002), I:347–76 (358); Pittock, *Enlightenment* (2019), 66, 87, 119; Rebecca Mason, 'Locating Women in the Early Modern Scottish Economy: Households, Commerce and Credit', unpublished paper, University of Glasgow Economic History Seminar, 4 March 2021.

14. Bob Harris and Charles McKean, *The Scottish Town in the Age of Enlightenment 1740–1820* (Edinburgh: Edinburgh University Press, 2014), 56; Leah Leneman and Rosalind Mitchison, *Sin in the City: Sexuality and Social Control in Urban Scotland 1660–1780* (Edinburgh: Scottish Cultural Press, 1998), 9.

15. Clarisse Godard Desmarest, 'Scottish and English Architecture: A "Provincial" Relationship?', *E–rea* (30 October 2019), 11; Margaret Stewart, *The Architectural,*

Landscape and Constitutional Plans of the Earl of Mar, 1700–32 (Dublin: Four Courts, 2016), 27, 113.

16. See Murray Pittock (General Editor), *The Edinburgh Edition of the Collected Works of Allan Ramsay* (Edinburgh: Edinburgh University Press, forthcoming).

17. Daniel Defoe, *A Tour Through the Whole Island of Great Britain*, ed. Pat Rogers (Harmondsworth: Penguin, 1971), 561.

18. Gordon Pentland, '"We Speak for the Ready": Images of Scots in Political Prints, 1707–1832', *Scottish Historical Review* XC (2011), 64–95 (67, 69, 72, 74).

19. Julian Hoppit, 'Scotland and the Taxing Union, 1707–1815', *Scottish Historical Review* XCVIII:1 (2019), 45–70 (46, 46, 49n, 51–52, 58–59, 64, 66, 68); Hoppit, *The Dreadful Monster and its Poor Relations: Taxing and Spending in the United Kingdom, 1707–2021* (London: Allen Lane, 2021), 40, 42, 56, 80, 85; Christopher A. Whatley, *Scottish Society 1707–1830* (Manchester: Manchester University Press, 2000), 54, 57, 69, 104, 111,116, 190–92, 194–96, 201.

20. Devine, *Scottish Clearances* (2019), 23, 53–54, 65, 75, 123; T.M Devine, *To the Ends of the Earth: Scotland's Global Diaspora* (London: Allen Lane, 2011), 3; T.M. Devine and Philipp R. Rosner, 'Scots in the Atlantic Economy 1600–1800' in John Mackenzie and T.M. Devine (eds), *Scotland and the British Empire* (Oxford: Oxford University Pres, 2011), 30–53 (42); Pittock, *Enlightenment* (2019), 73.

21. Whatley, *Scottish Society* (2000), 54, 57, 69, 104, 111,116, 190–92, 194–96, 201; Stéphane Robin, 'Jacobitism and Banditry', unpublished MA thesis (Université de Bretagne-Sud, 2014), 27, 32; Andrew Mackillop, *'More Fruitful than the Soil': Army, Empire and the Scottish Highlands, 1715–1815* (East Linton: Tuckwell Press, 2000), 22; Óscar Reio Morales, *Ireland and the Spanish Empire, 1600–1825* (Dublin: Four Courts, 2010), 185 and passim; Victoria E. Clark, *The Port of Aberdeen* (Aberdeen: D. Wyllie & Son, 1921), 66–68, 102.

22. Devine, *Scottish Clearances* (2019), 23, 53–54, 65, 75, 123; Frost in Devine and Hesse, *Scotland and Poland* (2012), 114; Whatley, *Scottish Society* (2000), 54, 57, 69, 104, 111, 116, 190–92, 194–96, 201; Pittock, *Enlightenment* (2019), 73; David Dobson, *Scottish Emigration to Colonial America, 1607–1785* (Athens and London: University of Georgia Press, 1994), 101; Jan Oosthoek, 'Worlds Apart: The Scottish Forestry Tradition and the Development of Forestry in India', *Journal of Irish and Scottish Studies* 3:1 (2010), 61–74 (65); Philip Long and Joanne Norman, *The Story of Scottish Design* (London: Thames& Hudson/V & A, 2018), 12; Douglas Hamilton, *Scotland, the Caribbean and the Atlantic World, 1750–1820* (Manchester: Manchester University Press, 2005), 13.

23. Devine, *Scottish Clearances* (2019), 23, 53–54, 65, 75, 123; Whatley, *Scottish Society* (2000), 54, 57, 69, 104, 111, 116, 190–92, 194–96, 201; Pittock, *Enlightenment* (2019), 73; Robin Law, 'The First Scottish Guinea Company, 1634–9', *Scottish Historical Review* LXXVI:2 (1998), 185–202 (189).

24. Devine, *Scottish Clearances* (2019), 83–84, 98–104, 106, 109, 111, 114; Whatley, *Scottish Society* (2000), 54, 193–94.

25. F. Peter Lole, *A Digest of the Jacobite Clubs*, Royal Stuart Society Paper LV (London: Royal Stuart Society, 1999), 19, 39–40, 45, 58, 66, 72; Karin Bowie, 'A 1706 Manifesto for an Armed Rising against Incorporating Union', *Scottish Historical Review* XCIV:2 (2015), 237–67 (259–60). For a more detailed discussion and theory of communication underpinning the use of Jacobite material culture to communicate political sympathy, see Murray Pittock, *Material Culture and Sedition* (Basingstoke: Macmillan, 2013).

26. Elizabeth Foyster and Christopher A. Whatley, 'Introduction', in Foyster and Whatley, *Everyday Life in Scotland* (2010), 1–26 (21); Jacqueline Riding, *Jacobites: A New History of the '45 Rebellion* (London: Bloomsbury, 2017 [2015]), 107, 145; Emile Durkheim, 'Symbolic Objects, Communicative Interaction and Social Creativity', in Jeremy Tanner (ed.), *The Sociology of Art: A Reader* (London and New York: Routledge, 2003), 63–68 (67); Graeme Morton, *William Wallace: A National Tale* (Edinburgh: Edinburgh University Press, 2014), 77; Nick Haynes, *Scotland's Sporting Buildings* (Edinburgh: Historic Scotland,

2014), 25–26; Pittock, *Material Culture and Sedition* (2013); Kidd, 'Conditional Britons' (2002), 1158; J. Balfour Paul, *History of the Royal Company of Archers* (Privately Printed, 1875).

27. John Parker Lawson, *History of the Scottish Episcopalian Church from the Revolution to the Present Time* (Edinburgh: Gallie and Bayley, 1843), xxxvi, 47, 101; Christopher A. Whatley, 'Reformed Religion, Regime Change, Scottish Whigs and the Struggle for the "Soul" of Scotland, *c.*1688–1788', *Scottish Historical Review* XCII (2013), 66–99 (71, 74); Jeffrey Stephen, *Defending the Revolution: The Church of Scotland 1689–1716* (Farnham: Ashgate, 2013), 165–70.

28. National Library of Scotland (NLS) Adv. MS 16.2.1; NLS MS 293; *Hearne's Remarks and Collections* Volume IV, ed. D.W. Rannie (Oxford: Clarendon Press, 1898), 203–04; *Lord Hervey's Memoirs*, ed. Romney Sedgwick (Harmondsworth: Penguin, 1984 [1963]), 191.

29. Mackillop, *'More Fruitful Than the Soil'* (2000), 21; Basil Skinner, *Scots in Italy in the 18th Century* (Edinburgh: National Galleries of Scotland, 1966), 32; John Ingamells, *A Dictionary of British and Irish Travelers in Italy, 1701–1800* (New Haven: Yale University Press, 1997), 573, 624, 641; Matthew Glozier, *Scottish Soldiers in France in the Reign of the Sun King: Nursery for Men of Honour* (Leiden, Boston: Brill, 2004), 232, 248; Stephen Wood, *The Scottish Soldier* (Edinburgh: Archive/National Museums of Scotland, 1987), 23; James G. Parker, 'Scottish Enterprise in India, 1750–1914' in R.A. Cage (ed.), *The Scots Abroad: Labour, Capital, Enterprise, 1750–1914* (London: Croom Helm, 1985), 191–219 (193); Andrew Phillips and J.C. Sharman, *Outsourcing Empire: How Company-States Made the Modern World* (Princeton and Oxford: Princeton University Press, 2020), 59, 103.

30. Dmitry Fedosov, *The Caledonian Connection* (Aberdeen, 1996), 13, 33, 37, 46, 62, 83; Duncan A. Bruce, *The Mark of the Scots* (New Jersey: Birch Lane Press, 1997 [1996]), 187.

31. Paul Dukes, 'Scottish Soldiers in Muscovy', *The Caledonian Phalanx: Scots in Russia* (Edinburgh: National Library of Scotland, 1987), 9–23 (16); R.G. Cross, 'Scoto-Russian Contacts in the Reign of Catherine the Great (1762–1796)', idem, 24–46 (37); John R. Bowles, 'From the Banks of the Neva to the Shores of Lake Baikal: Some Enterprising Scots in Russia', idem, 65–80 (67–68).

32. Robert Collis, 'Jacobite Networks, Freemasonry and Fraternal Sociability and their Influence in Russia', *Politica Hermetica* 24 (2016), 89–99 (89–90, 93–96, 97–99); Didier Ramelet Stuart, *Les Stuarts et la Corse* (Corsica: Alba Editions, 2020), 77–78; Atina L.K. Niktinen, 'Field-Marshal James Keith: Governor of the Ukraine and Finland, 1740–1743', in Andrew Mackillop and Steve Murdoch (eds), *Military Governors and Imperial Frontiers* (Leiden: Brill, 2002), 99–117 (102–03, 105–07).

33. John H. Appleby, 'Through the Looking-Glass: Scottish Doctors in Russia (1704–1854)', *Caledonian Phalanx,* 47 (47–48, 51); Rebecca Wills, *The Jacobites and Russia 1715–1750* (East Linton: Tuckwell Press, 2002), 77, 130; Fedosov, *Caledonian Connection* (1996),7, 17, 26, 33, 36, 46, 49, 54, 62, 67, 80, 81, 83, 94, 109.

34. Fedosov, *Caledonian Connection* (1996), 7, 8, 29, 71, 94, 108; Ian McGowan, ' "Caledonia and Rus": Some Literary Cross-References', in *Caledonian Phalanx* (1987), 81–89 (81); Cross in *Caledonian Phalanx* (1987), idem, 40–41; Cairns Craig, 'Empire of Intellect', in Mackenzie and Devine, *Scotland and the British Empire*, 84–116 (97).

35. *The Scots Magazine* (1739), I:4; Kieran German, 'Non-Jurors, Liturgy, and Jacobite Commitment, 1718–46', 74 (78–82); Wills, *Jacobites in Russia* (2002),15; Fedosov, *Caledonian Connection* (1996), 35; Steve Murdoch, 'Irish Entrepreneurs and Sweden in the First Half of the Eighteenth Century', in Thomas O'Connor and Mary Ann Lyons (eds), *Irish Communities in Early-Modern Europe* (Dublin: Four Courts, 2006), 348–66 (365); see H.W. Langford, 'The Non-Jurors and the Eastern Orthodox' (1965), at http://anglicanhistory.org/nonjurors/langford1.html

36. Wills, *Jacobites in Russia* (2002), 15, 22, 27–28; A.G. Cross, 'Scoto-Russian Contacts in the Reign of Catherine the Great (1762–1796)', in *Caledonian Phalanx* (1987), 24–46

(25–27); Steve Murdoch, 'Des reseaux de conspiration dans le Nord? Une étude de la franc-maçonnerie jacobite et hanovrienne en Scandinavie et en Russie, 1688–1746', *Politica Hermetica* 24 (2010), 29–56; Michael Brander, *Emigrant Scots* (New Jersey: Birch Hill Press, 1997 [1996]), 64; Thomas A. Fischer, *The Scots in Germany* (Edinburgh: Otto Schulze and Co., 1902), 128. Adam and Robert Armstrong are both family members.

37. Ingamells, *Dictionary* (1997), 329, 334, 476, 573, 690; Edward Corp, *The Stuarts in Italy, 1719–66* (Cambridge: Cambridge University Press, 2011), 4; Pittock, *Enlightenment* (2019), 142.

38. Ingamells, *Dictionary* (1997)),169, 174, 175, 184, 192, 214–15, 317, 685; Corp *Stuarts in Italy* (2011), 7, 97, 101–06, 332; Pittock, *Enlightenment* (2019), 140–50.

39. Ingamells, *Dictionary* (1997), 172, 334; Long and Norman, *Scottish Design* (2018), 13; Thierry Giappiconi, emails to the author, 8, 13 August 2018.

40. Steve Murdoch in O'Connor and Lyons, *Irish Communities* (2006), 348–66 (352, 365); Steve Murdoch, *Network North: Scottish Kin, Commercial and Covert Associations in Northern Europe, 1603*–1746 (Leiden and Boston: Brill, 2006), 333, 337; Alexander Murdoch, *Scotland and America, c.1600–c.1800* (Basingstoke: Palgrave Macmillan, 2010); Allan Mackenzie, *History of the Lodge Canongate Kilwinning No.2* (Edinburgh: James Hogg, 1888); Mark Colman Wallace, 'Scottish Freemasonry 1725–1810: Progress, Power, Politics', unpublished PhD (St Andrews, 2007), 105, 321, 328, 332; Lole, *Jacobite Clubs* (1999), 36; William James Hughan, *The Jacobite Lodge at Rome 1735–7* (Torquay, 1910), 15, 17, 19–21, 49–50; Pierre-Yves Beaurepaire, 'Le Parnasse de Chalmers et L'Art Royal Itinéraire d'un Duc', in *Politica Hermetica* 24 (2010), 100–109 (100); Steve Murdoch, 'Dés Reseaux de Conspiration dans le Nord?', idem, 29–56 (31, 53); José Antonio Ferrer Benimeli, 'La Présence de la Franc-Maçonnerie Stuartiste à Madrid et à Rome', idem, 68–88 (70, 84); Stuart, *Les Stuarts et la Corse* (2020), 72, 102, 111, 143, 149; Joe Rock, 'The Edinburgh Academy of St Luke at Work, *c.*1737–47', *Book of the Old Edinburgh Club* ns16 (2020), 47–62 (52).

41. Corp, *Stuart Court in Italy* (2011), 88; Johan Huizinga, *Homo Ludens* (London: Paladin, 1970 [1949]), 45.

42. Mackillop, *'More Fruitful Than the Soil'* (2000), 13.

43. National Records of Scotland (NRS) GD 241/380/14 (Copy Proclamation of the Earl of Mar); Whatley, 'Reformed Religion' (2013), 68, 94.

44. National Archives (TNA), SP 54/9/3B; Murray Pittock, *The Myth of the Jacobite Clans: The Jacobite Army in 1745* (Edinburgh: Edinburgh University Press, 2009 [1995]), 146–47.

45. Edward Corp, *Jacobites at Urbino* (Basingstoke: Palgrave Macmillan, 2009), 12, 154–55; Corp et al., *A Court in Exile: The Stuarts in France, 1689–1718* (Cambridge: Cambridge University Press, 2004); 'Volontaires écossais', Bibliotheque Universitaire de Poitiers Fonds d'Argenson X:60; Daniel Szechi, *The Jacobites: Britain and Europe, 1688–1788*, 2nd edition (Manchester: Manchester University Press, 2019 [1994]), 160.

46. James Buchan, *John Law* (London: Quercus/Maclehose Press, 2019 [2018]), 1, 18, 52, 103, 109.

47. Murray Pittock, 'John Law's Theory of Money and its Roots in Scottish Culture', *Proceedings of the Society of Antiquaries of Scotland* 133 (2003), 391–403.

48. Buchan, *John Law* (2019), 67, 277, 281.

49. Buchan, *John Law* (2019), 334.

50. Buchan, *John Law* (2019), 392, 413–15; Billy Kay, *The Scottish World: A Journey into the Scottish Diaspora* (Edinburgh and London: Mainstream, 2006), 92.

51. Buchan, *John Law* (2019), 45, 243, 261, 300.

52. Andrew S. Skinner, 'Sir James Steuart: The Market and the State', *History of Economic Ideas* I (1993), 1–42 (2, 3, 5, 6, 35, 38).

53. Margaret Lincoln, *British Pirates and Society, 1680–1730* (Farnham: Ashgate, 2014), 35, 77; Murdoch, *Network North* (2006), 322; Anne Bialuschewski, 'Thomas Bowrey's

Madagascar Manuscript of 1708', *History in Africa* 34 (2007), 31–42 (34); Virginia Bever Platt, 'The East India Company and the Madagascar Slave Trade', *William and Mary Quarterly* 26:4 (1969), 548–77 (549, 552); P. Bradley Nutting, 'The Madagascar Connection: Parliament and Piracy, 1690–1701', *The American Journal of Legal History* 22:3 (1978), 202–15 (203–04, 209); Jane Hooper, 'Pirates and Kings: Power on the Shores of Early Modern Madagascar and the Indian Ocean', *Journal of World History* 22:2 (2011), 215–42 (215, 222); Buchan, *John Law* (2019), 70; TNA RA State Papers (SP) Main 47, ff. 56–57 (William Morgan to King James, Paris, 4 June 1720); Robin, 'Jacobitism and Banditry' (2014), 38; E.T. Fox, 'Jacobitism and the "Golden Age" of Piracy', *International Journal of Maritime History* XXII:2 (2010), 277–303 (282–84, 287–88); Colin Woodard, *The Republic of Pirates* (London: Pan, 2014), 4, 196; Steve Murdoch, *The Terror of the Seas?* (Leiden: Brill, 2010), 291, 323; Eric J. Graham, *Seawolves: Pirates and the Scots* (Edinburgh: Birlinn, 2005), xxv, xxvi, xxx, 24, 133; Harry Lewis, 'Jacobites in the Caribbean', unpublished seminar paper, Jacobite Studies Trust, 9 March 2021.

54. Whatley, *Scottish Society* (2000), 74; Mackillop, *'More Fruitful Than the Soil'* (2000), 20, 25; Colin Calloway, *White People, Indians and Highlanders* (Oxford: Oxford University Press, 2008), 91. For the Atholl estates, see Leah Leneman, *Living in Atholl: A Social History of the Estates, 1685–1785* (Edinburgh: Edinburgh University Press, 1986).

55. George K. McGilvary, *East India Patronage and the British State* (London and New York: Tauris, 2008), ix, 65; Michael Brander and Iseabail Macleod, *World Dictionary of Scottish Associations* (Edinburgh and London: Johnston & Bacon, 1979), 1.

56. T.M. Devine, 'A Scottish Empire of Enterprise in the East, *c.*1700–1914', in T.M. Devine and Angela McCarthy (eds), *The Scottish Experience in Asia, c.1700 to the Present: Settlers and Sojourners* (Basingstoke: Palgrave Macmillan, 2017), 23–49 (24–27).

57. McGilvary, *East India Patronage* (2008), 1, 2, 5, 56, 65; Devine, *Scottish Empire* (2003), 251; Devine and Rossner in Mackenzie and Devine, *Scotland and the British Empire* (Oxford: Oxford University Press, 2011), 37; Janet Starkey, 'Food for Thought: Coffee, Coffee-Houses and le bon gout in Edinburgh during the Scottish Enlightenment', *Book of the Old Edinburgh Club* ns 14 (2018), 23–44 (37); Clark, *Port of Aberdeen* (1921), 90.

58. Buchan, *John Law* (2019), 27; Long and Norman, *Scottish Design* (2018), 32.

59. Ingamells, *Dictionary* (1997), 333; Rosemary Sweet, *Cities and the Grand Tour: The British in Italy, c.1690–1820* (Cambridge: Cambridge University Press, 2012), 23; Tobias Smollett, *Travels through France and Italy*, ed. Frank Felsenstein (Oxford: Oxford University Press, 1981), 52, 61, 241, 257, 263; Stuart, *Les Stuarts et la Corse* (2020), 40.

60. Hamilton, *Scotland, the Caribbean and the Atlantic World* (2005), 70, 85–86, 93; Ian Charles Cargill Graham, *Colonists from Scotland: Emigration to North America, 1707–1783* (Port Washington NY & London: Kennikat Press, 1972 [1956]), 14; David Dobson, *Scots in the West Indies*, Volume II (Baltimore: Clearfield, 2006), Introduction, 123–24; Andrew Phillips and J.C. Sherman, *Outsourcing Empire: How Company-States Made the Modern World* (Princeton and Oxford: Princeton University Press, 2020), 59, 70, 74. I am indebted to Jennifer Melville's research for the *Facing Our Past* National Trust for Scotland report for details on The Pineapple.

61. Hamilton, *Scotland, the Caribbean and the Atlantic World* (2005), 2–3; A. Murdoch, *Scotland and America* (2010), 64; Dobson, *Scots in West Indies* (2006), 123; Philip D. Morgan, 'British Encounters with Africans and African Americans, circa 1600–1780', in Bernard Balyn and Philip D. Morgan (eds), *Strangers within the Realm: Cultural Margins of the First British Empire* (Chapel Hill, NC: Omohundo Institute/University of North Carolina Press, 1991), 157–219 (197).

62. Whatley, *Scottish Society* (2000), 110; Hamilton, *Scotland, the Caribbean and the Atlantic World* (2005), 49, 50, 56, 60; Jonas Berg and Bo Lagercrantz, *Scots in Sweden*, intr. Eric Linklater (Edinburgh, 1962), 58, 60, 61; David Hancock, *Citizens of the World: London Merchants and the Integration of the British Atlantic Community, 1735–1785* (Cambridge: Cambridge University Press, 1995), 147; Michael Morris, 'Atlantic Archipelagos: A

Cultural History of Scotland, the Caribbean and the Atlantic World, *c*.1740–1833', unpublished Ph.D. (University of Glasgow, 2012), 54, 71.

63. T.M. Devine, 'Introduction: Scotland and Transatlantic Slavery', in T.M. Devine (ed.), *Recovering Scotland's Slavery Past: The Caribbean Connection* (Edinburgh: Edinburgh University Press, 2015), 1–20 (15); Devine and Rossner in Mackenzie and Devine, *Scotland and the British Empire* (2011) 49, 51–52; Devine, *Scottish Empire* (2003), 233, 237, 238, 244–46; Bruce Lenman, *Enlightenment and Change: Scotland 1746–1832* (Edinburgh: Edinburgh University Press, 2009)), 86–87; Hamilton, *Scotland, the Caribbean and the Atlantic World* (2005), 3–5, 58; A. Murdoch, *Scotland and America* (2010), 40; Dobson, *Scottish Emigration* (1994), 118, 125; Dobson, *Scots in West Indies* (2006), 122; Morgan in Bailyn and Morgan, *Strangers within the Realm* (1991), 193, 198.

64. T.M. Devine, *Recovering Scotland's Slavery Past* (2015), 15; Devine and Rossner in Mackenzie and Devine, *Scotland and the British Empire* 49, 51–52; David Alson, ' "The habits of these creatures in clinging one to the other": Enslaved Africans, Scots and the Plantations of Guyana', idem, 99–123; Devine, *Scottish Empire* (2003), 233, 237, 238, 244–46; Lenman, *Enlightenment and Change* (2009), 86–87; Hamilton, *Scotland, the Caribbean and the Atlantic World* (2005), 3–5, 58; A. Murdoch, *Scotland and America* (2010), 40; Giovanni Covi et al., *Caribbean-Scottish Relations* (London: Mango Publishing, 2007), 16; Dobson, *Scottish Emigration* (1994), 118, 125; Dobson, *Scots in the West Indies 1707–1857* (Baltimore: Clearfield, 2006), 122.

65. Philip D. Morgan, 'Foreword', in Devine, *Recovering Scotland's Slavery Past* (2015), xii–xv; Devine, 'Introduction' and Devine, 'Lost to History', idem, 3, 21–40 (28, 30); Devine and Rossner in Mackenzie and Devine, *Scotland and the British Empire,* 43–44; Hamilton, *Scotland, the Caribbean and the Atlantic World* (2005), 99; Devine, *Scottish Empire* (2003), 233, 237, 238, 244–46; Dobson, *Scots in West Indies* (2006), 1; Charles E. Orrer Jr, *An Archaeology of the English Atlantic World, 1600–1700* (Cambridge: Cambridge University Press, 2018), 151.

66. Phillips and Sherman, *Outsourcing Empire* (2020), 81–82, 87, 91–93; Hancock, *Citizens of the World* (1995), 1–2, 50–53, 56, 61–65, 125, 175, 177, 180, 184, 190, 194, 201–02; Morris, 'Atlantic Archipelagos' (2012), 36.

67. Hancock, *Citizens of the World* (1995), 1–2, 50–53, 56, 61–65, 125, 175, 177, 180, 184, 190, 194, 201–02.

68. Hancock, *Citizens of the World* (1995), 131, 134, 139, 203, 213, 222–23, 227, 251, 264.

69. Murdoch, *Scotland and America* (2010), 121, 123, 125; Linda Colley, 'What Happens When a Written Constitution Is Printed? A History across Boundaries', *Transactions of the Royal Historical Society* XXXI (2021), 75–88 (86); Colin Calloway, ' "Have the Scotch No Claim upon the Cherokee?" Scots, Indians and Scots Indians in the American South', in Angela McCarthy and John M. Mackenzie (eds), *Global Migrations: The Scottish Diaspora since 1600* (Edinburgh: Edinburgh University Press, 2016), 81–97 (81, 85, 88–89, 94); Tom Bryan, *Rich Man, Beggar Man, Indian Chief: Fascinating Scots in Canada and America* (Insch: Thistle Press, 1997), 50, 53, 54, 57; Michael Newton, *We're Indians Sure Enough: The Legacy of the Scottish Highlanders in the United States* (Auburn: Saorsa Media, 2001), 197; Matthew P. Dziennik, *The Fatal Land: War, Empire and the Highland Soldier in British America* (New York and London: Yale University Press, 2015), 101, 109, 111–12; Calloway, *White People, Indians and Highlanders* (2008), 149, 155; Jenni Calder, 'Perilous Enterprises: Scottish Explorers in the Arctic', in Calder (1986), 95–106 (96); Phillips and Sherman, *Outsourcing Empire* (2020), 15.

70. A. Murdoch, *Scotland and America* (2010), 44–45, 110–11, 115, and Alex Murdoch, 'John Glen and the Indians', in Mackillop and Murdoch, *Fighting for Identity* (2002), 141–59 (141); Dobson, *Scottish Emigration* (1994), 118–20; Graham, *Colonists from Scotland* (1972), 107; Ingamells, *Dictionary* (1997); Calloway, *White People, Indians and Highlanders* (2008), 99, 119, 135–36, 152, 155, 166; Phillips and Sherman, *Outsourcing Empire* (2020), 99.

71. David Brian Davis, *The Problem of Slavery in Western Culture* (Harmondsworth: Penguin, 1970 [1966]), 166–67, 166, 169; Dobson, *Scottish Emigration* (1994), 118–20; Harvey H. Jackson, 'The Darien Antislavery Petition of 1739 and the Georgia Plan', *William and Mary Quarterly* 34:4 (1977), 618–31 (619, 631); Marjory Harper, *Adventurers and Exiles: The Great Scottish Exodus* (London: Profile, 2004 [2003]), 115–16; Amanda Epperson, '"It would be my earnest desire that you all would come": Networks, the Migration Process and Highland Emigration', *Scottish Historical Review* LXXXVIII:2 (2009), 313–31 (321).

72. Calloway, *White People, Indians and Highlanders* (2008), 117; Tim Hanson, 'Gabriel Johnston and the Portability of Patronage in the Eighteenth-Century North Atlantic World', in Mackillop and Murdoch, *Fighting for Identity* (2002), 119–40 (119, 121–23, 130, 131, 139); Robert Cain, 'Governor Robert Dinwoodie and the Virginia Frontier', idem, 161–80 (163, 168, 175, 180). For Jacobitism in North America, see David Parrish, *Jacobitism and Anti-Jacobitism in the British Atlantic World, 1688–1727* (London, Royal Historical Society: Boydell and Brewer, 2017).

73. Philip Robinson Rossner, 'The 1738–41 Harvest Crisis in Scotland', *Scottish Historical Review* 90:1 (2011), 27–63 (27, 30–31, 34, 37–39, 41, 50, 51, 53, 60); Evans, *The Pursuit of Power* (2017).

74. Riding, *Jacobites* (2017), 20, 261; Lole, *Jacobite Clubs* (1999), 13; Pittock, *Myth of the Jacobite Clans* (2009), 151–52; James Allardyce (ed.), *Historical Papers Relating to the Jacobite Period 1699–1750*, 2 vols., (Aberdeen: New Spalding Club, 1895), I: 177, 188–89; 'Declaration of "LORD JOHN DRUMMOND Commander in Chief of his most Christian Majesty's Forces in SCOTLAND"', National Archives of Scotland (NAS) GD248/48/4/2.

75. T.M. Devine, 'Did Slavery Make Scotia Great? A Question Revisited', in Devine, *Recovering Scotland's Slavery Past* (2015), 225–45 (240). The figure of 200 Irish Brigade troops is based on the latest research from Daniel Szechi, which I am grateful for his sharing with me.

76. Murray Pittock, *Jacobitism* (Basingstoke: Macmillan, 1998), 97–98.

77. Riding, *Jacobites* (2017), 27, 188, 192, 199, 204; Sir Malcolm Innes of Edingight, 'Ceremonial in Edinburgh: The Heralds and the Jacobite Risings', *Book of the Old Edinburgh Club* NS 1 (1991), 1–6 (4); *The Scots Magazine* (31 December 1739), ii.

78. Pittock, *Jacobitism* (1998), 98.

79. See Murray Pittock, *Culloden* (Oxford: Oxford University Press, 2016) for a full account of the battle and its significance for historical memory.

80. Helen Wyld, 'Re-Framing Britain's Past: Paul Sandby and the Picturesque Tour of Scotland', *The British Art Journal* 12:1 (2011), 29–36 (29, 32, 34–35); Carolyn Anderson and Chris Fleet, *Scotland: Defending the Nation* (Edinburgh: Birlinn/National Library of Scotland, 2018), 118–29; Ann Macleod, 'The Highland Landscape: Visual Depictions, 1760–1883', in Dauvit Broun and Martin MacGregor (eds), *Mìorun Mòr nan Gall, 'The Great Ill-will of the Lowlander'? Lowland Perceptions of the Highlands, Medieval and Modern* (Glasgow: Centre for Scottish and Celtic Studies, 2009 [2007]), 128–57 (134).

81. William R. Brock and E. Helen Brock, *Scotus Americanus* (Edinburgh: Edinburgh University Press, 1982), 76; David Dobson, *Directory of Scots Banished to the American Plantations 1650–1775* (Baltimore: Genealogical Publishing Company, 1984), 10, 19, 20, 28, 85, 109, 121; Eric J. Graham, 'The Scots Penetration of the Jamaican Plantation Business', in Devine, *Recovering Scotland's Slavery Past* (2015), 82–98 (84); NLS MS 98.

82. Devine, *Scottish Clearances* (2019), 58–59; Bob Harris, *The Scottish People and the French Revolution* (London: Pickering & Chatto, 2008), 21; Bob Harris, *Politics and the Nation: Britain in the Mid-Eighteenth Century* (Oxford: Oxford University Press, 2002), 175, 177, 182; Haynes, *Scotland's Sporting Buildings* (2014), 37–38.

83. Pittock, *Inventing and Resisting Britain* (1997), 129.

CHAPTER 3: THE FORCE OF SENTIMENT

1. Corey E. Andrews, '"Caledonia's Bard, Brother Burns": Robert Burns and Scottish Freemasonry', in Jane Rendall and Mark Wallace (eds), *Association and Enlightenment: Scottish Clubs and Societies, 1700–1830* (Lewisburg: Bucknell University Press, 2021),143–60 (149); see Peter Garside (ed.), Walter Scott, *Waverley*, the Edinburgh Edition of the Waverley Novels (Edinburgh: Edinburgh University Press, 2007) for Scott's father's escapade.

2. Andrew Mackillop, 'Military Scotland in the Age of Proto-globalisation, *c.*1690–*c.*1815', in David Forsyth and Wendy Ugolini (eds), *A Global Force: War, Identities, and Scotland's Diaspora* (Edinburgh: Edinburgh University Press, 2016), 13–31 (24); Mackillop, '*More Fruitful Than the Soil': Army, Empire and the Scottish Highlands, 1715–1815* (East Linton: Tuckwell Press, 2000), 23; Bob Harris, *The Scottish People and the French Revolution* (London: Pickering & Chatto, 2008), 21; George Shepperson, 'Scotland: The World Perspective', in Jenni Calder (ed.), *The Enterprising Scot* (Edinburgh: National Museums of Scotland, 1986), 15–25 (18); Rowan G.W. Strong, 'Alexander Forbes of Brechin (1817–1875): The First Tractarian Bishop', unpublished PhD (Edinburgh, 1992), 14–15, 66–70, 83–84, 344.

3. Stephen Brumwell, *Redcoats: The British Soldier and War in the Americas, 1755–1763* (Cambridge: Cambridge University Press, 2002), 269; *Correspondence of William Pitt*, 2 vols (Fairford: Franklin Classics, 2018), II:364–65; Matthew P. Dziennik, *The Fatal Land: War, Empire and the Highland Soldier in British America* (New York and London: Yale University Press, 2015), 39; T.M. Devine, *The Scottish Clearances* (London: Allen Lane, 2019 [2018]), 257; Mackillop, '*More Fruitful Than the Soil'* (2000), 25; Eileen Cox (ed.), *Dunkeld Cathedral: Memorial Inscriptions* (Dunkeld: Dunkeld and Birnam Historical Society, 2003 [1993]), entry 155.

4. Dziennik, *Fatal Land* (2015), 33–36; Mackillop, '*More Fruitful Than the Soil'* (2000), 80.

5. Colin Calloway, *White People, Indians and Highlanders* (Oxford: Oxford University Press, 2008), 94, 98; Andrew Hill Clark, *Acadia: The Geography of Early Nova Scotia to 1760* (Madison, Milwaukee and London: University of Wisconsin Press, 1968), 350, 363; Mackillop, '*More Fruitful Than the Soil'* (2000), 29–30, 32–33, 44, 57, 79; Devine, *Scottish Clearances* (2019), 131, 258–59; Dziennik, *Fatal Land* (2015), 114; Peter Way, '"Not *Bull* Breed but *Mongrel* Race": Ethnic Identity in the British Army during the Seven Years' War', unpublished paper (2006), 6, 10; Calder, 'Introduction' in Calder, *Enterprising Scot* (1986), 9–13 (10); Philip Long and Joanne Norman (ed.), *The Story of Scottish Design* (London: Thames and Hudson/V&A, 2018), 30.

6. Mackillop, '*More Fruitful Than the Soil'* (2000), 29–30, 32–33, 44, 57, 79; Devine, *Scottish Clearances* (2019), 131, 258–59; Dziennik, *Fatal Land* (2015), 114; Way, 'Not *Bull* Breed' (2006), 6, 10; Calder, 'Introduction' in Calder, *Enterprising Scot* (1986), 9–13 (10); Long and Norman, *Scottish Design* (2018), 30; Stephen Wood, *The Scottish Soldier* (Edinburgh: Archive/National Museums of Scotland, 1987), 42.

7. Brian Lavery, *Shield of Empire: The Royal Navy and Scotland* (Edinburgh: Birlinn, 2007), 113, 131, 126, 149; John Bonehill, 'Theatre of War', in John Bonehill, Anne Dula Beveridge and Nigel Leask (eds), *Old Ways New Roads: Travels in Scotland 1720–1832* (Glasgow: Hunterian Museum and Art Gallery/Edinburgh: Birlinn, 2021), 21–43 (27); Nigel Leask, 'Antiquities', idem, 54–71 (55).

8. Lavery, *Shield of Empire* (2007), 113, 131, 126, 149; Dziennik (2015), 28, 39, 40–41, 47, 55–56; Way, 'Not *Bull* Breed' (2006), 10; Victoria E. Clerk, *The Port of Aberdeen* (Aberdeen: D. Wyllie & Son, 1921), 118–19.

9. Mackillop, '*More Fruitful Than the Soil'* (2000), 82, 84, 156–57, 166–67, 170–71; Mackillop, '"As Hewers of Wood, and Drawers of Water?" Scotland as an Emigrant Nation, *c.*1600–c1800', in Angela McCarthy and John M. Mackenzie (eds), *Global Migrations: The Scottish Diaspora since 1600* (Edinburgh: Edinburgh University Press, 2016), 23–45 (34–35); Mackillop, 'For King, Country and Regiment? Motive and

Identity within Highland Soldiering, 1746–1815', in Steve Murdoch and Andrew Mackillop (eds), *Fighting for Identity* (Leiden: Brill, 2002), 185–211 (189–94, 200–201, 204, 210); Calloway, *White People, Indians and Highlanders* (2008), 5–7; T.M. Devine, *The Scottish Clearances: A History of the Dispossessed 1600–1900* (London: Penguin, 2019 [2018]), 260, 263, 265–66, 300; Christopher A. Whatley, *Scotland 1707–1832* (Manchester: Manchester University Press, 2000), 111; Courts Martial Scotland 1751–53, National War Museum Edinburgh M1975.5.1; Way, 'Not *Bull* Breed' (2006), 11–12; Ian Charles Cargill Graham, *Colonists from Scotland: Emigration to North America, 1707–1783* (Port Washington, NY and London: Kennikat Press, 1972 [1956]), 71; H.P. Klepak, 'A Man's a Man Because of That: The Scots in the Canadian Military Experience' in Rider and McNabb (eds), *A Kingdom of the Mind* (Montréal, 2006), 40–59 (44).

10. Stephen Brumwell, 'The Scottish Military Experience in North America, 1756–63', in Edward Spiers, Jeremy A. Crang and Mathew J. Strickland (eds), *A Military History of Scotland* (Edinburgh: Edinburgh University Press, 2014 [2012]), 383–406 (386–87); Brumwell, *Redcoats* (2002), 9, 74, 265, 272; Michael Newton, *We're Indians Sure Enough: The Legacy of the Scottish Highlanders in the United States* (Auburn: Saorsa Media, 2001), 47; Mary Beacock Fryer, *Allan Maclean: Jacobite General* (Toronto: Dundurn Press, 1987); Devine, *Scottish Clearances* (2019), 256–57, 297–98; Dziennik, *Fatal Land* (2015), 195, 229–32; Dauvit Horsbroch, ' "Tae See Oursels as Ithers See Us": Scottish Military Identity from the Covenant to Victoria, 1637–1837', in Murdoch and Mackillop (eds), *Fighting for Identity* (2002), 105–29 (111, 118, 125); Calloway, *White People, Indians and Highlanders* (2008), 89.

11. Jeremy Black, *George III: Majesty and Madness* (London: Penguin, 2020), 35, 96.

12. Brumwell, *Redcoats* (2002), 9, 74, 265, 272; Murdoch and Mackillop, *Fighting for Identity* (2002) 'Introduction', xxiii–xliii (xxxvi); Dziennik, *Fatal Land* (2015), 27, 120–21; Tim Fulford and Kevin Hutchings, 'Introduction', in Fulford and Hutchings (eds), *Native Americans and Anglo-American Culture* (Cambridge: Cambridge University Press, 2009), 8; Lisa Sorensen, 'Savages and Men of Feeling: North American Indians in Adam Smith's *The Theory of Moral Sentiments* and Henry Mackenzie's *The Man of the World*', idem (2009), 74–93 (83); Calloway, *White People, Indians and Highlanders* (2008), 3–4, 67, 73, 75, 135–36.

13. Brumwell, *Redcoats* (2002), 266–68; Brumwell, 'Scottish Military Experience' (2014), 390; Dziennik, *Fatal Land* (2015), 68; Mackillop, 'Military Scotland' (2016), 34; 'Hewers of Wood' (2016), 17; Devine, *Scottish Clearances* (2019), 261.

14. Denis Frize, 'The Loyal Rebel', *History Scotland* 20:2 (2020), 32–39 (39); Devine, *Scottish Clearances* (2019), 313.

15. Dziennik, *Fatal Land* (2015), 27; Brumwell, 'Scottish Military Experience' (2014), 388; W.J. Rattray, *The Scot in British North America* (Toronto: Machear and Coy., 1880), 247; Lucille H. Campey, *Les Écossais: The Pioneer Scots of Lower Canada* (Toronto: Natural Heritage Books, 2006), 4–5.

16. Dziennik, *Fatal Land* (2015), 6, 37, 42, 59, 64; Mackillop, 'Military Scotland' (2016), 18, 25; Mackillop, *'More Fruitful Than the Soil'* (2000), 65, 225, 234, 244; Mackillop in Murdoch and MacKillop, *Fighting for Identity* (2002), 196, 199; Michael Morris, 'Atlantic Archipelagos: A Cultural History of Scotland, the Caribbean and the Atlantic World', *c.*1740–1833', unpublished Ph.D. (University of Glasgow, 2012), 53, 151; Devine, *Scottish Clearances* (2019), 263; *Memoir and Correspondence of Mrs Grant of Laggan*, ed. J.P. Grant, 3 vols (London, 1844), I:81–82; Omni Gust, 'Remembering and Forgetting the Scottish Highlands: Sir James Mackintosh and the Forging of a British Imperial Identity', *Journal of British Studies* 52 (2013), 1–23 (10); Matthew Dziennik and Michael Newton, 'Egypt, Empire, and the Gaelic Literary Imagination', *Journal of Irish and Scottish Studies* 43 (2018), 1–40 (1, 3); Nigel Leask, *Stepping Westward: Writing the Highland Tour, c.1720–1830* (Oxford: Oxford University Press, 2020), 9, 16; David Hesse, *Warrior Dreams: Playing Scotsmen in Mainland Europe* (Manchester: Manchester University Press, 2014), 54, 57, 58; Neil Davidson, 'Marx and Engels on the Highlands',

Science and Society 65:3 (2001), 286–326 (287); John Bonehill, 'The Theatre of War', in Bonehill, Beveridge and Leask, *Old Ways, New Roads* (2021), 39; Linda Colley, *The Gun, the Ship and the Pen* (London: Profile Books, 2021), 97–99. See Murray Pittock, *Culloden* (Oxford: Oxford University Press, 2016) for the way in which the memory of the battle exaggerated its remoteness in time.

17. Dziennik, *Fatal Land* (2015), 6, 37, 42, 59, 64; Mackillop, 'Military Scotland' (2016), 18, 25; Mackillop, *'More Fruitful Than the Soil'* (2000), 65, 225, 234, 244; Mackillop in Murdoch and MacKillop, *Fighting for Identity* (2002), 196, 199.

18. Devine, *Scottish Clearances* (2019), 70, 157–58; Celeste Ray, 'Scottish Immigration and Ethnic Organization in the United States', in Celeste Ray (ed.), *Transatlantic Scots* (Tuscaloosa: University of Alabama Press, 2005), 48–95 (51–54); William with C. Helen Brock, *Scotus Americanus* (Edinburgh: Edinburgh University Press, 1982), 84; Bruce Lenman, *Enlightenment and Change: Scotland 1746–1832* (Edinburgh: Edinburgh University Press, 2009), 8; Whatley, *Scottish Society* (2000), 104.

19. Alexander Murdoch, *Scotland and America c.1600–c.1800* (Basingstoke: Palgrave Macmillan, 2010), 40; David Dobson, *Scottish Emigration to Colonial America, 1607–1785* (Athens and London: University of Georgia Press, 1994), 81, 104, 145; Grant Jarvie, 'The North American Émigre, Highland Games, and Social Capital in International Communities', in Ray, *Transatlantic Scots* (2005), 198–214 (208); Ray, idem, 67; Emily Ann Donaldson, *The Scottish Highland Games in America* (Gretna: Pelican Publishing, 1986), 25; Douglas Hamilton, *Scotland, the Caribbean and the Atlantic World, 1750–1820* (Manchester: Manchester University Press, 2005), 48; Graham, *Colonists from Scotland* (1972), 173.

20. T.M. Devine, *To the Ends of the Earth: Scotland's Global Diaspora* (London: Allen Lane, 2011), 31; Devine, *Scottish Clearances* (2019), 165; Andrew Hook, *Scotland and America: A Study of Cultural Relations, 1750–1835*, 2nd ed., intr. Richard Sher (Glasgow: humming earth, 2008 [1975]), 19–21, 26; Archie Turnbull, 'Scotland and America, 1730–1790', in David Daiches, Peter and Jean Jones (eds), *The Scottish Enlightenment 1730–1790: A Hotbed of Genius* (Edinburgh: Saltire Society, 1996 [1986]), 137–52 (137–40, 142); Garry Wills, *Inventing America: Jefferson's Declaration of Independence* (New York: Doubleday, 1978), 176–77, 184, 201; Ronald Crawford, *Professor Anderson Dr Franklin and President Washington* (Glasgow: University of Strathclyde, 2014), 9, 12, 24, 56–57, 75; Troy O. Bickham, *Savages within the Empire: Representations of American Indians in Eighteenth-Century Britain* (Oxford: Clarendon Press, 2005), 172; Murray Pittock, 'Historiography', in Alexander Broadie and Craig Smith (eds), *The Cambridge Companion to the Scottish Enlightenment*, 2nd edition (Cambridge: Cambridge University Press, 2019 [2003]), 248–70; Brock, *Scotus Americanus* (1982), 92; Murdoch, *Scotland and America* (2010), 149. For the importance of rhetoric in Scotland and North America, see Lynee Lewis Gaillet (ed.), *Scottish Rhetoric and its Influences* (Mahwah, NJ; Lawrence Erlbaum, 1998), including Murray Pittock's essay on 'Staff and Student: The Teaching of Rhetoric in the Scottish Universities' (111–20) and Winifred Bryan Horner, *Nineteenth-Century Scottish Rhetoric: The American Connection* (Southern Illinois University Press, 2006 [1993]).

21. Edward J. Cowan, 'Tartan Day in America', in Ray, *Transatlantic Scots* (2005), 318–38 (333–35); Gideon Mailer, 'Anglo-Scottish Union and John Witherspoon's American Revolution', *William and Mary Quarterly* 67:4 (2010), 709–46 (710). See https://vimeo.com/492417702 for the 700th anniversary lecture on the Declaration in its global context for the Scottish Government.

22. Wills, *Inventing America* (1978), 180, 229; Mailer, 'Anglo-Scottish Union' (2010), 709, 742; Robert W. Galvin, *America's Founding Secret: What the Scottish Enlightenment Taught Our Founding Fathers* (New York and Oxford: Rowan & Littlefield, 2002), 33–34; Murdoch (2010), 149–50, 153–54; Turnbull, 'Scotland and America' (1996), 143–44.

23. Mailer, 'Anglo-Scottish Union' (2010), 735; Tom Bryan, *Rich Man, Beggar Man, Indian Chief: Fascinating Scots in Canada and* America (Insch: Thistle Press, 1997), 7, 133, 141;

Rattray, *Scot in British North America* (1880), 225; Dobson, *Scottish Emigration* (1994), 101; Hook, *Scotland and America* (2008), 133.

24. Hook, *Scotland and America* (2008), xi, 51, 64, 65; Wood, *Scottish Soldier* (1987), 38.

25. Ray, *Transatlantic Scots* (2005), 5; Hamilton, *Scotland, the Caribbean and the Atlantic World* (2005), 4; Alan Karras, *Sojourners in the Sun* (1992), 12, 32–33, 192, 193, 195–96, 200–01, 203, 209, 214–15; Lenman, *Enlightenment and Change* (2009), 65; Graham, *Colonists from Scotland* (1972), 92, 121, 153, 169; Giovanni Covi et al., *Caribbean-Scottish Relations* (London: Mango, 2007), 138; David Hancock, *Citizens of the World: London Merchants and the Integration of the British Atlantic Community, 1735–1785* (Cambridge: Cambridge University Press, 1995), 59, 385–87, 393.

26. Devine, *To the Ends of the Earth* (2011), 15; J.H. Bumstead, 'The Curious Tale of the Scots and the Fur Trade: An Historiographical Account', in Rider and McNabb, *Kingdom of the Mind* (2006), 60–75 (74); Campey, *L'Écossais* (2006), 13; Matthew Shaw, *Great Scots: How the Scots Created Canada* (Manitoba: Heartland Associates, n.d.), 19, 35, 140–41, 147, 216; 'Scots Skate on Thin Ice with Hockey Claim', *The Scotsman*, 31 January 2009.

27. Daniel Dobson, *Scots in West Indies*, Volume II (Baltimore: Clearfield, 2006), 7, 19, 86, 87–91, 96, 115, 120; Covi et al., *Caribbean-Scottish Relations* (2007), 119, 125–26; Hamilton, *Scotland, the Caribbean and the Atlantic World* (2005), 49; Douglas Hamilton, 'Robert Melville and the Frontiers of Empire in the British West Indies, 1763–1771', in Mackillop and Murdoch (eds), *Military Governors and Imperial Frontiers, c.1600–1800: A Study of Scotland and Empires* (Leiden: Brill, 2003), 181–204 (181–84, 201–02); Cairns Craig, 'Empire of Intellect', in John Mackenzie and T.M. Devine (eds), *Scotland and the British Empire* (Oxford: Oxford University Press, 2011), 84–116 (97); Stana Nenadic, 'Exhibiting India in Nineteenth-Century Scotland and the Impact on Commerce, Industry and Popular Culture', *Journal of the Scottish Historical Society* 34:1 (2014), 67–89 (73); Richard Andrew Berman, 'The Architects of Eighteenth-Century English Freemasonry, 1720–1740', unpublished Ph.D. (Exeter, 2010), 256–57, 338–39.

28. Daniel Dobson, *Scots in West Indies*, Volume II (Baltimore: Clearfield, 2006), 7, 19, 86, 87–91, 96, 115, 120; Covi et al., *Caribbean-Scottish Relations* (2007), 119, 125–26; Douglas Hamilton, *Scotland, the Caribbean and the Atlantic World, 1750–1820* (Manchester: Manchester University Press, 2005), 49; Douglas Hamilton, 'Robert Melville and the Frontiers of Empire in the British West Indies, 1763–1771', in Mackillop and Murdoch, *Military Governors* (2003) 181–84, 201–02; Cairns Craig, 'Empire of Intellect', in Mackenzie and Devine, *Scotland and the British Empire* (2011), 97; Frederick Albritton Jonsson, 'Natural History', in Bonehill, Beveridge and Leask (eds), *Old Ways, New Roads* (2021), 72–89 (73); Stana Nenadic, 'Exhibiting India', 73; Les Wilson, *Putting the Tea in Britain: The Scots Who Made Our National Drink* (Edinburgh: Birlinn, 2021) 92, 97–98, 107–09, 134; Julian Hoppit, *The Dreadful Monster and Its Poor Relations: Taxing and Spending in the United Kingdon, 1707–1821* (London: Allen Lane, 2021), 62.

29. David Dobson, *Scots in West Indies 1707–1857* (Baltimore: Clearfield, 2006), 7, 19, 86, 87–91, 96, 115, 120; Covi et al., *Caribbean-Scottish Relations* (2007), 119, 125–26.

30. Covi et al., *Caribbean-Scottish Relations* (2007), 26, 126, 150–51, 160, 176; Hamilton, *Scotland, the Caribbean and the Atlantic World* (2005), 209–10; Peter Linebaugh and Marcus Rediker, *The Many-Headed Hydra* (London and New York: Verso, 2000), 287.

31. Hamilton, *Scotland, the Caribbean and the Atlantic World* (2005), 205, 207–09; David Alston, '"Doll" Thomas and her Daughters', *History Scotland* 21:5 (2021), 24–28 (27–28).

32. Karras, *Sojourners* (1992), 11, 32–33, 49–50, 54; Hamilton, *Scotland, the Caribbean and the Atlantic World* (2005), 38; Covi et al., *Caribbean-Scottish Relations* (2007), 19; Devine, *To the Ends of the Earth* (2011), 44–45; Whatley, *Scottish Society* (2000), 110; Dobson, *Scots in West Indies* (2006), II:84.

33. Hamilton, *Scotland, the Caribbean and the Atlantic World* (2005), 141, 145, 173, 182; Dobson, *Scots in West Indies* (2006), II: 15, 20, 58; T.M. Devine and John M. Mackenzie, 'Scots in the Imperial Economy', in Mackenzie and Devine, *Oxford History of the British Empire* (2011), 227–54 (228); John Galt, 'Letters on West Indian Slavery', *Fraser's Magazine for Town and Country* (1830), 440.

34. Sudhir Hazareesingh, *Black Spartacus: The Epic Life of Toussaint Louverture* (London: Allen Lane, 2020), xxiii, 4, 30–31, 44, 68, 128, 135, 197, 200; Craig Lamont, *The Cultural Memory of Georgian Glasgow* (Edinburgh: Edinburgh University Press, 2021), 160–61; Michael Morris, 'Atlantic Archipelagos: A Cultural History of Scotland, the Caribbean and the Atlantic World, c.1740–1833' (unpublished Ph.D., University of Glasgow, 2013); Linda Colley, *The Gun the Ship and the Pen* (London: Profile Books, 2021), 166.

35. Finlay McKichen, 'Lord Seaforth: Highland Proprietor, Caribbean Governor and Slave Owner', *Scottish Historical Review* XC:2 (2011), 204–35 (204, 212); Morris, 'Atlantic Archipelagos' (2013), 169, 178, 180–83.

36. Ian Whyte, ' "The Upas Tree, Beneath Whose Pestiferous Shade All Intellect Languishes and All Virtue Dies": Scottish Public Perceptions of the Slave Trade and Slavery, 1756–1833', in T.M. Devine (ed.), *Recovering Scotland's Slavery Past: The Caribbean Connection* (Edinburgh: Edinburgh University Press, 2015), 187–205 (187–89); T.C. Smout, 'Scotland and Slavery Considered', *History Scotland* 20:5 (2020), 18–21 (19); Richard Evans, *The Pursuit of Power: Europe 1815–1914* (London: Penguin, 2017 [2016]), 88, 96; James Robertson, 'Slavery, Terrorism, Law and Justice', *The Bottle Imp* issue 14 (2013), https://www.thebottleimp.org.uk/2013/11/slavery-terrorism-law-and-justice/ .

37. Whyte, 'Upas Tree' (2015), 189–90; Murdoch, *Scotland and America* (2010), 94–95; László Kontler, 'William Robertson and His German Audience on European and Non-European Civilisations', *Scottish Historical Review* LXXXI: 1 (2001), 63–89 (67); Hume, *Essay* XI cited in Tanja Bueltmann, Andrew Hinson and Graeme Morton, *The Scottish Diaspora* (Edinburgh: Edinburgh University Press, 2013), 205; James Beattie, quoted in Murray Pittock, 'Contrasting Cultures: Town and Country', in Pat Dennison, David Ditchburn and Michael Lynch (eds), *A New History of Aberdeen*, 2 vols (East Linton: Tuckwell Press, 2002), I:347–76 (367); Stewart J. Brown, 'William Robertson, Early Orientalism and the *Historical Disquisition* on India of 1791', *Scottish Historical Review* LXXXVIII:2 (2009), 289–312 (299, 303, 309).

38. Catherine Jones, 'Travel Writing, 1707–1918', in Ian Brown, Thomas Clancy, Susan Manning and Murray Pittock (eds), *The Edinburgh History of Scottish Literature*, 3 vols (Edinburgh: Edinburgh University Press, 2006), II:277–85 (280); *Murdoch, Scotland and America* (2010), 97; Covi et al., *Caribbean-Scottish Relations* (2007), 174–76; Smout, 'Scotland and Slavery' (2020), 21; Whyte, 'Upas Tree' (2015), 194; Morris, 'Atlantic Archipelagos' (2013), 88–98, 109, 155.

39. T.M. Devine, 'A Scottish Empire of Enterprise in the East, c.1700–1914', in T.M. Devine and Angela McCarthy (eds), *The Scottish Experience in Asia, c.1700 to the Present: Settlers and Sojourners* (Basingstoke: Palgrave Macmillan, 2017), 23–49 (35); T.M. Devine, 'Introduction', 1–20 (10) and Nicholas Draper, 'Scotland and Colonial Slave Ownership: The Evidence of the Slave Compensation Records', in Devine, *Recovering Scotland's Slavery Past* (2015), 166–86 (167, 174); *The Caledonian Mercury*, 29 March 1792; Henry W. Meikle, *Scotland and the French Revolution* (Glasgow: James Maclehose, 1912), 78.

40. David Gilmour, *The British in India* (London: Allen Lane, 2019 [2018]), 99; Martha McLaren, *British India and British Scotland, 1780–1830* (Akron, Ohio: University of Akron Press, 2001), 7; Andrew Mackillop, 'Fashioning a "British Empire": Sir Archibald Campbell of Inverneil and Madras', in Mackillop and Murdoch, *Military Governors* (2003), 205–31 (207, 214); Mackillop, ' "The More Mischief, the Better for Us": Scots and Irish Officers and Predatory Imperialism in South Asia, c.1740–c.1820', unpublished paper, Scottish Centre for War Studies and Conflict Archaeology, 24 March 2021; Alastair Smart, *Allan Ramsay 1713–1784* (Edinburgh: Scottish National Portrait Gallery,

1982), 105; Lenman, *Enlightenment and Change* (2009), 254; 'Henry Dundas and the East India Company', at https://www.ed.ac.uk/india-institute/india-in-edinburgh/leaving-and-arriving/henry-dundas

41. Devine and McCarthy, 'Introduction', in *Scottish Experience in Asia* (2017), 1–22 (2, 3); T.M. Devine, idem, 27–32; John M. Mackenzie, 'Scottish Orientalists, Administrators and Missions: A Distinctive Scots Approach to Asia?' idem, 51–73 (54); George MacGilvary, 'Scottish Agency Houses in South-East Asia, *c.*1760–*c.*1813', idem, 75–96 (82); Joanna Frew, 'Scots and the Imposition of Improvement in South India' idem, 97–118 (98–99, 105); Devine, *Ends of the Earth* (2011), 21; Devine, *Scottish Clearances* (2019), 253; Mackillop, 'Fashioning a "British Empire"' in Mackillop and Murdoch, *Military Governors* (2003), 214, 219–20, 223–24, 231; Mackillop, 'Hewers of Wood' (2016), 18–19; McLaren, *British India and British Scotland* (2001), 1–2, 17, 33, 201, 231; Alan Tritton, *Scotland and the Indian Empire* (London: Bloomsbury Academic, 2020), xi, 3; Gilmour, *British India* (2019), 16, 23, 37, 97–98; Stewart J. Brown, 'William Robertson, Early Orientalism and the *Historical Disquisition* on India of 1791', *Scottish Historical Review* LXXXVIII:2 (2009), 289–312 (298); Mackillop, 'The More Mischief'; Viccy Coltman, 'Henry Raeburn's Portraits of Distant Sons in the Global British Empire', *The Art Bulletin* 95:2 (2013), 294–311 (294); Wilson, *Tea* (2021), 45; 'Sir Walter Scott's India Network', at https://www.ed.ac.uk/india-institute/india-in-edinburgh/leaving-and-arriving/sir-walter-scott

42. McLaren, *British India and British Scotland* (2001), 92; Colin Munro, 'Only He Could See', *London Review of Books*, 19 March 2020, 4–5.

43. Gilmour, *British India* (2019), 39, 419; McLaren, *British India and British Scotland* (2001), 6, 31, 32, 197, 198, 220, 229; Munro, 'Only He Could See' (2020), 4–5.

44. Brown, 'William Robertson' (2009), 289, 309, 312; Philip Constable, 'Scottish Missionaries, "Protestant Hinduism" and the Scottish Sense of Empire in Nineteenth- and Early Twentieth-Century India', *Scottish Historical Review* LXXXVI:2 (2007), 278–303 (286); Mackenzie in Devine and McCarthy, *Scottish Experience in Asia* (2017), 53.

45. Devine and McCarthy, *Scottish Experience in Asia* (2017), 2, 3, 27–32; Mackenzie, idem, 55–59, 60–61, 64–65; Devine, *To the Ends of the Earth* (2011), 21; Devine, *Scottish Clearances* (2019), 253; Mackillop, 'Hewers of Wood' (2016), 18–19; McLaren, *British India and British Scotland* (2001), 1–2, 17–18, 97, 201, 231; Helen Smailes, *Scottish Empire* (Edinburgh: Scottish National Portrait Gallery, 1981), 58; Constable, 'Scottish Missionaries' (2007), 282; Gust, 'Remembering and Forgetting the Scottish Highlands' (2013), 3.

46. Martha McLaren, *British India and British Scotland, 1780–1830* (2001), 1–2, 17, 201, 231; Alex M. Cain, *The Cornchest for Scotland: Scots in India* (Edinburgh: National Library for Scotland, 1986), 35; Smailes, *Scottish Empire* (1981), 58; Mackenzie, 55–59, 60–61, 64–65; Ellen Filor, 'Death or a Pension: Scottish Fortunes at the End of the East India Company, *c.*1800–57', 119–42 (120) both in Devine and McCarthy, *Scottish Experience in Asia* (2017); Jenni Calder, 'Paisley: A Textile Town' in Calder, *Enterprising Scot* (1986), 68–74 (70–71); Evans, *Pursuit of Power* (2018), 134 .

47. Devine and McCarthy, *Scottish Experience in Asia* (2017), 8; Cain, *Cornchest* (1986), 14; Smailes, *Scottish Empire* (1981), 63.

48. Mackenzie in Devine and McCarthy, *Scottish Experience in Asia* (2017), 62–64; Devine, *Ends of the Earth* (2011), 197, 200.

49. Matthew Dziennik and Michael Newton, 'Egypt, Empire, and the Gaelic Literary Imagination', *Journal of Irish and Scottish Studies* 43 (2018), 1–40 (1, 3); Smailes, *Scottish Empire* (1981), 29.

50. Cain, *Cornchest* (1986), 41–42; MacGilvary, 'Scottish Agency Houses' in Devine and McCarthy, *Scottish Experience in Asia* (2017), 78–82; Cairns Craig, *Intending Scotland: Explorations in Scottish Culture since the Enlightenment* (Edinburgh: Edinburgh University Press, 2009), 29–35; Brinsley Burbidge, 'Scottish Plantsmen', in Calder, *Enterprising Scot*

(1986), 52–58 (54–55); Hamilton, *Scotland, the Caribbean and the Atlantic World* (2005), 134.

51. Cain, *Cornchest* (1986), 41–42; MacGilvary, 'Scottish Agency Houses', in Devine and McCarthy, *Scottish Experience in Asia* (2017), 78–82; Craig, *Intending Scotland* (2009), 29–35; Benjamin Wilkie, 'Scotland and Australian Botany in the Colonial Era', *Australian Garden History* 29:2 (2017), 30–32 (31–32); Brinsley Burbidge, 'Scottish Plantsmen' (1986), 54–55; John M. Mackenzie, 'Scots and the Environment of Empire', in Mackenzie and Devine, *Oxford History of the British Empire* (2011), 147–75 (158, 160).

52. Steph Scholten, 'Foreword', 6–10 (9); Mungo Campbell, 'William Hunter and the Anatomy of the Modern Museum', 24–47 (34, 39–40,45); Nathan Flis, 'Skeletons in Hunter's Closet', 48–71 (51); María Dolores Sánchez-Jáuregui, 'Anatomical Jars and Butterflies: Curating Knowledge in William Hunter's Museum', 159–76 (166), all in Mungo Campbell and Nathan Flis (eds) with María Dolores Sánchez-Jáuregui, *William Hunter and the Anatomy of the Modern Museum* (New Haven and London: Yale University Press, 2018); Rachel Pike, 'Women Students at Anderson's Institution', https://www.strath.ac.uk/archives/iotm/june2012/; Calder, *Enterprising Scot* (1986), 62; Pittock, 'Historiography' (2019) for William Robertson's use of sentiment in the Scottish past.

53. Brian R.W. Lockhart and Arthur L. McCombie, *Bon Record: A History of Aberdeen Grammar School* (Edinburgh: John Donald, 2012); Theodore Watt, *Aberdeen Grammar School Roll of Pupils 1795–1919* (Aberdeen: The Rosemount Press, 1923); Brian R.W. Lockhart: *The Town School: A History of the High School of Glasgow* (Edinburgh: John Donald, 2010).

CHAPTER 4: SCOTTISH ROMANTICISM, TOURISM, CAPITALISM AND CLEARANCE

1. Clifford Siskin, *System* (Cambridge: MIT Press, 2016); Liza Picard, *Restoration London* (London: Weidenfeld & Nicolson, 2003 [1997]), 25, 43, 112, 155, 192; Murray Pittock, *Enlightenment in a Smart City: Edinburgh in the First Age of Enlightenment, 1660–1750* (Edinburgh: Edinburgh University Press, 2019).

2. Murray Pittock, 'Scotland the Brand', Scottish Government External Affairs awayday presentation, 5 June 2018; The Anholt–GfK Roper National Brands Index, https://www.gov.scot/binaries/content/documents/govscot/publications/statistics/2019/01/anholt-gfk-roper-nation-brands-indexsm-2018-report-scotland/documents/methodology-report/methodology-report/govscot%3Adocument/00545271.pdf

3. Pierre Nora, *Les lieux de mémoire* (Paris: Gallimard, 1984–92, translated in abridged form as *Realms of Memory*, Columbia University Press, 1996–1998); Mona Ozouf, *La fête révolutionnaire, 1789–1799* (Paris, Gallimard, 1976); Orlando Figes, *The Europeans: Three Lives and the Making of a Cosmopolitan Culture* (London: Penguin, 2020 [2019]), 116.

4. Nigel Leask, *Stepping Westward: Writing the Highland Tour, c.1720–1830* (Oxford: Oxford University Press, 2020), 80, 82, 90; Juliet Shields, 'Highland Emigration and the Transformation of Nostalgia in Romantic Poetry', *European Romantic Review* 23:6 (2012), 765–84 (766); Mona K. McLeod, *Agents of Change: Scots in Poland 1800–1918*, 71; David Hesse, *Warrior Dreams: Playing Scotsmen in Mainland Europe* (Manchester: Manchester University Press, 2014), 49–50; Dider Ramelet Stuart, *Les Stuart et la Corse* (Corsica: Alba, 2020), 139; Joep Leerssen, 'Introduction' in Leerssen (ed.), *The Encyclopedia of Romantic Nationalism in Europe* (Amsterdam: Amsterdam University Press, 2018), 18–44 (20, 30) and Leerssen, 'After *Ossian*: Editing Vernacular Classics' and 'Swiss: Historical Context', idem, 116, 1428–29; see also Leith Davis, 'Transnational Articulations in James Macpherson's *Poems of Ossian* and *The History and Management of the East-India Company*, *The Eighteenth Century,* 60:4 (2019), 441–60 (445); James Porter, *Beyond Fingal's Cave: Ossian in the Musical Imagination* (Rochester, NY: University of Rochester Press/Boydell and Brewer, 2019), xiii, 1, 7, 11, 72, 96, 102.

5. For a closer look at the Scots language, see https://dsl.ac.uk – the online dictionary of the Scots language. For Arndt, see https://www.youtube.com/watch?v=–9OUJcbgnXg

6. Murray Pittock, '"The real language of men": Fa's Speerin? Burns and the Scottish Romantic Vernacular', in D. Sergeant, D. and Fiona Stafford (eds.) *Burns and Other Poets* (Edinburgh: Edinburgh University Press, 2011), 91–106.

7. Murray Pittock, 'Introduction: Global Burns', in Pittock (ed.), *Robert Burns in Global Culture* (Lewisburg: Bucknell University Press, 2011), 13–24 (17–18).

8. M.W. Grant, *Auld Lang Syne: A Song and its Culture* (Cambridge: Open Book Publishers, 2021), xii, 78, 82, 89–91, 96, 104, 123, 124, 131–36, 144, 153, 158, 159, 160–61, 165–72, 193, 215, 227, 235–36; Clark McGinn, *The Burns Supper: A Comprehensive History* (Edinburgh: Luath Press, 2019), 339–41 (thanks also to Dr McGinn for the Bell reference); Daniel Cook, Review of Ian Brown and Gerard Carruthers (eds), *Performing Robert Burns, Burns Chronicle* 130:1 (2021), 120–24 (121, 123); David Cheal, 'The Life of a Song: Auld Lang Syne', *Financial Times*, 29 December 2015.

9. Ferenc Morton Szasz, *Abraham Lincoln and Robert Burns: Connected Lives and Legends* (Carbondale: Southern Illinois University Press, 2008), 32, 35–39, 86, 127; Murray Pittock (ed.), *Robert Burns in Global Culture* (Lewisburg: Bucknell University Press, 2011).

10. *The Edinburgh Herald*, 7 December 1791; James Buchan, *John Law* (London: Quercus/Maclehose Press, 2019 [2018]), 27; *Report of the Meeting, Held at Paisley, In the Saracen's Head Inn, on the 31ˢᵗ October 1822 in Celebration of Mr Hunt's Release from Ilchester Bastile* (Paisley: Neilson, 1822), 15–16; Leith Davis, 'The "Unfetter'd" Muse: Robert Burns, Pre-Confederation Poets and Transatlantic Circulation', *Studies in Canadian Literature* 44:1 (2019), 100–121 (100, 103).

11. T.M. Devine, *The Scottish Clearances* (London: Allen Unwin, 2019 [2018]), 362; Murray Pittock, *Robert Burns and the Scottish Economy* (Glasgow, 2020); Angela McCarthy, 'Scottish Migrant Ethnic Identities in the British Empire since the Nineteenth Century', in Mackenzie and Devine (eds), *Scotland and the British Empire* (Oxford: Oxford University Press, 2011), 118–43 (128); Email of Clark McGinn to Gerard Carruthers and the author, 7 May 2018.

12. Burns, 'Epistle to Davie' (1785); Pittock, *Burns in Global Culture* (2011), 20–21; Figes, *The Europeans* (2020), 332, 400–01; Joseph H. Jackson, *Writing Black Scotland: Race, Nation and the Devolution of Black Britain* (Edinburgh: Edinburgh University Press, 2021), 1; Clark McGinn, 'The Burns Supper in Hong Kong, China and the Far East', unpublished essay; Szasz, *Lincoln and Burns* (2008), 65.

13. See Robert Crawford, *The Bard* (London: Allen Lane, 2009).

14. Monika Báar, 'History Writing', in Leerssen, *Encyclopedia* (2018), 122–28 (122–23).

15. Leask, *Stepping Westward* (2020), 261; Christopher A. Whatley, *Scotland 1707–1832* (Manchester: Manchester University Press, 2000), 75; Murray Pittock, 'Scott and the British Tourist', in Gerard Carruthers and Alan Rawes (eds), *Romanticism and the Celtic World* (Cambridge: Cambridge University Press, 2003), 151–66; Rebecca Lenihan, *From Alba to Aotearoa: Profiling New Zealand's Scots Migrants 1840–1920* (Otago: Otago University Press, 2005), 43; Philip Long and Joanna Norman (eds), *The Story of Scottish Design* (London: V&A/Thames and Hudson, 2018), 46–48; Tim Worth, 'Ossianism in Britain and Ireland, 1760–1800', unpublished MA (Aberystwyth, 2012), 18; Julian Hoppit, 'Scotland and the Taxing Union, 1707–1815', *Scottish Historical Review* XCVIII:I (2019), 45–70 (51–52, 59, 70); Craig Lamont, *The Cultural Memory of Georgian Glasgow* (Edinburgh: Edinburgh University Press, 2021), 147; Christina Young, 'Panoramas and Landscapes' in John Bonehill, Anne Dulau Beveridge and Nigel Leask (eds), *Old Ways, New Roads* (Edinburgh: Birlinn, 2021), 180–93; Chris Whatley, *The Industrial Revolution in Scotland* (Cambridge: Cambridge University Press, 1997), 2, 12, 24, 33, 35, 48, 66, 81; Alastair J. Durie, *Scotland for the Holidays: Tourism in Scotland c.1780–1939* (East Linton: Tuckwell Press, 2003).

16. Durie, *Scotland for the Holidays* (2003), 3, 4, 26–27, 37–39. For a detailed study of the Highland Tour, see Leask, *Stepping Westward* (2020).

17. See Murray Pittock (ed.), *The Reception of Sir Walter Scott in Europe* (London: Bloomsbury, 2014 [2007]); Durie, *Scotland for the Holidays* (2003), 44–46, 140.

18. Pittock, 'Scott and the British Tourist' (2003), 151–66; Murray Pittock, 'Sir Walter Scott: Historiography Contested by Fiction', in Robert L. Caserio and Clement Hawes (eds), *The Cambridge History of the English Novel* (Cambridge: Cambridge University Press, 2012), 277–91 (277, 280).

19. Leask, *Stepping Westward* (2020), 275; Pittock, 'Sir Walter Scott' (2012), 286–87.

20. T.M. Devine, *To the Ends of the Earth: Scotland's Global Diaspora* (London: Allen Lane, 2011), 142; Billy Kay, *The Scottish World: A Journey into the Scottish Diaspora* (Edinburgh and London: Mainstream, 2006), 88.

21. Celeste Ray (ed.), *Transatlantic Scots*, 5; A.J. Mullay, *Streamlined Steam: Britain's 1930 Luxury Expresses* (n.p., David & Charles, 2002 [1994]), 105; Crosbie Smith, *Coal, Steam and Ships: Engineering, Enterprise and Empire on the Nineteenth-Century Seas* (Cambridge: Cambridge University Press, 2018), 35.

22. William Scrope, *The Art of Deerstalking* (London: John Murray, 1838), x, 311, 351–66; Murray Pittock, *The Invention of Scotland* (London: Routledge, 2014 [1991]), 103; Richard Ormond, *The Monarch of the Glen: Landseer in the Highlands* (Edinburgh: National Galleries of Scotland, 2005), 19, 25, 50, 79, 121.

23. Pittock, *Invention of Scotland* (2014); Ormond, *Monarch of the Glen* (2005), 15–16; Durie, *Scotland for the Holidays* (2003), 110, 112, 119; Ewen A. Cameron, *Land for the People? The British Government and the Scottish Highlands, c.1880–1925* (Edinburgh: John Donald, 2009 [1996]), 64–65, 77, 79, 80, 93.

24. D.T. Thomson Gray, *The Dogs of Scotland* (Dundee, 1891), 191, 208–09; Elizabeth Cumming, *Hand, Heart and Soul: The Arts and Crafts Movement in Scotland* (Edinburgh: Birlinn, 2006), 126–27; 'Thomas Duncan (1807–1845)', Oxford DNB; NG 604, National Galleries of Scotland. Duncan also depicted scenes from Scott's novels and Scott-related topics, such as *Jeanie Deans and the Robbers* (1831), *Prince Charles Edward and the Highlanders Entering Edinburgh after the Battle of Preston* (1840) and *Mary Queen of Scots Compelled to Sign Her Abdication* (1835), itself building on Gavin Hamilton's *The Abdication of Mary, Queen of Scots*; Nicola Gordon Bowe and Elizabeth Cumming, *The Arts and Crafts Movement in Dublin and Edinburgh 1885–1925* (Dublin: Irish Academic Press, 1998), 38–39.

25. William Donaldson, *Popular Literature in Victorian Scotland* (Edinburgh: Mercat Press, 1986), 25–26, 44; Ray, *Transatlantic Scots* (2005), 67, 69.

26. Alexander Murdoch, *Scotland and America c.1600–c.1800* (Basingstoke: Palgrave Macmillan, 2010), 156.

27. Murray Pittock, *Scottish and Irish Romanticism* (Oxford: Oxford University Press, 2011 [2008]), 235–58.

28. *Report of the Meeting, Held at Paisley* (1822), 17; Stuart, *Les Stuart et la Corse* (2020), 151; Murray Pittock, 'Byron's Networks and Scottish Romanticism', *The Byron Journal* 37:1 (2009), 5–14 (9); Pittock, *Scottish and Irish Romanticism* (2011), 250–52; Michael Morris, 'Atlantic Archipelagos: A Cultural History of Scotland, the Caribbean and the Atlantic World, c.1740–1833', unpublished Ph.D. (University of Glasgow, 2012), 214.

29. Pittock, 'Byron's Networks' (2009), 7–9, 11–12; Pittock, 'Scott and the British Tourist' (2003).

30. Leask, *Stepping Westward* (2020), 42, 126, 264.

31. Barbara Graham, 'Flora MacDonald', *The Jacobite* 159 (2019), 16–26 (25); Rosie Waine, 'Tartan History', *History Scotland* (Nov/Dec 2019), 8–11; Leask, *Stepping Westward* (2020), 76, 245; Jonathan Faiers, *Tartan* (Oxford and New York: Berg, 2008), 42, 111, 134,

32. Murray Pittock, 'Plaiding the Invention of Scotland', in Ian Brown (ed.), *From Tartan to Tartanry* (Edinburgh: Edinburgh University Press, 2012 [2010]), 32–47, in particular 41–43; Faiers, *Tartan* (2008), 27, 38, 116–17; Alex Tyrrell, 'The Queen's Little Trip: The Royal Visit to Scotland in 1842', *Scottish Historical Review* LXXXII:1 (2003), 47–73 (65, 68).

33. Donaldson, *Popular Literature* (1986), 25–26, 44; Ray, 'Scottish Immigration and Ethnic Organization in the United States' in *Transatlantic Scots* (2005), 48–95 (67, 69); Leask, *Stepping Westward* (2020), 76; David Duff (ed.), *Queen Victoria's Highland Journals* (London: Lomond Books, 1994 [1980]), 27; Tyrell, 'The Queen's Little Trip' (2003), 47, 63, 70; Grant Jarvie, *Highland Games: The Making of the Myth* (Edinburgh: Edinburgh University Press, 1991), 3, 6, 54, 58, 67, 72, 82.

34. Leask, *Stepping Westward* (2020), 42, 76; T.M. Devine, *Scottish Clearances* (2019), 3, 120–22, 164–66, 172–73; Whatley, *Scottish Society* (2000), 254; Shields, 'Highland Emigration' (2012), 770.

35. Leask, *Stepping Westward* (2020), 228, 261, 281; Devine, *Scottish Clearances* (2019), 123, 132–33, 140, 197, 228, 236, 239, 247; Whatley, *Scottish Society* (2000), 251, 292; Shields, 'Highland Emigration' (2012), 770; Douglas Hill, *Great Emigrations: The Scots to Canada* (London: Gentry Books, 1972), 49.

36. Amanda Epperson, '"It Would Be My Earnest Desire That You All Would Come": Network, the Migration Process and Highland Emigration', *Scottish Historical Review* LXXXVIII:2 (2009), 313–31 (315–17, 319); Richard Evans, *The Pursuit of Power: Europe 1815–1914* (London: Penguin, 2017 [2016]), 6, 8.

37. Devine, *Scottish Clearances* (2019), 320–23, 329, 342–43, 346, 359: Cameron, *Land for the People* (2008), 1, 10, 16–17, 20, 23, 37, 48, 52, 80; Hill, *Great Emigrations* (1972), 48, 51; T.M. Devine and Angela McCarthy (eds), 'Introduction', *The Scottish Experience in Asia, c.1700 to the Present: Settlers and Sojourners* (Basingstoke: PalgraveMacmillan, 2017), 1–22 (14).

38. Colin Kidd, '*The Strange Death of Scottish History* Revisited: Construction of the Past in Scotland, c.1790–c.1914', *Scottish Historical Review* LXXXVI (1997), 86–102 (93).

39. Murray Pittock, 'Historiography' in Alexander Broadie and Craig Smith (eds), *The Cambridge Companion to the Scottish Enlightenment*, 2nd ed (Cambridge: Cambridge University Press, 2019 [2003]), 248–70; Mike Davis, *Victorian Holocausts* (London and New York: Verso, 2017 [2001]), 446–47.

40. Devine, *Scottish Clearances* (2019), 316, 317, 320; Davis, *Victorian Holocausts* (2017), 7, 35, 42, 59, 64, 65, 119, 152, 163, 168, 175; Pittock, 'Historiography' (2019), 258; Pittock, *Scottish Nationality* (Basingstoke: Palgrave Macmillan, 2001), 74–75.

41. Devine, *Scottish Clearances* (2019), 143–44, 198–99, 201, 202, 207; Tanja Bueltmann, Andrew Hinson and Graeme Morton, *The Scottish Diaspora* (Edinburgh: Edinburgh University Press, 2013), 43; Richard Grace, *Opium and Empire* (Montréal: McGill–Queen's University Press, 2014), 313, 316.

42. Atle Wold, *Scotland and the French Revolutionary War, 1792–1802* (Edinburgh: Edinburgh University Press, 2015), 4–7, 73, 76–77, 84, 88–90, 94; Henry W. Meikle, *Scotland and the French Revolution* (Glasgow: John Maclehose, 1912), 163–64, 187; David Small, 'The Use of Police Spies in the Radical War of 1820', *History Scotland* 21:2 (2021), 14–19 (15, 16, 19).

43. Martha McLaren, *British India and British Scotland, 1780–1830: Career Building, Empire Building, and a Scottish School of Thought on Indian Governance* (Akron, OH: University of Akron Press, 2001), 6; Graeme Morton, *Unionist Nationalism: Governing Urban Scotland 1830–1860* (East Linton: Tuckwell Press, 1999), 21 ff, Pittock, *Scottish Nationality* (2001), 82, 90, 94; Eric J. Graham, *Seawolves: Pirates and the Scots* (Edinburgh: Birlinn, 2005), 203; Wold, *Scotland and the French Revolutionary War* (2015), 4, 10; Julian Hoppit, *The Dreadful Monster and Its Poor Relations: Taxing and Spending in the United Kingdom, 1707–2021* (London: Allen Lane, 2021), 104–05.

44. Whatley, *Scottish Society* (2000), 290, 308–9, 312, 315, 318, 325; Hill (1972), 75. For the Whig destruction of tradition, see Bruce Lenman, *Enlightenment and Change: Scotland 1746–1832* (Edinburgh: Edinburgh University Press, 2009 [1981]), 229, 232; Murray Pittock, 'Henry Hunt's White Hat: The Long Tradition of Mute Sedition', in Michael Demson and Regina Hewitt (eds), *Commemorating Peterloo* (Edinburgh: Edinburgh University Press, 2019), 84–99; Meikle, *Scotland and the French Revolution* (1912), 49.

45. Bob Harris, *The Scottish People and the French Revolution* (London: Pickering & Chatto, 2008), 3, 7, 11, 25, 82, 88; Whatley, *Scottish Society* (2000), 290, 308–9, 312, 315, 318, 325; Pittock, 'Henry Hunt's White Hat' (2019), 84–99'.

46. R.A. Cage, 'The Scots in England' in Cage (ed.), *The Scots Abroad: Labour, Capital, Enterprise, 1750–1914* (London: Croom Helm, 1985), 29–45 (38, 42); Lenman, *Enlightenment and Change* (2009), 237.

47. Cage, 'The Scots in England'(1985), 33–35, 37–38; Whatley, *The Industrial Revolution in Scotland* (1997), 55; Hoppit, *Dreadful Monster* (2021), 98, 107; Niall Ferguson, *The Ascent of Money* (London: Penguin, 2009 [2008]), 191.

48. Lenman, *Enlightenment and Change* (2009), 136, 229, 235, 239; Whatley, *The Industrial Revolution in Scotland* (1997), 54.

49. Lenman, *Enlightenment and Change* (2009), 4–6; Whatley, *Scottish Society* (2000), 228, 230, 233, 246, 251, 266; Devine, *Scottish Clearances* (2019), 222.

50. *The Scotsman*, 30 August 1817; Michael E. Vance, 'The Politics of Emigration: Scotland and Assisted Emigration to Upper Canada, 1815–26', in T.M. Devine (ed.), *Scottish Emigration and Scottish Society* (Edinburgh: John Donald, 1992), 37–60 (40); Devine, *Scottish Clearances* (2019), 281; Edward J. Cowan, 'The Scots' Imaging of Canada', 3–21 (3) and Marjory Harper, 'Exiles or Entrepreneurs: Snapshots of the Scots in Canada', 22–39 (23–26, 29–31), both in Peter Rider and Heather McNabb (eds), *A Kingdom of the Mind: How the Scots Helped Make Canada* (Montréal and Kingston: McGill–Queen's University Press, 2006); Michael Brander, *Emigrant Scots* (New Jersey: Birch Hill Press, 1997 [1996]), 62; Hans P. Rheinheimer, *Topo: The Story of a Scottish Colony near Caracas 1825–1827* (Edinburgh: Scottish Academic Press, 1988), 39, 46, 55, 58, 132–33.

CHAPTER 5: THE SCOTTISH WORLD

1. Quoted in Orlando Figes, *The Europeans: Three Lives and the Making of a Cosmopolitan Culture* (London: Penguin, 2020 [2019]), 41; John Brewer, *The Sinews of Power* (New Haven: Harvard University Press, 1989); John Darwin, *Unlocking the World: Port Cities and Globalization in the Age of Steam 1830–1930* (London: Allen & Unwin, 2020), xiv–xv, xxi, 81, 84–85, 241, 244, 347, 357–58.

2. Jenni Calder, *The Enterprising Scot* (Edinburgh: National Library of Scotland, 1986), 62–63, 67; Stewart Lamont, *When Scotland Ruled the World* (London: HarperCollins, 2001), 46–47, 97, 197; Richard Evans, *The Pursuit of Power: Europe 1815–1914* (London: Allen Lane, 2017 [2016]), 302, 390, 392; Elspeth Wills, *Scottish Firsts: Innovation and Achievement* (Glasgow: Scottish Development Agency, 1985), 50–52, 59, 63; A.D. Boney, *The Lost Gardens of Glasgow University* (Bromley: Christopher Helm, 1988), 87.

3. Wills, *Scottish Firsts* (1985), 18, 44, 68; Evans, *The Pursuit of Power* (2017), 391.

4. Lindsay Paterson, 'Traditions of Scottish Education', 21–46 (23–27); Donald J. Withrington, 'Church and State in Scottish Education Before 1872', 47–64 (47); Olive Checkland, 'Education in Scotland, Philanthropy and Private Enterprise', 65–83 (68–71, 81), all in Heather Holmes (ed.), *Scottish Life and Society: Education* (East Linton: Tuckwell Press, 2000); Joyce M. Wallace, *Historical Houses of Edinburgh*, with a Foreword by Basil Skinner (Edinburgh: John Donald, 1987), 126; Oliphant Smeaton, *Thomas Guthrie* (Edinburgh; Oliphant, Anderson and Ferrier, n.d), 60, 77.

5. R.G.W. Anderson, 'Industrial Enterprise and the Scottish Universities in the Eighteenth Century', in Calder, *Enterprising Scot* (1986), 59–67 (60).

6. Wills, *Scottish Firsts* (1985), 33; Lamont, *When Scotland Ruled the World* (2001), 99, 105.

7. John M. Mackenzie, 'Scots and Imperial Frontiers', *Journal of Irish and Scottish Studies* 3:1 (2011), 1–19 (9–12); Richard Ormond, *The Monarch of the Glen: Landseer in the Highlands* (Edinburgh: National Gallery of Scotland, 2005), 38; Jan Oosthoek, 'Worlds Apart: the Scottish Forestry Tradition and the Development of Forestry in India', *Journal*

of Irish and Scottish Studies 3:1 (2010), 61–74 (61, 66–70); Brinsley Burbidge, 'Scottish Plantsmen' in Calder, *Enterprising Scot* (1986), 52–58; Stana Nenadic, 'Exhibiting India in Nineteenth-Century Scotland and the Impact on Commerce, Industry and Popular Culture', *Journal of Scottish Historical Studies* 34:1 (2014), 67–89 (78).

8. For school boards, v. J.B. Barclay, *The Tounis Scule* (Edinburgh: Royal High School Club, 1974), 19–20; cf. *The Memoirs of Ernest Renan*, ed. J. Lewis May (London: Geoffrey Bles, 1935), 162; Billy Kay, *The Scottish World: A Journey into the Scottish Diaspora* (Edinburgh and London: Mainstream, 2006), 187–88.

9. Wills, *Scottish Firsts* (1985), 47, 50; Anthony Slaven, 'The Shipbuilders', in Calder, *Enterprising Scot* (1986), 114–29 (114); Alastair Durie, *Scotland for the Holidays: Tourism in Scotland c.1780–1939* (East Linton: Tuckwell Press, 2003), 49–50, 54, 59, 63; John Bonehill and Nigel Leask, 'Picturesque Prospects and Literary Landscapes', in John Bonehill, Anne Dulau Beveridge and Nigel Leask (eds), *Old Ways, New Roads: Travels in Scotland 1720–1832* (Edinburgh: Birlinn, 2021), 146–65 (157); Christina Young, 'Panoramas and Landscapes', idem, 180–93 (183); Darwin, *Unlocking the World* (2020), 86.

10. Crosbie Smith, *Coal, Steam and Ships: Engineering, Enterprise and Empire on the Nineteenth-Century Seas* (Cambridge: Cambridge University Press, 2018), 129–35, 141, 165; Darwin, *Unlocking the World* (2020), 87; Evans, *Pursuit of Power* (2017), 150.

11. Smith, *Coal, Steam and Ships* (2018), 227–28, 231, 263, 309, 312, 355; David Gilmour, *The British in India* (London: Allen Lane, 2019 [2018]), 130; Darwin, *Unlocking the World* (2020), 280–81; Richard J. Grace, *Opium and Empire: The Lives and Careers of William Jardine and James Matheson* (Montréal: McGil–Queen's University Press, 2016 [2014]), 296, 305; T.M. Devine and John M. Mackenzie, 'Scots in the Imperial Economy' in Devine and Mackenzie (eds), *Scotland and the British Empire* (Oxford: Oxford University Press, 2011), 227–54 (238).

12. Smith, *Coal, Steam and Ships* (2018), 89, 99, 295, 368; *The Fleet 1840–2008* (London: Cunard/The Open Agency, 2007 [2004]), 9, 14, 21–22; Darwin, *Unlocking the World* (2020), 107, 297; Devine and Mackenzie, 'Scots in the Imperial Economy' (2011), 246–47.

13. R.A. Cage, 'The Scots in England', in R.A. Cage (ed.), *The Scots Abroad: Labour, Capital, Enterprise, 1750–1914* (London: Croom Helm, 1985), 29–45 (36); Evans, *Pursuit of Power* (2017), 133, 635; Smith, *Coal, Steam and Ships* (2018), 325; *The Fleet* (2008), 134–58.

14. John Darwin, *Unlocking the World* (2020), xv, xxxiv, 91–93, 103–04, 132, 151; George Robertson, ' "The Captain": Alexander MacDougall of Islay', *History Scotland* 21:1 (March/April 2021), 28–29.

15. Grace, *Opium and Empire* (2016), 131; Philip Long and Jane Norman (eds), *Scottish Design* (London: Thames & Hudson/V&A, 2018), 64; Victoria E. Clerk, *The Port of Aberdeen* (Aberdeen: D. Wyllie & Son, 1921), 142, 145–47.

16. Darwin, *Unlocking the World* (2020), 141, 152; Clerk, *Port of Aberdeen* (1921), 152.

17. Wills, *Scottish Firsts* (1985), 52–53; Figes, *The Europeans* (2020), 152, 238; Brian Lavery, *Shield of Empire: The Royal Navy and Scotland* (Edinburgh: Birlinn, 2007), 151; Stana Nenadic, 'Exhibiting India in Nineteenth-Century Scotland and the Impact on Commerce, Industry and Popular Culture', *Journal of Scottish Historical Studies* 34:1 (2014), 67–89 (74); Julian Hoppit, 'Scotland and the Taxing Union, 1707–1815', *Scottish Historical Review* XCVIII:1 (2019), 45–70 (61, 70); Evans, *The Pursuit of Power* (2017), 292.

18. Wills, *Scottish Firsts* (1985), 77, 93; Angela McCarthy and John M. Mackenzie, 'Introduction', in McCarthy and Mackenzie (eds), *Global Migrations: The Scottish Diaspora since 1600* (Edinburgh: Edinburgh University Press, 2016), 10–22 (15); Devine and Mackenzie, 'Scots in the Imperial Economy' (2011), 252; Duncan A. Bruce, *The Mark of the Scots* (New York: Birch Lane Press, 1997 [1996]), 118; Sheila M. Brock, 'A Broad Strong Life: Dr Jane Waterston', in Calder, *Enterprising Scot* (1986), 75–87 (77, 79, 85–86).

19. T.M. Devine, *To the Ends of the Earth: Scotland's Global Diaspora* (London: Allen Lane, 2011), 231–32; T.M. Devine and Angela McCarthy (eds), *The Scottish Experience in Asia, c.1700 to the Present: Settlers and Sojourners* (Basingstoke: Palgrave Macmillan, 2017), 14; Evans, *The Pursuit of Power* (2017), 227; Les Wilson, *Putting the Tea in Britain: The Scots Who Made Our National Drink* (Edinburgh: Birlinn, 2021), 23–24, 146.

20. Ewan A. Cameron, *Impaled Upon a Thistle: Scotland Since 1880* (Edinburgh: Edinburgh University Press, 2008), 19–20; Long and Norman, *Scottish Design* (2018), 50–51, 56, 68–77; Devine and Mackenzie, 'Scots in the Imperial Economy' (2011), 232–33; Nenadic, 'Exhibiting India' (2014), 73–74; Craig Lamont, *The Cultural Memory of Georgian Glasgow* (Edinburgh: Edinburgh University Press, 2021), 169.

21. Tanja Bueltmann, *Clubbing Together: Ethnicity, Civility and Formal Sociability in the Scottish Diaspora to 1930* (Liverpool: Liverpool University Press, 2014), 22, 103; Cameron, *Impaled Upon a Thistle* (2008), 11, 15, 18; David Duff (ed.), *Queen Victoria's Highland Journals* (London: Lomond Books, 1994 [1980]), 6–7, 26, 28, 37, 72, 146, 149, 221; Evans, *Pursuit of Power* (2017), 304, 363; Howietoun Fish Farm exhibit, Smith Art Gallery and Museum, Stirling.

22. Grace, *Opium and Empire* (2016), 13, 14, 21, 131, 149–53, 155, 223, 230, 275, 290, 294, 296, 337, 341; Evans, *Pursuit of Power* (2017), 640; Wilson, *Putting the Tea in Britain* (2021), 37.

23. Devine and McCarthy, *Scottish Experience in Asia* (2017), 33; T.M. Devine, 'Addicting the Dragon? Jardine, Matheson & Co in the China Opium Trade' in Devine and McCarthy, *Scottish Experience in Asia* (2017), 213–33 (214, 219, 221, 223, 224–25; Grace, *Opium and Empire* (2016), 84–85, 101, 109; Iain Watson, 'The Right Kind of Migrants: Scottish Expatriates in Hong Kong Since 1950 and the Promotion of Human Capital', idem 283–307 (291, 300); Darwin, *Unlocking the World* (2020), 113; Mike Davis, *Victorian Holocausts* (London and New York: Verso, 2017 [2001]), 83, 366; Devine, *To the Ends of the Earth?* (2011), 256–57; Bueltmann, *Clubbing Together* (2014), 164, 168; Isabella Jackson, 'The Shanghai Scottish Volunteers with Scottish, Imperial and Local Identities, 1914–41', in Devine and McCarthy, *Scottish Experience in Asia* (2017), 235–57 (235); Vinod Moonesinghe, 'The Other Clerihew', *History Scotland* 21:1 (March/April 2021), 30–34; Anne de Courcy, *Chanel's Riviera* (London: Weidenfeld & Nicolson, 2019), 61; Wilson, *Putting the Tea in Britain* (2021), 35, 123.

24. Gilmour, *British in India* (2019), 82–83, 100, 103; Andrew Phillips and J.C. Sherman, *Outsourcing Empire: How Company-States Made the Modern World* (Princeton and Oxford: Princeton University Press, 2020), 146; Wilson, *Putting the Tea in Britain* (2021), 120, 122–23, 128, 170, 173, 177–81, 184–85; 'Balliol and Empire', *Floreat Domus* (June 2021), 6; see also www.balliol.ox.ac.uk/balliol-and-empire

25. Angela McCarthy in McCarthy and Mackenzie, *Global Migrations* (2016), 117–37; Patrick Peebles, 'Governor J.A. Stewart Mackenzie and the Making of Ceylon', in Devine and McCarthy, *Scottish Experience in Asia* (2017), 143–62 (143, 145, 155); T.J. Barron, 'Scots and the Coffee Industry in Nineteenth-Century Ceylon', idem, 163–85 (173–74); Angela McCarthy, 'Ceylon: A Scottish Colony?', idem, 187–211 (187, 188, 191, 195, 197, 202); Calder, *Enterprising Scot* (1986), 107; Devine and Mackenzie, 'Scots in the Imperial Economy' (2011), 233; Heshari Sothiraj Eddleston, 'Sri Lanka: An Outsider's Gaze', in Ben Reiss, Antonia Laurence, Allan and Jennifer Melville (eds), *E.A. Hornel: From Camera to Canvas* (Edinburgh: National Trust for Scotland/Birlinn, 2020), 93–108 (94); Bayly, *Birth of the Modern World* (2004), 407–08.

26. Avril A. Power, *Scottish Orientalists in India* (Woodbridge: Boydell Press, 2010), xiv, 6, 7, 9, 262, 270; Andrew Phillips and J.C. Sherman, *Outsourcing Empire: How Company-States Made the Modern World* (Princeton and Oxford: Princeton University Press, 2020), 146; Gioia Angeletti, 'A Scottish Migrant in India: John Leyden, Between Enlightenment and Orientalism', *La questione Romantica* 10: 1 and 2 (2018), 37–51 (37, 42).

27. Davis, *Victorian Holocausts* (2017), 59–60, 64, 168.

28. Bueltmann, *Clubbing Together* (2014), 133, 168; Michael Brander, *Emigrant Scots* (New Jersey: Birch Hill Press, 1997 [1996]), 69–71. For the significance of imperialist conflict over Persia in 1914, see Peter Frankopan, *The Silk Roads: A New History of the World* (London: Bloomsbury, 2016 [2015]), 317 and Chapters 16 and 17 more generally.

29. Davis, *Victorian Holocausts* (2017), 59–60, 64, 168.

30. Gilmour, *British India* (2019), 210–11; Frankopan, *The Silk Roads* (2016), 288.

31. Elizabeth Buettner, 'Haggis in the Raj: Private and Public Celebrations of Scottishness in Late Imperial India', *Scottish Historical Review* LXXXI:2 (2002), 212–39 (212).

32. Darwin, *Unlocking the World* (2020), 100.

33. John M. Mackenzie, 'Scottish Orientalists, Administrators and Missions: A Distinctive Scots Approach to Asia', in Devine and McCarthy, *The Scottish Experience in Asia* (2017), 51–74 (60); Bruce, *The Mark of the Scots* (1997), 96; G.R. Dalgleish, 'Scotland's Oriental Links: Scottish Pottery in South East Asia', in Calder, *Enterprising Scot* (1986), 108–13 (108, 111); Tanja Bueltmann, Andrew Hinson and Graeme Morton, *The Scottish Diaspora* (Edinburgh: Edinburgh University Press, 2013), 235; Norman Davies, *Beneath Another Sky: A Global Journey into History* (London: Penguin, 2018 [2017]), 178; Stana Nenadic, 'Exhibiting India in Nineteenth-Century Scotland and the Impact on Commerce, Industry and Popular Culture', in *Journal of the Scottish Historical Society* 34:1 (2014), 67–89 (72).

34. Angela McCarthy, 'The Importance of Scottish Origins in the Nineteenth Century: James Taylor and Ceylon Tea', in McCarthy and John M. Mackenzie (eds), *Global Migrations: The Scottish Diaspora since 1600* (Edinburgh: Edinburgh University Press, 2016), 117–37; Bueltmann, *Clubbing Together* (2014), 170–72, 175, 179, 187–91; Jackson in Devine and McCarthy, *Scottish Experience in Asia* (2017), 236.

35. Devine and McCarthy, *Scottish Experience in Asia* (2017), 'Introduction', 1–22 (4, 8, 9); 33, 35–38.

36. Bueltmann, *Clubbing Together* (2014), 16, 21, 91, 97, 105, 185, 187–88, 225, 230–35; Bueltmann, Hinson and Morton, *Scottish Diaspora* (2013), 118–19.

37. John Mackenzie, 'Irish, Scottish, Welsh and English Worlds? A Four-Nation Approach to the History of the British Empire', *History Compass* 6:5 (2008), 1244–63; Alex M. Cain, *The Cornchest for Scotland: Scots in India* (Edinburgh: National Library for Scotland, 1966), 90; Devine and McCarthy, *Scottish Experience* (2017), 270–72, 275–76; David Hesse, *Warrior Dreams: Playing Scotsmen in Mainland Europe* (Manchester: Manchester University Press, 2014), 86–87; Gilmour, *British in India* (2019), 195; Murdo Macdonald, *Patrick Geddes's Intellectual Origins* (Edinburgh: Edinburgh University Press, 2020), 83; Benjamin Wilkie, *The Scots in Australia 1788–1938* (Woodbridge: the Boydell Press, 2017), 82.

38. Alexander McKay, *Scottish Samurai: Thomas Blake Glove 1838–1911* (Edinburgh: Canongate, 2012 [1993]), 8, 12, 16, 18–19, 22–23, 31, 35, 40, 54, 190, 205; Michael Gardiner, *At the Edge of Empire: The Life of Thomas Blake Glover* (Edinburgh: Birlinn, 2007), 1, 9, 14.

39. Gardiner, *At the Edge of Empire* (2007), 1, 9, 14, 16–19, 25, 28, 43, 49, 58; McKay, *Scottish Samurai* (2012), 95–96, 107, 127, 156; Colin Calloway, *White People, Indians and Highlanders* (Oxford: Oxford University Press, 2008), 167; Bayly, *The Birth of the Modern World* (2004), 181; Linda Colley, *The Gun, the Ship and the Pen* (London: Profile Books, 2021), 370.

40. Gardiner, *At the Edge of Empire* (2007), 60–61, 69, 83, 115; McKay, *Scottish Samurai* (2012), 83, 119, 178, 191; Olive Checkland, 'The Scots in Meiji Japan, 1868–1912', in Cage, *Scots Abroad* (1985), 251–71 (260); Devine and McCarthy, *Scottish Experience in Asia* (2017), 39–42; David Egerton, *The Rise and Fall of the British Nation: A Twentieth-Century History* (London: Penguin, 2019 [2018]), 51; Wills, *Scottish Firsts* (1985), 72; Jennifer Melville, 'A Western Gaze on the Eastern Shore', in Ben Reiss, Antonia Laurence-Allan and Jennifer Melville (eds), *E.A. Hornel: From Camera to Canvas* (Edinburgh: National Trust for Scotland/Birlinn, 2020), 47–56 (52).

41. Ben Reiss, 'Introduction: From Camera to Canvas', 11–28 (15, 18, 20); Alix Agret, 'Hornel's Artistic Context', 29–46 (33); Jennifer Melville, 'A Western Gaze on the Eastern Shore', 47–56 (48); Luke Gartlan, 'Encounters with Modern Japan', 57–66 (58, 62); Ayako Ono, 'Hornel's Visit to Japan (1893–94) and His Use of Photography', 67–78 (68); all in Reiss et al (eds), *Hornel* (2020).

42. Michael Shaw, *The Fin-de-Siècle Scottish Revival: Romance, Decadence and Celtic Identity* (Edinburgh: Edinburgh University Press, 2020), 122–23, 128, 131, 136; Reiss in Reiss et al., *Hornel* (2020), 27; Jill Ruggett, 'Japan: A Sense of Inspiration for Historic Gardens in Scotland', in Reiss et al., *Hornel* (2020), 123–34 (124, 127).

43. McKay, *Scottish Samurai* (2012), 204, 214.

44. Douglas Reid, 'Sir Alexander Mackenzie: Canada's Forgotten Hero', *History Scotland* 20:1 (2020), 41–43; Initial seminar, 2nd World Congress of Scottish Literatures (Vancouver, 2017); Lucille H. Campey, *Les Écossais: The Pioneer Scots of Lower Canada, 1763–1855* (Toronto: Natural Heritage Books, 2006), 15; Matthew Shaw, *Great Scots: How the Scots Created Canada* (Manitoba: Heartland Associates, n.d.), 63.

45. Shaw, *Great Scots*, 79, 85, 114.

46. Christine Spicer, 'Set in Stone? Monuments, National Identity and John A. Macdonald', unpublished paper, National Forgetting and Memory Conference, NISE Antwerp, 11 March 2021; Alan R. Turner, 'Scottish Settlement in the West', in W. Stanford Reid (ed.) *The Scottish Tradition in Canada* (Ministry of Services and Supply, 1976), 76–91 (79, 85); Marjory Harper, *Adventurers and Exiles: The Great Scottish Exodus* (London: Profile, 2004 [2003]), 357–58; David S. Macmillan, 'Scottish Enterprise and Influences in Canada, 1620–1900', in Cage, *Scots Abroad* (1985), 46–79 (54–55, 66, 73); Michael Vance, 'A Brief History of Organized Scottishness in Canada' in Celeste Ray (ed.), *Transatlantic Scots*, 96–119 (96, 100, 105); Stuart Allan and David Forsyth, *Common Cause: Commonwealth Scots and the Great War* (Edinburgh: National Museums of Scotland, 2014), 8; Jenni Calder, 'Perilous Enterprises: Scottish Explorers in the Arctic' in Calder, *Enterprising Scot* (1986), 95–106 (96); Marjory Harper, 'Exiles or Entrepreneurs: Snapshots of the Scots in Canada', in Peter Rider and Heather McNabb (eds), *A Kingdom of the Mind: How the Scots Helped Make Canada* (Montréal-Kingston: McGill–Queen's University Press, 2006), 28; Bueltmann, *Clubbing Together* (2014), 67, 71, 89, 92; Bruce, *The Mark of the Scots* (1997), 11; Duncan Sim, *American Scots: The Scottish Diaspora and the USA* (Edinburgh: Dunedin Academic Press, 2011), 50, 52.

47. T.M. Devine, *The Scottish Clearances* (London: Allen & Unwin, 2019 [2018]), 214; Helen Smailes, *Scottish Empire* (Edinburgh: Scottish National Portrait Gallery, 1981), 21–22.

48. Tom Bryan, *Rich Man, Beggar Man, Indian Chief: Fascinating Scots in Canada and America* (Insch: Thistle Press, 1997), 12, 18, 25; Harper, *Adventurers and Exiles* (2004), 357; Devine, *To the Ends of the Earth* (2011), 275; Celeste Ray, 'Scottish Immigration and Ethnic Organization in the United States', in Ray, *Transatlantic Scots* (2005), 48–95 (77–78); Bueltmann, *Clubbing Together* (2014), 75, 81, 85, 91–95; Bueltmann, Hinson and Morton, *The Scottish Diaspora* (2013), 102; Michael Morris, 'Atlantic Archipelagos: A Cultural History of Scotland, the Caribbean and the Atlantic World, c.1740–1833', unpublished PhD (University of Glasgow, 2012), 131; Sim, *American Scots* (2011), xv, 33–35, 51–53

49. Sim, *American Scots* (2011), 27, 51; Bayly, *The Birth of the Modern World* (2004), 163; Mark Twain, *Life on the Mississipi*, eds. Fishkin, Morris and Howe (New York: Oxford University Press, 1996 [1883]), 465, 467–69. I am indebted to Jennifer Melville for some of the details on the Klan.

50. Tom Bryan, *Rich Man, Beggar Man, Indian Chief: Fascinating Scots in Canada and America* (Insch: Thistle Press, 1997), 12, 18, 25; Harper, *Adventurers and Exiles* (2004), 357; Devine, *To the Ends of the Earth* (2011), 275; Celeste Ray, 'Scottish Immigration and Ethnic Organization in the United States', in Ray, *Transatlantic Scots* (2005), 48–95 (77–78); Bueltmann, *Clubbing Together* (2014), 75, 81, 85, 91–95; Bueltmann, Hinson

and Morton, *The Scottish Diaspora* (2013), 102; Michael Morris, 'Atlantic Archipelagos: A Cultural History of Scotland, the Caribbean and the Atlantic World, *c.*1740–1833', unpublished Ph.D. (University of Glasgow, 2012), 131.

51. Manuel A. Fernandez, 'The Scots in Latin America: A Survey', in R.A. Cage (ed.), *The Scots Abroad: Labour, Capital, Enterprise, 1750–1914* (London: Croom Helm, 1985), 220–50 (230); Harper, *Adventures and Exiles* (2004), 361–62.

52. Harper, *Adventurers and Exiles* (2004), 356; John M. Mackenzie with Nigel R. Dalziel, *The Scots in South Africa* (Manchester: Manchester University Press, 2007), 41, 51, 54, 67, 68, 71, 73, 75, 77, 89, 242; E.W. McFarland, 'Commemoration of the South African War in Scotland, 1900–10', *Scottish Historical Review* LXXXIX:2 (2016), 194–223(204); John M. Mackenzie, in *Journal of Irish and Scottish Studies* 3:1 (2010), 1–18 (16); John M. Mackenzie, 'Scottish Diasporas and Africa', in Angela McCarthy and John M. Mackenzie (eds), *Global Migrations: The Scottish Diaspora since 1600* (Edinburgh: Edinburgh University Press, 2016), 63–80 (67–69); Bueltmann, *Clubbing Together* (2014), 133; Wilson, *Putting the Tea in Britain* (2021), 209.

53. Devine and Mackenzie, 'Scots in the Imperial Economy', in Mackenzie and Devine, *Scotland and the British Empire* (2011), 238; Bueltmann, *Clubbing Together* (2014), 137, 143–48, 153–55; Mackenzie, 'Scottish Diasporas and Africa', in McCarthy and Mackenzie, *Global Migrations* (2016), 65–67, 73, 75.

54. Joanna Lewis, *Empire of Sentiment: The Death of Livingstone and the Myth of Victorian Imperialism* (Cambridge: Cambridge University Press, 2018), 6, 7, 36–37, 46, 51, 97, 191, 201, 256–57; 261; Devine, *To the Ends of the Earth* (2011), 200; Jeremy Black (general editor), *Atlas of World History* (London, New York, Sydney: Dorling Kindersley, 1999), 85, 166; Bueltmann, Hinson and Morton, *Scottish Diaspora* (2013), 207–08. I am very grateful to Jennifer Melville for sharing her work on the Aberdeens as part of the Facing Our Past project of the National Trust for Scotland.

55. Mackenzie, 'Scottish Diaspora and Africa', in McCarthy and Mackenzie, *Global Migrations* (2016), 65–67, 73, 75; Bruce, *The Mark of the Scots* (1997), 97; Morris, 'Atlantic Archipelagos' (2012), 167n; David William Main, 'The Remarkable Career of Peter McLagan MP', *History Scotland* 21:3 (2021), 36–38.

56. Mackenzie, 'Scottish Orientalists' in Devine and McCarthy (2017), *Scottish Experience in Asia*, 64–65, 73n; Michael Marten, *Attempting to Bring the Gospel Home: Scottish Missions to Palestine 1839–1917* (London and New York: Tauris, 2006), 25; Cameron, *Impaled on a Thistle* (2008), 25, 60, 64; Harper in Rider and McNabb, *Empire of the Mind* (2006), 35; Charles D. Waterston, 'Hugh Miller', in Calder, *Enterprising Scots* (1986), 160–69 (169); Murray Pittock, *Scottish Nationality* (Basingstoke: Palgrave Macmillan, 2001), 8; Elizabeth Robertson, *Mary Slessor* (Edinburgh: National Museum of Scotland, 2001), 6, 10, 22; Gilmour, *British India* (2019), 224; Esther Breitenbach, 'Scots Churches and Missions', in Mackenzie and Devine (eds), *Scotland and the British Empire* (2011), 196–225 (198, 199, 201, 206, 214); Billy Kay, *The Scottish World: A Journey into the Scottish Diaspora* (Edinburgh and London: Mainstream, 2006), 212.

57. J. Douglas Porteous, 'Easter Island: The Scottish Connection', *Geographical Review* 68:2 (1978), 145–56; Kay, *Scottish World* (2006), 165–66. Stevenson's house had a ballroom that would hold a hundred and contained some 72 tons of furniture: see. https://www.frommers.com/destinations/samoa/attractions/robert-louis-stevenson-museum-grave

58. Jim Hewitson, *Far Off in Sunlit Places: Stories of the Scots in Australia and New Zealand* (Edinburgh: Canongate, 1998), vii, viii; Fiona Marsden, *Lachlan Macquarie* (Tobermory: Brow & Whitaker, 2001), 3, 13, 15–16, 18–19; Wilkie, *Scots in Australia* (2017), 30; Devine, *Scottish Clearances* (2019), 285; Ian Donnachie, 'The Making of "Scots on the Make": Scottish Settlement and Enterprise in Australia, 1830–1900', in T.M. Devine (ed.), *Scottish Emigration and Scottish Society* (Edinburgh: John Donald, 1992), 135–53 (135); Murray Pittock, *Scottish and Irish Romanticism* (Oxford: Oxford University Press, 2011 [2008]); Malcolm Prentiss, *The Scots in Australia* (Sydney: UNSW Press, 2008), 72; Wilson, *Putting the Tea in Britain* (2021), 155.

59. Hewitson, *Far Off in Sunlit Places* (1998), viii–ix, 154; Eric Richards, 'Australia and the Scottish Connection, 1788–1914', in Cage, *Scots Abroad* (1985), 111–155 (141–42); Prentiss, *Scots in Australia* (2008), 121; Colley, *Gun, the Ship and the Pen* (2021), 254–55, 258, 283.

60. Richards in Cage, *Scots Abroad* (1985), 116, 117, 120, 123, 133, 136, 141–42, 147; Andrew E.M. Wiseman, 'Chasing the Deer: Hunting Iconography, Literature and Tradition of the Scottish Highlands', unpublished Ph.D. (University of Edinburgh, 2007); Devine, *To the Ends of the Earth* (2011), 169; Lindsay Proudfoot and Diane Hall, 'Imaging the Frontier: Environment, Memory and Settlement: Narratives from Victoria (Australia), 1850–1890', *Journal of Irish and Scottish Studies* (2011), 19–39 (21, 34); Bueltmann, *Clubbing Together* (2014), 101, 108–09, 114, 119, 126; Brander, *Emigrant Scots* (1997), 65.

61. Eric Richards, 'Australia and the Scottish Connection 1788–1914' in Cage, *Scots Abroad* (1985), 111–55 (119, 129); Hewitson, *Far Off in Sunlit Places* (1998), 178, 180; Ann Curthoys, 'Conflicts of Interest, Crises of Conscience: Scots and Aboriginal Peoples in Eastern Australia, 1830s–1861', in McCarthy and Mackenzie, *Global Migrations* (2016), 98–116 (107); Wilkie, *Scots in Australia* (2017), 34, 54, 57, 59, 61.

62. Hewitson, *Far Off in Sunlit Places* (1998), viii, x; Tom Brooking, ' "Tam McCanny and Keith Clydeside": The Scots in New Zealand', in Cage, *Scots Abroad* (1985), 156–90 (158, 164, 168); Rebecca Lenihan, *From Alba to Aotearoa: Profiling New Zealand's Scots Migrants, 1840–1920* (Otago: Otago University Press, 2015), 25, 34; John M. Mackenzie, 'A Scottish Empire? The Scottish Diaspora and Interactive Identities', in Tom Brooking and Jennie Coleman (eds), *The Heather and the Fern: Scottish Migration and New Zealand Settlement* (Dunedin: University of Otago Press, 2003), 17–32 (25); John Wilson, 'Scots Education', *Te Ara: The Encyclopedia of New Zealand* (2011), https://teara.govt.nz/en/document/188/education-and-success

63. Davies (2018), 415, 422; Tom Brooking, ' "Green Scots and Golden Irish": The Environmental Impact of Scottish and Irish Settlers in New Zealand: Some Preliminary Ruminations', in *Journal for Irish and Scottish Studies* (2011), 41–59 (45–46, 49, 50, 53); Tom Brooking, ' "Tam McCanny and Kilty Clydeside": The Scots in New Zealand', in Cage, *Scots Abroad* (1985), 156–90 (184); Devine, *To the Ends of the Earth* (2011), 169; Bueltmann, *Clubbing Together* (2014), 101; Wilson, *Te Ara* (2011).

64. Tanja Bueltmann, 'Manly Games, Athletic Sports and the Commodification of Scottish Identity: Caledonian Gatherings in New Zealand to 1915', *Scottish Historical Review* LXXXIX:2 (2010), 224–47 (225, 233, 246–47); Allan and Forsyth, *Common Cause* (2014), 14; Hewitson, *Far Off in Sunlit Places* (1998), x; Hesse, *Warrior Dreams* (2014), 112; Wilson, *Te Ara* (2011); I am indebted to Liam McIlvanney for the information on the Dunedin Burns Club (message to the author, 24 February 2021).

65. R.N. Rudmose Brown, J.H. Pirie and R.C. Mossman, *The Voyage of the Scotia*, with a foreword by David Munro (Edinburgh: Mercat Press, 2002 [1906]), xi, 41, 112; Lamont, *When Scotland Ruled the World* (2001), 154–55.

66. David Forsyth and Wendy Ugolini, 'Introduction', in Forsyth and Ugolini (eds), *A Global Force: War, Identities and Scotland's Diaspora* (Edinburgh: Edinburgh University Press, 2016), 1–9 (6); Devine and McCarthy, *The Scottish Experience in Asia* (2017), 14.

67. David Stenhouse, *On the Make: How the Scots Took Over London* (Edinburgh and London: Mainstream, 2004), 11–12.

68. Stenhouse, *On the Make* (2004), 19, 25, 57, 66, 109–10, 123, 125; Bueltmann, *Clubbing Together* (2014), 34–35, 41–42, 202–03; Wallace, *Historic Houses of Edinburgh* (1987), 66.

69. Stenhouse, *On the Make* (2004), 16, 92; Bueltmann, *Clubbing Together* (2014), 48, 55–56; Bueltmann, Hinson and Morton, *Scottish Diaspora* (2013), 262.

70. Benjamin Colbert and Lucy Morrison, 'Introduction', in Colbert and Morrison (eds), *Continental Tourism, Travel Writing, and the Consumption of Culture, 1814–1900* (Basingstoke: Palgrave Macmillan, 2020), 1–13 (1).

71. Graeme Morton, *Ourselves and Others: Scotland 1832–1914* (Edinburgh: Edinburgh University Press, 2012), 79; Julie Holder, 'Collecting the Nation: Scottish History, Patriotism and Antiquarianism after Scott', unpublished Ph.D. (University of Glasgow, 2021), 172–75, 195–96.

72. Kirstie Blair, ' "Whose Cry is Liberty and Fatherland": Kossuth, Garibaldi and European Nationalism in Scottish Political Poetry', *Scottish Literary Review* 10:2 (2018), 71–94 (72–74, 81–82); Evans, *The Pursuit of Power* (2017), 123, 179; Morton, *Ourselves and Others* (2012), 3, 29; Janet Fyfe, 'Scottish Volunteers with Garibaldi', *Scottish Historical Review* 57 (1977), 168–81 (168, 173, 181); Devine, *To the Ends of the Earth* (2011), 171; Diana M. Henderson, 'The Scottish Soldier Abroad: The Sociology of Acclimatization', in Simpson, *Scottish Soldier Abroad* (1992), 122–31 (123); Brown, *Scotland on the Front Line* (2012), 19; M. Pittock with J. Ambroisine, *Robert Burns and the Scottish Economy* (Glasgow, 2019), 43; Pittock, *Scottish and Irish Romanticism* (Oxford, 2011 [2008]), 241. Scottish Local History Forum, Wallace Monument – the Historical Face of Crowd Funding (n.d), https://www.slhf.org/news/wallace-monument-%E2%80%93-historical-face-crowd-funding; The Wallace Memorial Cross (2011), https://www.geocaching.com/geocache/GC2N29F_the-wallace-memorial-cross?guid=b5f9d218-b519-4a33-b7ba-c7d66b4c3e0d. Morton's concept of 'Unionist Nationalism' was first developed in a book of that title in 1999.

73. Macdonald, *Geddes* (2020), 102, 108–09; Shaw, *Fin-de-Siècle Scottish Revival* (2020), 90, 97; Kay, *Scottish World* (2006), 90.

74. Stenhouse, *On the Make* (2004), 115–16; Pittock, *Scottish Nationality* (2001), 94–95; Lavery, *Shield of Empire* (2007), 157.

75. Eric Storm, 'World Fairs and (Inter)national Exhibitions', in Joep Leerssen (ed.), *Encyclopedia of Romantic Nationalism in Europe* (Amsterdam: Amsterdam University Press, 2018), 85–87; Steven Beller, *The Habsburg Monarchy 1815–1918* (Cambridge: Cambridge University Press, 2018), 156; Stana Nenadic, 'Exhibiting India', *Journal of Scottish Historical Studies* 34:1 (2014), 80, 82; Jenni Calder and S.M. Andrews, 'A Source of Inspiration: Robert Jameson', 26–33 (32) and Marinell Ash, 'New Frontiers: George and Daniel Wilson', 40–51 (43, 46), both in Calder, *Enterprising Scots* (1986); Murray Pittock, *Celtic Identity and the British Image* (Manchester: Manchester University Press, 1999), 58, 75; *The Official Guide to the Exhibition* (Edinburgh, 1886); Pittock, *Scottish Nationality* (2001), 96; Lamont, *Georgian Glasgow* (2021), 174, 178–79; Holder, 'Collecting the Nation' (2021), 98, 130; Nenadic, 'Exhibiting India' (2014), 82; *Scottish National Memorials* (Glasgow: James Maclehose, 1890).

76. Durie, *Scotland for the Holidays* (2003), 8; Nicola Gordon Bowe and Elizabeth Cumming, *The Arts & Crafts Movements in Dublin and Edinburgh, 1885–1925* (Dublin: Irish Academic Press, 1999), 80; Shaw, *The Fin-de-Siècle Scottish Revival* (2020), 10; Pittock, *Celtic Identity* (1999), 121; Holder, 'Collecting the Nation' (2021), 140.

77. Long and Norman, *Scottish Design* (2018), 88–89, 104–07; Andrew Newby, 'Edward McHugh, the National Land League of Great Britain and the "Crofters' War", 1879–1882', *Scottish Historical Review* LXXXII:1 (2003), 74–91; Brian Casey, 'Michael Davitt's Second Highland Tour, April 1887', *History Scotland* (July/August 2019), 38–45; Macdonald, *Geddes* (2020), 49, 55, 77; Murray Pittock and Isla Jack, 'Patrick Geddes and the Celtic Revival', in Ian Brown, Thomas Clancy, Susan Manning and Murray Pittock (eds), *The Edinburgh History of Scottish Literature*, 3 vols (Edinburgh: Edinburgh University Press, 2006), II:338–46; Bowe and Cumming, *Arts & Crafts Movements* (1999), 17, 20, 25, 52, 56; Elizabeth Cumming, *Hand, Heart and Soul: The Arts and Crafts Movement in Scotland* (Edinburgh: Birlinn, 2006), 38, 41–42, 135, 142, 180–81; Ian Brown, *Performing Scottishness* (Basingstoke: Palgrave Macmillan, 2020), 158; Pittock, *Celtic Identity* (1999), 62, 75; Ewen A. Cameron, *Land for the People: The British Government and the Scottish Highlands, c.1880–1925* (Edinburgh: John Donald, 2009 [1996]), 5, 20; Holder, 'Collecting the Nation' (2021),143.

78. Long and Norman, *Scottish Design* (2018), 88–89, 104–07; Macdonald, *Geddes* (2020), 66, 109; Bowe and Cumming, *Arts & Crafts Movements* (1999), 17, 20, 25, 52, 56; Cumming, *Hand, Heart and Soul* (2006), 38, 41–42, 135, 142, 180–81; Brown, *Performing Scottishness* (2020), 158; Pittock, *Celtic Identity* (1999), 62, 75.

79. Cameron, *Impaled Upon a Thistle* (2008), 61–62, 76–77, 97–98; Cameron, 'Poverty, Protest and Politics: Perceptions of the Scottish Highlands in the 1880s', in Dauvit Broun and Martin MacGregor (eds), *Mìorun Mòr nan Gall, 'The Great Ill-will of the Lowlander'? Lowland Perceptions of the Highlands, Medieval and Modern* (Glasgow: Centre for Scottish and Celtic Studies (2009 [2007]), 218–48 (227–29); Naomi Lloyd-Jones, 'Scottish Nationalism and the Home Rule Crisis, *c.*1886–93', *English Historical Review* CXXIX (2014), 862–87 (869–70, 881); Bowe and Cumming, *Arts & Crafts Movements* (1999), 15; Shaw, *The Fin-de-Siècle Scottish Revival* (2020), 46; Lachlan Munro, 'The Empire in Cunninghame Graham's Parliamentary Speeches and Early Writings, 1885–1900', in Carla Sassi and Silke Stroh (eds), *Empire and Revolution: Cunninghame Graham and His Contemporaries* (Glasgow: Association for Scottish Literary Studies, 2017), 128–43 (129, 134, 136–37); Pittock, *Scottish Nationality* (2001), 98–100; Lamont, *When Scotland Ruled the World* (2001), 218.

80. Shaw, *The Fin-de-Siècle Scottish Revival* (2020), 11–12, 202; Pittock, *Scottish Nationality* (2001), 99

81. Stenhouse, *On the Make* (2004), 106, 116–17; Bueltmann, *Clubbing Together* (2014), 215.

82. Edward M. Spiers, 'Forging Nationhood: Scottish Imperial Identity and the Construction of Nationhood in the Dominions, 1880–1914', in Forsyth and Ugolini, *A Global Force* (2016), 32–52 (33–35); Devine, *To the Ends of the Earth* (2011), 221; Chris Brown, *Scotland on the Frontline: A Photographic History of Scottish Forces, 1939–45* (Stroud: The History Press, 2012), 19.

83. Edward M. Spiers, *The Scottish Soldier and Empire, 1854–1902* (Edinburgh: Edinburgh University Press, 2006), 52, 71, 210, 213; Victor Kiernan, 'Scottish Soldiers and the Conquest of India', in Grant G. Simpson (ed.), *The Scottish Soldier Abroad 1247–1967* (Edinburgh: John Donald, 1992), 97–110 (97).

84. Ferenc Morton Szasz, *Abraham Lincoln and Robert Burns: Connected Lives and Legacies* (Carbondale: Southern Illinois University Press, 2008), 107–08; Allan and Forsyth, *Common Cause* (2014), 15, 27, 61, 77, 88–89, 124; Forsyth and Ugolini, *Global Force* (2016), 2, 4; Jeff Noakes, 'Canada, Military Scottishness and the First World War', 93–127 (95, 97, 102, 112); Jonathan Hyslop, 'South Africa and Scotland in the First World War', 150–67 (153); Séan Brosnahan, Ngāti Tūmatauenga and the Kilties: New Zealand's Ethnic Military Traditions', 168–92 (174), all in Forsyth and Ugolini, *Global Force* (2016); H.P. Klepak, 'A Man's a Man Because of That: The Scots in the Canadian Military Experience', in Rider and McNabb, *Empire of the Mind* (2006), 40–59 (48); Bueltmann, *Clubbing Together* (2014), 125–29, 156; Jackson in McCarthy and Devine, *Scottish Experience in Asia* (2017), 240–41; Hesse, *Warrior Dreams* (2014), 59; Brown, *Scotland on the Front Line* (2012), 18, 22, 31; Wilkie, *Scots in Australia* (2017), 93.

85. Christopher Harvie, *No Gods and Precious Few Heroes: Scotland 1914–1980* (London: Edward Arnold, 1981).

CHAPTER 6: WAR AND SUPPLY

1. Hew Strachan, 'The Scottish Soldier and Scotland, 1914–1918', in David Forsyth and Wendy Ugolini (eds), *A Global Force: War, Identities and Scotland's Diaspora* (Edinburgh: Edinburgh University Press, 2016), 53–70 (61–68); Richard Finlay, *Modern Scotland 1914–2000* (London: People Books, 2004), 7, 36–37; Stuart Allan and David Forsyth, *Common Cause: Commonwealth Scots and the Great War* (Edinburgh: National Museums

of Scotland, 2014), 4, 6; Ewan A. Cameron, *Impaled Upon a Thistle: Scotland Since 1880* (Edinburgh: Edinburgh University Press, 2008), 123, 128.

2. Christopher Harvie, *No Gods and Precious Few Heroes: Scotland Since 1914*, New Edition (Edinburgh: Edinburgh University Press, 1993 [1981]), 1–2, 13, 24–25, 27, 33, 41; Veronica Schreuder, 'The Harry Lauder Million Pound Fund', *History Scotland* (July/August 2019), 55; Murray Pittock, *The Road to Independence? Scotland in the Balance* (London: Reaktion, 2013 [2008]), 56; Finlay, *Modern Scotland* (2004), 9–11; Anne de Courcy, *Chanel's Riviera* (London: Weidenfeld & Nicolson, 2019), 40n; Julian Hoppit, *The Dreadful Monster and its Poor Relations: Taxing, Spending and the United Kingdom 1707–2021* (London: Allen Lane, 2021), 120, 129, 163; David Egerton, *The Rise and Fall of the British Nation: A Twentieth-Century History* (London: Penguin, 2019 [2018]), 53, 121; Victoria E. Clark, *The Port of Aberdeen* (Aberdeen: D. Wyllie, 1921), 162–64.

3. Cameron, *Impaled Upon a Thistle* (2008), 16, 194; Joseph M. Bradley, *Sport, Culture, Politics and Scottish Society: Irish Immigrants and the Gaelic Athletic Association* (Edinburgh: John Donald, 1998), 19, 25–27, 42, 52; Finlay, *Modern Scotland* (2004), 69, 95–6; 'Kirk "regret" over bigotry', BBC News 29 May 2002: http://news.bbc.co.uk/1/hi/scotland/2014961.stm.

4. Cameron, *Impaled Upon a Thistle* (2008), 16, 194; T.M. Devine and Angela McCarthy, 'Introduction', 1–20 (1); Nicholas J. Evans and Angela McCarthy, '"New" Jews in Scotland since 1945', 50–74 (50, 53); Stefan Bonnino, 'The Migration and Settlement of Pakistanis and Indians', 75–103 (81) and Eona Bell, 'Education and the Social Mobility of Chinese Families in Scotland', 150–75 (151), all in Devine and McCarthy (eds), *New Scots: Scotland's Immigrant Communities since 1945* (Edinburgh: Edinburgh University Press, 2018); Peter Gatrell, *The Unsettling of Europe: The Great Migration, 1945 to the Present* (London: Penguin, 2020 [2019]), 161.

5. Harvie, *No Gods and Precious Few Heroes* (1993), viii, 61; Finlay, *Modern Scotland* (2004), 171.

6. Pittock, *Road to Independence* (2013), 20–21, 49; Cameron, *Impaled Upon a Thistle* (2008), 48, 50–52, 203; Kajsa Louise Swaffer, 'The Politics of Population', *History Scotland* (July/August 2019), 28–37 (30); Stuart Allan and David Forsyth, *Common Cause: Commonwealth Scots and The Great War* (Edinburgh: National Museums of Scotland, 2014), 4, 6; John Darwin, *Unlocking the World* (London: Allen and Unwin, 2020), 334, 341; Harvie, *No Gods and Precious Few Heroes* (1993), 78; Finlay, *Modern Scotland* (2004), 69.

7. John Foster, 'Red Clyde, Red Scotland', in Ian Donnachie and Christopher Whatley (eds), *The Manufacture of Scottish History* (Edinburgh: Polygon, 1992), 106–24 (109, 112, 115, 119); James D. Young, *The Very Bastards of Creation* (Glasgow: Clydeside Press, 1996), 200.

8. Peter Lynch, *SNP: The History of the Scottish National Party* (Cardiff: Welsh Academic Press, 2002), 33, 38; Murray Pittock, *Celtic Identity and the British Image* (Manchester: Manchester University Press, 1999), 125; Pittock, *Scottish Nationality* (Basingstoke: Palgrave Macmillan, 2001), 103, 105; Stewart Lamont, *When Scotland Ruled the World* (London: HarperCollins, 2001), 226.

9. Richard J. Finlay, *Independent and Free: Scottish Politics and the Origins of the Scottish National Party, 1918–1945* (Edinburgh: John Donald, 1994), 1, 2, 4, 14; Lynch, *SNP* (2002), 33, 38; Pittock, *Celtic Identity and the British Image* (Manchester: Manchester University Press, 1999), 84; Pittock, *Scottish Nationality* (2001), 106; Harvie, *No Gods and Precious Few Heroes* (1993), 99, 127; Young, *Very Bastards* (1996), 201–03.

10. Pittock, *Road to Independence?* (2013), 21–22; Finlay, *Independent and Free* (1994), 30–32, 46, 93–94, 107, 126.

11. Cameron, *Impaled Upon a Thistle* (2008), 49–50, 189–90; Pittock, *Road to Independence?* (2013), 44; Harvie, *No Gods and Precious Few Heroes* (1993), 46, 51, 95–96, 140; Craig Lamont, *The Cultural Memory of Georgian Glasgow* (Edinburgh: Edinburgh University Press, 2021), 181–83; Young, *Very Bastards* (1996), 256; Lamont, *When Scotland Ruled*

the World (2001), 203; Ben Jackson, *The Case for Scottish Independence?* (Cambridge: Cambridge University Press, 2020), 39; George Elder Davie, *The Democratic Intellect* (Edinburgh: Edinburgh University Press, 1961); Hoppit, *Dreadful Monster* (2021), 166.

12. Finlay, *Independent and Free* (1994), 207, 209; Compton Mackenzie, 'Scotland and Home Rule', *Picture Post*, 8 July 1939, 54–60 (59).

13. Allan Carswell, 'Bonnie Fechters: The Polish Army and the Defence of Scotland, 1940–1942', 135–56 (135, 137, 146, 151, 153–54); Peter D. Stachura, ' "God, Honour, and Fatherland": The Poles in Scotland, 1940–1950, and the Legacy of the Second Republic', 157–72 (159–60, 163); Emily Pietka-Nyzaka, 'Polish Diaspora or Polish Migrant Communities? Polish Migrants in Scotland, 1945–2015', in Devine and McCarthy, *New Scots* (2018), 126–49 (127–28); Grazyra Fromi, 'The Polish Clan – A Personal View', in T.M. Devine and David Hesse (eds), *Scotland and Poland: Historical Encounters, 1500–2010* (Edinburgh: John Donald, 2011), 196–202 (199); Egerton, *Rise and Fall* (2019), 97.

14. Stephen Gethins, *Nation to Nation: Scotland's Place in the World* (2021), 41.

15. H.P. Klepak, 'A Man's a Man Because of That: The Scots in the Canadian Military Experience', in Rider and McNabb (eds), *A Kingdom of the Mind: How the Scots Helped Make Canada* (Montréal: McGill–Queen's University Press, 2006), 40–59 (40); Allan and Forsyth, *Common Cause* (2014), 43; Chris Brown, *Scotland on the Frontline: A Photographic History of Scottish Forces, 1939–45* (Stroud: The History Press, 2012), 46, 48–51, 56–57, 61, 86, 109, 135, 139, 140, 147.

16. Cameron, *Impaled Upon a Thistle* (2008), 184, 189.

17. Cameron, *Impaled Upon a Thistle* (2008), 184, 189; Jim Hewitson, *Far Off in Sunlit Places: Stories of the Scots in Australia and New Zealand* (Edinburgh: Canongate, 1998), 7; Peter Hennessy, *Never Again: Britain 1945–51*, 2nd ed (London: Penguin, 2006); Finlay, *Independent and Free* (1994), 222; Hoppit, *Dreadful Monster* (2021), 175, 183; Egerton, *Rise and Fall* (2019), 26, 28, 219. See for example the National Army Museum's 'Britain Alone' theme, https://www.nam.ac.uk/explore/britain-alone-1940

18. 'Zionism "Great Act of Justice", Buchan Says to London Jews', *Jewish Daily Bulletin*, 20 May 1934, 6.

19. Andrew Dewar Gibb, *Scottish Empire* (London: Alexander Maclehose, 1937), 314n; Pittock, *Road to Independence?* (2014), 21–22, 73; Harvie, *No Gods and Precious Few Heroes* (1993), 29; Finlay, *Independent and Free* (1994), 158, 236; *Modern Scotland* (2004), 195.

20. Pittock, *Road to Independence?* (2014), 11, 14–15, 28–29; Jackson, *Case for Scottish Independence?* (2020), 23; Egerton, *Rise and Fall* (2019), 220; Moya Jones, 'The Festival of Britain (1951) beyond London', *Mémoire(s), idéntite(s), marginalité(s) dans le monde occidental contemporain*, 20 (2019),

21. 'The 1951 Festival of Britain: A Brave New World', BBC2, 24 December 2011, https://www.bbc.co.uk/programmes/b015d486. Last repeated BBC4, 6 May 2021; Peter Gatrell, *The Unsettling of Europe: The Great Migration, 1945 to the Present* (London: Penguin, 2020 [2019]), 160.

22. Pittock, *Scottish Nationality* (2001), 113–14; Pittock, *Road to Independence?* (2014), 73–74; Harvie, *No Gods and Precious Few Heroes* (1993), 107; Finlay, *Modern Scotland* (2004), 231; Jackson, *Case for Scottish Independence?* (2020), 29, 132.

23. Pittock, *Road to Independence?* (2014), 22, 44, 46, 66; Harvie, *No Gods and Precious Few Heroes* (1993), 156–57.

24. Pittock, *Road to Independence?* (2014), 22, 44, 46, 66; Harvie, *No Gods and Precious Few Heroes* (1993), 57, 60, 66–67, 143, 150–51; Finlay, *Modern Scotland* (2004), 258.

25. Swaffer, 'The Politics of Population' (2019), 30, 33–34; Pittock, *Road to Independence?* (2014), 47; Tanja Bueltmann, *Scottish Ethnicity and the Making of New Zealand Society, 1850–1950* (Edinburgh: Edinburgh University Press, 2011), 29.

26. Pittock, *Scottish Nationality* (2001), 108, 136; *Road to Independence?* (2014), 65–66; William Donaldson, *Popular Literature in Victorian Scotland: Language, Fiction and the*

Press (Aberdeen: Aberdeen University Press, 1986); Harvie, *No Gods and Precious Few Heroes* (1993), 128, 141.

27. Bryan S. Gunn, *The Scottish Nation at Empire's End* (Basingstoke: Macmillan, 2014), 62–63, 100–02, 119, 140, 148; Peter Hennessey, *Winds of Change: Britain in the Early Sixties* (London: Penguin, 2020 [2019]), 13, 38, 49, 74, 180, 185, 208–09; Egerton, *Rise and Fall* (2019), 219, 350.

28. Brown, *Scotland on the Frontline* (2012), 10; David Hesse, *Warrior Dreams* (Manchester: Manchester University Press, 2014), 59; https://www.cwgc.org/non-commemoration-report/

29. Pittock, *Road to Independence?* (2014), 67.

30. Lynch, *SNP* (2002), 78; Brown, *Scotland on the Frontline* (2012), 183; Pittock, *Road to Independence?* (2014), 24–25, 27.

31. Pittock, *Road to Independence?* (2013), 25–27, 41–43, 46–47, 49–51. In preparation for a Radio 4 series on modern Scotland in 2013 it proved very difficult for the author to persuade senior figures in the BBC of the difference between the Conservative and Scottish Unionist parties in 1955.

32. Pittock, *Road to Independence?* (2014), 70.

33. Pittock, *Road to Independence?* (2014), 74–75, 82–83; John MacCormick, *The Flag in the Wind: The Story of the National Movement in Scotland* (London, 1955), 197; Jackson, *Case for Scottish Independence?* (2020), 41.

CHAPTER 7: WEST OF SUEZ TO OUT OF EUROPE, 1967–

1. Paul Goldsmith and Jason Farrell, 'How President de Gaulle's second veto of Britain's EC application fifty years ago led directly to the Leave vote in 2016', *UK in a Changing Europe*, https://ukandeu.ac.uk/how-president-de-gaulles-second-veto-of-britains-ec-application-fifty-years-ago-led-directly-to-the-leave-vote-in-2016/ (19 April 2021); Peter Hennessey, *Winds of Change: Britain in the Early Sixties* (London: Penguin, 2019 [2018]), 321.

2. Brian S. Glass, *The Scottish Nation at Empire's End* (Basingstoke: Macmillan, 2014), 162; David Egerton, *The Rise and Fall of the British Nation* (London: Penguin, 2019 [2018]), 356.

3. Len Freeman, 'How Britain converted to decimal currency', BBC 5 February 2011, https://www.bbc.co.uk/news/business-12346083; Murray Pittock, *Scottish Nationality* (Basingstoke: Palgrave Macmillan, 2001), 116–18; Hennessey, *Winds of Change* (2019), 341; Sir John Kay, '"The Road to the Bawbee": Currency Options for an Independent Scotland', Royal Society of Edinburgh lecture, 20 December 2021, https://www.youtube.com/watch?v=oCecyJUidkc

4. Murray Pittock, *The Road to Independence? Scotland in the Balance* (London: Reaktion, 2013), 47–48.

5. Pittock, *Scottish Nationality* (2001), 126; Pittock, *Road to Independence?* (2013), 76–77; Iain Macleay and Andrew Murray Scott, *Britain's Secret War: Tartan Terrorism and the Anglo-American State* (Edinburgh: Mainstream, 1990), 59; Andrew D. Devenney, 'Joining Europe: Ireland, Scotland, and the Celtic Response to European Integration, 1961–1975', *Journal of British Studies* 49:1 (2010), 97–116 (107); Peter Lynch, *SNP: The History of the Scottish National Party* (Cardiff: Welsh Academic Press, 2002), 94.

6. Pittock, *Road to Independence?* (2013), 76–77, 86–87; Lynch, *SNP* (2002), v, 147–49, 163–64, 243–45; Christopher Harvie, *No Gods and Precious Few Heroes: Scotland 1914–1980* (London: Arnold, 1981), 161–62; George McKechnie, 'The Decline of Britishness in Scotland since 1979', unpublished MA thesis (University of Swansea, 2007), 13–14, 23.

7. Pittock, *Road to Independence?* (2013), 56; Lindsay Paterson, Frank Beckhofer and David McCrone, *Living in Scotland: Social and Economic Change Since 1980* (Edinburgh: Edinburgh University Press, 2004), 83, 100, 108, 139.

8. Hesse, *Warrior Dreams* (2014), 65–67; Siobhan Synot, '*Outlander* is Scotland's *Game of Thrones*. Any Good?' *The Scotsman*, 18 August 2014: 'There has not been such a proud display of tartanalia since the opening of the 2014 Commonwealth Games'.

9. Ian Brown, *Performing Scottishness* (Basingstoke: Palgrave Macmillan, 2020), 194–95, 226–27; Hesse, *Warrior Dreams* (2014), 64.

10. Pittock, *Road to Independence?* (2013), 66, 150–54; see International Association for the Study of Scottish Literatures, https://www.iassl.org

11. Pittock, *Scottish Nationality* (2001), 8; Pittock, *Road to Independence?* (2013), 89–90, 97–99; Ben Jackson, *The Case for Scottish Independence* (Cambridge: Cambridge University Press, 2020), 142–43.

12. Jackson, *The Case for Scottish Independence* (2020), 156.

13. Pittock, *Road to Independence?* (2013), 100–03.

14. Pittock, *Road to Independence?* (2013), 103.

15. Pittock, *Scottish Nationality* (2001), 127.

16. For Ewing's speech in May 1999, see https://www.youtube.com/watch?v=PB_aOAO0c4g; Wendy Alexander, *Donald Dewar: Scotland's first First Minister* (Edinburgh: Mainstream, 2005), 5; https://archive2021.parliament.scot/EducationandCommunityPartnershipsresources/New_Parliament_Levels_A-F.pdf

17. Mark Brennock, 'Scots seek closer links with Ireland, Dewar says in Dublin', *Irish Times*, 30 October 1999.

18. Henry McLeish, *Scotland First: Truth and Consequences* (Edinburgh, 2004), 182, 192.

19. Pittock, *Road to Independence?* (2013), 62; Long and Norman, *Scottish Design* (2018), 160; Harvie, *No Gods and Precious Few Heroes* (1993), 123.

20. *The National*, 25 May 2021; Douglas Fraser, 'The battle for readers and viewers', BBC, 25 February 2020, https://www.bbc.co.uk/news/uk-scotland-51628954

21. Pittock, *Road to Independence?* (2013), 210–12; The Commission on Scottish Devolution: the 'Calman Commission', https://commonslibrary.parliament.uk/research-briefings/sn04744/

22. Tom Peterkin, *The Scotsman*, 12 October 2013, https://www.scotsman.com/news/politics/scottish-independence-support-25-cent-poll-1558251

23. See Murray Pittock, 'Referendum Rhetoric', Inaugural Lecture for the Network for Oratory and Politics, Glasgow, 25 February 2015: see https://www.youtube.com/watch?v=G_STSv8uUgs

24. Pittock, *Road to Independence?* (2013), 215, 221.

25. Polish Migrants in Scotland: Voting Behaviours and Engagement in the Scottish Independence Referendum', *ESRC Centre for Population Change Briefing* 20 (August 2014).

26. Mark Aitken, 'Cameron's regrets over Voice of England speech after indyref', *The Sunday Post*, 15 September 2019; Emilia Pietka-Nyzaka, 'Polish Diaspora or Polish Migrant Communities? Polish Migrants in Scotland, 1945–2015', in T.M. Devine and Angela McCarthy (eds), *New Scots: Scotland's Immigrant Communities since 1945* (Edinburgh: Edinburgh University Press, 2018), 126–49 (129); BBC, 'Election 2015: SNP wins 56 of 59 seats in Scots landslide', https://www.bbc.co.uk/news/election-2015-scotland-32635871 https://en.wikipedia.org/wiki/Opinion_polling_for_the_next_Scottish_Parliament_election

27. *After Brexit: The UK Internal Market Act and Devolution* (Edinburgh: Scottish Government, 2021), paras 25, 47–512, 90–92, 120; Richard Mason and Angus Cochran, 'Poll Predicts Tories Would Be Biggest Losers as Holyrood Gets 29-seat Yes Majority', *The National*, 5 April 2021; Laura Webster, 'Scottish Election: SNP on Track to Win Majority in Latest Ipsos MORI Poll', *The National*, 7 April 2021; Gregor Young, 'Election: Brexit "Pushing Voters towards Scottish Independence", Poll Shows', *The National*, 23 April 2021.

28. George McKechnie, 'The Decline of Britishness in Scotland since 1979', unpublished MA thesis (Swansea, 2007), 21.

29. Stuart Maxwell, *Arguing for Independence: Evidence, Risk and the Wicked Issues* (Edinburgh: Luath Press, 2012), 26, 123, 174; Pittock, *The Road to Independence?* (2013) 203, 223; X.-M. Núñez Seixas, 'Catalan Nationalism and the Quest for Independence in the Twenty-First Century: A Historical Perspective', *NISE Essays* 5 (Antwerp, 2020), 22–23, 32.

30. See Food and Drink Federation Scotland, http://www.fdfscotland.org.uk/sfdf/sfdf_comp.aspx; Scottish Enterprise, Economic Commentary, https://www.scottish-enterprise.com/learning-zone/research-and-publications/components-folder/research-and-publications-listings/scottish-economic-statistics; ReNews.biz on renewable energies, https://renews.biz/59350/renewable-electricity-reaches-90-of-scottish-supply/; *After Brexit* (2021) Annex C; Hennessey, *Winds of Change* (2019), 498; World Economic Forum, 'Scotland's New Target, https://www.weforum.org/agenda/2019/07/scotland-wind-energy-new-record-putting-country-on-track-for-100-renewable-electricity-in-2020 (19 April 2021); *Coherence and Sustainability: A Review of Tertiary Education and Research* (Edinburgh: Scottish Funding Council, 2021); Stephen Gethins, *Nation to Nation: Scotland's Place in the World* (Edinburgh: Luath, 2021), 76; David Ross, 'Technology: Europe Misled Over Wave Energy', *New Scientist* 10 November 1990; Scottish Government, Policy: Food and Drink, https://www.gov.scot/policies/food-and-drink/

31. Philip Long and Jane Norman (eds), *A History of Scottish Design* (London: Thames & Hudson, 2018), 164–65, 170, 184.

32. Stephen Maxwell, *Arguing for Independence: Evidence, Risk and the Wicked Issues* (Edinburgh: Luath, 2012), 85.

33. Paterson, Bechhofer and McCrone, *Living in Scotland* (2004), 73; Jeremy Peat and Stephen Boyle, *An Illustrated Guide to the Scottish Economy* (London, 1999), 57, 77; Fraser of Allander Institute, GDP per Capita, the Importance of Oil, https://fraserofallander.org/scottish-economy/gdp-per-capita-the-importance-of-oil-and-are-scots-actually-better-off/; Andrew Aiton, *Earnings in Scotland 2018*, Scottish Parliament Information Centre (SPICe), https://sp-bpr-en-prod-cdnep.azureedge.net/published/2018/11/29/Earnings-in-Scotland--2018/SB%2018-80.pdf; Insider.co.uk, 'Glasgow "set to lead economy growth in Scotland"', https://www.insider.co.uk/news/scottish-economic-growth-figures-glasgow-13698488; Scottish Financial Review, 'Edinburgh, Glasgow Economies To Grow Faster Than UK', https://scottishfinancialreview.com/2020/02/28/edinburgh-glasgow-economies-to-grow-faster-than-uk/

34. Pittock, *Scottish Nationality* (2001), 127; James Kellas, *Modern Scotland* (London, 1968), 124, 153, 234; Lindsay Paterson et al., *New Scotland, New Politics?* (Edinburgh: Edinburgh University Press, 2001), 105; *The Economist* (6–12 November 1999), 4.

35. Atsuko Ichijo, *Scottish Nationalism and the Idea of Europe* (London and New York, 2004), 145; Paterson et al, *New Scotland* (2001), 108, 124, 126; Ian McLean, Jim Gallagher and Guy Lodge, *Scotland's Choices: The Referendum and What Happens Afterwards* (Edinburgh: Edinburgh University Press, 2013), 71, 91; McKechnie, 'Decline of Britishness' (2007), 71–72.

36. Ian Brown, *Performing Scottishness: Enactment and National Identity* (Basingstoke: Palgrave Macmillan, 2020), 3.

37. Dennis Macleod and Michael Russell, *Grasping the Thistle* (Glendaruel: Argyll Publishing, 2006), 15; https://www.sustainablegrowthcommission.scot/about-1

38. Ben Jackson, *The Case for Scottish Independence* (Cambridge: Cambridge University Press, 2020), 179; 'FactCheck: Is 90% of Ireland's trade with the UK, as a former British trade minister claimed?' *The Journal.ie*, 31 July 2019.

39. Sir John Kay, '"The Road to the Bawbee": Currency Options for an Independent Scotland', Royal Society of Edinburgh Lecture, 20 December 2021; Christopher Harvie, *No Gods and Precious Few Heroes* (Edinburgh: Edinburgh University Press, 1993 [1981]), ix, 113; Tom Nairn, *After Britain* (London: Verso, 2000); Jackson, *Case for Scottish Independence* (2020), 124; Scottish Space, 'A Strategy for Space in Scotland', https://scottishspace.org/space-strategy/

40. *Guardian*, 'Britain's Role in the World', 6 December 1962, https://www.theguardian.com/century/1960–1969/Story/0,,105633,00.html
41. Hennessey, *Winds of Change* (2019), 307, 438–39.
42. *The Cultural and Creative Cities Monitor* (European Commission Joint Research Centre, 2019), 27, 66, 99; *The National*, 27 October 2020. The author organized one of this kind of hub event, the Dublin–Glasgow Creative Cities Summit at the Scottish Government Hub in the British Embassy in Dublin in 2019; Egerton, *Rise and Fall* (2019), 254. A Scottish Parliamentary Committee enquiry into external affairs strategy took place in late 2021, see https://www.youtube.com/watch?v=hBbL_a9r4wo
43. Stephen Gethins, *Nation to Nation: Scotland's Place in the World* (Edinburgh: Luath, 2021), 39, 64–65, 73–74, 184 (see also Mark Mueller Stuart, 'Foreword', 9–14 (12)); Lindsay Paterson, Frank Bechhofer and David McCrone, *Living in Scotland: Social and Economic Change Since 1980* (Edinburgh: Edinburgh University Press, 2004), 10; Dennis Macleod and Michael Russell, *Grasping the Thistle* (Glendaruel: Argyll Publishers, 2006), 153; Scotland: Scotland's International Hubs, https://www.scotland.org/about-scotland/scotland-around-the-world/scotlands-international-hubs; Scottish Government, Policy: International Development, https://www.gov.scot/policies/international-development/
44. Scotland's Census: At a Glance, https://www.scotlandscensus.gov.uk/ethnicity-identity-language-and-religion; T.M. Devine and Angela McCarthy, 'Introduction', 1–20 (5, 7, 11, 13, 17); Nicholas J. Evans and Angela McCarthy, '"New" Jews in Scotland since 1945', 50–74 (67); Stefan Bonnino, 'The Migration and Settlement of Pakistanis and Indians', 75–103 (84–85, 87, 89, 91, 93); Emilia Pietka-Nyzaka, 'Polish Diaspora or Polish Migrant Communities?', 132–33; Eona Bell, 'Education and the Social Mobility of Chinese Families in Scotland', 150–75 (152, 154); Teresa Piacentini, 'African Migrants, Asylum Seekers and Refugees: Tales of Settling in Scotland, 2000–15', 176–204 (189); Ashli Miller, '"Race", Place and Territorial Stigmatisation: The Construction of Roma Migrants in and through Govanhill, Scotland', 205–31 (208); Ailsa Henderson et al., 'Migration, Engagement and Constitutional Preferences: Evidence from the 2014 Scottish Independence Referendum', 232–51 (241–44); Enda Delaney, 'Conclusion', 252–62 (260), all in Devine and McCarthy, *New Scots: Scotland's Immigrant Communities since 1945* (Edinburgh: Edinburgh University Press, 2018).
45. Joseph H. Jackson, *Writing Black Scotland: Race, Nation and the Devolution of Black Britain* (Edinburgh: Edinburgh University Press, 2021), 15, 28, 36, 180.
46. Carol Craig, *The Scots' Crisis of Confidence* (Glasgow: BigThinking, 2003).
47. Murray Pittock, 'Culture and the National Brand: Selling Ourselves as Others See Us', Scottish Government External Affairs Awayday, Edinburgh, 5 June 2018; Scottish Government, Statistics, Anholt–Ipsos Nation Brands Index, https://www.gov.scot/publications/anholt-ipsos-nation-brands-indexsm-2020-report-scotland/; Gethins, *Nation to Nation* (2021), 130–31, 159.
48. The Bibliography of Scottish Literature (BOSLIT), previously hosted by the National Library of Scotland: a change in location is under discussion. See also 'The Global Burns Supper Database' compiled by Paul Magrati at the Centre for Robert Burns Studies, University of Glasgow, see https://burnsc21.glasgow.ac.uk/supper-map/ and elsewhere. The author has been engaged with colleagues at the Department of International Trade on publicizing the global reach of Burns in Burns season as well as briefing colleagues from the Scottish Government hubs abroad on the Romantic-era basis of the perception of Scotland (Scottish Government External Affairs Awayday, 5 June 2018); Josephine Dougal, 'In His Name: Burns Night Event Advertisements', *The Burns Chronicle* 130:1 (2021), 1–24 (13, 17, 18); Gethins, *Nation to Nation* (2021), 165, 181–82.
49. For Duolingo, see Jody Harrison, 'Duolingo Gaelic app deemed a huge success worldwide', *The Herald*, 1 December 2020.
50. J. Mark Percival, 'Rock, Pop and Tartan', 195–211 (197, 199–202) and Hugh O'Donnell, 'Class Warriors or Generous Men in Skirts? The Tartan Army in the Scottish and Foreign

Press', 212–31 (213–15, 217–18), both in Ian Brown (ed.), *From Tartan to Tartanry* (Edinburgh: Edinburgh University Press, 2010).

51. Anne de Courcy, *Chanel's Riviera* (London: Weidenfeld & Nicolson, 2019), 108, 115; Jonathan Faiers, *Tartan* (Oxford and New York: Berg, 2008), 57, 62, 74, 93, 95–98, 100, 147, 160; Alexander McQueen in *Time Out*, 24 September–1 October 1997; 'Stars check out tartan look from top to toe', *The Times*, 12 December 2020. See https://www.pinterest.co.uk/pin/183943966001938126/ for van Wyck's tartan room designs and https://www.youtube.com/watch?v=ZD3b03CK9tU and elsewhere for the *Widows of Culloden* catwalk, 2006.

52. David Hesse, *Warrior Dreams: Playing Scotsmen in Mainland Europe* (Manchester: Manchester University Press, 2014), 171–76; Duncan Sim, *American Scots: The Scottish Diaspora and the USA* (Edinburgh: Dunedin Academic Press, 2011), 193; BBC News Channel, 18 December 2008; BBC, 25 May 2010. For Dougie Maclean's song in advertising, see https://www.youtube.com/watch?v=SF9sG2bwImc

53. Gethins, *Nation to Nation* (2021), 50; John M. Mackenzie, 'A Scottish Empire: The Scottish Diaspora and Interactive Identities', in Tom Brooking and Jennie Coleman (eds), *The Heather and the Fern: Scottish Migration and New Zealand Settlement* (Dunedin: University of Otago Press, 2003), 17–32 (17); Sim, *American Scots* (2011), ix, 209, 216; Jim Hewitson, *Far Off in Sunlit Places: Stories of the Scots in Australia and New Zealand* (Edinburgh: Canongate, 1998), 1, 8, 10.

54. Sim, *American Scots* (2011), 61, 65, 93.

55. Sim, *American Scots* (2011), 56, 59–60, 67, 125.

56. Celeste Ray, 'Introduction', 1–20 (1, 4, 12) and 'Transatlantic Scots and Ethnicity' in Ray, *Transatlantic Scots* (2005), 21–47 (31, 36); Alexander Murdoch, *Scotland and America, c.1600–c.1800* (Basingstoke: Palgrave Macmillan, 2010), 145; Sim, *American Scots* (2011), 126; Senate Resolution 155, http://dctartanday.org/resolution-155/

57. Sim, *American Scots* (2011), 103, 113, 186.

58. T.M. Devine, *To the Ends of the Earth: Scotland's Global Diaspora* (London: Allen Lane, 2017), 275, 276, 279, 293–84; Devine, *The Scottish Clearances* (London: Penguin, 2019 [2018]), 11; Hesse, *Warrior Dreams* (2014), 113; Celeste Ray (ed.), *Transatlantic Scots*, 75, 79–80 (see also Margaret Bennett, 'From the Quebec-Hebrideans to "Les Écossais-Québécois"', in Ray, *Transatlantic Scots* (2005), 120–55 (149); Sims, *American Scots* (2011), 57–58; Tanja Bueltmann, *Clubbing Together: Ethnicity, Civility and Formal Sociability in the Scottish Diaspora to 1930* (Liverpool: Liverpool University Press, 2014), 61; Utah Scottish Association, utahscots.org

59. Bonnino, 'Migration and Settlement' (2018), 93. The idea that the best Scots had all left was a view heard by Sir Tom Devine while engaging with the US diaspora on behalf of the University of Strathclyde as Deputy Principal in the 1990s. See Hesse, *Warrior Dreams* (2014), 87, 89, 100, 108 for European pipe bands and Highland Games.

60. Billy Kay, 'The Declaration of Arbroath', BBC Radio Scotland, 6 April 2020; Devine, *To the Ends of the Earth* (2017), 282; Devine, *The Scottish Clearances* (London: Allen Unwin, 2019 [2018]) 11; Hesse, *Warrior Dreams* (2014), 1–4, 114–16, 136; *The National*, 1 March 2021; Bonnino, ' 'The Migration and Settlement of Pakistanis and Indians', in Devine and McCarthy, *New Scots* (2018), 93.

61. Hesse, *Warrior Dreams* (2014), 2.

62. Hesse, *Warrior Dreams* (2014), 3, 5–9, 17, 131–32, 136–37, 150, 157, 183.

CONCLUSION

1. Peter Gatrell, *The Unsettling of Europe* (London: Penguin, 2020 [2019]) addresses the postwar 'unsettling' of German and other European peoples in great detail.

2. Susan Reynolds, *Kingdoms and Communities in Western Europe 900–1300*, 2nd ed. (Oxford: Oxford University Press, 1997 [1984]).

3. There has – following the Balkan crises of the 1990s – been a trend towards some revisionist appraisal of the intractable problems faced by the Habsburgs and the efforts they made to address them: see for example Steven Beller, *The Habsburg Monarchy 1815–1918* (Cambridge: Cambridge University Press, 2018).

4. Coree Brown Swan and B. Petersohn, 'The Currency Issue', in Michael Keating (ed.), *Debating Scotland: Issues of Independence and Union in the 2014 Referendum* (Edinburgh: Edinburgh University Press, 2017), 66–83 (69–70).

5. Robert Liñeira, Ailsa Henderson and Liam Delaney, 'Voters' Response to the Campaign', in Keating, *Debating Scotland* (2017), 165–90 (170); John Kay, 'The Road to the Bawbee: Currency Options for an Independent Scotland', Royal Society of Edinburgh Lecture, 20 December 2021, https://www.youtube.com/watch?v=oCecyJUidkc.

6. Robert Macintyre, quoted in Jackson, *Case for Scottish Independence* (2020), 23; *The National*, 16 October 2020.

FURTHER READING

Bowie, Karen. *Public Opinion in Early Modern Scotland*. Cambridge: Cambridge University Press, 2020.

Broadie, Alexander and Smith, Craig, eds. *The Cambridge Companion to the Scottish Enlightenment*, 2nd edn. Cambridge: Cambridge University Press, 2019 [2003].

Brown, Ian. *Performing Scottishness*. Basingstoke: Palgrave Macmillan, 2020.

Brown, Ian (ed.). *From Tartan to Tartanry*. Edinburgh: Edinburgh University Press, 2012 [2010].

Brown, Stewart J. 'William Robertson, Early Orientalism and the *Historical Disquisition* on India of 1791', *Scottish Historical Review* LXXXVIII:2 (2009), 289–312.

Bueltmann, Tanja. *Clubbing Together: Ethnicity, Civility and Formal Sociability in the Scottish Diaspora to 1930*. Liverpool: Liverpool University Press, 2014.

Cage, R.A. (ed.). *The Scots Abroad: Labour, Capital, Enterprise, 1750–1914*. London: Croom Helm, 1985.

Corp, Edward. *The Stuarts in Italy, 1719–66*. Cambridge: Cambridge University Press, 2011.

Devine, T.M. *Scotland's Empire 1600–1815*. London: Allen Lane, 2003.

—— *To the Ends of the Earth: Scotland's Global Diaspora*. London: Allen Lane, 2011.

—— *The Scottish Clearances: A History of the Dispossessed 1600–1900*. London: Penguin, 2019 [2018].

Devine, T.M. (ed.). *Recovering Scotland's Slavery Past: The Caribbean Connection*. Edinburgh: Edinburgh University Press, 2015.

Devine, T.M. and McCarthy, Angela (eds). *New Scots: Scotland's Immigrant Communities since 1945*. Edinburgh: Edinburgh University Press, 2018.

Durie, Alastair J. *Scotland for the Holidays: Tourism in Scotland c.1780–1939*. East Linton: Tuckwell Press, 2003.

Dziennik, Matthew P. *The Fatal Land: War, Empire and the Highland Soldier in British America*. New York and London: Yale University Press, 2015.

Fedosov, Dmitry. *The Caledonian Connection*. Aberdeen: Centre for Scottish Studies, University of Aberdeen, 1996.

Galvin, Robert W. *America's Founding Secret: What the Scottish Enlightenment Taught Our Founding Fathers*. New York and Oxford: Rowan & Littlefield, 2002.

Gethins, Stephen. *Nation to Nation: Scotland's Place in the World*. Edinburgh: Luath Press, 2021.

Glass, Brian S. *The Scottish Nation at Empire's End*. Basingstoke: Macmillan, 2014.

Glozier, Matthew. *Scottish Soldiers in France in the Reign of the Sun King: Nursery for Men of Honour*. Leiden, Boston: Brill, 2004.

Grosjean, Alexia. *An Unofficial Alliance: Scotland and Sweden, 1569–1654*. Leiden: Brill, 2003.

Hamilton, Douglas. *Scotland, the Caribbean and the Atlantic World, 1750–1820*. Manchester: Manchester University Press, 2005.

Hesse, David. *Warrior Dreams: Playing Scotsmen in Mainland Europe*. Manchester: Manchester University Press, 2014.

Jackson, Ben. *The Case for Scottish Independence*. Cambridge: Cambridge University Press, 2020.

Jackson, Joseph H. *Writing Black Scotland: Race, Nation and the Devolution of Black Britain*. Edinburgh: Edinburgh University Press, 2021.

Kay, Billy. *The Scottish World: A Journey into the Scottish Diaspora*. Edinburgh and London: Mainstream, 2006.

Lamont, Craig. *The Cultural Memory of Georgian Glasgow*. Edinburgh: Edinburgh University Press, 2021.

Leask, Nigel. *Stepping Westward: Writing the Highland Tour, c.1720–1830*. Oxford: Oxford University Press, 2020.

McGilvary, George. *East India Patronage and the British State: The Scottish Elite and Politics in the Eighteenth Century*. London and New York: Tauris, 2008.

Macinnes, Allan I. *Clanship, Commerce and the House of Stuart*. East Linton: Tuckwell Press, 1996.

—— *Union and Empire*. Cambridge: Cambridge University Press, 2007.

McKay, Alexander. *Scottish Samurai: Thomas Blake Glove 1838–1911*. Edinburgh: Canongate, 2012 [1993].

MacKenzie, John M. with Dalziel, Nigel R. *The Scots in South Africa*. Manchester: Manchester University Press, 2007.

MacKenzie, John M. and Devine, T.M. (eds). *Scotland and the British Empire*. Oxford: Oxford University Press, 2011.

Mackillop, Andrew. *'More Fruitful Than the Soil': Army, Empire and the Scottish Highlands, 1715–1815*. East Linton: Tuckwell Press, 2000.

—— *Human Capital and Empire: Scotland, Ireland, Wales and British Imperialism in Asia, c.1690–c.1820*. Manchester: Manchester University Press, 2021.

Mackillop, Andrew and Murdoch, Steve (eds). *Military Governors and Imperial Frontiers c.1600–1800: A Study of Scotland and Empires*. Leiden: Brill, 2003.

McLean, Ian, Gallagher, Jim and Lodge, Guy. *Scotland's Choices: The Referendum and What Happens Afterwards*. Edinburgh: Edinburgh University Press, 2013.

McLeod, Mona. *Agents of Change: Scots in Poland, 1860–1918*. East Linton: Tuckwell Press, 2000.

Murdoch, Steve. *Network North: Scottish Kin, Commercial and Covert Associations in Northern Europe 1603–1746*. Leiden: Brill, 2006.

Pittock, Murray. *Celtic Identity and the British Image*. Manchester: Manchester University Press, 1999.

—— *A New History of Scotland*. Stroud: The History Press, 2003.

—— *Scottish and Irish Romanticism*. Oxford: Oxford University Press, 2008.

—— *Culloden*. Oxford: Oxford University Press, 2021 [2016].

Pittock, Murray (ed). *Robert Burns in Global Culture*. Lewisburg: Bucknell UP, 2011.

Porter, James. *Beyond Fingal's Cave: Ossian in the Musical Imagination*. Martlesham: Boydell and Brewer, 2019.

Rigney, Ann. *The Afterlives of Walter Scott*. Oxford: Oxford University Press, 2012.

Shaw, Michael. *The Fin-de-Siècle Scottish Revival: Romance, Decadence and Celtic Identity*. Edinburgh: Edinburgh University Press, 2020.

Sim, Duncan. *American Scots: The Scottish Diaspora and the USA*. Edinburgh: Dunedin Academic Press, 2011.

Szechi, Daniel. *Britain's Lost Revolution?* Manchester: Manchester University Press, 2015.

—— *The Jacobites*. 2nd edn. Manchester: Manchester University Press, 2019 [1994].

Whatley, Christopher A. with Patrick, Derek. *The Scots and the Union*. Edinburgh: Edinburgh University Press, 2006.

Wills, Rebecca. *The Jacobites and Russia 1715–1750*. East Linton: Tuckwell Press, 2002.

INDEX